Workshop on Text Simplification, Accessibility and Readability (TSAR 2022)

Online
8 December 2022

ISBN: 978-1-7138-9150-5

Printed from e-media with permission by:

Curran Associates, Inc.
57 Morehouse Lane
Red Hook, NY 12571

Some format issues inherent in the e-media version may also appear in this print version.

Printed with permission by Curran Associates, Inc. (2024)

For permission requests, please contact the Association for Computational Linguistics at the address below.

Association for Computational Linguistics
209 N. Eighth Street
Stroudsburg, Pennsylvania 18360

Phone: 1-570-476-8006
Fax: 1-570-476-0860

acl@aclweb.org

Additional copies of this publication are available from:

Curran Associates, Inc.
57 Morehouse Lane
Red Hook, NY 12571 USA
Phone: 845-758-0400
Fax: 845-758-2633
Email: curran@proceedings.com
Web: www.proceedings.com

TSAR 2022

Workshop on Text Simplification, Accessibility, and Readability

Proceedings of the Workshop

December 8, 2022

The TSAR organizers gratefully acknowledge the support from the following sponsors.

We acknowledge Frontiers as an official sponsor of TSAR 2022

Introduction

Welcome to the proceedings of the 1st edition of the Workshop on Text Simplification, Accessibility and Readability (TSAR).

We have received 35 submissions to the workshop's main track and 11 submissions describing the systems that participated in the shared task on lexical simplification for English, Spanish, and Portuguese, held in conjunction with the TSAR workshop.

The submissions to the main track covered various topics: readability assessment, user studies, creation of datasets for text simplification in several domains and languages, novel text simplification architectures, use of complexity assessment in machine translation, as well as other related topics. Interestingly, most submissions focussed on languages other than English. The lexical simplification systems that participated in the shared task explored various architectures, ranging from non-neural (dictionary-based) approaches to those using the latest GPT-3 models. The best systems outperformed the previous state-of-the-art lexical simplification system on the shared task benchmark dataset.

All submissions were peer-reviewed by the members of the program committee which includes distinguished specialists in text simplification, accessibility, and readability. Out of the 35 submissions to the workshop's main track, one submission was withdrawn by the authors, 15 were rejected and 19 were accepted. Out of 19 accepted papers, 8 were selected to be presented orally and 11 as posters. Out of 11 submissions submitted to the shared task system description track, one was desk-rejected, and 10 were accepted.

The workshop is held fully virtually. The program encompasses two sessions with a total of 9 oral presentations, a poster session with 21 poster presentations, two invited talks, and a round table discussion. The oral presentations feature 8 papers submitted to the workshop's main track and one system demonstration paper which describes the winning system in the English track of the shared task. The poster session features 12 papers from the workshop's main track and 9 papers which describe the participating systems of the shared task on lexical simplification for English, Spanish, and Portuguese.

We would like to thank the members of the program committee for their timely help in reviewing the submissions, all the authors for submitting their papers to the workshop, and all teams that participated in the shared task and submitted the outputs of their systems. We also thank Frontiers for sponsoring the workshop.

TSAR Organizing Committee
Sanja Štajner, Horacio Saggion, Daniel Ferrés, Matthew Shardlow, Kim Cheng Sheang, Kai North, Marcos Zampieri, and Wei Xu

Organizing Committee

Organizers

Sanja Štajner, Karlsruhe, Germany
Horacio Saggion, Universitat Pompeu Fabra, Spain
Daniel Ferrés, Universitat Pompeu Fabra, Spain
Matthew Shardlow, Manchester Metropolitan University, United Kingdom
Kim Cheng Sheang, Universitat Pompeu Fabra, Spain
Kai North, George Mason University, USA
Marcos Zampieri, George Mason University, USA
Wei Xu, Georgia Institute of Technology, USA

Program Committee

Program Committee

Raksha Agarwal, Indian Institute of Technology Delhi, India
Sweta Agrawal, University of Maryland, USA
Rodrigo Alarcon, Universidad Carlos III de Madrid, Spain
Oliver Alonzo, Rochester Institute of Technology, USA
Fernando Alva-Manchego, Cardiff University, United Kingdom
Yuki Arase, Osaka University, Japan
Susana Bautista, Universidad Francisco de Vitoria, Spain
Rémi Cardon, Université Catholique de Louvain, Belgium
Felice Dell'orletta, Institute for Computational Linguistics "Antonio Zampolli", Italy
Anna Dmitrieva, University of Helsinki, Finland
Sarah Ebling, University of Zurich, Switzerland
Richard Evans, University of Wolverhampton, United Kingdom
Núria Gala, Aix Marseille Université, France
Itziar Gonzalez-Dios, University of the Basque Country UPV/EHU, Spain
Natalia Grabar, Université de Lille, France
Raquel Hervas, Universidad Complutense de Madrid, Spain
Tomoyuki Kajiwara, Ehime University, Japan
Jaap Kamps, University of Amsterdam, Netherlands
David Kauchak, Pomona College, USA
Tannon Kew, University of Zurich, Switzerland
Reno Kriz, Johns Hopkins University, USA
Philippe Laban, Salesforce Research, USA
Bruce W. Lee, University of Pennsylvania, USA
Mounica Maddela, Georgia Institute of Technology, USA
Lourdes Moreno, Universidad Carlos III de Madrid, Spain
Nhung Nguyen, The University of Manchester, United Kingdom
Christina Niklaus, University of St. Gallen, Switzerland
Tadashi Nomoto, National Institute of Japanese Literature, Japan
Brian Ondov, National Library of Medicine, USA
Maja Popović, Dublin City University, Ireland
Piotr Przybyła, Institute of Computer Science, Polish Academy of Sciences, Poland
Jipeng Qiang, Yangzhou University, China
Evelina Rennes, Linköping University, Sweden
Regina Stodden, Heinrich Heine University Düsseldorf, Germany
Giulia Venturi, Institute of Computational Linguistics "Antonio Zampolli", Italy
Gayatri Venugopal, Symbiosis International (Deemed University), India
Laura Vásquez-Rodríguez, University of Manchester, United Kingdom
Daniel Wiechmann, Institute for Logic Language and Computation, Netherlands
Victoria Yaneva, University of Wolverhampton, United Kingdom

Secondary Reviewers

Omar Hassan
David Heineman
Michael Ryan

Keynote Talk: Human-Computer Interaction and Automatic Text Simplification: Understanding the Perspective of Deaf and Hard of Hearing Users

Matt Huenerfauth
Rochester Institute of Technology, New York

Abstract: While there have been major advances in automatic text simplification and other related natural language processing technologies, there has been much less research conducted with direct participation of users, to understand their needs for this technology nor how it can be best evaluated through their participation in studies. In this talk, I will discuss how research methods from human-computer interaction and computing accessibility for people with disabilities can illuminate the potential benefits of this technology for a specific user group who has been the focus of research at our laboratory: Deaf and Hard of Hearing adult readers. In prior research presented at the ACM CHI and ASSETS conferences, we have learned that reading-assistance tools that incorporate lexical simplification benefit DHH adult readers, and we have also found that these users prefer designs in which they have greater autonomy over which portions of text have been simplified and transparency as to whether text has been modified. Focusing specifically on DHH adults working in the computing and information technology professions, we have also conducted research on users' current reading practices, approaches they use when encountering difficult text, their interest in reading-assistance technologies, and specific design considerations that would affect their interest (e.g., sense of autonomy, privacy, or social acceptability of this technology in the workplace). Finally, our most recent work has been methodological in nature, in which we have identified specific types of questions that can be asked in studies with DHH adults, of various English literacy levels, to effectively measure the complexity and fluency of English texts that have been simplified. Beyond our specific findings for DHH readers, our work illustrates how human-computer interaction researchers can contribute to progress in the field of automatic text simplification and provide useful guidance and methodological tools for other researchers.

Bio: Matt Huenerfauth is a Professor and Dean of the Golisano College of Computer and Information Sciences at Rochester Institute of Technology (RIT). He studies the design of technology to benefit people who are Deaf or Hard of Hearing or who have low written-language literacy, and his team of research students operates bilingually in English and American Sign Language (ASL). He has secured $5.25 million in external research funding since 2007, including a U.S. National Science Foundation CAREER Award in 2008. He has authored over 115 peer-reviewed scientific journal articles, book chapters, and conference papers, including at top venues in human-computer interaction and computing accessibility. He is a five-time recipient of the Best Paper Award at the top computing research conference in the field of computing accessibility, the ACM SIGACCESS Conference on Computers and Accessibility (ASSETS), which is more than any other individual in the conference history. In 2021, he was elected Chair of the ACM SIGACCESS special interest group on accessible computing for a three-year term, and in 2019, he completed a maximum six-year term as editor-in-chief of the ACM Transactions on Accessible Computing (TACCESS) journal. In 2018, RIT awarded him the Trustees Scholarship Award, the university's highest honor for faculty research.

Keynote Talk: Beyond the state-of-the-art models: What is complex text, and what are we simplifying?

Sowmya Vajjala
National Research Council, Canada

Abstract: We have seen over two decades of NLP research on readability assessment and text simplification by now. But, what do we really mean by "readability", and how is a "simplified" text different from an unsimplified one? In this talk, I will try to explore this question by looking into relevant literature in education and psychology research, and attempt to connect them with NLP research. I will also explore whether the current explainable AI research will help in addressing this question. Through this **non-technical** talk, I hope to initiate a discussion on what else should we be doing apart from building state of the art readability and simplification models with standard datasets.

Bio: Sowmya Vajjala is a researcher in the Multilingual Text Processing group , within the Digital Technologies Research Center at National Research Council, Canada. She has worked extensively on automatic readability assessment in the past, and is currently interested in developing and studying methods to understand the generalizability of NLP systems. She is also a co-author of "Practical Natural Language Processing", published by O'Reilly Media (2020).

Table of Contents

Program

Thursday, December 8, 2022

09:30 - 09:45 *Opening Remarks*

09:45 - 10:30 *Session 1*

Parallel Corpus Filtering for Japanese Text Simplification
Koki Hatagaki, Tomoyuki Kajiwara and Takashi Ninomiya

Patient-friendly Clinical Notes: Towards a new Text Simplification Dataset
Jan Trienes, Jörg Schlötterer, Hans-Ulrich Schildhaus and Christin Seifert

IrekiaLF_es: a New Open Benchmark and Baseline Systems for Spanish Automatic Text Simplification
Itziar Gonzalez-Dios, Iker Gutiérrez-Fandiño, Oscar M. Cumbicus-Pineda and Aitor Soroa

10:30 - 11:00 *Coffee Break*

11:00 - 12:30 *Session 2*

Lexically Constrained Decoding with Edit Operation Prediction for Controllable Text Simplification
Tatsuya Zetsu, Tomoyuki Kajiwara and Yuki Arase

(Psycho-)Linguistic Features Meet Transformer Models for Improved Explainable and Controllable Text Simplification
Yu Qiao, Xiaofei Li, Daniel Wiechmann and Elma Kerz

A Dataset of Word-Complexity Judgements from Deaf and Hard-of-Hearing Adults for Text Simplification
Oliver Alonzo, Sooyeon Lee, Mounica Maddela, Wei Xu and Matt Huenerfauth

Eye-tracking based classification of Mandarin Chinese readers with and without dyslexia using neural sequence models
Patrick Haller, Andreas Säuberli, Sarah Kiener, Jinger Pan, Ming Yan and Lena Jäger

Findings of the TSAR-2022 Shared Task on Multilingual Lexical Simplification
Horacio Saggion, Sanja Štajner, Daniel Ferrés, Kim Cheng Sheang, Matthew Shardlow, Kai North and Marcos Zampieri

	UniHD at TSAR-2022 Shared Task: Is Compute All We Need for Lexical Simplification? Dennis Aumiller and Michael Gertz
12:30 - 14:00	*Lunch Break*
14:00 - 15:30	*Session 3 (Posters)*
15:30 - 16:00	*Coffee Break*
16:00 - 16:30	*Round Table Discussion*
16:30 - 17:30	*Invited Talk 1: Matt Huenerfauth*
17:45 - 18:45	*Invited Talk 2: Sowmya Vajjala*
18:45 - 19:00	*Closing Statements*

The Fewer Splits are Better: Deconstructing Readability in Sentence Splitting

Tadashi Nomoto
National Institute of Japanese Literature
Tachikawa, Tokyo 190-0014, Japan
nomoto@acm.org

Abstract

In this work, we focus on sentence splitting, a subfield of text simplification, motivated largely by an unproven idea that if you divide a sentence in pieces, it should become easier to understand. Our primary goal in this paper is to find out whether this is true. In particular, we ask, does it matter whether we break a sentence into two or three? We report on our findings based on Amazon Mechanical Turk.

More specifically, we introduce a Bayesian modeling framework to further investigate to what degree a particular way of splitting the complex sentence affects readability, along with a number of other parameters adopted from diverse perspectives, including clinical linguistics, and cognitive linguistics. The Bayesian modeling experiment provides clear evidence that bisecting the sentence leads to enhanced readability to a degree greater than when we create simplification by trisection.

1 Introduction

In text simplification, one question people often fail to ask is, whether the technology they are driving truly helps people better understand texts. This curious indifference may reflect the tacit recognition of the partiality of datasets covered by the studies (Xu et al., 2015) or some murkiness that surrounds the goal of text simplification.

As a way to address the situation, we examine a role of simplification in text readability, with a particular focus on sentence splitting. The goal of sentence splitting is to break a sentence into small pieces in a way that they collectively preserve the original meaning. A primary question we ask in this paper is, does a splitting of text affect readability? In the face of a large effort spent in the past on sentence splitting, it comes as a surprise that none of the studies put this question directly to people; in most cases, they ended up asking whether generated texts 'looked simpler' than the original unmodified versions (Zhang and Lapata, 2017), which of course does not say much about their readability. We are not even sure whether there was any agreement among people on what constituted simplification.

Another related question is, how many pieces should we break a sentence into? Two, three, or more? In the paper, we focus on a particular setting where we ask whether there is any difference in readability between two- and three-sentence splits. We also report on how good or bad sentence splits are that are generated by a fine-tuned language model, compared to humans'.

A general strategy we follow in the paper is to elicit judgments from people on whether simplification made a text anyway readable for them (Section 4), and do a Bayesian analysis of their responses to identify factors that may have influenced their decisions (Section 5).[1]

2 Related Work

Historically, there have been extensive efforts in ESL (English as a Second Language) to explore the use of simplification as a way to improve reading performance of L2 (second language) students. Crossley et al. (2014) presented an array of evidence showing that simplifying text did lead to an improved text comprehension by L2 learners as measured by reading time and and accuracy of their responses to associated questions. They also noticed that simple texts had less lexical diversity, greater word overlap, greater semantic similarity among sentences than more complicated texts. Crossley et al. (2011) argued for the importance of cohesiveness as a factor to influence the readability. Meanwhile, an elaborative modification of text was found to play a role in enhancing readability, which involves adding information

[1]We will make available on GitHub the data we created for the study soon after the paper's publication (they should be found under https://github.com/tnomoto).

Proceedings of the Workshop on Text Simplification, Accessibility, and Readability (TSAR-2022), pages 1 - 11
December 8, 2022 ©2022 Association for Computational Linguistics

to make the language less ambiguous and rhetorically more explicit. Ross et al. (1991) reported that despite the fact that it made a text longer, the elaborative manipulation of a text produced positive results, with L2 students scoring higher in comprehension questions on modified texts than on the original unmodified versions.

While there have been concerted efforts in the past in the NLP community to develop metrics and corpora purported to serve studies in simplification (Zhang and Lapata, 2017; Sulem et al., 2018a; Narayan et al., 2017; Botha et al., 2018; Niklaus et al., 2019; Kim et al., 2021; Xu et al., 2015), they fell far short of addressing how their work contributes to improving the text comprehensibility by readers. Part of our goal is to break away from a prevailing view that relegates the readability to a sideline.

3 Method

The data come from two sources, the Split and Rephrase Benchmark (v1.0) (SRB, henceforth) (Narayan et al., 2017) and WikiSplit (Botha et al., 2018). SRB consists of complex sentences aligned with a set of multi-sentence simplifications varying in size from two to four. WikiSplit follows a similar format except that each complex sentence is accompanied only by a two-sentence simplification.[2] We asked Amazon Mechanical Turk workers (Turkers, henceforth) to score simplifications on linguistic qualities as well as to indicate whether they have any preference between two-sentence and three-sentence versions in terms of readability.

We randomly sampled a portion of SRB, creating test data (call it $\mathcal{H}$), which consisted of triplets of the form: $\langle S_0, A_0, B_0\rangle, \ldots, \langle S_i, A_i, B_i\rangle, \ldots, \langle S_m, A_m, B_m\rangle$, where S_i is a complex sentence, A_i a corresponding two-sentence simplification, and B_i its three-sentence version. While A alternates between versions created by BART and by human, B deals only with manual simplifications.[3] See Table 1 for a further explanation.

[2]We used WikiSplit, together with part of SRB, exclusively to fine tune BART to give a single split (bipartite) simplification model, and SRB to develop test data to be administered to humans for linguistic assessments. SRB was derived from WebNLG (Gardent et al., 2017) by making use of RDFs associated with textual snippets to assemble simplifications.

[3]HSplit (Sulem et al., 2018a) is another dataset (based on Zhang and Lapata (2017)) that gives multi-split simplifications. We did not adopt it here as the data came with only 359 sentences with limited variations in splitting.

	BART	HUM
A (TWO-SENTENCE SPLIT)	113	108
B (THREE-SENTENCE SPLIT)	–	221

Table 1: A break down of $\mathcal{H}$. 113 of them are of type A (bipartite split) generated by BART-large; 108 are of type A created by humans. There were 221 of type B (tripartite split), all of which were produced by humans.

TRAIN	DEV
1,135,009 (989,944)	13,797(5,000)

Table 2: A training setup for BART. The data comes from SRB (Narayan et al., 2017) and WikiSplit (Botha et al., 2018). The parenthetical numbers indicate amounts of data that originate in WikiSplit (Botha et al., 2018).

Separately, we extracted from WikiSplit and SRB, another dataset $\mathcal{B}$ consisting of complex sentences as a source and two-sentence simplifications as a target (Table 2) i.e. $\mathcal{B} = \{\langle S'_0, A'_0\rangle, \ldots, \langle S'_n, A'_n\rangle\}$, to use it to fine-tune a language model (BART-large).[4] The fine-tuning was done using a code available at GitHub.[5]

A task (or a HIT in Amazon's parlance) we asked Turkers to do was to work on a three-part language quiz. The initial problem section introduced a worker to three short texts, corresponding to a triplet $\langle S_i, A_i, B_i\rangle$; the second section asked about linguistic qualities of A_i and B_i along three dimensions, *meaning*, *grammar*, and *fluency*; and in the third, we asked two comparison questions: (1) whether A_i and B_i are more readable than S_i, and (2) which of A_i and B_i is easier to understand.

Figure 1 gives a screen capture of an initial section of the task. Shown Under **Source** is a complex sentence or S_i for some i . **Text A** and **Text B** correspond to A_i and B_i, which were displayed in a random order.

In total, there were 221 HITs (Table 1), each administered to seven people. All of the participants were self-reported native speakers of English with a degree from college or above. The participation was limited to residents in US, Canda, UK, Australia, and New Zealand.

[4]`https://huggingface.co/facebook/bart-large`

[5]`https://github.com/huggingface/transformers/blob/master/examples/pytorch/translation/run_translation.py`

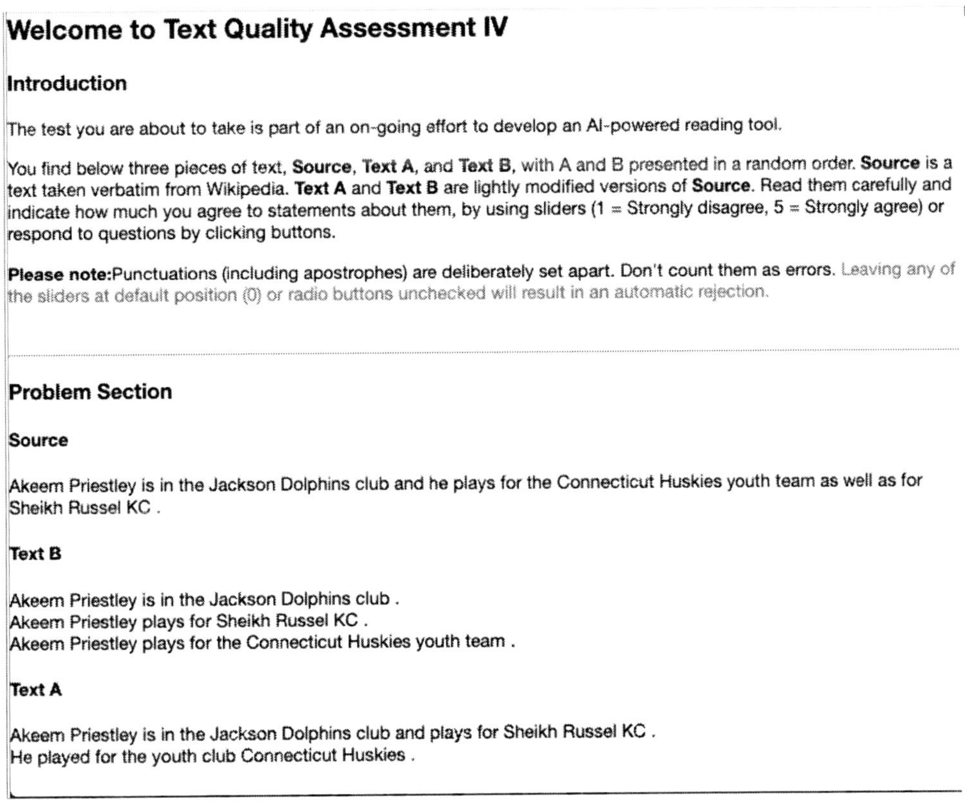

Welcome to Text Quality Assessment IV

Introduction

The test you are about to take is part of an on-going effort to develop an AI-powered reading tool.

You find below three pieces of text, **Source**, **Text A**, and **Text B**, with A and B presented in a random order. **Source** is a text taken verbatim from Wikipedia. **Text A** and **Text B** are lightly modified versions of **Source**. Read them carefully and indicate how much you agree to statements about them, by using sliders (1 = Strongly disagree, 5 = Strongly agree) or respond to questions by clicking buttons.

Please note: Punctuations (including apostrophes) are deliberately set apart. Don't count them as errors. Leaving any of the sliders at default position (0) or radio buttons unchecked will result in an automatic rejection.

Problem Section

Source

Akeem Priestley is in the Jackson Dolphins club and he plays for the Connecticut Huskies youth team as well as for Sheikh Russel KC .

Text B

Akeem Priestley is in the Jackson Dolphins club .
Akeem Priestley plays for Sheikh Russel KC .
Akeem Priestley plays for the Connecticut Huskies youth team .

Text A

Akeem Priestley is in the Jackson Dolphins club and plays for Sheikh Russel KC .
He played for the youth club Connecticut Huskies .

Figure 1: A screen capture of HIT. This is what a Turker would be looking at when taking the test.

4 Preliminary Analysis

Table 3 summarizes results from comparison questions. A question, labelled $\langle\langle$S, BART-A$\rangle\rangle_{|q}$, asks a Turker, which of Source and BART-A he or she finds easier to understand, where BART-A is a BART generated two-sentence simplification. We had 791 (113×7) responses, out of which 32% said they preferred Source, 67% liked BART better, and 1% replied they were not sure. Another question, labelled $\langle\langle$S, HUM-A$\rangle\rangle_{|q}$, compares Source to HUM-A, a two-sentence split by human. It got 756 responses (108×7). The result is generally parallel to $\langle\langle$S, BART-A$\rangle\rangle_{|q}$. The majority of people favored a two-sentence split over a complex sentence. The fact that three sentence versions are also favored over complex sentences suggests that breaking up a complex sentence improves readability, regardless of how many pieces it ends up with.

Table 4 gives a tally of responses to comparison questions on two- and three-sentence splits. More people voted for bipartite over tripartite simplifications. Tables 5 and 6 show scores on fluency, grammar, and meaning retention of simplifications, comparing BART-A and HUM-B,[6] on one hand, and HUM-A and HUM-S, on another, on a scale of 1 (poor) to 5 (excellent). In either case, we did not see much divergence between A and B in grammar and meaning, but they diverged the most in fluency. A T-test found the divergence statistically significant. Two-sentence simplifications generally scored higher on fluency (over 4.0) than three sentence counterparts (below 4.0).

Table 7 gives an example showing what generated texts looked like in BART-A and HUM-A/B.

[6]As Tables 5 and 6 indicate, BART-A is generally comparable to HUM-A in the quality of its outputs, suggesting that what it generates is mostly indistinguishable from those by humans.

QUESTION	AVAILABLE CHOICES				
	S	BART-A	HUM-B	NOT SURE	TOTAL
⟪S, BART-A⟫$_{\|q}$	254 (0.32)	527 (0.67)	–	10 (0.01)	791
⟪S, HUM-B⟫$_{\|q}$	290 (0.37)	–	490 (0.62)	11 (0.01)	791
	S	HUM-A	HUM-B	NOT SURE	TOTAL
⟪S, HUM-A⟫$_{\|q}$	253 (0.33)	494 (0.65)	–	9 (0.01)	756
⟪S, HUM-B⟫$_{\|q}$	288 (0.38)	–	463 (0.61)	5 (0.01)	756

Table 3: Results from the Comparison Section. We are showing how many Turkers went with each available choice. S: source. BART-A: BART-generated two-sentence simplification. HUM-A: manual two-sentence simplification. HUM-B: manual three-sentence simplification. ⟪S, BART-A⟫$_{|q}$ asked Turkers which of S and BART-A they found easier to understand. 67% said they would favor BART-A, and 32% S, with 1% not sure. ⟪S, HUM-B⟫$_{|q}$ compares S and HUM-B for readability. ⟪S, HUM-A⟫$_{|q}$ looks at S and HUM-A.

QUESTION	AVAILABLE CHOICES			
	BART-A	HUM-B	NOT SURE	TOTAL
⟪BART-A, HUM-B⟫$_{\|q}$	460 (0.58)	316 (0.40)	15 (0.02)	791
	HUM-A	HUM-B	NOT SURE	TOTAL
⟪HUM-A, HUM-B⟫$_{\|q}$	439 (0.58)	301 (0.40)	16 (0.02)	756

Table 4: Comparison of two- vs three-sentence simplifications. The majority went with two-sentence simplifications regardless of how they were generated.

category	HUM-A	HUM-B
**fluency	4.04 (0.39)	3.75 (0.38)
grammar	4.12 (0.32)	4.10 (0.32)
meaning	4.31 (0.36)	4.33 (0.28)

Table 5: Average scores and standard deviations for HUM-A and HUM-B. HUM-A is more fluent than HUM-B. Note: ** = $p < 0.01$.

category	BART-A	HUM-B
**fluency	4.04 (0.37)	3.72 (0.36)
grammar	4.07 (0.30)	4.05 (0.34)
meaning	4.21 (0.38)	4.25 (0.35)

Table 6: Average scores and standard deviations of BART-A and the corresponding HUM-B. BART-A is significantly more fluent than HUM-B. '**' indicates the two groups are distinct at the 0.01 level.

5 A Bayesian Perspective

A question we are curious about at this point is what are the factors that led Turkers to decisions that they made. We answer the question by way of building a Bayesian model based on predictors assembled from the past literature on readability and in related fields.

5.1 Model

We consider a Bayesian logistic regression.[7]

$$
\begin{aligned}
Y_j &\backsim Ber(\lambda), \\
\text{logit}(\lambda) &= \beta_0 + \sum_i^m \beta_i X_i, \\
\beta_i &\backsim \mathcal{N}(0, \sigma_i) \ \ (0 \leq i \leq m)
\end{aligned}
\tag{1}
$$

$Ber(\lambda)$ is a Bernoulli distribution with a parameter λ. β_i represents a coefficient tied to a random variable (predictor) X_i, where β_0 is an intercept. We assume that β_i, including the intercept, follows a normal distribution with the mean at 0 and the variance at σ_i. Y_i takes either 1 or 0. $Y = 1$ if a Turker finds a two-sentence simplification more readable, and $Y = 0$ if a three-sentence version is preferred.

[7]Equally useful in explaining relationships between potential causes and the outcome are Bayesian tree-based methods (Chipman et al., 2010; Linero, 2017; Nuti et al., 2019), which we do not explore here. The latter could become a viable choice when an extensive non-linearity exists between predictors and the outcome.

[8]https://github.com/jasonyux/FastKASSIM

[9]https://github.com/luozhouyang/python-string-similarity

[10]https://github.com/shivam5992/textstat

TYPE	TEXT
ORIGINAL	The Alderney Airport serves the island of Alderney and its 1st runway is surfaced with poaceae and has a 497 meters long runway .
BART-A	Alderney Airport serves the island of Alderney . The 1st runway at Aarney Airport is surfaced with poaceae and has 497 meters long .
HUM-A	The runway length of Alderney Airport is 497.0 and the 1st runway has a poaceae surface . The Alderney Airport serves Alderney .
HUM-B	The surface of the 1st runway at Alderney airport is poaceae . Alderney Airport has a runway length of 497.0 . The Alderney Airport serves Alderney .

Table 7: Original vs. Modified

CATEGORY	VAR NAME	DESCRIPTION	VALUE
synthetic	**bart**	true if the simplification is generated by BART; false otherwise.	categorical
cohesion	**ted1**	the trcc edit distance (TED) between a source and its proposed simplification.[8] where TED represents the number of editing operations (*insert*, *delete*, *replace*) required to turn one parse tree into another; the greater the number, the less the similarity (Boghrati et al., 2018; Zhang and Shasha, 1989).	continuous
	ted2	TED across sentences contained in the simplification.	continuous
	subset	Subset based Tree Kernel (Collins and Duffy, 2002; Moschitti, 2006; Chen et al., 2022)[8]	continuous
	subtree	Subtree based Tree Kernel (Collins and Duffy, 2002; Moschitti, 2006; Chen et al., 2022)[8]	continuous
	overlap	Szymkiewicz-Simpson coefficient, a normalized cardinality of an intersection of two sets of words (Vijaymeena and Kavitha, 2016).[9]	continuous
cognitive	**frazier**	the distance from a terminal to the root or the first ancestor that occurs leftmost (Frazier, 1985).	continuous
	yngve	per-token count of non-terminals that occur to the right of a word in a derivation tree (Yngve, 1960)	continuous
	dep length	per-token count of dependencies in a parse (Magerman, 1995; Roark et al., 2007).	continuous
	tnodes	per-token count of nodes in a parse tree (Roark et al., 2007)	continuous
classic	**dale**	Dale-Chall readability score (Chall and Dale, 1995)[10]	continuous
	ease	Flesch Reading Ease (Flesch, 1979)[10]	continuous
	fk grade	Flesch-Kincaid Grade Level (Kincaid et al., 1975)[10]	continuous
perception	**grammar**	grammatical integrity (manually coded)	continuous
	meaning	semantic fidelity (manually coded)	continuous
	fluency	language naturalness (manually coded)	continuous
structural	**split**	true if the sentence is bisected; false otherwise.	categorical
informational	**samsa**	measures how much of the original content is preserved in the target (Sulem et al., 2018b).	continuous

Table 8: Predictors

5.2 Predictors

We use predictors shown in Table 8. They come in six categories: *synthetic*, *cohesion*, *cognitive*, *classic*, *perception* and *structural*. A *synthetic* feature indicates whether the simplification was created with BART or not, taking *true* if it was and *false* otherwise. Those found under *cohesion* are our adaptions of SYNSTRUT and CRFCWO, which are among the diverse features McNamara et al. (2014) created to measure cohesion across sentences. SYSTRUCT gauges the uniformity and consistency across sentences by looking at their syntactic similarities, or by counting nodes in a common subgraph shared by neighboring sentences. We substituted SYSTRUCT with **tree edit distance** (Boghrati et al., 2018), as it allows us to handle multiple subgraphs, in contrast to SYSTRUCT, which only looks for a single common subgraph. CRFCWO gives a normalized count of tokens found in common between two neighboring sentences. We emulated it here with the Szymkiewicz-Simpson coefficient, given as $O(X,Y) = \frac{|X \cap Y|}{\min(|X|,|Y|)}$.

Predictors in the *cognitive* class are taken from works in clinical and cognitive linguistics (Roark et al., 2007; Boghrati et al., 2018). They reflect various approaches to measuring the cognitive complexity of a sentence. For example, **yngve** scoring defines a cognitive demand of a word as the number of non-terminals to its right in a derivation rule that are yet to be processed.

5.2.1 yngve

Consider Figure 2. **yngve** gives every edge in the parse a number reflecting its cognitive cost. NP gets '1' because it has a sister node VP to its right. The cognitive cost of a word is defined as the sum of numbers on a path from the root to the word. In Figure 2, 'Vanya' would get $1 + 0 + 0 = 1$, whereas 'home' 0. Averaging words' costs gives us an Yngve complexity.

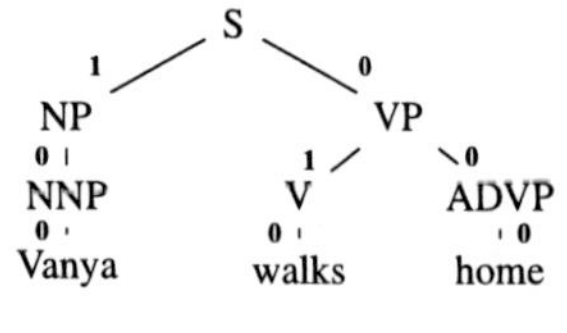

Figure 2: Yngve scoring

5.2.2 frazier

frazier scoring views the syntactic depth of a word (the distance from a leaf to a first ancestor that occurs leftmost in a derivation rule) as a most important factor to determining the sentence complexity. If we run **frazier** on the sentence in Figure 2, it will get the score like one shown in Figure 3. 'Vanya' gets $1 + 1.5 = 2.5$, 'walks' 1 and 'home' 0 (which has no leftmost ancestor). Roark et al. (2007) reported that both **yngve** and **frazier** worked well in discriminating subjects with mild memory impairement.

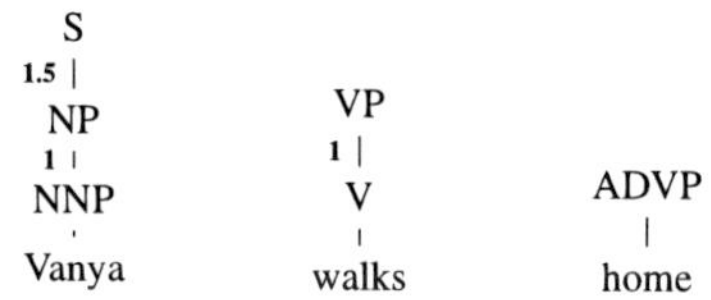

Figure 3: Frazier scoring

5.2.3 dep length

dep length (dependency length) and **tnodes** (tree nodes) are also among the features that Roark et al. (2007) found effective. The former measures the number of dependencies in a dependency parse, and the latter the number of nodes in a phrase structure tree.

5.2.4 subset and subtree

subset and **subtree** are both measures based on the idea of *Tree Kernel* (Collins and Duffy, 2002; Moschitti, 2006; Chen et al., 2022).[11] The former considers how many subgraphs two parses share, while the latter how many subtrees. Note that subtrees are those structures that end with terminal nodes.

5.2.5 Classic readability features

We also included features that have long been established in the readability literature as standard, i.e. Dale-Chall Readability, Flesch Reading Ease, and Flesch-Kincaid Grade Level (Chall and Dale, 1995; Flesch, 1979; Kincaid et al., 1975).

[11] Tree Kernel is a function defined as $K(T_1, T_2) = \sum_{n_1 \in N(T_1)} \sum_{n_2 \in N(T_2)} \Delta(n_1, n_2)$ where

$$\Delta(a,b) = \begin{cases} 0 & \text{if } a \neq b; \\ 1 & \text{if } a = b; \\ \prod_i^{C(a)} (\sigma + \Delta(c_a^{(i)}, c_b^{(i)})) & \text{otherwise.} \end{cases}$$

$C(a)$ = the number of children of a, $c_a^{(i)}$ represents the i-th child of a. We let $\sigma > 0$.

5.2.6 Perceptual features

Those found in the *perception* category are from judgments Turkers made on the quality of simplifications we asked them to evaluate. We did not provide any specific definition or instruction as to what constitutes grammaticality, meaning, and fluency during the task. So, it is most likely that their responses were spontaneous and perceptual.

5.2.7 split and samsa

Finally, we have **split**, which records whether or not the simplification is bipartite: it takes *true* if it is, and *false* if not. **samsa** is a recent addition to a battery of simplification metrics, which looks at how much of a propositional content in the source remains after a sentence is split (Sulem et al., 2018b). (The greater, the better.) We standardized all of the features, except for **bart** and **split**, by turning them into z-scores, where $z = \frac{x-\bar{x}}{\sigma}$.

5.3 Evaluation

We trained the model (Eqn. 1) using BAMBI (Capretto et al., 2020),[12] with the burn-in of 50,000 while making draws of 4,000, on 4 MCMC chains (Hamiltonian). As a way to isolate the effect (or importance) of each predictor, we did two things: one was to look at a posterior distribution of each factor, i.e. a coefficient β tied with a predictor, and see how far it is removed from 0; another was to conduct an ablation study where we looked at how the absence of a feature affected the model's performance, which we measured with a metric known as 'Watanabe-Akaike Information Criterion' (WAIC) (Watanabe, 2010; Vehtari et al., 2016), a Bayesian incarnation of AIC (Burnham and Anderson, 2003).[13]

Figure 4 shows what posterior distributions of parameters associated with predictors looked like after 4,000 draw iterations with MCMC. None of the chains associated with the parameters exhibited divergence. We achieved $\hat{R}$ between 1.0 and 1.02, for all β_i, a fairly solid stability (Gelman and Rubin, 1992), indicating that all the relevant parameters had successfully converged.[14]

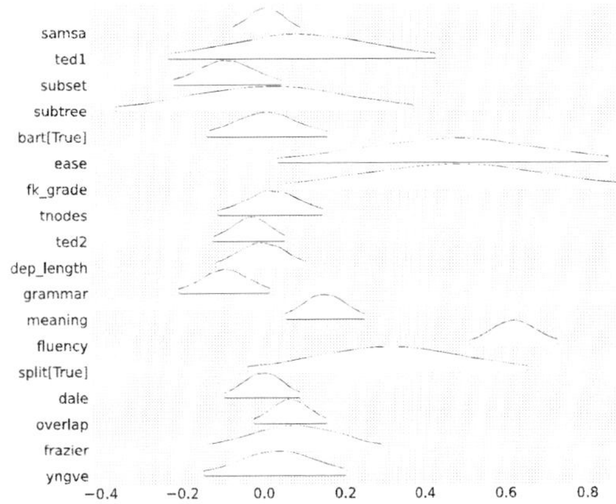

Figure 4: Posterior distributions of coefficients (β's) in the full model. The further the distribution moves away from 0, the more relevant it becomes to predicting the outcome.

At a first glance, it is a bit challenging what to make of Figure 4, but a generally accepted rule of thumb is to assume distributions that center around 0 as of less importance in terms of explaining observations, than those that appear away from zero. If we go along with the rule, then the most likely candidates that affected readability are: **ease**, **subset**, **fk grade**, **grammar**, **meaning**, **fluency**, **split**, and **overlap**. What remains unclear is, to what degree the predictors affected readability.

One good way to find out is to do an ablation study, a method to isolate the effects of an individual factor by examining how seriously its removal from a model degrades its performance. The result of the study is shown in Table 9. Each row represents performance in WAIC of a model with a particular predictor removed. Thus, 'ted1' in Table 9 represents a model that includes all the predictors in Table 8, except for **ted1**. A row in blue represents a full model which had none of the features disabled. Appearing above the base model means that a removal of a feature had a positive effect, i.e. the feature is redundant. Appearing below means that the removal had a negative effect, indicating that we should not forgo the feature. A

[12] `https://bambinos.github.io/bambi/main/index.html`

[13] WAIC is given as follows.

$$\text{WAIC} = \sum_i^n \log \mathbb{E}[p(y_i|\theta)] - \sum_i^n \mathbb{V}[\log p(y_i|\theta)]. \quad (2)$$

$\mathbb{E}[p(y_i|\theta)]$ represents the average likelihood under the posterior distribution of θ, and $\mathbb{V}[\alpha]$ represents the sample variance of α, i.e. $\mathbb{V}[\alpha] = \frac{1}{S-1}\sum_1^S(\alpha_s - \bar{\alpha})$, where α_s is a sample draw from $p(\alpha)$. A higher WAIC score indicates a better model. n is the number of data points.

[14] $\hat{R}$ = the ratio of within- and between-chain variances, a standard tool to check for convergence (Lambert, 2018). The closer the ratio is to the unity, the more likely MCMC chains have converged.

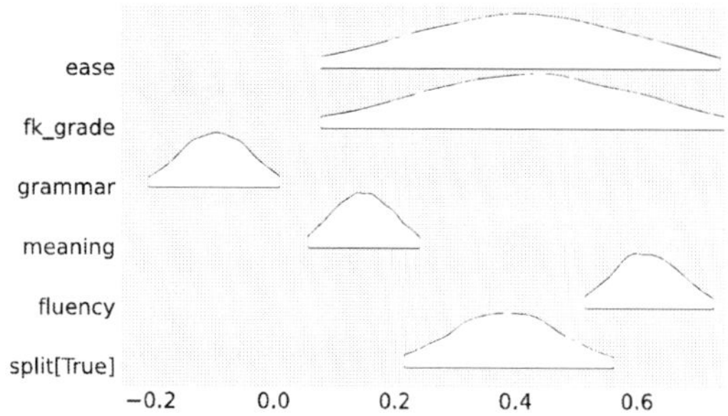

Figure 5: Posterior distributions of the coefficient parameters in the reduced model.

feature becomes more relevant as we go down, and becomes less relevant as we go up the table. Thus the most relevant is **fluency**, followed by **meaning**, the least relevant is **subtree**, followed by **dale**, and so forth. We can tell from Table 9 what predictors we need to keep to explain the readability: they are **grammar**, **split**, **fk grade**, **ease**, **meaning** and **fluency** (call them 'select features'). Note that **bart** is in the negative realm, meaning that from a perspective of readability, people did not care about whether the simplification was done by human or machine. **samsa** was also found in the negative domain, implying that for a perspective of information, a two-sentence splitting carries just as much information as a three way division of a sentence.

To further nail down to what extent they are important, we ran another ablation experiment involving the select features alone. The result is shown in Table 10. At the bottom is **fluency**, the second to the bottom is **split**, followed by **meaning**, and so forth. As we go up the table, a feature becomes less and less important. The posterior distributions of these features are shown in Figure 5.[15] Not surprisingly, they are found away from zero, with **fluency** furtherest away. The result indicates that contrary to the popular wisdom that classic readability metrics such as **ease**, and **fk grade**, are of little use, they had a large sway on decisions people made when they were asked about readability.

6 Conclusions

In this work, we asked two questions: does cutting up a sentence help the reader better understand the text? and if so, does it matter how many pieces we break it into? We found that splitting does allow the reader to better interact with the text (Table 3) and moreover, two-sentence simplifications are clearly favored over three-sentence simplifications (Tables 3,9,10). Why two-sentence splits make a better simplification is something of a mystery. A possible answer may lie in a potential disruption splitting may have caused in a sentence-level discourse structure, whose integrity Crossley et al. (2011, 2014) argued, constitutes a critical part of simplification, a topic that we believe is worth a further exploration in the future.

7 Limitations

- We did not consider cases where a sentence is split into more than three. This is mainly due to our failure to find a dataset containing manual simplifications of length greater than three in a large number. While it is unlikely that our claim in this work does not hold for cases beyond three, testing the hypothesis on cases that involve more than three sentences would be desirable.

- A cohort of people we solicited for the current work are generally well educated adults who speak English as the first language. Therefore, the results we found in this work may not necessarily hold for L2-learners, minors, or those who do not have college level education.

8 Acknowledgement

We thank anonymous reviewers for sharing with us their comments and ideas. We note their effort with much gratitude and appreciation.

References

Reihane Boghrati, Joe Hoover, Kate M. Johnson, Justin Garten, and Morteza Dehghani. 2018. Conversation level syntax similarity metric. *Behavior Research Methods*, 50(3):1055–1073.

Jan A. Botha, Manaal Faruqui, John Alex, Jason Baldridge, and Dipanjan Das. 2018. Learning to split and rephrase from Wikipedia edit history. In *Proceedings of the 2018 Conference on Empirical Methods in Natural Language Processing*, pages 732–737, Brussels, Belgium. Association for Computational Linguistics.

K.P. Burnham and D.R. Anderson. 2003. *Model Selection and Multimodel Inference: A Practical*

[15]We found that they had $1.0 \leq \hat{R} \leq 1.01$, a near-perfect stability. Settings for MCMC, i.e. the number of burn-ins and that of draws, were set to the same as before.

effect	predictor	rank↑	waic↑	p_waic↓	d_waic↓	se↓	dse↓
	subtree	0	-1899.249	17.797	0.000	17.787	0.000
	dale	1	-1899.287	17.852	0.038	17.791	0.207
	dep_length	2	-1899.362	17.916	0.113	17.777	0.211
	yngve	3	-1899.406	17.904	0.157	17.777	0.464
	tnodes	4	-1899.414	17.898	0.165	17.797	0.408
	bart	5	-1899.421	17.967	0.172	17.786	0.216
−	samsa	6	-1899.450	18.018	0.201	17.776	0.315
	ted1	7	-1899.557	17.996	0.308	17.771	0.575
	ted2	8	-1899.632	18.019	0.383	17.782	0.624
	frazier	9	-1899.740	18.096	0.492	17.779	0.708
	subset	10	-1900.069	17.811	0.820	17.741	1.282
	overlap	11	-1900.431	17.966	1.182	17.750	1.511
ref.	base	12	-1900.532	19.089	1.283	17.787	0.208
	grammar	13	-1900.780	17.979	1.531	17.698	1.657
	split	14	-1900.852	18.030	1.603	17.697	1.776
	ease	15	-1901.657	17.962	2.408	17.670	2.064
+	fk_grade	16	-1901.710	18.030	2.462	17.685	2.049
	meaning	17	-1903.795	17.885	4.546	17.425	3.071
	fluency	18	-1965.386	17.938	66.137	14.067	11.349

Table 9: Comparison in WAIC. *p_waic* = the effective number of parameters (Spiegelhalter et al., 2002), a measure to estimate the complexity of the model: the greater, the more complex. *d_waic* = the distance in WAIC to the top model. *se* = standard error of WAIC estimates. *dse* = standard error of differences in WAIC estimates between the top model and each of the rest. ↑ means that higher is better. ↓ indicates the opposite.

predictor	rank↑	waic↑	p_waic↓	d_waic↓	se↓	dse↓
base	0	-1891.901	7.181	0.000	17.485	0.000
grammar	1	-1892.235	6.183	0.335	17.365	1.672
ease	2	-1893.515	6.137	1.614	17.350	2.324
fk_grade	3	-1893.626	6.161	1.726	17.366	2.358
meaning	4	-1895.308	6.145	3.407	17.111	3.059
split	5	-1900.028	6.169	8.127	17.038	4.247
fluency	6	-1956.041	5.935	64.140	13.784	11.289

Table 10: Results in WAIC for the reduced model

Information-Theoretic Approach. Springer New York.

Tomás Capretto, Camen Piho, Ravin Kumar, Jacob Westfall, Tal Yarkoni, and Osvaldo A. Martin. 2020. Bambi: A simple interface for fitting bayesian linear models in python.

J.S. Chall and E. Dale. 1995. *Readability Revisited: The New Dale-Chall Readability Formula.* Brookline Books.

Maximillian Chen, Caitlyn Chen, Xiao Yu, and Zhou Yu. 2022. Fastkassim: A fast tree kernel-based syntactic similarity metric. *arXiv preprint arXiv:2203.08299.*

Hugh A. Chipman, Edward I. George, and Robert E. McCulloch. 2010. BART: Bayesian additive regression trees. *The Annals of Applied Statistics*, 4(1).

Michael Collins and Nigel Duffy. 2002. New ranking algorithms for parsing and tagging: Kernels over discrete structures, and the voted perceptron. In *Proceedings of the 40th Annual Meeting of the Association for Computational Linguistics*, pages 263–270, Philadelphia, Pennsylvania, USA. Association for Computational Linguistics.

Scott A. Crossley, David B. Allen, and Danielle S. McNamara. 2011. Text readability and intuitive simplification: A comparison of readability formulas. *Reading in a Foreign Language*, 23(1):84–101.

Scott A. Crossley, Hae Sung Yang, and Danielle S. McNamara. 2014. What's so simple about simplified texts? A computational and psycholinguistic investigation for text comprehension and text processing. *Reading in a Foreign Language*, 26(1):92–113.

R. Flesch. 1979. *How to Write Plain English: A Book for Lawyers and Consumers.* Harper & Row.

Lyn Frazier. 1985. Syntactic complexity. In David R. Dowty, Lauri Karttunen, and Arnold M.Editors Zwicky, editors, *Natural Language Parsing: Psychological, Computational, and Theoretical Perspectives*, Studies in Natural Language Processing, pages 129–189. Cambridge University Press.

Claire Gardent, Anastasia Shimorina, Shashi Narayan, and Laura Perez-Beltrachini. 2017. Creating training corpora for NLG micro-planners. In *Proceedings of the 55th Annual Meeting of the Association for Computational Linguistics (Volume 1: Long Papers)*, pages 179–188, Vancouver, Canada. Association for Computational Linguistics.

Andrew Gelman and Donald B. Rubin. 1992. Inference from iterative simulation using multiple sequences. *Statistical Science*, 7(4):457–472.

Joongwon Kim, Mounica Maddela, Reno Kriz, Wei Xu, and Chris Callison-Burch. 2021. BiSECT: Learning to split and rephrase sentences with bitexts. In *Proceedings of the 2021 Conference on Empirical Methods in Natural Language Processing*, pages 6193–6209, Online and Punta Cana, Dominican Republic. Association for Computational Linguistics.

J. Peter Kincaid, Robert P. Fishburne Jr., Richard L. Rogers, and Brad S. Chissom. 1975. Derivation of new readability formulas (automated readability index, fog count and flesch reading ease formula) for navy enlisted personnel. Technical report, Naval Technical Training Command.

Ben Lambert. 2018. *A Student's Guide to Bayesian Statistics.* SAGE.

Antonio R. Linero. 2017. A review of tree-based bayesian methods. *Communications for Statistical Applications and Methods*, 24:543–559.

David M. Magerman. 1995. Statistical decision-tree models for parsing. In *33rd Annual Meeting of the Association for Computational Linguistics*, pages 276–283, Cambridge, Massachusetts, USA. Association for Computational Linguistics.

Danielle S. McNamara, Arthur C. Graesser, Philip M. McCarthy, and Zhiqiang Cai. 2014. *Automated Evaluation of Text and Discourse with Coh-Metrix.* Cambridge University Press.

Alessandro Moschitti. 2006. Making tree kernels practical for natural language learning. In *11th Conference of the European Chapter of the Association for Computational Linguistics*, pages 113–120, Trento, Italy. Association for Computational Linguistics.

Shashi Narayan, Claire Gardent, Shay B. Cohen, and Anastasia Shimorina. 2017. Split and rephrase. In *Proceedings of the 2017 Conference on Empirical Methods in Natural Language Processing*, pages 606–616, Copenhagen, Denmark. Association for Computational Linguistics.

Christina Niklaus, André Freitas, and Siegfried Handschuh. 2019. MinWikiSplit: A sentence splitting corpus with minimal propositions. In *Proceedings of the 12th International Conference on Natural Language Generation*, pages 118–123, Tokyo, Japan. Association for Computational Linguistics.

Giuseppe Nuti, Lluís Antoni Jiménez Rugama, and Andreea-Ingrid Cross. 2019. An explanable bayesian decision tree algorithm. *arXiv:1901.03214v3 [stat.ML].*

Brian Roark, Margaret Mitchell, and Kristy Hollingshead. 2007. Syntactic complexity measures for detecting mild cognitive impairment. In *Biological, translational, and clinical language processing*, pages 1–8, Prague, Czech Republic. Association for Computational Linguistics.

Steven Ross, Michael H. Long, and Yasukata Yano. 1991. Simplification or elaboration? the effects of two types of text modifications on foreign language reading comprehension. *University of Hawai'i Working Papers in ESL*, 10(22):1–32.

David J Spiegelhalter, Nicola G Best, Bradley P Carlin, and Angelika Van Der Linde. 2002. Bayesian measures of model complexity and fit. *Journal of the Royal Statistical Society: Series B (Statistical Methodology)*, 64(4):583–639.

Elior Sulem, Omri Abend, and Ari Rappoport. 2018a. BLEU is not suitable for the evaluation of text simplification. In *Proceedings of the 2018 Conference on Empirical Methods in Natural Language Processing*, pages 738–744. Association for Computational Linguistics.

Elior Sulem, Omri Abend, and Ari Rappoport. 2018b. Semantic structural evaluation for text simplification. In *Proceedings of the 2018 Conference of the North American Chapter of the Association for Computational Linguistics: Human Language Technologies, Volume 1 (Long Papers)*, pages 685–696, New Orleans, Louisiana. Association for Computational Linguistics.

Aki Vehtari, Andrew Gelman, and Jonah Gabry. 2016. Practical bayesian model evaluation using leave-one-out cross-validation and WAIC. *Statistics and Computing*, 27(5):1413–1432.

M. K. Vijaymeena and K. Kavitha. 2016. A survey on similarity measures in text mining. *Machine Learning and Applications: An International Journal*, 3(1):19–28.

Sumio Watanabe. 2010. Asymptotic equivalence of bayes cross validation and widely applicable information criterion in singular learning theory. *Journal of Machine Learning Research*, pages 3571–3594.

Wei Xu, Chris Callison-Burch, and Courtney Napoles. 2015. Problems in current text simplification research: New data can help. *Transactions of the Association for Computational Linguistics*, 3:283–297.

Victor H. Yngve. 1960. A model and an hypothesis for language structure. *Proceedings of the American Philosophical Society*, 104(5):444–466.

Kaizhong Zhang and Dennis Shasha. 1989. Simple fast algorithms for the editing distance between trees and related problems. *SIAM Journal on Computing*, 18(6):1245–1262.

Xingxing Zhang and Mirella Lapata. 2017. Sentence simplification with deep reinforcement learning. In *Proceedings of the 2017 Conference on Empirical Methods in Natural Language Processing*, pages 584–594, Copenhagen, Denmark. Association for Computational Linguistics.

Parallel Corpus Filtering for Japanese Text Simplification

Koki Hatagaki **Tomoyuki Kajiwara** **Takashi Ninomiya**
Graduate School of Science and Engineering, Ehime University, Japan
hatagaki@ai.cs.ehime-u.ac.jp {kajiwara, ninomiya}@cs.ehime-u.ac.jp

Abstract

We propose a method of parallel corpus filtering for Japanese text simplification. The parallel corpus for this task contains some redundant wording. In this study, we first identify the type and size of noisy sentence pairs in the Japanese text simplification corpus. We then propose a method of parallel corpus filtering to remove each type of noisy sentence pair. Experimental results show that filtering the training parallel corpus with the proposed method improves simplification performance.

1 Introduction

The number of foreign residents in Japan is increasing yearly due to government policies and the progress of globalization. Iwata (2010) reported that many of them can partially understand Japanese, more than the number who can understand other languages such as English or Chinese. Therefore, many information such as disaster information and daily news (Tanaka et al., 2013) are provided in "easy Japanese" in Japan today.

Recent research in text simplification has focused on data-driven approaches (Alva-Manchego et al., 2020) based on parallel corpora (Coster and Kauchak, 2011; Xu et al., 2015; Zhang and Lapata, 2017; Jiang et al., 2020). For Japanese, a parallel corpus with tens of thousands of sentence pairs (Maruyama and Yamamoto, 2018; Katsuta and Yamamoto, 2018) is available for the study of text simplification. However, the Japanese text simplification corpus contains 16% of noisy sentence pairs, as shown in Table 1, which hinders the simplification performance.

In this study, we first identify the type and size of noisy sentence pairs in the Japanese text simplification corpus. As shown in Table 1, there are three main types of noise: sentence pairs with large differences in sentence length, sentence pairs with different meanings, and sentence pairs with low fluency. We then propose a method of parallel corpus filtering to remove each type of noisy sentence pair. For noisy sentence pairs with large differences in sentence length, we design methods of parallel corpus filtering based on differences in the number of tokens or Levenshtein distance. For noisy sentence pairs with different meanings, we design methods of parallel corpus filtering based on word embeddings or sentence embeddings. For noisy sentence pairs with low fluency, we design methods of parallel corpus filtering based on the perplexity of language models.

Type of noise	Ratio
large difference in sentence length	4% (20/500)
different meanings	8% (42/500)
low fluency	8% (41/500)
other noise	1% (2/500)
sentence pairs without noise	84% (419/500)

Table 1: Types of noisy sentence pairs and their ratios in the Japanese text simplification corpus.

We conducted experiments to evaluate the effectiveness of parallel corpus filtering for Transformer- and BART-based text simplification models (Vaswani et al., 2017; Lewis et al., 2020). Experimental results show that our methods are more effective for the BART-based text simplification model. Specifically, parallel corpus filtering based on differences in sentence lengths enables BART to achieve the best simplification performance for both metrics of BLEU (Papineni et al., 2002) and SARI (Xu et al., 2016).

2 Related Work

Parallel corpus filtering (Koehn et al., 2020) is a technique that has been studied primarily in machine translation tasks where a large parallel training corpus is available, and contributes to improving the quality of the generated text by removing

Proceedings of the Workshop on Text Simplification, Accessibility, and Readability (TSAR-2022), pages 12 - 18
December 8, 2022 ©2022 Association for Computational Linguistics

Type of noise	Original sentence	Simplified sentence
large difference in sentence length	それの代金を仕払うことによって 確立する所有権 (You establish the property right by paying for it.)	買う
	このひもは強い (This string is strong.)	この物を制限するための 長いものは強い
	洪水がおさまり始めた (The flood began to subside.)	水の量が増えて川から出る 状態が静かになり始めた
different meanings	くじで誰が勝つか決めよう (Let's decide the winner by lot.)	勝ったか負けたか 決めることができない
	熱はたいていの物を膨張させる (Heat expands most things.)	あらゆる物は熱で増える
	彼女はみんなをうんざりさせます (She drives everybody up the wall.)	彼女はみんなを飽きさせます
low fluency	豆腐は良い酒の肴になる (Tofu goes well with good sake.)	植物で作った白い柔らかい物を 食べると，うまい酒が たくさん飲むことができる
	金融引き締めで金利が上昇するだろう (Interest rates will rise due to monetary tightening.)	金の流れを厳しくすることで 金を借りる際に返す時につける 金が占める率のが上がるだろう
	酸が金属を腐食した (The acid ate into the metal.)	酸っぱい特徴を持つ水が 金属を腐らせた

Table 2: Examples of noisy sentence pairs in the Japanese text simplification corpus.

noisy sentence pairs from the training data. Text simplification tasks use relatively small training data. Therefore, parallel corpus mining (Hwang et al., 2015; Kajiwara and Komachi, 2016; Jiang et al., 2020) has been actively studied, but there is no prior research on parallel corpus filtering for text simplification.

3 Methodology

We propose a method of parallel corpus filtering for noise in Japanese simplification corpus (Maruyama and Yamamoto, 2018; Katsuta and Yamamoto, 2018) to improve the performance of Japanese text simplification. Parallel corpus filtering is performed on the training data using multiple methods, and the resulting subset of training data is used to train the text simplification model. Transformer (Vaswani et al., 2017) and pre-trained BART (Lewis et al., 2020) are used for the model, and a text simplification model is constructed by fine-tuning using a subset of the Japanese simplification corpus. First, in Section 3.1, we analyze noise in the Japanese simplification corpus and define three representative types of noise that we target. In Sections 3.2 to 3.4, we then describe our proposed method for detecting each of the noises.

3.1 Definition of Noise

We manually classified the noise type in 500 randomly selected sentence pairs from the Japanese simplification corpus, and the results are shown in Table 1. The Japanese simplification corpus is a parallel corpus in which given sentences are paraphrased to make them simpler. Since these are manually paraphrased, most of the sentence pairs are expected to be noise-free.

Our analysis confirms that 84% of the sentence pairs do not contain noise. We manually classified the noisy sentence pairs and found that the three main types of noise were sentence pairs with large sentence length differences, low synonymy, and low fluency. Table 2 shows examples of these noises. Sentence pairs with large differences in sentence length often contain examples in which complex phrases were replaced with expressions similar to dictionary definitions. Sentence pairs with low synonymy often contain errors in rewriting, in which related but non-synonymous expressions are used. Sentence pairs with low fluency often contain redundant expressions due to over-simplification and simple errors such as incorrect particles.

3.2 Methods for Sentence Length Difference

This method performs parallel corpus filtering by detecting noise with large sentence length differences between complex and simple sentences. These noise types include cases in which excessive information is lost due to extreme simplification and cases in which complex phrases are replaced with dictionary definition-like expressions. To determine the sentence length difference between sentence pairs, we propose two methods: one is to use the absolute value of the difference in the number of tokens, and the other is to use the edit distance per token. Three types of tokens are used: characters, words, and subwords. In this paper, words with the best performance are used as tokens. Sentence pairs with a sentence length difference larger than a threshold are detected as noise and removed from the training data.

3.3 Methods for Sentence Meaning

This method performs parallel corpus filtering by detecting noise with the small semantic similarity between complex and simple sentences. These noises include rewritings that use related but not identical expressions, such as "most things" and "all things". To estimate the semantic similarity between sentences, we propose three methods based on word and sentence embeddings. The method based on word embeddings uses the Japanese model of fastText (Bojanowski et al., 2017). The method based on sentence embeddings uses mUSE (Chidambaram et al., 2019), which is a multilingual version of Universal Sentence Encoder (Cer et al., 2018). Sentence pairs whose semantic similarity between sentences is lower than a threshold are detected as noise and removed from the training data.

First, we use a method (Shen et al., 2018) which constructs sentence embeddings by mean pooling of word embeddings. This method is also used as a baseline method in the previous study (Kajiwara and Komachi, 2016). The cosine similarity between the sentence variates obtained in this way is used to estimate the semantic similarity between sentences.

Second, we use the word variate alignment method (Song and Roth, 2015), which is also used in the previous study (Kajiwara and Komachi, 2016). This method considers the problem of word alignment between sentences as a weighted complete bipartite graph matching problem, where the word variates are nodes and the edge weights are the cosine similarity between the word variates, and word alignment is obtained by maximum matching. Then, the cosine similarity of the word embeddings between the aligned words are averaged to estimate the semantic similarity between the sentences.

Third, we use the cosine similarity of the sentence embeddings by mUSE. Recent general-purpose sentence encoders such as BERT (Devlin et al., 2019) are difficult to properly estimate semantic similarity between sentences without fine-tuning. Since there is no labeled corpus available for estimating semantic similarity between sentences in Japanese, we use mUSE, which can estimate semantic similarity between sentences without fine-tuning.

3.4 Methods for Sentence Fluency

To estimate sentence fluency, we propose two methods based on language models. The method based on the unidirectional language model uses the Japanese model of GPT-2 (Radford et al., 2019). The method based on the bidirectional language model uses the Japanese model of BERT. Sentence pairs containing sentences with perplexity higher than a threshold are detected as noise and removed from the training data.

First, we use perplexity based on a unidirectional language model. While the N-gram language model is used in the previous study (Zhang and Lapata, 2017; Kriz et al., 2019), this study uses the GPT-2 neural language model to consider all intra-sentence contexts.

Second, we use pseudo perplexity (Salazar et al., 2020) based on a bidirectional language model. The perplexity based on the bidirectional language model is the sum of the log-likelihoods of the conditional probabilities of estimating a masked word from surrounding words.

4 Experiments

To evaluate the effectiveness of the proposed method, we conduct experiments on Japanese text simplification. First, we describe the dataset and evaluation metrics in Section 4.1, then our experimental setup including models and hyperparameters in Section 4.2, and threshold setting on the validation set in Section 4.3. Finally, Section 4.4 presents our experimental results.

Method	Threshold	deleted sentence	Transformer		BART	
			BLEU	SARI	BLEU	SARI
Baseline (w/o parallel corpus filtering)	-	0	75.29	64.17	81.56	62.88
Difference in the number of tokens	12	5,173	73.63	62.95	**<u>83.60</u>**	**<u>63.69</u>**
Levenshtein Distance	10	4,065	**76.47**	63.92	**83.38**	**63.13**
Average of Word Embeddings	0.85	1,553	**75.90**	63.41	80.68	59.80
Word Alignment	0.7	12,533	73.81	63.48	80.93	62.31
Sentence Embeddings	0.5	2,312	73.63	62.70	81.50	61.32
Unidirectional Language Model	60	894	**<u>77.26</u>**	**<u>64.19</u>**	**82.34**	**63.00**
Bidirectional Language Model	200	4,979	74.28	63.34	**82.15**	**63.05**

Table 3: Experimental results. The upper, middle, and lower rows are our parallel corpus filtering methods based on differences in sentence length, synonymy, and fluency, respectively. Bolded letters indicate scores that outperform the baseline model without parallel corpus filtering, and underlined letters indicate the best performance.

4.1 Dataset and Evaluation Metrics

In our experiments, we used the Japanese simplification corpus[1,2] (Maruyama and Yamamoto, 2018; Katsuta and Yamamoto, 2018). The Japanese simplification corpus consists of 85,000 manually paraphrased sentence pairs of complex and simple sentences. Among them, 50,000 sentence pairs were annotated by university students who are native speakers of Japanese. The other 35,000 sentence pairs were annotated by native Japanese speakers hired via a crowdsourcing service. We used multi-reference 100-sentence pairs annotated with seven types of reference sentences for testing. For validation, 2,000 sentence pairs were randomly selected from other sentence pairs annotated with a single reference sentence. The other 82,300 sentence pairs were for training and were targeted for parallel corpus filtering.

The performance of the text simplification models is automatically evaluated by BLEU (Papineni et al., 2002) and SARI (Xu et al., 2016), which are commonly used in this task. These metrics are implemented in EASSE[3] (Alva-Manchego et al., 2019). As a pre-processing step for automatic evaluation, we performed word segmentation with MeCab[4] (Kudo et al., 2004). The effectiveness of parallel corpus filtering is evaluated by comparing the performance of text simplification models trained on the entire training set and a subset of the training corpus extracted by the proposed method, using BLEU and SARI, respectively.

[1]https://www.jnlp.org/GengoHouse/snow/t15
[2]https://www.jnlp.org/GengoHouse/snow/t23
[3]https://github.com/feralvam/easse
[4]http://taku910.github.io/mecab/

4.2 Settings

For the text simplification model, we used Transformer (Vaswani et al., 2017) and BART[5] (Lewis et al., 2020), which was pre-trained Transformer on Japanese Wikipedia. We implemented these models using fairseq[6] (Ott et al., 2019) and used Adam (Kingma and Ba, 2015) as the optimization method for fine-tuning, setting $\beta_1 = 0.9$, $\beta_2 = 0.99$, and the learning rate as 5e-4. The batch size was set to 4,096 tokens, and label smoothing and dropout were used for regularization. The dropout probability was set to 0.2. Training was terminated when the cross-entropy loss in the validation set did not improve for five checkpoints.

As pre-processing for Transformer, we performed word segmentation with MeCab. As pre-processing for BART, we performed word segmentation with Juman++[7] (Morita et al., 2015) and subword segmentation with SentencePiece[8] (Kudo and Richardson, 2018). The vocabulary size for subword segmentation was set to 8,000.

Following models were used for parallel corpus filtering of the proposed method. Japanese fastText[9] (Bojanowski et al., 2017) was used for word embeddings. MeCab was used for word segmentation. For sentence embeddings, we used mUSE, a multilingual version of Universal Sentence Encoder[10] (Cer et al., 2018). For the unidirectional

[5]https://github.com/utanaka2000/fairseq/tree/japanese_bart_pretrained_model
[6]https://github.com/pytorch/fairseq
[7]https://github.com/ku-nlp/jumanpp
[8]https://github.com/google/sentencepiece
[9]https://fasttext.cc/
[10]https://tfhub.dev/google/universal-sentence-encoder-multilingual/3

language model, we used Japanese GPT-2.[11] For the bidirectional language model, we used Japanese BERT.[12] The GPT-2 and BERT language models were implemented using HuggingFace Transformers (Wolf et al., 2020).

4.3 Thresholds

We set thresholds for each method for parallel corpus filtering through the evaluation of simplification performance on the validation set. In this experiment, we set our thresholds with respect to SARI, the primary automatic evaluation metric for text simplification.

4.4 Results

Table 3 shows the experimental results. Transformer improved BLEU by parallel corpus filtering on edit distance, and improved both BLEU and SARI by parallel corpus filtering on unidirectional language models. In BART, parallel corpus filtering for sentence length difference and fluency improved both BLEU and SARI. On the other hand, parallel corpus filtering for synonymy worsened both BLEU and SARI in both models.

5 Conclusion

To improve the performance of Japanese text simplification, we proposed methods of parallel corpus filtering to remove noisy sentence pairs from the training dataset in terms of differences in sentence length, synonymy, and fluency. Experiments on text simplification models based on Transformer and BART showed that parallel corpus filtering based on differences in sentence length and perplexity of language models improved both metrics of BLEU and SARI over the baseline model without parallel corpus filtering.

Acknowledgments

This work was supported by JSPS KAKENHI Grant Number JP22H03651. This research was also obtained from the commissioned research (No. 225) by National Institute of Information and Communications Technology (NICT), Japan.

[11]https://huggingface.co/rinna/japanese-gpt2-medium

[12]https://huggingface.co/cl-tohoku/bert-base-japanese-whole-word-masking

References

Fernando Alva-Manchego, Louis Martin, Carolina Scarton, and Lucia Specia. 2019. EASSE: Easier Automatic Sentence Simplification Evaluation. In *Proceedings of the 2019 Conference on Empirical Methods in Natural Language Processing and the 9th International Joint Conference on Natural Language Processing : System Demonstrations*, pages 49–54.

Fernando Alva-Manchego, Carolina Scarton, and Lucia Specia. 2020. Data-Driven Sentence Simplification: Survey and Benchmark. *Computational Linguistics*, 46(1):135–187.

Piotr Bojanowski, Edouard Grave, Armand Joulin, and Tomas Mikolov. 2017. Enriching Word Vectors with Subword Information. *Transactions of the Association for Computational Linguistics*, 5:135–146.

Daniel Cer, Yinfei Yang, Sheng-yi Kong, Nan Hua, Nicole Limtiaco, Rhomni St. John, Noah Constant, Mario Guajardo-Cespedes, Steve Yuan, Chris Tar, Brian Strope, and Ray Kurzweil. 2018. Universal Sentence Encoder for English. In *Proceedings of the 2018 Conference on Empirical Methods in Natural Language Processing: System Demonstrations*, pages 169–174.

Muthu Chidambaram, Yinfei Yang, Daniel Cer, Steve Yuan, Yunhsuan Sung, Brian Strope, and Ray Kurzweil. 2019. Learning Cross-Lingual Sentence Representations via a Multi-task Dual-Encoder Model. In *Proceedings of the 4th Workshop on Representation Learning for NLP*, pages 250–259.

William Coster and David Kauchak. 2011. Simple English Wikipedia: A New Text Simplification Task. In *Proceedings of the 49th Annual Meeting of the Association for Computational Linguistics: Human Language Technologies*, pages 665–669.

Jacob Devlin, Ming-Wei Chang, Kenton Lee, and Kristina Toutanova. 2019. BERT: Pre-training of Deep Bidirectional Transformers for Language Understanding. In *Proceedings of the 2019 Conference of the North American Chapter of the Association for Computational Linguistics: Human Language Technologies*, pages 4171–4186.

William Hwang, Hannaneh Hajishirzi, Mari Ostendorf, and Wei Wu. 2015. Aligning Sentences from Standard Wikipedia to Simple Wikipedia. In *Proceedings of the 2015 Conference of the North American Chapter of the Association for Computational Linguistics: Human Language Technologies*, pages 211–217.

Kazunari Iwata. 2010. The Preference for English in Linguistic Services: 'Japanese for Living: Country wide Survey' and Hiroshima. *The Japanese Journal of Language in Society*, 13(1):81–94.

Chao Jiang, Mounica Maddela, Wuwei Lan, Yang Zhong, and Wei Xu. 2020. Neural CRF Model for

Sentence Alignment in Text Simplification. In *Proceedings of the 58th Annual Meeting of the Association for Computational Linguistics*, pages 7943–7960.

Tomoyuki Kajiwara and Mamoru Komachi. 2016. Building a Monolingual Parallel Corpus for Text Simplification Using Sentence Similarity Based on Alignment between Word Embeddings. In *Proceedings of COLING 2016, the 26th International Conference on Computational Linguistics: Technical Papers*, pages 1147–1158.

Akihiro Katsuta and Kazuhide Yamamoto. 2018. Crowdsourced Corpus of Sentence Simplification with Core Vocabulary. In *Proceedings of the Eleventh International Conference on Language Resources and Evaluation*, pages 461–466.

Diederik P. Kingma and Jimmy Ba. 2015. Adam: A Method for Stochastic Optimization. In *Proceedings of the 3rd International Conference on Learning Representations*.

Philipp Koehn, Vishrav Chaudhary, Ahmed El-Kishky, Naman Goyal, Peng-Jen Chen, and Francisco Guzman. 2020. Findings of the WMT 2020 Shared Task on Parallel Corpus Filtering and Alignment. In *Proceedings of the Fifth Conference on Machine Translation*, pages 726–742.

Reno Kriz, Joao Sedoc, Marianna Apidianaki, Carolina Zheng, Gaurav Kumar, Eleni Miltsakaki, and Chris Callison-Burch. 2019. Complexity-Weighted Loss and Diverse Reranking for Sentence Simplification. In *Proceedings of the 2019 Conference of the North American Chapter of the Association for Computational Linguistics: Human Language Technologies*, pages 3137–3147.

Taku Kudo and John Richardson. 2018. Sentencepiece: A Simple and Language Independent Subword Tokenizer and Detokenizer for Neural Text Processing. In *Proceedings of the 2018 Conference on Empirical Methods in Natural Language Processing: System Demonstrations*, pages 66–71.

Taku Kudo, Kaoru Yamamoto, and Yuji Matsumoto. 2004. Applying Conditional Random Fields to Japanese Morphological Analysis. In *Proceedings of the 2004 Conference on Empirical Methods in Natural Language Processing*, pages 230–237.

Mike Lewis, Yinhan Liu, Naman Goyal, Marjan Ghazvininejad, Abdelrahman Mohamed, Omer Levy, Veselin Stoyanov, and Luke Zettlemoyer. 2020. BART: Denoising Sequence-to-Sequence Pretraining for Natural Language Generation, Translation, and Comprehension. In *Proceedings of the 58th Annual Meeting of the Association for Computational Linguistics*, pages 7871–7880.

Takumi Maruyama and Kazuhide Yamamoto. 2018. Simplified Corpus with Core Vocabulary. In *Proceedings of the Eleventh International Conference on Language Resources and Evaluation*, pages 1153–1160.

Hajime Morita, Daisuke Kawahara, and Sadao Kurohashi. 2015. Morphological Analysis for Unsegmented Languages using Recurrent Neural Network Language Model. In *Proceedings of the 2015 Conference on Empirical Methods in Natural Language Processing*, pages 2292–2297.

Myle Ott, Sergey Edunov, Alexei Baevski, Angela Fan, Sam Gross, Nathan Ng, David Grangier, and Michael Auli. 2019. fairseq: A Fast, Extensible Toolkit for Sequence Modeling. In *Proceedings of the 2019 Conference of the North American Chapter of the Association for Computational Linguistics*, pages 48–53.

Kishore Papineni, Salim Roukos, Todd Ward, and Wei-Jing Zhu. 2002. BLEU: a Method for Automatic Evaluation of Machine Translation. In *Proceedings of the 40th Annual Meeting of the Association for Computational Linguistics*, pages 311–318.

Alec Radford, Jeff Wu, Rewon Child, David Luan, Dario Amodei, and Ilya Sutskever. 2019. Language Models are Unsupervised Multitask Learners. *Technical Report, OpenAI*, pages 1–24.

Julian Salazar, Davis Liang, Toan Q. Nguyen, and Katrin Kirchhoff. 2020. Masked Language Model Scoring. In *Proceedings of the 58th Annual Meeting of the Association for Computational Linguistics*, pages 2699–2712.

Dinghan Shen, Guoyin Wang, Wenlin Wang, Martin Renqiang Min, Qinliang Su, Yizhe Zhang, Chunyuan Li, Ricardo Henao, and Lawrence Carin. 2018. Baseline Needs More Love: On Simple Word-Embedding-Based Models and Associated Pooling Mechanisms. In *Proceedings of the 56th Annual Meeting of the Association for Computational Linguistics*, pages 440–450.

Yangqiu Song and Dan Roth. 2015. Unsupervised Sparse Vector Densification for Short Text Similarity. In *Proceedings of the 2015 Conference of the North American Chapter of the Association for Computational Linguistics: Human Language Technologies*, pages 1275–1280.

Hideki Tanaka, Hideya Mino, Tadashi Kumano, Ochi, and Shibata. 2013. News Service in Simplified Japanese and Its Production Support Systems. In *Proceedings of the IBC2013 Conference*.

Ashish Vaswani, Noam Shazeer, Niki Parmar, Jakob Uszkoreit, Llion Jones, Aidan N Gomez, Ł ukasz Kaiser, and Illia Polosukhin. 2017. Attention is All you Need. In *Advances in Neural Information Processing Systems 30*, pages 5998–6008.

Thomas Wolf, Lysandre Debut, Victor Sanh, Julien Chaumond, Clement Delangue, Anthony Moi, Pierric Cistac, Tim Rault, Remi Louf, Morgan Funtowicz, Joe Davison, Sam Shleifer, Patrick von Platen, Clara

Ma, Yacine Jernite, Julien Plu, Canwen Xu, Teven Le Scao, Sylvain Gugger, Mariama Drame, Quentin Lhoest, and Alexander Rush. 2020. Transformers: State-of-the-Art Natural Language Processing. In *Proceedings of the 2020 Conference on Empirical Methods in Natural Language Processing: System Demonstrations*, pages 38–45.

Wei Xu, Chris Callison-Burch, and Courtney Napoles. 2015. Problems in Current Text Simplification Research: New Data Can Help. *Transactions of the Association for Computational Linguistics*, 3:283–297.

Wei Xu, Courtney Napoles, Ellie Pavlick, Quanze Chen, and Chris Callison-Burch. 2016. Optimizing Statistical Machine Translation for Text Simplification. *Transactions of the Association for Computational Linguistics*, 4:401–415.

Xingxing Zhang and Mirella Lapata. 2017. Sentence Simplification with Deep Reinforcement Learning. In *Proceedings of the 2017 Conference on Empirical Methods in Natural Language Processing*, pages 584–594.

Patient-friendly Clinical Notes: Towards a new Text Simplification Dataset

Jan Trienes[†] **Jörg Schlötterer**[†] **Hans-Ulrich Schildhaus**[‡] **Christin Seifert**[†]
[†]University of Duisburg-Essen, Germany
[‡]University Hospital Essen, Germany
[‡]Discovery Life Sciences, Kassel, Germany
{jan.trienes, joerg.schloetterer, christin.seifert}@uni-due.de
hans-ulrich.schildhaus@dls.com

Abstract

Automatic text simplification can help patients to better understand their own clinical notes. A major hurdle for the development of clinical text simplification methods is the lack of high quality resources. We report ongoing efforts in creating a parallel dataset of professionally simplified clinical notes. Currently, this corpus consists of 851 document-level simplifications of German pathology reports. We highlight characteristics of this dataset and establish first baselines for paragraph-level simplification.

1 Introduction

Many hospitals worldwide give patients access to their own clinical notes with the goal to strengthen patient autonomy and increase transparency of the care process (Delbanco et al., 2012). Yet, clinical notes are seldomly written with the patient in mind. Being a communication tool for doctors, clinical notes must use a precise and unambiguous medical vocabulary. With limited health literacy, these notes are therefore practically inaccessible to most patients (Sørensen et al., 2015). The urgency of making clinical notes accessible to patients is underlined by initiatives like *"What's my diagnosis?"* where medical doctors and students volunteer to translate patient notes into a simple language (Bittner et al., 2015). Approaches to automatic text simplification (TS) have the potential to assist with this time consuming manual process (Shardlow, 2014; Alva-Manchego et al., 2020).

However, there is a lack of resources to develop TS methods for clinical notes. Most commonly used resources for TS include, on the one hand, professionally simplified news articles such as Newsela (Xu et al., 2015) and OneStopEnglish (Vajjala and Lučić, 2018), and on the other hand, large scale but potentially noisy alignments of Wikipedia (Zhu et al., 2010; Jiang et al., 2020). In the medical domain, datasets cover consumer health lexicons (Cao et al., 2020), laymen summaries of scientific articles (Devaraj et al., 2021) and medical subsets of Wikipedia (Grabar and Cardon, 2018; van den Bercken et al., 2019; Van et al., 2020). In addition, there is a lack of parallel document-level TS datasets (with the notable exception of Newsela and OneStopEnglish). This makes it difficult to study document-level phenomena of TS such as sentence reordering, deletion and explanation generation (Alva-Manchego et al., 2019b; Zhong et al., 2020; Srikanth and Li, 2021).

Contributions. As a response to the lack of resources, we report initial results towards a parallel dataset of patient-friendly clinical notes. Currently, the dataset covers 851 German surgical pathology reports with document-level simplifications by medical professionals. We describe a lightweight simplification protocol that encourages an intuitive simplification style and medical correctness, while not demanding linguistic training on the side of the editors. Furthermore, we conduct first analyses of the dataset and establish baselines for automatic simplification. Overall, we find that the source text is dense, with partly incomplete sentences and a highly specialized vocabulary, while manually produced simplifications are on average longer with a more constrained vocabulary. We observe a variety of simplification operations in the references including lexical substitution, syntactic simplification, explanations and content selection. We believe that this dataset can be an interesting testbed for research on document-level TS.

Our goal with this dataset is to increase the diversity of resources that TS research has available in terms of the text types, domains and languages. Sharing this dataset with the research community while respecting ethical, legal and privacy standards is currently underway.[1]

[1]We share the experiment code and provide updates on the dataset at github.com/jantrienes/simple-patho.

Proceedings of the Workshop on Text Simplification, Accessibility, and Readability (TSAR-2022), pages 19 - 27
December 8, 2022 ©2022 Association for Computational Linguistics

Original (German)	Translation (English)
1. Klinische Angaben	1. Background
Original: Unklare Raumforderung proximaler Oberschenkel links. V.a. Lymphom, DD Weichteilsarkom. Entität?	Original: Undefined mass proximal thigh left. Suspicion of lymphoma. DDx soft tissue sarcoma. Entity?
Human Reference: Bei der vorliegenden Gewebeentnahme handelt es sich um eine unklare Gewebeneubildung des oberen linken Oberschenkels. Es wird die Frage nach einer Diagnose gestellt.	Human Reference: The present tissue sample is an undefined tissue growth of the upper left thigh. The question of a diagnosis is raised.
System Output (mBART): Anhand der histologischen Untersuchungen wurde die Diagnose gesichert und dabei geht es um eine unklare Raumforderung am oberen Anteil des linken Oberschenkels. Es besteht der Verdacht auf ein Lymphom, ein Weichteilsarkom. Ein Weichteilsarkom ist ein bösartiger Tumor des Weichteilgewebes, welcher Merkmale von Fettzellen aufweist bzw. aus diesen hervorgeht.	System Output (mBART): By means of histological examinations the diagnosis was confirmed and it is about an undefined mass on the upper part of the left thigh. There is a suspicion of a lymphoma, a soft tissue sarcoma. A soft tissue sarcoma is a malignant tumor of the soft tissue, which has characteristics of fat cells or develops from them.
R-1/2/L: 33.33/11.43/30.56, BLEU: 7.25, SARI: 39.28	
2. Makroskopie	2. Macroscopy
Original: Proximaler Oberschenkel ventral links: mehrteilig beige-braunes, teils gelbliches Gewebe von zusammengelegt 2 x 2 bis 0,3 cm.	Original: Proximal thigh ventral left: several fragments of beige-brown, partly yellowish tissue of 2 x 2 to 0.3 cm when put together.
Human Reference: Eine makroskopische Untersuchung wird mit bloßem Auge durchgeführt und gibt eine erste Einschätzung über krankhafte Veränderungen. Außerdem soll diese Untersuchung eine Auswahl von Abschnitten für eine genauere Untersuchung mithilfe des Mikroskops liefern. Es handelt sich um eine Gewebeentnahme der Vorderseite des linken Oberschenkels. Das Präparat besteht aus mehreren Teilen, die beige-braun bis gelblich gefärbt sind und zusammengelegt 2 x 2 x 0,3 cm messen.	Human Reference: A macroscopic examination is done with the naked eye and allows an initial assessment of pathological changes. In addition, this examination shall provide a selection of slices suitable for a more detailed examination under the microscope. It is a tissue sample of the front of the left thigh. The specimen consists of several fragments that are beige-brown to yellowish in color and measure 2 x 2 x 0.3 cm when put together.
System Output (mBART): Die makroskopische Beurteilung beinhaltet eine Untersuchung und Beurteilung von eingesandten Proben mit dem bloßen Auge. Zur Untersuchung steht ein mehrereteilig beige-braunes, teils gelbliches Gewebe von zusammengelegt 2 x 2 bis 0,3 cm.	System Output (mBART): The macroscopic assessment includes an examination and assessment of submitted specimens with the naked eye. The specimen to be examined is a several parts beige-brown, partly yellowish tissue of 2 x 2 to 0.3 cm when put together.
R-1/2/L: 34.86/9.35/31.19, BLEU: 3.92, SARI: 36.56	

Table 1: Example pathology report from the validation set including human reference and system output (mBART). Reports typically consist of four sections (background, macroscopy, microscopy and conclusion) and each section is one input for the paragraph-level simplification model. We color-code summarization/deletion, explanation and lexical simplification/paraphrasing. For each section, we also give the ROUGE, BLEU and SARI scores. The example is continued in Appendix Table 5.

2 Dataset Creation and Analysis

We describe our design decisions for the creation of a parallel corpus of clinical notes. An example report is given in Table 1.

2.1 Data Selection

We decided to focus on pathology reports of sarcoma patients since clinicians noted particularly high amounts of questions concerning these reports. Sarcomas are a rare type of cancer with many subtypes which can affect people of all ages. The pathology report describes an analysis of tumor tissue and establishes the main diagnosis.

We sample reports from the electronic health records of the University Hospital Essen, a large research hospital in Germany. Each year, about 60,000 pathology reports are written by the pathology department. We identify suitable reports based on clinical codings (ICD-O-M). A query for the period of January 2019 until August 2021 yielded 1,644 reports on sarcoma patients. All reports were fully anonymized and we received ethics approval from our institutional review board.[2]

2.2 Simplification Protocol

To create a parallel corpus of original and simplified clinical notes, we ask medical experts how they would *intuitively explain* a given report to a patient. We take a decidedly inductive approach here: while guidelines for simplified language exist,[3] it is not clear to what extent these are suitable for clinical notes, and if annotators without formal linguistic training could operationalize them. In the terminology of Allen (2009), we use an intuitive rather than a structural simplification process.

It is commonly accepted that a good simplification depends on the target audience (Xu et al., 2015; Bingel et al., 2018; Gooding, 2022). To better define the audience and ensure a common simplification goal among editors, we developed

[2]University of Duisburg-Essen; Reference: 21-10198-BO

[3]For example Basic English (Ogden, 1930); we refer to Saggion (2017) and Štajner (2021) for more examples.

Statistic	Document-Level Original	Document-Level Simplified	Paragraph-Level Original	Paragraph-Level Simplified
Documents	851	851	3,280	3,280
Sentences	23,554	28,155	22,191	26,551
Tokens	327,466	462,994	299,365	433,027
Types	10,292	11,229	9,843	10,798
Words/doc	385	544	91	132
Words/sent	14	16	13	16
Avg. TTR	0.47	0.42	0.69	0.63
Avg. FRE	32.90	40.30	27.65	40.05
Novelty	63/84/91%		70/87/92%	
CMP	1.55		2.75	

Table 2: Statistics for a document-level and paragraph-level alignment of our dataset. TTR = type-token ratio, FRE = Flesch Reading-Ease, CMP = average compression. Novelty is the average percentage of 1/2/3-grams that appear in the simplified text but not in the original.

a *patient persona*. A persona is a rich description of a prototypical user of a software system, a tool often used in human-computer interaction research (Cooper, 1999). With this persona at hand, editors were asked *"What questions would this patient have about the report?"* Additionally, we provided following simplification guidelines to further increase consistency across editors: (i) preserve the section structure of the reports, (ii) use the same tense as the original report, and (iii) do not add any interpretations that go beyond the stated facts.

We hired a team of 9 medical students in their fourth year of studies. A senior pathologist provided guidance on clinical questions during regular meetings and through email. All reports were simplified by one editor at the document-level using a plain text editor with grammar and spellchecking functionality. We implemented several quality gates for consistency and medical correctness of simplifications. First, we used an initial trial period of 10 reports to refine the guidelines and to allow editors to get familiar with the task. Second, we held monthly meetings to discuss simplification challenges and examples. A chat platform was setup to resolve urgent questions in a timely manner. Over the span of one year, we simplified 851 reports with a total effort of 812 hours (median 50 min./report). The students were compensated for their work with 10.5€ per hour corresponding to the usual rate for student assistants in Germany.

2.3 Preprocessing

For studying the characteristics of our TS corpus, we apply minimal pre-processing. We segment each document into sentences and tokens using NLTK. To establish a reliable vocabulary size, we lemmatize the text using spaCy and replace tokens that only consist of digits, punctuation or combinations thereof with a special token.[4]

We found that most reports consist of four core sections: background, microscopy, macroscopy, and conclusion. Therefore, we also compile a section-aligned version of the dataset where we keep reports that have a one-to-one alignment for all core sections (820 out of 851 reports). This makes our dataset also amenable for paragraph-level simplification (Devaraj et al., 2021) in addition to document-level simplification.

2.4 Dataset Characteristics

To better characterize the dataset, we analyze several surface-level properties (see Table 2 for an overview). We focus on measures that were commonly reported in prior work (Xu et al., 2015; Dmitrieva and Tiedemann, 2021) including the number of sentences and tokens, the vocabulary size (types), the length of documents and sentences, and the n-gram novelty. The type-token ratio (TTR) is used as a measure of lexical diversity and the Flesch Reading-Ease (FRE, Flesch, 1948) serves as a first indication of changes in readability.[5]

Simplifications are on average 41% longer than the original text (Table 2). Through manual inspection, we identified two potential reasons. First, the original reports tend to use a brief writing style with partly incomplete sentences. These were expanded to full sentences by the editors. Second, editors often added contextual information and explanations (e.g., why an examination was done, and what the result mean to a patient). The most striking difference in length can be observed for the background section (Figure 1). We assume that simplifications are "setting the scene" in this section by simplifying terminology and explaining concepts which do not have to be repeated again in the remainder of the report.

Simplifications select and summarize content. While simplifications are longer than their original counterpart, we also note a form of summarization (see example in Table 1). In some cases, particularly technical concepts were not included in the simplification, presumably because there is no simple explanation or because an explanation

[4] `nltk.org` and `spacy.io`

[5] We use constants adapted to German text (Amstad, 1978). Implementation in `github.com/textstat/textstat`.

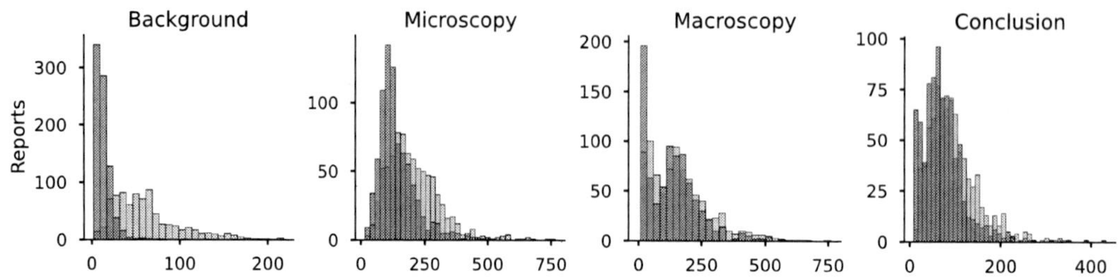

Figure 1: Comparing section length in the number of tokens for the Original and Simplified text. We observe largest expansion in the Background section. Simplifications for other sections follow the original length more closely.

would not help a user to better understand the report. This is in line with prior work which argues that document-level TS also requires summarization (Zhong et al., 2020; Aumiller and Gertz, 2022).

Simplifications have a different and more constrained vocabulary. While the simplified corpus is substantially larger in the number of tokens, the vocabulary size has only slightly increased. This is reflected in the lexical diversity measure (TTR: 0.47→0.42, Table 2). A decrease in TTR indicates that simplifications use a more constrained vocabulary which might translate to better readability. Furthermore, we observe a high average rate of unigram novelty (around 63%), which signals that large parts of the vocabulary are not shared.

Simplifications have a slightly higher readability. We observe a small increase in the readability measure (FRE: 32.9→40.3, Table 2). However, the overall readability is low according to this measure. By means of comparison, Aumiller and Gertz (2022) reported FRE values of 40 for the original and 67 for the simplified parts of a document-level TS dataset collected from German Wikipedia. There are inherent limitations with readability measures like FRE, so this finding has to be interpreted with care (Tanprasert and Kauchak, 2021).

3 Simplification Baselines

We next establish a first baseline for pathology report simplification using paragraph-level sequence-to-sequence methods (Devaraj et al., 2021).

3.1 Modeling Considerations

As discussed in Section 2.4, our dataset features multiple simplification operations including lexical simplification, paraphrasing, summarization and explanation generation. Therefore, we focus on monolingual neural machine translation models which can learn these operations simultaneously (Nisioi et al., 2017). Prior work on medical text investigated lexical simplification (Abrahamsson et al., 2014; Kloehn et al., 2018) or hybrid systems that combine pre-trained translation models with domain-specific phrase tables (Shardlow and Nawaz, 2019). With our parallel dataset, fine-tuning large general-purpose language models becomes a realistic option (Rothe et al., 2020).

Inspired by Devaraj et al. (2021), we train a paragraph-level simplification model. Compared with sentence-level methods, a paragraph-level model has the benefit that we do not need sentence alignments (Štajner et al., 2018) and that we can capture simplification phenomena like syntactic simplification and summarization (Alva-Manchego et al., 2019b). Our dataset has a natural paragraph-level alignment in the form of four core sections, so we consider this a suitable first baseline.

Methods. We experiment with four instantiations of paragraph-level methods. (1) **Identity**: A simple baseline which outputs the original text as simplification. (2) **Bert2Bert**: A transformer-based encoder-decoder where both parts are initialized with BERT (Devlin et al., 2019; Rothe et al., 2020). (3) **Bert2Share**: Same as Bert2Bert, but weights of the encoder and decoder are shared. (4) **mBART**: A sequence-to-sequence transformer, pre-trained on a sentence reconstruction objective (Liu et al., 2020). We include hyperparameters and replication details in Appendix A.

Evaluation. We report the standard TS metrics SARI (Xu et al., 2016), BLEU (Papineni et al., 2002) and ROUGE F_1 (Lin, 2004) for unigram (R-1) and bigram (R-2) matches, and the longest common subsequence between the reference and system output (R-L). To calculate SARI and BLEU, we use the implementation in EASSE (Alva-Manchego et al., 2019a) with default settings. For ROUGE,

Model	R-1	R-2	R-L	BLEU	SARI	Len.	Nov.
Identity	29.6	14.3	28.6	10.8	11.2	92	0%
Bert2Bert	26.5	8.3	25.0	7.3	41.4	103	79%
Bert2Share	28.3	9.5	26.6	8.2	42.7	102	78%
mBART	**35.2**	**15.3**	**33.4**	**14.2**	**46.2**	129	65%

Table 3: Automatic simplification results on paragraph-aligned data. The identity baseline simply returns the input as simplification. For the reference simplification, the average length (Len.) is 132 tokens and the average unigram novelty (Nov.) is 70% (cf. Table 2).

	Identity			**mBART**		
Section	BLEU	SARI	Len.	BLEU	SARI	Len.
Background	0.1	6.2	15	6.5	47.9	86
Macroscopy	17.2	12.5	136	18.0	48.2	131
Microscopy	8.7	10.7	146	13.0	44.3	213
Conclusion	13.9	10.5	72	13.6	43.6	88
Micro Avg.	10.8	11.2	92	14.2	46.2	129

Table 4: Evaluation by report section. Micro averaged metrics over all sections are reproduced from Table 3.

we use the rouge-score package with stemming disabled. We randomly split reports into training/validation/test sets with an 80/10/10 ratio.

3.2 Results and Discussion

Quantitative Results. According to automatic metrics, the generated simplifications have a substantially higher simplicity (SARI) but only slightly higher adequacy (ROUGE and BLEU) than an identity baseline (Table 3). mBART provides best results with an average simplification length and novelty close to the reference (129 vs. 132 tokens, and 65% vs. 70% novelty, Table 3). While not directly comparable, metrics are in a similar range as the paragraph-level simplification results on English medical abstracts by Devaraj et al. (2021).

For a better intuition of where the models can be improved, we report metrics by section type in Table 4. We see that the background section is most difficult to simplify. The low BLEU score of the identity baseline (0.1 in Table 4) indicates that there is little overlap between the original and simplified vocabulary. We hypothesize that simplifications for the background section include explanations and contextual domain knowledge which are difficult to generate with sequence-to-sequence methods (Srikanth and Li, 2021).

Qualitative Observations. By manual inspection, we found that system outputs are mostly fluent, grammatical and subjectively easier to read (Table 1). Furthermore, we observe that models generate elaborations and perform a certain degree of content selection. We also found factual errors in the automatically generated simplifications. In the example in Table 5, a clinical result was reported as positive in the original report but negative in the generated simplification (STAT6 positive vs. negative). The subsequently generated sentence (*"This combination of tumor markers is suggestive of GIST"*) is a clinically conceivable statement, but in the context of this report wrong. We anticipate that factual correctness will be of high importance for any practical deployment of a TS system for clinical notes and consider the evaluation of factual correctness as a significant avenue for future work on this dataset (Devaraj et al., 2022).

4 Conclusion and Future Work

We present ongoing work towards a dataset of professionally simplified clinical notes. Currently, the corpus consists of 851 parallel documents totaling close to 790k tokens. Quantitative and qualitative analyses show potential challenges for paragraph-level and document-level TS research. Despite a moderately sized training set, fine-tuning general language models led to promising results.

In future work, we will increase the size of the dataset and conduct a formal analysis of the simplification operations in the data to better understand the challenges for TS on clinical notes. Human evaluations with a focus on factual correctness, as well as user studies with end-users such as patients and patient advocacy groups are also envisioned.

Acknowledgements

We thank Celina Bandowski, Theresa Bernsmann, Monika Coers, Lisa Gödde, Hannah Göke, Lisa Meißner, Ral Merjanah, Justin Roschlak and Chiara Wedekind for writing the simplifications. We also thank Andrea Tonk for helping to translate the example report into English.

References

Emil Abrahamsson, Timothy Forni, Maria Skeppstedt, and Maria Kvist. 2014. Medical text simplification using synonym replacement: Adapting assessment of word difficulty to a compounding language. In *Proceedings of the 3rd Workshop on Predicting and Improving Text Readability for Target Reader Populations (PITR)*, pages 57–65.

David Allen. 2009. A study of the role of relative clauses in the simplification of news texts for learners of English. *System*, 37(4):585–599.

Fernando Alva-Manchego, Louis Martin, Carolina Scarton, and Lucia Specia. 2019a. EASSE: Easier automatic sentence simplification evaluation. In *Proceedings of the 2019 Conference on Empirical Methods in Natural Language Processing and the 9th International Joint Conference on Natural Language Processing (EMNLP-IJCNLP)*, pages 49–54.

Fernando Alva-Manchego, Carolina Scarton, and Lucia Specia. 2019b. Cross-sentence transformations in text simplification. In *Proceedings of the 2019 Workshop on Widening NLP*, pages 181–184.

Fernando Alva-Manchego, Carolina Scarton, and Lucia Specia. 2020. Data-driven sentence simplification: Survey and benchmark. *Computational Linguistics*, 46(1):135–187.

Toni Amstad. 1978. *Wie verständlich sind unsere Zeitungen?* Ph.D. thesis.

Dennis Aumiller and Michael Gertz. 2022. Klexikon: A german dataset for joint summarization and simplification. In *Proceedings of the 13th Language Resources and Evaluation Conference (LREC)*, pages 2693–2701.

Joachim Bingel, Gustavo H. Paetzold, and Anders Søgaard. 2018. Lexi: A tool for adaptive, personalized text simplification. In *Proceedings of the 27th International Conference on Computational Linguistics (COLING)*, pages 245–258.

Anja Bittner, Johannes Bittner, and Ansgar Jonietz. 2015. *"Was hab' ich?" Makes Medical Specialist Language Understandable for Patients*, pages 331–338. Springer International Publishing.

Yixin Cao, Ruihao Shui, Liangming Pan, Min-Yen Kan, Zhiyuan Liu, and Tat-Seng Chua. 2020. Expertise style transfer: A new task towards better communication between experts and laymen. In *Proceedings of the 58th Annual Meeting of the Association for Computational Linguistics (ACL)*, pages 1061–1071.

Alan Cooper. 1999. The inmates are running the asylum. In *Software-Ergonomie '99*, volume 53 of *Berichte des German Chapter of the ACM*.

Tom Delbanco, Jan Walker, Sigall K. Bell, Jonathan D. Darer, Joann G. Elmore, Nadine Farag, Henry J. Feldman, Roanne Mejilla, Long Ngo, James D. Ralston, Stephen E. Ross, Neha Trivedi, Elisabeth Vodicka, and Suzanne G. Leveille. 2012. Inviting patients to read their doctors' notes: A quasi-experimental study and a look ahead. *Annals of internal medicine*, 157(7):461–470.

Ashwin Devaraj, Iain J. Marshall, Byron C. Wallace, and Junyi Jessy Li. 2021. Paragraph-level simplification of medical texts. In *Proceedings of the 2021 Conference of the North American Chapter of the Association for Computational Linguistics: Human Language Technologies (NAACL)*, pages 4972–4984.

Ashwin Devaraj, William Sheffield, Byron Wallace, and Junyi Jessy Li. 2022. Evaluating factuality in text simplification. In *Proceedings of the 60th Annual Meeting of the Association for Computational Linguistics (ACL)*, pages 7331–7345.

Jacob Devlin, Ming-Wei Chang, Kenton Lee, and Kristina Toutanova. 2019. BERT: Pre-training of deep bidirectional transformers for language understanding. In *Proceedings of the 2019 Conference of the North American Chapter of the Association for Computational Linguistics: Human Language Technologies (NAACL)*, pages 4171–4186.

Anna Dmitrieva and Jörg Tiedemann. 2021. Creating an aligned Russian text simplification dataset from language learner data. In *Proceedings of the 8th Workshop on Balto-Slavic Natural Language Processing*, pages 73–79.

Rudolph Flesch. 1948. A new readability yardstick. *Journal of applied psychology*, 32(3):221.

Sian Gooding. 2022. On the ethical considerations of text simplification. In *Ninth Workshop on Speech and Language Processing for Assistive Technologies (SLPAT)*, pages 50–57.

Natalia Grabar and Rémi Cardon. 2018. CLEAR – simple corpus for medical French. In *Proceedings of the 1st Workshop on Automatic Text Adaptation (ATA)*, pages 3–9.

Chao Jiang, Mounica Maddela, Wuwei Lan, Yang Zhong, and Wei Xu. 2020. Neural CRF model for sentence alignment in text simplification. In *Proceedings of the 58th Annual Meeting of the Association for Computational Linguistics (ACL)*, pages 7943–7960.

Diederik P. Kingma and Jimmy Lei Ba. 2015. Adam: A method for stochastic optimization. In *Proceedings of the 3rd International Conference on Learning Representations (ICLR)*.

Nicholas Kloehn, Gondy Leroy, David Kauchak, Yang Gu, Sonia Colina, Nicole P. Yuan, and Debra Revere. 2018. Improving consumer understanding of medical text: Development and validation of a new SubSimplify algorithm to automatically generate term explanations in English and Spanish. *Journal of Medical Internet Research*, 20(8).

Chin-Yew Lin. 2004. ROUGE: A package for automatic evaluation of summaries. In *Text Summarization Branches Out*, pages 74–81.

Yinhan Liu, Jiatao Gu, Naman Goyal, Xian Li, Sergey Edunov, Marjan Ghazvininejad, Mike Lewis, and Luke Zettlemoyer. 2020. Multilingual denoising pretraining for neural machine translation. *Transactions of the Association for Computational Linguistics*, 8:726–742.

Ilya Loshchilov and Frank Hutter. 2019. Decoupled weight decay regularization. In *Proceedings of the 7th International Conference on Learning Representations (ICLR)*.

Sergiu Nisioi, Sanja Štajner, Simone Paolo Ponzetto, and Liviu P. Dinu. 2017. Exploring neural text simplification models. In *Proceedings of the 55th Annual Meeting of the Association for Computational Linguistics (ACL)*, pages 85–91.

Charles Kay Ogden. 1930. Basic English: A general introduction with rules and grammar.

Kishore Papineni, Salim Roukos, Todd Ward, and Wei-Jing Zhu. 2002. Bleu: A method for automatic evaluation of machine translation. In *Proceedings of the 40th Annual Meeting of the Association for Computational Linguistics (ACL)*, pages 311–318.

Annette Rios, Nicolas Spring, Tannon Kew, Marek Kostrzewa, Andreas Säuberli, Mathias Müller, and Sarah Ebling. 2021. A new dataset and efficient baselines for document-level text simplification in German. In *Proceedings of the Third Workshop on New Frontiers in Summarization*, pages 152–161.

Sascha Rothe, Shashi Narayan, and Aliaksei Severyn. 2020. Leveraging pre-trained checkpoints for sequence generation tasks. *Transactions of the Association for Computational Linguistics*, 8:264–280.

Horacio Saggion. 2017. *Automatic Text Simplification*. Synthesis Lectures on Human Language Technologies. Morgan & Claypool Publishers.

Matthew Shardlow. 2014. A survey of automated text simplification. *International Journal of Advanced Computer Science and Applications (IJACSA)*, 4(1).

Matthew Shardlow and Raheel Nawaz. 2019. Neural text simplification of clinical letters with a domain specific phrase table. In *Proceedings of the 57th Annual Meeting of the Association for Computational Linguistics (ACL)*, pages 380–389.

Neha Srikanth and Junyi Jessy Li. 2021. Elaborative simplification: Content addition and explanation generation in text simplification. In *Findings of the Association for Computational Linguistics (ACL-IJCNLP)*, pages 5123–5137.

Sanja Štajner. 2021. Automatic text simplification for social good: Progress and challenges. In *Findings of the Association for Computational Linguistics (ACL-IJCNLP)*, pages 2637–2652.

Sanja Štajner, Marc Franco-Salvador, Paolo Rosso, and Simone Paolo Ponzetto. 2018. CATS: A tool for customized alignment of text simplification corpora. In *Proceedings of the Eleventh Language Resources and Evaluation Conference (LREC)*.

Kristine Sørensen, Jürgen M. Pelikan, Florian Röthlin, Kristin Ganahl, Zofia Slonska, Gerardine Doyle, James Fullam, Barbara Kondilis, Demosthenes Agrafiotis, Ellen Uiters, Maria Falcon, Monika Mensing, Kancho Tchamov, Stephan van den Broucke, and on behalf of the HLS-EU Consortium Brand, Helmut. 2015. Health literacy in europe: Comparative results of the european health literacy survey (HLS-EU). *European Journal of Public Health*, 25(6):1053–1058.

Teerapaun Tanprasert and David Kauchak. 2021. Flesch-Kincaid is not a text simplification evaluation metric. In *Proceedings of the 1st Workshop on Natural Language Generation, Evaluation, and Metrics (GEM)*, pages 1–14.

Sowmya Vajjala and Ivana Lučić. 2018. OneStopEnglish corpus: A new corpus for automatic readability assessment and text simplification. In *Proceedings of the Thirteenth Workshop on Innovative Use of NLP for Building Educational Applications*, pages 297–304.

Hoang Van, David Kauchak, and Gondy Leroy. 2020. AutoMeTS: The autocomplete for medical text simplification. In *Proceedings of the 28th International Conference on Computational Linguistics (COLING)*, pages 1424–1434.

Laurens van den Bercken, Robert-Jan Sips, and Christoph Lofi. 2019. Evaluating neural text simplification in the medical domain. In *The World Wide Web Conference (WWW)*, pages 3286–3292.

Thomas Wolf, Lysandre Debut, Victor Sanh, Julien Chaumond, Clement Delangue, Anthony Moi, Pierric Cistac, Tim Rault, Remi Louf, Morgan Funtowicz, Joe Davison, Sam Shleifer, Patrick von Platen, Clara Ma, Yacine Jernite, Julien Plu, Canwen Xu, Teven Le Scao, Sylvain Gugger, Mariama Drame, Quentin Lhoest, and Alexander M. Rush. 2020. Transformers: State-of-the-art natural language processing. In *Proceedings of the 2020 Conference on Empirical Methods in Natural Language Processing (EMNLP)*, pages 38–45.

Wei Xu, Chris Callison-Burch, and Courtney Napoles. 2015. Problems in current text simplification research: New data can help. *Transactions of the Association for Computational Linguistics*, 3:283–297.

Wei Xu, Courtney Napoles, Ellie Pavlick, Quanze Chen, and Chris Callison-Burch. 2016. Optimizing statistical machine translation for text simplification. *Transactions of the Association for Computational Linguistics*, 4:401–415.

Yang Zhong, Chao Jiang, Wei Xu, and Junyi Jessy Li. 2020. Discourse level factors for sentence deletion in text simplification. In *Proceedings of the AAAI Conference on Artificial Intelligence*, pages 9709–9716.

Zhemin Zhu, Delphine Bernhard, and Iryna Gurevych. 2010. A monolingual tree-based translation model for sentence simplification. In *Proceedings of the 23rd International Conference on Computational Linguistics (COLING)*, pages 1353–1361.

A Implementation Details

Hyperparameters. All simplification models were trained for 25 epochs using the AdamW optimizer with an initial learning rate of 3e−5 (Kingma and Ba, 2015; Loshchilov and Hutter, 2019). We use a learning rate schedule with an initial warmup period of 10% of the training steps and a linear decay afterwards. Checkpoints are taken every epoch and the checkpoint with lowest validation loss is kept. For Bert2Bert and Bert2Share, we set the batch size to 16 and for mBART to 4. During inference, we use beam search decoding with 5 beams. Generation ends when an end-of-sequence token is generated. We did not perform any manual or automatic hyperparameter tuning.

Implementation. To adapt mBART for the task of monolingual translation, we follow recommendations by Rios et al. (2021) and add a special language token for the original text and for the simplified text. We implement the models using the Transformers library (Wolf et al., 2020). Models are initialized with the bert-base-multilingual-cased and facebook/mbart-large-cc25 checkpoints.

Computation Cost. All models are trained on a single NVIDIA RTX A6000 GPU with 48GB of memory. Training duration is 2:45h for mBART, 1:30h for Bert2Bert and 1:16h for Bert2Share.

Original (German)	Translation (English)
3. Mikroskopie	3. Microscopy
Original: Mikroskopisch zeigt die Biopsie Anteile eines spindelzellig gestalteten Tumors. Dieser zeigt ein relativ monomorphes Bild mit einem hämangioperizytomartigem Gefäßmuster. Die Tumorzellen besitzen vergrößerte, leicht vesikuläre Zellkerne. Mitosefiguren sind kaum erkennbar (1/10 HPF). Das Stroma ist relativ fein und enthält einzelne Kollagenfasern. Nekrosen sieht man nicht. Ergänzend wurden immunhistochemische Untersuchungen durchgeführt. Der Tumor zeigt eine kräftige Positivität für CD34 und eine kräftige nukleäre Expression von STAT6. Die folgenden Antigene werden vom Tumor nicht exprimiert: Aktin, Caldesmon, Panzytokeratin (CKplus), Desmin, EMA, MUC4, S100, SOX10 und TLE1.	**Original:** Microscopically, the biopsy shows portions of a spindle-cell shaped tumor. The tumor has a relatively monomorphic appearance, with a hemangiopericytoma-like vascular pattern. The tumor cells have enlarged, slightly vesicular nuclei. Mitotic figures are barely visible (1/10 HPF). The stroma is relatively fine and contains single collagen fibers. Necroses are not detectable. Additionally, immunohistochemical examinations were conducted. The tumor shows strong positivity for CD34 and strong nuclear expression of STAT6. The following antigens are not expressed by the tumor: Actin, caldesmon, pancytokeratin (CKplus), desmin, EMA, MUC4, S100, SOX10, and TLE1.
Human Reference: Nachdem die Gewebeproben in schmale Schnitte weiterverarbeitet wurden, können sie nach weiterer Aufarbeitung (z.B Färbung) unter dem Mikroskop betrachtet werden. Unter dem Mikroskop erkennt Anteile eines Tumors aus spindelförmigen Zellen. Der Tumor zeigt in sich ein recht gleichartiges Bild. Die Blutgefäße wachsen in einem speziellen Muster. Man erkennt viele kleine, verzweigte Gefäße. Die Tumorzellen weisen vergrößerte, leicht blasenförmige Zellkerne auf. Zellkerne sind der Ort in einer Zelle, in der das Erbgut in Form von DNA gespeichert wird. Mitosefiguren stellen unter dem Mikroskop sichtbare Chromosomenstrukturen dar, die während der Zellteilung auftreten. Damit geben Sie Aufschluss über die Teilungsfähigkeit der Tumorzellen. Sie kommen nur vereinzelt vor. Das die Zellen umgebende Gewebe ist fein und enthält einzelne Kollagenfasern. Abgestorbene Gewebebereiche sind nicht sichtbar. Die Schnitte der Gewebeproben wurden außerdem immunhistochemisch angefärbt. Dies bedeutet, dass spezielle Stoffe genutzt wurden, welche eine Farbreaktion auslösen, sobald diese an bestimmte Strukturen an der Oberfläche und im Inneren der Tumorzellen binden. Durch diese Anfärbemethode kann die Art des Tumors weiter bestimmt werden. Es wurde CD34 und STAT6 nachgewiesen. Die Kombination aus diesen beiden Markern ist ein Kriterium für die Diagnose eines solitären fibrösen Tumors. Dies bezeichnet einen bösartigen Tumor mit Bindegewebseigenschaften. Bösartige Tumore unterscheiden sich von gutartigen vor allem in der Fähigkeit Tochtertumore ausbilden zu können und über Gewebegrenzen hinaus zu wachsen.	**Human Reference:** After being processed into narrow slices and further preprocessing (e.g. staining), the tissue samples can be viewed under the microscope. Under the microscope, parts of a tumor consisting of spindle-shaped cells can be seen. The tumor itself shows a rather homogeneous picture. The blood vessels grow in a particular pattern. Many small, branched vessels are visible. The tumor cells show enlarged, slightly vesicular nuclei. Nuclei are the place in a cell where genetic material is stored as DNA. Mitotic figures are chromosome structures that appear during cell division and are visible under the microscope. They thus provide information about the ability of the tumor cells to divide. There is only an isolated number of them. The tissue surrounding the cells is fine and contains single collagen fibers. Dead tissue areas are not visible. Moreover, the slice of the tissue samples were immunohistochemically stained. This means that special substances were used which trigger a color reaction as soon as they bind to certain structures on the surface and inner parts of tumor cells. This staining method can further determine the type of tumor. CD34 and STAT6 were detected. The combination of these two markers is a criterion for the diagnosis of a solitary fibrous tumor. This is a malignant tumor characterized by connective tissue. Malignant tumors differ from benign ones mainly in their ability to develop secondary tumors and to grow beyond tissue boundaries.
System Output (mBART): Die präparierten Gewebeproben wurden zur Aufklärung der Gewebeart und der Ausbreitung des Tumors mikroskopisch untersucht. Es wurden zusätzlich Antikörperuntersuchungen (Immunhistochemische Untersuchungen) für die weitere Bestimmung des Tumors durchgeführt. In der mikroskopischen Untersuchung zeigen sich Anteile eines Tumors aus spindelförmigen Zellen. Die Tumorzellen sehen im Vergleich zu gesunden Zellen verändert aus und weichen von der Norm ab. Es sind nur wenige Zellen im Prozess der Zellteilung zu erkennen (1 Mitosefigur/ 10HPF), was für ein langsames Wachstum des Tumors spricht. Ergänzend wurden immunhistochemische Untersuchungen durchgeführt. Hierbei werden mithilfe von Antikörpern Zellbestandteile nachgewiesen, welche in Tumoren typischerweise vorkommen und somit Informationen über die Art und Herkunft des Tumors liefern. Von den getesteten Tumormarkern (CD34, STAT6, Aktin, Caldesmon, Panzytokeratin (CKplus), Desmin, EMA, MUC4, S100, SOX10 und TLE1) sind CD34 positiv ausgefallen und STAT6 negativ ausgefallen. Diese Kombination aus Tumormarkern spricht für das Vorliegen eines Gastrointestinalen Stromatumors (GIST) oder einer Metastase eines GIST.	**System Output (mBART):** The prepared tissue samples were examined microscopically to elucidate the type of tissue and the spread of the tumor. Additionally, antibody examinations (immunohistochemical examinations) were performed to further determine the tumor. A microscopic examination revealed portions of a tumor consisting of spindle-shaped cells. The tumor cells look altered compared to healthy cells and deviate from the norm. Only a small number of cells are in the process of cell division (1 mitotic figure/ 10HPF), suggesting that the tumor grows slowly. In addition, immunohistochemical examinations were performed. In these examinations, antibodies are used to detect cellular components that are typically found in tumors and thus provide information about the type and origin of the tumor. Of the tumor markers tested (CD34, STAT6, actin, caldesmon, pancytokeratin (CKplus), desmin, EMA, MUC4, S100, SOX10 and TLE1), CD34 was positive and STAT6 was negative. This combination of tumor markers is suggestive of the presence of a gastrointestinal stromal tumor (GIST) or a metastasis of GIST.
R-1/2/L: 30.92/9.02/27.93, **BLEU:** 5.12, **SARI:** 35.94	
4. Epikritische Stellungnahme	4. Conclusion
Original: PE (proximaler Oberschenkel ventral links) mit einem solitären fibrösen Tumor (SFT), klassischer Typ. Zur Validierung des Befundes wurde ergänzend eine molekularpathologische Untersuchung (Fusionspanel) eingeleitet. Diesbezüglich folgt ein Nachbericht.	**Original:** BX (proximal thigh ventral left) with a solitary fibrous tumor (SFT), classic type. A supplementary molecular pathological examination (fusion panel) was initiated to validate the findings. There will be a follow-up report on this topic.
Human Reference: Es handelt sich um eine Probenentnahme der Oberschenkelvorderseite mit einem solitären fibrösen Tumor. Zum Nachweis dieser Diagnose wurden weitere Untersuchungen eingeleitet. Die Ergebnisse werden in einem Nachbericht geliefert.	**Human Reference:** This is a tissue sample of the thigh front with a solitary fibrous tumor. Further examinations were initiated to confirm this diagnosis. The results will be provided in a follow-up report.
System Output (mBART): Anhand der histologischen Untersuchungen wurde die Diagnose gesichert und dabei geht es um einen solitären fibrösen Tumor (SFT), klassischer Typ. Zur Validierung des Befundes wurde ergänzend eine molekularpathologische Untersuchung (Fusionspanel) eingeleitet. Diesbezüglich folgt ein Nachbericht.	**System Output (mBART):** By means of histological examinations the diagnosis was confirmed and it is about a solitary fibrous tumor (SFT), classic type. A supplementary molecular pathological examination (fusion panel) was initiated to validate the findings. There will be a follow-up report on this topic.
R-1/2/L: 40.58/11.94/34.78, **BLEU:** 5.07, **SARI:** 20.59	

Table 5: Example report (continued from Table 1).

Target-Level Sentence Simplification as Controlled Paraphrasing

Tannon Kew **Sarah Ebling**
Department of Computational Linguistics,
University of Zurich
{kew,ebling}@cl.uzh.ch

Abstract

Automatic text simplification aims to reduce the linguistic complexity of a text in order to make it easier to understand and more accessible. However, simplified texts are consumed by a diverse array of target audiences and what might be appropriately simplified for one group of readers may differ considerably for another. In this work we investigate a novel formulation of sentence simplification as paraphrasing with controlled decoding. This approach aims to alleviate the major burden of relying on large amounts of in-domain parallel training data, while at the same time allowing for modular and adaptive simplification. According to automatic metrics, our approach performs competitively against baselines that prove more difficult to adapt to the needs of different target audiences or require significant amounts of complex-simple parallel aligned data.

1 Introduction

Automatic text simplification (ATS) aims to reduce the linguistic complexity of a text while preserving its meaning in order to make it easier to understand and more accessible to a wider array of potential readers (Bingel and Søgaard, 2016; Sikka and Mago, 2020). These readers might include children or adults with low literacy levels, cognitive impairments, or a lack of specialist knowledge in certain topics, as well as non-native language learners (Štajner, 2021; Saggion, 2017). However, the notion of exactly what constitutes 'simplified' text is highly subjective and can differ considerably between different types of readers. Thus it is important to tailor solutions appropriately in order to accommodate the needs of specific target audiences.

Research on ATS, or more specifically sentence simplification (SS), has been spurred on by performance gains in neural sequence-to-sequence (seq2seq) language generation methods (Zhang and Lapata, 2017; Scarton and Specia, 2018), which aim to do away with complex hand-crafted rules (De Belder and Moens, 2010; Siddharthan and Mandya, 2014) and improve on earlier statistical approaches (Wubben et al., 2012; Xu et al., 2016). However, fully supervised seq2seq SS approaches require a large amount of sentence-aligned parallel training data (Koehn and Knowles, 2017), which remains relatively scarce and difficult to attain.

For this reason, much work has focused on certain aspects of ATS such as lexical (Glavaš and Štajner, 2015; Kriz et al., 2018) or structural simplification (Niklaus et al., 2019; Garain et al., 2019; Narayan et al., 2017; Gao et al., 2021). Others have aimed to make better use of limited parallel complex-simple training sentences by using more sample-efficient modelling techniques that aim to predict and execute in-place edit operations (Omelianchuk et al., 2021; Dong et al., 2019). Meanwhile, despite considerable similarities between SS and paraphrasing, the task of reformulating a sentence while maintaining an equivalent meaning (Bhagat and Hovy, 2013), relatively few works have aimed to exploit paraphrases to bootstrap seq2seq-based simplification (Martin et al., 2020; Maddela et al., 2021).

We investigate this last line of work and consider an alternative framing of SS as the task of *controlled* paraphrasing. We train a large-scale paraphrase model capable of producing high-quality and diverse paraphrases and combine it with future discriminators for generation (FUDGE) (Yang and Klein, 2021) to control decoding and steer the generated paraphrase towards a specific target level for text simplification. Our experiments show that this proves to be an effective approach for generating simplified sentences for different target audiences without requiring any parallel data in the form of complex-simple aligned sentence pairs. The code and model outputs from this work are made available at `https://github.com/ZurichNLP/SimpleFUDGE`.

Proceedings of the Workshop on Text Simplification, Accessibility, and Readability (TSAR-2022), pages 28 - 42
December 8, 2022 ©2022 Association for Computational Linguistics

2 Background & Motivation

Perhaps the largest hurdle for seq2seq-based simplification is the collection of appropriately aligned complex-simple parallel data required for training robust and reliable systems (Laban et al., 2021). Furthermore, as discussed by Štajner (2021), ATS systems should be developed to support a variety of target readers and would thus benefit from modular approaches that allow for easy customisation and adaption. Recently, however, large pre-trained generation models have continued to demonstrate impressive performance when finetuned on conditional language generation tasks (Raffel et al., 2020; Lewis et al., 2020). Along with this, there has been considerable work done on exploring ways to better control the outputs of large generative models in order to achieve certain communicative goals (Dathathri et al., 2020; Krause et al., 2021; Liu et al., 2021; Yang and Klein, 2021; Pascual et al., 2021). We see a clear link between these recent developments and the challenges associated with SS and set out to investigate a modular approach suitable for simplifying text for different target audiences and that relaxes the need for complex-simple parallel training data.

3 Method

Given a complex source sentence, our goal is to transform it into a simplified target sequence[1] that preserves its meaning. Under the traditional seq2seq framework, a target sequence $y = \{y_1, ..., y_T'\}$ can be generated autoregressively as a series of conditional probabilities over the vocabulary, whereby each target token y_i is conditioned on the source sentence $x = \{x_1, ..., x_T\}$ and any preceding target tokens $y_{1:i-1}$,

$$P(y) = \prod_{i=1}^{n} P(y_i|x, y_{1:i-1}). \quad (1)$$

To ensure that the generated target sequence is appropriately simplified, we employ FUDGE (Yang and Klein, 2021), which has been shown to be effective for various controlled generation tasks. FUDGE introduces a lightweight classifier $\mathcal{B}$ to control for a desired target attribute a during autoregressive generation with a model $\mathcal{G}$. In essence, it modifies the conditional probability in Equation 1 with the following Bayesian factorisation:

$$P(y_i|x, y_{1:i-1}, a) \propto P(a|y_{1:i})P(y_i|x, y_{1:i-1}). \quad (2)$$

Here, the second term is the unmodified prediction from $\mathcal{G}$ which is combined with the conditional probability of a given all possible continuations at the current timestep i according to $\mathcal{B}$. For further details on FUDGE, we refer the reader to Yang and Klein (2021).

3.1 FUDGE for Target-Level Simplification

To leverage FUDGE for target-level SS, we train a classifier for *each* target level, i.e. $\mathcal{B}_{Simp-l}$, and combine them with the same underlying generator model $\mathcal{G}$. Following Yang and Klein (2021), each classifier is trained as a binary predictor on labelled subsequences of complex (Simp-0) and simple (Simp-l) texts. Since SS often involves breaking down a long complex sentence into smaller atomic sentences (Honeyfield, 1977), we train each classifier to predict labels on subsequences pertaining to consecutive sentences within a paragraph. This ensures that the classifier's predictions do not unduly bias the generation of the end of sentence symbol '</s>' after producing sentence-final punctuation.

For the underlying generator, $\mathcal{G}$, we fine-tune BART-large on approximately 1.4 million paraphrase sentence pairs mined from the web.[2] This model has no explicit knowledge of complex vs. simple language. To ensure a fair comparison to previous work, we use the exact same training data as Martin et al. (2021) and aim to keep training hyperparameters as consistent as possible (detailed in Appendix C).

In practice, combining the predictions from $\mathcal{G}$ and $\mathcal{B}$ relies on a single weight parameter λ. For our experiments, we derive suitable values for each target-level by sweeping over possible whole number values in the range [0,10] and selecting the best according to SARI on the validation set (see Appendix D).

4 Experimental Setup

4.1 Data

We conduct our experiments on the Newsela corpus of simplified news articles.[3] In its current form, the

[1] Since an appropriate simplified formulation may consist of multiple shorter sentences we refer to it as a sequence.

[2] In theory, given BART's denoising autoencoding pre-training, it could also be possible to avoid fine-tuning altogether. However, initial experiments showed that the probability distribution of the off-the-shelf BART model is far too peaked for the classifier's predictions to have any effect.

[3] `https://newsela.com/data/`.

	# articles	# manually aligned sentences			
		Simp-1	Simp-2	Simp-3	Simp-4
train	1,862	-	-	-	-
train	35	1,341	1,245	1,042	841
test	10	365	353	309	256
valid	5	180	163	134	87

Table 1: Newsela English corpus articles and their *manually* aligned sentences from Jiang et al. (2020) for Simp-0 to Simp-*l*.

corpus contains 1,912 English news articles that have been professionally re-written according to readability guidelines for children at multiple grade levels (Xu et al., 2015). Article versions range from Simp-0 to Simp-4, with the former referring to the original, unsimplified article, suitable for upper secondary school grades, and the latter indicating the simplest versions, suitable for lower primary school grades.[4]

While Newsela provides complex-simple alignments at the document level, it must be emphasised that this alignment is *not* a requirement for our approach and thus training examples are randomly shuffled each epoch. Nevertheless, we reason that this type of alignment is beneficial since it ensures that attribute classifiers are trained on comparable examples covering the same domains. As a consequence, each classifier must learn to distinguish between complex and simple text based on relevant characteristics, such as the lexical choices and grammatical structures for a target level, rather than exploiting potentially misleading differences in topical content (Kumar et al., 2019).

For automatic evaluation purposes, however, sentence-level alignments are a must. To this end, we make use of the manually aligned test and validation splits provided by Jiang et al. (2020). Setting aside all sentence pairs from these splits ensures that no unwanted data leakage occurs. An overview of the corpus and manually aligned sentence pairs is provided in Table 1.

4.2 Baselines

We compare our approach to two recently proposed techniques for controlled SS and a naive baseline that only uses paraphrasing.

[4]In this work, we assume that article versions (0-4) are reliable indicators of level-appropriate simplifications and provide a detailed discussion on this assumption in Appendix B.

MUSS Martin et al. (2021) leveraged large-scale paraphrase data to fine-tune BART-large in combination with the ACCESS control method for simplification (Martin et al., 2020). This method relies on four control tokens which are prepended to the source sequence and used to indicate the desired length, edit distance, lexical complexity and syntactic complexity as a ratio between the source and the output sequence. At inference time, these special tokens act as 'control knobs' for the simplification. Following Martin et al. (2021), we derive optimal control values through a parameter search on the validation split (see Appendix C.4).

SUPER Following Scarton and Specia (2018), we also train a level-aware supervised baseline with a single special token indicating the target level (e.g. `<L3>` = Simp-3) prepended to each source sentence. For a fair comparison, we initialise this model from the same BART-large checkpoint as the other two models and fine-tune on the manually aligned training sentences for all Newsela levels simultaneously. This amounts to a low resource setting with a total of 4,469 training instances.

PARA In addition, we also compare to a straightforward paraphrase generated by our underlying generation model $\mathcal{G}$ with no controls or intervention.

4.3 Evaluation Metrics

Reliably evaluating SS is an open challenge (Alva-Manchego et al., 2021). However, a range of both reference-based and reference-less automatic metrics have been proposed (Martin et al., 2018). We make use of the open-source EASSE package (Alva-Manchego et al., 2019), which implements relevant metrics such as SARI, BERTScore, Flesch-Kincaid Grade Level (FKGL) and a host of quality estimation measures for more fine-grained analysis (these metrics are detailed in Appendix A).

5 Results & Discussion

Table 2 presents the results of our experiments on the Newsela corpus. According to SARI, our primary metric, SS with FUDGE outperforms both MUSS and the supervised baseline for all target levels except for Simp-4. Our simplifications tend to exhibit lower rates of compression and higher rates of sentence splitting and additions, particularly as the degree of simplification increases. This could be considered advantageous for certain target au-

Method	SARI	BERTScore	FKGL	Comp. ratio	Sent. splits	Lev. sim.	Copies	Add prop.	Del prop.
Target Level: Simp-1			7.97	1.01	1.19	0.90	0.44	0.10	0.10
PARA	36.61	81.68	9.15	0.97	1.02	**0.89**	**0.18**	**0.08**	**0.11**
MUSS	35.69	75.95	**7.75**	0.81	1.00	0.84	0.01	0.07	0.24
SUPER	32.49	88.19	9.36	**0.99**	**1.04**	0.99	0.89	0.01	0.01
$\mathcal{B}_{Simp-1}$	36.10	80.45	8.81	0.94	1.01	0.88	0.13	0.07	0.13
Target Level: Simp-2			6.41	0.98	1.42	0.82	0.23	0.17	0.20
PARA	35.01	73.53	9.12	**0.97**	1.02	0.89	**0.18**	0.08	0.11
MUSS	36.57	65.91	**7.27**	0.78	1.03	0.75	0.00	**0.15**	0.35
SUPER	31.12	78.22	8.88	0.99	1.10	0.98	0.80	0.02	0.03
$\mathcal{B}_{Simp-2}$	38.32	70.75	7.42	0.96	**1.25**	**0.84**	0.08	0.12	**0.17**
Target Level: Simp-3			4.91	0.92	1.55	0.73	0.13	0.24	0.31
PARA	30.87	65.06	9.09	0.98	1.01	0.89	**0.18**	0.08	0.11
MUSS	38.05	56.03	**5.19**	0.62	1.01	**0.68**	0.00	0.12	0.45
SUPER	37.89	66.60	6.65	**0.93**	1.34	0.90	0.48	0.06	0.13
$\mathcal{B}_{Simp-3}$	39.56	61.46	6.44	1.00	**1.45**	0.81	0.02	**0.20**	**0.20**
Target Level: Simp-4			3.40	0.85	1.79	0.65	0.09	0.30	0.43
PARA	25.61	56.21	9.41	0.98	1.01	0.89	0.18	0.08	0.11
MUSS	39.63	51.73	5.61	0.65	1.04	**0.68**	0.00	0.13	**0.44**
SUPER	43.22	55.00	5.09	**0.78**	**1.45**	0.74	0.24	0.12	0.32
$\mathcal{B}_{Simp-4}$	37.03	49.60	**4.60**	1.02	2.14	0.76	**0.00**	**0.28**	0.28

Table 2: Target-level results on the manually aligned Newsela test set (Jiang et al., 2020). For reference-based metrics (SARI, BERTScore), where higher values are better, we highlight systems according to their performance. For FKGL and reference-less quality estimation metrics we embolden the systems that perform closest to the level-specific references (provided in the intermediary rows).

diences and in settings where the loss of too much information could be detrimental for the reader. That said, it is also possible that not all additions and sentence splits are warranted. For example, degenerate repetitions or hallucinations could potentially skew these results (see tables in Appendix G for examples). Still, the positive influence of FUDGE's classifier is indeed most visible when comparing against the paraphrase baseline, which fails to generate more readable texts according to FKGL.

We also note that the superior performance of the fully supervised method for level Simp-4 is consistent with the findings from Spring et al. (2021), where a similar approach proved most effective for simplifying ordinary German to A1-level German, despite it being the target level with the least amount of parallel data in both studies. For other target levels, however, where the differences between source and target are perhaps more subtle, this supervised model has a strong tendency to simply copy the input sentence.

While the MUSS baseline produces decent simplifications according to SARI and FKGL, the lower compression ratio and a higher proportion of deleted N-grams indicate that this model also tends to severely summarise the input. This information loss causes model outputs to diverge from the ground truth references and it is thus penalised heavily by BERTScore.

FUDGE's simplification operations are performed actively during decoding by modifying the generator's prediction logits at each timestep, with each decision being informed by the currently generated prefix and its potential continuations $y_{1:i}$. Therefore, this approach does not enforce a transformation of the input text. This is an important and desirable feature for SS as oftentimes not all parts of a sentence need to be simplified (Garbacea et al., 2021). Thus, assuming a well-trained classifier $\mathcal{B}$, simplification operations should occur only when appropriate given the source sentence and the generation context.[5]

Finally, using FUDGE for SS also makes use of a single hyperparameter λ which controls the

[5] In an attempt to define 'well-trained', we demonstrate the effect of the amount of classifier training data on simplification performance in Appendix F.

contribution from the classifier. In contrast, MUSS requires setting an appropriate value for each of the four control tokens to attain a suitable simplification. These are not only difficult to determine for each target level (see Appendix E), but the way in which these tokens interact with each other is still unclear (Martin et al., 2020), making it difficult to set these values according to any underlying intuition.

6 Conclusion & Future Work

We have explored a modular and adaptable approach to SS by reframing it as controlled paraphrasing. We used FUDGE (Yang and Klein, 2021) to steer the generation of paraphrastic sequences toward different target levels. According to automatic metrics, this approach performs competitively when compared to state-of-the-art methods. In future work we aim to conduct a more detailed analysis of the model outputs in order to better understand the qualitative differences and potential shortcomings, as well as applying this method to larger textual units beyond sentences.

Limitations

In this work we aimed to generate level-appropriate sentence simplifications without the need for parallel aligned training data which is expensive to produce and difficult to come by. Due to a lack of existing work addressing simplification for specific target levels, the number of comparable approaches and relevant evaluation data sets are inherent limitations of this work. While the approach proposed by Martin et al. (2021) is not explicitly designed to generate level-specific simplifications, we searched for the most appropriate control tokens for each target level and selected the best values according to validation performance. To this end, we used the code provided by Martin et al. (2021) but note that we did not investigate potential improvements to this parameter search. Secondly, to the best of our knowledge, the Newsela English corpus constitutes the only available resource containing simplifications for readers at specific levels. Thus, this current work does not seek to assess how well this method generalises to other domains and languages.

Finally, our system evaluation relies on automatic metrics. While we have strived to report metrics that cover the degree of simplification (SARI, FKGL) and meaning preservation (BERTScore), we acknowledge that extensive human evaluation with the target audience is crucial in assessing the viability and validity of any system intended to adapt and rewrite text. On the one hand, degenerate outputs may lead to even more confusion and less understandability, while, on the other hand, erroneous additions and deletions could be dangerous in certain contexts (e.g. when applied to medical or legal domain texts). Therefore, a thorough qualitative analysis of the proposed approach is still required and planned for future work.

Acknowledgements

In addition to the anonymous reviewers, we would like to thank Martin Volk and Rico Sennrich for helpful comments on an earlier version of this paper.

References

Fernando Alva-Manchego, Louis Martin, Carolina Scarton, and Lucia Specia. 2019. EASSE: Easier automatic sentence simplification evaluation. In *Proceedings of the 2019 Conference on Empirical Methods in Natural Language Processing and the 9th International Joint Conference on Natural Language Processing (EMNLP-IJCNLP): System Demonstrations*, pages 49–54, Hong Kong, China. Association for Computational Linguistics.

Fernando Alva-Manchego, Carolina Scarton, and Lucia Specia. 2021. The (un)suitability of automatic evaluation metrics for text simplification. *Computational Linguistics*, 47(4):861–889.

Rahul Bhagat and Eduard Hovy. 2013. Squibs: What is a paraphrase? *Computational Linguistics*, 39(3):463–472.

Joachim Bingel and Anders Søgaard. 2016. Text simplification as tree labeling. In *Proceedings of the 54th Annual Meeting of the Association for Computational Linguistics (Volume 2: Short Papers)*, pages 337–343, Berlin, Germany. Association for Computational Linguistics.

Sumanth Dathathri, Andrea Madotto, Janice Lan, Jane Hung, Eric Frank, Piero Molino, Jason Yosinski, and Rosanne Liu. 2020. Plug and Play Language Models: A Simple Approach to Controlled Text Generation. *arXiv:1912.02164 [cs]*.

Jan De Belder and Marie-Francine Moens. 2010. Text simplification for children. Prroceedings of the SIGIR Workshop on Accessible Search Systems, pages 19–26. ACM; New York.

Yue Dong, Zichao Li, Mehdi Rezagholizadeh, and Jackie Chi Kit Cheung. 2019. EditNTS: An neural programmer-interpreter model for sentence simplification through explicit editing. In *Proceedings of the 57th Annual Meeting of the Association for Computational Linguistics*, pages 3393–3402, Florence, Italy. Association for Computational Linguistics.

Yanjun Gao, Ting-Hao Huang, and Rebecca J. Passonneau. 2021. ABCD: A graph framework to convert complex sentences to a covering set of simple sentences. In *Proceedings of the 59th Annual Meeting of the Association for Computational Linguistics and the 11th International Joint Conference on Natural Language Processing (Volume 1: Long Papers)*, pages 3919–3931, Online. Association for Computational Linguistics.

Avishek Garain, Arpan Basu, Rudrajit Dawn, and Sudip Kumar Naskar. 2019. Sentence Simplification using Syntactic Parse trees. In *2019 4th International Conference on Information Systems and Computer Networks (ISCON)*, pages 672–676, Mathura, India. IEEE.

Cristina Garbacea, Mengtian Guo, Samuel Carton, and Qiaozhu Mei. 2021. Explainable Prediction of Text Complexity: The Missing Preliminaries for Text Simplification. *arXiv:2007.15823 [cs]*.

Goran Glavaš and Sanja Štajner. 2015. Simplifying lexical simplification: Do we need simplified corpora? In *Proceedings of the 53rd Annual Meeting of the Association for Computational Linguistics and the 7th International Joint Conference on Natural Language Processing (Volume 2: Short Papers)*, pages 63–68, Beijing, China. Association for Computational Linguistics.

John Honeyfield. 1977. Simplification. *TESOL Quarterly*, 11(4):431–440.

Chao Jiang, Mounica Maddela, Wuwei Lan, Yang Zhong, and Wei Xu. 2020. Neural CRF model for sentence alignment in text simplification. In *Proceedings of the 58th Annual Meeting of the Association for Computational Linguistics*, pages 7943–7960, Online. Association for Computational Linguistics.

Philipp Koehn and Rebecca Knowles. 2017. Six challenges for neural machine translation. In *Proceedings of the First Workshop on Neural Machine Translation*, pages 28–39, Vancouver. Association for Computational Linguistics.

Ben Krause, Akhilesh Deepak Gotmare, Bryan McCann, Nitish Shirish Keskar, Shafiq Joty, Richard Socher, and Nazneen Fatema Rajani. 2021. GeDi: Generative discriminator guided sequence generation. In *Findings of the Association for Computational Linguistics: EMNLP 2021*, pages 4929–4952, Punta Cana, Dominican Republic. Association for Computational Linguistics.

Reno Kriz, Eleni Miltsakaki, Marianna Apidianaki, and Chris Callison-Burch. 2018. Simplification using paraphrases and context-based lexical substitution. In *Proceedings of the 2018 Conference of the North American Chapter of the Association for Computational Linguistics: Human Language Technologies, Volume 1 (Long Papers)*, pages 207–217, New Orleans, Louisiana. Association for Computational Linguistics.

Sachin Kumar, Shuly Wintner, Noah A. Smith, and Yulia Tsvetkov. 2019. Topics to avoid: Demoting latent confounds in text classification. In *Proceedings of the 2019 Conference on Empirical Methods in Natural Language Processing and the 9th International Joint Conference on Natural Language Processing (EMNLP-IJCNLP)*, pages 4153–4163, Hong Kong, China. Association for Computational Linguistics.

Philippe Laban, Tobias Schnabel, Paul Bennett, and Marti A. Hearst. 2021. Keep it simple: Unsupervised simplification of multi-paragraph text. In *Proceedings of the 59th Annual Meeting of the Association for Computational Linguistics and the 11th International Joint Conference on Natural Language Processing (Volume 1: Long Papers)*, pages 6365–6378, Online. Association for Computational Linguistics.

Mike Lewis, Yinhan Liu, Naman Goyal, Marjan Ghazvininejad, Abdelrahman Mohamed, Omer Levy, Veselin Stoyanov, and Luke Zettlemoyer. 2020. BART: Denoising sequence-to-sequence pre-training for natural language generation, translation, and comprehension. In *Proceedings of the 58th Annual Meeting of the Association for Computational Linguistics*, pages 7871–7880, Online. Association for Computational Linguistics.

Alisa Liu, Maarten Sap, Ximing Lu, Swabha Swayamdipta, Chandra Bhagavatula, Noah A. Smith, and Yejin Choi. 2021. DExperts: Decoding-time controlled text generation with experts and anti-experts. In *Proceedings of the 59th Annual Meeting of the Association for Computational Linguistics and the 11th International Joint Conference on Natural Language Processing (Volume 1: Long Papers)*, pages 6691–6706, Online. Association for Computational Linguistics.

Mounica Maddela, Fernando Alva-Manchego, and Wei Xu. 2021. Controllable text simplification with explicit paraphrasing. In *Proceedings of the 2021 Conference of the North American Chapter of the Association for Computational Linguistics: Human Language Technologies*, pages 3536–3553, Online. Association for Computational Linguistics.

Louis Martin, Éric de la Clergerie, Benoît Sagot, and Antoine Bordes. 2020. Controllable sentence simplification. In *Proceedings of the 12th Language Resources and Evaluation Conference*, pages 4689–4698, Marseille, France. European Language Resources Association.

Louis Martin, Angela Fan, Éric de la Clergerie, Antoine Bordes, and Benoît Sagot. 2021. MUSS: Multilingual Unsupervised Sentence Simplification by Mining Paraphrases. *arXiv:2005.00352 [cs]*.

Louis Martin, Samuel Humeau, Pierre-Emmanuel Mazaré, Éric de La Clergerie, Antoine Bordes, and Benoît Sagot. 2018. Reference-less quality estimation of text simplification systems. In *Proceedings of the 1st Workshop on Automatic Text Adaptation (ATA)*, pages 29–38, Tilburg, the Netherlands. Association for Computational Linguistics.

Shashi Narayan, Claire Gardent, Shay B. Cohen, and Anastasia Shimorina. 2017. Split and rephrase. In *Proceedings of the 2017 Conference on Empirical Methods in Natural Language Processing*, pages 606–616, Copenhagen, Denmark. Association for Computational Linguistics.

Christina Niklaus, Matthias Cetto, André Freitas, and Siegfried Handschuh. 2019. DisSim: A discourse-aware syntactic text simplification framework for English and German. In *Proceedings of the 12th International Conference on Natural Language Generation*, pages 504–507, Tokyo, Japan. Association for Computational Linguistics.

Kostiantyn Omelianchuk, Vipul Raheja, and Oleksandr Skurzhanskyi. 2021. Text Simplification by Tagging. In *Proceedings of the 16th Workshop on Innovative Use of NLP for Building Educational Applications*, pages 11–25, Online. Association for Computational Linguistics.

Myle Ott, Sergey Edunov, Alexei Baevski, Angela Fan, Sam Gross, Nathan Ng, David Grangier, and Michael Auli. 2019. fairseq: A fast, extensible toolkit for sequence modeling. In *Proceedings of the 2019 Conference of the North American Chapter of the Association for Computational Linguistics (Demonstrations)*, pages 48–53, Minneapolis, Minnesota. Association for Computational Linguistics.

Damian Pascual, Beni Egressy, Clara Meister, Ryan Cotterell, and Roger Wattenhofer. 2021. A plug-and-play method for controlled text generation. In *Findings of the Association for Computational Linguistics: EMNLP 2021*, pages 3973–3997, Punta Cana, Dominican Republic. Association for Computational Linguistics.

Jeffrey Pennington, Richard Socher, and Christopher Manning. 2014. Glove: Global Vectors for Word Representation. In *Proceedings of the 2014 Conference on Empirical Methods in Natural Language Processing (EMNLP)*, pages 1532–1543, Doha, Qatar. Association for Computational Linguistics.

Colin Raffel, Noam Shazeer, Adam Roberts, Katherine Lee, Sharan Narang, Michael Matena, Yanqi Zhou, Wei Li, and Peter J. Liu. 2020. Exploring the Limits of Transfer Learning with a Unified Text-to-Text Transformer. *arXiv:1910.10683 [cs, stat]*.

Horacio Saggion. 2017. *Automatic Text Simplification*. Synthesis Lectures on Human Language Technologies. Morgan & Claypool.

Carolina Scarton and Lucia Specia. 2018. Learning simplifications for specific target audiences. In *Proceedings of the 56th Annual Meeting of the Association for Computational Linguistics (Volume 2: Short Papers)*, pages 712–718, Melbourne, Australia. Association for Computational Linguistics.

Thomas Scialom, Louis Martin, Jacopo Staiano, Éric Villemonte de la Clergerie, and Benoît Sagot. 2021. Rethinking Automatic Evaluation in Sentence Simplification. *arXiv:2104.07560 [cs]*.

Advaith Siddharthan and Angrosh Mandya. 2014. Hybrid text simplification using synchronous dependency grammars with hand-written and automatically harvested rules. In *Proceedings of the 14th Conference of the European Chapter of the Association for Computational Linguistics*, pages 722–731, Gothenburg, Sweden. Association for Computational Linguistics.

Punardeep Sikka and Vijay Mago. 2020. A Survey on Text Simplification. *arXiv:2008.08612 [cs]*.

Nicolas Spring, Annette Rios, and Sarah Ebling. 2021. Exploring German multi-level text simplification. In *Proceedings of the International Conference on Recent Advances in Natural Language Processing (RANLP 2021)*, pages 1339–1349, Held Online. INCOMA Ltd.

Sanja Štajner. 2021. Automatic Text Simplification for Social Good: Progress and Challenges. In *Findings of the Association for Computational Linguistics: ACL-IJCNLP 2021*, pages 2637–2652, Online. Association for Computational Linguistics.

Teerapaun Tanprasert and David Kauchak. 2021. Flesch-kincaid is not a text simplification evaluation metric. In *Proceedings of the 1st Workshop on Natural Language Generation, Evaluation, and Metrics (GEM 2021)*, pages 1–14, Online. Association for Computational Linguistics.

Sowmya Vajjala and Ivana Lučić. 2018. OneStopEnglish corpus: A new corpus for automatic readability assessment and text simplification. In *Proceedings of the Thirteenth Workshop on Innovative Use of NLP for Building Educational Applications*, pages 297–304, New Orleans, Louisiana. Association for Computational Linguistics.

Thomas Wolf, Lysandre Debut, Victor Sanh, Julien Chaumond, Clement Delangue, Anthony Moi, Pierric Cistac, Tim Rault, Remi Louf, Morgan Funtowicz, Joe Davison, Sam Shleifer, Patrick von Platen, Clara Ma, Yacine Jernite, Julien Plu, Canwen Xu, Teven Le Scao, Sylvain Gugger, Mariama Drame, Quentin Lhoest, and Alexander Rush. 2020. Transformers: State-of-the-art natural language processing. In *Proceedings of the 2020 Conference on Empirical Methods in Natural Language Processing: System Demonstrations*, pages 38–45, Online. Association for Computational Linguistics.

Sander Wubben, Antal van den Bosch, and Emiel Krahmer. 2012. Sentence simplification by monolingual machine translation. In *Proceedings of the 50th Annual Meeting of the Association for Computational Linguistics (Volume 1: Long Papers)*, pages 1015–1024, Jeju Island, Korea. Association for Computational Linguistics.

Wei Xu, Chris Callison-Burch, and Courtney Napoles. 2015. Problems in current text simplification research: New data can help. *Transactions of the Association for Computational Linguistics*, 3:283–297.

Wei Xu, Courtney Napoles, Ellie Pavlick, Quanze Chen, and Chris Callison-Burch. 2016. Optimizing statistical machine translation for text simplification. *Transactions of the Association for Computational Linguistics*, 4:401–415.

Kevin Yang and Dan Klein. 2021. FUDGE: Controlled text generation with future discriminators. In *Proceedings of the 2021 Conference of the North American Chapter of the Association for Computational Linguistics: Human Language Technologies*, pages 3511–3535, Online. Association for Computational Linguistics.

Xingxing Zhang and Mirella Lapata. 2017. Sentence simplification with deep reinforcement learning. In *Proceedings of the 2017 Conference on Empirical Methods in Natural Language Processing*, pages 584–594, Copenhagen, Denmark. Association for Computational Linguistics.

A Evaluation Metrics for Sentence Simplification

Simplicity SARI is intended to measure simplicity by considering N-gram overlap between the model output, source sentence and one or more reference sentences. It rewards model outputs that involve edit operations, such as deletions, additions and copies, which correspond with the provided references.

Fluency and meaning preservation BERTScore uses BERT's contextualised representations to compute the similarity between tokens in the model output and one or more references. It has been shown to correlate better than BLEU for assessing meaning preservation and fluency in SS (Scialom et al., 2021).

Readability Flesch-Kincaid Grade Level (FKGL) is often used as a proxy for estimating text simplicity without a reference. Originally developed for grading technical materials for military personnel, it considers surface-level statistics such as word and sentence length to provide a single score. However, these scores should be interpreted carefully as it has recently been shown that this metric can be mislead by degenerate and disfluent outputs (Tanprasert and Kauchak, 2021).

Quality Estimation Measures For a more fine-grained analysis of model outputs, we also report quality estimation measures which are computed between the source sentence and the model's output. These include the compression ratio, Levenshtein similarity, average number of sentence splits performed, exact copies between source and target, and the proportion of added and deleted N-grams.

B Target Levels in Newsela

Newsela contains articles written for different graded reading levels (2-12) corresponding to primary and secondary school grades in the United States. These grades can be considered true indicators of an simplicity. However, assessing target-level simplification for all available grades is challenging due to the sheer number of them and the fact that not all of them are equally well represented in the corpus. For example, there are 1,853 articles for grade 12 but only 20 articles for grade 10 and 2 for grade 11.

To simplify our target-level analysis, we follow Xu et al. (2015) and assume that Newsela's article version IDs (0-4) are reliable indicators of a text's simplicity and thus adopt these as our target levels (Simp-l). Figure 1 shows how the graded reading levels are distributed over our target levels. As can be seen, the article versions do not provide a clear cut aggregation of all grades since there is a limited degree of overlap, particularly between the lower Simp-l levels. Nevertheless, a rough aggregation is discernible; Simp-4 covers grades 2 to 4, Simp-3 consists predominately of grade 5, Simp-2 contains grades 6 and 7, and Simp-1 covers grades 7 and 8. Finally, Simp-0 (the complex sources articles in our study) is mostly restricted to grade 10 and up.

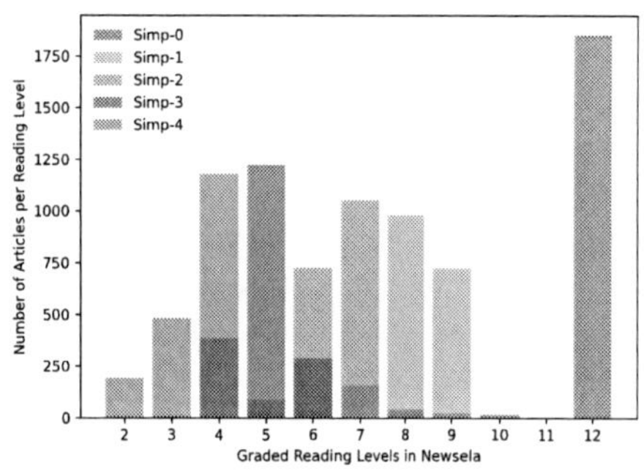

Figure 1: The distribution of graded reading levels among article versions in Newsela. For simplicity, we use as article versions our target levels for simplification.

C Details on Model Training and Inference

C.1 Resources

Model training and inference experiments were performed on NVIDIA GeForce GTX TITAN X GPUs with 12GB of memory.

C.2 Training Generation Models

For our underlying generator model $\mathcal{G}$ and the level-aware supervised baseline, we fine-tuned BART-large using Hugging Face's Transformers library[6] (Wolf et al., 2020). Training parameters used for $\mathcal{G}$ aim to replicate the settings used by Martin et al. (2021) who trained their models using Fairseq[7] (Ott et al., 2019). For the level-aware supervised baseline, we aimed to replicate the settings used by Spring et al. (2021) who trained their models with Sockeye[8]. Note, in contrast to the paraphrase model, the effective batch size and maximum training steps for this model are considerably smaller to account for the differences in the size of the relevant training data (1.4M paraphrase sentence pairs vs. 4k aligned simplifications).

Paraphrase Model $\mathcal{G}$	
hyperparameter	value
max src length	1024
max tgt length	256
eff. batch size	64
learning rate	3e-05
weight decay	0.01
optim	adamw_hf
adam betas	0.9 - 0.999
adam epsilon	1e-8
lr scheduler	polynomial
warmup steps	500
label smoothing	0.1
max steps	20000
num beams for pred	4
optim metric	loss
Level-Aware Supervised Model	
hyperparameter	value
max src length	256
max tgt length	128
eff. batch size	16
learning rate	3e-05
weight decay	0.01
optim	adamw_hf
adam betas	0.9 - 0.999
adam epsilon	1e-8
lr scheduler	polynomial
warmup steps	500
label smoothing	0.1
max steps	5000
num beams for pred	4
optim metric	rougel

Table 3: Hyperparameters for training generation models.

C.3 Training FUDGE Classifiers

Our FUDGE classifiers $\mathcal{B}_{simp-l}$ are unidirectional three-layer LSTM-based RNNs with hidden layer dimensionality of 512. These settings differ slightly from the original implementation by Yang and Klein (2021), who used smaller classifiers for their tasks. The embedding matrix is constructed to cover the vocabulary of the underly-

[6] https://github.com/huggingface/transformers.

[7] https://github.com/facebookresearch/fairseq.

[8] https://github.com/awslabs/sockeye.

ing generator model (i.e. the tokenizer is shared between $\mathcal{G}$ and $\mathcal{B}$) and token embeddings are initialised using 300d pre-trained GloVe embeddings (`glove-wiki-gigaword-300`) (Pennington et al., 2014). For certain subwords and rare words that are OOV in GloVe, we initialise their embeddings randomly.

C.4 Inference

For all models except MUSS we run inference with beam search (k=5). A manual inspection of the model outputs revealed that our underlying paraphraser $\mathcal{G}$ showed a tendency to produce repetitions in the target sequence. To counter this, we set the repetition penalty equal to 1.2 when performing inference with $\mathcal{G}$. All other inference hyperparameters use the default values set in Hugging Face. For each source sentence in the test set, we generate the top five model hypotheses according to the model and select the first non-empty string as the final model output.

For MUSS, we kept inference settings the same as the default set by Martin et al. (2021). The only differences are the control token values used for performing inference on each of the Newsela simplification levels, which we derive via a parameter sweep on 50 items from the respective development sets. Table 4 shows the relevant values used. Note that these values are rounded up to the nearest 0.05 inside the model.

	Comp. Ratio	Levenshtein Sim.	Word Rank Ratio	Dep. Tree Depth Ratio
Simp-1	0.30	0.99	0.54	1.45
Simp-2	0.75	0.82	0.94	0.22
Simp-3	0.52	0.85	0.45	0.62
Simp-4	0.47	0.79	0.43	0.42

Table 4: Values used for target-level inference on the Newsela English corpus with MUSS.

D Parameter Sweep for FUDGE

FUDGE has two hyperparameters which need to be set at inference time. The first is a weight λ that controls the strength of $\mathcal{B}$'s contribution, while the second aims to keep the cost associated with classifying all possible continuations at each decoding timestep down by only considering the best k predictions at each step (i.e. the most probable k tokens according to the model). Initial experiments showed that λ is indeed useful for controlling the degree of simplification and finding a suitable λ is essential. Meanwhile, using different pre-selection k values (e.g. [50, 200]) had almost no effect on the resulting generation sequence when using argmax decoding techniques such as beam search. Therefore, we followed the recommendation by Yang and Klein (2021) and fixed the pre-selection k=200.

To get the best target-level simplifications, we searched for the optimum λ value for each combination of Newsela simplification levels and each target-level FUDGE on 50 sentences from the manually aligned validation set (Jiang et al., 2020). Figure 2 shows the resulting SARI scores. For our experiments, we selected the best scoring λ values for each simplification level and its corresponding FUDGE (i.e. plots along the diagonal). For cases where more than one possible λ delivered good results, we selected the lowest value > 0 (marked with a vertical dotted line).

It is clear from Figure 2 that cross-matching target simplification levels with FUDGEs trained on a different target level would also yield good, and in some cases even better, results according to SARI (e.g. target-level Simp-2 with $\mathcal{B}_{Simp-3}$). We hypothesise that this is likely due to it being easier for the classifier to correctly distinguish between the positive (simple) and negative (complex) classes when the stylistic differences between simplification levels are larger. Indeed, ROC-AUC scores for each target-level classifier on the respective test sets increase from 0.67 to 0.96 going from Simp-1 to Simp-4, indicating that FUDGEs trained on higher simplification levels are better at distinguishing between the classes.

E ACCESS Attributes on Newsela Corpus

While parameter sweeps are helpful, deciding on optimal attribute values for target-level simplification with ACCESS is non-trivial, especially if limited validation data is on hand. Furthermore, control values that might be suitable for one input sentence, may not be suitable for another input sentence. For example, it may not be possible to reduce an already short input sentence to half of its original length. To examine potentially suitable control values, we computed the ratio scores on source-target pairs from the manually aligned training split from Jiang et al. (2020) for all four simplification levels of the Newsela English corpus. Figure 3 shows that for most attributes the

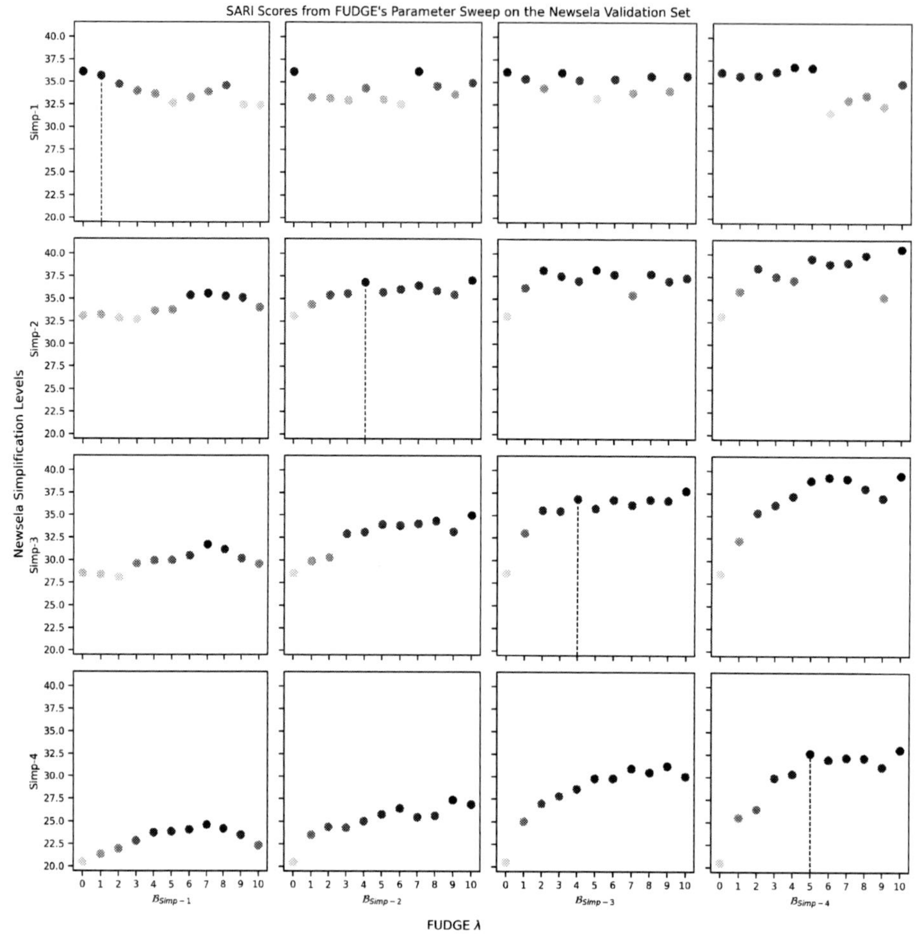

Figure 2: SARI scores from parameter sweep over different λ values for FUDGE at inference time.

largest density is on a value of 1.0, indicating no difference between the source and target. For many attribute values, the distributions are also relatively wide and flat indicating that there could be many potentially valid values, especially for the higher simplification levels (e.g. Simp-2 - Simp-4).

F Ablation Experiment

Unlike a fully-supervised seq2seq approach, FUDGE for SS does not require parallel complex-simple sentence pairs for training. Instead, it relies on contrastive instances to train its target-level classifiers. Such data is significantly easier to collect from comparable corpus resources in many languages, e.g. language learning materials (Vajjala and Lučić, 2018) or news articles produced specifically for certain target groups.[9]

However, an open question remains as to how much data is required to train a suitable classifier. While this may depend heavily on the target-level simplified text both in topical and stylistic features, we examined this question for Newsela's Simp-4 target level. In contrast to our main experiments, here, we fix the weighted contribution from the classifier as $\lambda = 1.0$ (i.e. the minimum amount of influence). Figure 4 depicts the relationship between the amount of contrastive data used to train $\mathcal{B}_{Simp-4}$ and the primary metrics for simplification and quality estimation.

On these plots, a strong correlation is visible between increasing the amount of contrastive data

[9] For example, Ligetil from the Danish Broadcasting Corporation (https://www.dr.dk/ligetil/) and Japan's News Web Easy (https://www3.nhk.or.jp/news/easy/).

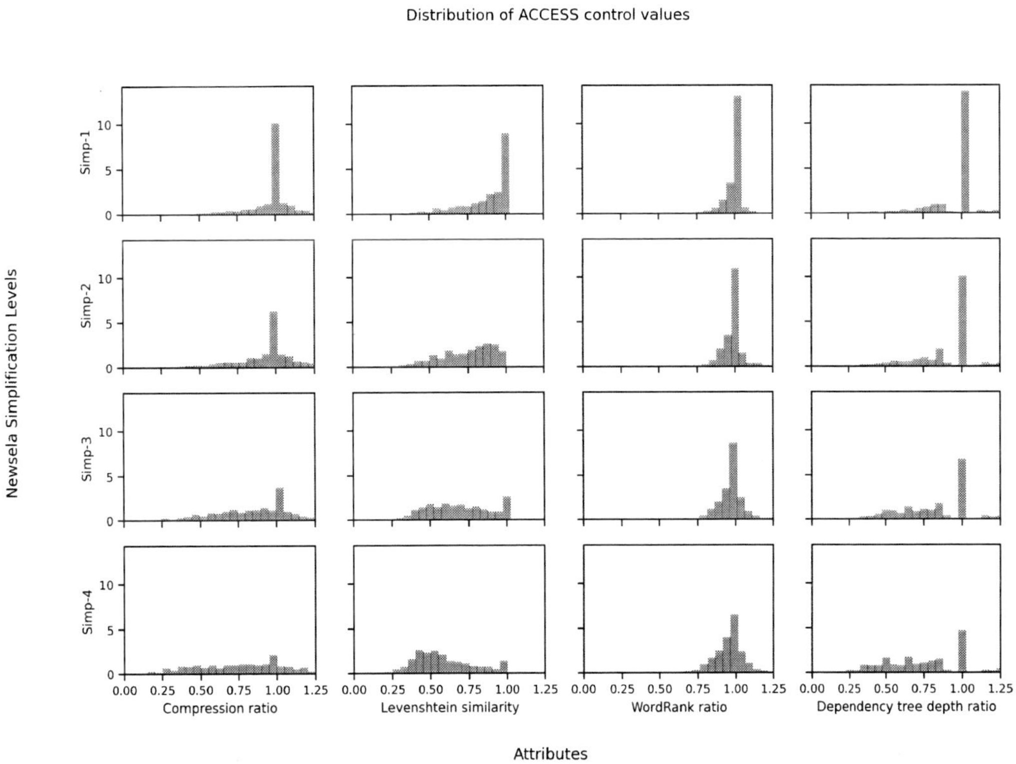

Figure 3: Density of attribute values for the four control tokens used in the ACCESS simplification method (Martin et al., 2020) and employed by MUSS (Martin et al., 2021).

and the degree to which the model simplifies the input sentences. Clearly, while more data is helpful, even small amounts of contrastive data (e.g. 500-1000 examples) can already be effective in steering the generations towards the target attribute.

G Model Output Examples

On closer inspection of the model outputs, we observed some undesirable trends among all model outputs. Firstly, the supervised approach (SUPER) tends to keep edit operations to a minimum, resulting in model outputs that are very similar to the input text. In cases where the ground truth simplification also happens to be a copy of the source, overlap metrics are unduly maximised. Secondly, MUSS tends to produce highly fluent simplifications yet these often resemble short summaries. For longer sentences, outputs can be densely packed, leading to even more complex sentences, or significant amounts of information are simply dropped from the input. It remains an open question as to whether or not this information loss is suitable for simplifying towards a target level. Finally, we also observed that FUDGE's model outputs (B_{simp-l}) are more susceptible to disfluencies such as redundant punctuation, subwords and phrases. This suggests that the attribute classifier can unfortunately have a negative impact on the generator in some cases.

The tables below provide randomly sampled examples of model outputs for each target-level in the Newsela English corpus. We colour parts of the simplified texts based on the edit operations applied to the source text. Blue indicates additions or explanations not in the source text. Green is used to highlight lexical and punctuation substitutions. Yellow shows operations on contractions (either creating or deconstructing). Pink indicates phrases that have been truncated or lexical deletions from the source text. Violet is used for larger paraphrastic segments or positionally shuffled phrases. Undesirable repetitions or hallucinations are italicised.

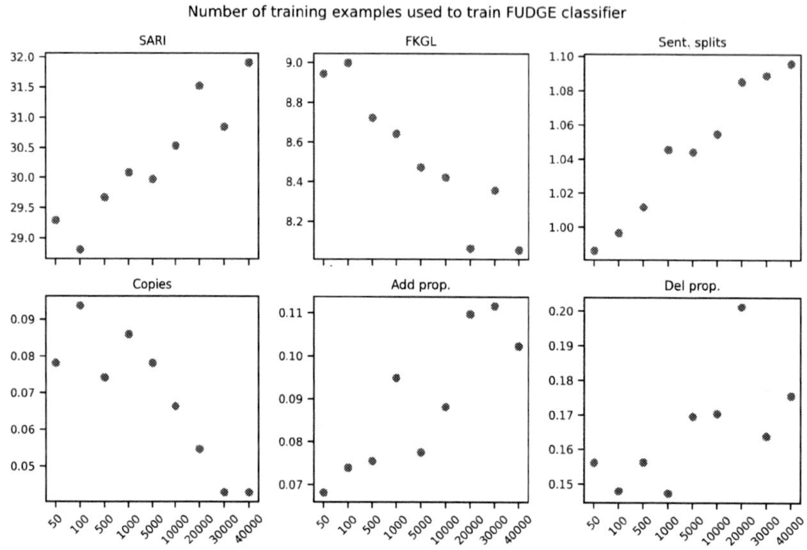

Figure 4: Automatic simplification metrics for simplification as a function of the number of contrastive complex-simple paragraphs from the Newsela English corpus used to train a FUDGE classifier $\mathcal{B}_{Simp-4}$.

Target Level: Simp-1	
Simp-0 (source)	They found that there was indeed a pattern in their motion — though it wasn't quite what they expected.
Simp-1 (reference)	They found that there was indeed a pattern in their motion — though it was not quite what they expected.
MUSS	They found that there was a pattern in their motion - but it wasn't what they expected.
SUPER	They found that there was indeed a pattern in their motion — though it wasn't quite what they expected.
$\mathcal{B}_{simp-1}$	They found that there was a pattern in their movement, though it wasn't what they expected.
Simp-0 (source)	The tribes helped members of the expedition through the winter, bringing them food and assisting with navigation.
Simp-1 (reference)	The tribes helped members of the expedition through the winter, bringing them food and assisting with navigation.
MUSS	The tribes helped members of the expedition by bringing them food and helping with navigation.
SUPER	The tribes helped members of the expedition through the winter, bringing them food and assisting with navigation.
$\mathcal{B}_{simp-1}$	The tribes helped members of the expedition through the winter, bringing food and helping with navigation.

Target Level: Simp-2

Simp-0 (source)	The feat should be possible based on Einstein's theory of general relativity, which describes gravity as the warping of spacetime by energy and matter.
Simp-2 (reference)	It should be possible based on Einstein's theory of general relativity. His famous theory describes gravity as the bending of space and time, which are one thing called "spacetime."
MUSS	Einstein's theory, called general relativity, describes gravity as the warping of spacetime by energy and matter.
SUPER	The feat should be possible based on Einstein's theory of general relativity, which describes gravity as the warping of spacetime by energy and matter.
$\mathcal{B}_{simp-2}$	The feat is based on Einstein's theory of general relativity. It describes gravity as the warping of spacetime by matter and energy.
Simp-0 (source)	Changes include moving the earliest date from which tribes must provide documentation of their existence into the 1930s and allowing tribes to reapply for federal recognition under certain circumstances, something previously prohibited.
Simp-2 (reference)	The revisions include establishing the 1930s as the earliest date from which tribes must provide documentation of their existence. Also, tribes may reapply for federal recognition under certain situations, something previously prohibited.
MUSS	Changes include moving the earliest date for tribes to provide documentation of existence into the 1930s, and allowing under certain circumstances tribes to reapply for federal recognition.
SUPER	Changes include moving the earliest date from which tribes must provide documentation of their existence into the 1930s and allowing tribes to reapply for federal recognition under certain circumstances, something previously prohibited.
$\mathcal{B}_{simp-2}$	Changes include moving the earliest date from which tribes must provide documentation of their existence. Tribes will also be allowed to reapply for federal recognition.

Target Level: Simp-3

Simp-0 (source)	Cafes, restaurants and bakeries around the nation are feeling the pain from recent outbreaks of bird flu, or avian influenza, expanding through the Midwest.
Simp-3 (reference)	The rising prices is caused by recent outbreaks of bird flu.
MUSS	Restaurants and bakeries around the nation are feeling the effects of the recent bird flu outbreak in the Midwest.
SUPER	Cafes, restaurants and bakeries around the nation are feeling the pain from recent outbreaks of bird flu. The disease is spreading through the Midwest.
$\mathcal{B}_{simp-3}$	Cafes, restaurants and bakeries around the nation are feeling the pain of bird flu outbreaks that have spread in the Midwest.
Simp-0 (source)	"That is, a time traveler who emerges from a Deutschian CTC enters a universe that has nothing to do with the one she exited in the future.
Simp-3 (reference)	Lloyd says a time traveler coming from Deutsch's CTC "enters a universe that has nothing to do with the one she exited."
MUSS	A Deutschian CTC traveler enters a universe that has nothing to do with the one she left.
SUPER	"That is, a time traveler who emerges from a Deutschian CTC enters a universe that has nothing to do with the one she exited in the future.
$\mathcal{B}_{simp-3}$	"That is, a time traveler who emerges from a Deutschian CTC enters a universe. This universe has nothing to do with the one she exited in the future. *The universe she enters into has nothing to do with the one she exited in the future.*

Target Level: Simp-4	
Simp-0 (source)	If the particle flips the switch, the machine emits a particle—the particle—back into the CTC; if the switch isn't flipped, the machine emits nothing.
Simp-4 (reference)	If the particle flips the switch, the machine shoots a particle — the particle — back into the CTC. If the switch isn't flipped, the machine shoots out nothing.
MUSS	If the particle turns, the machine sends a particle back to the CTC. If it doesn't, it sends nothing.
SUPER	If the particle flips the switch, the machine emits a particle—the particle—back into the CTC. If the switch isn't flipped, the machine emits nothing.
$\mathcal{B}_{simp-4}$	If the switch is turned, the machine emits a particle-like stateBack into the CTC. If the switch is not turned, the machine emits nothing.
Simp-0 (source)	Deutsch's insight was to postulate self-consistency in the quantum realm, to insist that any particle entering one end of a CTC must emerge at the other end with identical properties.
Simp-4 (reference)	Deutsch assumes that tiny quantum particles are stable and fixed.
MUSS	In quantum theory, Deutsch insisted that any particle entering one end of a CTC must emerge at the other end with equal properties.
SUPER	Deutsch's idea was to show that any particle entering one end of a CTC must emerge at the other end *of a CTC must emerge at the other end* with identical properties.
$\mathcal{B}_{simp-4}$	Deutsch's idea was to postulate a very nature. He was claiming that any particle entering one end of a CTC must emerge at the other end with identical properties.

Conciseness: An Overlooked Language Task

Felix Stahlberg and **Aashish Kumar** and **Chris Alberti** and **Shankar Kumar**
Google Research
{fstahlberg,kumaraashish,chrisalberti,shankarkumar}@google.com

Abstract

We report on novel investigations into training models that make sentences concise. We define the task and show that it is different from related tasks such as summarization and simplification. For evaluation, we release two test sets, consisting of 2000 sentences each, that were annotated by two and five human annotators, respectively. We demonstrate that conciseness is a difficult task for which zero-shot setups with large neural language models often do not perform well. Given the limitations of these approaches, we propose a synthetic data generation method based on round-trip translations. Using this data to either train Transformers from scratch or fine-tune T5 models yields our strongest baselines that can be further improved by fine-tuning on an artificial conciseness dataset that we derived from multi-annotator machine translation test sets.

1 Introduction

> *"Vigorous writing is concise. A sentence should contain no unnecessary words, a paragraph no unnecessary sentences, for the same reason that a drawing should have no unnecessary lines and a machine no unnecessary parts."*
>
> Strunk and White (1918)
> The Elements of Style

Conciseness is a writing principle of removing redundant information in text. Even though conciseness is highly valued in expository English writing and is often considered good writing style (Brock and Walters, 1992; Zinsser, 2016), it is still an understudied topic in the natural language processing (NLP) community, mainly due to the lack of annotated data sets. However, automatic methods for improving conciseness have the potential to improve the writing experience even for native speakers, or to provide useful tools for editorial tasks. In this work we take initial steps towards conciseness from an NLP perspective. We release[1] two hand-annotated test sets for conciseness – *Concise-Lite* (2-way annotated) and *Concise-Full* (5-way annotated). *Concise-Lite* annotators were asked to make minimal changes to the original sentence, whereas *Concise-Full* annotators were given the option to make larger rewrites. Table 1 contains examples from both test sets. For evaluation, we compute $F_{0.5}$-scores of edit spans, a metric that is also commonly used for grammatical error correction (GEC) (Dahlmeier and Ng, 2012; Felice et al., 2016; Bryant et al., 2017). Given that both the test sets and the evaluation tool we employ are publicly available, we hope our setup will encourage NLP researchers to investigate models for conciseness.

We evaluate a range of models on our newly collected conciseness test sets. Our initial approach follows the recent paradigm of using massively pre-trained neural models with either no or very little task-specific training data. Inspired by Brown et al. (2020) we report on zero-shot experiments with the large language model LaMDA (Thoppilan et al., 2022). We also fine-tune the large sequence model T5 (Raffel et al., 2020) on small conciseness data sets. We achieve our best results using an unsupervised synthetic data generation method based on round-trip translations, i.e. sentence pairs that were generated by translating an English sentence into another language (e.g. German) and back, a technique that was previously proposed for GEC pre-training (Lichtarge et al., 2019). We construct additional data sets by creating mappings from the longest to the shortest reference in multi-reference machine translation (MT) test sets. Our experiments suggest that conciseness is a hard task for current NLP models. We conclude with a thorough investigation into the similarities and differences of our systems and map out the challenges ahead.

[1] https://github.com/google-research-datasets/wiki-conciseness-dataset

Proceedings of the Workshop on Text Simplification, Accessibility, and Readability (TSAR-2022), pages 43 - 56
December 8, 2022

Input sentence	Concise-Lite	Concise-Full
Gemco had a version called Memco, also owned by Lucky Stores, that operated stores in the Chicago and Washington, D.C., areas.	Gemco had a version called Memco, **owned** by Lucky Stores, **operating** stores in the Chicago and Washington, D.C.	**Memco was** a version of Gemco **operated by** Lucky Stores in Chicago and Washington, D.C.
The film was adapted from a best-selling biography of the brothers, and was well presented and well received.	The film was adapted from a best-selling biography of the brothers, and was well presented **and received**.	The **film, adapted** from the **brothers'** best-selling biography, was well presented **and received**.

Table 1: Example sentences from our *Concise-Lite* and *Concise-Full* test sets.

Input sentence	Abstractive sentence summarization	Conciseness model output
Exxon corp. and Mobil corp. have held discussions about combining their business operations, a person involved in the talks said Wednesday.	Exxon and Mobil discuss combining business operations; possible merger.	Exxon Corp. and Mobil Corp. **have discussed** combining their business operations, a person involved in the talks said Wednesday.
Chuck Knoblauch and Tino Martinez were as popular as squeegee men a week ago, the speculation rampant that one or the other or both might be exiled if the Yankees' historic year crumbled in the post-season.	Knoblauch and Martinez home run hits cinch Yankee's First World Series game	Chuck Knoblauch and Tino Martinez were as popular as squeegee men a week ago, the speculation rampant that **either or both could** be exiled if the Yankees' historic year crumbled in the **postseason**.

Table 2: Example outputs of one of our conciseness models on sentences from an abstractive sentence summarization data set (Over et al., 2007, DUC2004).

Input sentence	Sentence simplification	Conciseness model output
A mutant is a type of fictional character that appears in comic books published by Marvel comics.	A mutant is a **form** of **imaginary** character that **is seen** in comic books published by Marvel comics.	A mutant **is a fictional** character that appears in **comics** published by Marvel comics.
It will then dislodge itself and sink back to the river bed in order to digest its food and wait for its next meal.	It will then **get away from its place** and sink back **into** the river bed in order to digest its food and wait for its next meal.	It will then dislodge and **return** to the riverbed to digest its food and wait for the next meal.

Table 3: Example outputs of one of our conciseness models on sentences from a text simplification data set (Zhang and Lapata, 2017, WikiLarge).

2 The conciseness task

In this work we define the conciseness task as *applying the required edits to make a sentence less wordy without changing its meaning, intent or sentiment.* We will shed more light on the limitations of this definition in Sec. 6. We expect conciseness models to be useful mainly for native or advanced non-native writers who wish to improve their writing style. Conciseness is related to several other NLP tasks, but we argue below that each of these tasks has a different focus and deserves an independent treatment.

Summarization and sentence compression Abstractive sentence summarization (Over et al., 2007) attempts to produce a condensed version of the input text. Summaries are similar to headlines with a maximum length that is independent of the input sentence length (Rush et al., 2015). Thus, generating a summary often requires a much more severe compression compared to conciseness. Unlike summarization, conciseness is faithful to the input and aims to avoid the loss of any information – the goal is to generate a shorter sentence that can replace the original sentence within continuous text (see Table 2 for examples). Furthermore, most work on summarization focuses on the compression of entire documents or paragraphs (Zhang et al., 2020) and not on single sentences.

Similarly to sentence summarization, *sentence compression* also aims to generate a shorter version of the input text. Many sentence compression models only allow the deletion of words without the ability to rephrase parts of the sentence (Knight and Marcu, 2000; Jing, 2000; Filippova et al., 2015). Perhaps closest to our work, Mallinson et al. (2018) trained sentence compression models on round-trip translations and thereby avoided this restriction. The main difference to us is that we evaluate a broader range of methods on human-annotated test sets which we release for future research.

Sentence simplification The task of reducing the linguistic complexity of text to improve readability is known as *sentence simplification* (Saggion, 2017). It can be subdivided into lexical (e.g. replacing uncommon words with synonyms) and syntactic (e.g. changing passive to active) simplification (Devlin, 1999; Carroll et al., 1999). Most forms of syntactic simplification result in concise outputs,[2] but lexical simplification may yield even more verbose outputs. For example, replacing 'to portray' with a simpler but verbose phrase such as 'to describe very vividly' would be an instance of lexical simplification but not of conciseness. Conversely, a conciseness system may substitute a phrase with another that is concise but less common and thereby deteriorate readability. Another difference is that simplification often targets people with cognitive disabilities (Devlin, 1999; Carroll et al., 1999; Rello et al., 2013) or low literacy (Watanabe et al., 2009) or second language learners (Petersen and Ostendorf, 2007; Siddharthan, 2002; Xia et al., 2016) whereas conciseness can be thought as writing assistance for proficient writers. Table 3 contrasts simplification and conciseness with the help of example sentences.

Style transfer Text style is an important consideration for several NLP tasks (Fu et al., 2018). For example, it is desirable for MT output to match the stylistic properties of the source sentence (Sennrich et al., 2016; Lohar et al., 2017). Natural language generation systems not only need to take into account the content of generated utterances but also other attributes such as style and sentiment (Li et al., 2018). Text-to-text style transfer systems have been used to change Shakespearean English to modern English (Jhamtani et al., 2017). We consider conciseness as a special case of style transfer with a single source style (wordy) and one target style (concise). However, while most style transfer systems attempt to change attributes like sentiment or political slant (Li et al., 2018; Fu et al., 2018; Prabhumoye et al., 2018; Shen et al., 2017), our conciseness models aim to keep them unchanged.

Paraphrasing Paraphrasing databases such as PPDB (Ganitkevitch et al., 2013; Pavlick et al., 2015) that store pairs of phrases with the same meaning have proven useful for various NLP tasks such as textual entailment (Bjerva et al., 2014) and semantic similarity (Han et al., 2013). In this work we include a paraphrasing system for comparison.

[2]An exception would be *sentence splitting* since it is a syntactic simplification strategy that often makes the text longer.

3 Modeling conciseness

The approaches in this section cover a wide range of NLP models to convey a better sense for the task. They are intended to serve as baselines to compare against, and as a starting point for future research.

3.1 Giant language models (LaMDA)

Large language models (LMs) such as OpenAI's GPT-3 (Radford et al., 2019), Google's Meena (Adiwardana et al., 2020) and PaLM (Chowdhery et al., 2022) and Microsoft's Turing NLG[3] have recently captured the interest of the general public through their ability to generate text that is sometimes astonishingly difficult to distinguish from text written by humans. While these models are useful for building open-domain dialog agents, they also have the potential to solve specific NLP problems when provided with an appropriate preamble (LM history) (Brown et al., 2020). We expect general dialog agents to understand the nuances of language such as grammar, conciseness, etc. Thus, we explored using the large LM LaMDA (Thoppilan et al., 2022) with a zero-shot preamble that steers the model towards making a sentence more concise. We use the following template to provide the LM context:

> *Here is some text:*
> *"*`[INPUT_SENTENCE]`*". Rewrite it to be more concise.*

where `[INPUT_SENTENCE]` is replaced by the source sentence.[4] We post-process the output to a) discard any additional comment that the model generated besides the rewrite, and b) retain only the first suggestion if multiple rewrites are generated.

3.2 Transformers pre-trained on round-trip translations

This method employs synthetic training data generated using MT. Fig. 1 illustrates the approach. First, we translate an English sentence into a pivot language such as German, and then translate it back

[3]`https://msturing.org/`

[4]This prompt was best among a small number of zero-shot and few-shot prompts we explored. Systematic prompt engineering could potentially improve LaMDA results at a significantly higher computational cost, but we have not explored this option in this work since we focus on conciseness as an NLP task.

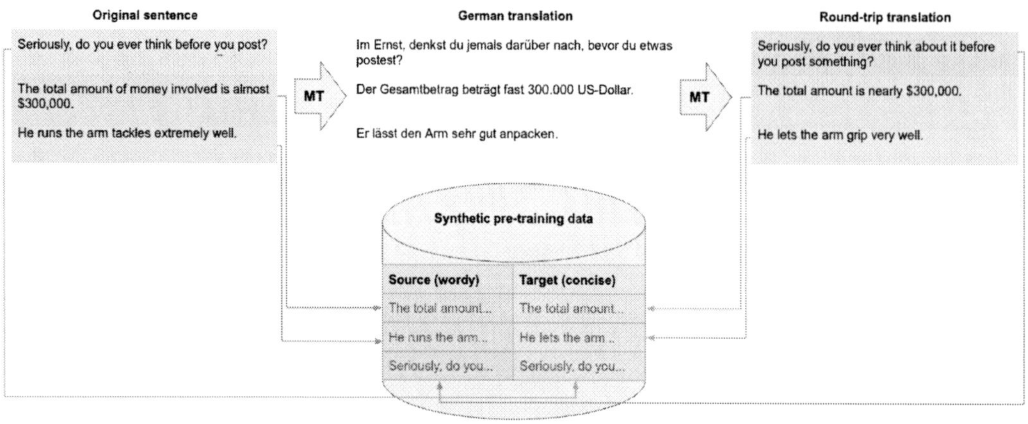

Figure 1: Synthetic pre-training data generation using round-trip translations.

Name	Number of sentence pairs	Average source sentence length in words	Average target sentence length in words	Compression ratio
Pre-training and fine-tuning data sets				
RoundTrip-French	169M	20.6	19.4	0.94
RoundTrip-German	169M	20.4	19.4	0.95
RoundTrip-Japanese	169M	20.4	17.9	0.88
RoundTrip-Russian	169M	20.9	19.5	0.93
MultiRefMT-FineTune	9K	31.9	26.1	0.82
Development sets				
MultiRefMT-Dev	820	33.3	25.8	0.77
Hand-annotated test sets				
Concise-Lite	2K	23.7	21.2	0.89
Concise-Full	2K	23.7	20.1	0.85

Table 4: Data set statistics. The compression ratio is the number of target words divided by the number of source words.

into English. This idea of generating sentence pairs via round-trip translation was initially proposed by Lichtarge et al. (2019) to pre-train GEC systems. In this work, we construct synthetic parallel data for conciseness by using the longer sentence as the source and the shorter sentence as the target sentence. We then train a standard neural sequence-to-sequence Transformer (Vaswani et al., 2017) on the synthetic data until convergence.[5] This approach is simple and enables us to generate large quantities of data, but the resulting data set contains noise. For example, round-trip translation pairs often contain synonym substitutions (see the replacement of *almost* with *nearly* in the second sentence in Fig. 1) that do not help conciseness. Furthermore, MT may fail to translate the sentence properly, resulting in an undesirable change of meaning (see the third sentence in Fig. 1). Another problem is that it is hard to control the compression ratio in the data set. Despite these limitations we show in Sec. 5 that round-trip translations are useful for pre-training.

3.3 Fine-tuning T5

The final method considered in this work employs T5 (Raffel et al., 2020). Very large sequence-to-sequence models have been found to be extremely powerful, even for challenging language tasks with a limited amount of training data. We fine-tuned the publicly available 11B parameter version (xxl) of T5[6], with a batch size of 1,024 sentences and a learning rate of 10^{-4}.

4 Data sets

Table 4 lists the data sets used in this work. Table 5 contains information about their provenance.

Round-trip translations (RoundTrip-*) Our Transformer system is pre-trained on round-trip translations of sentences crawled from news websites following the recipe of Lichtarge et al. (2019)

[5] More details about the Transformer model implementation are provided in Appendix A.

[6] https://github.com/google-research/text-to-text-transfer-transformer/blob/main/released_checkpoints.md

Name	Reference	Type
RoundTrip-*	Lichtarge et al. (2019)	Round-trip translations (news)
MultiRefMT-FineTune	LDC2010T10, LDC2010T11, LDC2010T12, LDC2010T14	4-annotator MT test sets (Arabic-English, Chinese-English)
MultiRefMT-Dev	LDC2013T03	4-annotator MT test set (Chinese-English)
Concise-Lite	This work	2-way hand-annotated conciseness test set
Concise-Full	This work	5-way hand-annotated conciseness test set

Table 5: Synthetic and hand-annotated conciseness data sets used in this work.

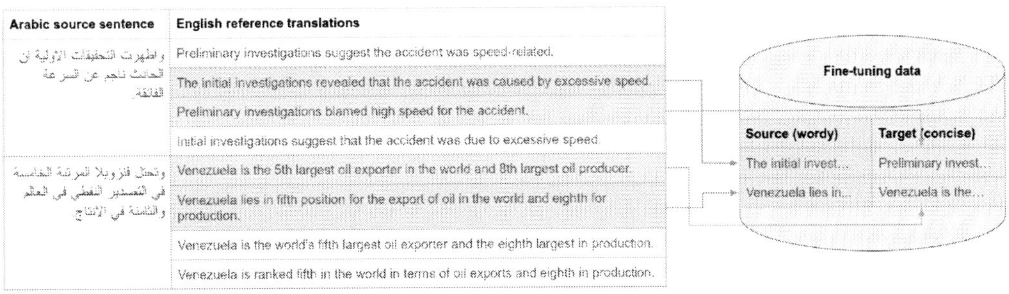

Figure 2: Fine-tuning data generation using multi-reference MT test sets.

that were prepared as described in Sec. 3.2. For fine-tuning T5 on round-trip translations we randomly sample 1M sentence pairs from the full data set to limit computation.

OpenMT-based fine-tuning and development sets (MultiRefMT-*) We derive fine-tuning and development sets from existing publicly available MT test sets. It is common practice in several NLP areas to collect reference sentences from multiple annotators to increase the trustworthiness of automatic evaluation measures, for example in grammatical error correction (Ng et al., 2014; Bryant and Ng, 2015; Napoles et al., 2017), MT (Freitag et al., 2020), and image caption generation (Zheng et al., 2018). Multi-reference MT test sets have been used in the past to evaluate paraphrasing or sentence compression systems (Ganitkevitch et al., 2011; Pang et al., 2003). We make use of these multi-annotator test sets by selecting the longest reference sentence as the (wordy) source sentence and the shortest reference sentence as the golden (concise) target sentence (Fig. 2). Our MultiRefMT-FineTune set uses all Arabic-English and Chinese-English NIST Open Machine Translation (OpenMT) evaluation sets from 2002-2005. The MultiRefMT-Dev set is based on the Chinese-English 2012 OpenMT evaluation set.

Hand-annotated test sets (Concise-*) Deriving conciseness test sets from multi-reference MT evaluation sets is viable as a first approximation given that all references have similar meaning, intent, and sentiment by design (apart from annotation errors). However, it does not allow us to determine how wordy the sentence is in the first place. If all MT references agreed, it would suggest that the original source sentence has a single obvious translation, not that the references are already concise.

Therefore, we collected two new data sets, consisting of 2000 sentences each, that were explicitly annotated for conciseness – *Concise-Lite* and *Concise-Full*. Both data sets used the same set of source sentences drawn from Wikipedia. Sentences that a) were ungrammatical, b) contained fewer than 15 words or c) included mismatched quotation marks were not selected. While *Concise-Lite* annotators were asked to make minimal changes to the original sentence, *Concise-Full* annotators were given the flexibility to make larger changes to the original sentence. The exact annotator guidelines are listed in Appendix B.

We will make the test sets publicly available to establish a benchmark for researchers to evaluate conciseness models.

5 Results

We use the GEC evaluation toolkit ERRANT (Bryant et al., 2017; Felice et al., 2016) to compute $F_{0.5}$-scores on spaCy[7]-tokenized text. Like in GEC, precision is weighted twice as high as recall using the $F_{0.5}$-score, which matches our intuition

[7]https://spacy.io/

System	Concise-Lite			Concise-Full		
	P	R	$F_{0.5}$	P	R	$F_{0.5}$
Other NLP tasks						
a Summarization: Pegasus	0.8	1.4	0.9	2.0	3.9	2.2
b Summarization: Long-T5	1.7	6.3	2.0	3.5	11.7	4.1
c Simplification: T5	7.4	5.4	6.9	13.8	9.9	12.8
d Paraphrasing: ParaNMT	9.3	21.4	10.4	15.4	25.1	16.7
Conciseness models						
e Giant-LM (zero-shot LaMDA)	4.4	13.5	5.1	8.5	20.0	9.6
f Transformer (RT)	13.6	21.3	14.6	21.1	25.5	21.9
g Transformer (RT→MT)	15.0	25.8	16.4	24.4	29.6	25.2
h T5 (RT)	18.4	19.5	18.6	29.1	24.2	28.0
i T5 (RT→MT)	16.0	26.8	17.4	26.6	30.6	27.3

Table 6: System comparison on our two conciseness test sets. "RT" denotes models trained on round-trip translations. "RT→MT" configurations are subsequently fine-tuned on MultiRefMT-FineTune.

System	Number of parameters
Giant-LM (LaMDA)	137B
T5	11B
Transformer	313M

Table 7: Number of model parameters.

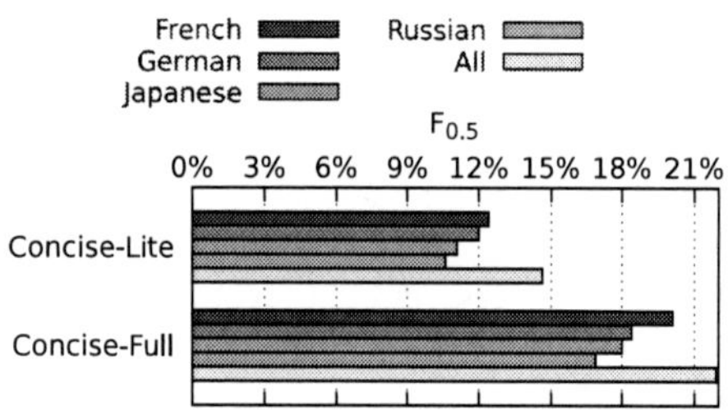

Figure 3: Transformer models trained from scratch on round-trip translations via different pivot languages.

that a conciseness system should act as a minimally intrusive writing assistant for which false positives are far worse than false negatives.

5.1 System comparison

Table 6 compares all approaches from Sec. 3 and the following baselines from other NLP tasks:

- Summarization: Long-T5 (Guo et al., 2022) and Pegasus (Zhang et al., 2020).
- Simplification: T5 fine-tuned on the WikiLarge simplification dataset (Zhang and Lapata, 2017) using a procedure similar to our T5-conciseness system from Sec. 3.3.[8]
- Paraphrasing: A Transformer model trained on the full ParaNMT-50M (Wieting and Gimpel, 2018) training set using the hyper-parameters in Appendix A.

The summarization baselines (rows a and b) perform poorly since they are mostly trained on full documents. The simplification system achieves a slightly higher performance but is weaker than the paraphrasing or the Transformer/T5 based conciseness systems. The paraphrasing system (row d) achieved a recall of over 20% on both test sets, but the precision is relatively low because the ParaNMT training set contains various types of edits such as synonym replacements or word reorderings that do not necessarily help conciseness.

The zero shot Giant-LM (LaMDA) setup (row e) was not able to match either the precision or recall of the other conciseness systems. Round-trip translations are useful for both training a Transformer model from scratch (row f) and fine-tuning T5 (row h). Subsequent fine-tuning on MultiRefMT-FineTune yields large precision and recall gains for the Transformer model (row g). MultiRefMT-FineTune also improves the recall for T5, but the precision suffers (row i).[9] T5 outperforms the Transformers in terms of $F_{0.5}$-score by achieving higher precision on both sets but has many more parameters (Table 7).

5.2 Ablation studies and analyses

The following analyses were carried out on the *Concise-Lite* and *Concise-Full* test sets.

Round-trip translation languages Our final models in Table 6 use round-trip translations from four different pivot languages: French, German,

[8]Our simplification baseline achieves 33.1 SARI on the WikiLarge test set.

[9]T5 is fine-tuned for 4K steps on the 1M round-trip translations and for 1K steps on the smaller MultiRefMT-FineTune set.

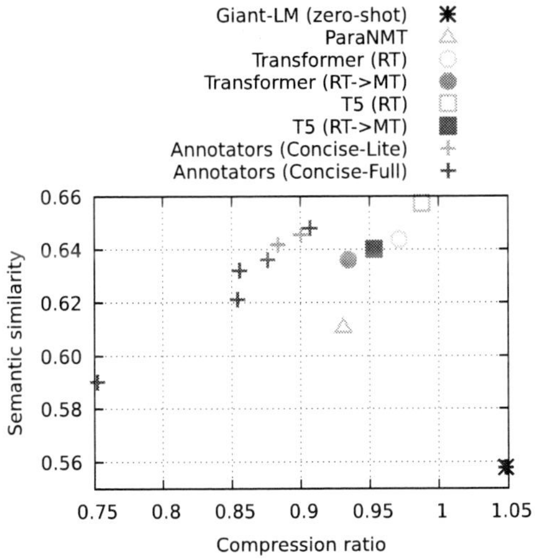

Figure 4: Trade-off between semantic similarity and the sentence compression ratio.

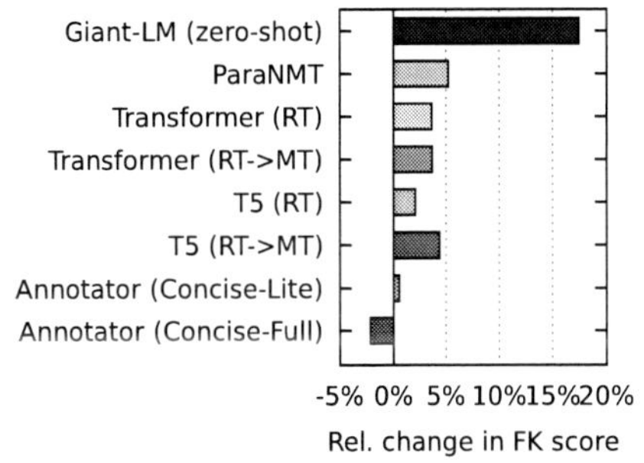

Figure 5: Relative change in Flesch–Kincaid readability scores (Kincaid et al., 1975).

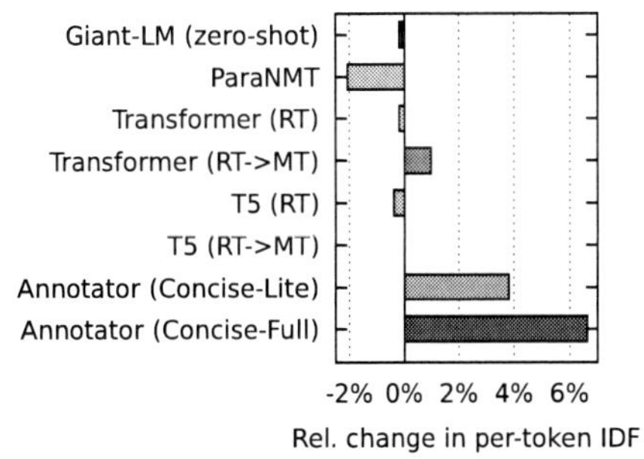

Figure 6: Relative change in information density.

Japanese, and Russian. Fig. 3 shows that combining all languages yields consistent gains on both test sets over using any single language.

Preserving semantics To measure how well our systems retain the meaning of the original sentence we computed semantic similarity scores between the input and the output sentences using the models provided by the Semantic Reactor toolkit (Yang et al., 2018; Cer et al., 2018). Systems and annotators trade off compression against semantic similarity differently (Figure 4). There is a large variability in compression ratio (i.e. the number of target words divided by the number of source words) and semantic similarity between the *Concise-Full* annotators (dark purple). The Giant-LM (blue) is more prone to meaning change than other systems, and is not effective in reducing the sentence length. Fine-tuning on MultiRefMT-FineTune (empty vs. filled circle/square) improves the compression ratio but hurts semantic similarity. T5 (red) preserves semantics better than the Transformer but outputs slightly longer sentences.

Readability Fig. 5 shows that our systems often improve the readability of the sentence, in particular the Giant-LM system. The Giant-LM prefers simpler language as it was originally designed for dialog applications (Thoppilan et al., 2022). In contrast, the *Concise-Full* annotators tend to achieve concision using longer and more complex words, resulting in a decline in readability (dark purple).

Information density We expect the outputs of a high-performing conciseness system to have a high information content per word. This information density can be measured using per-token inverse document frequency (Jones, 1973):

$$\text{idf}(t) = \log \frac{N}{|\{d \in D : t \in d\}|},$$

where t is the token, N is the total number of documents, and D is the document collection. In our case, the document frequencies are derived from the C4 corpus (Raffel et al., 2020). Fig. 6 shows that the reference sentences from the *Concise-Lite* and *Concise-Full* annotators indeed have a higher per-token IDF than the input sentences (pink and dark purple bars). The results on the system outputs are mixed, but fine-tuning on MultiRefMT-FineTune improves the per-token IDF for the Transformer and T5 ("RT" vs. "RT→ MT").

Synonym substitutions One problem with using round-trip translations for training and multi-reference test sets for evaluation is that both may contain synonym substitutions that do not help conciseness. We counted synonym substitutions by extracting all 1:1 substitutions and checking

	Without A1			Without A2			Without A3			Without A4			Without A5		
	P	R	$F_{0.5}$	P	R	$F_{0.5}$	P	R	$F_{0.5}$	P	R	$F_{0.5}$	P	R	$F_{0.5}$
Annotator A1	45.8	52.0	46.9												
Annotator A2				16.3	32.0	18.1									
Annotator A3							51.5	48.4	50.9						
Annotator A4										23.1	32.6	24.5			
Annotator A5													33.5	27.1	32.0
Transformer	22.7	27.6	23.5	19.7	28.6	21.0	23.6	27.7	24.3	20.8	26.8	21.8	23.0	25.9	23.6
T5	25.3	28.9	26.0	20.7	29.2	22.0	25.7	28.9	26.3	23.1	28.0	23.9	25.4	27.0	25.7

Table 8: Measuring annotator agreement on *Concise-Full* by evaluating each single annotator using the other four annotations as references. We list the Transformer and T5 system outputs ("RT→MT") for comparison.

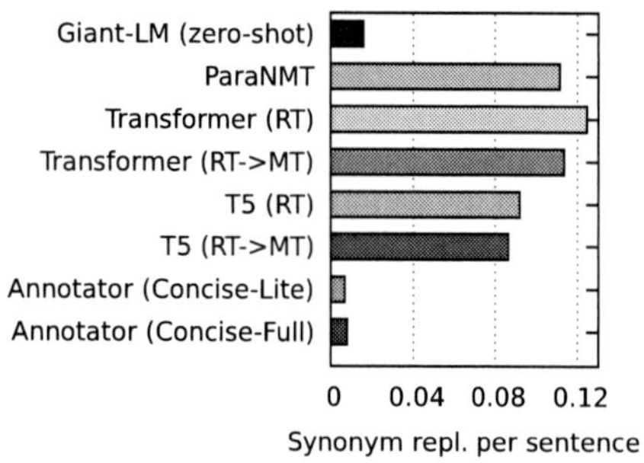

Figure 7: Number of 1:1 synonym substitutions.

whether these were marked as synonyms in WordNet (Miller, 1995). Fig. 7 shows that most of our systems replace synonyms on an average in every 10th sentence. Fine-tuning the Transformer or T5 on MultiRefMT-FineTune reduces the number of synonym substitutions. Synonyms are much less of a problem with the Giant-LM (blue bar) which was not trained on round-trip translations.

6 Limitations

In terms of both information density (Fig. 6) and number of unnecessary synonym replacements (Fig. 7), the annotators are clearly separated from most of our automatic systems, illustrating the gap to human performance on this task.

Our experiments showed that the Giant-LM (zero-shot) underperformed the other approaches. Preliminary experiments using few-shot learning did not yield improvements over the zero-shot setting. We expect the performance of Giant-LM to improve via systematic prompt engineering.

Another challenge lies in the intrinsic uncertainty (Ott et al., 2018; Stahlberg et al., 2022) of the conciseness task, i.e. the existence of multiple viable ways to make a sentence more concise. Table 8 demonstrates that the five *Concise-Full* annotators usually did not agree on a single concise version of a sentence, leading to great variability in $F_{0.5}$-scores when evaluated against each other.[10] Therefore, adequate system outputs may get penalized if they do not agree with one of the human references. We mitigate this concern by using multiple annotators, but – like in other intrinsically uncertain NLP tasks such as MT – a certain level of noise remains in our evaluation.

Limitations of our task definition We acknowledge that there are various aspects of conciseness that are not covered by our definition in Sec. 2 ("*applying the required edits to make a sentence less wordy without changing its meaning, intent or sentiment*"). First, we intentionally did not include the use of context in our definition. In practice, however, appropriate levels of conciseness can be highly context dependent. Treating the problem on the sentence-level is limiting because using inter-sentential cross-references for conciseness requires access to the document-level context such as the previous sentence. Furthermore, the sentence-level restriction prevents the systems from improving conciseness through sentence splitting (Botha et al., 2018) or merging (Geva et al., 2019). In real-life situations, the context may also be provided through other channels such as physical medium (e.g. pointing to things) or social factors (e.g. does person B know person A?). We also noticed that our *Concise-Full* annotators occasionally relied on common knowledge to shorten sentences (see Appendix C for examples), a strategy that is *not* covered by our definition and thus makes our evaluation slightly more noisy. Exploring the various forms of context for conciseness is a promising potential direction for future research.

Another limitation of our definition is that it does

[10]On some of the setups in Table 8 (e.g. "Without A2" or "Without A4"), T5 achieves scores comparable to the human annotators. We emphasize that this is a sign of low inter-annotator agreement and does not allow us to claim human parity since this pattern is not consistent across annotators.

not allow for a change of semantics, intent, or sentiment. In practice, however, conciseness or the lack of it may reflect the intent of the speaker, for example in indicating emergency situations (signalling urgency through brevity) or in detecting lying (Vrij, 2005). Another manner in which conciseness can carry meaning is when used as a rhetorical device to persuade or inspire the audience, a well-known strategy in legal writing (Osbeck, 2011) that was perhaps most famously demonstrated by Abraham Lincoln in the Gettysburg Address (Oseid, 2009). Furthermore, our ablation studies in Sec. 5.2 revealed that systems and human annotators alike sometimes accepted a minor loss of (irrelevant) information to achieve better compression, which, despite being contrary to our definition, may be acceptable in practice.

7 Conclusion

Our work is an initial exploration of conciseness from an NLP point of view. We compared a variety of approaches to the problem using popular techniques based on synthetic data generation or giant pre-trained sequence models. Round-trip translations provide a useful data source for training conciseness models but can introduce undesirable synonym substitutions.[11] Our analyses show that our systems trade off the objectives in conciseness differently (e.g. reducing the sentence length vs. preserving semantics vs. improving readability vs. increasing information density). Further experiments are necessary to understand how these tradeoffs would impact the user experience or potential downstream NLP tasks. We expect our study and our annotated test sets to provide impetus for researchers to explore this field further.

References

Daniel Adiwardana, Minh-Thang Luong, David R So, Jamie Hall, Noah Fiedel, Romal Thoppilan, Zi Yang, Apoorv Kulshreshtha, Gaurav Nemade, Yifeng Lu, et al. 2020. Towards a human-like open-domain chatbot. *arXiv preprint arXiv:2001.09977*.

Johannes Bjerva, Johan Bos, Rob van der Goot, and Malvina Nissim. 2014. The meaning factory: Formal semantics for recognizing textual entailment and determining semantic similarity. In *Proceedings of the 8th International Workshop on Semantic Evaluation (SemEval 2014)*, pages 642–646, Dublin, Ireland. Association for Computational Linguistics.

[11]Appendix C illustrates the strengths and weaknesses of our current systems with the help of some example outputs.

Jan A. Botha, Manaal Faruqui, John Alex, Jason Baldridge, and Dipanjan Das. 2018. Learning to split and rephrase from Wikipedia edit history. In *Proceedings of the 2018 Conference on Empirical Methods in Natural Language Processing*, pages 732–737, Brussels, Belgium. Association for Computational Linguistics.

James Bradbury, Roy Frostig, Peter Hawkins, Matthew James Johnson, Chris Leary, Dougal Maclaurin, George Necula, Adam Paszke, Jake VanderPlas, Skye Wanderman-Milne, and Qiao Zhang. 2021. JAX: composable transformations of Python+NumPy programs.

Mark Newell Brock and Larry Walters. 1992. *Teaching composition around the pacific rim: Politics and pedagogy*, volume 88. Multilingual matters.

Tom B Brown, Benjamin Mann, Nick Ryder, Melanie Subbiah, Jared Kaplan, Prafulla Dhariwal, Arvind Neelakantan, Pranav Shyam, Girish Sastry, Amanda Askell, et al. 2020. Language models are few-shot learners. *arXiv preprint arXiv:2005.14165*.

Christopher Bryant, Mariano Felice, and Ted Briscoe. 2017. Automatic annotation and evaluation of error types for grammatical error correction. In *Proceedings of the 55th Annual Meeting of the Association for Computational Linguistics (Volume 1: Long Papers)*, pages 793–805, Vancouver, Canada. Association for Computational Linguistics.

Christopher Bryant and Hwee Tou Ng. 2015. How far are we from fully automatic high quality grammatical error correction? In *Proceedings of the 53rd Annual Meeting of the Association for Computational Linguistics and the 7th International Joint Conference on Natural Language Processing (Volume 1: Long Papers)*, pages 697–707, Beijing, China. Association for Computational Linguistics.

John Carroll, Guido Minnen, Darren Pearce, Yvonne Canning, Siobhan Devlin, and John Tait. 1999. Simplifying text for language-impaired readers. In *Ninth Conference of the European Chapter of the Association for Computational Linguistics*, pages 269–270, Bergen, Norway. Association for Computational Linguistics.

Daniel Cer, Yinfei Yang, Sheng-yi Kong, Nan Hua, Nicole Limtiaco, Rhomni St John, Noah Constant, Mario Guajardo-Céspedes, Steve Yuan, Chris Tar, et al. 2018. Universal sentence encoder. *arXiv preprint arXiv:1803.11175*.

Aakanksha Chowdhery, Sharan Narang, Jacob Devlin, Maarten Bosma, Gaurav Mishra, Adam Roberts, Paul Barham, Hyung Won Chung, Charles Sutton, Sebastian Gehrmann, Parker Schuh, Kensen Shi, Sasha Tsvyashchenko, Joshua Maynez, Abhishek Rao, Parker Barnes, Yi Tay, Noam Shazeer, Vinodkumar Prabhakaran, Emily Reif, Nan Du, Ben Hutchinson, Reiner Pope, James Bradbury, Jacob Austin, Michael Isard, Guy Gur-Ari, Pengcheng

Yin, Toju Duke, Anselm Levskaya, Sanjay Ghemawat, Sunipa Dev, Henryk Michalewski, Xavier Garcia, Vedant Misra, Kevin Robinson, Liam Fedus, Denny Zhou, Daphne Ippolito, David Luan, Hyeontaek Lim, Barret Zoph, Alexander Spiridonov, Ryan Sepassi, David Dohan, Shivani Agrawal, Mark Omernick, Andrew M. Dai, Thanumalayan Sankaranarayana Pillai, Marie Pellat, Aitor Lewkowycz, Erica Moreira, Rewon Child, Oleksandr Polozov, Katherine Lee, Zongwei Zhou, Xuezhi Wang, Brennan Saeta, Mark Diaz, Orhan Firat, Michele Catasta, Jason Wei, Kathy Meier-Hellstern, Douglas Eck, Jeff Dean, Slav Petrov, and Noah Fiedel. 2022. Palm: Scaling language modeling with pathways. *CoRR*.

Daniel Dahlmeier and Hwee Tou Ng. 2012. Better evaluation for grammatical error correction. In *Proceedings of the 2012 Conference of the North American Chapter of the Association for Computational Linguistics: Human Language Technologies*, pages 568–572, Montréal, Canada. Association for Computational Linguistics.

Siobhan Devlin. 1999. *Simplifying natural language text for aphasic readers*. Ph.D. thesis, Ph. D. thesis, University of Sunderland, UK.

Mariano Felice, Christopher Bryant, and Ted Briscoe. 2016. Automatic extraction of learner errors in ESL sentences using linguistically enhanced alignments. In *Proceedings of COLING 2016, the 26th International Conference on Computational Linguistics: Technical Papers*, pages 825–835, Osaka, Japan. The COLING 2016 Organizing Committee.

Katja Filippova, Enrique Alfonseca, Carlos A. Colmenares, Lukasz Kaiser, and Oriol Vinyals. 2015. Sentence compression by deletion with LSTMs. In *Proceedings of the 2015 Conference on Empirical Methods in Natural Language Processing*, pages 360–368, Lisbon, Portugal. Association for Computational Linguistics.

Markus Freitag, David Grangier, and Isaac Caswell. 2020. BLEU might be guilty but references are not innocent. In *Proceedings of the 2020 Conference on Empirical Methods in Natural Language Processing (EMNLP)*, pages 61–71, Online. Association for Computational Linguistics.

Zhenxin Fu, Xiaoye Tan, Nanyun Peng, Dongyan Zhao, and Rui Yan. 2018. Style transfer in text: Exploration and evaluation. *Proceedings of the AAAI Conference on Artificial Intelligence*, 32(1).

Juri Ganitkevitch, Chris Callison-Burch, Courtney Napoles, and Benjamin Van Durme. 2011. Learning sentential paraphrases from bilingual parallel corpora for text-to-text generation. In *Proceedings of the 2011 Conference on Empirical Methods in Natural Language Processing*, pages 1168–1179, Edinburgh, Scotland, UK. Association for Computational Linguistics.

Juri Ganitkevitch, Benjamin Van Durme, and Chris Callison-Burch. 2013. PPDB: The paraphrase database. In *Proceedings of the 2013 Conference of the North American Chapter of the Association for Computational Linguistics: Human Language Technologies*, pages 758–764, Atlanta, Georgia. Association for Computational Linguistics.

Mor Geva, Eric Malmi, Idan Szpektor, and Jonathan Berant. 2019. DiscoFuse: A large-scale dataset for discourse-based sentence fusion. In *Proceedings of the 2019 Conference of the North American Chapter of the Association for Computational Linguistics: Human Language Technologies, Volume 1 (Long and Short Papers)*, pages 3443–3455, Minneapolis, Minnesota. Association for Computational Linguistics.

Mandy Guo, Joshua Ainslie, David Uthus, Santiago Ontañón, Jianmo Ni, Yun-Hsuan Sung, and Yinfei Yang. 2022. LongT5: Efficient text-to-text transformer for long sequences. In *Findings of the Association for Computational Linguistics: NAACL 2022*, pages 724–736.

Lushan Han, Abhay L. Kashyap, Tim Finin, James Mayfield, and Jonathan Weese. 2013. UMBC_EBIQUITY-CORE: Semantic textual similarity systems. In *Second Joint Conference on Lexical and Computational Semantics (*SEM), Volume 1: Proceedings of the Main Conference and the Shared Task: Semantic Textual Similarity*, pages 44–52, Atlanta, Georgia, USA. Association for Computational Linguistics.

Harsh Jhamtani, Varun Gangal, Eduard Hovy, and Eric Nyberg. 2017. Shakespearizing modern language using copy-enriched sequence to sequence models. In *Proceedings of the Workshop on Stylistic Variation*, pages 10–19, Copenhagen, Denmark. Association for Computational Linguistics.

Hongyan Jing. 2000. Sentence reduction for automatic text summarization. In *Sixth Applied Natural Language Processing Conference*, pages 310–315, Seattle, Washington, USA. Association for Computational Linguistics.

K. Sparck Jones. 1973. Index term weighting. *Information Storage and Retrieval*, 9(11):619–633.

J Peter Kincaid, Robert P Fishburne Jr, Richard L Rogers, and Brad S Chissom. 1975. Derivation of new readability formulas (automated readability index, fog count and Flesch reading ease formula) for Navy enlisted personnel. Technical report, Naval Technical Training Command Millington TN Research Branch.

Kevin Knight and Daniel Marcu. 2000. Statistics-based summarization - step one: Sentence compression. In *Proceedings of the Seventeenth National Conference on Artificial Intelligence and Twelfth Conference on Innovative Applications of Artificial Intelligence*, page 703–710. AAAI Press.

Taku Kudo and John Richardson. 2018. SentencePiece: A simple and language independent subword tokenizer and detokenizer for neural text processing. In *Proceedings of the 2018 Conference on Empirical Methods in Natural Language Processing: System Demonstrations*, pages 66–71, Brussels, Belgium. Association for Computational Linguistics.

Juncen Li, Robin Jia, He He, and Percy Liang. 2018. Delete, retrieve, generate: a simple approach to sentiment and style transfer. In *Proceedings of the 2018 Conference of the North American Chapter of the Association for Computational Linguistics: Human Language Technologies, Volume 1 (Long Papers)*, pages 1865–1874, New Orleans, Louisiana. Association for Computational Linguistics.

Jared Lichtarge, Chris Alberti, Shankar Kumar, Noam Shazeer, Niki Parmar, and Simon Tong. 2019. Corpora generation for grammatical error correction. In *Proceedings of the 2019 Conference of the North American Chapter of the Association for Computational Linguistics: Human Language Technologies, Volume 1 (Long and Short Papers)*, pages 3291–3301, Minneapolis, Minnesota. Association for Computational Linguistics.

Pintu Lohar, Haithem Afli, and Andy Way. 2017. Maintaining sentiment polarity in translation of user-generated content. *Prague Bulletin of Mathematical Linguistics*, pages 73–84.

Jonathan Mallinson, Rico Sennrich, and Mirella Lapata. 2018. Sentence compression for arbitrary languages via multilingual pivoting. In *Proceedings of the 2018 Conference on Empirical Methods in Natural Language Processing*, pages 2453–2464, Brussels, Belgium. Association for Computational Linguistics.

George A. Miller. 1995. WordNet: A lexical database for English. *Commun. ACM*, 38(11):39–41.

Courtney Napoles, Keisuke Sakaguchi, and Joel Tetreault. 2017. JFLEG: A fluency corpus and benchmark for grammatical error correction. In *Proceedings of the 15th Conference of the European Chapter of the Association for Computational Linguistics: Volume 2, Short Papers*, pages 229–234, Valencia, Spain. Association for Computational Linguistics.

Hwee Tou Ng, Siew Mei Wu, Ted Briscoe, Christian Hadiwinoto, Raymond Hendy Susanto, and Christopher Bryant. 2014. The CoNLL-2014 shared task on grammatical error correction. In *Proceedings of the Eighteenth Conference on Computational Natural Language Learning: Shared Task*, pages 1–14, Baltimore, Maryland. Association for Computational Linguistics.

Mark K Osbeck. 2011. What is good legal writing and why does it matter. *Drexel L. Rev.*, 4:417.

Julie A Oseid. 2009. The power of brevity: Adopt Abraham Lincoln's habits. *J. Ass'n Legal Writing Directors*, 6:28.

Myle Ott, Michael Auli, David Grangier, and Marc'Aurelio Ranzato. 2018. Analyzing uncertainty in neural machine translation. In *International Conference on Machine Learning*, pages 3956–3965. PMLR.

Paul Over, Hoa Dang, and Donna Harman. 2007. DUC in context. *Information Processing & Management*, 43(6):1506–1520. Text Summarization.

Bo Pang, Kevin Knight, and Daniel Marcu. 2003. Syntax-based alignment of multiple translations: Extracting paraphrases and generating new sentences. In *Proceedings of the 2003 Human Language Technology Conference of the North American Chapter of the Association for Computational Linguistics*, pages 181–188.

Ellie Pavlick, Pushpendre Rastogi, Juri Ganitkevitch, Benjamin Van Durme, and Chris Callison-Burch. 2015. PPDB 2.0: Better paraphrase ranking, fine-grained entailment relations, word embeddings, and style classification. In *Proceedings of the 53rd Annual Meeting of the Association for Computational Linguistics and the 7th International Joint Conference on Natural Language Processing (Volume 2: Short Papers)*, pages 425–430, Beijing, China. Association for Computational Linguistics.

Sarah E Petersen and Mari Ostendorf. 2007. Text simplification for language learners: a corpus analysis. In *Workshop on Speech and Language Technology in Education*.

Shrimai Prabhumoye, Yulia Tsvetkov, Ruslan Salakhutdinov, and Alan W Black. 2018. Style transfer through back-translation. In *Proceedings of the 56th Annual Meeting of the Association for Computational Linguistics (Volume 1: Long Papers)*, pages 866–876, Melbourne, Australia. Association for Computational Linguistics.

Alec Radford, Jeff Wu, Rewon Child, David Luan, Dario Amodei, and Ilya Sutskever. 2019. Language models are unsupervised multitask learners. *OpenAI blog*.

Colin Raffel, Noam Shazeer, Adam Roberts, Katherine Lee, Sharan Narang, Michael Matena, Yanqi Zhou, Wei Li, and Peter J. Liu. 2020. Exploring the limits of transfer learning with a unified text-to-text Transformer. *Journal of Machine Learning Research*, 21(140):1–67.

Luz Rello, Ricardo Baeza-Yates, Stefan Bott, and Horacio Saggion. 2013. Simplify or help? text simplification strategies for people with dyslexia. In *Proceedings of the 10th International Cross-Disciplinary Conference on Web Accessibility*, W4A '13, New York, NY, USA. Association for Computing Machinery.

Alexander M. Rush, Sumit Chopra, and Jason Weston. 2015. A neural attention model for abstractive sentence summarization. In *Proceedings of the 2015 Conference on Empirical Methods in Natural Language Processing*, pages 379–389, Lisbon, Portugal. Association for Computational Linguistics.

Horacio Saggion. 2017. Automatic text simplification. *Synthesis Lectures on Human Language Technologies*, 10(1):1–137.

Rico Sennrich, Barry Haddow, and Alexandra Birch. 2016. Controlling politeness in neural machine translation via side constraints. In *Proceedings of the 2016 Conference of the North American Chapter of the Association for Computational Linguistics: Human Language Technologies*, pages 35–40, San Diego, California. Association for Computational Linguistics.

Tianxiao Shen, Tao Lei, Regina Barzilay, and Tommi Jaakkola. 2017. Style transfer from non-parallel text by cross-alignment. In *Advances in Neural Information Processing Systems*, volume 30. Curran Associates, Inc.

A. Siddharthan. 2002. An architecture for a text simplification system. In *Language Engineering Conference, 2002. Proceedings*, pages 64–71.

Felix Stahlberg, Ilia Kulikov, and Shankar Kumar. 2022. Uncertainty determines the adequacy of the mode and the tractability of decoding in sequence-to-sequence models. In *Proceedings of the 60th Annual Meeting of the Association for Computational Linguistics (Volume 1: Long Papers)*, pages 8634–8645, Dublin, Ireland. Association for Computational Linguistics.

William Strunk and E. B. White. 1918. *The Elements of style*. W.F. Humphrey, Ithaca, N.Y.

Romal Thoppilan, Daniel De Freitas, Jamie Hall, Noam Shazeer, Apoorv Kulshreshtha, Heng-Tze Cheng, Alicia Jin, Taylor Bos, Leslie Baker, Yu Du, et al. 2022. Lamda: Language models for dialog applications. *arXiv preprint arXiv:2201.08239*.

Ashish Vaswani, Noam Shazeer, Niki Parmar, Jakob Uszkoreit, Llion Jones, Aidan N Gomez, Ł ukasz Kaiser, and Illia Polosukhin. 2017. Attention is all you need. In I. Guyon, U. V. Luxburg, S. Bengio, H. Wallach, R. Fergus, S. Vishwanathan, and R. Garnett, editors, *Advances in Neural Information Processing Systems 30*, pages 5998–6008. Curran Associates, Inc.

Aldert Vrij. 2005. Criteria-based content analysis: A qualitative review of the first 37 studies. *Psychology, Public Policy, and Law*, 11(1):3.

Willian Massami Watanabe, Arnaldo Candido Junior, Vinícius Rodriguez Uzêda, Renata Pontin de Mattos Fortes, Thiago Alexandre Salgueiro Pardo, and Sandra Maria Aluísio. 2009. Facilita: Reading assistance for low-literacy readers. In *Proceedings of the 27th ACM International Conference on Design of Communication*, SIGDOC '09, page 29–36, New York, NY, USA. Association for Computing Machinery.

John Wieting and Kevin Gimpel. 2018. ParaNMT-50M: Pushing the limits of paraphrastic sentence embeddings with millions of machine translations. In *Proceedings of the 56th Annual Meeting of the Association for Computational Linguistics (Volume 1: Long Papers)*, pages 451–462, Melbourne, Australia. Association for Computational Linguistics.

Menglin Xia, Ekaterina Kochmar, and Ted Briscoe. 2016. Text readability assessment for second language learners. In *Proceedings of the 11th Workshop on Innovative Use of NLP for Building Educational Applications*, pages 12–22, San Diego, CA. Association for Computational Linguistics.

Yinfei Yang, Steve Yuan, Daniel Cer, Sheng-yi Kong, Noah Constant, Petr Pilar, Heming Ge, Yun-Hsuan Sung, Brian Strope, and Ray Kurzweil. 2018. Learning semantic textual similarity from conversations. In *Proceedings of The Third Workshop on Representation Learning for NLP*, pages 164–174, Melbourne, Australia. Association for Computational Linguistics.

Yang You, Jing Li, Sashank Reddi, Jonathan Hseu, Sanjiv Kumar, Srinadh Bhojanapalli, Xiaodan Song, James Demmel, Kurt Keutzer, and Cho-Jui Hsieh. 2020. Large batch optimization for deep learning: Training BERT in 76 minutes. In *International Conference on Learning Representations*.

Jingqing Zhang, Yao Zhao, Mohammad Saleh, and Peter Liu. 2020. PEGASUS: Pre-training with extracted gap-sentences for abstractive summarization. In *Proceedings of the 37th International Conference on Machine Learning*, volume 119 of *Proceedings of Machine Learning Research*, pages 11328–11339. PMLR.

Xingxing Zhang and Mirella Lapata. 2017. Sentence simplification with deep reinforcement learning. In *Proceedings of the 2017 Conference on Empirical Methods in Natural Language Processing*, pages 584–594, Copenhagen, Denmark. Association for Computational Linguistics.

Renjie Zheng, Mingbo Ma, and Liang Huang. 2018. Multi-reference training with pseudo-references for neural translation and text generation. In *Proceedings of the 2018 Conference on Empirical Methods in Natural Language Processing*, pages 3188–3197, Brussels, Belgium. Association for Computational Linguistics.

William Zinsser. 2016. *On writing well: The classic guide to writing nonfiction*. Harper Perennial, New York, N.Y.

Parameter	Value
Attention dropout rate	0.1
Attention layer size	1,024
Batch size	256
Beam size	10
Dropout rate	0.1
Embedding size	1,536
Learning rate	0.4
MLP dimension	4,096
Number of attention heads	4
Number of layers	6
Number of fine-tuning iterations	100-2,000 (early stopping)
Number of pre-training iterations	100,000
TPU topology	4x4

Table 9: Transformer hyper-parameters.

A Transformer hyper-parameters

Our round-trip translation based models (Sec. 3.2) are trained on TPUs with the LAMB optimizer (You et al., 2020) in JAX (Bradbury et al., 2021). We used the Transformer (Vaswani et al., 2017) implementation from the MT example in Flax[12] with the 32K SentencePiece vocabulary (Kudo and Richardson, 2018) from T5 (Raffel et al., 2020). Model hyper-parameters are listed in Table 9.

B Annotator instructions

The *Concise-Lite* annotators received the following instructions:

> *Rewrite the sentence to make it more concise, without changing the sentence structure. By sentence structure, we mean the general order of words in the sentence should not change, some sub-phrases could be rewritten/replaced/deleted (3-5 words). These should be relatively minor rewrites, such that you can replace a phrase with a shorter alternative without reorganizing the entire sentence. The sentences should be annotated in isolation without any assumptions on preceding or succeeding sentences.*

The *Concise-Full* instructions are:

> *Rewrite the sentence to achieve maximum conciseness. These can be major rewrites that alter the sentence structure to make it as concise as possible. The annotator needs to make sure that the sentence stays the same semantically (meaning, intent & sentiment) and there is no loss of any critical information. The sentences should be annotated in isolation without any assumptions on preceding or succeeding sentences.*

C Example outputs

Table 10 shows some example outputs of our systems and the baselines. The summarization (Long T5) system frequently changes the meaning of the source sentence. The simplification (Simplify T5) system performs slightly better but still changes the meaning in some instances (example c). The T5 system is mostly faithful to the meaning of the source sentence. We observe occasional slight meaning shifts with the Transformer and ParaNMT systems (see e.g. examples b) and g)). The Giant-LM often changes or expands the information in the source sentence (e.g. examples b) and d), f)) or adds certain artefacts (e.g. "*Here is a revision: '... '* " in example a)) that stem from its main use case as a user-facing dialog agent. Being a paraphrasing system, ParaNMT often falls short of actually improving the conciseness (examples c) and f)), and often uses unnecessary synonyms. Synonym replacements can also be found sometimes in Transformer and T5 outputs (examples a) and c)), but not in Giant-LM and human-annotated sentences. The pre-trained models Giant-LM and T5 are sometimes able to compress sentences by relying

[12] `https://github.com/google/flax/tree/master/examples/wmt/`

Example a)	
Source	A few other men fell and sneaked back, but I don't know their names.
Long T5	A few other men fell and sneaked back.
Simplify T5	A few other men fell and sneaked back, but I don't know their names.
Giant-LM	Here is a revision: Other men fell and snuck back, but their names I do not know.
ParaNMT	several other men fell and crept back, but I don't know their names.
Transformer	Some other men fell and sneaked, but I do not know their names.
T5	A few other men fell and escaped, but I do not know their names.
Human (C.-Lite)	Some other men fell and sneaked back, but I don't know their names.
Human (C.-Full)	Others fell and snuck back, but I don't know their names.
Example b)	
Source	"Helplessly Hoping" is a 1969 song by the American folk rock group Crosby, Stills, and Nash.
Long T5	Helplessly Hoping is a 1969 song by the American folk rock group Crosby, Stills and Nash.
Simplify T5	Helplessly Hoping is a song by the American folk rock group Crosby, Stills & Nash .
Giant-LM	"Helplessly Hoping" is a 1969 song by the American folk rock group Crosby, Stills, and Nash. The song was written for Stephen Stills' wife.
ParaNMT	"helpless Hoping" is a 1969 song from the American rock band Crosby, Stills and Nash.
Transformer	"Helpless Hoping" is a 1969 song by American folk rock group Crosby, Stills and Nash.
T5	"Helplessly Hoping" is a 1969 song by the American folk rock group Crosby, Stills and Nash.
Human (C.-Lite)	"Helplessly Hoping" is a 1969 song by American folk rock group Crosby, Stills, and Nash.
Human (C.-Full)	Crosby, Stills, and Nash's "Helplessly Hoping" was released in 1969.
Example c)	
Source	The NLA Tower, Britain's 88th tallest tower, is an example of original 1970s architecture in the town.
Long T5	The NLA Tower, Britain's 88th tallest tower, is an example of original 1970s architecture in the town.
Simplify T5	The NLA Tower is an example of original 1970s architecture in the town .
Giant-LM	NLA Tower, Britain's 88th tallest tower, is a 1970s example of architecture in the town.
ParaNMT	the NLA Tower, the 88th highest British tower, is an example of the architecture of the 1970s in the city.
Transformer	The NLA Tower, Britain's 88th tallest tower, is an example of the city's original 1970s architecture.
T5	The NLA Tower, Britain's 88th tallest building, is an example of the town's original 1970s architecture.
Human (C.-Lite)	The NLA Tower, Britain's 88th tallest tower, is an original 1970s architecture in town.
Human (C.-Full)	Britain's 88th tallest tower, the NLA Tower, is an original 1970s architecture.
Example d)	
Source	There are some claims that even the kaiser had been amused by the incident.
Long T5	Police say the kaiser used a special case kaiser to cover the snafu on a McDonald's breakfast.
Simplify T5	There are some claims that even the kaiser had been amused by the incident.
Giant-LM	the kaiser was reportedly amused by the incident – This is a pretty vague phrase, in fact. Was the kaiser laughing? Grinning?
ParaNMT	there are some claims that even the kaiser was amused by the incident.
Transformer	There are some claims that even Kaiser was amused by the incident.
T5	Some claim that even the Kaiser was amused by the incident.
Human (C.-Lite)	There are claims that even the Kaiser was amused by the incident.
Human (C.-Full)	Some claim that the incident amused even the kaiser.
Example e)	
Source	Approximately 50% of viewers spend between one and three hours watching TV per day.
Long T5	TV Viewership Up to 50%.
Simplify T5	Approximately 50% of viewers spend between one and three hours watching TV per day.
Giant-LM	About half of viewers watch TV for 1 to 3 hours each day.
ParaNMT	approximately 50% of viewers spend one to three hours watching TV every day.
Transformer	About 50% of viewers spend between one and three hours watching TV a day.
T5	About 50% of viewers watch TV for one to three hours a day.
Human (C.-Lite)	Approximately 50% of viewers spend between one and three hours watching TV daily.
Human (C.-Full)	50% of viewers spend 1-3 hours watching TV daily.
Example f)	
Source	He studied at Tübingen, Freiburg, Berlin, and Heidelberg, where he earned his medical degree in 1910.
Long T5	German Doctor Emil Henckel von Donnersmarck Dies at 87
Simplify T5	He studied at Tübingen, Freiburg, Berlin, and Heidelberg, where he earned his medical degree in 1910.
Giant-LM	He studied medicine in Tübingen, Freiburg, Berlin and Heidelberg.
ParaNMT	he studied at Tübingen, Freiburg, Berlin, and Heidelberg, where he earned a medical degree in 1910.
Transformer	He studied in Tübingen, Freiburg, Berlin and Heidelberg, where he graduated in medicine in 1910.
T5	He studied in Tübingen, Freiburg, Berlin and Heidelberg, where he received his medical degree in 1910.
Human (C.-Lite)	He studied at Tübingen, Freiburg, Berlin, and Heidelberg, where he earned his medical degree in 1910.
Human (C.-Full)	He studied at Tübingen, Freiburg, Berlin, and Heidelberg, earning his medical degree in 1910.
Example g)	
Source	Almost without exception, the Keetoowahs sided with the Northern States during the Civil War.
Long T5	Keetoowahs Speak Out on Civil War.
Simplify T5	Almost without exception, the Keetoowahs sided with the Northern States during the Civil War.
Giant-LM	Almost without exception, the Keetoowahs sided with the Union.
ParaNMT	almost without exception, Keetoowah sailed with the Northern States during the Civil War.
Transformer	Almost without exception, the Keetoowahs joined the northern states during the civil war.
T5	Almost without exception, the Keetoowahs sided with the North during the Civil War.
Human (C.-Lite)	The Keetoowahs sided with the Northern States during the Civil War.
Human (C.-Full)	During the Civil War, the Keetoowahs sided with the North.

Table 10: Example sentences from our conciseness systems and other baselines (summarization: Long T5, simplification: Simplify T5, ParaNMT). We use the "RT→ MT" setups for the Transformer and T5 systems. We show one *Concise-Lite* and one *Concise-Full* human reference.

on background knowledge, e.g. by replacing "the Northern States" with "the Union" or "the North" in example g).

Revision for Concision: A Constrained Paraphrase Generation Task

Wenchuan Mu   Kwan Hui Lim
Singapore University of Technology and Design
{wenchuan_mu,kwanhui_lim}@sutd.edu.sg

Abstract

Academic writing should be concise as concise sentences better keep the readers' attention and convey meaning clearly. Writing concisely is challenging, for writers often struggle to revise their drafts. We introduce and formulate revising for concision as a natural language processing task at the sentence level. Revising for concision requires algorithms to use only necessary words to rewrite a sentence while preserving its meaning. The revised sentence should be evaluated according to its word choice, sentence structure, and organization. The revised sentence also needs to fulfil semantic retention and syntactic soundness. To aide these efforts, we curate and make available a benchmark parallel dataset that can depict revising for concision. The dataset contains 536 pairs of sentences before and after revising, and all pairs are collected from college writing centres. We also present and evaluate the approaches to this problem, which may assist researchers in this area.

1 Introduction

Concision and clarity[1] are important in academic writing as wordy sentences will obscure good ideas (Figure 1). Concise writing encourages writers to choose words deliberately and precisely, construct sentences carefully to eliminate deadword, and use grammar properly (Stanford University), which often requires experience and time. A first draft often contains far more words than necessary, and achieving concise writing requires revisions (MON, 2020). As far as we know, currently this revision process can only be done manually, or semi-manually with the help of some rule-based wordiness detectors (Adam and Long, 2013). We therefore introduce and formulate revising for concision as a natural language processing (NLP) task

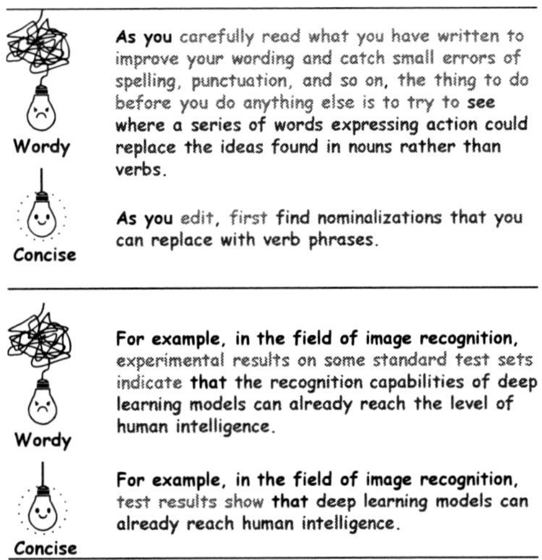

Figure 1: Wordy sentences are more boring to read than concise sentences. But how do we turn lengthy sentences into concise ones? We show two examples. The above sentence pair is taken from the Purdue Writing Lab, which suggests how college students should succinctly revise their writing (PU). In the other example, the wordy sentence comes from a scientific paper (Chen et al., 2020), and its concise counterpart is predicted from the concise revisioner we developed (Section 5). In each pair, text with the same colour delivers the same information.

and address it. In this study, we make the following contributions:

1. We formulate the revising for concision NLP task at the sentence level, which reflects the revising task in academic writing. We also survey the differences between this task and sentence compression, paraphrasing, etc.

2. We release a corpus of 536 sentence pairs, curated from 72 writing centres and additionally coded with the various linguistic rules for concise sentence revision.

3. We propose an gloss-based Seq2Seq approach

[1]We treat *concision* and *conciseness* as equivalent, and *clarity* as part of *concision*

Proceedings of the Workshop on Text Simplification, Accessibility, and Readability (TSAR-2022), pages 57 - 76

to this problem, and conduct automatic and human evaluations. We observed promising preliminary results and we believe that our findings will be useful for researchers working in this area.

2 Problem Statement

2.1 Revision as an English Writing Task

Concise writing itself is a lesson that is often emphasized in colleges, and revision is crucial in writing. The following definitions are helpful when we set out to formulate the task.

Definition 2.1 (Concise). Marked by brevity of expression or statement: free from all elaboration and superfluous detail (Merriam-Webster).

Definition 2.2 (Concise writing, English). Writing that is clear and does not include unnecessary or vague/unclear words or language (UOA).

Revising for concision at paragraph level, or even article level, may be the best practice. However, sentence-level revising usually suffices. We focus on revising for concision at the sentence level now. Indeed, in many college academic writing tutorials, revisions for concision are for individual sentences, and this process is defined as follows.

Definition 2.3 (Revise for concision at the sentence level, English[2]). Study a sentence in draft, use specific strategies[3] to edit the sentence concisely without losing meaning.

If someone, such as a college student, wants to concisely modify a sentence, specific strategies (*e.g.*, *delete* weak modifiers, *replace* phrasal verbs with single verbs, or *rewrite* in active voice, etc.) tell us how to locate wordiness and how to edit it (PU; WU; UALR; UNZ; MON, 2020). The rule is to repeatedly detect wordiness and revise it until no wordiness is detected or it cannot be removed without adding new wordiness. The final product serves as a concise version of the original sentence, if it does not lose its meaning.

2.2 Task Definition in NLP

Now that we know how humans can revise a sentence, what about programs? Each strategy is clear to a trained college student, but not clear enough to program in code. On the one hand, existing verbosity detectors may suggest which part of a sentence is too "dense" (Adam and Long, 2013), but fail to expose fine-grained wordiness details. On the other hand, how programs can edit sentences without losing their meaning remains challenging. In short, no existing program can generate well-modified sentences in terms of concision.

Eager for a program that revises sentences nicely and concisely, we set out to formulate this modification process as a sequence-to-sequence (Seq2Seq) NLP task. In this task, the input is any English sentence and the output should be its concise version. We define it as follows.

Definition 2.4 (Revise for concision at the sentence level, NLP). Produce a sentence where minimum wordiness can be identified. (And,) the produced sentence delivers the same information as input does. (And,) the produced sentence is syntactically correct.

As many other NLP tasks, *e.g.*, machine translation, named-entity recognition, etc., Definition 2.4 describes the product (text) of a process, not the process itself, *i.e.*, how the text is produced. This perspective is different from that of Definition 2.3.

Among the three components in Definition 2.4, both the first and the third are clear and self-contained. They are related to syntax; hence, at least human experts would think it straightforward to determine the soundness of a sentence on both. For example, the syntax correctness of an English sentence will not be judged differently by different experts, unless the syntax itself changes. Unfortunately, the second component is neither clear nor self-contained. This component asks for information retention, which is a rule inherited from Definition 2.3. Determining the semantic similarity between texts has long been challenging, even for human experts (Rus et al., 2014).

We then clarify the definition by assuming that combining the second and third components in Definition 2.4 meet the definition of the paraphrase generation task (Rus et al., 2014). Henceforth, Definition 2.4 can be simplified to Definition 2.5.

Definition 2.5 (Revise for concision at the sentence level, NLP, simplified). Produce a *paraphrase* where minimum wordiness can be identified.

The revising[4] task is well-defined, as long as "paraphrase generation" is well-defined. It is a paraphrase generation task with a syntactic constraint.

[2]Adapted from notes of PU Writing Lab and Rambo (2019)

[3]Presented in Appendix (Table 4) as a periphery of this study.

[4]stands for *(machine) revising for concision* if not otherwise specified, so does *revision*

2.3 Task Performance Indicator

How does one approximately measure revision performance? In principle, Definition 2.4 should be used as a checklist. A good sample requires correct grammar (γ), complete information (ρ) and reduced wordiness ($1-\omega$), assuming each component as a float number between 0 and 1. The overall assessment (χ) of the three components is as follows,

$$\chi = \alpha^2 \cdot (\gamma - 1) + \alpha \cdot (\rho - 1) + (1 - \omega), \quad (1)$$

where $\alpha \in \mathbb{R}_{>1}$ is a large enough number, as we believe that γ and ρ overweigh $1-\omega$. Intuitively, if a revised sentence does not paraphrase the original one, assessing the reduction of wordiness makes little sense. Concision χ would always be negative if $\gamma < 1$ or $\rho < 1$.

Corresponding to the three components is a mix of three tasks, including grammatical error correction for g, textual semantic similarity for r, and wordiness detection for w. Unfortunately, both a reference-free metric good enough to characterize the paraphrase and a robust wordiness detector are rare. Therefore, such assessment of concision is now only feasible through human evaluation.

To enable automatic evaluation for faster feedback, we currently follow Papineni's viewpoint (Papineni et al., 2002). The closer a machine revision is to a professional human revision, the better it is. To judge the quality of a machine revision, one measures its closeness to one or more reference human revisions according to a numerical metric. Thus, our revising evaluation system requires two main components:

1. A numerical "revision closeness" metric.
2. A corpus of good quality human reference revisions.

Different from days when Papineni needed to propose a closeness metric, we can adopt various metrics from machine translation and summarization community (Lin, 2004; Banerjee and Lavie, 2005). Since it is certain which criterion correlates best, we take multiple relevant and reasonable metrics into account to estimate quality of revision. These metrics include those measuring higher order n-grams precision (BLEU, Papineni et al., 2002), explicit Word-matching, stem-matching, or synonym-matching (METEOR, Banerjee and Lavie, 2005), surface bigram units overlapping (ROUGE-2-F1, Lin, 2004), cosine similarity between matched contextual words embeddings (BERTScore-F1, Zhang et al., 2020b), edit distance with single-word insertion, deletion, or replacement (word error rate, Su et al., 1992), edit distance with block insertion, deletion, or replacement (translation edit rate, Snover et al., 2006), and explicit goodness of words editing against reference and source (SARI, Xu et al., 2016). In short, BLEU, METEOR, ROUGE-2-F1, SARI, word error rate and translation edit rate estimate sentence well-formedness lexically; METEOR and BERTScore-F1 consider semantic equivalence. Comparing grammatical relations found in prediction with those found in references can also measure semantic similarity (Clarke and Lapata, 2006b; Riezler et al., 2003; Toutanova et al., 2016). Grammatical relations are extracted from dependency parsing, and F1 scores can then be used to measure overlap.

In contrast, the lack of good parallel corpus impedes (machine) revising for concision. To address this limitation, we curate and make available such a corpus as benchmark. Each sample in the corpus contains a wordy sentence, and at least one sentence revised for concision. Samples are from English writing centres of 57 universities, ten colleges, four community colleges, and a postgraduate school.

3 Related Work

Manual revision operations include delete, replace, and rewrite. Intuitively, a revising program should do similar jobs, too. In fact, these actions are implemented individually in various NLP tasks. For example, sentence compression requires programs to delete unnecessary words, and paraphrasing itself is a matter of replacement. Machine revision for concision could also share traits with them. Practically, when a neural model learns in a Seq2Seq manner, the difference among these tasks is the parallel dataset. We are also interested in whether programs developed for these tasks can work in machine revision.

3.1 Deleting as in Sentence Compression

When revising, deleting redundant words is common. For example, we can revise "*research is increasing in the field of nutrition and food science*" to "*research is increasing in nutrition and food science*" (URI, 2019), simply by deleting "*the field of*". Deleting is canonical in sentence compression, a task aiming to reduce sentence length from source sentences while retaining basic meaning (Jing, 2000; Knight and Marcu, 2000; McDonald, 2006). For example, the compression task has been formulated as integer linear programming optimization using syntactic trees (Clarke and Lapata, 2006a), or as a sequence labelling optimization problem using the recurrent neural networks (RNN) (Filippova et al., 2015; Klerke et al., 2016; Kamigaito et al., 2018). They explicitly or implicitly use dependency grammar. Pre-trained language models such as ELMo (Peters et al., 2018) and BERT (Devlin et al., 2019) can encode features apart from dependency parsing (Kamigaito and Okumura, 2020), bringing prediction and reference sentences closer.

All methods rely on parallel datasets labelling parts to be deleted. However, the deleting part in sentence compression differs from that in revision. Filippova and Altun (2013) created Google dataset from titles and first sentence of news articles. The information retained in the first sentence depends on the title. While this creation is useful for reducing excessive information, the deleted part is probably not wordiness.

Deleting does not solve everything in revision. We can revise "*in this report I will conduct a study of ants and the setup of their colonies*" to "*in this report I will study ants and their colonies*", taking advantage of noun-and-verb homograph. However, a more concise version "*this report studies ants*" (Commnet) requires changing "*study*" to third-person singular.

3.2 Replacing as in Paraphrase Generation

Word choice matters as well, thus we revise by paraphrasing to stronger words. Paraphrase generation changes a sentence grammatically and reselects words, while retaining meaning. Paraphrasing matters in academic writing, for it helps avoid plagiarism. Rule-based or statistical machine paraphrasing substitutes words by finding synonyms from lexical databases, and decodes syntax according to template sentences. This rigid method may undermine creativity (Bui et al., 2021). Pre-trained neural language models like GPT (Radford et al., 2019) or BART (Lewis et al., 2020) paraphrase more accurately (Hegde and Patil, 2020). Through paraphrasing, we can replace verb phrase "*conduct a study*" to verb "*study*" in the example above, rather than delete and rely on noun-and-verb homographs to keep the sentence syntactically correct.

Machine revision is a kind of paraphrase generation, and vice versa is not true. Current paraphrase generation does not require concision in generated sentences. Automatically annotated datasets for paraphrasing include ParaNMT (Wieting and Gimpel, 2018), Twitter (Lan et al., 2017), or repurposed noisy datasets such as MSCOCO (Lin et al., 2014) and WikiAnswers (Fader et al., 2013). We may adapt paraphrase parallel datasets to train revising models, as investigated in Section 5.

3.3 Other related tasks

Summarization produces a shorter text of one or several documents, while retaining most of meaning (Paulus et al., 2018). This is similar to sentence compression. In practice, summarization welcomes novel words, allows specifying output length (Kikuchi et al., 2016), and removes much more information than sentence compression does. Datasets include XSum (Narayan et al., 2018) , CNN/DM (Hermann et al., 2015), WikiHow (Koupaee and Wang, 2018), NYT (Sandhaus, 2008), DUC-2004 (Over et al., 2007), and Gigaword (Rush et al., 2015), where summaries are generally shorter than one-tenth of documents. On the other hand, sentence summarization (Chopra et al., 2016) uses summarization methods on sentence compression datasets, retaining more information and possibly generating new words.

Text simplification modifies vocabulary and syntax for easier reading, while retaining approximate meaning (Omelianchuk et al., 2021). Handcrafted syntactic rules (Siddharthan, 2006; Carroll et al., 1999; Chandrasekar et al., 1996) and aligned sentences-driven simplification (Yatskar et al., 2010) have been explored. Corpora such as Turk (Xu et al., 2016) and PWKP (Zhu et al., 2010) are compiled from Wikipedia and Simple English Wikipedia (Coster and Kauchak, 2011). Rules for simplification may deviate from that for revision, *e.g.*, text simplification sometimes encourages prepositional phrases (Xu et al., 2016). Still, adapting these approaches may benefit academic revising for concision.

Fluency editing (Napoles et al., 2017) not only corrects grammatical errors but paraphrases text to be more native sounding as well. Its paraphrasing section is constrained such that outputs represent a higher level of English proficiency than inputs. As a constrained paraphrase task, fluency editing may alleviate ill-posed problems in paraphrase generation (Cao et al., 2020; Rus et al., 2014). However, such constraints may not be consistent with those required for concision.

In general, machine revision for academic writing requires new methods. Rules for revision can be adapted from these related tasks, so do training strategies.

4 Benchmark Corpus

The collated corpus, named **Concise-536**, contains 536 pairs of sentences. This is a fair starting size, comparable with 385 of RST-DT (semantic parsing, Carlson et al., 2003), 500 of DUC 2004 (summarization[5]), or 575 by Cohn and Lapata (2008) (sentence compression). Each concise sentence is revised from its wordy counterpart by English specialists from the 72 universities, colleges, or community colleges. Sentence ID, category and original link are available for each data point[6], and a 120-point validation split from other sources is attached.

Revising different sentences can go through a completely different process. As seen below, simply crossing out a few words revises Example 4.1; a new word is needed in revising Example 4.2; and even the sentence structure needs changing in Example 4.3.

Corpus Example 4.1 (Delete). Any ~~particular type of~~ dessert is fine with me. (PU)

Corpus Example 4.2 (Replace). She ~~has the ability to~~ can influence the outcome. (PU)

Corpus Example 4.3 (Rewrite). ~~The 1780 constitution of Massachusetts was written by John Adams.~~ John Adams wrote the 1780 Massachusetts Constitution. (UNC, 2021)

In Concise-536, we do not identify fine-grained wordiness because a phrase can have more than one type of verbosity at the same time. For instance, we can revise "*Her poverty also helped in the formation of her character.*" to "*Her poverty also helped form her character.*" (George Mason University, 2021), treating "*in the formation of*" as either a wordy prepositional phrase, or nominalization. Rather, we focus on editing.

In editing, the three actions are not complementary, and instead have varying degrees of power. Deleting can be covered by replacing (See Section 3.1), which could be again covered by rewriting, *i.e.*, rewriting is the most flexible. However, Occam's razor pushes us to prioritize the actions requiring lower effort to complete, *i.e.*, delete < replace < rewrite. Supposedly, the difficulty for implement each action with programs shares the same trend. In addition, some sentences contain multiple wordiness occurrences, each of which may need a different action, *e.g.*, delete + replace.

Interested in how well a revising algorithm resembles each action, we label revisions in each sentence pair and divide them into seven categories. Revisions that require the same set of actions will be assigned to the same category. Each revision is assigned to one of seven categories in Table 1.

For convenience, we standardize categorizing rules as follows where each sentence is a word-level sequence. For each pair, we have a wordy sequence (w) and a concise sequence (c).

1. If c is a (not necessarily consecutive) subsequence of w, we consider revision only requires deletion (category I).

2. If not, we only delete redundancy from w to get w', *i.e.*, w' paraphrases w, and w' is a subsequence of w. Then, we make local[7] replacement(s) to w' to get w^*, and every individual state from w' to w^* (*i.e.*, after each local replacement) paraphrases w'. If $w^* = c$ and $w' = w$, we consider revision only requires replacement (category II). If $w^* = c$ and $w' \neq w$, we consider revision only requires deletion and replacement (category IV).

3. If $w^* = w$, we consider revision relies solely on rewriting (category III).

Corpus Example 4.4 (category I). ~~There are~~ four rules ~~that~~ should be observed. (PU)

Corpus Example 4.5 (category III). ~~Regular reviews of~~ online content should be ~~scheduled~~ reviewed regularly. (MON, 2020)

Corpus Example 4.6 (category IV). She fell ~~down due to the fact that~~ because she hurried. (PU)

Example 4.4 used to be wordy in the running start, but deleting suffices in revision. Therefore, although counter intuitive, it belongs to category I. An adjective-noun pair is the wordiness in Example 4.5, yet its revision is more complex than replacing a verb. Usually, revision involves multiple

[5]https://duc.nist.gov/duc2004/

[6]https://huggingface.co/datasets

[7]Empirically, in a sentence or clause, we do not replace the subject and predicate verb together.

Category	Action	# sents.	Mean words wordy sent.	Mean words concise sent.	Translation Edit Rate
I	Delete	169	13.16	9.17	4.72
II	Replace	116	12.37	9.02	5.1
III	Rewrite	153	14.43	9.73	9.54
IV	Delete + Replace	42	23.81	11.57	15.16
V	Replace + Rewrite	33	21.52	12.85	14.88
VI	Delete + Rewrite	14	24.5	11.36	17.71
VII	Delete + Replace + Rewrite	9	32.56	14.56	25.56
All	-	536	15.32	9.86	8.31

Table 1: Revising a sentence can involve either one of the three strategies (category I, II, III), or a combination of them (category IV, V, VI, VII). Sample sizes, average word counts before and after revisions, and average edit distance (translate edit rate, TER) for revision are listed.

strategies, as seen in Example 4.6 (delete "*down*" + replace "*due to the fact that with*" with "*because*").

Human annotators implement the rules, as we need to check whether the meaning is still the same at each step.

Usually, category III sentences are the hardest to revise as the easier strategies of deleting and replacing are not applicable. In fact, revising category V, VI, and VII sentences are more challenging, as these sentences are longer, more complex, and more deliberate than category III sentences (Figure 4, Table 9, 10), which is a bias in this corpus.

5 Approaches to Revisions

We approach the raised problem in this study. Solutions to machine revision for concision can be diverse. Neural model solutions include tree-to-tree transduction models (Cohn and Lapata, 2008), or general Seq2Seq models. We present a Seq2Seq approach, for it is flexible and straightforward. The model architecture is BART (Lewis et al., 2020).

Ideally, training corpora tune statistical models or neural models, such that we can test tuned models on the benchmark corpus. However, lacking authoritative revisions prompted us to let models fit relevant task data. We also use public external knowledge, *e.g.*, WordNet (Fellbaum, 2010). This section describes how we build an ad hoc training corpus to initiate this task.

The BART base model (124,058,116 parameters) is then used to fit *each* training set in this section. Training settings are fixed (batch size at 32, PyTorch Adam optimizer (Paszke et al., 2019; Kingma and Ba, 2015) with initial learning rate at 5×10^{-5}, validated every 5,000 iterations). We then evaluate trained models on Concise-536.

5.1 Baselines

We prepare training samples by adjusting data from paraphrase generation (ParaNMT, Wieting and Gimpel, 2018), sentence simplification (WikiSmall, Zhang and Lapata, 2017), or sentence compression (Gigaword, Rush et al., 2015; Google News datasets, Filippova and Altun, 2013; MSR Abstractive Text Compression Dataset, Toutanova et al., 2016).

5.2 Approach 1: WordNet as Booster

Baseline methods are useful, but they are not developed for revision tasks after all. To replace a verb or noun phrase with a single word, we leverage word glosses in public dictionaries, *i.e.*, WordNet (Fellbaum, 2010). Word semantics are close to semantics in their glosses. This feature is usually used to improve word embedding (Bosc and Vincent, 2018) or evaluate analogy of word embedding (Mikolov et al., 2013). We use this feature to replace a verb or noun phrase with a single word.

We create data samples using WordNet and a language modelling corpus. For each sentence s in the corpus, we use WordNet vocabulary glosses to inflate it and obtain s'. Resulted parallel data approximate phrase replacement in sentence revision.

We first pick a unigram u, one of nouns, verbs, adjectives, or adverbs in s. At the same time, we avoid common words, *e.g.*, "*old*", or collocations and compounds, *e.g.*, "*united*" in "*United Kingdom*". Next, we apply Lesk's dictionary-based word sense disambiguation (WSD) algorithm (Lesk, 1986) on u and s to get gloss g. Then, we parse s and g to obtain respective dependency trees T_s and T_g; r_g denotes root node in T_g. Usually, if u is a noun, r_g is a noun, and if u is an adjective, r_g is a verb. Eight $u \rightarrow r_g$ patterns account for over 90% of the WordNet vocabulary (Table 5). In Algorithm 1, we modify dependency trees (T_s and T_g) according to the eight patterns. The remaining six patterns are NOUN→VERB, ADJ(-S) → ADJ, ADJ → ADP, ADJ → VERB, and ADV → ADP.

Finally, we filter and post-process synthesized sentences. We parse s' again and compare it with

Algorithm 1 Rule-based Gloss Substitution

Require: T_s, T_g **return** s'
  Copy-children(from u, to r_g)
  Locate h_u ▷ head node of u
  Delete (u with children, from T_s)
  if $u \in$ NOUN **then**
    Insert-child-node (r_g with children, to h_u)
    if $r_g \in$ VERB **then**
      $u \leftarrow$ Gerund(u)
    end if
    Correct inflections (singular and plural forms)
    Remove duplicate determiners
  else if $u \in$ VERB **then**
    Insert-child-node (r_g with children, to h_u)
    Correct inflections (person and tense)
    Add/Remove prepositions according to verb transitivity
  else
    Insert-right-child-node (r_g with children, to h_u) ▷ Post attributive
  end if
  $s' \leftarrow$ Linearize(T_s)

the dependency tree from which s' is linearized. We drop those with more than three mismatches, or with accuracy lower than 0.9. We "smooth" synthesized sentences with parroting[8], to mitigate overfitting. We also drop those sharing low semantic similarity (BERTScore $\leq$ 0.82) with original s.

We take the first 0.2 million sentences from WikiText-103 corpus (Merity et al., 2017) and around 71 thousand data points after filtration are available to train the BART base model.

5.3 Approach 2: Multi-Task Learning

Each dataset in baselines and Approach 1 handles part of task. However, sentence compression or simplification does not emphasize complete information retention; paraphrase generation hardly encourages deletion; synthetic data limit editing scope because word glosses are limited. We hypothesize that mixing the good samples among these datasets could more closely approximate the revision task. Therefore, we adjust datasets again. We keep every sample in MSR as it is small (21,145, see Appendix). Semantic similarity lower bound for sentence compression and simplification datasets is set at BERTScore = 0.9. For ParaNMT, we discard samples with less than 10 words. As a result, ablation of mixed and shuffled data samples shows that a mixture of MSR, filtered ParaNMT, and synthetic WordNet dataset leads to the strongest approach. This approach uses transfer learning from multiple datasets to learn revising strategies such as deletion and phrase replacement.

5.4 Experiment and Result

Table 2 shows test results in each category. Our approach 2 has the highest overall score and is more robust than baseline models on category I, IV, and VII. The same architecture trained only on MSR outperforms any other baseline for deletion (category I) and ranks second for replacement (category II). The top-ranked baseline for replacement (category II) is trained on ParaNMT. In category V, the model trained on WordNet scores highest, slightly outperforming other baselines. Trends in category III, IV, VI, VII are less clear. Datasets Gigaword, Google News, and WikiSmall may be quite different from the benchmark corpus, and thus models trained on these datasets do not score well.

Our approach 2 suffers from two shortcomings common to all baselines. First, the model relies on transfer learning from MSR and ParaNMT and struggle to rewrite (category III) or to handle composite wordiness (category V, VI, VII). Second, the approach 2 outputs score worse than the input text on many metrics in many categories, especially on category III. These shortcomings suggest challenges in revision. We take the 5th and 95th percentile from all 536 samples to qualitatively illustrate the best proposed approach in Table 3. Apart from samples in Concise-536, Figure 1 shows an arbitrary sentence by non-English native speakers (Chen et al., 2020). The proposed revisioner removes repetition and unnecessary prepositional phrases, illustrating its potential in academic writing.

For human evaluation, we adopt an approach similar to Hsu et al. (2018); Zhang et al. (2020a); Ravaut et al. (2022). We (1) rank the samples by overall automatic evaluation on the model in descending order; (2) divide the examples in *each category* into two buckets; (3) randomly pick one example from each bucket. For each picked sample, we ask three graduate students (IELTS 7.0 or equivalent) to rank the predictions of seven systems, and the average ranking of each system is shown in **H** column in Table 2.

For top three systems, human evaluators then assess information retention (ρ) and wordiness (ω), since system outputs are in good syntax. Particularly, human assessment on wordiness engages the Paramedic Method (Lanham and Stodel, 1992) to highlight the wordy part and ω = (# wordy words)

[8] https://huggingface.co/prithivida/parrot_paraphraser_on_T5

Methods	I	II	III	IV	V	VI	VII	All	H	ρ	ω
ParaNMT (Wieting and Gimpel, 2018)	0.46	**0.62**	0.46	*0.53*	0.44	0.45	*0.38*	0.55	3.40		
MSR (Toutanova et al., 2016)	*0.74*	0.58	0.44	0.51	0.41	0.44	0.37	0.57	*2.79*	0.78	**0.40**
G. News (Filippova and Altun, 2013)	*0.61*	0.46	0.39	0.40	0.35	0.39	0.33	0.48	5.74		
Gigaword (Rush et al., 2015)	0.30	0.29	0.28	0.31	0.25	0.29	0.23	0.29	6.74		
WikiSmall (Zhang and Lapata, 2017)	0.70	0.59	**0.48**	0.52	0.44	**0.46**	*0.38*	0.57	3.31		
Our Approach 1	0.70	0.60	*0.47*	0.52	**0.46**	*0.45*	0.37	*0.58*	*2.79*	**0.99**	0.47
Our Approach 2	**0.75**	0.60	*0.47*	**0.55**	0.40	*0.45*	**0.41**	**0.59**	**2.62**	*0.82*	*0.41*

Table 2: We average BLEU, METEOR, ROUGE-2-F1, SARI, Parsed relation F1, BERTScore-F1, *and* (negative) translation edit rate of (pre-)baseline methods. The most favorable score in each column is in bold, the second most favorable in italics. This table estimates the strengths and weaknesses of each variants. System ranking from human evaluation (**H**), information retention (ρ), and wordiness (ω) are presented in the right-most columns.

Category	Reference(s)	Prediction
5th percentile	Bob ~~provided an explanation of~~ explained the computer to his grandmother.	Bob ~~provided an explanation of~~ explained the computer to his grandmother.
95th percentile	~~Rather than taking the bull by the horns,~~ she ~~was quiet as a church mouse~~ avoided confrontation by remaining silent.	~~Rather than taking the bull by the horns,~~ she was quiet as a church mouse.

Table 3: Well/poorly revised samples in the corpus. Shorter sentences that require simpler actions are perfectly revised. Rewriting clichés is difficult, in which case the approach tends to use deletion.

/ (# all words). The model trained adapted WordNet data preserves information better, which also accounts for its good human ranking.

We observe general correlation between automatic score ranking and human evaluation ranking. However, information retention is not sufficiently represented by semantic similarity scores like BERTScore. These findings suggest further investigation on the evaluation scheme of this task.

6 Discussion

Comparing the proposed revisioner's effectiveness for different categories, we understand deleting and replacing are much easier sub-tasks than rewriting is. The former two actions, especially deletion, are less ill-posed, while rewriting is open. Still, revision for concision requires an algorithm that is able to use all three actions in combination. Its goal is to resolve all seven categories of cases, marking distinction between revision and other tasks such as sentence compression.

We use seven metrics to estimate a revisioner's effectiveness, since each metric has its shortcomings. For example, METEOR does not adequately penalize nominalization, and thus wordy input texts typically score higher on METEOR than algorithm outputs. More targeted metrics for this task, including reference-free structural metrics (Sulem et al., 2018), might help. We do not include word counts. Although concision is marked by brevity and wordiness often correlates to high word count, concise writing does not always require the fewest words (PU). Optimizing a lower word count may be misleading even if it is constrained to zero information loss (Siddharthan, 2006). For example, abusing pronouns and ellipses can result in shorter sentences that are harder to read.

Transferring knowledge from other tasks to approximate revising is a stopgap measure. Specialized revising methods exist, *e.g.*, the Paramedic Method (Lanham and Stodel, 1992). Automated specialized methods may be more efficient.

7 Conclusion

We formulate sentence-level revision for concision as a constrained paraphrase generation task. The revision task not only requires semantics preservation as in usual paraphrasing tasks, but also specifies syntactic changes. A revised sentence is free of wordiness and as informative. Revising sentences is challenging and requires coordinated use of delete, replace, and rewrite. To benchmark revising algorithms, we collect 536 sentence pairs before and after revising from 72 college writing centres. We then propose a Seq2Seq revising model and evaluate it on this benchmark. Despite scarcity of training data, the proposed approaches offer promising results for revising academic texts. We believe this corpus will drive specialized revision algorithms that benefit both authors and readers.

Ethical considerations

The release of Concise-536 is intended only for "not-for-profit" educational purposes or private research and study in accordance with the Copyright Act 1994; all original text content is acknowledged as the property of each educational institution. All text content in Concise-536 (and the 120-point validation split) are public, and our release details their original links, thus making the release no different from a list of outbound links.

Limitations

The transfer of knowledge from other tasks to the rough revision is an emergency solution. There are specialised revision methods. For example, automating the Paramedic method (Lanham and Stodel, 1992) could possibly lead to a more efficient revisioner.

Acknowledgements

We would like to thank the reviewers for thoughtful comments and efforts to improve our manuscript.

References

Adam and Ben Long. 2013. Hemingway editor.

Satanjeev Banerjee and Alon Lavie. 2005. METEOR: An automatic metric for MT evaluation with improved correlation with human judgments. In *Proceedings of the ACL Workshop on Intrinsic and Extrinsic Evaluation Measures for Machine Translation and/or Summarization*, pages 65–72, Ann Arbor, Michigan. Association for Computational Linguistics.

Tom Bosc and Pascal Vincent. 2018. Auto-encoding dictionary definitions into consistent word embeddings. In *Proceedings of the 2018 Conference on Empirical Methods in Natural Language Processing*, pages 1522–1532, Brussels, Belgium. Association for Computational Linguistics.

Tien-Cuong Bui, Van-Duc Le, Hai-Thien To, and Sang Kyun Cha. 2021. Generative pre-training for paraphrase generation by representing and predicting spans in exemplars. In *2021 IEEE International Conference on Big Data and Smart Computing (BigComp)*, pages 83–90. IEEE.

Ruisheng Cao, Su Zhu, Chenyu Yang, Chen Liu, Rao Ma, Yanbin Zhao, Lu Chen, and Kai Yu. 2020. Unsupervised dual paraphrasing for two-stage semantic parsing. In *Proceedings of the 58th Annual Meeting of the Association for Computational Linguistics*, pages 6806–6817, Online. Association for Computational Linguistics.

Lynn Carlson, Daniel Marcu, and Mary Ellen Okurowski. 2003. Building a discourse-tagged corpus in the framework of rhetorical structure theory. In *Current and new directions in discourse and dialogue*, pages 85–112. Springer.

John Carroll, Guido Minnen, Darren Pearce, Yvonne Canning, Siobhan Devlin, and John Tait. 1999. Simplifying text for language-impaired readers. In *Ninth Conference of the European Chapter of the Association for Computational Linguistics*, pages 269–270, Bergen, Norway. Association for Computational Linguistics.

R. Chandrasekar, Christine Doran, and B. Srinivas. 1996. Motivations and methods for text simplification. In *COLING 1996 Volume 2: The 16th International Conference on Computational Linguistics*.

Kai Chen, Haoqi Zhu, Leiming Yan, and Jinwei Wang. 2020. A survey on adversarial examples in deep learning. *Journal on Big Data*, 2(2):71.

Sumit Chopra, Michael Auli, and Alexander M. Rush. 2016. Abstractive sentence summarization with attentive recurrent neural networks. In *Proceedings of the 2016 Conference of the North American Chapter of the Association for Computational Linguistics: Human Language Technologies*, pages 93–98, San Diego, California. Association for Computational Linguistics.

James Clarke and Mirella Lapata. 2006a. Constraint-based sentence compression: An integer programming approach. In *Proceedings of the COLING/ACL 2006 Main Conference Poster Sessions*, pages 144–151, Sydney, Australia. Association for Computational Linguistics.

James Clarke and Mirella Lapata. 2006b. Models for sentence compression: A comparison across domains, training requirements and evaluation measures. In *Proceedings of the 21st International Conference on Computational Linguistics and 44th Annual Meeting of the Association for Computational Linguistics*, pages 377–384, Sydney, Australia. Association for Computational Linguistics.

Trevor Cohn and Mirella Lapata. 2008. Sentence compression beyond word deletion. In *Proceedings of the 22nd International Conference on Computational Linguistics (Coling 2008)*, pages 137–144, Manchester, UK. Coling 2008 Organizing Committee.

Commnet. The guide to grammar and writing.

William Coster and David Kauchak. 2011. Simple English Wikipedia: A new text simplification task. In *Proceedings of the 49th Annual Meeting of the Association for Computational Linguistics: Human Language Technologies*, pages 665–669, Portland, Oregon, USA. Association for Computational Linguistics.

Marie-Catherine De Marneffe and Christopher D Manning. 2008. Stanford typed dependencies manual. Technical report, Technical report, Stanford University.

Jacob Devlin, Ming-Wei Chang, Kenton Lee, and Kristina Toutanova. 2019. BERT: Pre-training of deep bidirectional transformers for language understanding. In *Proceedings of the 2019 Conference of the North American Chapter of the Association for Computational Linguistics: Human Language Technologies, Volume 1 (Long and Short Papers)*, pages 4171–4186, Minneapolis, Minnesota. Association for Computational Linguistics.

Anthony Fader, Luke Zettlemoyer, and Oren Etzioni. 2013. Paraphrase-driven learning for open question answering. In *Proceedings of the 51st Annual Meeting of the Association for Computational Linguistics (Volume 1: Long Papers)*, pages 1608–1618, Sofia, Bulgaria. Association for Computational Linguistics.

Christiane Fellbaum. 2010. Wordnet. In *Theory and applications of ontology: computer applications*, pages 231–243. Springer.

Katja Filippova, Enrique Alfonseca, Carlos A. Colmenares, Lukasz Kaiser, and Oriol Vinyals. 2015. Sentence compression by deletion with LSTMs. In *Proceedings of the 2015 Conference on Empirical Methods in Natural Language Processing*, pages 360–368, Lisbon, Portugal. Association for Computational Linguistics.

Katja Filippova and Yasemin Altun. 2013. Overcoming the lack of parallel data in sentence compression. In *Proceedings of the 2013 Conference on Empirical Methods in Natural Language Processing*, pages 1481–1491, Seattle, Washington, USA. Association for Computational Linguistics.

The Writing Center George Mason University. 2021. Writing concisely.

Chaitra V. Hegde and Shrikumar Patil. 2020. Unsupervised paraphrase generation using pre-trained language models. *CoRR*, abs/2006.05477.

Karl Moritz Hermann, Tomás Kociský, Edward Grefenstette, Lasse Espeholt, Will Kay, Mustafa Suleyman, and Phil Blunsom. 2015. Teaching machines to read and comprehend. In *Advances in Neural Information Processing Systems 28: Annual Conference on Neural Information Processing Systems 2015, December 7-12, 2015, Montreal, Quebec, Canada*, pages 1693–1701.

Wan-Ting Hsu, Chieh-Kai Lin, Ming-Ying Lee, Kerui Min, Jing Tang, and Min Sun. 2018. A unified model for extractive and abstractive summarization using inconsistency loss. In *Proceedings of the 56th Annual Meeting of the Association for Computational Linguistics (Volume 1: Long Papers)*, pages 132–141, Melbourne, Australia. Association for Computational Linguistics.

Hongyan Jing. 2000. Sentence reduction for automatic text summarization. In *Sixth Applied Natural Language Processing Conference*, pages 310–315, Seattle, Washington, USA. Association for Computational Linguistics.

Hidetaka Kamigaito, Katsuhiko Hayashi, Tsutomu Hirao, and Masaaki Nagata. 2018. Higher-order syntactic attention network for longer sentence compression. In *Proceedings of the 2018 Conference of the North American Chapter of the Association for Computational Linguistics: Human Language Technologies, Volume 1 (Long Papers)*, pages 1716–1726, New Orleans, Louisiana. Association for Computational Linguistics.

Hidetaka Kamigaito and Manabu Okumura. 2020. Syntactically look-ahead attention network for sentence compression. In *The Thirty-Fourth AAAI Conference on Artificial Intelligence, AAAI 2020, The Thirty-Second Innovative Applications of Artificial Intelligence Conference, IAAI 2020, The Tenth AAAI Symposium on Educational Advances in Artificial Intelligence, EAAI 2020, New York, NY, USA, February 7-12, 2020*, pages 8050–8057. AAAI Press.

Yuta Kikuchi, Graham Neubig, Ryohei Sasano, Hiroya Takamura, and Manabu Okumura. 2016. Controlling output length in neural encoder-decoders. In *Proceedings of the 2016 Conference on Empirical Methods in Natural Language Processing*, pages 1328–1338, Austin, Texas. Association for Computational Linguistics.

Diederik P. Kingma and Jimmy Ba. 2015. Adam: A method for stochastic optimization. In *3rd International Conference on Learning Representations, ICLR 2015, San Diego, CA, USA, May 7-9, 2015, Conference Track Proceedings*.

Sigrid Klerke, Yoav Goldberg, and Anders Søgaard. 2016. Improving sentence compression by learning to predict gaze. In *Proceedings of the 2016 Conference of the North American Chapter of the Association for Computational Linguistics: Human Language Technologies*, pages 1528–1533, San Diego, California. Association for Computational Linguistics.

Kevin Knight and Daniel Marcu. 2000. Statistics-based summarization - step one: Sentence compression. In *Proceedings of the Seventeenth National Conference on Artificial Intelligence and Twelfth Conference on on Innovative Applications of Artificial Intelligence, July 30 - August 3, 2000, Austin, Texas, USA*, pages 703–710. AAAI Press / The MIT Press.

Mahnaz Koupaee and William Yang Wang. 2018. Wikihow: A large scale text summarization dataset. *CoRR*, abs/1810.09305.

Wuwei Lan, Siyu Qiu, Hua He, and Wei Xu. 2017. A continuously growing dataset of sentential paraphrases. In *Proceedings of the 2017 Conference on Empirical Methods in Natural Language Processing*, pages 1224–1234, Copenhagen, Denmark. Association for Computational Linguistics.

Richard A Lanham and James Stodel. 1992. *Revising prose*. Macmillan Publishing Company.

Michael Lesk. 1986. Automatic sense disambiguation using machine readable dictionaries: how to tell a pine cone from an ice cream cone. In *Proceedings of the 5th Annual International Conference on Systems Documentation, SIGDOC 1986, Toronto, Ontario, Canada, 1986*, pages 24–26. ACM.

Mike Lewis, Yinhan Liu, Naman Goyal, Marjan Ghazvininejad, Abdelrahman Mohamed, Omer Levy, Veselin Stoyanov, and Luke Zettlemoyer. 2020. BART: Denoising sequence-to-sequence pre-training for natural language generation, translation, and comprehension. In *Proceedings of the 58th Annual Meeting of the Association for Computational Linguistics*, pages 7871–7880, Online. Association for Computational Linguistics.

Chin-Yew Lin. 2004. ROUGE: A package for automatic evaluation of summaries. In *Text Summarization Branches Out*, pages 74–81, Barcelona, Spain. Association for Computational Linguistics.

Tsung-Yi Lin, Michael Maire, Serge Belongie, James Hays, Pietro Perona, Deva Ramanan, Piotr Dollár, and C Lawrence Zitnick. 2014. Microsoft coco: Common objects in context. In *European conference on computer vision*, pages 740–755. Springer.

Zhouhan Lin, Minwei Feng, Cícero Nogueira dos Santos, Mo Yu, Bing Xiang, Bowen Zhou, and Yoshua Bengio. 2017. A structured self-attentive sentence embedding. In *5th International Conference on Learning Representations, ICLR 2017, Toulon, France, April 24-26, 2017, Conference Track Proceedings*. OpenReview.net.

Ryan McDonald. 2006. Discriminative sentence compression with soft syntactic evidence. In *11th Conference of the European Chapter of the Association for Computational Linguistics*, pages 297–304, Trento, Italy. Association for Computational Linguistics.

Stephen Merity, Caiming Xiong, James Bradbury, and Richard Socher. 2017. Pointer sentinel mixture models. In *5th International Conference on Learning Representations, ICLR 2017, Toulon, France, April 24-26, 2017, Conference Track Proceedings*. OpenReview.net.

Merriam-Webster. Concise definition.

Tomás Mikolov, Kai Chen, Greg Corrado, and Jeffrey Dean. 2013. Efficient estimation of word representations in vector space. In *1st International Conference on Learning Representations, ICLR 2013, Scottsdale, Arizona, USA, May 2-4, 2013, Workshop Track Proceedings*.

Monash University (MON) Writing Department MON. 2020. Writing clearly, concisely and precisely.

Courtney Napoles, Keisuke Sakaguchi, and Joel Tetreault. 2017. JFLEG: A fluency corpus and benchmark for grammatical error correction. In *Proceedings of the 15th Conference of the European Chapter of the Association for Computational Linguistics: Volume 2, Short Papers*, pages 229–234, Valencia, Spain. Association for Computational Linguistics.

Shashi Narayan, Shay B. Cohen, and Mirella Lapata. 2018. Don't give me the details, just the summary! topic-aware convolutional neural networks for extreme summarization. In *Proceedings of the 2018 Conference on Empirical Methods in Natural Language Processing*, pages 1797–1807, Brussels, Belgium. Association for Computational Linguistics.

Kostiantyn Omelianchuk, Vipul Raheja, and Oleksandr Skurzhanskyi. 2021. Text Simplification by Tagging. In *Proceedings of the 16th Workshop on Innovative Use of NLP for Building Educational Applications*, pages 11–25, Online. Association for Computational Linguistics.

Paul Over, Hoa Dang, and Donna Harman. 2007. Duc in context. *Information Processing & Management*, 43(6):1506–1520.

Kishore Papineni, Salim Roukos, Todd Ward, and Wei-Jing Zhu. 2002. Bleu: a method for automatic evaluation of machine translation. In *Proceedings of the 40th Annual Meeting of the Association for Computational Linguistics*, pages 311–318, Philadelphia, Pennsylvania, USA. Association for Computational Linguistics.

Adam Paszke, Sam Gross, Francisco Massa, Adam Lerer, James Bradbury, Gregory Chanan, Trevor Killeen, Zeming Lin, Natalia Gimelshein, Luca Antiga, Alban Desmaison, Andreas Kopf, Edward Yang, Zachary DeVito, Martin Raison, Alykhan Tejani, Sasank Chilamkurthy, Benoit Steiner, Lu Fang, Junjie Bai, and Soumith Chintala. 2019. Pytorch: An imperative style, high-performance deep learning library. In H. Wallach, H. Larochelle, A. Beygelzimer, F. d'Alché-Buc, E. Fox, and R. Garnett, editors, *Advances in Neural Information Processing Systems 32*, pages 8024–8035. Curran Associates, Inc.

Romain Paulus, Caiming Xiong, and Richard Socher. 2018. A deep reinforced model for abstractive summarization. In *6th International Conference on Learning Representations, ICLR 2018, Vancouver, BC, Canada, April 30 - May 3, 2018, Conference Track Proceedings*. OpenReview.net.

Matthew E. Peters, Mark Neumann, Mohit Iyyer, Matt Gardner, Christopher Clark, Kenton Lee, and Luke Zettlemoyer. 2018. Deep contextualized word representations. In *Proceedings of the 2018 Conference of the North American Chapter of the Association for Computational Linguistics: Human Language Technologies, Volume 1 (Long Papers)*, pages 2227–2237, New Orleans, Louisiana. Association for Computational Linguistics.

Purdue University (PU) Writing Lab PU. Concision.

Avinesh P.V.S and Christian M. Meyer. 2019. Data-efficient neural text compression with interactive learning. In *Proceedings of the 2019 Conference of the North American Chapter of the Association for Computational Linguistics: Human Language Technologies, Volume 1 (Long and Short Papers)*, pages 2543–2554, Minneapolis, Minnesota. Association for Computational Linguistics.

Alec Radford, Jeffrey Wu, Rewon Child, David Luan, Dario Amodei, Ilya Sutskever, et al. 2019. Language models are unsupervised multitask learners. *OpenAI blog*, 1(8):9.

Randy Rambo. 2019. English composition 1.

Mathieu Ravaut, Shafiq Joty, and Nancy F. Chen. 2022. Summareranker: A multi-task mixture-of-experts re-ranking framework for abstractive summarization. *CoRR*, abs/2203.06569.

Stefan Riezler, Tracy H. King, Richard Crouch, and Annie Zaenen. 2003. Statistical sentence condensation using ambiguity packing and stochastic disambiguation methods for Lexical-Functional Grammar. In *Proceedings of the 2003 Human Language Technology Conference of the North American Chapter of the Association for Computational Linguistics*, pages 197–204.

Vasile Rus, Rajendra Banjade, and Mihai Lintean. 2014. On paraphrase identification corpora. In *Proceedings of the Ninth International Conference on Language Resources and Evaluation (LREC'14)*, pages 2422–2429, Reykjavik, Iceland. European Language Resources Association (ELRA).

Alexander M. Rush, Sumit Chopra, and Jason Weston. 2015. A neural attention model for abstractive sentence summarization. In *Proceedings of the 2015 Conference on Empirical Methods in Natural Language Processing*, pages 379–389, Lisbon, Portugal. Association for Computational Linguistics.

Evan Sandhaus. 2008. The new york times annotated corpus.

Advaith Siddharthan. 2006. Syntactic simplification and text cohesion. *Research on Language and Computation*, 4(1):77–109.

Matthew Snover, Bonnie Dorr, Rich Schwartz, Linnea Micciulla, and John Makhoul. 2006. A study of translation edit rate with targeted human annotation. In *Proceedings of the 7th Conference of the Association for Machine Translation in the Americas: Technical Papers*, pages 223–231, Cambridge, Massachusetts, USA. Association for Machine Translation in the Americas.

Engineering Stanford University. Writing style guide.

Keh-Yih Su, Ming-Wen Wu, and Jing-Shin Chang. 1992. A new quantitative quality measure for machine translation systems. In *COLING 1992 Volume 2: The 14th International Conference on Computational Linguistics*.

Elior Sulem, Omri Abend, and Ari Rappoport. 2018. Semantic structural evaluation for text simplification. In *Proceedings of the 2018 Conference of the North American Chapter of the Association for Computational Linguistics: Human Language Technologies, Volume 1 (Long Papers)*, pages 685–696, New Orleans, Louisiana. Association for Computational Linguistics.

Kristina Toutanova, Chris Brockett, Ke M. Tran, and Saleema Amershi. 2016. A dataset and evaluation metrics for abstractive compression of sentences and short paragraphs. In *Proceedings of the 2016 Conference on Empirical Methods in Natural Language Processing*, pages 340–350, Austin, Texas. Association for Computational Linguistics.

University of Arkansas at Little Rock (UALR) Writing Center UALR. Somes steps toward concise writing.

University of North Carolina (UNC) Chapel Hill Writing Center UNC. 2021. Writing concisely.

Massey University (UNZ) The Online Writing & Learning Link (OWLL) UNZ. Writing concisely.

Learning Hub UOA, The University of Auckland (UOA). Concise writing.

The Graduate Writing Center URI, The University of Rhode Island (URI). 2019. Concise writing: Tips and tricks.

John Wieting and Kevin Gimpel. 2018. ParaNMT-50M: Pushing the limits of paraphrastic sentence embeddings with millions of machine translations. In *Proceedings of the 56th Annual Meeting of the Association for Computational Linguistics (Volume 1: Long Papers)*, pages 451–462, Melbourne, Australia. Association for Computational Linguistics.

Walden University (WU) Writing Center WU. Scholarly voice: Writing concisely.

Wei Xu, Courtney Napoles, Ellie Pavlick, Quanze Chen, and Chris Callison-Burch. 2016. Optimizing statistical machine translation for text simplification. *Transactions of the Association for Computational Linguistics*, 4:401–415.

Zhilin Yang, Zihang Dai, Yiming Yang, Jaime Carbonell, Russ R Salakhutdinov, and Quoc V Le. 2019. Xlnet: Generalized autoregressive pretraining for language understanding. *Advances in neural information processing systems*, 32.

Mark Yatskar, Bo Pang, Cristian Danescu-Niculescu-Mizil, and Lillian Lee. 2010. For the sake of simplicity: Unsupervised extraction of lexical simplifications from Wikipedia. In *Human Language Technologies: The 2010 Annual Conference of the North American Chapter of the Association for Computational Linguistics*, pages 365–368, Los Angeles, California. Association for Computational Linguistics.

Jingqing Zhang, Yao Zhao, Mohammad Saleh, and Peter J. Liu. 2020a. PEGASUS: pre-training with extracted gap-sentences for abstractive summarization. In *Proceedings of the 37th International Conference on Machine Learning, ICML 2020, 13-18 July 2020, Virtual Event*, volume 119 of *Proceedings of Machine Learning Research*, pages 11328–11339. PMLR.

Tianyi Zhang, Varsha Kishore, Felix Wu, Kilian Q. Weinberger, and Yoav Artzi. 2020b. Bertscore: Evaluating text generation with BERT. In *8th International Conference on Learning Representations, ICLR 2020, Addis Ababa, Ethiopia, April 26-30, 2020*. OpenReview.net.

Xingxing Zhang and Mirella Lapata. 2017. Sentence simplification with deep reinforcement learning. In *Proceedings of the 2017 Conference on Empirical Methods in Natural Language Processing*, pages 584–594, Copenhagen, Denmark. Association for Computational Linguistics.

Zhemin Zhu, Delphine Bernhard, and Iryna Gurevych. 2010. A monolingual tree-based translation model for sentence simplification. In *Proceedings of the 23rd International Conference on Computational Linguistics (Coling 2010)*, pages 1353–1361, Beijing, China. Coling 2010 Organizing Committee.

A Linguistic Rules in Revising for Concision

We collate and present a set of practical linguistic rules for concise sentence revision, which we synthesize based on guidelines from writing centres at numerous major universities and educational institutes. Table 4 illustrates how wordiness can be fine-grained, and what action is required once a wordiness is identified (UNC, 2021; PU; MON, 2020).

Wordiness identified	**Action**
Weak modifiers (qualifiers / intensifiers)	Delete
Redundant pairs	
Grouped synonyms	
Stock phrases	
Unnecessary hedging	
Implied information	
Yourself	
Informal language	Replace
Vague pronoun references	
Possessive constructions using "of"	
Prepositional phrases	
All-purpose nouns	
Vague Swamp	
Fancy words	
Helping verbs ("to be" verbs, "be" + adjective)	
Adjective-noun pairs	
Phrasal verbs	
Verb-adverb pairs	
Nominalisation / noun strings	
Cliches and Euphemisms	
Empty phrases	
Expletive constructions	
long sentences (>25 words)	Rewrite
Running starts (with "there / it" + "be")	
Long opening phrases / clauses	
Needless transitions	
Interrupted subjects and verbs	
Interrupted verbs and objects	
Negatives (opposite to affirmatives)	
and anything violating:	
A blend of active and passive verbs	
Elliptical constructions / parallelism	
Only one main idea per sentence	

Table 4: Revising rules collated from college writing centers. Three actions are available. Redundancy can be deleted; short, specific, concrete and stronger expressions shall replace vague ones; sentences should be rewritten if neither deleting nor replacing helps.

B Technical Difficultics in Reference-free Revision Evaluation

Had we chosen not to follow Papineni's viewpoint, reference-free evaluation is the way to go. However, it is technically not trivial to use programs to detect wordiness or syntax errors these days (See Section 2.3), let alone detect semantic similarity. Progress in sentence embedding (Lin et al., 2017) and semantic textual similarity (Yang et al., 2019) enables meaning comparison between sentences, but relying on one developing system to evaluate another is risky. Moreover, information delivered by a sentence is sometimes beyond its textual meaning. Concise writing can suggest eliminating first-person narratives; *e.g.*, "*I feel that the study is significant*" is revised to "*The study is significant*" (WU). Here, the first-person statement used to be the main clause, and removing it will shift sentence embedding. Nevertheless, in academic writing, these two sentences deliver identical information.

C Balance between Syntax, Information, and Wordiness

The coefficient α tells how much syntax overweighs information, or information overweighs reduced wordiness. Empirically, minimum of α can be around the word count in a standard sentence. In other words, even if a single key word is missing, the decrease in ρ is bigger than the increase in $1 - \omega$.

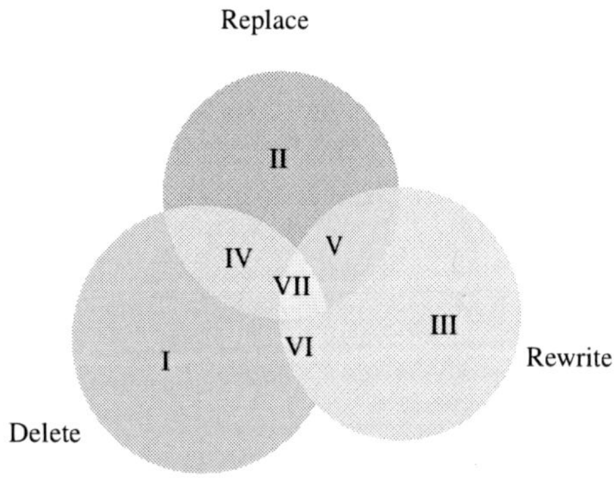

Figure 2: Revising a sentence can involve either one of the three strategies (category I, II, III), or a combination of them (category IV, V, VI, VII).

D Explaining Categories in the Corpus

There are seven categories, as seen in Figure 2. Note that although three actions (delete, replace, rewrite) are put side-by-side, they are with different levels of flexibility. In fact, every revision made with deleting can be done through replace, *e.g.*, the fourth example in Table 9, "*fell down*" could be replaced to "*fell*", but we would simply consider the cheapest revision, which is to delete "*down*"[9]. Similarly, rewriting is even more expensive and ambiguous. Therefore, our rule of Occam's razor is that only when a cheaper revision fails, will we use a more expensive one.

Here, we give examples of which category a revision corresponds to. Indeed, many sentence revisions are categorized in original websites. See the two examples from Purdue Writing Lab (PU) below. The strategies applied are to "eliminate words that explain the obvious or provide excessive detail" (category I) and to "replace several vague words with more powerful and specific words" (category II), respectively.

Corpus Example D.1 (category I). Imagine ~~a mental picture of~~ someone ~~engaged in the intellectual activity of~~ trying to learn ~~what~~ the rules ~~are for how to play the game~~ of chess.

Corpus Example D.2 (category II). The politician ~~talked about several of the merits of~~ touted after-school programs in his speech

For revisions not categorized in sources, we first align the segments of a pair of sentences by their meaning, as seen in Figure 1. This is intuitively straightforward when the revised sentence is given[10].

Then, we determine the actions to revise. For example, in the fourth example (category IV) in Table 9, we find that we cannot delete any words in "*due to the fact that*" without violating the second and third components in Definition 2.4. Thus, we have to put some more concise conjunction to take its place, *i.e.*, "*because*".

Another example is the sixth one (category IV) in Table 10. Though it looks that the entire wordy sentence can only be written to reach the concise form, a cheaper revision is actually to first delete some redundancy, *e.g.*, "*sent ~~to you~~ by us*", and then rewrite the necessary part.

Whether the subject and predicate of a sentence (clause) is changed together determines the border between replacing and rewriting. In the fifth example (category IV) in Table 9, "*it was necessary*" is aligned to "*had to*", and "*us*" to "*we*". However, we cannot change either of them individually without violating the third component in Definition 2.4. Therefore, when two or more replacements intertwine, we rewrite.

E Explaining Rule-based Gloss Substitution

A demonstration of Algorithm 1 is shown in Fig.3, where a verb that appears in the past participle is replaced. By running this rule-based gloss replacement multiple times, we can recursively expand a sentence because the words used in a gloss have their associated glosses (Bosc and Vincent, 2018). Table 5 describes $u \rightarrow r_g$ in the WordNet vocabulary.

F Details in Datasets Used to Train baselines

We prepare training samples by adjusting data from paraphrase generation, sentence simplification, or sentence compression. ParaNMT (Wieting and Gimpel, 2018) contains over five million paraphrase pairs annotated from machine translation tasks; we sort each pair by sentence length. This is a rough approximation, since shorter sentences are not necessarily more concise. Google News datasets (News, Filippova and Altun, 2013) contains 0.2 million pairs of sentences, where the longer one is the leading sentence of each article, and the shorter one is a subsequence of the

[9]"*fell*" means "*fell down*", as one never "*fell up*".

[10]If the revised sentences were not from a trustworthy site, this process could have been less intuitive.

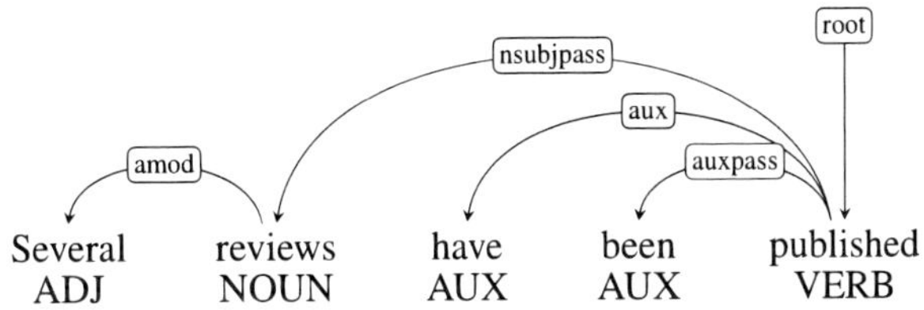

(a) Sentence "*Several reviews have been published*" and its dependency tree. We expand the word "*publish*" below.

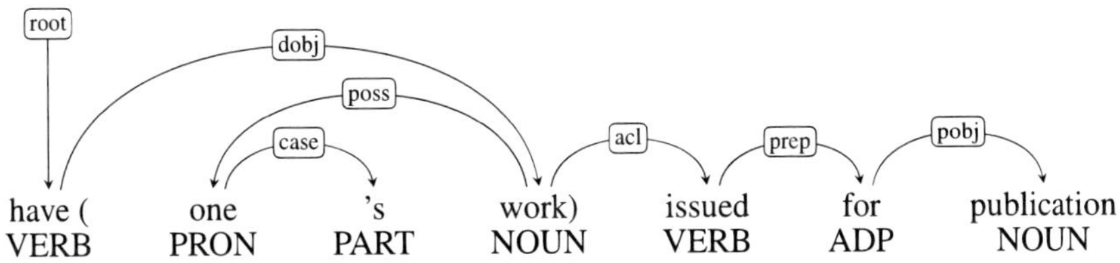

(b) Gloss of "*publish*" from WordNet(Fellbaum, 2010); the root node is the verb "*have*".

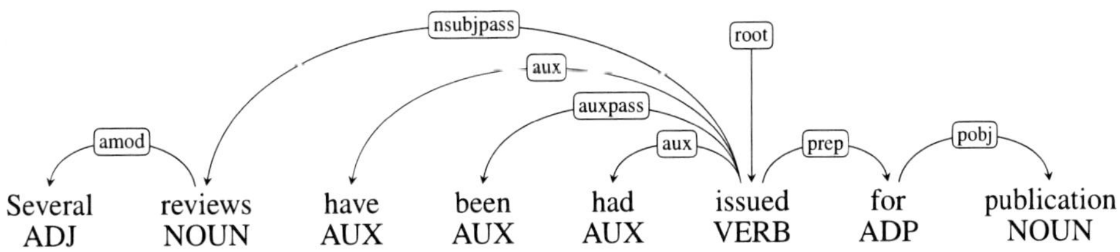

(c) Synthesized sentence with the first stage of our approach; r_g node "*have/had*" is grafted onto the original sentence in (a).

Figure 3: Demonstration of dependency tree grafting in sentence synthesis. The dependency in (c) is obtained by re-parsing the synthesized sentence. As we can see, the POS tag of "*have/had*" has changed from a verb to an auxiliary word, and the synthesized sentence is still syntactically and semantically correct, which shows that dependency changes may be unavoidable in the process of sentence synthesis. We also dealt with inflections to reduce grammatical errors.

longer one. Gigaword (Rush et al., 2015) contains four million pairs of article headline and the first sentence. Although these datasets are mainly for generating news headlines (P.V.S and Meyer, 2019), they approximate the deletion aspect of sentence revision. MSR Abstractive Text Compression Dataset (Toutanova et al., 2016) contains six thousand sentence pairs from business letters, newswire, journals, and technical documents sampled from the Open American National Corpus[11]; humans rewrite sentences at a fixed compression ratio. WikiSmall (Zhang and Lapata, 2017) contains sentence pairs from Wikipedia articles and corresponding Simple English Wikipedia. We adopt training splits of these datasets, and Table 6 lists their sizes.

G Random Sample Selection in Human Evaluation

```
import random
random.seed(0)
for k in [169, 116, 153, 42, 33, 14, 9]:
    print(random.randint(0, k//2))
    print(random.randint(k//2, k))
```

[11]https://www.anc.org/data/oanc

H Evaluation on Individual Metrics

For each sample in the benchmark corpus, we compute individual metric score for its best-revised sentence and average the corpus ranking of its individual metric scores to obtain the final ranking for that sample. Table 9 lists the well-treated samples (at the third percentile) in each category. Table 10 lists the cases that were not well resolved (at the 97th percentile).

Figure 4 shows the difficulty of revising sentences for each category. The data in Figure 4, while demonstrating strengths and weaknesses of the proposed approach, can also serve as an approximation of the difficulty of the corpus itself. The proposed approach is better at deleting and replacing than rewriting due to heavy reliance on transfer learning.

POS	ADJ	ADJS	ADV	NOUN	VERB
VERB	**3627**	**6354**	221	**3349**	**11586**
DET	1	6	4	1594	0
ADJ	1053	**2825**	50	544	316
NOUN	155	405	57	**73527**	1739
CCONJ	0	0	0	24	0
PUNCT	0	1	0	6	0
PART	0	5	4	4	6
ADV	10	84	235	37	52
ADP	**2615**	972	**3019**	222	29
AUX	5	5	4	108	1
PRON	0	3	2	1516	1
SCONJ	4	10	14	3	10
PROPN	0	6	0	534	15
X	2	2	2	16	19
NUM	1	16	8	658	0
INTJ	1	1	3	13	12
SYM	0	0	0	0	0

Table 5: Part-of-speech (POS) tags for a word w and its corresponding r_g. Representation of POS tags follows the Stanford typed dependencies manual (De Marneffe and Manning, 2008) (except for ADJ-S, which stands for 'adjective satellite' in WordNet (Fellbaum, 2010)). POS tags of r_g are closely related to the POS tags of w, and we bold the pairs that appear frequently. In particular, among nearly 117,000 word-gloss ($w \rightarrow r_g$) pairs, NOUN $\rightarrow$ NOUN is most frequent, accounting for more than three fifths. We have now studied the eight most frequently occurring pairs.

Dataset	Size
MSR (2016)	21,145
ParaNMT (2018)	5,306,522
Google News (G. News 2013)	200,000
Gigaword (2015)	3,803,957
WikiSmall (2017)	89,042
Approach 2 fine-tuning set (Section 5.3)	182,330

Table 6: Sample numbers of training sets. MSR dataset has multiple references, we take each reference as a sample point. The mixed fine-tuning set in Section 5.3 is composed of 89,712 samples from ParaNMT, 21,145 from MSR, and 71,473 from our synthesized dataset from WordNet.

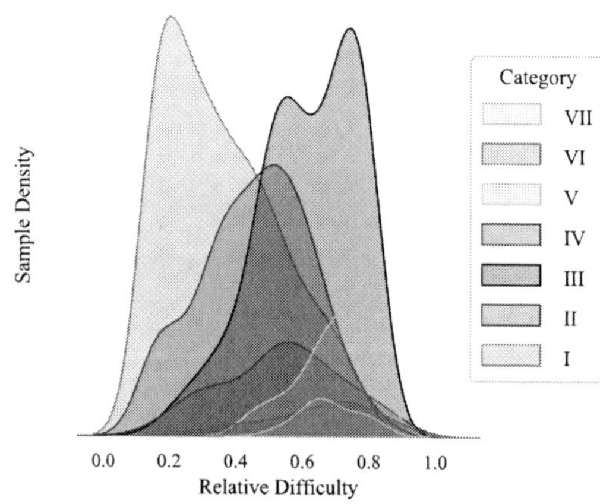

Figure 4: Difficulty faced by the proposed approachs when dealing with sentences from different categories. This difficulty is relative to other samples in the corpus of 536 sentences. Deletion (category I) is the least challenging. The most challenging samples are most likely from category III. Handling sentences requiring more than one revising strategies (category IV-VII) is usually more challenging.

	BL	M	R	S	P	BS	T
ParaNMT	.40	.78	.56	.49	.55	.96	.53
MSR	.55	.86	.69	.62	.73	**.97**	.39
News	.36	.67	.56	.52	.62	.95	.51
Gigaword	.04	.27	.19	.25	.16	.89	.92
WikiSmall	.47	**.91**	.65	.59	.63	.95	.82
Approach 1	.48	.90	.65	.59	.66	.94	.82
Approach 2	**.57**	.87	**.71**	**.66**	**.74**	**.97**	**.37**

(a) Category I, 169 / 536, Delete

	BL	M	R	S	P	BS	T
ParaNMT	**.38**	.75	**.54**	**.54**	**.51**	**.97**	**.50**
MSR	.33	.73	.51	.45	.47	.96	.56
News	.17	.56	.39	.35	.37	.94	.64
Gigaword	.01	.26	.17	.28	.15	.89	.92
WikiSmall	.33	.80	.51	.48	.44	.95	.92
Approach 1	.36	**.80**	**.54**	.51	.46	.95	.91
Approach 2	.36	.76	.53	.50	.50	.96	.53

(b) Category II, 116 / 536, Replace

	BL	M	R	S	P	BS	T
ParaNMT	.16	.60	.33	.44	.28	**.94**	.94
MSR	.15	.56	.31	.38	.28	.93	.92
News	.10	.44	.26	.37	.25	.92	.85
Gigaword	.03	.20	.12	.38	.09	.88	1.00
WikiSmall	**.19**	**.66**	.35	**.45**	.29	.93	1.26
Approach 1	.17	.65	**.36**	.43	.29	.93	1.27
Approach 2	.18	.60	.35	.42	**.30**	**.94**	**.91**

(c) Category III, 153 / 536, Rewrite

	BL	M	R	S	P	BS	T
ParaNMT	.27	.68	.40	**.48**	.41	.94	1.22
MSR	.26	.63	.39	.44	.39	.94	1.09
News	.12	.41	.29	.37	.31	.92	**.77**
Gigaword	.03	.24	.16	.35	.16	.89	.86
WikiSmall	.24	.71	.39	.46	.37	.93	1.69
Approach 1	.23	**.72**	.39	.44	.39	.92	1.70
Approach 2	**.32**	.67	**.44**	.47	**.43**	**.95**	.94

(d) Category IV, 42 / 536, Delete + Replace

	BL	M	R	S	P	BS	T
ParaNMT	.16	.55	.27	**.44**	.26	**.94**	1.18
MSR	.14	.49	.28	.37	.24	.93	1.05
News	.08	.34	.21	.35	.22	.92	**.85**
Gigaword	.01	.15	.09	.34	.06	.87	.90
WikiSmall	.17	.58	.30	.40	.27	.93	1.40
Approach 1	**.20**	**.59**	**.31**	.43	**.29**	.93	1.37
Approach 2	.14	.49	.26	.35	.25	**.93**	1.04

(e) Category V, 33 / 536, Replace + Rewrite

	BL	M	R	S	P	BS	T
ParaNMT	.21	.56	.30	**.43**	.27	**.93**	1.35
MSR	.19	.53	.30	.40	.30	**.93**	1.23
News	.12	.39	.26	.37	.25	.92	**.81**
Gigaword	.04	.20	.12	.38	.10	.87	.87
WikiSmall	.17	.62	**.31**	.43	**.30**	.92	1.92
Approach 1	.16	**.62**	**.31**	.41	.29	.92	1.96
Approach 2	**.22**	.55	**.31**	.41	**.30**	**.93**	1.23

(f) Category VI, 14 / 536, Delete + Rewrite

	BL	M	R	S	P	BS	T
ParaNMT	.06	.50	.17	.40	.20	.92	1.61
MSR	.06	.49	.17	.39	.17	.92	1.34
News	.03	.28	.15	.38	.21	.91	**.79**
Gigaword	.00	.11	.04	.36	.02	.86	.95
WikiSmall	**.08**	.54	.20	.38	.18	.91	2.02
Approach 1	.04	.53	.18	.39	.17	.91	1.96
Approach 2	**.08**	**.55**	**.23**	**.43**	**.24**	**.93**	1.18

(g) Category VII, 9 / 536, Delete + Replace + Rewrite

	BL	M	R	S	P	BS	T
ParaNMT	.29	.69	.44	.48	.42	**.95**	.77
MSR	.32	.69	.48	.48	.47	**.95**	.71
News	.20	.53	.38	.41	.40	.93	.69
Gigaword	.03	.23	.15	.31	.13	.88	.94
WikiSmall	.31	.76	.48	.49	.43	.94	1.12
Approach 1	.31	**.76**	.49	.50	.45	.94	1.12
Approach 2	**.35**	.72	**.50**	**.51**	**.49**	**.95**	**.68**

(h) Overall

Table 7: BLEU (**BL**), METEOR (**M**) , ROUGE-2-F1 (**R**), SARI (**S**), Parsed relation F1 (**P**), BERTScore-F1 (**BS**), *and* translation edit rate (**T**) of pre-Approach 2s and Approach 2 method. Numbers are shown in categories. Smaller edit distance is more favorable. The most favorable score(s) in each column is bold. In category V, the model trained on Approach 1 has the highest scores on three metrics, slightly outperforming other pre-Approach 2s. In category III,IV, VI, VII, no particular pre-Approach 2 scores well on all metrics.

	W	R1	RL
ParaNMT	.65	.75	.71
MSR	.43	.85	.8
News	.54	.73	.7
Gigaword	.97	.39	.37
WikiSmall	.89	.82	.77
Approach 1	.96	.82	.77
Approach 2	**.42**	**.86**	**.81**

(a) Category I, 169 / 536, Delete

W	R1	RL
.61	**.73**	**.72**
.58	.71	.7
.66	.6	.59
.98	.37	.35
.93	.71	.7
1.03	**.73**	**.72**
.54	**.73**	**.72**

(b) Category II, 116 / 536, Replace

	W	R1	RL
ParaNMT	1.04	.61	.50
MSR	.99	.60	.48
News	.88	.52	.43
Gigaword	1.03	.32	.29
WikiSmall	1.35	.63	.50
Approach 1	1.40	.63	.50
Approach 2	**.97**	.63	**.51**

(c) Category III, 153 / 536, Rewrite

W	R1	RL
1.28	.59	.58
1.14	.59	.57
.81	.48	.46
.90	.37	.32
1.74	.58	.56
1.79	.59	.56
.97	**.63**	**.62**

(d) Category IV, 42 / 536, Delete + Replace

	W	R1	RL
ParaNMT	1.36	.52	.45
MSR	1.17	.51	.43
News	**.91**	.42	.36
Gigaword	.96	.28	.24
WikiSmall	1.58	.53	.44
Approach 1	1.59	**.55**	**.46**
Approach 2	1.15	.52	.43

(e) Category V, 33 / 536, Replace + Rewrite

W	R1	RL
1.54	.49	.41
1.37	.51	.41
.87	.45	.38
.89	.30	.30
2.04	.51	.43
2.10	.51	.43
1.39	**.54**	**.45**

(f) Category VI, 14 / 536, Delete + Rewrite

	W	R1	RL
ParaNMT	1.64	.44	.35
MSR	1.38	.47	.35
News	**.81**	.38	.34
Gigaword	.97	.25	.20
WikiSmall	2.04	.44	.33
Approach 1	1.98	.45	.34
Approach 2	1.24	**.53**	**.43**

(g) Category VII, 9 / 536, Delete + Replace + Rewrite

W	R1	RL
.88	.66	.61
.76	.69	.63
.72	.59	.55
.98	.35	.33
1.19	.69	.63
1.25	.70	.63
.73	**.71**	**.65**

(h) Overall

Table 8: Other metrics include word error rate (**W**), ROUGE-1-F1 (**R1**), *and* ROUGE-L-F1 (**RL**) . Numbers are shown in categories. Smaller edit distance is more favorable. The most favorable score(s) in each column is bold.

Category	Reference(s)	Prediction
I	~~The reason~~ she moved ~~is~~ because she was offered a better position.	~~The reason~~ she moved ~~is~~ because she was offered a better position.
II	We outlined the letters for the banner ~~in a careful way~~ carefully.	We outlined the letters for the banner ~~in a careful way~~ carefully.
III	~~The current focus of the medical profession is~~ The medical profession currently focuses on disease prevention.	~~The current focus of the medical profession is~~ The medical profession focuses on disease prevention.
IV	She fell ~~down~~ ~~due to the fact that~~ because she hurried.	She fell ~~down~~ ~~due to the fact that~~ because she hurried.
V	We didn't renew the contract with our supplier ~~on account of the fact that~~ because ~~it was necessary for us to~~ we had to find a cheaper ~~supplier~~ one.	We didn't renew the contract ~~with our supplier~~ ~~on account of the fact that~~ because it was necessary for us to find a cheaper supplier.
VI	Research is increasing in ~~the field of~~ nutrition and food science. *OR* Research within nutrition and food science is increasing ~~the field of nutrition and food science~~.	Research is increasing in ~~the field of~~ nutrition and food science.
VII	Joe found ~~that~~ ~~the fictional novel by~~ Alcott's book, Little Women, ~~conveyed a sense of emotion and feeling~~ both delightful and tragic.	Joe found that ~~the fictional novel by~~ Alcott's novel, Little Women, conveyed ~~a sense of~~ emotion and feeling.

Table 9: Well-revised samples in each category (about the third percentile). Shorter sentences that require simpler actions are perfectly revised. When sentence length increases, not all wordiness can be resolved. The baseline method tends to delete and replace, even if sentences need to be rewritten.

Category	Reference(s)	Prediction
I	~~I would call your attention to the fact that~~ our President, ~~who was~~ formerly the Governor of Arkansas, is ~~basically~~ a Southerner.	I would call your attention to the fact that our President ~~, who was formerly the Governor of Arkansas,~~ is a ~~basically~~ Southerner.
II	We have ~~conducted an investigation~~ investigated and ~~arrived at the conclusion~~ concluded.	We ~~have~~ conducted an investigation and arrived at the conclusion.
III	~~As far as my professor is concerned, the problem of wordiness is the thing she'd really like to see us involved with actually eliminating.~~ My professor wants us to focus on eliminating wordiness.	~~As far as my professor is concerned,~~ the problem of wordiness is the thing she'd ~~really~~ like to see us involved with ~~actually~~ eliminating.
IV	~~The existence of~~ computers ~~and computer technology~~ ~~has~~ have improved ~~commercial enterprise~~ business ~~and information exchange~~ communication.	The existence of computers and ~~computer~~ technology has ~~greatly~~ influenced commercial enterprise and information exchange.
V	~~It has come to my attention that~~ I have noticed ~~there is a vast proliferation of undesirable vegetation~~ many weeds growing ~~surrounding the periphery of~~ around ~~this facility~~ the building	It has come to my attention that there is a vast proliferation of undesirable vegetation ~~surrounding the periphery of this facility~~.
VI	~~Your statement in your letter that has the contention that the information submitted and sent to you by us contained certain inaccuracies and errors has prompted us to embark on a careful and thorough reevaluation of the information submitted, with the result that the original informative data has been determined to be accurate and correct in all instances and aspects of the information.~~ As you suggested, we have checked our information and confirmed its accuracy.	Your statement in your letter that ~~has the contention that~~ the information submitted and sent to you by us contained ~~certain~~ some inaccuracies and errors has prompted us to embark on a ~~careful and~~ thorough reevaluation of the information ~~submitted~~, with the result that the original informative data has been determined to be accurate and correct ~~in all instances and aspects of the information.~~
VII	~~In the event that~~ If you get ~~some~~ any information ~~concerning~~ about Mr. Smith ~~should be brought to your attention, it should be forwarded via mail or courier or telephone to us~~ please contact us ~~in view of the possibility that~~ in case ~~the information may reveal any attempt on the part of Mr. Smith to depart from the United States~~ he tries to leave the country.	~~In the event that~~ If ~~some~~ any information concerning Mr. Smith should be brought to your attention, it should be forwarded via mail or courier or telephone to us in view of the possibility that the information may reveal any attempt ~~on the part of Mr. Smith~~ to depart from the United States.

Table 10: Badly-revised samples in each category (about the 97th percentile). These sentences are longer than sentences in Table 9. Informative part may be trimmed. Replacing nominalizations with verbs is hard. For severely wordy sentences (category VI, VII), the model fails to rewrite, and resorts to deletion. A lot of improvement is needed.

Controlling Japanese Machine Translation Output by Using JLPT Vocabulary Levels

Alberto Poncelas and **Ohnmar Htun**
Rakuten Institute of Technology
Rakuten Group, Inc.
{alberto.poncelas, ohnmar.htun}@rakuten.com

Abstract

In Neural Machine Translation (NMT) systems, there is generally little control over the lexicon of the output. Consequently, the translated output may be too difficult for certain audiences. For example, for people with limited knowledge of the language, vocabulary is a major impediment to understanding a text.

In this work, we build a complexity-controllable NMT for English-to-Japanese translations. More particularly, we aim to modulate the difficulty of the translation in terms of not only the vocabulary but also the use of kanji. For achieving this, we follow a sentence-tagging approach to influence the output.

1 Introduction

In the Natural Language Processing research, text simplification aims to find variants of a text which convey the same meaning but are expressed in a simpler form. This process includes modifications such as reducing the length, decreasing the use of infrequent words, etc. Simplification systems are useful for helping certain populations such as children, non native speakers, and people with a low level of literacy or language disorders (Štajner and Popović, 2016).

In this work, we apply simplification to the translation task. In particular, we aim to control the lexicon complexity of English-to-Japanese Neural Machine Translation (NMT) models. The output generated by an NMT system in Japanese may be too difficult to understand for a person with more limited knowledge of the language. An example of this is the use of kanji ideograms. Certain kanji are learned in the later stages of education[1], which causes some people not to be entirely familiarized with all of them. This implies that both vocabulary and kanji may represent an accessibility problem. Accordingly, we focus on influencing the output of an NMT system to control whether it should produce more or less difficult words. This can be measured based on the vocabulary lists provided for different levels of the Japanese Language Proficiency Test (JLPT). A more detailed explanation of this can be found in Section 2.

For modulating the translation, our approach is inspired by other works consisting of influencing the generation of sentences for certain domains or languages. This can be achieved by including a tag at the beginning of each sentence stating how the output should be. For our approach, we use tags to indicate the level of lexicon complexity expected in the output. We first insert a token at the beginning of each training sentence according to the complexity of the Japanese target side. Then, at decoding time, we can influence the output by using such tags.

This paper describes such an approach, and explores the following Research Questions (RQ):

RQ1: Can the vocabulary complexity of the output be controlled adding tags in the source sentences?

The addition of tags in the source sentences to control the output of the NMT models has been explored not only for different domains (Chu et al., 2017) but also for different languages (Johnson et al., 2017). We want to explore these techniques for Japanese translation and investigate how could it be used to control the complexity level of the output.

RQ2: How much does the output level agree with the complexity level indicated in the input?

Although adding tags could bias the complexity of the translation, it has limitations. For example, some translations may require the use of complex vocabulary despite the restrictions. We analyze to what extent the complexity of the sentences generated by the NMT corresponds to those indicated in the input.

[1] https://en.wikipedia.org/wiki/Ky%C5%8Diku_kanji

Proceedings of the Workshop on Text Simplification, Accessibility, and Readability (TSAR-2022), pages 77 - 85
December 8, 2022 ©2022 Association for Computational Linguistics

RQ3: How much does the restrictions in complexity impact the translation quality?

Introducing tags to restrict the complexity could lead also to degradation of the performance of the NMT in terms of adequacy. Our third research question aims to investigate how much these restrictions impact the translation.

2 Japanese Language and JLPT

The Japanese language has three writing systems[2]: hiragana (46 characters); katakana (46 characters); and kanji (more than 2000 characters).

Hiragana is mainly used for native Japanese words whereas katakana is used for foreign words or onomatopoeia. For example, the translation for the word "hat" is ぼうし (read as "boushi") which is written in hiragana. Alternatively, some people may use the term borrowed from English "ハット" ("hatto") which is a transliteration of "hat". As it is a loanword, it is written in the katakana syllabary.

Despite that, native Japanese speakers would use more frequently the kanji ideogram 帽子 (which is also read as "boushi") for "hat".

Although it is possible to fully express in Japanese using hiragana or katakana exclusively, kanji is usually used. Despite that, as there exists more than 2000 kanji, a Japanese learner would assimilate them gradually, and therefore be more comfortable using hiragana for writing or reading certain words.

A popular criterion to measure the level of proficiency in Japanese for non-native speakers is the Japanese Language Proficiency Test (JLPT). It is a five-level grading system that ranges from JLPT 5 (the most basic) to JLPT 1 (the most advanced). These five levels are also referred to as N5, N4, N3, N2, and N1.[3]

In this work we use both notations, "JLPT" or "N" , indistinctly. Additionally, we may refer to *higher levels* to those JLPT levels closer to N1, and *lower levels* to those closer to N5.

3 Related Work

In the text simplification field, several approaches alter the complexity of the lexicon. For example, Glavaš and Štajner (2015) propose replacing difficult words with a simpler synonym. Furthermore, Hading et al. (2016) perform the complex-word replacement applied for Japanese language.

Alternatively, Wang et al. (2016) build a monolingual NMT system to transform sentences into a simplified version in the same language.

Nishihara et al. (2019) propose a similar monolingual sequence-to-sequence system with several levels of complexity in English. These are based on the grade level of US education system. Similarly to our work, they control the complexity by using special tokens for each grade.

Performing text simplification in combination with translation has also been explored by Štajner and Popović (2019). They focus on using automatically simplified sentences as the input of an NMT model.

Regarding the complexity-controllable translation, Spring et al. (2021) aim to produce translations based on different levels established by the Common European Framework of Reference for Languages (CEFR).

Shardlow and Alva-Manchego (2022) also performs combinations of simplification and translation (*Translate then Simplify*, *Simplify then Translate* and *Direct*) to generate simplified translations.

There are previous works that use tags to control the output. Martin et al. (2020) extract different characteristics that measure the complexity and include them as tags in the source to condition the output. Similarly, Agrawal and Carpuat (2019) also use a tagging system, training the model with a dataset where the same sentences have been rewritten at different complexity level. Finally, Marchisio et al. (2019) use two tags (i.e. "simple" and "complex") to classify the sentences by difficulty.

Some difference with our research is that we use a five-tag system based on the JLPT framework. In addition, as we explore the Japanese language, the definition of complexity also considers spelling. Therefore, depending on the writing system, some words may have different complexity levels.

4 Complexity-Controllable Translation

Our proposal consists of building an English-to-Japanese NMT model with a controllable lexicon complexity. In this work, the *complexity* is measured based solely on the vocabulary of the different JLPT levels.

There are two main processes involved: (i) determine the JLPT level of a sentence (Section 4.1); and (ii), include the complexity level in the training

[2]https://en.wikipedia.org/wiki/Japanese_writing_system

[3]This notation comes from the first letter of Japanese name of the JLPT, "Nihongo Nōryoku Shiken"

Word	JLPT level
友達	3
ともだち	5

Table 1: Example of the word mapping. Each word is assigned a JLPT level. Although both words convey the same meaning, they belong to different JLPT levels due to the writing system.

process of the NMT model (Section 4.2).

4.1 Sentence Classification

Initially, we build a classifier to estimate what is the JLPT level of a sentence. Following the proposal of Ramkissoon, a sentence can be classified with the level of that of the most difficult (highest level) word of the sentence. This approach assumes that one can understand a sentence if one is capable of understanding each word. This is not necessarily true, as usually there are other components involved such as the length of the sentence, the grammar, or the number of clauses. For future work, we propose to expand this assumption of complexity and include a more detailed classification.

Deciding the level of a word can be done based on the vocabulary lists of JLPT levels. We use the resources from Waller (2010)[4].

For each JLPT level, we obtain a list of words and a list of kanji that a Japanese student should be familiar with. We combine this information to build a mapping between each word and its JLPT level as in Table 1. This map also takes into consideration the spelling of the words as follows:

- The word is spelled using hiragana: Its corresponding JLPT level will be that of the vocabulary list.
- The word is spelled using kanji: The JLPT level of this word is that of the level of the most difficult kanji.

Note that the same word can be classified as two different levels depending on the spelling. For example, the words we see in Table 1, 友達 and ともだち, are both the same word ("tomodachi", which means "friend" in English). They have different JLPT levels because ともだち only contains hiragana which is readable by the lowest levels of fluency (JLPT 5) whereas the word 友達 is formed by the kanji 友 (JLPT 5) and 達 (JLPT 3), and therefore that word is categorized as JLPT 3.

Considering a sentence t a sequence of words $(t_1, ..., t_{|t|})$, the JLPT level of the sentence will be that of the word t_i with the highest difficulty according to the mapping. If a word is not in the mapping, such as an English or an out-of-vocabulary term, we assume it is a proper name and it will be ignored (equivalent to assuming that it is in the level JLPT 5).

4.2 Machine Translation Training

The models we build should generate translations biased towards the complexity levels established in the input. The method we follow is by adding a complexity tag to the sentences.

Including a special token in the source to control the output of an NMT technique has demonstrated good results for translating into different domains (Chu et al., 2017) or even into different languages (Johnson et al., 2017).

This technique consists of preprocessing each sentence pair (s, t) in the training and dev set as follows:

1. Classify the Japanese sentence t as described in Section 4.1 and retrieve the JLPT level l.
2. Build a token N_l according to the level l. To avoid using just numeric values our tag consists of concatenating the letter N with the level together. For example, the token N_l for JLPT 1 we build would be "$N1$".
3. Expand the English source-side sentence by adding the token in the beginning $s' = (N_l, s_1, ..., s_{|s|})$.
4. Retrieve the pair with the expanded source (s', t).

The processed data is used to train an NMT model. By doing this, the system should learn the relation between the first token in the source and the vocabulary on the target side. Later, at decoding time, we include a tag with the desired JLPT level so the model should generate sentences including the vocabulary of such level.

5 Experiments

We build NMT models in the English-to-Japanese direction using Marian NMT (Junczys-Dowmunt

[4]https://www.tanos.co.uk/jlpt/

et al., 2018). These models consist of a transformer (Vaswani et al., 2017) model with 6 layers both in the encoder and 6 in the decoder. We train it for a maximum of 500K steps (18 epochs).

We use one of the biggest English-Japanese corpus, JParaCrawl v3.0 (Morishita et al., 2020), as train set (25.7M sentences) and 10K randomly-selected sentences from Tatoeba (Tiedemann, 2012) as dev set.

For the experiments, we build two models. One model is built with plain data without any modification that serves as a reference for comparison purposes. The second model is built by including tags as described in Section 4.2. We use kytea (Neubig et al., 2011) to split sentences and extract the vocabulary of the Japanese side.

For testing the models, we randomly selected 5000 sentences from Tatoeba (from those not included in the dev set). This dataset is built for educational purposes and therefore there are sentences of different complexities.

First, we translate these sentences with the plain model. Then, for the model that uses tags, we replicated each sentence five times and added a different tag (from N1 to N5) to each of them. By doing this we encourage the model to produce translations of different levels for each input.

This means that we generate six alternative translations from a single test set. One output is the translation of the plain NMT model trained without tags ("no-tag" output). The other five outputs correspond to the translation when one of the tags is added at the beginning of the sentence. In the following, we name each output with the tag added in the source. For example, we refer as *N2 output* to the translations when the tag "N2" was added in the input sentences.

6 Experimental Results

We divide the analysis of the results of the experiments into four different sections: (i) Section 6.1, where we explore the simplification capabilities of the NMT model (RQ1); (ii) Section 6.2, where we analyze the agreement between the output level and that stated in the input (RQ2); (iii) Section 6.3, where we investigate the translation quality (RQ3); and (iv), Section 6.4, where we provide translation examples that illustrate the effect of constraining complexity in the output.

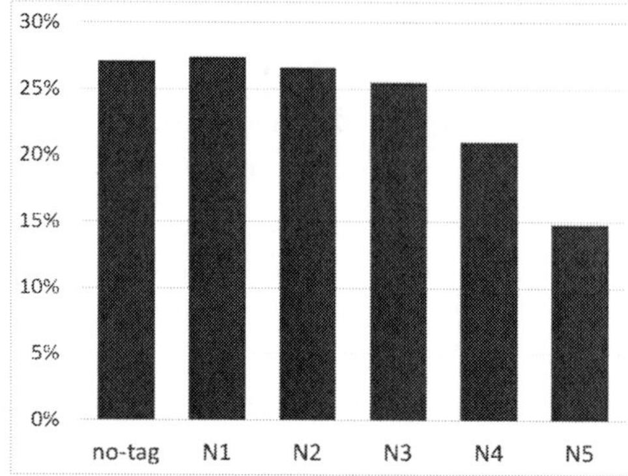

Figure 1: Average percentage of kanji

6.1 RQ1: Can the vocabulary complexity of the output be controlled adding tags in the source sentences?

The tags used to modulate the complexity are based on the vocabulary and kanji in Japanese. Accordingly, we explore whether the outputs of the model are simplified in terms of these.

First, we explore the usage of kanji. For someone with limited knowledge of Japanese, it is expected the kanji comprehension to be lower also. Therefore, the outputs in the lower levels should contain a smaller proportion of kanji. In Figure 1 we present what is the proportion of kanji in the outputs. In the reference 27.5% of the characters are kanji, which is similar to the output of the NMT model with no tags. This is also the proportion in the outputs of higher levels of JLPT (in fact, the N1 output has a slightly higher usage of kanji than the plain model).

The proportion of kanji decreases gradually as lower JLPT levels are stated in the input. For the N5 output, the percentage of characters that are kanji is just 14.8%. Therefore we can say that in terms of kanji usage, the inclusion of tags is beneficial to decrease the complexity.

In addition to that, we compare the vocabulary sizes of the translations. In general, the more restricted the generation is, the lower the size of the vocabulary is expected to be. In Figure 2 we present the number of distinct words in each output.

In the plot, we see that the size of the vocabulary for the model with no tags is similar to those of higher levels such as N1 or N2. The number of words tends to decrease the more restricted the complexity is.

The N5 output seems to be an exception to that,

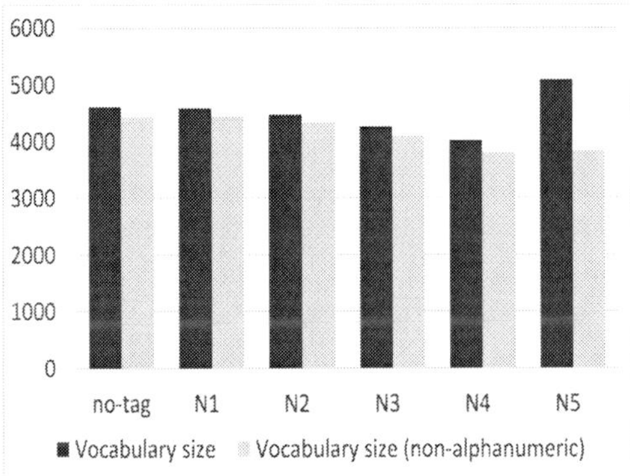

Figure 2: Vocabulary size of the output.

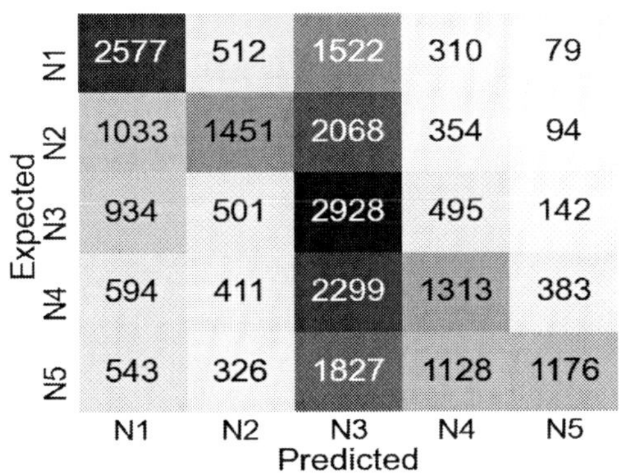

Figure 3: Confusion matrix of the classification of the output

as the vocabulary size exceeds that of the N1 output. However, upon inspection of the translations, we discovered that many words were just copied directly from the source instead of being a translation. We decided to include in that plot the size of vocabulary after removing the alphanumeric terms (e.g. English words, numbers) from the output as it may distort the analysis. Under these circumstances, we observe that the number of words also decreases for the N5 output. In this case, the vocabularies of the translations range from 4400 words (for less restricted outputs such as no-tag or N1) to 3800 words (for N5 output).

Consequently, the sizes of the vocabularies also indicate that the complexity tag is useful to limit the diversity of words.

6.2 RQ2: How much does the output level agree with the complexity level indicated in the input?

For answering the second RQ, we want to estimate whether the outputs match the levels stated on the test set. Therefore, we classified the outputs of the model (25000 sentences) and compare them to the level that was prepended as a tag on the source side. In Figure 3 we present the heatmap of the confusion matrix.

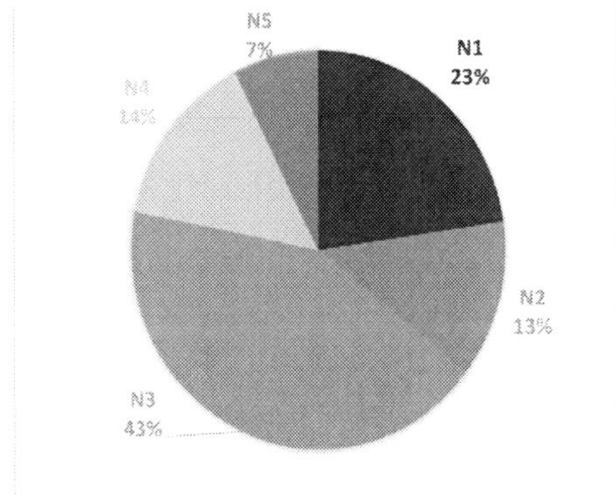

Figure 4: Proportion of sentences of each JLPT level (output file).

We found that only 38% of the sentences in the output had an exact match with the proposed tag on their source side. Most of the sentences in the output of the model are predicted to be JLPT 3 level as can be seen in Figure 4.

In addition, we also see that many disagreements occur in sentences where lower complexity is expected. Many sentences in the N5 output include kanji of more advanced levels. We find two main reasons for that.

One reason is that certain terms may not exist in the vocabulary of lower JLPT levels. For example, even when attaching an N5 tag to a sentence, the model may not be able to translate difficult concepts such as "monopolize" or "corruption" that do not exist in the vocabulary of such a low level.

Another reason is that the model does not have enough information to generate an adequate translation. For example, the word "window" is a basic word that would be categorized as JLPT 5 (lowest complexity level) if it is spelled in hiragana as "まど". However, in the N5 output, this was spelled using the kanji "窓" instead, which is considered to be in level JLPT 3. This occurs because it is unlikely to find the hiragana spelling in most texts. Upon the inspection of the training data, we did not find any occurrence of translation of "window" spelled in hiragana.

Answering this RQ, we find that the model is not very accurate in terms of generating translation in the JLPT level as expected in the input.

Added tag	BLEU (full)	BLEU (hiragana)
no-tag	23.3	24.8
N1	22.4	23.8
N2	21.8	23.1
N3	21.8	22.8
N4	18.9	20.8
N5	13.8	15.2

Table 2: Translation quality of the outputs measured with BLEU metric. The column *BLEU (full)* presents the scores of the output when compared to the original reference. The column *BLEU (hiragana)* presents the scores after both output and reference have been converted into a single writing system (i.e. hiragana).

Alternatively, one may consider that the knowledge of vocabulary should be cumulative. In the experiments, we used the hardest word to tag the sentence, which implies that sentences classified as JLPT 1 or 2, also contain the vocabulary of lower levels. This is coherent with the problem of different literacy levels, as an advanced reader is also capable of reading sentences with simpler vocabulary. In such a case, we could consider that the output should be at either the same or lower level than that stated in the input. Then, the number of correctly classified sentences ascends to 62%. Despite that, the problem of lower-level sentences containing difficult kanji remains.

6.3 RQ3: How much does the restrictions in complexity impact the translation quality?

On top of the simplification capabilities of the model, also the adequacy of the translations is important. In this section, we investigate the translation quality of the model. We expect that the more we limit the complexity, the less accurate the translation will be. To measure the quality, we use the BLEU (Papineni et al., 2002) metric to compare the output sentences with those in the reference. We present the results in Table 2.

According to the scores, the model trained without tags achieved the highest translation quality. This indicates that it is preferable not to limit the complexity of the output at all. Even the less restricted output (i.e. the N1 output) does not outperform the model with no tags.

Additionally, we validate our hypothesis that constraining the output deteriorates the quality. In the table, the lower the JLPT level is the lower the BLEU scores are. Moreover, we find a significant difference, 9.5 BLEU points, between the highest and lowest level outputs.

As BLEU is an n-gram matching metric, some sentences may convey the same meaning of the reference although they use different spellings (such as the two spellings of "friend" mentioned before). We understand that the reference uses the spelling that is the most comfortable for a Japanese native speaker. However, in the table, we have also included the BLEU scores when both the set of outputs and the reference were converted into hiragana (i.e. column *BLEU (hiragana)* to avoid mixed spelling.

By doing this, the BLEU scores are higher as there is a higher n-gram overlap with the reference. However, the conclusions are the same: the model without tags performs the best, and the lower the JLPT level the lower the quality is (with 8.6 BLEU points difference between N1 and N5).

6.4 Translation Examples

In the previous section, we introduced that a reason for lower-level outputs to have poor translation quality is due to the lack of information to correctly translate certain terms. For example, as the vocabulary of N5 is more limited, in several sentences of N5 output we find translation mistakes such as wrong translations, or even terms copied directly from the source. We provide examples of these in the following section. Here we present some sentences that illustrate some of the advantages and disadvantages of using tags to control the complexity of the vocabulary. These are included in Table 3.

We see that the word "hat" is translated as "ハット" which is read as "hatto" and corresponds to a transliteration from English using katakana alphabet. For upper levels (i.e. N3 to N1) the terms generated is "帽子" (read as "bōshi") which is written in kanji.

Something similar can be seen with "noses and cheeks". This is translated as "ノーズとチーク" ("Nōzu to chīku") by the N5 output, and it is also closer to a transliteration of the English terms. In the other outputs, this is translated as "鼻と頬", which contain kanji.

Regarding the translation of "companions", in the outputs of upper levels we found "仲間" which is the same as in the reference. The N3 output produces "同行者", which is also spelled in kanji.

Interestingly, the N4 output we find "友だち"

Source	My companions, who weren't wearing hats, apparently had their noses and cheeks turn red.
Ref	帽子をかぶってなかった仲間は、鼻とほっぺが赤くなっているようでした。
no-tag	帽子を被っていない仲間は、鼻や頬が赤くなっていたそうです。
N1	帽子をかぶっていない仲間は、鼻や頬が赤くなったそうです。
N2	帽子をかぶっていない仲間は、鼻や頬が赤くなったそうです。
N3	帽子をかぶっていなかった私の同行者は、見たところ、彼らの鼻と頬が赤くなりました。
N4	ハットをかぶっていなかった私のお友だちは、鼻と頬が赤くなったようです。
N5	ハットをかぶっていなかったお姉さんは、ノーズとチークが赤くなっていたそうです。
Source	Tom and Mary have gone hunting
Ref	トムとメアリーは狩りに行ったよ。
no-tag	トムとメアリーは狩りに行きました
N1	トムとメアリーは狩りに行った。
N2	トムとメアリーはハンティングに行きました。
N3	トムとメアリーはハンティングに行った。
N4	トムとメアリーはハンティングに行きました。
N5	Tom と Mary メアリー have gone 行った hunting ハンティング

Table 3: Translation Examples.

which means "friend". As seen in Section 4.1, this word could be written as "友達". However, only the kanji 友 belongs to N4. The other kanji, "達", belongs to a higher level than that stated in the input. Therefore, the model produced the hiragana spelling of that part.

In the N5 output, as the tag is the most restrictive, the word "companions" is too complex to be translated. In this case, the word generated is "お姉さん" which means "older sister", and do not convey the same meaning.

In the second example, we present different ways of how the word "hunting" has been translated by the models. First, "no-tag" and N1 outputs correctly produce the kanji "狩". This kanji belongs to the N1 level, therefore these are the outputs where we find it. The rest of the outputs produce the term "ハンティング" which is a transliteration, in katakana, of the English term.

Regarding the N5 output, this is another example of how limiting the complexity could harm the translation. Many words have been copied from the source instead of being translated. In this sentence, the word "hunting" has been generated twice: one copied from the English side, and the other one as transliteration.

7 Conclusion and Future Work

In this work, we have used the addition of tags to control the complexity of the output of an English-to-Japanese MT model. The complexity has been established based on the vocabulary and kanji of JLPT exams.

Our results show that the complexity of the lexicon in the translation can be modulated with these tags. Despite that, although it can be influenced to a certain extent, the output may contain vocabulary of higher levels than that stated. This is not only because in the lower levels the vocabulary is too limited, but also because of the lack of translation occurrences in the train data.

We have also shown that restricting the output harms the translation quality. None of the outputs obtained using a complexity tag was better than that of a model trained without any restriction. In addition, enforcing too much simplicity causes the model not to be able to translate accurately and in some cases, it ends up copying words from the source.

One limitation of this work is that the classification of difficulty is decided solely based on the vocabulary. In future work, we want to expand this to also consider other factors such as the grammar or length of the sentences.

Another aspect that we want to investigate is using alternative configurations. For example, text simplification or paraphrasing models (Maddela et al., 2021) could be included to change the distribution of the complexity in the training data.

References

Sweta Agrawal and Marine Carpuat. 2019. Controlling text complexity in neural machine translation. In *Proceedings of the 2019 Conference on Empirical Methods in Natural Language Processing and the 9th International Joint Conference on Natural Language Processing (EMNLP-IJCNLP)*, pages 1549–1564, Hong Kong, China.

Chenhui Chu, Raj Dabre, and Sadao Kurohashi. 2017. An empirical comparison of domain adaptation methods for neural machine translation. In *Proceedings of the 55th Annual Meeting of the Association for Computational Linguistics (Volume 2: Short Papers)*, pages 385–391, Vancouver, Canada.

Goran Glavaš and Sanja Štajner. 2015. Simplifying lexical simplification: Do we need simplified corpora? In *Proceedings of the 53rd Annual Meeting of the Association for Computational Linguistics and the 7th International Joint Conference on Natural Language Processing (Volume 2: Short Papers)*, pages 63–68, Beijing, China.

Muhaimin Hading, Yuji Matsumoto, and Maki Sakamoto. 2016. Japanese lexical simplification for non-native speakers. In *Proceedings of the 3rd Workshop on Natural Language Processing Techniques for Educational Applications (NLPTEA2016)*, pages 92–96, Osaka, Japan.

Melvin Johnson, Mike Schuster, Quoc V Le, Maxim Krikun, Yonghui Wu, Zhifeng Chen, Nikhil Thorat, Fernanda Viégas, Martin Wattenberg, Greg Corrado, et al. 2017. Google's multilingual neural machine translation system: Enabling zero-shot translation. *Transactions of the Association for Computational Linguistics*, 5:339–351.

Marcin Junczys-Dowmunt, Roman Grundkiewicz, Tomasz Dwojak, Hieu Hoang, Kenneth Heafield, Tom Neckermann, Frank Seide, Ulrich Germann, Alham Fikri Aji, Nikolay Bogoychev, André F. T. Martins, and Alexandra Birch. 2018. Marian: Fast neural machine translation in C++. In *Proceedings of ACL 2018, System Demonstrations*, pages 116–121, Melbourne, Australia.

Mounica Maddela, Fernando Alva-Manchego, and Wei Xu. 2021. Controllable text simplification with explicit paraphrasing. In *Proceedings of the 2021 Conference of the North American Chapter of the Association for Computational Linguistics: Human Language Technologies*, pages 3536–3553.

Kelly Marchisio, Jialiang Guo, Cheng-I Lai, and Philipp Koehn. 2019. Controlling the reading level of machine translation output. In *Proceedings of Machine Translation Summit XVII: Research Track*, pages 193–203, Dublin, Ireland.

Louis Martin, Éric de la Clergerie, Benoît Sagot, and Antoine Bordes. 2020. Controllable sentence simplification. In *Proceedings of the Twelfth Language Resources and Evaluation Conference*, pages 4689–4698, Marseille, France.

Makoto Morishita, Jun Suzuki, and Masaaki Nagata. 2020. JParaCrawl: A large scale web-based English-Japanese parallel corpus. In *Proceedings of The 12th Language Resources and Evaluation Conference*, pages 3603–3609, Marseille, France.

Graham Neubig, Yosuke Nakata, and Shinsuke Mori. 2011. Pointwise prediction for robust, adaptable Japanese morphological analysis. In *Proceedings of the 49th Annual Meeting of the Association for Computational Linguistics: Human Language Technologies*, pages 529–533, Portland, Oregon, USA.

Daiki Nishihara, Tomoyuki Kajiwara, and Yuki Arase. 2019. Controllable text simplification with lexical constraint loss. In *Proceedings of the 57th Annual Meeting of the Association for Computational Linguistics: Student Research Workshop*, pages 260–266, Florence, Italy.

Kishore Papineni, Salim Roukos, Todd Ward, and Wei-Jing Zhu. 2002. Bleu: a method for automatic evaluation of machine translation. In *Proceedings of 40th Annual Meeting of the Association for Computational Linguistics*, pages 311–318, Philadelphia, Pennsylvania, USA.

Nicholas Ramkissoon. Japanese reading difficulty classification for non-native language learners.

Matthew Shardlow and Fernando Alva-Manchego. 2022. Simple tico-19: A dataset for joint translation and simplification of covid-19 texts. In *Proceedings of the 13th Language Resources and Evaluation Conference*, pages 3093–3102, Marseille, France.

Nicolas Spring, Annette Rios Gonzales, and Sarah Ebling. 2021. Exploring german multi-level text simplification. In *Proceedings of the International Conference on Recent Advances in Natural Language Processing (RANLP 2021)*, pages 1339–1349.

Sanja Štajner and Maja Popović. 2016. Can text simplification help machine translation? In *Proceedings of the 19th Annual Conference of the European Association for Machine Translation*, pages 230–242, Riga, Latvia.

Sanja Štajner and Maja Popović. 2019. Automated text simplification as a preprocessing step for machine translation into an under-resourced language. In *Proceedings of the International Conference on Recent Advances in Natural Language Processing (RANLP 2019)*, pages 1141–1150, Varna, Bulgaria.

Jörg Tiedemann. 2012. Parallel data, tools and interfaces in opus. In *Proceedings of the Eight International Conference on Language Resources and Evaluation (LREC'12)*, pages 2214–2218, Istanbul, Turkey.

Ashish Vaswani, Noam Shazeer, Niki Parmar, Jakob Uszkoreit, Llion Jones, Aidan N Gomez, Łukasz Kaiser, and Illia Polosukhin. 2017. Attention is all you need. In *Advances in neural information processing systems*, pages 5998–6008, Long Beach, USA.

Jonathan Waller. 2010. Japanese language proficiency test resources.

Tong Wang, Ping Chen, John Rochford, and Jipeng Qiang. 2016. Text simplification using neural machine translation. In *Proceedings of the AAAI Conference on Artificial Intelligence*, volume 30, pages 4270–4270.

IrekiaLF_es: a new open benchmark and baseline systems for Spanish Automatic Text Simplification

Itziar Gonzalez-Dios
HiTZ Center - Ixa, University of the Basque Country (UPV/EHU)
itziar.gonzalezd@ehu.eus

Iker Gutiérrez-Fandiño
University of Deusto
ikergutierrez@opendeusto.es

Oscar M. Cumbicus-Pineda
Univ. Nac. de Loja and Ixa (UPV/EHU)
oscar.cumbicus@unl.edu.ec

Aitor Soroa
HiTZ Center - Ixa, University of the Basque Country (UPV/EHU)
a.soroa@ehu.eus

Abstract

Automatic Text simplification (ATS) seeks to reduce the complexity of a text for a general or a target audience. In the last years, deep learning methods have become the most used systems in ATS research, but these systems need large and good-quality datasets to be evaluated. Moreover, these data are available on a large scale only for English and in some cases with restrictive licenses. In this paper, we present IrekiaLF_es, an open-license benchmark for Spanish text simplification. It consists of a document-level corpus and a sentence-level test set that has been manually aligned. We also conduct a neurolinguistically-based evaluation of the corpus in order to reveal its suitability for text simplification. This evaluation follows the Lexicon-Unification-Linearity (LeULi) model of neurolinguistic complexity assessment. Finally, we present a set of experiments and baselines of ATS systems in a zero-shot scenario.

1 Introduction

According to the UN, illiteracy affects 16 per cent of the world population (759 million adults)[1] and the number of children experiencing reading difficulties has increased from 460 million to 584 million after the COVID-19 pandemic.[2] Moreover, in the OECD countries, between 4.9 % and 27.7 % of adults only has proficiency at the lowest levels in literacy (OECD, 2013) and regarding the young people 10 % of new graduates have low literacy skills (OECD, 2015).

Due to these facts, plain language[3] and easy-to-read initiatives[4] give some guidelines to make texts more accessible. Basically, their recommendations can be summarised in writing for the audience, organising the information, using short and positive sentences, using active instead of passive voice, choosing words carefully, being concise, employing an appropriate design for smooth reading and, in the case of online communication, following the web standards.

In this line, text simplification seeks to reduce the complexity of texts (at the lexical, syntactic and discourse levels) for a general public or a target audience. As adapting the texts manually is a hard-working task, researchers in Natural Language Processing (NLP) have tried to automatise it since the mid 90s. The pioneers were Chandrasekar et al. (1996) and their main motivation was related to the problems that long and complex sentences caused in advanced NLP applications. Nowadays, however, most of the research on Automatic Text Simplification (ATS) focuses on human target audience (Štajner, 2021).

As other NLP tasks, ATS has evolved from rule-based systems, statistic systems, hybrid systems mixing hand-crafted rules and machine learning, to the present deep learning paradigm. The interested reader is referred to the following state-of-the-art reports for more information about the evolution of ATS (Gonzalez-Dios et al., 2013; Shardlow, 2014; Siddharthan, 2014; Saggion, 2017; Alva-Manchego et al., 2020b).

Current deep learning techniques, however, need extensive data and these data are mainly available for English. Moreover, some corpora do not have open licenses. There are NLP techniques to alleviate this problem such as transfer learning and cross-lingual learning, but, even in these cases, high-quality evaluation benchmarks are needed.

In this paper, we present IrekiaLF_es, an open corpus and benchmark for Spanish ATS systems. IrekiaLF_es compiles texts published by the Basque Government in both original and easy-to-read format. The corpus is divided in a document-

[1] https://www.un.org/en/chronicle/article/education-all-rising-challenge
[2] https://news.un.org/en/story/2021/03/1088392
[3] https://www.plainlanguage.gov/
[4] https://www.inclusion-europe.eu/easy-to-read/

Proceedings of the Workshop on Text Simplification, Accessibility, and Readability (TSAR-2022), pages 86 - 97
December 8, 2022

level version containing 288 documents, and a sentence-level version, where 35 of them have been manually aligned. The corpus is available with an open license.[5] Furthermore, in order to reveal its quality and suitability for ATS, we have evaluated neurolinguistic complexity of the corpus following the Lexicon-Unification-Linearity (LeULi) model (Gutiérrez-Fandiño, 2022). This model of neurolinguistic complexity assessment is entirely inspired by Hagoort (2005, 2013, 2014, 2017, 2019, 2020)'s Memory, Unification, Control (MUC) model of language neurobiology. Finally, we have evaluated three different systems that will serve as baselines for future research in this corpus.

This paper is structured as follows: right after this introduction (Section 2), we present the related work on simplified corpora; in Section 3 we describe the methodology to build the IrekiaLF_es corpus; in Section 4 we summarise the LeULi model and provide the rationale for its use; in Section 5 we carry out a LeULi-based complexity evaluation of the corpus; in Section 6 we show the experiments with the three baseline systems; and we conclude with the take-home messages and outline the future work in Section 7.

2 Related work

Corpora or datasets for ATS are built with two main objectives: on the one hand, to study the process and operations carried out when simplifying texts e.g. by annotating the operations (Caseli et al., 2009; Bott and Saggion, 2014; Brunato et al., 2015; Gonzalez-Dios et al., 2018), and, on the other hand, to use them as resources to build and evaluate machine learning systems (see next paragraph for references). When creating and compiling corpora of simplified texts, the strategies (intuitive or structural) and the target audiences can be different (Gonzalez-Dios et al., 2018). Hence, there is no unique answer or simplified correct sentence for a given complex or original sentence. A recent overview on the creation of ATS corpora can be found in Brunato et al. (2022).

The main research in text simplification, both from an educational perspective and from an NLP perspective, has focused on English and, therefore, the majority of corpora as well as the largest ones are in such language (Petersen and Ostendorf, 2007; Pellow and Eskenazi, 2014; Vajjala and Lučić, 2018). The most used datasets for NLP are i) those derived from Wikipedia and Simple Wikipedia (and therefore with open licences): WikiSmall, originally created by Zhu et al. (2010) and adapted by Zhang and Lapata (2017), WikiLarge, compiled by Zhang and Lapata (2017) and usually used for training, TurkCorpus (Xu et al., 2016) and Asset (Alva-Manchego et al., 2020a) used for evaluation and ii) Newsela (Xu et al., 2015), which has proprietary licence but can be obtained for research. In order to study the document level simplification, D-Wikipedia dataset has been proposed (Sun et al., 2021).

However, there are also corpora for other languages such as Brazilian Portuguese (Caseli et al., 2009; Hartmann et al., 2018, 2020), Danish (Klerke and Søgaard, 2012), German (Klaper et al., 2013; Battisti et al., 2020; Säuberli et al., 2020), Italian (Brunato et al., 2015; Tonelli et al., 2016; Brunato et al., 2016), Basque (Gonzalez-Dios et al., 2018) and French (Gala et al., 2020). Recently, a multilingual corpus of news has been compiled that includes Finnish, French, Italian, Swedish, English and German (Hauser et al., 2022).

Regarding Spanish, the first ATS corpus was developed in Saggion et al. (2011)'s project, which aimed to build an ATS system guided by the so-called easy-to-read principles. The corpus, named Simplext, was created manually by trained experts and the target audience were students with Down Syndrome. An analysis of the operations needed to simplify the original text revealed that the most frequent operations in Simplext were change (transformation), delete, insert and split (Bott and Saggion, 2011, 2014). This corpus is available upon request from the authors. The Newsela corpus (Xu et al., 2015), which is also available upon request, contains a portion in Spanish, but there is no information about the particulars of the Spanish subset. There are three resources for Spanish focusing on lexical simplification: the LexSiS corpus (Bott et al., 2012) (obtained upon request), and the EASIER corpus (Alarcón García, 2022) (available at GitHub, but without explicit license), and ALEXSIS (Ferrés and Saggion, 2022), which will be available after what the authors call *embargo period* (but so far there is no explicit license). Finally, a bilingual (EN/ES) dataset about Covid-19 texts (Simple TICO-19) has been released (Shardlow and Alva-Manchego, 2022) and a corpus for Spanish medical text simplification, the CLARA-MeD comparable corpus, is made up of 24 298 pairs of pro-

[5] `https://github.com/itziargd/IrekiaLF`

	orig	e2r
Word number	185,070	135,659
Token number	231,332	177,402
Sentence number	5,389	2,408

Table 1: Basic statistics of the document level corpus.

fessional and simplified texts (Campillos-Llanos et al., 2022).

3 Building IrekiaLF_es

Irekia is the open-government communication channel of the Basque Government. This web site contains, among others, news about the Government, written in a non-administrative language, both in Spanish and Basque. Some of the news are adapted to the easy-to-read format, thereby making the site very valuable as a source to compile complex-simple parallel texts, which, moreover, can be bilingual. The portal has CC-BY license, so that its content can be used to derive research datasets.[6] Based on this resource, the aim of this work is to create a good-quality corpus of Spanish, IrekiaLF_es, with original and adapted/simplified texts. We release the corpus under an open license, thus expanding the options for ATS researchers to train and test systems for Spanish.

IrekiaLF_es is built by crawling all the Spanish news that have an easy-to-read counterpart until 17/11/2021 (unfortunately the last adapted version was published in 28/12/2021). The first document's date is 1/04/2017. After removing the duplicates, we have compiled a document-level corpus comprising 288 parallel documents. The dataset is publicly available[7] under CC BY-SA 4.0 license.

Table 1 shows the number of words, tokens and sentences of the complex and simple parts of the corpus.[8] As it can be seen, the *orig* texts are much longer than the *e2r*. This is in line with what is found for example in English corpora (Amancio and Specia, 2014), where simplified texts have also fewer words.[9]

As in the original web site, some complex and unfamiliar words in the documents are linked to their definitions (see Figure 1). We keep these definitions at the document level dataset so that they can serve for both complex word identification and generation of explanations (elaboration). There are 1624 definitions in the corpus that explain complex legal denominations, named entities, and complex words.

In addition to the document-level corpus, we have created a subcorpus, a part of the document-level corpus, that is manually aligned at a sentence level,[10] and which comprises 705 aligned sentences from 35 documents.[11] We have followed this methodology to align the sentences:

1. Preliminary alignment: As a preliminary step, two persons (a computational linguist expert in ATS and a linguistics student) aligned the sentences in five documents and discussed the doubts and unclear cases. As a result, the following guidelines were defined:
   - Align sentences according to information preservation.
   - Do not manipulate easy-to-read texts to improve the simplifications.
   - Regarding sentence boundaries: periods (.) and ellipses (...) indicate the end of a declarative sentence; exclamation marks (!) indicate the end of an exclamative or imperative sentence; question marks (?) indicate the end of an interrogative sentence. Colons (:) are also sentence boundaries, but only when they are used to introduce new paragraphs, not when they link two clauses in a subordinate relationship.
2. Agreement alignment: once the guidelines were fixed, the annotators aligned ten additional documents, so that inter-annotator agreement could be calculated. The resulting percentage of agreement (or observed agreement) was 80.5 % and Cohen's kappa was 0.7. We considered this as a substantial agreement and, therefore, as a good basis to align the rest of the corpus.

[6] We are not aware of other governmental initiatives that could serve as data source under the same conditions. Research should be done at local and regional levels to consider the possibility of adding other data sources to augment the dataset.

[7] https://github.com/itziargd/IrekiaLF

[8] In this paper, we will call *orig* to the original, complex text and *e2r* to the simplified, easy-to-read counterpart.

[9] We do not have the data of the other Spanish corpora to make this comparison.

[10] We have also assessed the possibility of using ATS alignment tools for an automatic alignment, but none of them was good enough to maintain the quality of the alignments.

[11] The definitions of complex words are not considered when aligning the sentences.

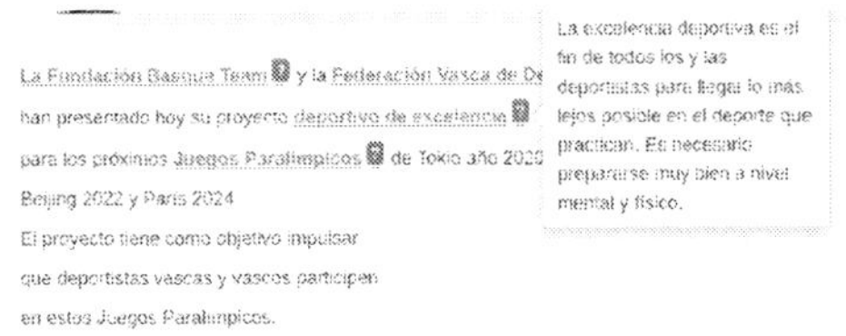

Figure 1: Example of words with hyperlinks to definitions.

3. General alignment: one of the annotators has aligned the rest of the documents in the sentence-aligned subcorpus (20 documents).

In Table 2 we present an example of two sentences aligned to their *e2r* counterparts. The translations of the examples are provided in Table 7 (Appendix A).

In Table 3 we present the number and percentage of the alignment scales, that is, how many sentences have been created/removed out of the original one. The percentage of merge operations is remarkable, close to the Italian *Teacher* subcorpus (Brunato et al., 2015), but high in comparison to the Basque CBST (Gonzalez-Dios et al., 2018) and the Italian *Terence* subcorpus (Brunato et al., 2015).[12] Most alignments are at scale 1:1, that is, when no splitting is performed, followed by 1:0, where the sentence has no equivalent *e2r* version. In the vast majority of splitting cases, the original sentence has been split into two (1:2), or into three (1:3) *e2r* sentences. Splitting into more than three sentences is residual.

4 LeULi model of complexity assessment

Evaluation of simplified corpora and ATS systems is more often than not largely based on formal, purely linguistic complexity metrics. However, determining the so-called readability can only be achieved in terms of neurolinguistic complexity: text comprehension takes place in the brain, and as such it requires a cognitive assessment.

On the basis of Hagoort (2005, 2013, 2014, 2017, 2019, 2020)'s Memory, Unification, Control (MUC) model of language neurobiology, Gutiérrez-Fandiño (2022)[13] proposes a model of three categories of neurolinguistic complexity assessment: Lexicon-Unification-Linearity (LeULi). Complexity assessment of IrekiaLF_es has therefore been conducted according to the LeULi model, which is synthesised in Table 4.

Regarding Lexical complexity, it has been shown that the less frequent a word is, the more effortful it is retrieve from long-term memory (LTM), resulting in higher levels of neural activation (Fiebach et al., 2002; Nakic et al., 2006). Infrequent words are not just more difficult to access, they are also more likely to be unknown to the reader, in which case they do not even exist in the mental lexicon and are hence impossible to retrieve from LTM.

The Unification of information from different language modules of the brain is a costly operation in language processing. Accordingly, to lighten complexity of the Unification category, linguistic phenomena involving several language modules should be strongly avoided in ATS: for instance, coreference (principally measured by pronoun incidence) demands the integration of information from the syntactic and semantic language modules.[14] Similarly, the large presence of elements that help avoid the presence of coreference is also an indicator of the lack of Unification complexity: the ratio of proper nouns for all nouns and content word overlap, for example, are metrics showing how often referents are repeated, instead of being pronominalised, coreferenced.

Lastly, linearity affects sentence comprehension as it determines both the temporal separation of chunks provisionally stored in working memory (WM) and the number of chunks stored in such temporary buffer during the processing of a sentence. It is primarily measured by sentence length, but also by non-selected constituents (adjunction and coordination), since selected constituents such as complements are effortlessly retrieved from LTM as part of the syntactic template of any lexical item.

5 Complexity assessment of IrekiaLF_es

In this section we present the results of the complexity evaluation of the whole IrekiaLF_es (document-level corpus). As explained in Section 4, we wanted

[12] We compare the alignments to these works because they are the only available to our knowledge. We show the statistics of the other datasets in the Appendix, in Table 8.

[13] This project will be soon publicly available at `https://dkh.deusto.es/en/community/learning/tfg`. Yet, anyone interested can obtain it in advance upon request to the author via email (ikergutierrez@opendeusto.es).

[14] The present analysis focuses on the syntactic-semantic Unification, since phenomena involving the remaining phonological module seem to have no significant presence in text processing.

orig	e2r
La Consejera de Empleo y Políticas Sociales, Beatriz Artolazabal, y el Consejero de Hacienda y Economía, Pedro Azpiazu, se han reunido con los responsables de EHLABE-Euskal Herriko Lan Babestuaren Elkartea-Asociación vasca de entidades no lucrativas que fomentan la inclusión sociolaboral de las personas con discapacidad, en la sede de Lantegi Batuak, en Loiu, Bizkaia.	Beatriz Artolazabal es la Consejera de Empleo y Políticas Sociales del Gobierno Vasco. Pedro Azpiazu es el Consejero de Hacienda y Economía del Gobierno Vasco. Euskal Herriko Lan Babestuaren Elkartea (EHLABE) es una asociación que impulsa la inclusión en la sociedad y en el trabajo de las personas con discapacidad. Beatriz Artolazabal y Pedro Azpiazu se han reunido con los responsables de EHLABE en la sede de Lantegi Batuak, en Bizkaia.
En el encuentro se ha analizado el trabajo de estas empresas y se han propuesto nuevas fórmulas de colaboración.	En la reunión han estudiado el trabajo de estas empresas y se han propuesto nuevas maneras de colaborar.

Table 2: Examples of aligned sentences (English translations in Table 7 in the Appendix).

Alignment scale	Sentences	Percentage
Merge (2:1)	53	7.6%
1:0	154	22.0%
1:1	310	44.0%
1:2	123	17.5%
1:3	50	7.1%
1:4	14	2.0%
1:5	1	0.1%

Table 3: Statistics of the alignment scales (the sentences created/removed out of the original sentences).

to base our complexity evaluation on recent evidence on sentence and text processing complexity, and thus we have decided to follow the metrics provided by the LeULi model (Gutiérrez-Fandiño, 2022). For the automatic measurement of complexity metrics, we have employed MultiAzterTest (Bengoetxea and Gonzalez-Dios, 2021), an open-source multilingual text analysis tool which examines more than 130 features at various linguistic levels. To calculate word frequencies we have used Python's *wordfreq* package (Speer et al., 2018). Specifically, we have grouped words in eight bins according to the logarithm of their frequencies.[15] Next, we present histograms and violin plots (Hintze and Nelson, 1998) comparing the scores of *orig* and *e2r* texts according to the neurolinguistic complexity metrics of the LeULi model.

Regarding the Lexicon category, there are substantially more infrequent words (0-4 levels) in *orig*

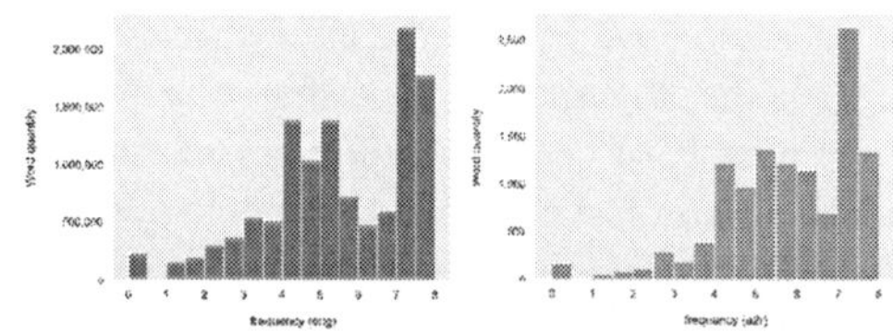

Figure 2: Histograms of word frequencies, grouped in eight bins according to the frequency logarithm.

than in *e2r* texts (Figure 2), where words around frequency level 6 are more regularly distributed, as a result of the conscious, purposeful use of frequent words.

When it comes to the Unification category, in Figure 3 it can be observed that there is a positive but too slight difference in the incidence of pronouns: *e2r* texts should have a markedly lower score than *orig* in this metric. The higher the pronoun incidence, the higher the Unification complexity.

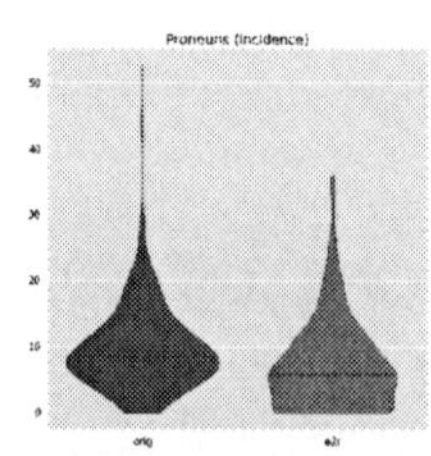

Figure 3: Incidence of pronouns.

As previously explained, the ratio of proper nouns for all nouns and content word overlap are metrics that show the extent to which coreference

[15] Which corresponds to the `zipf_frequency` of the *wordfreq* package.

Category	Constrainer	Constrainee	Metrics
Lexicon	LTM	Infrequent words: hard to access or not stored	**Word frequency**
Unification	WM	The integration of information from different modules	**Multi-module phenomena** (mainly coreference in syntactic-semantic Unification)
Linearity	WM	Time and volume of temporary storage	**Sentence length** mainly, but also adjunction and coordination

Table 4: Constrainers and constrainees of the LeULi categories of neurolinguistic complexity and their metrics.

is being avoided. Ratio/Mean scores in these metrics should therefore be notably higher in *e2r* than in *orig* texts (contrary to pronoun incidence), and standard deviation should be the lowest possible (as in any *e2r* metric). Thus, coreference would be avoided in a consistent manner and the easy-to-read principle "use the same word for the same term" would be observed.

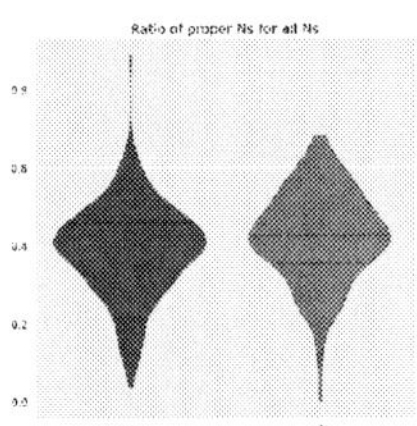

Figure 4: Plots of the ratio of proper nouns for all nouns (mean).

In this corpus, the ratio of proper nouns for all nouns is just slightly and hence insufficiently higher in *e2r* texts (Figure 4). Content word overlap (c.f. Figure 5) should not have a higher mean in *e2r* than in *orig* texts. Besides, it should not have a higher standard deviation in *e2r* than in *orig* texts.

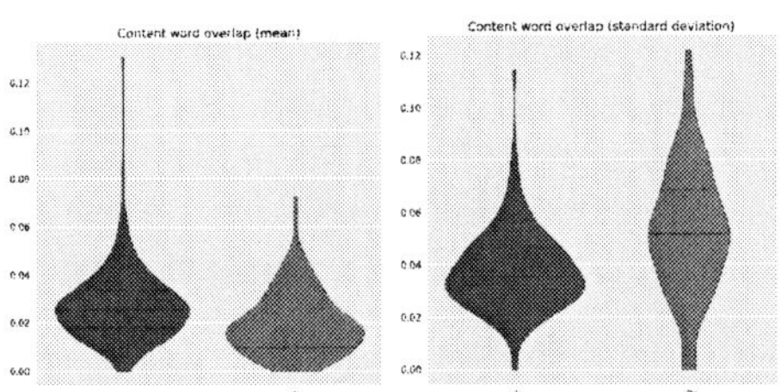

Figure 5: Plot of the content word overlap: mean (left) and standard deviation (right).

With respect to the Linearity category, Figure 6 displays the plots of sentence length and sentence depth. In both cases, there are lower mean scores in *e2r* texts and the difference between *orig* and *e2r* texts is similarly large for both metrics. These two are highly correlated metrics (Gutiérrez-Fandiño, 2022) and their plots are accordingly similar, but only sentence length actually contributes to processing complexity. This is because hierarchical structures (sentence depth, subordinate clauses) are effortlessly processed whereas linear phenomena that contribute to sentence length (number of words per sentence, coordination) are costly: WM consumption occurs in the horizontal extension of the syntactic tree, not in the vertical one.

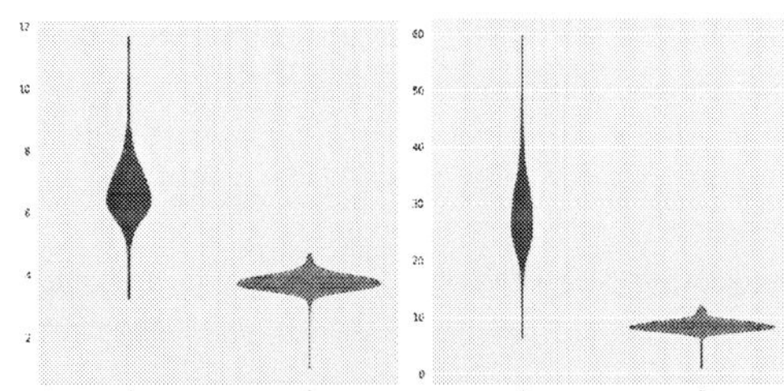

Figure 6: Plots of sentence depth (mean) (left) and words per sentence (mean) (right).

In Figure 7, it is shown that there is a large difference between *orig* and *e2r* texts in propositions per sentence than in subordinate clauses. Such difference accords with neurolinguistic simplicity since coordinated clauses should always be split into different sentences, to lighten the processing load, whereas subordinate clauses are not a problem themselves, as long as they do not include coreference.

In Figure 8, we see that there is a bigger difference in NP decendents (adjuncts+complements) than in NP modifiers (adjuncts) between *orig* and *e2r*. In terms of neurolinguistic simplicity, however, such difference should be bigger in adjuncts,

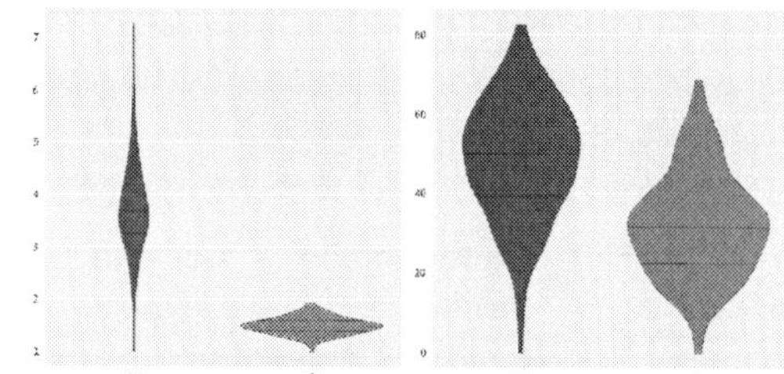

Figure 7: Plots of propositions per sentence (mean) (left) and subordinate clauses (incidence) (right).

which are non-selected constituents incurring an extra processing cost.

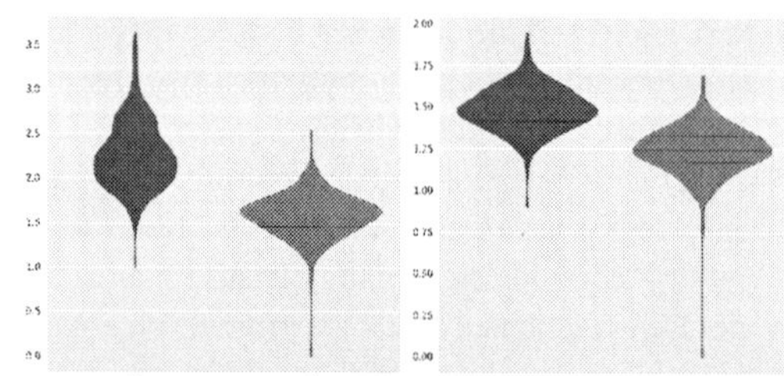

Figure 8: Plots of decendents per NP (mean) (left) and modifiers per NP (mean) (right).

In sum, taking into account the LeULi framework (Table 5), results on the word frequency metric are positive and hence the IrekiaLF_es corpus harmonises with neurolinguistic simplification as regards the Lexicon category of complexity. Regarding the Unification category, results are considerably worse: scores on 2 out of 3 metrics are halfway —not negative but highly improvable— and scores on the remaining metric are negative. Finally, results of the LeULi-based evaluation show positive scores in 2 out of 3 metrics of the Linearity category and negative scores on the remaining metric. Consequently, the text simplifications of the IrekiaLF_es corpus are good at the lexical and sentence level, but not at the discourse level owing to the substantial presence of multi-module phenomena (Unification category).

6 Experiments

In this section we report the results of three neural-based ATS systems when evaluated in the sentence-level IrekiaLF_es dataset. Given its small size, we followed a zero-shot scenario where the neural ATS systems are trained using Simplext (Saggion et al., 2015), and tested on IrekiaLF_es. Simplext comprises 200 manually simplified news texts from

Category	Metric	Assessment
Lexicon	Word frequency	POSITIVE
Unification	Ratio of proper nouns per all nouns	HALFWAY
	Pronouns (incidence)	HALFWAY
	Content word overlap (mean)	NEGATIVE
Linearity	Words per sentence	POSITIVE
	Coordination	POSITIVE
	NP adjunction	NEGATIVE

Table 5: Results of the LeULi-based evaluation of IrekiaLF_es.

different domains in Spanish. We have decided to train the baseline systems on Simplext because the text genre and the Spanish variety (peninsular Spanish) are similar. We followed Martin et al. (2020) and split the corpus in 574 sentences for training, 143 for development, and 693 for testing. We used the training set for finetuning, and the development set for model selection (the test split of Simplext was not used). Regarding IrekiaLF_es, we discarded the 1:0 alignments as well as the merge operations (29.3 % of the sentence level corpus), which results in a test set with 498 sentence pairs. The ATS systems are the following:

Edit+Synt is an edit-based seq2seq system that adds syntactic information at the word level (Cumbicus-Pineda et al., 2021). In the preprocessing stage, the training dataset was lowercased and the sentences were tokenised and parsed with SpaCy,[16] using the large model. The model was trained for 50 epochs, with a batch size of 64, a learning rate of 10^{-3}, a hidden dimension of 200, a decay factor of 10^{-6}.

mBART is a multilingual encoder-decoder model based on the transformers architecture, which is pretrained on 25 languages using the cc5 corpus (Liu et al., 2020). We used mBART-large, and fine-tuned it on Simplext (train set) for 50 epochs following default hyperparameters.[17]

mT5 is an encoder-decoder system similar to mBART but pre-trained using a different learning function and corpora (Xue et al., 2021). We used

[16]`https://spacy.io/`

[17]Learning rate of 5^{-5}, number of beams for beam search of 4, number of steps between val check of 500, number of steps between logs of 50, batch size of 2

System	BLUE	SARI
Edit+synt	5.44	37.95
mBART	4.38	38.90
mT5	7.12	42.19

Table 6: Results of the baseline systems.

the large version of mT5, and pretrained it on Simplext train using the same hyperparameters used in mBART.

We used default values for the hyperparameters, and did not perform any hyperparameter tuning. Regarding model selection, we selected the checkpoints that obtained the best SARI (Xu et al., 2016) score in the Simplext development test. To evaluate the models, we followed usual practice[18] and computed the BLUE (Papineni et al., 2002) and SARI metrics, using EASSE (Alva-Manchego et al., 2019).

In Table 6 we present the results obtained by the ATS systems. In general, all systems obtain SARI values that are similar to other ATS datasets, and in particular, to Simplext (Cumbicus-Pineda et al., 2021), with mT5 yielding the best results. While comparing figures across datasets cannot be used to draw meaningful conclusions, the relatively high SARI values might suggest the suitability of IrekiaLF_es for evaluating Spanish ATS systems. BLUE scores are however low in all systems, which we attribute to the followed zero-shot approach. Because Simplext simplifications are very short and highly compressed, the ATS systems produce sentences that are much shorter than the reference simplifications of IrekiaLS_es.

7 Conclusion and future work

In this paper, we have presented IrekiaLF_es, a new open corpus for Automatic Text Simplification in Spanish. The corpus compiles a document-level version with 288 parallel original and easy-to-read texts and a sentence-level version, where 35 of the documents have been manually aligned to create a test set of 705 sentences. The aim of this test set is to serve as a benchmark to evaluate ATS systems at the sentence level.

We have evaluated the neurolinguistic complexity of the corpus by following the Lexicon-Unification-Linearity (LeULi) model. The evaluation yields positive results regarding the Lexicon category of complexity, mostly negative regarding the Unification category and mostly positive regarding the Linearity category. Therefore, we can conclude that this corpus is suitable for ATS training and evaluation regarding lexical simplification and sentence simplification, but it may hinder end users' comprehension when it comes to discourse simplification due to the significant presence of multi-module phenomena (Unification category). This important drawback should be considered for future work. A specific quantitative benchmark for establishing the boundaries of the qualitative assessment (positive/halfway/negative) of the LeULi-based evaluation results should also be addressed in future work.

We have also evaluated three different systems that will serve as baselines for future research with this corpus. Results show good SARI values for all systems, but very low BLUE scores, which we attribute to the used zero-shot approach. Such results suggest the need of simplification datasets in Spanish where ATS systems can be trained or finetuned on.

In the future, we plan to align automatically the rest of the corpus by developing/adapting specific tools. From a linguistic point of view, we also foresee to study the operations carried out to simplify the texts. From an experimental point of view, we would like to carry out crosslingual experiments and test them in this corpus. Finally, we plan to create the Basque version of the corpus.

Acknowledgements

This research has been partially funded by the Basque Government (Ixa excellence research center, IT1570-22) and the Spanish government (DeepKnowledge project, PID2021-127777OB-C21).

References

Rodrigo Alarcón García. 2022. Lexical simplification for the systematic support of cognitive accessibility guidelines. *https://doi.org/10.1145/3471391.3471400*.

Fernando Alva-Manchego, Louis Martin, Antoine Bordes, Carolina Scarton, Benoît Sagot, and Lucia Specia. 2020a. ASSET: A dataset for tuning and evaluation of sentence simplification models with multiple rewriting transformations. In *Proceedings of the 58th Annual Meeting of the Association for Computational*

[18]We are aware that these metrics are flawed and may not be suitable for the quality evaluation of automatic simplifications but they are used as reference by the community (Sulem et al., 2018; Alva-Manchego et al., 2021).

Linguistics, pages 4668–4679, Online. Association for Computational Linguistics.

Fernando Alva-Manchego, Louis Martin, Carolina Scarton, and Lucia Specia. 2019. Easse: Easier automatic sentence simplification evaluation. In *EMNLP-IJCNLP 2019-Conference on Empirical Methods in Natural Language Processing and 9th International Joint Conference on Natural Language Processing (demo session)*, pages 49–54.

Fernando Alva-Manchego, Carolina Scarton, and Lucia Specia. 2020b. Data-driven sentence simplification: Survey and benchmark. *Computational Linguistics*, 46(1):135–187.

Fernando Alva-Manchego, Carolina Scarton, and Lucia Specia. 2021. The (un) suitability of automatic evaluation metrics for text simplification. *Computational Linguistics*, 47(4):861–889.

Marcelo Adriano Amancio and Lucia Specia. 2014. An analysis of crowdsourced text simplifications. In *Proceedings of the 3rd Workshop on Predicting and Improving Text Readability for Target Reader Populations (PITR)*, pages 123–130.

Alessia Battisti, Dominik Pfütze, Andreas Säuberli, Marek Kostrzewa, and Sarah Ebling. 2020. A corpus for automatic readability assessment and text simplification of german. In *Proceedings of the 12th Language Resources and Evaluation Conference*, pages 3302–3311.

Kepa Bengoetxea and Itziar Gonzalez-Dios. 2021. Multiaztertest: a multilingual analyzer on multiple levels of language for readability assessment. *arXiv preprint arXiv:2109.04870*.

Stefan Bott, Luz Rello, Biljana Drndarević, and Horacio Saggion. 2012. Can spanish be simpler? lexsis: Lexical simplification for spanish. In *Proceedings of COLING 2012*, pages 357–374.

Stefan Bott and Horacio Saggion. 2011. An unsupervised alignment algorithm for text simplification corpus construction. In *Proceedings of the Workshop on Monolingual Text-To-Text Generation*, pages 20–26.

Stefan Bott and Horacio Saggion. 2014. Text simplification resources for spanish. *Language Resources and Evaluation*, 48(1):93–120.

Dominique Brunato, Andrea Cimino, Felice Dell'Orletta, and Giulia Venturi. 2016. Paccss-it: A parallel corpus of complex-simple sentences for automatic text simplification. In *Proceedings of the 2016 Conference on Empirical Methods in Natural Language Processing*, pages 351–361.

Dominique Brunato, Felice Dell'Orletta, and Giulia Venturi. 2022. Linguistically-based comparison of different approaches to building corpora for text simplification: A case study on italian. *Frontiers in Psychology*, 13.

Dominique Brunato, Felice Dell'Orletta, Giulia Venturi, and Simonetta Montemagni. 2015. Design and annotation of the first italian corpus for text simplification. In *Proceedings of The 9th Linguistic Annotation Workshop*, pages 31–41.

Leonardo Campillos-Llanos, Ana Rosa Terroba Reinares, Sofía Zakhir Puig, Ana Valverde Mateos, and Adrián Capllonch Carrión. 2022. Building a comparable corpus and a benchmark for spanish medical text simplification.

Helena M Caseli, Tiago F Pereira, Lucia Specia, Thiago AS Pardo, Caroline Gasperin, and Sandra M Aluisio. 2009. Building a brazilian portuguese parallel corpus of original and simplified texts. *Advances in Computational Linguistics*, page 59.

Raman Chandrasekar, Christine Doran, and Srinivas Bangalore. 1996. Motivations and methods for text simplification. In *COLING 1996 Volume 2: The 16th International Conference on Computational Linguistics*.

Oscar M Cumbicus-Pineda, Itziar Gonzalez-Dios, and Aitor Soroa. 2021. A syntax-aware edit-based system for text simplification. In *Proceedings of the International Conference on Recent Advances in Natural Language Processing (RANLP 2021)*, pages 324–334.

Daniel Ferrés and Horacio Saggion. 2022. Alexsis: A dataset for lexical simplification in spanish. In *Proceedings of the 13th Conference on Language Resources and Evaluation (LREC 2022)*, page 3582–3594.

Christian J Fiebach, Angela D Friederici, Karsten Müller, and D Yves Von Cramon. 2002. fmri evidence for dual routes to the mental lexicon in visual word recognition. *Journal of cognitive neuroscience*, 14(1):11–23.

Núria Gala, Anaïs Tack, Ludivine Javourey-Drevet, Thomas François, and Johannes C Ziegler. 2020. Alector: A parallel corpus of simplified french texts with alignments of misreadings by poor and dyslexic readers. In *Language Resources and Evaluation for Language Technologies (LREC)*.

Itziar Gonzalez-Dios, María Jesús Aranzabe, and Arantza Díaz de Ilarraza. 2013. Testuen sinplifikazio automatikoa: arloaren egungo egoera. *Linguamática*, 5(2):43–63.

Itziar Gonzalez-Dios, María Jesús Aranzabe, and Arantza Díaz de Ilarraza. 2018. The corpus of basque simplified texts (cbst). *Language Resources and Evaluation*, 52(1):217–247.

Iker Gutiérrez-Fandiño. 2022. Toward complexity assessment in automatic text simplification: Evidence from neurobiological models of language. Bachelor's thesis. University of Deusto.

Peter Hagoort. 2005. On broca, brain, and binding: a new framework. *Trends in cognitive sciences*, 9(9):416–423.

Peter Hagoort. 2013. Muc (memory, unification, control) and beyond. *Frontiers in psychology*, 4:416.

Peter Hagoort. 2014. Nodes and networks in the neural architecture for language: Broca's region and beyond. *Current opinion in Neurobiology*, 28:136–141.

Peter Hagoort. 2017. The core and beyond in the language-ready brain. *Neuroscience & Biobehavioral Reviews*, 81:194–204.

Peter Hagoort. 2019. The neurobiology of language beyond single-word processing. *Science*, 366(6461):55–58.

Peter Hagoort. 2020. The core and beyond in the language-ready brain. Talk presented at Abralin ao Vivo – Linguists Online.

Nathan Hartmann, Gustavo Paetzold, and Sandra Aluísio. 2020. Simplex-pb 2.0: A reliable dataset for lexical simplification in brazilian portuguese. In *Proceedings of the The Fourth Widening Natural Language Processing Workshop*, pages 18–22.

Nathan S Hartmann, Gustavo H Paetzold, and Sandra M Aluísio. 2018. Simplex-pb: A lexical simplification database and benchmark for portuguese. In *International Conference on Computational Processing of the Portuguese Language*, pages 272–283. Springer, Cham.

Renate Hauser, Jannis Vamvas, Sarah Ebling, and Martin Volk. 2022. A multilingual simplified language news corpus. In *2nd Workshop on Tools and Resources for REAding DIfficulties (READI)*, page 25.

Jerry L. Hintze and Ray D. Nelson. 1998. Violin plots: A box plot-density trace synergism. *The American Statistician*, 52(2):181–184.

David Klaper, Sarah Ebling, and Martin Volk. 2013. Building a german/simple german parallel corpus for automatic text simplification. In *Proceedings of the Second Workshop on Predicting and Improving Text Readability for Target Reader Populations*, pages 11–19.

Sigrid Klerke and Anders Søgaard. 2012. Dsim, a danish parallel corpus for text simplification. In *Proceedings of the Eighth International Conference on Language Resources and Evaluation (LREC'12)*, pages 4015–4018.

Yinhan Liu, Jiatao Gu, Naman Goyal, Xian Li, Sergey Edunov, Marjan Ghazvininejad, Mike Lewis, and Luke Zettlemoyer. 2020. Multilingual denoising pretraining for neural machine translation.

Louis Martin, Angela Fan, Éric de la Clergerie, Antoine Bordes, and Benoît Sagot. 2020. Multilingual unsupervised sentence simplification. *CoRR*, abs/2005.00352.

Marina Nakic, Bruce W Smith, Sarah Busis, Meena Vythilingam, and R James R Blair. 2006. The impact of affect and frequency on lexical decision: the role of the amygdala and inferior frontal cortex. *Neuroimage*, 31(4):1752–1761.

OECD. 2013. *OECD Skills Outlook 2013*.

OECD. 2015. *OECD Skills Outlook 2015*.

Kishore Papineni, Salim Roukos, Todd Ward, and Wei-Jing Zhu. 2002. Bleu: a method for automatic evaluation of machine translation. In *Proceedings of the 40th annual meeting of the Association for Computational Linguistics*, pages 311–318.

David Pellow and Maxine Eskenazi. 2014. An open corpus of everyday documents for simplification tasks. In *Proceedings of the 3rd Workshop on Predicting and Improving Text Readability for Target Reader Populations (PITR)*, pages 84–93.

Sarah E Petersen and Mari Ostendorf. 2007. Text simplification for language learners: a corpus analysis. In *Workshop on speech and language technology in education*. Citeseer.

Horacio Saggion. 2017. Automatic text simplification. *Synthesis Lectures on Human Language Technologies*, 10(1):1–137.

Horacio Saggion, Elena Gómez-Martínez, Esteban Etayo, Alberto Anula, and Lorena Bourg. 2011. Text simplification in simplext: Making texts more accessible. *Procesamiento del lenguaje natural*, (47):341–342.

Horacio Saggion, Sanja Štajner, Stefan Bott, Simon Mille, Luz Rello, and Biljana Drndarevic. 2015. Making it simplext: Implementation and evaluation of a text simplification system for spanish. *ACM Transactions on Accessible Computing (TACCESS)*, 6(4):1–36.

Andreas Säuberli, Sarah Ebling, and Martin Volk. 2020. Benchmarking data-driven automatic text simplification for german. In *Proceedings of the 1st Workshop on Tools and Resources to Empower People with REAding DIfficulties (READI)*, pages 41–48.

Matthew Shardlow. 2014. A survey of automated text simplification. *International Journal of Advanced Computer Science and Applications*, 4(1):58–70.

Matthew Shardlow and Fernando Alva-Manchego. 2022. Simple tico-19: A dataset for joint translation and simplification of covid-19 texts. In *Proceedings of the 13th Language Resources and Evaluation Conference, Marseille, France, June. European Language Resources Association.*

Advaith Siddharthan. 2014. A survey of research on text simplification. *ITL-International Journal of Applied Linguistics*, 165(2):259–298.

Robyn Speer, Joshua Chin, Andrew Lin, Sara Jewett, and Lance Nathan. 2018. Luminosoinsight/wordfreq: v2.2.

Sanja Štajner. 2021. Automatic text simplification for social good: Progress and challenges. *Findings of the Association for Computational Linguistics: ACL-IJCNLP 2021*, pages 2637–2652.

Elior Sulem, Omri Abend, and Ari Rappoport. 2018. BLEU is not suitable for the evaluation of text simplification. In *Proceedings of the 2018 Conference on Empirical Methods in Natural Language Processing*, pages 738–744, Brussels, Belgium. Association for Computational Linguistics.

Renliang Sun, Hanqi Jin, and Xiaojun Wan. 2021. Document-level text simplification: Dataset, criteria and baseline. In *Proceedings of the 2021 Conference on Empirical Methods in Natural Language Processing*, pages 7997–8013.

Sara Tonelli, Alessio Palmero Aprosio, and Francesca Saltori. 2016. Simpitiki: a simplification corpus for italian. In *Proceedings of Third Italian Conference on Computational Linguistics (CLiC-it 2016) & Fifth Evaluation Campaign of Natural Language Processing and Speech Tools for Italian. Final Workshop (EVALITA 2016)*.

Sowmya Vajjala and Ivana Lučić. 2018. Onestopenglish corpus: A new corpus for automatic readability assessment and text simplification. In *Proceedings of the thirteenth workshop on innovative use of NLP for building educational applications*, pages 297–304.

Wei Xu, Chris Callison-Burch, and Courtney Napoles. 2015. Problems in current text simplification research: New data can help. *Transactions of the Association for Computational Linguistics*, 3:283–297.

Wei Xu, Courtney Napoles, Ellie Pavlick, Quanze Chen, and Chris Callison-Burch. 2016. Optimizing statistical machine translation for text simplification. *Transactions of the Association for Computational Linguistics*, 4:401–415.

Linting Xue, Noah Constant, Adam Roberts, Mihir Kale, Rami Al-Rfou, Aditya Siddhant, Aditya Barua, and Colin Raffel. 2021. mT5: A massively multilingual pre-trained text-to-text transformer. In *Proceedings of the 2021 Conference of the North American Chapter of the Association for Computational Linguistics: Human Language Technologies*, pages 483–498, Online. Association for Computational Linguistics.

Xingxing Zhang and Mirella Lapata. 2017. Sentence simplification with deep reinforcement learning. In *Proceedings of the 2017 Conference on Empirical Methods in Natural Language Processing*, pages 584–594, Copenhagen, Denmark. Association for Computational Linguistics.

Zhemin Zhu, Delphine Bernhard, and Iryna Gurevych. 2010. A monolingual tree-based translation model for sentence simplification. In *Proceedings of the 23rd International Conference on Computational Linguistics (Coling 2010)*, pages 1353–1361.

A Translation of the examples

In Table 7 we provide the translations into English of the examples of aligned sentences in Table 2.

B Alignment scales of the Italian and Basque corpora

In Table 8 we show the statistics in percentages of the Italian (IT) and Basque (EU) corpora as reported by Brunato et al. (2015) and Gonzalez-Dios et al. (2018) respectively.

orig	e2r
The Councilor for Employment and Social Policies, Beatriz Artolazabal, and the Councilor for Finance and Economy, Pedro Azpiazu, met with the heads of EHLABE-Euskal Herriko Lan Babestuaren Elkartea-Basque Association of non-profit organisations that promote the social and labor inclusion of people with disabilities, at the headquarters of Lantegi Batuak, in Loiu, Bizkaia.	Beatriz Artolazabal is the Councilor of Employment and Social Policies of the Basque Government. Pedro Azpiazu is the Councilor of Finance and Economy of the Basque Government. Euskal Herriko Lan Babestuaren Elkartea (EHLABE) is an association that promotes the inclusion of people with disabilities in society and at work. Beatriz Artolazabal and Pedro Azpiazu met with the heads of EHLABE at the headquarters of Lantegi Batuak, in Bizkaia.
During the meeting, the work of these companies was analyzed and new formulas for collaboration were proposed.	At the meeting they studied the work of these companies and proposed new ways to collaborate.

Table 7: English translations of the examples of aligned sentences in Table 2.

Alignment scale	Terence (IT)	Teacher (IT)	CBST- structural (EU)	CBST- intuitive (EU)
Merge (2:1)	2.88	13.74	0.88	0.44
1:0	0.67	1.15	-	-
1:1	92.1	68.32	76.21	73.25
1:2	3.75	11.45	18.50	19.74
1:3	0.19	0.76	3.52	4.39
Other	0.38	-	0.88	2.19

Table 8: Statistics (percentage) of the alignment scales of the Italian and Basque corpora.

Lexical Simplification in Foreign Language Learning: Creating Pedagogically Suitable Simplified Example Sentences

Jasper Degraeuwe
LT[3] / MULTIPLES
Ghent University
Belgium
Jasper.Degraeuwe@UGent.be

Horacio Saggion
LaSTUS / TALN
Universitat Pompeu Fabra
Spain
horacio.saggion@upf.edu

Abstract

This study presents a lexical simplification (LS) methodology for foreign language (FL) learning purposes, a barely explored area of automatic text simplification (TS). The method, targeted at Spanish as a foreign language (SFL), includes a customised complex word identification (CWI) classifier and generates substitutions based on masked language modelling. Performance is calculated on a custom dataset by means of a new, pedagogically-oriented evaluation. With 43% of the top simplifications being found suitable, the method shows potential for simplifying sentences to be used in FL learning activities. The evaluation also suggests that, though still crucial, meaning preservation is not always a prerequisite for successful LS. To arrive at grammatically correct and more idiomatic simplifications, future research could study the integration of association measures based on co-occurrence data.

1 Introduction

The rise of digital corpora has been steadily transforming the FL learning domain. As corpora are an easy-to-compile source of natural text which can be consulted in a highly efficient fashion (Granger et al., 2007; Pilán et al., 2016), they are arriving at a stage of being seamlessly embedded in several aspects of the everyday language learning practice (Chambers, 2019). This "normalisation" (Bax, 2003) of corpora is especially evidenced in the growing interest in data-driven learning (DDL; Johns, 1990). In its broadest sense, this area refers to both teachers and learners "using the tools and techniques of corpus linguistics for pedagogical purposes" (Gilquin and Granger, 2010, p. 359). While learner-led DDL activities tend to consist in analysing concordance lines (e.g. to discover collocations), teacher-focused DDL usually corresponds to accessing corpora directly in order to generate resources such as vocabulary lists and fill-the-gap exercises, which has led to the concept of "corpus-informed language teaching" (Jablonkai and Csomay, 2022).

However, working with corpora also entails challenges and limitations, for instance with regard to learner proficiency levels. To begin with, DDL has been found to be beneficial for intermediate and advanced learners (Boulton and Cobb, 2017), but with lower levels the credentials of using corpora still have to be established (Boulton and Vyatkina, 2021). Furthermore, also between intermediate and advanced learners considerable differences can exist, for example with respect to vocabulary knowledge: the lower one's language proficiency, the less extensive one's vocabulary will be (Laufer and Nation, 1995). In DDL, this can lead to the following scenario: while preparing a language for specific purposes (LSP) class on economics, an SFL teacher is using a corpus query tool to create a fill-the-gap exercise for the target item *arancel* and finds sentence (a) below in the query output. However, if this sentence were to be included in the final exercise, low- or intermediate-proficiency learners could find themselves unable to solve it, as their limited vocabulary knowledge might prevent them from understanding essential parts of the context, such as the word *esquivar*.

(a) La planta local también permitirá **esquivar** los <u>aranceles</u>. ('The local plant will also allow **evading** <u>tariffs</u>.')

To overcome this limitation, (part of) the corpus data can be simplified according to the needs of the target audience (Gilquin and Granger, 2010). As manual simplification constitutes a time-consuming task, automating the simplification procedure could provide a more viable solution, especially when large corpora are involved. This study aims to contribute to this barely explored area of automatic TS for FL learning purposes (Section 2.1). We specifically focus on the natural language processing (NLP) technique of lexical

Proceedings of the Workshop on Text Simplification, Accessibility, and Readability (TSAR-2022), pages 98 - 110
December 8, 2022

simplification (Section 2.2), which will be used to adapt DDL activities to the needs of Dutch-speaking B2-level SFL learners. Apart from presenting this novel LS method (Section 3), the study also introduces a new type of human-based evaluation, distinguished by its particular pedagogical focus (Section 4).

2 Related Research

2.1 Text Simplification

Automatic TS, usually subdivided into syntactic and lexical simplification, is the computer-driven operation of "transforming a text into another text which, ideally conveying the same message, will be easier to read and understand by a broader audience" (Saggion, 2017). TS methods have been applied in a wide range of areas, where they have been proven useful for developing reading aids for children and people with cognitive disabilities (Rello et al., 2013; Watanabe et al., 2009), and for improving NLP tasks such as information extraction and machine translation in the form of a preprocessing step (Evans, 2011; Štajner and Popović, 2016).

The field of FL learning, however, has seen little attention being devoted to automatic TS, despite having a long tradition in manual TS (Shardlow, 2014a; Siddharthan, 2014). As one of the few existing studies related to automatic TS, Paetzold and Specia (2016) focus on unsupervised word embedding-based LS for non-native English speakers. Their aim is to satisfy the needs of this target audience by constructing a custom evaluation dataset based on a user study. Uchida et al. (2018) also present a language learning-oriented dataset for English, containing sentences taken from university textbooks. All B2+ words in those sentences were marked as complex, and substitution candidates were identified after manually revising a thesaurus-based selection of possible replacements. Finally, Martin et al. (2020) propose a controllable sentence simplification system based on Sequence-to-Sequence models, in which attributes such as sentence length and lexical complexity can be conditioned by the user. Although they do not specifically target FL learners, the controllable nature of their system can enable adjusting the simplification procedure to this target audience.

Even though TS is sometimes tackled as a generic task with a one-size-fits-all simplified output, it is agreed that different user groups often require different simplification methodologies (Martin et al., 2020; Shardlow, 2014a; Uchida et al., 2018). Datasets annotated by native speakers, for instance, have shown to be unsuitable for evaluating a TS system for non-native speakers, since word complexity as perceived by mother-tongue speakers does not correspond to word complexity for non-natives (Paetzold and Specia, 2016). Moreover, to further define this "non-native word complexity" (and to identify the simplification needs of FL learners in general), linguistic and pedagogical insights could be taken into account, such as Krashen's (1985) theory that learners acquire language when the input they are exposed to is comprehensible, but just somewhat beyond their current knowledge. It is, however, also important to highlight that manipulating corpus data is an intervention which needs to be undertaken with caution, since it may jeopardise the authentic character of the DDL activities (Boulton, 2009; Siddharthan, 2014).

Finally, by choosing Spanish as the target language, this study aims to continue the line of TS research which focuses on languages other than English. Since LexSis (the first implemented LS system for Spanish; Bott et al., 2012), Spanish has been included in more and more studies (Alarcón et al., 2021; Sheang, 2019; Saggion et al., 2015) and shared tasks (Yimam et al., 2018). The methodology and models presented in this study will contribute to further developing the Spanish TS domain.

2.2 Lexical Simplification

In LS, the goal is to replace "words in a given sentence in order to make it simple, without applying any modifications to its syntactic structure" (Paetzold and Specia, 2017, p. 549). LS systems can have different types of architectures, ranging from rule-based pipelines in which a predefined set of complex words is linked to synonyms (Devlin and Tait, 1998), over systems which exploit parallel corpora and the corresponding edit information (Biran et al. 2011), to word embedding approaches, which are designed to be less resource-dependent (Glavaš and Štajner, 2015). The LS process typically consists of four steps, presented below.

2.2.1 Complex Word Identification

A first important step within the CWI process is the definition of "complexity", as this concept may refer to absolute/objective or relative/agent-related complexity (North et al., 2022). While the former type refers to the linguistic properties of a word (e.g. word length, number of diphthongs and number of senses), the latter reports how individuals perceive a word based on their individual experiences or psycholinguistic factors (e.g. cognitive load and level of familiarity with a particular typography). In the field of CWI, however, a more general definition is adopted which combines elements from both complexity types. Therefore, when using the terms "complex" and "complexity" in this paper, we refer to the difficulty an individual may have in understanding a particular target word as a result of the target word's linguistic properties as well as factors belonging to the individual (North et al., 2022).

As for types of CWI methods, four categories can be discerned: threshold-based, lexicon-based, implicit and machine-learning assisted CWI. In threshold-based strategies, words are usually categorised as simple or complex based on word frequency. However, despite being intuitive and easy to implement, they lead to many simple words being unnecessarily labelled as complex (Shardlow, 2014b). Next, lexicon-based approaches look up words in human-curated lexicons, a strategy which yields good results but suffers from low coverage. Third, implicit CWI integrates this step into later stages of the simplification process, for example by only replacing words for which the top substitution candidate has a higher frequency (Glavaš and Štajner, 2015). In machine learning strategies, finally, classifiers such as support vector machines (Shardlow, 2013) or convolutional neural networks (Sheang, 2019) are trained based on training data with word embeddings, morphological data (word frequency, word length, number of syllables, etc.) and (psycho)linguistic information (age-of-acquisition value, part-of-speech [POS] tag, dependency relation, etc.) as features. As can be concluded from the 2018 CWI shared task (Yimam et al., 2018), of all strategies machine-learning assisted approaches obtain the best results.

Finally, it should be highlighted that as an alternative for CWI, the task of lexical complexity prediction (LCP) is also attracting more attention, as appears from the corresponding SemEval 2021 task (Shardlow et al., 2021). In LCP, a word's complexity is evaluated by assigning a value from a continuous scale, instead of providing a binary complex versus non-complex judgement as in CWI.

2.2.2 Substitution Generation

In the substitution generation step, candidate substitutions for the complex words are proposed. The generation can take two forms: linguistic database querying or automatic generation (Paetzold and Specia, 2017). In the former scenario, synonyms and/or other related words are looked up in human-curated databases such as WordNet (Fellbaum, 1998). Although the approach generally leads to suitable substitution candidates, both its coverage and potential to be extended to other languages are limited, since building such databases constitutes an expensive and time-consuming process (Shardlow, 2014b).

As for automatic generation, parallel resources such as English Wikipedia and Simple English Wikipedia can be exploited to automatically generate simplification pairs. Recently, the introduction of first static word embedding models such as word2vec (Mikolov et al., 2013) and later contextualised word embedding models such as BERT (Devlin et al., 2019) opened a whole new range of opportunities for the automatic generation of substitution candidates. Especially the masked language modelling feature of BERT and other models with transformer-based architectures has proven to bear great potential (Qiang et al., 2021; Zhou et al., 2019), as it is able to predict a masked word in a sentence such as (b) below while attending to both its left and right context. Introducing this sequence into the base, cased version of RoBERTa-BNE (Gutiérrez-Fandiño et al., 2021) results in *reducir* (0.09 probability; 'to reduce'), *cobrar* (0.05; 'to collect') and *bajar* (0.05; 'to decrease') as the top predictions. Finally, it should be noted that a hybrid approach, which combines embeddings with database information, can further improve performance (Paetzold and Specia, 2017).

(b) La planta local también permitirá <mask> los aranceles.

2.2.3 Substitution Selection

To determine which candidate substitutions fit the sentence context, a selection process needs to be carried out. The most common approaches to substitute selection are sense labelling (Baeza-Yates et al., 2015), POS tag filtering (Aluísio and Gasperin, 2010) and semantic similarity filtering (Biran et al., 2011). In the resource-dependent sense labelling approach, substitution selection is modelled as a word sense disambiguation task, in which classification methods are used to check which candidates have the same sense label as the original complex word in a given database. Next, POS tag filtering consists in excluding all substitution candidates which do not have the same POS as the word to be simplified. For semantic similarity filtering, finally, the similarity between the substitution candidate and the word to be simplified is measured, after which all candidates which do not pass a certain threshold are removed.

2.2.4 Substitution Ranking

The fourth and final LS step encompasses ranking the selected candidates, for which three main strategies can be adopted: frequency-based, simplicity-based or machine learning-assisted (Paetzold and Specia, 2017). The first approach draws on the notion that the more frequent the word, the more familiar it will be to readers. Ranking from highest to lowest frequency is a very intuitive and straightforward operation, but the calculation of the frequency values can take many forms (token-based vs. lemma-based, raw frequencies vs. "transformed" logarithmic frequencies, extracting frequencies from different corpora, etc.). Simplicity measures and machine learning-assisted approaches expand on this frequency-based strategy by incorporating word frequency together with other features such as word length into, respectively, handcrafted metrics (Biran et al., 2011) or machine learning methods (Horn et al., 2014). The output of these metrics or machine learning models are designed to capture the complexity of words, after which candidates are ranked from lowest to highest complexity. Finally, substitution ranking can also be obtained by combining several ranking strategies and calculating one single average ranking score in the end (Glavaš and Štajner, 2015). In this case, aspects of the substitution selection stage (e.g. cosine similarity scores) can also be used as an additional ranker, instead of serving as a threshold-based selection parameter (Qiang et al., 2021).

3 Methodology

3.1 Setting

As mentioned in the introduction, a DDL-flavoured Spanish LSP course for Dutch-speaking B2-level learners is taken as the target setting, with business vocabulary as the specific purpose. The DDL character of the course is twofold: on the one hand, it includes a series of DDL activities in which learners analyse concordance lines of a selection of target vocabulary items they have to learn. On the other, the teacher of the course uses a corpus to create fill-the-gap exercises for another series of target vocabulary items. We specifically adopt a teacher-focused perspective on DDL, meaning that the goal of this study is to tailor the corpus data (i.e. the concordance lines and the sentences used for the fill-the-gap exercises) to the (lexical) needs of the B2-level target audience as perceived by the teacher. However, it is important to highlight that, in an ideal scenario, this operation is complemented by data on how SFL learners themselves perceive their lexical needs.

3.2 Datasets

Given the specific FL learning setting, we cannot make use of general benchmarking datasets such as ALEXSIS (Ferrés and Saggion, 2022). Instead, we generate datasets from a 11M tokenised, POS-tagged and lemmatised corpus containing newspaper articles on economics available within the pedagogically-oriented Spanish Corpus Annotation Project (SCAP; scap.ugent.be; Goethals, 2018). To arrive at the selection of target vocabulary items to be learned in the DDL activities, we first extract all candidate key vocabulary items from the corpus by means of a keyness calculation methodology (Gabrielatos, 2018). We use the Log Ratio metric (Hardie, 2014) to compare the frequency of each lemma in the economic corpus with its frequency in a 94M reference corpus and calculate the effect size of the difference in frequencies. Next, only the candidate items with a statistically significant effect size according to the Bayesian Information Criterion (values ≥2; Wilson, 2013) are maintained. Finally, the resulting list is ranked from highest to lowest keyness and all items are assigned a difficulty level by the dictionary-based difficulty level classifier of SCAP, after which the top 25 nouns of a C1 level (i.e. the proficiency level to be acquired) are selected as the final set of target vocabulary items.

Lemma (Log Ratio)	Original	Selection	≥1 CW	1 CW (noun/verb)	Changed
Arancel (7.72)	837	65	46	16	16
Desaceleración (7.68)	272	39	23	3	3
Competitividad (7.34)	699	83	58	16	14
Depreciación (7.31)	258	36	26	12	12
Competidor (6.61)	1272	113	67	27	25
Revalorización (6.34)	313	58	24	12	12
Liberalización (5.71)	347	25	15	3	3
Puja (5.59)	311	51	27	11	11
Remuneración (559)	645	93	57	23	21
Robótica (5.47)	150	24	12	3	3
Carburante (5.22)	173	25	14	10	10
Anunciante (5.14)	169	27	20	6	6
Canje (5.11)	232	31	24	13	13
Cancelación (4.73)	364	37	21	11	11
Emprendedor (4.62)	389	49	25	9	8
Encarecimiento (4.57)	128	16	13	4	4
Fomento (4.52)	167	19	15	5	5
Dígito (4.5)	353	44	18	12	12
Solvencia (4.23)	673	67	48	16	14
Factoría (4.17)	331	24	16	8	8
Plusvalía (4.1)	412	45	25	12	11
Homologación (4.05)	140	15	12	3	3
Normativa (3.73)	1680	148	112	31	29
Captación (3.71)	274	45	29	16	15
Provisión (3.59)	881	117	83	23	22
	11 470	1296	830	305	291

Table 1: Dataset statistics.

For each of the 25 selected target items, all sentences in which the lemma of the item occurs are then extracted from the 11M economic corpus.

3.3 Example Selection

Prior to performing LS on them, the datasets can already be brought one step closer to the needs of FL learners by filtering out unsuitable sentences, an intervention which has often been neglected in previous research (Pilán et al., 2016). This filtering consists in applying a series of criteria sentences need to comply with in order to be comprehensible in isolation (Kilgarriff, 2009). To perform this automatic sentence selection for FL learning purposes, we develop an example sentence selection methodology based on the HitEx framework for Swedish (Pilán et al., 2016). A complete overview of the criteria and the definition of the corresponding parameters is to be found in Appendix A. Table 1 presents the dataset sizes before ("Original") and after ("Selection") applying the example selection methodology.

3.4 Lexical Simplification

3.4.1 Complex Word Identification

To tailor the CWI strategy to the teacher-focused DDL setting, we build a classifier which is able to predict, for all words in a given sentence, different complexity labels based on the proficiency levels described in the Common European Framework of Reference (CEFR). To this end, we first build a lexicon based on the PortaVoces (Buyse et al., 2005) and Thematische Woordenschat (Navarro and Navarro Ramil, 2010) SFL vocabulary learning resources for Dutch-speaking learners, whose contents we combine into a single lexicon of 2823 A-level lemmas, 1557 B1 lemmas, 1998 B2 lemmas and 3584 C lemmas. Drawing on insights from FL learning research and taking into account criteria ranging from frequency to learner-specific features such as familiarity, these vocabulary learning resources are often taken as reference points in many SFL curricula for Dutch-speaking learners, and can thus serve as an indicator for the lexical needs of SFL students at a given stage of their language learning careers. In other words, the output of the classifier can help teachers identify

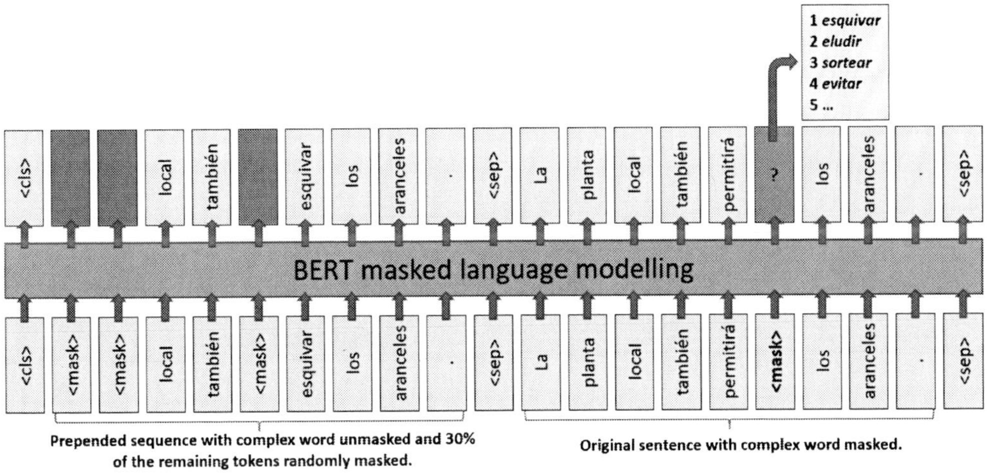

Figure 1: Illustration of masked language modelling using next sentence prediction (the special "<cls>" and "<sep>" tokens are used to initiate the input sequence and separate the items of the sentence pair, respectively). For the masked complex word *esquivar* in the original sentence, the top candidates from the probability distribution of the model's vocabulary (50 262 entries) are collected. For the randomly masked tokens in the prepended sentence no predictions are generated.

potentially complex words for a B2 target audience.

To train the classifier, we fine-tune the base, cased version of RoBERTa-BNE for token classification, thus adopting a machine learning-assisted approach. Apart from the pretrained model weights, training the token classifier also requires labelled sequences as input. To obtain this labelled data, all sentences from the SCAP corpora in which every content word has a matching entry in the previously elaborated lexicon are gathered (all non-content words receive the A label) and split into a training (1 511 387 sentences), validation and test set (both 188 924 sentences). We train the token classifier for 3 epochs with a learning rate of $2e^{-5}$, AdamW as the optimiser and a weight decay of 0.01, and obtain a 0.9983 macro F1 score on the test set.

The classifier [1], which thus offers unlimited coverage, is then applied to the 25 datasets. Every C-labelled token is identified as complex, unless it has a Dutch cognate[2] or appears amongst the 25 target items. As cognates have shown to be easily processed and learned by foreign language learners (De Groot and Keijzer, 2000), they usually possess low lexical complexity and thus should not be identified as such. In total, 64% of the selected sentences contain one or more potentially complex content words for a B2 target audience (see "≥1 CW" in Table 1), which highlights the need for LS in a FL learning setting. Next, the column "1 CW (noun/verb)" presents the number of sentences in which exactly one complex noun or verb was found: these sentences constitute the final dataset to be used in this study, as a one-per-sentence setup is most suitable to measure the exact impact of the simplification procedure.

3.4.2 Substitution Generation

To generate substitution candidates, we build upon the line of research of Qiang et al. (2021). Their automatic generation method, which offers potentially unlimited coverage, exploits the masked language modelling and next sentence prediction features of BERT models to get the probability distribution of the model's vocabulary $p(\cdot|S\backslash\{w\})$ corresponding to the masked word w in sentence S. The input introduced into the BERT model is a sequence pair: the original sequence with the complex word being masked, preceded by the exact same sequence, but now with the complex word unmasked and a given percentage of the remaining tokens randomly masked (see Figure 1).

In this study we use RoBERTa-BNE, apply 0.3 as the ratio for randomly masking tokens in the prepended sequence, and bring the top 25

[1] huggingface.co/JasperD-UGent/roberta-base-bne-complexity-classifier-v1

[2] A pair of words in different languages which are related and look similar, or which have the same origin. Spanish – Dutch example: 'proyecto' – 'project' (EN 'project').

Number	Criterion
1	Probability value obtained from masked language modelling
2	Language model score (Qiang et al., 2021)
3	Lemma frequency in SCAP corpora
4	Token frequency in SUBTLEX-ESP (Cuetos et al., 2011)
5	Cosine similarity with complex word using word2vec and fastText (fasttext.cc) pretrained static word embeddings
6	Cosine similarity with complex word using RoBERTa-BNE contextualised word embeddings

Table 2: Substitution ranking criteria.

candidates from the probability distribution to the substitution selection phase. As a novel aspect, we also add contextual information to the sequence in the form of the previous and following sentence of the corpus text from which the target sentence was taken. This adjustment is particularly useful in cases where the complex word is situated at the sentence-final position. In fact, when the previous and following sentence are not added, for 17 of the 25 target sentences with the complex word at the sentence-final position no suitable substitution candidate is found, because almost all of the 25 suggestions appeared to be punctuation marks. With the extra contextual information being added, this number decreases to 7 out of 25.

3.4.3 Substitution Selection

The first component of our substitution selection strategy is a POS filter, which excludes every candidate whose POS tag does not correspond to the POS tag of the complex word. Next, given the morphological richness of the Spanish language, an additional filter is applied: using spaCy's (spacy.io) v3.3.1 morphologiser ("es_core_news_lg" model), the morphological features of the complex word are determined, after which all substitution candidates without matching features are discarded. The feature set consists of gender (masculine, feminine) and number (singular, plural) for nouns, and mood (indicative, subjunctive, imperative), person (1, 2, 3), number (singular, plural) and verb form (finite, infinitive, past participle, gerund) for verbs. To tailor the selection strategy to our FL learning context, a third component replaces the complex word by the substitution candidates, introduces each of these modified sentences into the CWI classifier (see Section 3.4.1) and eliminates every candidate for which the classifier predicted C as the complexity label. Finally, all morphological variants of the complex word are also excluded, as well as words whose lemma appears in the target sentence.

3.4.4 Substitution Ranking

In the last phase, all remaining substitution candidates are ranked based on the criteria described in Table 2. The six individual rankings are averaged to obtain one single final ranking.

4 Results

4.1 Evaluation of Suitability

The LS method changed 291 of the 305 complex words included in the final datasets (see "Changed" in Table 1), corresponding to a 95.41% score on the "changed" metric (Horn et al., 2014). Apart from the 7 sentence-final cases mentioned earlier, the main reason for which no candidates are found is that the morphological filter appears to be too strict for, amongst others, sentence structures which allow both singular and plural replacements for a complex noun. If in such case none of the generated candidates shares the number of the complex noun, no candidates pass the selection phase.

To evaluate the 291 simplified sentences, a novel evaluation method with SFL teachers as evaluators is applied, which is in line with the teacher-focused DDL perspective we adopted. After presenting them the background information explained in Section 3.1, we ask them to indicate, for each of the 3 top-ranked substitution candidates of a given sentence, if replacing the complex word by the candidate results in a better, similar or worse example sentence (see Table 3). For each sentence, responses from 3 different teachers are collected (2619 annotations in total). Importantly, in the instructions we explicitly mention that changes in

Sentence	Substitution	Better	Similar	Worse
La planta local también permitirá **esquivar** los aranceles.	evitar			
	escapar			
	olvidar			

Table 3: Illustration of the annotation task, with *aranceles* as the vocabulary item to be learned. Teachers are asked to indicate if the substitutions for the complex word *esquivar* result in a more ("Better"), equally ("Similar") or less ("Worse") suitable example sentence to be used in the setting described in Section 3.1.

Metric	All	R1	R2	R3
IAA	.26	.28	.24	.26
% 3/3 agreement	35.4	36.08	32.65	37.46
% better (≥2/3)	33.68	37.46	35.74	27.84
% similar (≥2/3)	11.57	12.37	12.37	9.97
% worse (≥2/3)	44.9	40.21	42.96	51.55
% suitable (binary)	38.95	42.96	40.89	32.99

Table 4: Performance results. "IAA" reports the inter-annotator agreement as measured by Fleiss' Kappa, "≥2/3" refers to agreement between at least 2 participants, and "binary" refers to the results of classifying the annotations into suitable (at least 2 "better" annotations or 1 "better" and 2 "similar" annotations) and non-suitable (all other cases) simplifications. Percentages for "binary" correspond to the precision metric of Horn et al. (2014).

meaning should not be taken into account during evaluation, as long as the end result is a pedagogically suitable example sentence. This enabled us to analyse if FL learning as the target setting affects the importance of the meaning preservation criterion (see Section 4.2).

Table 4 presents the main descriptive statistics taken from the experiment, with the "All" column reporting the results for all annotations combined and the three "R" columns showing the results broken down according to ranking position. Overall, the results show moderate agreement between the teachers (IAA of 0.26 and 35.4% of the sentences annotated equally by all 3 annotators), without any considerable differences between the ranking groups. Although these statistics suggest that evaluating the added value of LS for FL learning purposes is not a straightforward task, we consider the number of times in which at least two of the three teachers coincide (90.15% across all labels in "All") as an indication that agreement is sufficiently high to draw valuable conclusions.

First of all, the statistics reveal mixed performance results: when converting the annotations into a binary classification, 42.96% of the "R1" simplifications come out as suitable, a score which highlights both the potential of the method and its room for improvement. Next, the ranking component seems to perform well, as the first-ranked substitutions are considerably more annotated as better and considerably less as worse compared to "R3". Third, the CWI classifier can still be improved: despite being found pedagogically suitable, 11.57% of the sentences are not evaluated as more simple compared to the original text, which indicates that the classifier labelled an equally complex word as more simple.

4.2 Evaluation of Meaning Preservation

For this supplementary analysis, we annotate all substitutions according to meaning preservation (see Table 5). The results suggest that meaning preservation is not a sine qua non for successful LS in a FL learning context, as replacing the complex word by an unrelated or even opposite concept does not prevent 45 sentences from being found suitable. However, meaning preservation does remain a key criterion, as is evidenced by the majority of the suitable sentences having the same meaning as the original word (189 sentences), or at least being related to it (106 sentences). Finally, it should be noted that substitutions which share the meaning of the complex word do not necessarily result in better example sentences. Many of those cases can be linked to the "idiomaticity" of the simplified sentence, which comes to the fore as an additional important criterion. This is evidenced in the results for sentence (c) in Table 5: despite being semantically equal to *aliviar*, none of the 3 teachers

Label	Total	Suitable (binary)	Example
Preserved	311	189	(c) Los aranceles pueden **aliviar** la presión que sufren los fabricantes. ('Tariffs can **alleviate** pressure on manufacturers.') → *reducir* ('to reduce')
Related	258	106	(d) Estoy muy contento con los 100.000 millones de dólares en aranceles que llenan nuestras **arcas**. ('I am very happy with the $100 billion in tariffs that fill our **treasury**.') → *cuentas* ('bank accounts')
Unrelated	257	42	(e) Las importaciones de **baldosas** chinas se cargarán con aranceles del 30% al 69%. ('Chinese **tile** imports will be charged tariffs from 30% to 69%.') → *alfombras* ('carpets')
Opposite	47	3	(f) Sus principales competidores presentan **retrocesos** anuales muy fuertes. ('Its main competitors show very strong annual **declines**.') → *incremento* ('increase')

Table 5: Overview of meaning preservation annotations.

annotated the substitution candidate *relajar* ('to relax') as "better", because *relajar la presión* is a rather uncommon collocation. A similar case is that of multiword expressions, in which often only one formulation sounds idiomatic (e.g. *agrupación de acciones* → *?unión de acciones*; 'consolidation of shares → ?union of shares').

4.3 Evaluation of Grammaticality

Finally, a manual grammaticality check of the output reveals that 50 simplifications result in incorrect sentences, with preposition issues being the main cause. The *escapar* prediction in Table 3 is such an example, as this verb needs to be followed by the preposition *de*. Non-surprisingly, virtually all of these substitutions were annotated as "worse", which suggests that, in a future version of the method, excluding non-grammatical simplifications alone can lead to considerable increases in performance.

5 Discussion and Conclusion

In this study, we presented a Spanish LS method tailored to FL learning as the target setting. By simplifying all potentially complex words except the vocabulary item to be studied, the method adapts DDL activities to a given proficiency level while also taking into account the language acquisition theory of providing comprehensible input which is just somewhat beyond the current knowledge of the target audience (Krashen, 1985). As we specifically focused on SFL learners with Dutch as their mother tongue, the findings of this study primarily contribute to LS for this particular language combination. However, if equivalent resources (graded vocabulary learning resources, language models, etc.) are available, the methodological design of the LS pipeline can be applied to any language.

To analyse performance, a new type of human-based evaluation was carried out, which revealed the potential of the system (43% of the top-ranked predictions being found suitable) and suggested that meaning preservation is an important though not always necessary condition for obtaining both successfully simplified and pedagogically suitable example sentences. However, the results also showed that the custom-made CWI classifier leaves room for improvement, that many simplifications lack idiomaticity and that the substitution selection component is not yet able to exclude all non-grammatical replacements.

To overcome these limitations in the future, we first of all aim to further develop the CWI classifier and evaluate it in a separate experiment. Next, to arrive at grammatically correct and more idiomatic substitution candidates, we also plan to implement "typicality"-related measures (e.g. association measures based on co-occurrence data; Gries, 2013) into the substitution selection and ranking components. Finally, we will study the addition of weights to the ranking calculation, in order to balance the relative importance of the criteria.

As a final observation, it should be highlighted that the teacher-focused DDL perspective adopted in this study also comes with its limitations. The expert knowledge of teachers and the contents of scientifically grounded vocabulary learning resources (as the ones used in this study to train the CWI classifier) can be valuable indicators of lexical complexity, but they often exhibit a lack of systematicity and do not capture how FL learners perceive lexical complexity themselves (Tack et al., 2021). Therefore, in future research we will also collect "non-native data" and integrate them into the LS methodology. The pedagogically oriented evaluation, for instance, could be performed by SFL learners in the form of a best-worst scaling experiment in which learners have to indicate the best and worst item in a set of four versions of the same sentence (the original sentence plus three sentences with the complex word being replaced by the three top-ranked substitution candidates).

Acknowledgements

The first author acknowledges the support from the IVESS project (file number 11D3921N), a PhD fellowship funded by the Research Foundation – Flanders (FWO). The second author acknowledges support from the project Context-aware Multilingual Text Simplification (ConMuTeS) PID2019-109066GB-I00/AEI/10.13039/501100011033 individual grant awarded by the Ministerio de Ciencia, Innovación y Universidades (MCIU) and by the Agencia Estatal de Investigación (AEI) of Spain. Finally, both authors also wish to express their sincere gratitude to the reviewers for their valuable comments.

References

Alarcón Rodrigo, Moreno Lourdes, & Martínez Paloma (2021). Exploration of Spanish Word

Embeddings for Lexical Simplification. *Proceedings of the First Workshop on Current Trends in Text Simplification (CTTS 2021)*, 29–41.

Aluísio Sandra, & Gasperin Caroline (2010). Fostering Digital Inclusion and Accessibility: The PorSimples project for Simplification of Portuguese Texts. *Proceedings of the NAACL HLT 2010 Young Investigators Workshop on Computational Approaches to Languages of the Americas*, 46–53.

Baeza-Yates Ricardo, Rello Luz, & Dembowski Julia (2015). CASSA: A Context-Aware Synonym Simplification Algorithm. *Proceedings of the 2015 Conference of the North American Chapter of the Association for Computational Linguistics: Human Language Technologies*, 1380–1385.

Bax Stephen (2003). CALL—past, present and future. *System*, *31*(1), 13–28.

Biran Or, Brody Samuel, & Elhadad Noémie (2011). Putting it Simply: A Context-Aware Approach to Lexical Simplification. *Proceedings of the 49th Annual Meeting of the Association for Computational Linguistics: Human Language Technologies*, 496–501.

Bott Stefan, Rello Luz, Drndarevic Biljana, & Saggion Horacio (2012). Can Spanish Be Simpler? LexSiS: Lexical Simplification for Spanish. *Proceedings of COLING 2012*, 357–374.

Boulton Alex (2009). Data-driven learning: reasonable fears and rational reassurance. *Indian Journal of Applied Linguistics*, 2009, *35*(1), 1–28.

Boulton Alex, & Cobb Tom (2017). Corpus Use in Language Learning: A Meta-Analysis. *Language Learning*, *67*(2), 348–393.

Boulton Alex, & Vyatkina Nina (2021). Thirty years of data-driven learning: Taking stock and charting new directions over time. *Language Learning & Technology*, *25*(3), 66–89.

Buyse Kris, Delbecque Nicole, & Speelman Dirk (2005). *Portavoces: Thematische woordenschat Spaans*. Wolters Plantyn.

Chambers Angela (2019). Towards the corpus revolution? Bridging the research–practice gap. *Language Teaching*, *52*(4), 460–475.

Cuetos Fernando, Glez-Nosti Maria, Barbon Analia, & Brysbaert Marc (2011). SUBTLEX-ESP: Spanish word frequencies based on film subtitles. *PSICOLOGICA*, *32*(2), 133–143.

De Groot Annette M.B., & Keijzer Rineke (2000). What Is Hard to Learn Is Easy to Forget: The Roles of Word Concreteness, Cognate Status, and Word Frequency in Foreign-Language Vocabulary Learning and Forgetting. *Language Learning*, *50*(1), 1–56.

Devlin Jacob, Chang Ming-Wei, Lee Kenton, & Toutanova Kristina (2019). BERT: Pre-training of Deep Bidirectional Transformers for Language Understanding. *Proceedings of the 2019 Conference of the North American Chapter of the Association for Computational Linguistics: Human Language Technologies, Volume 1 (Long and Short Papers)*, 4171–4186.

Devlin Siobhan, & Tait John (1998). The use of a psycholinguistic database in the simplification of text for aphasic readers. *Linguistic Databases*, *1*, 161–173.

Evans Richard (2011). Comparing methods for the syntactic simplification of sentences in information extraction. *Literary and Linguistic Computing*, *26*(4), 371–388.

Fellbaum Christiane (Ed.). (1998). *WordNet: An Electronic Lexical Database*. The MIT Press.

Ferrés Daniel, & Saggion Horacio (2022). ALEXSIS: A Dataset for Lexical Simplification in Spanish. *Proceedings of the 13th Conference on Language Resources and Evaluation (LREC 2022)*, 3582–3594.

Gabrielatos Costas (2018). Keyness analysis: Nature, metrics and techniques. In Charlotte Taylor & Anne Marchi (Eds.), *Corpus Approaches To Discourse* (pp. 225–258). Routledge.

Gilquin Gaëtanelle, & Granger Sylviane (2010). How can data-driven learning be used in language teaching? In *The Routledge Handbook of Corpus Linguistics*. Routledge.

Glavaš Goran, & Štajner Sanja (2015). Simplifying Lexical Simplification: Do We Need Simplified Corpora? *Proceedings of the 53rd Annual Meeting of the Association for Computational Linguistics and the 7th International Joint Conference on Natural Language Processing (Volume 2: Short Papers)*, 63–68.

Goethals Patrick (2018). Customizing vocabulary learning for advanced learners of Spanish. In Read, Timothy and Sedano Cuevas, Beatriz and Montaner-Villalba, Salvador (Eds.), *Technological innovation for specialized linguistic domains: Languages for digital lives and cultures, proceedings of TISLID'18* (pp. 229–240). Éditions Universitaires Européennes.

Granger Sylviane, Kraif Olivier, Ponton Claude, Antoniadis Georges, & Zampa Virginie (2007). Integrating learner corpora and natural language processing: A crucial step towards reconciling technological sophistication and pedagogical effectiveness. *ReCALL*, *19*(3), 252–268.

Gries Stefan (2013). 50-something years of work on collocations: What is or should be next ….

International Journal of Corpus Linguistics, 18(1), 137–166.

Gutiérrez-Fandiño Asier, Armengol-Estapé Jordi, Pàmies Marc, Llop-Palao Joan, Silveira-Ocampo Joaquín, Carrino Casimiro Pio, Gonzalez-Agirre Aitor, Armentano-Oller Carme, Rodriguez-Penagos Carlos, & Villegas Marta (2021). *MarIA: Spanish Language Models*. Computer Science Repository, arXiv:2107.07253, Version 5.

Hardie Andrew (2014). Log ratio: An informal introduction. *ESRC Centre for Corpus Approaches to Social Science (CASS)*, 1–2.

Horn Colby, Manduca Cathryn, & Kauchak David (2014). Learning a Lexical Simplifier Using Wikipedia. *Proceedings of the 52nd Annual Meeting of the Association for Computational Linguistics (Volume 2: Short Papers)*, 458–463.

Jablonkai Reka, & Csomay Eniko (Eds.). (2022). *The Routledge handbook of corpora and English language teaching and learning*. Routledge.

Johns Tim (1990). From printout to handout: Grammar and vocabulary teaching in the context of data-driven learning. *CALL Austria, 10*, 14–34.

Kilgarriff Adam (2009). Corpora in the classroom without scaring the students, *Proceedings from the 18th International Symposium on English Teaching*.

Krashen Stephen (1985). *The input hypothesis: Issues and implications*, Vol. 1. London: Longman.

Laufer Batia, & Nation Paul (1995). Vocabulary Size and Use: Lexical Richness in L2 Written Production. *Applied Linguistics, 16*(3), 307–322.

Martin Louis, de la Clergerie Éric, Sagot Benoît, & Bordes Antoine (2020). Controllable Sentence Simplification. *Proceedings of the 12th Language Resources and Evaluation Conference*, 4689–4698.

Mikolov Tomas, Chen Kai, Corrado Greg, & Dean Jeffrey (2013). *Efficient Estimation of Word Representations in Vector Space*. Computer Science Repository, arXiv:1301.3781, Version 1.

Navarro José María, & Navarro Ramil Axel (2010). *Thematische woordenschat Spaans*. Intertaal.

North Kai, Zampieri Marcos, & Shardlow Matthew (2022). Lexical Complexity Prediction: An Overview. *ACM Computing Surveys*, 3557885.

Paetzold Gustavo, & Specia Lucia (2016). Unsupervised Lexical Simplification for Non-Native Speakers. *Proceedings of the AAAI Conference on Artificial Intelligence, 30*(1).

Paetzold Gustavo, & Specia Lucia (2017). A Survey on Lexical Simplification. *Journal of Artificial Intelligence Research, 60*, 549–593.

Pilán Ildikó, Volodina Elena, & Borin Lars (2016). Candidate sentence selection for language learning exercises: From a comprehensive framework to an empirical evaluation. *Revue Traitement Automatique Des Langues, 57*(3), 67–91.

Qiang Jipeng, Li Yun, Zhu Yi, Yuan Yunhao, Shi Yang, & Wu Xindong (2021). LSBert: Lexical Simplification Based on BERT. *IEEE/ACM Transactions on Audio, Speech, and Language Processing, 29*, 3064–3076.

Rello Luz, Baeza-Yates Ricardo, Bott Stefan, & Saggion Horacio (2013). Simplify or help?: Text simplification strategies for people with dyslexia. *Proceedings of the 10th International Cross-Disciplinary Conference on Web Accessibility - W4A '13*, 1.

Saggion Horacio (2017). *Automatic Text Simplification*. Springer International Publishing.

Saggion Horacio, Štajner Sanja, Bott Stefan, Mille Simon, Rello Luz, & Drndarevic Biljana (2015). Making It Simplext: Implementation and Evaluation of a Text Simplification System for Spanish. *ACM Transactions on Accessible Computing, 6*(4), 1–36.

Shardlow Matthew (2013). A Comparison of Techniques to Automatically Identify Complex Words. *51st Annual Meeting of the Association for Computational Linguistics Proceedings of the Student Research Workshop*, 103–109.

Shardlow Matthew (2014a). A Survey of Automated Text Simplification. *International Journal of Advanced Computer Science and Applications, 4*(1).

Shardlow Matthew (2014b). Out in the Open: Finding and Categorising Errors in the Lexical Simplification Pipeline. *Proceedings of the Ninth International Conference on Language Resources and Evaluation (LREC'14)*, 1583–1590.

Shardlow Matthew, Evans Richard, Paetzold Gustavo, & Zampieri Marcos (2021). SemEval-2021 Task 1: Lexical Complexity Prediction. *Proceedings of the 15th International Workshop on Semantic Evaluation (SemEval-2021)*, 1–16.

Sheang Kim Cheng (2019). Multilingual Complex Word Identification: Convolutional Neural Networks with Morphological and Linguistic Features. *Proceedings of the Student Research Workshop Associated with RANLP 2019*, 83–89.

Siddharthan Advaith (2014). A survey of research on text simplification. *ITL - International Journal of Applied Linguistics, 165*(2), 259–298.

Štajner Sanja, & Popovic Maja (2016). Can Text Simplification Help Machine Translation? *Proceedings of the 19th Annual Conference of the European Association for Machine Translation*, 230–242.

Tack Anaïs, Desmet Piet, Fairon Cédrick, & François Thomas (2021). *Mark My Words! On the Automated Prediction of Lexical Difficulty for Foreign Language Readers.*

Uchida Satoru, Takada, Shohei & Arase Yuki (2018). CEFR-based Lexical Simplification Dataset. *Proceedings of the Eleventh International Conference on Language Resources and Evaluation (LREC 2018).*

Watanabe Willian Massami, Junior Arnaldo Candido, Uzêda Vinícius Rodriguez, Fortes Renata Pontin de Mattos, Pardo Thiago Alexandre Salgueiro, & Aluísio Sandra (2009). Facilita: Reading assistance for low-literacy readers. *Proceedings of the 27th ACM International Conference on Design of Communication - SIGDOC '09*, 29.

Wilson Andrew (2013). Embracing Bayes factors for key item analysis in corpus linguistics. In Markus Bieswanger & Amei Koll-Stobbe (Eds.), *New Approaches to the Study of Linguistic Variability* (pp. 3–11). Peter Lang.

Yimam Seid Muhie, Biemann Chris, Malmasi Shervin, Paetzold Gustavo, Specia Lucia, Štajner Sanja, Tack Anaïs, & Zampieri Marcos (2018). A Report on the Complex Word Identification Shared Task 2018. *Proceedings of the Thirteenth Workshop on Innovative Use of NLP for Building Educational Applications*, 66–78.

Zhou Wangchunshu, Ge Tao, Xu Ke, Wei Furu, & Zhou Ming (2019). BERT-based Lexical Substitution. *Proceedings of the 57th Annual Meeting of the Association for Computational Linguistics*, 3368–3373.

Appendix A. Example Selection Criteria

Table 6 in this appendix includes the criteria and values applied in the example sentence selection methodology (Section 3.3). Custom criteria which have been added to take into account the particularities of Spanish as the target language are indicated as "(CUSTOM)". The tools used to process the corpus are the SCAP tokeniser, POS tagger (list of POS tags available at scap.ugent.be/static/SCAP_POS-tags_details.pdf) and lemmatiser, as well as spaCy's v3.3.1 dependency parser ("es_core_news_lg" model).

Criterion	Values applied
Search term	
Number of matches	= 1
Position of search term	Anywhere in the sentence
Well-formedness	
Dependency root	= 1
Ellipsis	Not allowed: sentence has to contain a finite verb, a subject and a verbal root
Incompleteness	Sentence has to start with a capital letter and end with a punctuation mark
Non-lemmatised tokens	≤ 5% of the tokens (non-lemmatised tokens are identified as tokens without a matching entry in the SCAP lemma list)
Non-alphabetical tokens	≤ 5% of the tokens (non-alphabetical tokens are identified as tokens which have been assigned the "SYM" POS tag)
Subject type (CUSTOM)	Sentence has to contain an explicit subject, not an implicit subject integrated into the verb form
Context independence	
Structural connective in isolation	Not allowed: sentence cannot contain connectives in sentence-initial position unless it consists of more than one clause
Pronominal anaphora	Not allowed: sentence cannot contain tokens which have been assigned the "DM" tag or which have *eso*, *esto*, *aquello* or *tal* as their lemma
Adverbial anaphora	Not allowed: sentence cannot contain time or location adverbs which behave anaphorically, such as *entonces* ('then')
L2 complexity	
L2 complexity in CEFR level	This criterion is excluded, as complex words are supposed to be identified in the CWI step and replaced by simpler alternatives
Additional structural criteria	
Negative formulations	Not allowed: sentence cannot contain tokens which have been assigned the "CCNEG" or "NEG" tag
Interrogative sentence	Not allowed: sentence cannot contain question marks
Direct speech	Allowed
Answer to closed questions	Not allowed: sentence cannot start with adverbs or interjections such as *sí* ('yes') or *no* ('no') preceded and followed by delimiters such as commas
Modal verbs	Allowed
Sentence length	≤ 40 tokens
Additional lexical criteria	
Difficult vocabulary	This criterion is excluded, as complex words are supposed to be identified in the CWI step and replaced by simpler alternatives
Word frequency	No limitations
Sensitive vocabulary	Not allowed: sentence cannot contain tokens which appear in a self-compiled list of swear words
Typicality	No limitations
Proper names	Not allowed: sentence cannot contain tokens which have been assigned the "XP" tag
Abbreviations	Not allowed: sentence cannot contain tokens which have been assigned the "ACRNM" or "UMMX" tag

Table 6: Example selection criteria.

Eye-tracking based classification of Mandarin Chinese readers with and without dyslexia using neural sequence models

Patrick Haller[1], **Andreas Säuberli**[1], **Sarah E. Kiener**[1]
Jinger Pan[3], **Ming Yan**[4], **Lena A. Jäger**[1,2]
[1]University of Zurich [2]University of Potsdam
[3]The Education University of Hong Kong [4]University of Macau
haller@cl.uzh.ch andreas@cl.uzh.ch sarahelisabeth.kiener@uzh.ch
jpan@eduhk.hk mingyan@um.edu.mo jaeger@cl.uzh.ch

Abstract

Eye movements are known to reflect cognitive processes in reading, and psychological reading research has shown that eye gaze patterns differ between readers with and without dyslexia. In recent years, researchers have attempted to classify readers with dyslexia based on their eye movements using Support Vector Machines (SVMs). However, these approaches (i) are based on highly aggregated features averaged over all words read by a participant, thus disregarding the sequential nature of the eye movements, and (ii) do not consider the linguistic stimulus and its interaction with the reader's eye movements. In the present work, we propose two simple sequence models that process eye movements on the entire stimulus without the need of aggregating features across the sentence. Additionally, we incorporate the linguistic stimulus into the model in two ways—contextualized word embeddings and manually extracted linguistic features. The models are evaluated on a Mandarin Chinese dataset containing eye movements from children with and without dyslexia. Our results show that (i) even for a logographic script such as Chinese, sequence models are able to classify dyslexia on eye gaze sequences, reaching state-of-the-art performance, and (ii) incorporating the linguistic stimulus does not help to improve classification performance.[1]

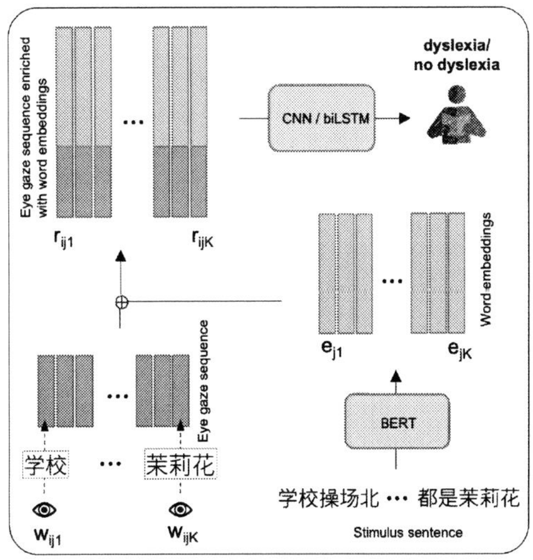

Figure 1: Proposed approach. Each eye-movement reading measure vector is concatenated with contextualized word embeddings and used as input for the sequence models to infer whether a reader suffers from dyslexia.

1 Introduction

Reading effortlessly constitutes a key skill in modern society. Individuals suffering from developmental dyslexia are characterized by specific and persistent reading problems. Global prevalence estimates range from 3 to 7% (Landerl et al., 2013; Peterson and Pennington, 2012). Previous research has consistently shown that early diagnosis and intervention is key to mitigate the resulting long-term consequences (Vaughn et al., 2010).

Psychological and clinical research on eye movement patterns has revealed that individuals with dyslexia exhibit gaze patterns that differ significantly from the patterns observed in individuals without dyslexia (Rayner, 1998; Pan et al., 2014). In particular, scanpaths of individuals with dyslexia are characterized by longer fixation durations, more fixations, decreased saccade durations and a higher proportion of regressions. In recent years, increasing effort has been spent on utilizing these findings and applying supervised classification methods such as SVMs and Random Forests on eye movement data (see Kaisar 2020 for an overview) to infer the presence or absence of dyslexia. There are several reasons why automatized approaches for assistance in dyslexia detection are desirable. Currently, paper-pencil diagnostic tools are conducted by trained speech therapists. These tools are time-intensive and are typically only considered after a suspected case has been reported by

[1]Model code is publicly available and can be found under `https://github.com/hallerp/dyslexia-seqmod`.

Proceedings of the Workshop on Text Simplification, Accessibility, and Readability (TSAR-2022), pages 111 - 118
December 8, 2022

observant educational staff, leaving many cases overlooked. Eye-movement-based diagnostic tools have the potential to be deployed in schools in a relatively inexpensive manner and as part of a standard procedure aimed at early and comprehensive detection of dyslexia; making an important contribution to educational equity.

Although the aforementioned approaches provide promising results, they suffer from specific drawbacks: (i) The model input consists of eye movement features, aggregated for each subject over the presented stimulus material (text), thus disregarding the sequential nature of the eye movements; (ii) both the linguistic stimulus and its interaction with the reader's eye movements are not considered. For classification purposes, this does not pose a problem *per se*. However, it does not allow us to investigate questions such as: Which words (or, more specifically, what linguistic properties of the stimulus) are particularly informative to discriminate between individuals with and without dyslexia?

In the present work, we propose two neural sequence models, depicted in Figure 1, that process the eye movements on the entire stimulus without the necessity of feature aggregation over the sentence. To incorporate the linguistic stimulus into the model, we use pre-trained contextualized word embeddings. We evaluate our model on an eye-tracking-while-reading dataset from children with and without dyslexia reading Mandarin Chinese sentences by Pan et al. (2014).

2 Related Work

2.1 ML-based detection of dyslexia

To date, various data types and signals have been utilized to solve the task of automated detection of dyslexia such as text, MRI scans (Cui et al., 2016), EEG recordings (Frid and Breznitz, 2012), student engagement data (Abdul Hamid et al., 2018) as well as eye-tracking data (Rello and Ballesteros, 2015; Raatikainen et al., 2021; Benfatto et al., 2016). Benfatto et al. (2016) train a *Support Vector Machine with recursive feature elimination* (SVM-RFE) on 168 eye-tracking features obtained from an eye-tracking-while-reading dataset from 185 Swedish children (aged 9-10 years). Their best SVM-RFE model selected 48 features and achieved an accuracy score of 95.6% ± 4.5% (sic!) on a balanced dataset. We reimplement this method and use it as a reference method (cf. 4.1). Jothi Prabha and Bhargavi (2020), using the same dataset as Benfatto et al. (2016), experiment with various feature selection algorithms and machine learning models. They find that feature selection via Principle Component Analysis (PCA) in combination with a Particle Swarm Optimization based Hybrid Kernel SVM classifier yields the best accuracy.

Raatikainen et al. (2021) combine a Random Forest classifier for feature selection with an SVM, achieving an accuracy of 89.7%. They expand their feature space with transition matrices that represent the number of transitions between the different segments (question, answer selection) in a trial as well as the number of gaze shifts within one segment.

2.2 Modeling eye-tracking data with deep neural sequence models

Eye movement data for task inference. Deep neural sequence models have been deployed to solve inference tasks based on eye movements such as reader (Jäger et al., 2019) and viewer identification (Lohr et al., 2020; Makowski et al., 2020, 2021), ADHD detection (Deng et al., 2022) as well as the prediction of reading comprehension (Reich et al., 2022).

Integrating the linguistic stimulus. There has been growing interest in combining language and eye movement models to predict gaze patterns during naturalistic reading (Hollenstein et al., 2021; Merkx and Frank, 2021; Hollenstein et al., 2022). Wiechmann et al. (2022) investigate the role of general text features and their interaction with eye movement patterns in predicting human reading behavior and find that models incorporating the linguistic stimulus improves prediction accuracy.

3 Problem Setting

We investigate the two closely related tasks of classifying (i) whether a given eye gaze sequence on one sentence is from a reader with or without dyslexia and (ii) whether a given eye gaze sequence on a set of sentences is from a reader with or without dyslexia. Formally, our training data can be represented as a set $\mathcal{D} = \{(\mathbf{W}_{11}, y_1), \dots, (\mathbf{W}_{NM}, y_N)\}$, where $\mathbf{W}_{ij} = \langle \mathbf{w}_{ij1} \dots \mathbf{w}_{ijK} \rangle$ is a sequence of reading measure vectors[2] for each word $k \in 1 \dots K_j$ obtained from subject i reading sentence j, where N is the number of participants, M is the number of stimulus sentences read by each of the participants and K_j

[2]Cf. the list of reading measures in Appendix B.

the number of words in a given sentence j. Each reading measure vector consists of R reading measures, i.e., $\mathbf{w}_{ijk} = (r_{ijk1} \dots r_{ijkR})$. The binary target label y_i denotes whether participant i is a reader with or without dyslexia. For (i), our goal is to train a binary classifier g_θ such that

$$\widehat{y}_i = \begin{cases} 1, & \text{if } g_\theta(\mathbf{W}_{ij}) \geq \delta \\ 0, & \text{else,} \end{cases}$$

where δ denotes the decision threshold and θ the set of hyperparameters. Accordingly, for (ii), $\widehat{y}_i = 1$, if $\frac{1}{M} \sum_{j=1}^{M} g_\theta(\mathbf{W}_{ij}) \geq \delta$.
The performance of a binary model can be characterized by a false-positive and a true-positive rate. By altering the decision threshold δ, a receiver operator characteristic (ROC) curve can be derived, with the area under the curve providing an aggregated measure for all possible values of δ.

4 Methods

4.1 Reference method

As a baseline method, we train an SVM-RFE, following the procedure described by Benfatto et al. (2016). We use the *scikit-learn* implementation (Pedregosa et al., 2011) of the SVM-RFE with a linear kernel. In the *subject-prediction* setting, we use eye movement features from each subject aggregated (mean and standard deviation) across trials and sentences as input vectors. In the *sentence-prediction* setting, we use aggregates of each sentence over all trials, yielding $2 \times 12 = 24$ features per instance in both settings.[3]

4.2 Proposed neural sequence models

Both models take as input an enriched reading measure vector $\mathbf{r}_{ij}$ (cf. Section 4.2.1) of a sentence j read by participant i, normalized for each train/test set separately, and predict a label y_i. We tune both models using random search.

LSTM. We implement a bidirectional recurrent neural network with LSTM cells. The mean of the hidden states is fed into a linear layer projecting it down to a single sigmoid output to represent the label prediction. Optimized hyperparameters and search space are reported in Appendix 2.

[3]We also experimented with training random forests as baseline, however, they were outperformed by the SVM-RFE.

CNN. We implement a CNN that convolves the input accross the word sequence axis. It consists of two convolutional layers, each followed by a pooling layer, two dense layers, and a sigmoid output unit. Hyperparameters are listed in Appendix 2.

4.2.1 Incorporating the linguistic stimulus

Using contextualized word embeddings. To incorporate the linguistic stimulus (the words occurring in the current sentence), we first extract 768-dimensional BERT embeddings $\mathbf{e}_{jk}$ for each word w in a given sentence j, using the pre-trained $\text{BERT}_{\text{BASE}}$-embeddings, provided by Hugging Face (Wolf et al., 2020), and concatenate them with the reading measure vector $\mathbf{w}_{ijk}$, resulting in an enriched reading measure vector $\mathbf{r}_{ijk}$. Concatenating the full embedding to the feature vectors results in $768 + R$ dimensions, resulting in a substantial increase in parameters to be estimated. Given the small amount of available training data, we test two methods of dimensionality reduction: (i) We perform PCA on the word embeddings and use the first 20 principal components. (ii) *Mean-difference-encoding*: In order to capture domain-specific information from the word embeddings relating to differences in reading behaviour exhibited by individuals with and without dyslexia, we propose an alternative method, which we call *mean-difference-encoding*: We train a feed-forward neural network with one hidden layer of size 20 to predict differences between the mean values of each eye movement feature between the two groups for each word based on its original word embedding. The values of the hidden layer are a compressed representation of the original embedding that is optimized to encode information that discriminates between children with and without dyslexia. In order to avoid train-test data leakage, in each fold, the mean-difference-encoder is trained from scratch on the respective training set.

Using manually extracted features. As an alternative way to incorporate the linguistic stimulus, we add a range of *manually extracted linguistic features* for each token w_{jk} in sentence j: Surprisal, i.e., $-\log p(w_{jk} \mid \mathbf{w}_{j<k})$, estimated with GPT-2 (Radford et al., 2019), part of speech, dependency relation type, distance to syntactic head, extracted using spaCy (Honnibal et al., 2020), mean character frequency and lexical frequency extracted from SUBTLEX-CH (Cai and Brysbaert, 2010).

5 Experiments

Data. We employ eye-tracking-while-reading data from 62 Mandarin Chinese children (33 with dyslexia) provided by Pan et al. (2014). Participants were instructed to read 60 sentences out loud while their eye movements were recorded. 40 sentences were selected from fifth grade textbooks and 20 additional control sentences were extracted from the Beijing Sentence Corpus (Pan et al., 2022). The dyslexia label had been assigned when a child scored at least 1.5 standard deviations below their corresponding age mean in standard character recognition test (Shu et al., 2003).

5.1 Evaluation procedure

We evaluate our models using 10-fold nested cross-validation in two settings. In the *sentence prediction* setting, we predict the label from a single sentence, read by a given subject. In the *subject prediction* setting, we average the sigmoid outputs from all sentences read by a given subject in order to obtain a subject-level prediction. In both settings, sentences are stratified over 10 folds, balanced by group. Data from the same subject is always constrained to one fold, thus, the model always makes predictions for unseen subjects.

Hyperparameter tuning. For each test fold, we iterate through 9 validation folds, training 50 LSTM and 100 CNN models using randomly sampled parameter combinations for each fold. We select the highest scoring parameter set over all 9 validation folds and train a final model using 8 training folds. We use one left-out fold for early stopping and evaluate it on the test fold.

5.2 Results

For all methods, we report AUC as well as accuracy, recall, precision and the harmonic precision-recall mean F_1 for a decision threshold of 0.5 on subject- and sentence-level. As can be seen in Table 1, our proposed models reach but do not outperform state-of-the art performance. While on subject-level, the CNN architecture enriched with PCA-reduced word embeddings achieves the highest AUC, on sentence-level, the best results are obtained by the LSTM that solely includes eye-movement features. Overall, we note that classification performance on subject-level is higher than on sentence-level and that adding the linguistic stimulus does not aid classification performance, neither as contextualized word embeddings nor as manually-extracted

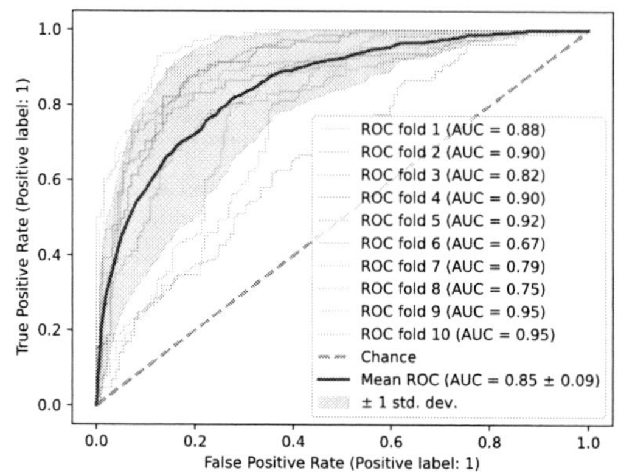

Figure 2: ROC curves over all test sets for best performing model (LSTM with no linguistic stimulus representation) on sentence-level.

features. Furthermore, as can be seen in Figure 2, performance varies considerably with respect to different test sets. We also observe that the variance in AUC for models enriched with the linguistic stimulus is larger for LSTMs compared to CNNs. Lastly, our domain-specific dimensionality reduction method (cf. Section 4.2.1) has no advantage over PCA, although the former is explicitly trained on differences between the two groups.

6 Discussion

Our proposed neural sequence models reach state-of-the-art performance on solving the task of detecting dyslexia from eye gaze sequences, for the first time investigated for a logographic script such as Chinese. Our results suggest that for our dataset, (i) neural architectures processing eye-movement sequences along the sentence have no advantage over the parsimonious SVM-baseline where features are aggregated over the sentence, and (ii) enabling the interaction between stimulus input and eye movements does not improve classification performance. However, after having shown that our approach is able to reach SOTA performance, we aim to exploit its properties to investigate the informativeness of particular sentences, words, and other linguistic sub-units for dyslexia detection in the future.

Furthermore, for all investigated models, the overall performance appears to be driven by a small subset of individuals who presumably exhibit less typical reading behavior among their group and were more difficult to classify. Given that dyslexia is a spectrum disorder—not binary as it is often perceived—it is to be expected that individuals that are not located at the two extremes (clearly dyslexic

	Architecture		Evaluation Metrics				
	Model	Stimulus representation	AUC	Accuracy	Recall	Precision	F_1
SUBJECT-LEVEL	*Baseline*		**0.93** (±0.03)	**0.90** (±0.03)	0.87 (±0.04)	0.97 (±0.03)	0.91 (±0.03)
	LSTM	None	0.91 (±0.03)	**0.90** (±0.03)	**0.88** (±0.05)	0.98 (±0.02)	**0.92** (±0.03)
		BERT meandiff	0.88 (±0.03)	0.80 (±0.06)	0.78 (±0.06)	0.93 (±0.06)	0.83 (±0.06)
		BERT PCA	0.90 (±0.03)	0.83 (±0.05)	0.81 (±0.06)	0.97 (±0.03)	0.87 (±0.04)
		Manually extracted	0.87 (±0.04)	0.87 (±0.05)	0.84 (±0.05)	0.97 (±0.03)	0.89 (±0.04)
	CNN	None	0.91 (±0.04)	0.90 (±0.03)	0.86 (±0.04)	**1.00** (±0.00)	**0.92** (±0.02)
		BERT meandiff	0.91 (±0.03)	0.90 (±0.03)	0.88 (±0.04)	0.97 (±0.03)	0.91 (±0.02)
		BERT PCA	**0.93** (±0.03)	0.87 (±0.02)	0.86 (±0.04)	0.93 (±0.04)	0.88 (±0.02)
		Manually extracted	0.89 (±0.04)	0.83 (±0.04)	0.80 (±0.05)	0.97 (±0.03)	0.86 (±0.03)
SENTENCE-LEVEL	*Baseline*		**0.85** (±0.03)	**0.78** (±0.02)	**0.79** (±0.04)	0.76 (±0.02)	0.77 (±0.02)
	LSTM	None	**0.85** (±0.03)	0.77 (±0.03)	0.74 (±0.04)	0.83 (±0.03)	**0.78** (±0.03)
		BERT meandiff	0.81 (±0.04)	0.68 (±0.04)	0.65 (±0.04)	**0.86** (±0.05)	0.72 (±0.03)
		BERT PCA	0.79 (±0.04)	0.66 (±0.04)	0.64 (±0.04)	0.85 (±0.05)	0.71 (±0.03)
		Manually extracted	0.77 (±0.05)	0.71 (±0.03)	0.67 (±0.03)	0.85 (±0.05)	0.74 (±0.03)
	CNN	None	0.84 (±0.02)	0.76 (±0.02)	0.73 (±0.02)	0.83 (±0.04)	0.77 (±0.02)
		BERT meandiff	0.82 (±0.03)	0.75 (±0.02)	0.72 (±0.02)	0.82 (±0.04)	0.76 (±0.02)
		BERT PCA	0.82 (±0.03)	0.74 (±0.02)	0.70 (±0.02)	0.85 (±0.04)	0.76 (±0.02)
		Manually extracted	0.82 (±0.03)	0.74 (±0.02)	0.69 (±0.02)	**0.86** (±0.03)	0.76 (±0.02)

Table 1: Classification results using 10-fold cross validation on subject- and sentence-level. We report AUC, accuracy, recall, precision and $F1$ [results ± standard error]. The latter four were computed for a decision threshold of 0.5.

or clearly not dyslexic) are more difficult to classify in a binary environment.
Our study was able to show that an SVM-based approach, previously applied to alphabetic languages such as Swedish and Spanish, also works well on a logographic script such as Chinese. In future work, we would like to test our approach on alphabetic language data sets. This is particularly interesting given the fact that young Chinese readers are faced with different challenges, e.g., the absence of orthographic word boundaries, therefore requiring word segmentation, and the much larger number of characters required to be memorized.

Limitations. It should be noted that our dataset contained very little data. Considering that the number of parameters of our sequence models exceeded the one of the baseline model by orders of magnitude, it might be worth comparing the approaches again, once more data is available. The problem of data scarcity might be alleviated by pre-training on domain general eye-tracking datasets or with data augmentation methods[4]. Furthermore, we did not have access to the raw scores of the character recognition task. While our methods did not outperform the baseline in this binary environment, it would be interesting to assess their performance on a regression task.

[4]In a preliminary experiment, we pre-trained our models on the Beijing Sentence Corpus (Pan et al., 2022) and found that it did not increase classification performance.

7 Conclusion

For the first time, we deploy models to detect dyslexia from eye gaze sequences on data from Mandarin Chinese readers. We propose two sequence classification approaches that (i) take as input the full, non-aggregated linguistic stimulus and (ii) model the interaction of the stimulus with the eye movements. As a comparison, we adapt a previously proposed SVM-based approach for Mandarin Chinese. We find that all models reach SOTA performance for data based on a logographic script such as Chinese. In addition, we find that incorporating the linguistic stimulus does not improve the models' performance. Given that we reach SOTA performance on a very small dataset, our approach has proven worthwhile to be pursued, expanded, and further tested (e.g., on alphabetic language data sets). It has the potential to be successfully deployed in the context of automatized approaches for dyslexia detection with the final objective being the improvement of educational equity.

Acknowledgments

We thank David Reich for his continuous feedback on the model architectures as well as our anonymous reviewers for their invaluable feedback on the manuscript for this work. Lena Jäger was partially funded by the German Federal Ministry of Education and Research under grant 01|S20043.

References

Siti Suhaila Abdul Hamid, Novia Admodisastro, Noridayu Manshor, Azrina Kamaruddin, and Abdul Azim Abd Ghani. 2018. Dyslexia adaptive learning model: Student engagement prediction using machine learning approach. In *International Conference on Soft Computing and Data Mining*, pages 372–384. Springer.

Mattias Nilsson Benfatto, Gustaf Öqvist Seimyr, Jan Ygge, Tony Pansell, Agneta Rydberg, and Christer Jacobson. 2016. Screening for dyslexia using eye tracking during reading. *PLoS ONE*, 11(12):e0165508.

Qing Cai and Marc Brysbaert. 2010. SUBTLEX-CH: Chinese word and character frequencies based on film subtitles. *PLoS ONE*, 5(6):e10729.

Zaixu Cui, Zhichao Xia, Mengmeng Su, Hua Shu, and Gaolang Gong. 2016. Disrupted white matter connectivity underlying developmental dyslexia: A machine learning approach. *Human Brain Mapping*, 37(4):1443–1458.

Shuwen Deng, Paul Prasse, David R. Reich, Sabine Dziemian, Maja Stegenwallner-Schütz, Daniel Krakowczyk, Silvia Makowski, Nicolas Langer, Tobias Scheffer, and Lena A. Jäger. 2022. Detection of ADHD based on eye movements during natural viewing. In *Joint European Conference on Machine Learning and Knowledge Discovery in Databases*.

Alex Frid and Zvia Breznitz. 2012. An SVM based algorithm for analysis and discrimination of dyslexic readers from regular readers using ERPs. In *2012 IEEE 27th Convention of Electrical and Electronics Engineers in Israel*, pages 1–4. Institute of Electrical and Electronics Engineers.

Nora Hollenstein, Itziar Gonzalez-Dios, Lisa Beinborn, and Lena A. Jäger. 2022. Patterns of text readability in human and predicted eye movements. In *Proceedings of the Workshop on the Cognitive Aspects of the Lexicon*. Association for Computational Linguistics.

Nora Hollenstein, Marius Tröndle, Martyna Plomecka, Samuel Kiegeland, Yilmazcan Özyurt, Lena A. Jäger, and Nicolas Langer. 2021. Reading task classification using EEG and eye-tracking data. *arXiv:2112.06310*.

Matthew Honnibal, Ines Montani, Sofie Van Landeghem, and Adriane Boyd. 2020. spaCy: Industrial-strength natural language processing in Python. Zenodo. https://spacy.io/.

Lena A. Jäger, Silvia Makowski, Paul Prasse, Sascha Liehr, Maximilian Seidler, and Tobias Scheffer. 2019. Deep Eyedentification: Biometric identification using micro-movements of the eye. In *Joint European Conference on Machine Learning and Knowledge Discovery in Databases*, Lecture Notes in Computer Science, pages 299–314. Springer.

Appadurai Jothi Prabha and Renta Bhargavi. 2020. Predictive model for dyslexia from fixations and saccadic eye movement events. *Computer Methods and Programs in Biomedicine*, 195:105538.

Shahriar Kaisar. 2020. Developmental dyslexia detection using machine learning techniques: A survey. *ICT Express*, 6(3):181–184.

Karin Landerl, Franck Ramus, Kristina Moll, Heikki Lyytinen, Paavo H.T. Leppänen, Kaisa Lohvansuu, Michael O'Donovan, Julie Williams, Jürgen Bartling, Jennifer Bruder, Sarah Kunze, Nina Neuhoff, Dénes Tõth, Ferenc Honbolygõ, Valéria Csépe, Caroline Bogliotti, Stéphanie Iannuzzi, Yves Chaix, Jean François Démonet, Emilie Longeras, Sylviane Valdois, Camille Chabernaud, Florence Delteil-Pinton, Catherine Billard, Florence George, Johannes C. Ziegler, Isabelle Comte-Gervais, Isabelle Soares-Boucaud, Christophe Loïc Gérard, Leo Blomert, Anniek Vaessen, Patty Gerretsen, Michel Ekkebus, Daniel Brandeis, Urs Maurer, Enrico Schulz, Sanne Van Der Mark, Bertram Müller-Myhsok, and Gerd Schulte-Körne. 2013. Predictors of developmental dyslexia in European orthographies with varying complexity. *Journal of Child Psychology and Psychiatry and Allied Disciplines*, 54(6):686–694.

Dillon Lohr, Henry Griffith, Samantha Aziz, and Oleg Komogortsev. 2020. A metric learning approach to eye movement biometrics. In *2020 IEEE International Joint Conference on Biometrics*, pages 1–7. Institute of Electrical and Electronics Engineers.

Silvia Makowski, Lena A. Jäger, Paul Prasse, and Tobias Scheffer. 2020. Biometric identification and presentation-attack detection using micro- and macro-movements of the eyes. In *2020 IEEE International Joint Conference on Biometrics*, pages 1–10. Institute of Electrical and Electronics Engineers.

Silvia Makowski, Paul Prasse, David R. Reich, Daniel Krakowczyk, Lena A. Jäger, and Tobias Scheffer. 2021. DeepEyedentificationLive: Oculomotoric biometric identification and presentation-attack detection using deep neural networks. *IEEE Transactions on Biometrics, Behavior, and Identity Science*, 3(4):506–518.

Danny Merkx and Stefan L. Frank. 2021. Human sentence processing: Recurrence or attention? In *Proceedings of the Workshop on Cognitive Modeling and Computational Linguistics*, pages 12–22. Association for Computational Linguistics.

Jinger Pan, Ming Yan, Jochen Laubrock, Hua Shu, and Reinhold Kliegl. 2014. Saccade-target selection of dyslexic children when reading Chinese. *Vision Research*, 97:24–30.

Jinger Pan, Ming Yan, Eike M. Richter, Hua Shu, and Reinhold Kliegl. 2022. The Beijing Sentence Corpus: A Chinese sentence corpus with eye movement data and predictability norms. *Behavior Research Methods*, 54(4):1989–2000.

Fabian Pedregosa, Gaël Varoquaux, Alexandre Gramfort, Vincent Michel, Bertrand Thirion, Olivier Grisel, Mathieu Blondel, Peter Prettenhofer, Ron Weiss, Vincent Dubourg, Jake Vanderplas, Alexandre Passos, David Cournapeau, Matthieu Brucher, Matthieu Perrot, and Edouard Duchesnay. 2011. Scikit-learn: Machine learning in Python. *Journal of Machine Learning Research*, 12:2825–2830.

Robin L. Peterson and Bruce F. Pennington. 2012. Developmental dyslexia. *The Lancet*, 379(9830):1997–2007.

Peter Raatikainen, Jarkko Hautala, Otto Loberg, Tommi Kärkkäinen, Paavo Leppänen, and Paavo Nieminen. 2021. Detection of developmental dyslexia with machine learning using eye movement data. *Array*, 12:100087.

Alec Radford, Jeff Wu, Rewon Child, David Luan, Dario Amodei, and Ilya Sutskever. 2019. Language models are unsupervised multitask learners. *OpenAI Blog*, 1(8):9.

Keith Rayner. 1998. Eye movements in reading and information processing: 20 years of research. *Psychological Bulletin*, 124(3):372–422.

David R. Reich, Paul Prasse, Chiara Tschirner, Patrick Haller, Frank Goldhammer, and Lena A. Jäger. 2022. Inferring native and non-native human reading comprehension and subjective text difficulty from scanpaths in reading. In *2022 Symposium on Eye Tracking Research and Applications*, ETRA '22, pages 1–8. Association for Computing Machinery.

Luz Rello and Miguel Ballesteros. 2015. Detecting readers with dyslexia using machine learning with eye tracking measures. In *Proceedings of the 12th International Web for All Conference*, W4A '15, pages 1–8. Association for Computing Machinery.

Hua Shu, Xi Chen, Richard C. Anderson, Ningning Wu, and Yue Xuan. 2003. Properties of school Chinese: Implications for learning to read. *Child Development*, 74(1):27–47.

Sharon Vaughn, Paul T. Cirino, Jeanne Wanzek, Jade Wexler, Jack M. Fletcher, Carolyn D. Denton, Amy Barth, Melissa Romain, and David J. Francis. 2010. Response to intervention for middle school students with reading difficulties: Effects of a primary and secondary intervention. *School Psychology Review*, 39(1):3–21.

Daniel Wiechmann, Yu Qiao, Elma Kerz, and Justus Mattern. 2022. Measuring the impact of (psycho-)linguistic and readability features and their spill over effects on the prediction of eye movement patterns. In *Proceedings of the 60th Annual Meeting of the Association for Computational Linguistics*, pages 5276–5290. Association for Computational Linguistics.

Thomas Wolf, Lysandre Debut, Victor Sanh, Julien Chaumond, Clement Delangue, Anthony Moi, Pierric Cistac, Tim Rault, Rémi Louf, Morgan Funtowicz, Joe Davison, Sam Shleifer, Patrick von Platen, Clara Ma, Yacine Jernite, Julien Plu, Canwen Xu, Teven Le Scao, Sylvain Gugger, Mariama Drame, Quentin Lhoest, and Alexander M. Rush. 2020. Transformers: State-of-the-art natural language processing. In *Proceedings of the 2020 Conference on Empirical Methods in Natural Language Processing: System Demonstrations*, pages 38–45. Association for Computational Linguistics.

A Pan et al.'s (2014) dataset

Each sentence was composed of seven to 13 words and each word consisted out of one to three characters, with 38 one-character words, 372 two-character words and 22 three-character words. Sentences in which a child blinked while reading a word, except the first and last one, are not included in the final dataset. The set therefore contains the data for between 24 up to 59 sentences for each child.

B Reading Measures

Word-level reading measures used as input for both the baseline models (aggregated over text or subject, respectively) and the neural models. All durations are in ms. Saccade distances refer to distances with respect to x/y-axis coordinates. Landing position refers to character index within a fixated word.

- Horizontal location of fixation on screen
- Total gaze duration (sum of all fixations landing on the word before moving away from it)
- Landing position of first fixation within the word
- Landing position of last fixation within the word
- Duration of first fixation
- Duration of outgoing saccade
- Horizontal distance of outgoing saccade
- Vertical distance of outgoing saccade
- Total distance of outgoing saccade
- Duration of incoming saccade
- Horizontal distance of incoming saccade
- Vertical distance of incoming saccade

C Hyperparameter tuning

Model	Hyperparameter	Range
Both	Batch size	$[8, 16, 32, 64, 128]$
	Learning rate	$15 \times \mathcal{U} \sim (1e^{-5}, 1e^{-1})$
	Decision boundary	$20 \times \mathcal{U} \sim (0.35, 0.65)$
LSTM	Hidden layer size	$[10, 20, \ldots, 70]$
CNN	C1 # channels	$[5, 10, \ldots, 30]$
	C1 kernel	$[3, 5]$
	C1 pooling	[average, max]
	C2 # channels	$[10, 20, \ldots, 50]$
	C2 kernel	$[3, 5]$
	C2 pooling	[average, max]
	L1 size	$[10, 20, \ldots, 60]$
	dropout	$[0.1, 0.2, \ldots 0.7]$

Table 2: Hyperparameter space for LSTMs and CNNs.

A Dataset of Word-Complexity Judgements from Deaf and Hard-of-Hearing Adults for Text Simplification

Oliver Alonzo
Rochester Institute of Technology
Rochester, NY 14623
oa7652@rit.edu

Sooyeon Lee
New Jersey Institute of Technology
Newark, NJ 07102
sooyeon.lee@njit.edu

Mounica Maddela and **Wei Xu**
Georgia Institute of Technology
Atlanta, GA 30332
mmaddela3@gatech.edu, wei.xu@cc.gatech.edu

Matt Huenerfauth
Rochester Institute of Technology
Rochester, NY 14623
matt.huenerfauth@rit.edu

Abstract

Research has explored the use of automatic text simplification (ATS), which consists of techniques to make text simpler to read, to provide reading assistance to Deaf and Hard-of-hearing (DHH) adults with various literacy levels. Prior work in this area has identified interest in and benefits from ATS-based reading assistance tools. However, no prior work on ATS has gathered judgements from DHH adults as to what constitutes complex text. Thus, following approaches in prior NLP work, this paper contributes new word-complexity judgements from 11 DHH adults on a dataset of 15,000 English words that had been previously annotated by L2 speakers, which we also augmented to include automatic annotations of linguistic characteristics of the words. Additionally, we conduct a supplementary analysis of the interaction effect between the linguistic characteristics of the words and the groups of annotators. This analysis highlights the importance of collecting judgements from DHH adults for training ATS systems, as it revealed statistically significant interaction effects for nearly all of the linguistic characteristics of the words.

1 Introduction

Automatic text simplification (ATS) consists of computing techniques that make text simpler to read, while preserving the meaning of the original text (Shardlow, 2014; Siddharthan, 2014; Al-Thanyyan and Azmi, 2021). ATS can be applied at the lexical level by replacing complex words with simpler synonyms, at the syntactic level by rewriting sentences to reduce their syntactic complexity, or by doing both at the same time (Shardlow, 2014; Siddharthan, 2014; Al-Thanyyan and Azmi, 2021). Prior work has explored the use of ATS to provide reading assistance to different user groups, including non-native speakers (henceforth referred to as *L2 speakers*) and Deaf and Hard-of-hearing (DHH) adults because of their diversity in literacy skill (e.g., Azab et al., 2015; Alonzo et al., 2020; Kushalnagar et al., 2018; Ehara et al., 2010).

While there have been many efforts into the use of ATS for assistive applications, most ATS research from a natural language processing (NLP) perspective focuses on improving the machine learning models supporting those applications. However, training data for these models is scarce as texts are not usually written at various levels of linguistic complexity and thus the access to the needed corpora is limited (e.g., Simple Wikipedia or Newsela) (Coster and Kauchak, 2011; Xu et al., 2015).

In recent work, researchers created a dataset of 15,000 English words from a general lexicon, obtaining word-complexity judgement on all 15,000 words from adult L2 speakers (Maddela and Xu, 2018). Using this dataset to train simplification models provided promising results (Maddela and Xu, 2018). However, considering that research has identified that various linguistic characteristics may affect text complexity differently for different reader groups (Paetzold and Specia, 2016b), researchers have called for the creation of datasets with judgements from intended target audiences (Gooding, 2022; Maddela and Xu, 2018). Prior work identified benefits from lexical simplification among DHH adults (Alonzo et al., 2020); thus, we collect judgements from DHH adults on the lexicon previously created in Maddela and Xu (2018). Then, to understand whether there is indeed value in gathering these judgements from annotators from target reader groups, we conduct an analysis of complexity judgements, to determine

Proceedings of the Workshop on Text Simplification, Accessibility, and Readability (TSAR-2022), pages 119 - 124
December 8, 2022 ©2022 Association for Computational Linguistics

whether there was an interaction effect between the annotator groups and various linguistic characteristics of words, which had been identified as relevant for word complexity in prior work.

As the main contribution of this paper, we collect and publicly release[1] word-complexity judgements from DHH adults (and automatically-computed linguistic characteristics) on a set of 15,000 words, which had previously been annotated by L2 speakers in prior work. As a supplementary contribution, we provide an additional analysis of the interaction effects between the groups of annotators and the linguistic characteristics identified, which highlight the importance of collecting word-complexity judgements with annotators from different reader groups.

2 Related Work

Advances in ATS have motivated research into its use to support the reading tasks of various groups of people, including people with disabilities such as dyslexia or aphasia (e.g., Rello et al., 2013a; Devlin and Unthank, 2006) , or people who are DHH (e.g., Alonzo et al., 2020), as well as children (e.g., De Belder and Moens, 2010; Xu et al., 2015) or foreign language learners (e.g., Azab et al., 2015; Ehara et al., 2010.) A key challenge in the field, however, is obtaining access to datasets (Xu et al., 2015) and there have been calls in the community for the collection of datasets from people from the intended audiences for the systems (Paetzold and Specia, 2016b; Maddela and Xu, 2018; Gooding, 2022). In the next section, we summarize work on obtaining datasets for ATS and motivate our approach.

2.1 Datasets for Automatic Text Simplification

As mentioned in the introduction, there are various approaches to automatic text simplification, including lexical and syntactic approaches (Shardlow, 2014; Al-Thanyyan and Azmi, 2021), and there have been efforts to create datasets for both of these tasks (Xu et al., 2015; Al-Thanyyan and Azmi, 2021). When it comes to syntactic simplification, most approaches require sentence-aligned training data. Thus, researchers have typically created datasets based on aligning the sentences of existing resources that provide texts at different levels of complexity. These include the articles provided in Simple English in Wikipedia (Kauchak, 2013; Jiang et al., 2020), as well as news articles from Newsela, a website that provides news articles with human-produced simplifications (Xu et al., 2015).

When it comes to lexical simplification, the two main tasks that require the use of datasets are the complex word identification (CWI) stage, where systems identify potential words to simplify, and the substitution generation (SG) stage, where systems identify potential synonyms to replace a complex word (Shardlow, 2014; Paetzold and Specia, 2016b). While sentence-aligned datasets can also be used for lexical simplification by identifying complex words that have been replaced, most datasets created specifically for lexical simplification are obtained by having readers judge individual isolated word forms (e.g., Maddela and Xu, 2018; Gooding and Tragut, 2022) or identify complex words in sentences (e.g., Paetzold and Specia, 2016b). There are trade-offs with these approaches, including the fact that judging individual words is less time consuming, but identifying complex words in sentences may also provide insights into how a reader may judge a particular word in context, which is especially relevant for polysemous words.

As prior work has highlighted, many of the datasets presented in the literature are not targeted to any specific group (Xu et al., 2015; Gooding, 2022). However, evidence supports the need for collecting datasets with people from specific target audiences for ATS, including the fact that what makes text complex may vary depending on various characteristics of a reader group (Paetzold and Specia, 2016b). While prior work has identified benefits from both syntactic and lexical simplification for people who are DHH (Kushalnagar et al., 2018; Alonzo et al., 2020), to the best of our knowledge no prior work has gathered datasets of judgements from DHH adults.

3 The Dataset

Our dataset was originally gathered by researchers in Maddela and Xu (2018) by selecting the 15,000 most frequent words in Google's IT Ngram Corpus. Word-complexity judgements on all 15,000 words were also obtained from 11 L2 English speakers using a 6-point scale, going from "very simple" (1) to "very complex" (6), and using 6 points to avoid a neutral choice (Maddela and Xu, 2018). In this new work, we expand this dataset by obtaining word-

[1] https://github.com/oliveralonzo/DHH-lexical-dataset

complexity judgements from 11 DHH annotators following that prior approach, and we also compute several linguistic characteristics of the words. The selection of these linguistic characteristics was based on prior work, which had identified linguistic characteristics (e.g., word length or number of syllables) that had affected text complexity for various reader groups (Paetzold and Specia, 2016b).

3.1 Annotators and Annotation Process

Our 11 annotators were hired as part-time research assistants over 3 academic years at the Rochester Institute of Technology. All annotators identified as DHH, and their reported first languages included: ASL alone, English alone, ASL and English, and Chinese. At the beginning of their employment, our annotators completed the sentence-comprehension sub-test from the Wide Range Achievement Test 4 (WRAT-4), which had previously been validated as a measure of DHH's adults literacy skill. Their average WRAT-4 scores were 81 (SD = 11.62, range = 73 - 111), which is slightly below the U.S. average of 100.

Following the approach of Maddela and Xu (2018), we provided our annotators with the list of individual words, and asked them to provide a complexity judgement for each word using a 6-point scale where 1 meant "very simple" and 6 meant "very complex." A 6-point scale was employed to avoid a neutral choice. Furthermore, participants were instructed to rate a word as -1 if they considered that it was not a word.

3.2 Linguistic Characteristics

Prior work (Paetzold and Specia, 2016b) had identified that the relationship between various linguistic characteristics of words and their perceived complexity for a reader may vary depending upon the reader group. Thus, to investigate whether perceptions of word complexity among DHH annotators differed from those of non-DHH annotators in prior work (Maddela and Xu, 2018), we computed various linguistic characteristics for each word in the dataset. Notably, these characteristics were computed separately from the annotation process, so our annotators did not see those characteristics during the annotation process described above in section 3.1. Similar to linguistic properties investigated in prior work (e.g., Paetzold and Specia, 2016b), our characteristics were grouped into three categories: morphological, semantic and lexical features. These characteristics were computed using a Python script and employing publicly-available libraries as detailed below.

3.2.1 Morphological Features

The morphological features included **word length** and the **number of syllables**. Word length was computed using Python's built-in function for string variables, while the number of syllables was computed using the 'pronouncing' Python module[2], which provides an interface for the CMU Pronouncing Dictionary.

3.2.2 Semantic Features

The semantic features included the number of **senses** (possible meanings for a word), **synonyms** (words with the same meaning), **hypernyms** (words that a specific word is a type of, e.g., 'number' is a hypernym of 'five') and **hyponyms** (words that are a type of a specific word, e.g., 'five' is a hyponym of 'number'). All of these semantic features were computed using the Natural Language ToolKit (NLTK) implementation of WordNet[3].

3.2.3 Lexical Features

These lexical features consisted of **unigram log-probabilities** based on their frequency on three corpora used in: **SubIMDB**, a dataset comprised of 38,102 subtitles obtained from OpenSubtitles and IMDB (Paetzold and Specia, 2016a); **Subtlex**, a dataset of 50 million English words containing their word frequencies based on American movies and TV shows (Brysbaert and New, 2009); and **Simple Wikipedia**, a dataset of articles from Wikipedia written in the Simple English language (Kauchak, 2013). The unigram log-probabilities were computed using the NLTK toolkit.

4 Dataset Analysis and Results

4.1 Descriptive Statistics

When combining all the data from all of the DHH annotators, their average word-complexity judgements were 2.2 (SD = 0.67), where 1 meant "very simple" and 6, "very complex." The average word-complexity judgements previously obtained from L2 speakers in Maddela and Xu (2018), in turn, were 2.7 (SD = 0.83). Table 1a provides descriptive statistics for each of the linguistic characteristics.

Following the approach of Maddela and Xu (2018) and Agirre et al. (2014), we computed the average of the Pearson correlation between each

[2]https://pronouncing.readthedocs.io/en/latest/
[3]https://www.nltk.org/howto/wordnet.html

	a) Descriptive Statistics			b) Interaction Effect	
Linguistic Characteristics	**Average**	**SD**	**Range**	**F Value**	**Statistical Significance**
Length	7.1	2.4	1 to 18	15.42	Yes; p < 0.001
Syllables	2.3	1	0 to 7	26.64	Yes; p < 0.001
Senses	4.5	5.5	0 to 75	1.84	Yes; p < 0.001
Synonyms	6.9	8.9	0 to 100	0.82	No; p = 0.87
Hyponyms	3.4	4.6	0 to 59	0.55	No; p = 1
Hypernyms	11.5	28.7	0 to 693	1.81	Yes; p < 0.001
SubIMDB Unigram Log-probability	-17.5	3.2	-26.4 to -6.5	3.01	Yes; p < 0.001
Subtlex Unigram Log-probability	-17.6	3.5	-24.4 to -6.2	2.85	Yes; p < 0.001
Simple Wikipedia Unigram Log-probability	-16.5	2.6	-22.2 to -7.5	2.18	Yes; p < 0.001

Table 1: A summary of a) the descriptive statistics for each of the linguistic characteristics for all words in the dataset of the 15,000 most frequent English words (Maddela and Xu, 2018), and b) the results of the interaction effect between the group of annotators (DHH or L2 speakers) and each linguistic characteristic.

annotator's annotations and the average of the rest of the annotators, to assess the quality of the annotations. The average inter-annotator agreement for the annotations was 0.53, which is in line with the agreement observed in Maddela and Xu (2018) before removing outliers. Following their approach to identify outliers (i.e. defining an outlier as an annotation that had an absolute difference ≥ 2 from the average of the rest of the annotators) resulted in 11.2% of the annotations being identified as outliers. After removing those, the average agreement was 0.55. However, we release our dataset and present our results *without* removing any outliers as the definition of an outlier may vary depending on the application.

4.2 Interaction Effects

While it is possible to conduct significant difference testing between the overall judgements of DHH and L2 annotators (which, in fact, revealed significant differences), it may not be meaningful as it may simply suggest that the way the two groups of annotators calibrated to the scale was different. Furthermore, we were not concerned with identifying exactly what features *correlate* with word complexity in our dataset as those would be better identified through machine-learning models trained using this dataset. Instead, we were interested in whether, when conducting a two-factor analysis of the average judgements obtained from both groups, there is an interaction effect between the group and the linguistic characteristics outlined above. An interaction effect occurs when the effect of one independent variable on a dependent variable depends on another independent variable. Thus, an interaction effect would suggest that the way these various linguistic characteristics affect word complexity may be different for these two groups of annotators, thereby further motivating the need to collect datasets from specific groups of annotators who, in our case, were DHH adults.

Thus, we conducted two-way analyses of variance (ANOVA) where the dependent variable was the average judgements from annotators, and the independent variables were each of the linguistic characteristics of the words and the group of annotators. Overall, we observed interaction effects between the group of annotators and nearly all of the linguistic characteristics, with the exception of the number of synonyms and hyponyms. Table 1b provides the detailed results for these analyses.

5 Discussion and Conclusion

Our results provide further evidence for the importance of gathering judgments from intended audiences to train systems using datasets based on those judgements. Prior work had suggested that the linguistic characteristics that affect text complexity for different user groups may vary (e.g. word length may affect word complexity for people with dyslexia but less so for L2 speakers) (Rello et al., 2013b; Paetzold and Specia, 2016b). Through our analysis of interaction effects, we observed that the way *several* linguistic characteristics affect word-complexity judgements depends indeed on the group of annotators that provide those judgements. Thus, it is important to gather judgements from target audiences and build models based on those judgements, which may better capture the nuanced relations between how these different features impact word complexity for target audiences.

Limitations and Future Work

Our work presented in this paper had various limitations, and opens several avenues for future work:

1. There are different approaches to gather word-complexity judgements. Our dataset is limited in that it provides out-of-context judgements from DHH annotators. Thus, it may miss the influence of context on word complexity. Future work should gather additional datasets that obtain in-context judgements.

2. Our supplementary analysis focused mainly on whether the group of annotators affected how the various linguistic characteristics affect word complexity, which served to validate the importance of our dataset. However, we do not discuss why or how those relationships work (e.g., why synonyms or hyponyms did not reveal significant differences) as our analysis did not provide insights into these aspects and thus our discussion would involve speculation. Future work based on our dataset can focus on providing further insights into these issues.

3. Our annotators were recruited from a university campus. While we still observed diversity in their literacy skills, as measured by their WRAT-4 scores, future work should expand our dataset by collecting judgements from a broader group of DHH adults with varying levels of education.

4. The main contribution of this paper consists of the release of the word-complexity dataset. However, future work should explore the utility of this dataset for the various stages of lexical simplification (e.g. CWI, or substitution generation and ranking). Furthermore, future work should explore how the use of this dataset to train ATS systems may impact the utility of these systems for DHH adults.

Ethics Statement

Our annotators were hired as research assistants for our study. However, we still followed the traditional considerations expected for an IRB-approved study. In addition, we took all the necessary steps to remove any personal identifiable information to preserve the privacy of our annotators.

Acknowledgements

We thank the anonymous reviewers for their thoughtful comments. We also thank Abraham Glasser and Jinlan Li for their contributions in managing the annotation process, as well as our colleagues who supported us in recruiting annotators.

This material is based upon work supported by the National Science Foundation under award No. 1822747.

References

Eneko Agirre, Carmen Banea, Claire Cardie, Daniel Cer, Mona Diab, Aitor Gonzalez-Agirre, Weiwei Guo, Rada Mihalcea, German Rigau, and Janyce Wiebe. 2014. SemEval-2014 task 10: Multilingual semantic textual similarity. In *Proceedings of the 8th International Workshop on Semantic Evaluation (SemEval 2014)*, pages 81–91, Dublin, Ireland. Association for Computational Linguistics.

Suha S. Al-Thanyyan and Aqil M. Azmi. 2021. Automated text simplification: A survey. *ACM Comput. Surv.*, 54(2).

Oliver Alonzo, Matthew Seita, Abraham Glasser, and Matt Huenerfauth. 2020. Automatic text simplification tools for deaf and hard of hearing adults: Benefits of lexical simplification and providing users with autonomy. In *Proceedings of the 2020 CHI Conference on Human Factors in Computing Systems*, CHI '20, page 1–13, New York, NY, USA. Association for Computing Machinery.

Mahmoud Azab, Chris Hokamp, and Rada Mihalcea. 2015. Using word semantics to assist English as a second language learners. In *Proceedings of the 2015 Conference of the North American Chapter of the Association for Computational Linguistics: Demonstrations*, pages 116–120, Denver, Colorado. Association for Computational Linguistics.

Marc Brysbaert and Boris New. 2009. Moving beyond kučera and francis: A critical evaluation of current word frequency norms and the introduction of a new and improved word frequency measure for american english. *Behavior research methods*, 41(4):977–990.

William Coster and David Kauchak. 2011. Simple english wikipedia: A new text simplification task. In *Proceedings of the 49th Annual Meeting of the Association for Computational Linguistics: Human Language Technologies: Short Papers - Volume 2*, HLT '11, page 665–669, USA. Association for Computational Linguistics.

Jan De Belder and Marie-Francine Moens. 2010. Text simplification for children. In *Proceedings of the SIGIR workshop on accessible search systems*, pages 19–26. ACM; New York.

Siobhan Devlin and Gary Unthank. 2006. Helping aphasic people process online information. In *Proceedings of the 8th International ACM SIGACCESS Conference on Computers and Accessibility*, Assets '06, pages 225–226, New York, NY, USA. ACM.

Yo Ehara, Nobuyuki Shimizu, Takashi Ninomiya, and Hiroshi Nakagawa. 2010. Personalized reading support for second-language web documents by collective intelligence. In *Proceedings of the 15th international conference on Intelligent user interfaces*, pages 51–60.

Sian Gooding. 2022. On the ethical considerations of text simplification. In *Ninth Workshop on Speech and Language Processing for Assistive Technologies (SLPAT-2022)*, pages 50–57, Dublin, Ireland. Association for Computational Linguistics.

Sian Gooding and Manuel Tragut. 2022. One size does not fit all: The case for personalised word complexity models.

Chao Jiang, Mounica Maddela, Wuwei Lan, Yang Zhong, and Wei Xu. 2020. Neural crf model for sentence alignment in text simplification. In *Proceedings of the 58th Annual Meeting of the Association for Computational Linguistics*, pages 7943–7960.

David Kauchak. 2013. Improving text simplification language modeling using unsimplified text data. In *Proceedings of the 51st Annual Meeting of the Association for Computational Linguistics (Volume 1: Long Papers)*, pages 1537–1546, Sofia, Bulgaria. Association for Computational Linguistics.

Poorna Kushalnagar, Scott Smith, Melinda Hopper, Claire Ryan, Micah Rinkevich, and Raja Kushalnagar. 2018. Making cancer health text on the internet easier to read for deaf people who use american sign language. *Journal of Cancer Education*, 33(1):134–140.

Mounica Maddela and Wei Xu. 2018. A word-complexity lexicon and a neural readability ranking model for lexical simplification. In *Proceedings of the 2018 Conference on Empirical Methods in Natural Language Processing*, pages 3749–3760, Brussels, Belgium. Association for Computational Linguistics.

Gustavo Paetzold and Lucia Specia. 2016a. Collecting and exploring everyday language for predicting psycholinguistic properties of words. In *Proceedings of COLING 2016, the 26th International Conference on Computational Linguistics: Technical Papers*, pages 1669–1679, Osaka, Japan. The COLING 2016 Organizing Committee.

Gustavo Paetzold and Lucia Specia. 2016b. Understanding the lexical simplification needs of non-native speakers of English. In *Proceedings of COLING 2016, the 26th International Conference on Computational Linguistics: Technical Papers*, pages 717–727, Osaka, Japan. The COLING 2016 Organizing Committee.

Luz Rello, Ricardo Baeza-Yates, Stefan Bott, and Horacio Saggion. 2013a. Simplify or help?: Text simplification strategies for people with dyslexia. In *Proceedings of the 10th International Cross-Disciplinary Conference on Web Accessibility*, W4A '13, pages 15:1–15:10, New York, NY, USA. ACM.

Luz Rello, Ricardo Baeza-Yates, Laura Dempere-Marco, and Horacio Saggion. 2013b. Frequent words improve readability and short words improve understandability for people with dyslexia. In *IFIP Conference on Human-Computer Interaction*, INTERACT 2013, pages 203–219. Springer.

Matthew Shardlow. 2014. A survey of automated text simplification. *International Journal of Advanced Computer Science and Applications*, 4(1):58–70.

Advaith Siddharthan. 2014. A survey of research on text simplification. *ITL - International Journal of Applied Linguistics*, 165(2):259–298.

Wei Xu, Chris Callison-Burch, and Courtney Napoles. 2015. Problems in current text simplification research: New data can help. *Transactions of the Association for Computational Linguistics*, 3:283–297.

(Psycho-)Linguistic Features Meet Transformer Models for Improved Explainable and Controllable Text Simplification

Yu Qiao[1], **Xiaofei Li**[1], **Daniel Wiechmann**[2], **Elma Kerz**[1]
[1] RWTH Aachen University
[2] University of Amsterdam
{yu.qiao, xiaofei.li1}@rwth-aachen.de
d.wiechmann@uva.nl, elma.kerz@ifaar.rwth-aachen.de

Abstract

State-of-the-art text simplification (TS) systems adopt end-to-end neural network models to directly generate the simplified version of the input text, and usually function as a black-box. Moreover, TS is usually treated as an all-purpose generic task under the assumption of homogeneity, where the same simplification is suitable for all. In recent years, however, there has been increasing recognition of the need to adapt the simplification techniques to the specific needs of different target groups. In this work, we aim to advance current research on explainable and controllable TS in two ways: First, building on recently proposed work to increase the transparency of TS systems (Garbacea et al., 2021), we use a large set of (psycho-)linguistic features in combination with pre-trained language models to improve explainable complexity prediction. Second, based on the results of this preliminary task, we extend a state-of-the-art Seq2Seq TS model, ACCESS (Martin et al., 2020), to enable explicit control of ten attributes. The results of experiments show (1) that our approach improves the performance of state-of-the-art models for predicting explainable complexity and (2) that explicitly conditioning the Seq2Seq model on ten attributes leads to a significant improvement in performance in both within-domain and out-of-domain settings.

1 Introduction

Text simplification (henceforth TS) is a natural language generation task aimed at transforming a text into an equivalent that is more readable and understandable for a target audience, while preserving the original information and underlying meaning. It involves a number of transformations applied at different linguistic levels, including lexical, syntactic and discourse aimed at reducing the complexity of content for the purpose of accessibility and readability (see Siddharthan, 2011; Shardlow, 2014; Alva-Manchego et al., 2020; Al-Thanyyan and Azmi, 2021; Jin et al., 2022, for overviews). Simplification techniques have been shown to be beneficial as reading supports across a wide range of populations, from children (De Belder and Moens, 2010; Kajiwara et al., 2013), individuals with language disorders such as aphasia (Carroll et al., 1999; Devlin and Unthank, 2006), dyslexia (Rello et al., 2013a,b) or autism (Evans et al., 2014); language learners and non-native English speakers (Petersen and Ostendorf, 2007; Paetzold and Specia, 2016), and people with low literacy skills (Max, 2006; Candido Jr et al., 2009; Watanabe et al., 2009). Moreover, TS techniques have also been successfully employed as a preprocessing step to improve the performance of various downstream NLP tasks such as parsing (Chandrasekar et al., 1996), machine translation (Gerber and Hovy, 1998; Hasler et al., 2017), summarization (Beigman Klebanov et al., 2004; Silveira and Branco, 2012), semantic role labeling (Vickrey and Koller, 2008), and information extraction (Miwa et al., 2010). TS approaches typically learn simplification transformations using parallel corpora of matched original and simplified sentences and can be classified into six categories (for recent overviews see Alva-Manchego et al., 2020; Al-Thanyyan and Azmi, 2021): Early approaches relied on either (1) manually generated rules for splitting and reordering sentences (Candido Jr et al., 2009; Siddharthan, 2011) or (2) learned simple lexical simplifications, i.e., one-word substitutions (Devlin, 1998; Carroll et al., 1998). Subsequent work has introduced (3) phrase-based and syntax-based statistical machine translation techniques (Wubben et al., 2012; Xu et al., 2016), (4) grammar induction (Paetzold and Specia, 2013; Feblowitz and Kauchak, 2013), and (5) semantics-assistance, i.e., obtaining semantic representations of the original sentences (Narayan and Gardent, 2014; Štajner and Glavaš, 2017). More recently, TS tasks have been approached with (6)

Proceedings of the Workshop on Text Simplification, Accessibility, and Readability (TSAR-2022), pages 125 - 146
December 8, 2022 ©2022 Association for Computational Linguistics

neural machine translation methods, in particular sequence-to-sequence (Seq2Seq) models using an attention-based encoder-decoder architecture (Nisioi et al., 2017; Alva-Manchego et al., 2017; Zhang et al., 2017). While the performance of Seq2Seq TS models is impressive, most of these models are black-box models characterized by the lack of interpretability of their procedures (Alva-Manchego et al., 2020). In recent years, there have been growing calls to a move away from black-box models toward explainable (white-box) models (Loyola-Gonzalez, 2019; Qiao et al., 2020; Aguilar et al., 2022). Moreover, recent work in TS suggests that the performance of state-of-the-art TS systems can be improved by conducting explainable complexity prediction as a preliminary step (Garbacea et al., 2021).

Another important trend in current TS research is the growing recognition that the concept of 'text complexity' is not homogeneous for different target populations (Gooding et al., 2021). That is, rather than viewing TS as a general task where the same simplification is appropriate for everyone (one-fits-all approach), researchers are placing a greater emphasis on the need to develop TS systems that can flexibly adapt to the needs of different audiences: For example, while second language learners might struggle with texts with rare or register-specific vocabulary, aphasic patients might be overwhelmed by a high cognitive load associated with long, syntactically complex sentence structures. In response, recent TS research has begun to adopt methods proposed in controllable text generation research (see the 2 section for further discussion). Controllable text generation refers to the task of generating text according to a given controlled property of a text. More generally, the development of controllable text generation systems makes an important contribution to the general development of ethical AI applications. This requires the ability to avoid biased content such as gender bias, racial discrimination, and toxic words. In addition, it is widely seen as critical to the development of advanced text generation technologies that better address specific needs in real-world applications (Prabhumoye et al., 2020; Zhang et al., 2022). For example, the task of dialog response generation requires effective control over text attributes associated with emotions (Li et al., 2021) and persona (Zhang et al., 2018). In the context of TS, the relevant attributes involve various linguistic aspects of text complexity (Siddharthan, 2011). By combining multiple attributes, a natural language generation system can theoretically achieve not only greater controllability but also greater interpretability. This requires the inclusion not only of surface features, but also of more sophisticated features. Traditionally, TS has used readability measures that consider only surface features. For example, the Flesch Reading Ease Score (Flesch, 1948), a commonly used surface feature, measures the length of words (in syllables) and sentences (in words). While readability has been shown to correlate to some degree with such features (Just and Carpenter, 1980), there is general consensus that they are insufficient to capture the full complexity of a text.

In a nutshell, despite significant progress in data-driven text simplification, the development of explainable and controllable models for automatic text simplification remains a challenge. In this paper, we advance current research on explainable and controllable text simplification in two ways:

1. First, we use what is, to our knowledge, the most comprehensive set of (psycho-)linguistic features that goes beyond traditional surface measures and includes features introduced in the recent literature on human (native and non-native) language learning and processing. These encompass lexical, syntactic, register-specific ngram, readability and psycholinguistic features and are used in combination with pre-trained language models to improve explainable complexity prediction proposed in Garbacea et al. (2021).

2. Second, based on the results of this preliminary task, we extend a state-of-the-art Seq2Seq TS model, ACCESS (Martin et al., 2020), to provide explicit control over ten attributes so that simplifications can be adapted to the linguistic needs of different audiences.

The remainder of the paper is organized as follows: Section 2 provides a concise overview of related work in the field of explainable and controllable text generation with a focus on TS. Section 3 outlines the experimental setup including the description of three benchmark datasets used (Section 3.1), the type of features extracted from these datasets (Section 3.2), and the models performed to improve explainable and controllable TS (Sections 3.3-3.5). Section 4 presents and discusses the results of our experiments before presenting conclusions and future work in Section 5. Sections 6 and 7 address the limitations of the study and point out ethical considerations.

2 Related work

State-of-the-art systems for controllable text generation typically use a Sequence-to-Sequence (Seq2Seq) architecture. These systems follow either a learning-based or a decoding-based approach: In the learning-based approaches, the Seq2Seq model is conditioned on the attribute under consideration at training time and then used to control the output at inference time. Within this approach, controlled text generation can be achieved by disentangling the latent space representations of a variational autoencoder between the text representation and the controlled attributes (Hu et al., 2017). Decoding-based methods, on the other hand, are based on a Seq2Seq training setup that is modified to control specific attributes of the output text (Kikuchi et al., 2016; Scarton and Specia, 2018). For instance, Kikuchi et al. (2016) controlled the length of the text output in the encoder-decoder framework by preventing the decoder from generating the end-of-sentence token before the desired length was reached, or by selecting only hypotheses of a certain length during the beam search. Recently, Martin et al. (2020) adapted a discrete parameterization mechanism to the task of sentence simplification by conditioning on relevant attributes. Building on the earlier work of TS (Scarton and Specia, 2018), their model, called ACCESS – short for AudienCe-CEntric Sentence Simplification – provides explicit control of TS by conditioning the output returned by the model on specific attributes. These attributes and their values are prepended as additional inputs to the source sentences at train time as plain text 'parameter tokens'. Results of experiments on the WikiLarge corpus (Zhang and Lapata, 2017) show that with carefully chosen values of three attributes - (i) character length ratio between source sentence and target sentence, (ii) normalized character-level Levenshtein similarity between source and target, and (iii) WordRank, a proxy to lexical complexity, the ACCESS model outperformed previous TS systems on simplification benchmarks, achieving state-of-the-art at 41.87 SARI, corresponding to a +1.42 improvement over the best previously reported score.

Another recently introduced line of research, on which the present work builds, explores how the transparency and explainability of the TS process can be facilitated by decomposing the task into several carefully designed subtasks. More specifically, Garbacea et al. (2021) propose that TS benefits from a preparatory task aimed at the explainable prediction of text complexity, which in turn is divided into two subtasks: (1) classifying whether a given text needs to be simplified or not (complexity prediction) and (2) highlighting the part of the text that needs to be simplified (complexity explanation). Garbacea et al. (2021) focuses on empirical analysis of the two subtasks of explicable prediction of text complexity. Specifically, they conduct experiments using a broad portfolio of deep and shallow classification models in combination with model-agnostic explanatory techniques, in particular LIME (Ribeiro et al., 2016) and SHAP (Lundberg and Lee, 2017). The results of their experiment show that a combination of a Long Short-Term Memory network at the word level and LIME explanations can achieve strong performance on datasets. As a next step, they conduct follow-up experiments with state-of-the-art controllable end-to-end text generation systems, including ACCESS. The results of these experiments suggest that the performance of state-of-the-art TS models can be significantly improved in out-of-sample text simplification simply by applying explainable complexity prediction as a preliminary step.

3 Experimental Setup

In this section, we first introduce the three datasets used in our experiments (Section 3.1) and the type of (psycho-)linguistic features used in our models (Section 3.2). We then describe the methods used to address the three subtasks, i.e., (1) complexity prediction, (2) complexity explanation, and (3) simplification generation. For subtask (1), we perform experiments with five complexity prediction models described in Section 3.3: (1) A word-level Long Short-Term Memory (LSTM) network, (2) a fine-tuned pre-trained BERT-based model, (3) and (4) two hybrid Bidirectional Long-Term Memory (BLSTM) classifiers that integrate GloVe word embeddings with (psycho-)linguistic features using different fusion methods, and (5) A hybrid classifier that integrates the those features with BERT representations. In subtask (2), we apply these five models to identify the complex parts of a given input set to facilitate model validation and evaluation (section 3.4). In Section 3.5, we turn to subtask (3) and introduce an extended ACCESS model, which we refer to as ACCESS-XL, containing a total of ten control features (parameter tokens) covering several dimensions of linguistic complexity.

3.1 Datasets

We conducted our experiments with three benchmark datasets and ground truth complexity labels that were also used in Garbacea et al. (2021): (1) the WikiLarge corpus Zhang et al. (2017), composed of parallel-aligned "Wikipedia-simple-Wikipedia" sentence pairs, (2) the Newsela corpus (Xu et al., 2015), comprised of news articles simplified by professional news editors, and (3) the Biendata dataset, comprising matches of research papers from different scientific disciplines with press releases describing them[1]. The size of the three datasets and their distribution among training, validation, testing datasets are shown in Table 1.

Dataset	Training	Validation	Test
Newsela	94,944	1,131	1,079
WiKiLarge	207,480	30,632	59,639
Biendata	29,710	4,244	8,490

Table 1: Number of aligned complex-simple sentence pairs by dataset

3.2 (Psycho-)Linguistic Features

The textual data of the three datasets were automatically analyzed using CoCoGen (short for Complexity Contour Generator), a computational tool that implements a sliding window technique to calculate sentence-level measurements for a given feature (for recent applications of the tool, see Kerz et al., 2020, 2022; Wiechmann et al., 2022). We extracted 107 features that fall into five categories: (1) measures of syntactic complexity (N=16), (2) measures of lexical richness (N=14), (3) register-based n-gram frequency measures (N=25), (4) readability measures (N=14), and (5) psycholinguistic measures (N=38). The first category comprises (i) surface measures that concern the length of production units, such as the mean length clauses and sentences, or (ii) measures of the type and incidence of embeddings, such as dependent clauses per T-Unit or verb phrases per sentence. These features are implemented based on descriptions in Lu (2010) using the Tregex tree pattern matching tool (Levy and Andrew, 2006) with syntactic parse trees for extracting specific patterns. The second category comprise several distinct sub-types, including (i) measures of lexical variation, i.e. the range of vocabulary as displayed in language use, captured by text-size corrected type-token ratio and (ii) lexical sophistication, i.e. the proportion of relatively unusual or advanced words in the learner's text. The operationalizations of these measures follow those described in Lu (2012) and Ströbel et al. (2016). The register-based n-gram frequency measures of the third category are derived from the five register sub-components of the Contemporary Corpus of American English (COCA, Davies, 2009): spoken, magazine, fiction, news and academic language (see Kerz et al., 2020, for details). The fourth category combine a word familiarity variable defined by pre-specified vocabulary resource to estimate semantic difficulty together with a syntactic variable, such as average sentence length. Examples of these measures are the Fry index (Fry, 1968) or the SMOG formula (McLaughlin, 1969). The psycholinguistic measures of the fifth category capture cognitive aspects of human language processing not directly addressed by the surface vocabulary and syntax features of traditional formulas. These measures include a word's average age-of-acquisition (Kuperman et al., 2012) or prevalence, which refers to the number of people knowing the word (Brysbaert et al., 2019; Johns et al., 2020). For an overview of all features, see Table 3 in the Appendix. Tokenization, sentence splitting, part-of-speech tagging, lemmatization and syntactic PCFG parsing were performed using Stanford CoreNLP (Manning et al., 2014).

3.3 Complexity prediction

For complexity prediction, i.e. the preliminary task of classifying whether a given text needs to be simplified or not, we performed experiments with five (hybrid) deep neural network architectures. Two of these prediction models are reimplementations of models used in Garbacea et al. (2021) and serve as baselines: The first model, LSTM, is a 2-layer word-level BLSTM classifier that uses GloVe word embeddings as input. The second baseline model is a 12-layer BERT model for sequence classification using a pre-trained BERT, with the first 8 layers frozen during fine-tuning.

We also conducted experiments with three hybrid models that integrate the (psycho-)linguistic features described in Section 3.2 into neural networks. GloVe-PSYLING A and GloVe-PSYLING B are hybrid BLSTM with attention models (Wu et al., 2019) that differ in how the integration was

[1]https://www.biendata.com/competition/ hackathon

performed: In model A, the linguistic features were concatenated with word embeddings before being fed into a BLSTM. In the B model, the linguistic features were concatenated with the last layer hidden state of the BLSTM. In the third hybrid model, referred to as BERT-PSYLING, we concatenated the linguistic features with the last layer output for [CLS] token from BERT. The vector representation of a sentence was then fed into a MLP classifier with ReLu as activation function. For all classifiers, Best hyperparameters were found by grid search: For BERT on WiKiLarge, the best results were obtained with a learning rate of 3×10^{-5} and a batch size of 64. For LSTM on Newsela, the learning rate was 2×10^{-4} and the batch size was 32. For BERT-PYSLING on Biendata, the learning rate was 2e-5 and the batch size was 32. We used Adam as the optimizer with $\beta = (0.9, 0.999)$ and $\epsilon = 10^{-8}$. Early stopping, where accuracy did not increase for more than 4 epochs, was used as the stopping criterion. All models were evaluated using precision, recall, F1, and classification accuracy on balanced training, validation, and testing datasets.

3.4 Complexity Explanation

The objective of the complexity explanation subtask is to highlight the part of the text that needs to be simplified. In Garbacea et al. (2021) this was achieved by quantifying the relative importance of the features in the of complexity prediction models (unigrams, bigrams, trigrams, GloVe word embeddings) using model-agnostic explanatory techniques, in particular LIME (Ribeiro et al., 2016) and SHAP (Lundberg and Lee, 2017). To afford complexity explanation of the five complexity prediction models described in section 3.3, we utilized BERT attention outputs: Since BERT uses byte-pair tokenization, we converted token attentions to word attentions by averaging the token attention weights per word. For a given attention head, the attention weights from the [CLS] token to other words at the first layer were considered as weights of those words for a given sentence. For each individual word, its final weight was the average of the weights from the 12 heads of BERT. The decision whether or not to highlight a particular word was based on a comparison of its final weight and the average of the final weights of all words in a given sentence: a word was considered complex, and thus highlighted, if its final weight fell below sentence average (see Figure 2 in the Appendix). We compare these complexity explanatory approaches with LSTM-LIME, random highlighting, and lexicon-based highlighting based on words that appear in the Age-of-Acquisition (AoA) lexicon Garbacea et al. (see 2021, for details on these basic methods). Following Garbacea et al. (2021), we evaluated the models using token-wise precision (P), recall (R), and translation edit rate (TER) (Snover et al., 2006), which assesses the minimum number of edits needed to the unhighlighted part of a source sentence so that it exactly matches the target sentence.

3.5 Simplification Generation

The original AudienCe-CEntric Sentence Simplification (ACCESS) model, introduced by Martin et al. (2020), provides explicit control of TS by conditioning the output returned by the model on specific attributes. The ACCESS model used four such parameter tokens as control features: (1) NbChars, the character length ratio between source sentence and target sentence, (2) LevSim, the normalized character-level Levenshtein similarity between source and target, which quantifies the amount of modification operated on the source sentence, (3) WordRank, a proxy to lexical complexity measured as the third-quartile of log-ranks of all words in a sentence. To get a ratio the WordRank of the target was divided by that of the source. The Seq2Seq model is parametrized on the control features by prepending a these attributes and their values as additional inputs to the source sentences as plain text 'parameter tokens'. The special token values are the ratio of this parameter token calculated on the target sentence with respect to its value on the source sentence. For example to control the number of characters of a generated simplification, the compression ratio between the number of characters in the source and the number of characters in the target sentence is computed. Ratios are discretized into bins of fixed width of 0.05 and capped to a maximum ratio of 2. Special tokens are then included in the vocabulary. At inference time, we the ratio is set a fixed value for all samples. For example, to generate simplifications that are 80% of the length of the source sentence, the token <NbChars 0.8> is prepended to each source sentence. As the Seq2Seq model, a Transformer model with a base architecture (Vaswani et al., 2017) was trained utilizing FairSeq toolkit (Ott et al., 2019a).

Our extended model, referred to here as ACCESS-XL, integrates ten of the 107 features examined in the complexity prediction step. These ten measures were selected to cover all feature groups. Within the lexical richness group, which is the largest of the five groups, features were selected to represent all subcategories of the group, i.e. length of production unit, lexical diversity, lexical sophistication, n-gram frequency, and both crowdsourcing-based and corpus-based word prevalence. Figure 4 in the Appendix shows the differences in mean standardized feature scores between 'normal' and 'simple' sentences in Wikipedia, highlighting in blue the features selected in our model. Following (Martin et al., 2020), we then trained a base transformer (Vaswani et al., 2017) using the FairSeq toolkit (Ott et al., 2019b). Both encoder and decoder consist of 6 layers. For the encoder, each of the 6 layers consists of an 8-head self-attention sub-layer and a position-wise fully connected sub-layer with a dimensionality of 2048. Each decoder layer has a similar structure, but with an additional 8-head self-attention layer that performs multi-head attention over the output of the encoder stack. The embedding size is 512. Dropout with a rate 0.2 was used for regularization. The optimizer used is the Adam optimizer with a learning rate of 0.00011, $\beta = (0.9, 0.999)$, $\epsilon = 10^{-8}$. Label smoothing with a uniform prior distribution of $\epsilon = 0.54$ was applied. Early stopping was used to prevent overfitting, with non-increasement of SARI score for more than 5 epochs as the stopping criterion. Sentencepiece with a vocabulary size of 10k was used as the tokenizer (Kudo and Richardson, 2018). Beam search with a beam size of 8 for searching for the best possible simplified sentence. A fixed combination of control tokens (a control feature along with its binned value) was used in text generation. To find the best combination, we applied the greedy forward select algorithm; we progressively added the control token from a candidate set that, in combination with the previously added control tokens, leads to the largest performance improvement in terms of SARI score on the validation set of WiKiLarge. After adding a control token to the combination, all control tokens sharing the same control feature with the newly added token were removed from the candidate set. The algorithm stopped when no control token led to an improvement in SARI score or no control token was left in the candidate set. The 5 most frequent control tokens from the WiKi-Large training set were used as the initial candidate set for each control feature, resulting in a reduction of the total search space from about 40^{10} to 5^{10}. We evaluated the output of the text simplification models using the FKGL (Flesch-Kincaid Grade Level) readability metric (Kincaid et al., 1975) to evaluate simplicity and SARI (Xu et al., 2016) as an overall performance metric, since FKGL does not take into account grammaticality and meaning preservation (Wubben et al., 2012)[2]. All scores were calculated using the EASSE python package for sentence simplification (Alva-Manchego et al., 2019)[3]. We selected the model with the best SARI on the validation set and report its score on the test set. The best combination of control tokens was as follows: $\text{MLS}_{0.50}$, $\text{Fry}_{0.85}$, $\text{FORCAST}_{0.90}$, $\text{WPCorp}_{0.95}$, $\text{WPCrowd}_{0.90}$, $\text{BigramNews}_{2.00}$, $\text{ANC}_{0.85}$, $\text{AoA}_{1.00}$, $\text{MLWs}_{0.90}$, $\text{CTTR}_{0.85}$.

4 Results

An overview of the results of the three subtasks – complexity prediction, complexity explanation and simplification generation – is presented in Table 2. We discuss the results of each subtask in turn.

Complexity prediction: Our best-performing models outperformed the classification accuracy of explainable model – the word-level LSTM - predicting complexity in all three benchmark datasets reported in Garbacea et al. (2021). Since the pattern of results is consistent across all evaluation metrics, we focus here on classification accuracy: On WikiLarge, we improve on the word-level LSTM presented in Garbacea et al. (2021) by +8.08% by extracting attention weights from the pre-trained BERT model. On Newsela, our GloVe-based LSTM model outperforms the word-level LSTM by +6.68%. On the Biendata dataset, our hybrid model that integrates BERT representations with linguistic features leads to an improvement of +4.43%. Overall, our results replicate the general pattern of results reported in Garbacea et al. (2021) in that the best-performing models achieve approximately 80% accuracy on the WikiLarge and Newsela datasets and much higher – approximately 95% accuracy – on the Biendata dataset. These results support the conclusion drawn in Garbacea et al. (2021) that complexity prediction is influenced by the application domain, with the distinction between scientific content and public domain press releases (Biendata) being much easier

[2]See Appendix for definitions and more details on these evaluation metrics.

[3]https://github.com/feralvam/easse

	Complexity Prediction											
	WikiLarge				Newsela				Biendata			
Model	P	R	F1	Acc	P	R	F1	Acc	P	R	F1	Acc
LSTM (Garbacea et al., 2021)	-	-	-	0.716	-	-	-	0.733	-	-	-	0.898
BLSTM GloVe	0.731	0.710	0.721	0.725	0.867	**0.703**	**0.776**	**0.797**	0.923	0.889	0.906	0.907
BERT	**0.794**	**0.807**	**0.800**	**0.799**	**0.973**	0.572	0.720	0.778	0.934	**0.947**	0.940	0.940
GloVe-PSYLING A (ours)	0.766	0.781	0.773	0.771	0.929	0.609	0.736	0.781	0.930	0.915	0.922	0.923
GloVe-PSYLING B (ours)	0.762	0.783	0.772	0.769	0.925	0.604	0.731	0.778	0.924	0.928	0.926	0.926
BERT-PYSLING (ours)	0.779	**0.807**	0.793	0.789	0.972	0.580	0.727	0.782	**0.942**	0.945	**0.943**	**0.943**
	Complexity Explanation											
	WikiLarge				Newsela				Biendata			
	P	R	F1	TER↓	P	R	F1	TER↓	P	R	F1	TER↓
Random highlighting	0.410	0.463	0.457	1.084	0.550	0.488	0.504	1.029	0.803	0.424	0.550	1.011
AoA lexicon	0.407	0.549	**0.500**	1.026	0.550	0.620	0.572	0.858	0.770	0.629	0.678	0.989
LSTM+LIME	0.404	0.639	0.419	0.997	0.520	0.615	0.506	1.062	0.805	**0.826**	**0.796**	0.983
BERT	0.405	**0.660**	0.434	**0.936**	0.542	**0.729**	**0.597**	0.817	0.784	0.635	0.688	0.965
GloVe-PSYLING A (ours)	**0.454**	0.596	0.426	1.010	**0.579**	0.481	0.501	0.827	0.806	0.552	0.641	0.959
GloVe-PSYLING B (ours)	0.453	0.643	0.440	0.999	0.544	0.554	0.524	**0.816**	**0.813**	0.556	0.646	**0.951**
BERT-PSYLING (ours)	0.400	0.619	0.419	0.949	0.540	0.701	0.586	0.818	0.781	0.638	0.688	0.966
	Simplification Generation											
	WikiLarge (wd)				Newsela (OOD)				Biendata (OOD)			
	SARI↑		FK↓		SARI↑		FK↓		SARI↑		FK↓	
ACCESS	41.87		7.22		29.44		6.45		20.21		12.53	
ACCESS-XL (ours)	**43.34**		**4.39**		**34.91**		**3.96**		**27.25**		**10.71**	

Table 2: **Prediction**: Scores represent out-of-sample precision (P), recall (R), F1 and accuracy (Acc) scores. **Explanation**: P, R, and and F1 values represent token-level scores. TER scores represent Translation Edit Rates (Snover et al., 2006) **Simplification**: Scores represent out-of-sample SARI and Flesch-Kinkaid Grade Level (FK)

than the distinction between regular and simplified news articles (Newsela) or Wikepedia articles (WikiLarge).

On the WikiLarge dataset, the BERT model performed the best, with a +7.4% performance increase over the LSTM. On the Newsela dataset, however, the LSTM achieved the highest accuracy, outperforming both the BERT and BERT-HYBRID models by +1.9% and +1.5%, respectively. On the Biendata dataset, the highest performance was achieved by our BERT-HYBRID model, which improved the already high performance of the LSTM by +3.6%. Across all datasets, the GloVe word embedding-based models consistently ranked between the LSTM and BERT-based models, suggesting that the use of contextualized word embeddings of the BERT-based model may reduce the generalizability of the model, leading to variations in model performance across datasets.

Complexity explanation: The second part of Table 2 presents the results of the subtask designed to evaluate how well complexity classification can be explained, as measured by how accurately the complex parts of a sentence can be identified (highlighted). In general, all of our models showed better recall than precision, meaning that they were better at identifying words that were removed in the simplified version of a pair than words that were truly removed from the complex version. This pattern is opposite to what is reported in Garbacea et al. (2021), where precision is strongly favoured over recall. This may indicate that using average attention as a threshold may not be optimal: While this approach is the de facto standard in text style transfer research, recent work has pointed out the limitations of this approach, such as its inability of handling flat attention distributions (Lee et al., 2021)[4]. Future research may address this issue. As in the case of complexity prediction, we found that the performance of the models is dataset-specific and also varies with respect to the rank order across evaluation metrics: For WikiLarge, the BERT model achieved the best recall and TER scores, while precision was highest for the GloVE-based hybrid models (+4.5% compared to BERT). For Newsela, the BERT-based models outperformed the other models in terms of recall and F1, while the GloVe-based hybrid models achieved higher precision. All of our models significantly outperformed the three base models in terms of TER values, with the best performing model, Glove-PSYLING B, reducing the TER of the AoA method by 4.2% and that of the LSTM by as much as -24.4%. For Biendata, Glove-PSYLING B achieved the best values for precision and TER. However, the LSTM dominated the ranking in terms of recall and F1

[4]Figure 2 in the Appendix illustrates the differences in attention weight distributions among our models.

with improvements of the next best model (BERT-PSYLING) by up to 18%.

Simplification Generation We establish the state-of-the-art at 43.34 SARI on the WikiLarge test set, an improvement of +1.47 over the best previously reported result. Our ACCESS-XL text simplification model consistently outperforms the original ACCESS model (Martin et al., 2020) on all datasets and performance metrics. The performance improvement was even greater in the out-of-domain settings – with a +5.47% increase in SARI in the Newsela dataset and +7.04% in the Biendata dataset – suggesting that increased controllability also leads to increased model robustness and generalizability. For FK readability, the performance gain is even more pronounced: in the within-domain setting (WikiLarge), the ACCESS-XL model achieves a Flesch-Kinkaid score of 4.39, an improvement of -2.88. To put this number in perspective, the original ACCESS model improved previous state-of-the-art models, SBMT+PPDB+SARI (Xu et al., 2016) and PBMT-R (Wubben et al., 2012), by only -0.07 and -1.11, respectively. As in the case of SARI, the improvement in FK performance extends to both out-of-domain settings with an improvement of -2.49 for Newsela and -1.82 for Biendata. To shed more light on the textual characteristics of the outputs of the two text simplification models, we compared their average scores on the ten parameter tokens. A visualization of the results along with the scores obtained for the target and source sentences of the testset for each dataset is shown in Figure 3 in the Appendix. The comparisons revealed several important facts about the behavior of the models as well as the training data: (1) For the WikiLarge dataset, on which the model was trained, we found that the differences in average scores between the 'complex' source sentences and the 'simple' target sentences varied in magnitude: On some measures, such as mean sentence length (MLS) – a proxy of syntactic complexity, the difference between simple and complex sentences is very pronounced ($\text{MLS}_{\text{simple}}$=14.9 words, $\text{MLS}_{\text{complex}}$=22.4 words). For others, e.g. LS.ANC – a measure of lexical sophistication, the difference between the standard versions and their simplified counterparts is minimal ($\text{LS.ANC}_{\text{simple}}$=0.411, $\text{LS.ANC}_{\text{complex}}$=0.414). These results are consistent with previous indications of limitations in the WikiLarge dataset related to the high proportion of inappropriate simplifications (Xu et al., 2016). We further observed (2) that the ACCESS-XL model successfully learned to control the attributes and achieved the desired effect on the generated simplifications: For example, its outputs are characterized by much lower MLS values ($\text{MLS}_{\text{ACCESS-XL}}$ = 10.8 words) compared to the source. We note that shorter MLS values were achieved by splitting the sentence (rather than simply deleting content), which has been shown to be a weakness of current seq2seq TS models (Maddela et al., 2020). This is illustrated in the sentence set in Table 5 in the Appendix. And (3) we found that the ACCESS-XL model was able to successfully generalize its ability to control the target attributes to out-of-domain settings. For example, the learned control over the MLS parameter led to the generation of Newsela simplifications that almost matched almost perfectly the mean value of the simple sentence targets in this dataset.

Lastly, we address the question of whether explainable prediction of text complexity is still a necessary preliminary step in the pipeline when using a strong, end-to-end simplification system. We found that for all datasets – and for both the original ACCESS model and the extended ACCESS-XL model – using of preliminary complexity prediction did not improve simplification performance (see Figure 6 in the Appendix): For both SARI and FKGL evaluation metrics the best performance was invariably achieved by a model without prior indication of what sentences should undergo simplification. These results stand in stark contrast to the results reported in Garbacea et al. (2021), where prior complexity prediction was found to improve the performance of the original ACCESS model. Rather than evaluating performance using SARI and FKGL, as was the case here and in the original ACCESS publication (Martin et al., 2020), Garbacea et al. (2021) evaluated model performance using edit distance (ED), TER, and Frechet Embedding Distance. For ED alone, the reported improvements ranged from 30% to 50%. Follow up experiments based on ED, conducted to determine if the discrepancy was related to the choice of evaluation metric only confirmed the pattern of results reported here for SARI and FKGL (see Tables 7 and 8 in the Appendix). Follow-up experiments based on ED, conducted to determine if the discrepancy was related to the choice of scoring metric, only confirmed the pattern of results reported here for SARI and FKGL (see Tables 7 and 8 in the Appendix). Garbacea et al. (2021) conclude that the ACCESS model – and also the DMLMTL presented in (Guo et al., 2018), which had the highest performance for Newsela (33.22 SARI) – tends to simplify even simple inputs. Moreover, (Garbacea et al., 2021) report that over 70% of the 'simple' sentences in the test data were modified (and thus oversimplified) by the ACCESS model. Note, however, that 'simple' here means that the input sentence in question was classified as such by a preliminary complexity prediction model. Since these classifiers in WikiLarge only achieve a classification accuracy of 80%, the true percentage of oversimplification cannot be accurately estimated.

5 Conclusion and Future Work

In this work, we have advanced research on explainable and controllable text simplification in two ways: First, we have shown that performance on a prior task of explainable complexity prediction can be significantly improved by the combined use of (psycho-)linguistic features and pre-trained neural language models. And second, by extending the AudienCe-CEntric sentence simplification model to explicitly control ten text attributes, we have achieved a new state of the art in text simplification in both within-domain and out-of domain settings. In future work, we plan to apply our modeling approach to another key text style transfer task, that of formality transfer, and evaluate it on existing benchmark datasets such as the GYAFC dataset (Rao and Tetreault, 2018). Moreover, we intend to explore the role of (psycho-)linguistic features for controllable TS in unsupervised settings using a variational auto-encoder and a content predictor in combination with attribute predictors (Liu et al., 2020).

6 Limitations

The current work relies exclusively on automatic evaluation metrics for text simplification. While such metrics provide a cost-effective, reproducible, and scalable way to gauge the quality of text generation results, they also have their own weaknesses. Human scoring is necessary to address some of the inherent weaknesses of automatic evaluation (for more details, see Jin et al., 2022)

Furthermore, the performance of the proposed text simplification methods was tested on informational texts in English. While we assume that the methods can be applied to other domains and languages, we have not tested this assumption experimentally and limit our conclusions to English and the types of language registers represented in the three datasets used in this work.

References

Diana Laura Aguilar, Miguel Angel Medina Perez, Octavio Loyola-Gonzalez, Kim-Kwang Raymond Choo, and Edoardo Bucheli-Susarrey. 2022. Towards an interpretable autoencoder: a decision tree-based autoencoder and its application in anomaly detection. *IEEE Transactions on Dependable and Secure Computing*.

Suha S Al-Thanyyan and Aqil M Azmi. 2021. Automated text simplification: A survey. *ACM Computing Surveys (CSUR)*, 54(2):1–36.

Fernando Alva-Manchego, Joachim Bingel, Gustavo Paetzold, Carolina Scarton, and Lucia Specia. 2017. Learning how to simplify from explicit labeling of complex-simplified text pairs. In *Proceedings of the Eighth International Joint Conference on Natural Language Processing (Volume 1: Long Papers)*, pages 295–305.

Fernando Alva-Manchego, Louis Martin, Carolina Scarton, and Lucia Specia. 2019. EASSE: Easier automatic sentence simplification evaluation. In *Proceedings of the 2019 Conference on Empirical Methods in Natural Language Processing and the 9th International Joint Conference on Natural Language Processing (EMNLP-IJCNLP): System Demonstrations*, pages 49–54, Hong Kong, China. Association for Computational Linguistics.

Fernando Alva-Manchego, Carolina Scarton, and Lucia Specia. 2020. Data-driven sentence simplification: Survey and benchmark. *Computational Linguistics*, 46(1):135–187.

Beata Beigman Klebanov, Kevin Knight, and Daniel Marcu. 2004. Text simplification for information-seeking applications. In *OTM Confederated International Conferences" On the Move to Meaningful Internet Systems"*, pages 735–747. Springer.

Marc Brysbaert, Paweł Mandera, Samantha F McCormick, and Emmanuel Keuleers. 2019. Word prevalence norms for 62,000 english lemmas. *Behavior research methods*, 51(2):467–479.

Arnaldo Candido Jr, Erick Galani Maziero, Lucia Specia, Caroline Gasperin, Thiago Pardo, and Sandra Aluisio. 2009. Supporting the adaptation of texts for poor literacy readers: a text simplification editor for brazilian portuguese. In *Proceedings of the Fourth Workshop on Innovative Use of NLP for Building Educational Applications*, pages 34–42.

John Carroll, Guido Minnen, Yvonne Canning, Siobhan Devlin, and John Tait. 1998. Practical simplification of english newspaper text to assist aphasic readers. In *Proceedings of the AAAI-98 Workshop on Integrating Artificial Intelligence and Assistive Technology*, pages 7–10. Citeseer.

John A Carroll, Guido Minnen, Darren Pearce, Yvonne Canning, Siobhan Devlin, and John Tait. 1999. Simplifying text for language-impaired readers. In *Ninth Conference of the European Chapter of the Association for Computational Linguistics*, pages 269–270.

Raman Chandrasekar, Christine Doran, and Srinivas Bangalore. 1996. Motivations and methods for text simplification. In *COLING 1996 Volume 2: The 16th International Conference on Computational Linguistics*.

Mark Davies. 2009. The 385+ million word corpus of contemporary american english (1990–2008+): Design, architecture, and linguistic insights. *International journal of corpus linguistics*, 14(2):159–190.

Jan De Belder and Marie-Francine Moens. 2010. Text simplification for children. In *Prroceedings of the SIGIR workshop on accessible search systems*, pages 19–26. ACM; New York.

Siobhan Devlin. 1998. The use of a psycholinguistic database in the simplification of text for aphasic readers. *Linguistic databases*.

Siobhan Devlin and Gary Unthank. 2006. Helping aphasic people process online information. In *Proceedings of the 8th International ACM SIGACCESS Conference on Computers and Accessibility*, pages 225–226.

Richard Evans, Constantin Orasan, and Iustin Dornescu. 2014. An evaluation of syntactic simplification rules for people with autism. Association for Computational Linguistics.

Dan Feblowitz and David Kauchak. 2013. Sentence simplification as tree transduction. In *Proceedings of the second workshop on predicting and improving text readability for target reader populations*, pages 1–10.

Rudolph Flesch. 1948. A new readability yardstick. *Journal of applied psychology*, 32(3):221.

Edward Fry. 1968. A readability formula that saves time. *Journal of reading*, 11(7):513–578.

Cristina Garbacea, Mengtian Guo, Samuel Carton, and Qiaozhu Mei. 2021. Explainable prediction of text complexity: The missing preliminaries for text simplification. In *Proceedings of the 59th Annual Meeting of the Association for Computational Linguistics and the 11th International Joint Conference on Natural Language Processing (Volume 1: Long Papers)*, pages 1086–1097, Online. Association for Computational Linguistics.

Laurie Gerber and Eduard Hovy. 1998. Improving translation quality by manipulating sentence length. In *Conference of the Association for Machine Translation in the Americas*, pages 448–460. Springer.

Sian Gooding, Ekaterina Kochmar, Seid Muhie Yimam, and Chris Biemann. 2021. Word complexity is in the eye of the beholder. In *Proceedings of the 2021 Conference of the North American Chapter of the Association for Computational Linguistics: Human Language Technologies*, pages 4439–4449. Association for Computational Linguistics.

Han Guo, Ramakanth Pasunuru, and Mohit Bansal. 2018. Dynamic multi-level multi-task learning for sentence simplification. *arXiv preprint arXiv:1806.07304*.

Eva Hasler, Adrià de Gispert, Felix Stahlberg, Aurelien Waite, and Bill Byrne. 2017. Source sentence simplification for statistical machine translation. *Computer Speech & Language*, 45:221–235.

Zhiting Hu, Zichao Yang, Xiaodan Liang, Ruslan Salakhutdinov, and Eric P Xing. 2017. Toward controlled generation of text. In *International conference on machine learning*, pages 1587–1596. PMLR.

Di Jin, Zhijing Jin, Zhiting Hu, Olga Vechtomova, and Rada Mihalcea. 2022. Deep learning for text style transfer: A survey. *Computational Linguistics*, 48(1):155–205.

Brendan T Johns, Melody Dye, and Michael N Jones. 2020. Estimating the prevalence and diversity of words in written language. *Quarterly Journal of Experimental Psychology*, 73(6):841–855.

Marcel A Just and Patricia A Carpenter. 1980. A theory of reading: from eye fixations to comprehension. *Psychological review*, 87(4):329.

Tomoyuki Kajiwara, Hiroshi Matsumoto, and Kazuhide Yamamoto. 2013. Selecting proper lexical paraphrase for children. In *Proceedings of the 25th Conference on Computational Linguistics and Speech Processing (ROCLING 2013)*, pages 59–73.

Elma Kerz, Yu Qiao, Daniel Wiechmann, and Marcus Ströbel. 2020. Becoming linguistically mature: Modeling English and German children's writing development across school grades. In *Proceedings of the Fifteenth Workshop on Innovative Use of NLP for Building Educational Applications*. Association for Computational Linguistics.

Elma Kerz, Yu Qiao, Sourabh Zanwar, and Daniel Wiechmann. 2022. Pushing on personality detection from verbal behavior: A transformer meets text contours of psycholinguistic features. *arXiv preprint arXiv:2204.04629*.

Yuta Kikuchi, Graham Neubig, Ryohei Sasano, Hiroya Takamura, and Manabu Okumura. 2016. Controlling output length in neural encoder-decoders. *arXiv preprint arXiv:1609.09552*.

J Peter Kincaid, Robert P Fishburne Jr, Richard L Rogers, and Brad S Chissom. 1975. Derivation of new readability formulas (automated readability index, fog count and flesch reading ease formula) for navy enlisted personnel. Technical report, Naval Technical Training Command Millington TN Research Branch.

Taku Kudo and John Richardson. 2018. Sentencepiece: A simple and language independent subword tokenizer and detokenizer for neural text processing. *arXiv preprint arXiv:1808.06226*.

Victor Kuperman, Hans Stadthagen-Gonzalez, and Marc Brysbaert. 2012. Age-of-acquisition ratings for 30,000 english words. *Behavior research methods*, 44(4):978–990.

Dongkyu Lee, Zhiliang Tian, Lanqing Xue, and Nevin L Zhang. 2021. Enhancing content preservation in text style transfer using reverse attention and conditional layer normalization. *arXiv preprint arXiv:2108.00449*.

Roger Levy and Galen Andrew. 2006. Tregex and tsurgeon: Tools for querying and manipulating tree data structures. In *LREC*, pages 2231–2234. Citeseer.

Shifeng Li, Shi Feng, Daling Wang, Kaisong Song, Yifei Zhang, and Weichao Wang. 2021. Emoelicitor: an open domain response generation model with user emotional reaction awareness. In *Proceedings of the Twenty-Ninth International Conference on International Joint Conferences on Artificial Intelligence*, pages 3637–3643.

Dayiheng Liu, Jie Fu, Yidan Zhang, Chris Pal, and Jiancheng Lv. 2020. Revision in continuous space: Unsupervised text style transfer without adversarial learning. In *Proceedings of the AAAI Conference on Artificial Intelligence*, volume 34, pages 8376–8383.

Octavio Loyola-Gonzalez. 2019. Black-box vs. white-box: Understanding their advantages and weaknesses from a practical point of view. *IEEE Access*, 7:154096–154113.

Xiaofei Lu. 2010. Automatic analysis of syntactic complexity in second language writing. *International journal of corpus linguistics*, 15(4):474–496.

Xiaofei Lu. 2012. The relationship of lexical richness to the quality of esl learners' oral narratives. *The Modern Language Journal*, 96(2):190–208.

Scott M Lundberg and Su-In Lee. 2017. A unified approach to interpreting model predictions. *Advances in neural information processing systems*, 30.

Mounica Maddela, Fernando Alva-Manchego, and Wei Xu. 2020. Controllable text simplification with explicit paraphrasing. *arXiv preprint arXiv:2010.11004*.

Christopher D Manning, Mihai Surdeanu, John Bauer, Jenny Rose Finkel, Steven Bethard, and David McClosky. 2014. The stanford corenlp natural language processing toolkit. In *Proceedings of 52nd annual meeting of the association for computational linguistics: system demonstrations*, pages 55–60.

Louis Martin, Éric de la Clergerie, Benoît Sagot, and Antoine Bordes. 2020. Controllable sentence simplification. In *Proceedings of the 12th Language Resources and Evaluation Conference*, pages 4689–4698, Marseille, France. European Language Resources Association.

Aurélien Max. 2006. Writing for language-impaired readers. In *International Conference on Intelligent Text Processing and Computational Linguistics*, pages 567–570. Springer.

G Harry McLaughlin. 1969. Clearing the smog. *J Reading*.

Makoto Miwa, Rune Saetre, Yusuke Miyao, and Jun'ichi Tsujii. 2010. Entity-focused sentence simplification for relation extraction. In *Proceedings of the 23rd International Conference on Computational Linguistics (Coling 2010)*, pages 788–796.

Shashi Narayan and Claire Gardent. 2014. Hybrid simplification using deep semantics and machine translation. In *The 52nd annual meeting of the association for computational linguistics*, pages 435–445.

Sergiu Nisioi, Sanja Štajner, Simone Paolo Ponzetto, and Liviu P Dinu. 2017. Exploring neural text simplification models. In *Proceedings of the 55th annual meeting of the association for computational linguistics (volume 2: Short papers)*, pages 85–91.

Myle Ott, Sergey Edunov, Alexei Baevski, Angela Fan, Sam Gross, Nathan Ng, David Grangier, and Michael Auli. 2019a. fairseq: A fast, extensible toolkit for sequence modeling. In *NAACL*.

Myle Ott, Sergey Edunov, Alexei Baevski, Angela Fan, Sam Gross, Nathan Ng, David Grangier, and Michael Auli. 2019b. fairseq: A fast, extensible toolkit for sequence modeling.

Gustavo Paetzold and Lucia Specia. 2013. Text simplification as tree transduction. In *Proceedings of the 9th Brazilian Symposium in Information and Human Language Technology*.

Gustavo Paetzold and Lucia Specia. 2016. Unsupervised lexical simplification for non-native speakers. In *Proceedings of the AAAI Conference on Artificial Intelligence*, volume 30.

Sarah E Petersen and Mari Ostendorf. 2007. Text simplification for language learners: a corpus analysis. In *Workshop on speech and language technology in education*. Citeseer.

Shrimai Prabhumoye, Alan W Black, and Ruslan Salakhutdinov. 2020. Exploring controllable text generation techniques. *arXiv preprint arXiv:2005.01822*.

Yu Qiao, Daniel Wiechmann, and Elma Kerz. 2020. A language-based approach to fake news detection through interpretable features and brnn. In *Proceedings of the 3rd international workshop on rumours and deception in social media (RDSM)*, pages 14–31.

Sudha Rao and Joel Tetreault. 2018. Dear sir or madam, may i introduce the gyafc dataset: Corpus, benchmarks and metrics for formality style transfer. *arXiv preprint arXiv:1803.06535*.

Luz Rello, Ricardo Baeza-Yates, Stefan Bott, and Horacio Saggion. 2013a. Simplify or help? text simplification strategies for people with dyslexia. In *Proceedings of the 10th International Cross-Disciplinary Conference on Web Accessibility*, pages 1–10.

Luz Rello, Ricardo Baeza-Yates, and Horacio Saggion. 2013b. The impact of lexical simplification by verbal paraphrases for people with and without dyslexia. In *International Conference on Intelligent Text Processing and Computational Linguistics*, pages 501–512. Springer.

Marco Tulio Ribeiro, Sameer Singh, and Carlos Guestrin. 2016. Model-agnostic interpretability of machine learning. *arXiv preprint arXiv:1606.05386*.

Carolina Scarton and Lucia Specia. 2018. Learning simplifications for specific target audiences. In *Proceedings of the 56th Annual Meeting of the Association for Computational Linguistics (Volume 2: Short Papers)*, pages 712–718.

Matthew Shardlow. 2014. A survey of automated text simplification. *International Journal of Advanced Computer Science and Applications*, 4(1):58–70.

Advaith Siddharthan. 2011. Text simplification using typed dependencies: A comparision of the robustness of different generation strategies. In *Proceedings of the 13th European Workshop on Natural Language Generation*, pages 2–11.

Sara Botelho Silveira and António Branco. 2012. Combining a double clustering approach with sentence simplification to produce highly informative multi-document summaries. In *2012 IEEE 13th International Conference on Information Reuse & Integration (IRI)*, pages 482–489. IEEE.

Matthew Snover, Bonnie Dorr, Richard Schwartz, Linnea Micciulla, and John Makhoul. 2006. A study of translation edit rate with targeted human annotation. In *Proceedings of the 7th Conference of the Association for Machine Translation in the Americas: Technical Papers*, pages 223–231.

Sanja Štajner and Goran Glavaš. 2017. Leveraging event-based semantics for automated text simplification. *Expert systems with applications*, 82:383–395.

Marcus Ströbel, Elma Kerz, Daniel Wiechmann, and Stella Neumann. 2016. CoCoGen - complexity contour generator: Automatic assessment of linguistic complexity using a sliding-window technique. In *Proceedings of the Workshop on Computational Linguistics for Linguistic Complexity (CL4LC)*, pages 23–31, Osaka, Japan. The COLING 2016 Organizing Committee.

Ashish Vaswani, Noam M. Shazeer, Niki Parmar, Jakob Uszkoreit, Llion Jones, Aidan N. Gomez, Lukasz Kaiser, and Illia Polosukhin. 2017. Attention is all you need. *ArXiv*, abs/1706.03762.

David Vickrey and Daphne Koller. 2008. Sentence simplification for semantic role labeling. In *Proceedings of ACL-08: HLT*, pages 344–352.

Willian Massami Watanabe, Arnaldo Candido Junior, Vinícius Rodriguez Uzêda, Renata Pontin de Mattos Fortes, Thiago Alexandre Salgueiro Pardo, and Sandra Maria Aluísio. 2009. Facilita: reading assistance for low-literacy readers. In *Proceedings of the 27th ACM international conference on Design of communication*, pages 29–36.

Daniel Wiechmann, Yu Qiao, Elma Kerz, and Justus Mattern. 2022. Measuring the impact of (psycho-) linguistic and readability features and their spill over effects on the prediction of eye movement patterns. *arXiv preprint arXiv:2203.08085*.

Xing Wu, Tao Zhang, Liangjun Zang, Jizhong Han, and Songlin Hu. 2019. "mask and infill" : Applying masked language model to sentiment transfer.

Sander Wubben, Antal Van Den Bosch, and Emiel Krahmer. 2012. Sentence simplification by monolingual machine translation. In *Proceedings of the 50th Annual Meeting of the Association for Computational Linguistics (Volume 1: Long Papers)*, pages 1015–1024.

Wei Xu, Chris Callison-Burch, and Courtney Napoles. 2015. Problems in current text simplification research: New data can help. *Transactions of the Association for Computational Linguistics*, 3:283–297.

Wei Xu, Courtney Napoles, Ellie Pavlick, Quanze Chen, and Chris Callison-Burch. 2016. Optimizing statistical machine translation for text simplification. *Transactions of the Association for Computational Linguistics*, 4:401–415.

Hanqing Zhang, Haolin Song, Shaoyu Li, Ming Zhou, and Dawei Song. 2022. A survey of controllable text generation using transformer-based pre-trained language models. *arXiv preprint arXiv:2201.05337*.

Saizheng Zhang, Emily Dinan, Jack Urbanek, Arthur Szlam, Douwe Kiela, and Jason Weston. 2018. Personalizing dialogue agents: I have a dog, do you have pets too? *arXiv preprint arXiv:1801.07243*.

Xingxing Zhang and Mirella Lapata. 2017. Sentence simplification with deep reinforcement learning. *arXiv preprint arXiv:1703.10931*.

Yaoyuan Zhang, Zhenxu Ye, Yansong Feng, Dongyan Zhao, and Rui Yan. 2017. A constrained sequence-to-sequence neural model for sentence simplification. *ArXiv*, abs/1704.02312.

7 Appendix

Table 3: Overview of the 107 features investigated in the work

Feature group	Number of features	Features	Example/Description
Syntactic complexity	16	MLC	Mean length of clause (words)
		MLS	Mean length of sentence (words)
		MLT	Mean length of T-unit (words)
		C/S	Clauses per sentence
		C/T	Clauses per T-unit
		DepC/C	Dependent clauses per clause
		T/S	T-units per sentence
		CompT/T	Complex T-unit per T-unit
		DepC/T	Dependent Clause per T-unit
		CoordP/C	Coordinate phrases per clause
		CoordP/T	Coordinate phrases per T-unit
		NP.PostMod	NP post-mod (word)
		NP.PreMod	NP pre-mod (word)
		CompN/C	Complex nominals per clause
		CompN/T	Complex nominals per T-unit
		VP/T	Verb phrases per T-unit
Lexical richness	14	MLWc	Mean length per word (characters)
		MLWs	Mean length per word (sylables)
		LD	Lexical density
		NDW	Number of different words
		CNDW	NDW corrected by Number of words
		TTR	Type-Token Ration (TTR)
		cTTR	Corrected TTR
		rTTR	Root TTR
		AFL	Sequences Academic Formula List
		ANC	LS (ANC) (top 2000, inverted)
		BNC	LS (BNC) (top 2000, inverted)
		NAWL	LS New Academic Word List
		NGSL	LS (General Service List) (inverted)
		NonStopWordsRate	Ratio of words in NLTK non-stopword list
Register-based	25	Spoken ($n \in [1,5]$)	Frequencies of uni-, bi-
		Fiction ($n \in [1,5]$)	tri-, four-, five-grams
		Magazine ($n \in [1,5]$)	from the five sub-components
		News ($n \in [1,5]$)	(genres) of the COCA
		Academic ($n \in [1,5]$)	

Feature group	Number of features	Features	Example/Description
Readability	14	ARI	Automated Readability Index
		ColemanLiau	Coleman-Liau Index
		DaleChall	Dale-Chall readability score
		FleshKincaidGradeLevel	Flesch-Kincaid Grade Level
		FleshKincaidReadingEase	Flesch Reading Ease score
		Fry-x	x coord. on Fry Readability Graph
		Fry-y	y coord. on Fry Readability Graph
		Lix	Lix readability score
		SMOG	Simple Measure of Gobbledygook
		GunningFog	Gunning Fog Index readability score
		DaleChallPSK	Powers-Sumner-Kearl Variation of the Dale and Chall Readability score
		FORCAST	FORCAST readability score
		Rix	Rix readability score
		Spache	Spache readability score
Psycholinguistic	38	WordPrevalence	See Brysbaert et al. (2019)
		Prevalence	Word prevalence list incl. 35 categories (Johns et al. (2020))
		AoA-mean	avg. age of acquisition (Kuperman et al. (2012))
		AoA-max	max. age of acquisition

Table 4: Means and standard deviations of all engineered languge features across the 'normal' and 'simple' sentences in the three benchmark datasets

	Biendata				Newsela				WikiLarge			
	normal		simple		normal		simple		normal		simple	
Feature	M	SD	M	SD	M	SD	M	SD	M	SD	M	SD
LexDens	0.73	0.1	0.76	0.12	0.58	0.1	0.58	0.11	0.58	0.12	0.6	0.17
CTTR	3.9	0.66	3.53	0.56	4.69	0.83	3.94	0.67	4.33	0.92	3.71	1.06
RTTR	2.65	0.42	2.39	0.37	3.21	0.57	2.69	0.44	2.96	0.63	2.54	0.7
TTR	0.97	0.05	0.99	0.04	0.91	0.07	0.95	0.06	0.88	0.1	0.92	0.1
MLWc	6.59	1.09	5.87	1.03	4.89	0.61	4.67	0.67	4.98	0.83	4.95	1.19
MLWs	2.02	0.36	1.73	0.35	1.47	0.2	1.39	0.21	1.52	0.25	1.49	0.37
Prev.AllAP	6.25	1.07	7.12	0.74	7.3	0.59	7.38	0.68	6.54	1.25	6.51	1.5
Prev.AllBP	7.48	1.31	8.58	0.95	8.98	0.75	9.11	0.87	8	1.56	7.96	1.86
Prev.AllCD	9.43	1.73	10.65	1.4	11.98	1.13	12.25	1.3	10.66	2.14	10.6	2.59
Prev.AllSD	7.55	1.35	8.79	1	9.14	0.77	9.32	0.89	8.14	1.57	8.14	1.89
Prev.AllSDAP	3.63	0.69	4.23	0.5	4.44	0.38	4.51	0.44	3.95	0.77	3.93	0.93
Prev.AllSDBP	5.06	0.98	5.91	0.75	6.34	0.57	6.47	0.66	5.61	1.12	5.59	1.36
Prev.AllWF	10.03	1.85	11.18	1.51	12.74	1.22	13.01	1.41	11.39	2.3	11.31	2.79
Prev.FemAP	5.58	1.02	6.45	0.71	6.67	0.55	6.75	0.64	5.95	1.15	5.93	1.38
Prev.FemBP	6.72	1.26	7.81	0.92	8.26	0.71	8.4	0.83	7.32	1.45	7.3	1.74
Prev.FemCD	8.79	1.69	9.98	1.39	11.37	1.1	11.65	1.27	10.09	2.05	10.04	2.49
Prev.FemSD	6.96	1.31	8.18	0.99	8.6	0.74	8.79	0.86	7.64	1.49	7.64	1.8
Prev.FemSDAP	3.01	0.62	3.56	0.46	3.79	0.34	3.86	0.39	3.34	0.67	3.33	0.81
Prev.FemSDBP	4.35	0.91	5.16	0.72	5.63	0.53	5.76	0.61	4.94	1.02	4.93	1.24
Prev.FemWF	9.2	1.78	10.32	1.48	11.91	1.18	12.19	1.36	10.62	2.18	10.55	2.66
Prev.MaleAP	5.69	0.97	6.47	0.67	6.63	0.53	6.7	0.62	5.95	1.13	5.92	1.36
Prev.MaleBP	6.99	1.23	8.01	0.89	8.38	0.7	8.51	0.81	7.48	1.45	7.45	1.74
Prev.MaleCD	9.01	1.67	10.18	1.36	11.5	1.09	11.76	1.26	10.23	2.06	10.18	2.5
Prev.MaleSD	7.23	1.3	8.41	0.97	8.79	0.74	8.96	0.86	7.82	1.51	7.82	1.82
Prev.MaleSDAP	2.92	0.56	3.39	0.4	3.57	0.3	3.62	0.35	3.18	0.62	3.16	0.75
Prev.MaleSDBP	4.45	0.87	5.18	0.66	5.59	0.51	5.7	0.58	4.95	0.99	4.93	1.2
Prev.MaleWF	9.48	1.78	10.56	1.46	12.11	1.18	12.37	1.36	10.84	2.2	10.75	2.68
Prev.UKAP	4.97	0.9	5.73	0.63	5.93	0.49	6	0.56	5.31	1.02	5.29	1.23
Prev.UKBP	6.22	1.16	7.2	0.85	7.61	0.66	7.73	0.76	6.78	1.33	6.75	1.6
Prev.UKCD	8.26	1.59	9.38	1.33	10.72	1.05	10.99	1.21	9.52	1.94	9.47	2.36
Prev.UKSD	6.46	1.22	7.6	0.93	7.97	0.69	8.15	0.81	7.07	1.38	7.08	1.67
Prev.UKSDAP	2.42	0.5	2.85	0.38	3.05	0.28	3.1	0.32	2.71	0.54	2.7	0.66
Prev.UKSDBP	3.79	0.79	4.47	0.63	4.89	0.47	5.01	0.54	4.32	0.89	4.31	1.08
Prev.UKWF	8.72	1.7	9.75	1.43	11.33	1.14	11.59	1.31	10.11	2.09	10.03	2.55
Prev.USAAP	5.84	1.01	6.68	0.7	6.86	0.55	6.94	0.64	6.14	1.18	6.11	1.41
Prev.USABP	7.08	1.27	8.15	0.92	8.56	0.72	8.69	0.84	7.61	1.49	7.58	1.78
Prev.USACD	9.12	1.7	10.33	1.39	11.67	1.11	11.95	1.29	10.38	2.09	10.33	2.54
Prev.USASD	7.25	1.33	8.49	0.99	8.86	0.75	9.04	0.88	7.87	1.52	7.88	1.84
Prev.USASDAP	3.24	0.63	3.8	0.46	4.01	0.35	4.07	0.4	3.54	0.7	3.53	0.85
Prev.USASDBP	4.67	0.93	5.49	0.72	5.94	0.54	6.06	0.63	5.23	1.06	5.21	1.28
Prev.USAWF	9.55	1.81	10.68	1.48	12.24	1.19	12.51	1.38	10.93	2.23	10.85	2.71
AFL	0	0	0	0.01	0	0.01	0	0.01	0	0.01	0	0.01
ANC	0.53	0.15	0.46	0.17	0.32	0.12	0.29	0.14	0.42	0.16	0.42	0.22
BNC	0.7	0.12	0.67	0.14	0.53	0.11	0.51	0.14	0.6	0.14	0.62	0.18
NAWL	0.07	0.08	0.05	0.08	0.01	0.03	0.01	0.03	0.02	0.04	0.01	0.05
NGSL	0.43	0.16	0.29	0.16	0.22	0.12	0.19	0.13	0.35	0.18	0.35	0.23

	Biendata				Newsela				WikiLarge			
	normal		simple		normal		simple		normal		simple	
Feature	M	SD	M	SD	M	SD	M	SD	M	SD	M	SD
ngram1acad	100.3	45.99	82.6	30.9	218.21	97.56	134.33	54.24	191.58	106.77	134.35	89.59
ngram1fic	80.26	39.83	73.47	29.2	211.26	93.65	132.17	53.26	179.99	101.04	127.55	85.76
ngram1mag	94.13	43.86	82.86	30.58	222.63	98.35	137.77	54.8	191.85	106.55	135.32	89.95
ngram1news	86.11	43.24	78.63	30.42	222.82	98.5	137.91	54.84	190.63	105.75	134.58	89.44
ngram1spok	84.23	42.43	77.21	30.28	218.49	97.09	136.38	54.85	183.53	103.33	130.18	87.59
ngram2acad	11.07	12.58	8.13	9.15	41.46	30.02	27.72	21.32	32.37	28.85	24.59	24.74
ngram2fic	3.55	5.37	4.26	6.69	33.83	25.95	25.47	20.46	22.31	21.55	18.68	19.98
ngram2mag	7.87	9.44	8.24	9.36	45.95	31.26	31.95	22.9	32.18	27.69	25.37	24.67
ngram2news	6.25	8.25	6.35	8.02	47.49	32.39	32.88	23.57	31.52	27.44	24.99	24.53
ngram2spok	5.45	7.44	6.04	7.99	42.87	31	31.11	23.43	26.57	24.46	22.08	22.77
ngram3acad	0.82	1.97	0.56	1.5	3.81	5.23	2.89	4.53	3.12	5.06	2.72	4.67
ngram3fic	0.15	0.65	0.24	0.96	2.58	4.17	2.37	4.07	1.4	2.68	1.44	2.88
ngram3mag	0.47	1.3	0.58	1.57	4.52	5.8	3.65	5.25	2.87	4.53	2.67	4.41
ngram3news	0.36	1.12	0.42	1.26	4.91	6.19	3.96	5.61	2.85	4.62	2.68	4.53
ngram3spok	0.28	1	0.36	1.22	3.87	5.68	3.41	5.33	1.95	3.58	2.05	3.86
ngram4acad	0.09	0.42	0.06	0.32	0.41	1.06	0.34	1.02	0.35	1.04	0.32	0.97
ngram4fic	0.01	0.13	0.02	0.2	0.24	0.76	0.24	0.82	0.12	0.42	0.13	0.5
ngram4mag	0.05	0.26	0.07	0.35	0.52	1.21	0.45	1.21	0.31	0.89	0.31	0.91
ngram4news	0.04	0.23	0.04	0.26	0.57	1.29	0.5	1.28	0.3	0.92	0.29	0.94
ngram4spok	0.03	0.19	0.04	0.25	0.41	1.13	0.4	1.17	0.19	0.69	0.21	0.79
ngram5acad	0.01	0.16	0.01	0.09	0.07	0.33	0.05	0.35	0.05	0.3	0.05	0.29
ngram5fic	0	0.03	0	0.06	0.03	0.18	0.03	0.2	0.01	0.1	0.02	0.14
ngram5mag	0.01	0.09	0.01	0.1	0.09	0.38	0.07	0.38	0.05	0.25	0.04	0.24
ngram5news	0	0.07	0.01	0.08	0.09	0.37	0.08	0.38	0.05	0.28	0.04	0.28
ngram5spok	0	0.06	0	0.07	0.06	0.31	0.06	0.32	0.03	0.18	0.03	0.21
NonStopW	0.74	0.1	0.78	0.12	0.6	0.1	0.59	0.12	0.63	0.12	0.64	0.17
AoA.max	12.64	2.47	10.89	2.53	10.19	2.33	8.4	2.16	10.36	2.78	8.96	3.25
AoA.mean	7.43	1.34	6.8	1.31	5.55	0.72	5.22	0.74	5.73	1.16	5.45	1.68
WordPrev	1.62	0.42	2.04	0.29	1.99	0.28	2.01	0.33	1.62	0.49	1.59	0.58
KolDef	0.85	0.12	0.93	0.12	0.77	0.12	0.89	0.13	0.8	0.23	0.93	0.35
NPPostMod	6.41	5.6	2.8	3.3	3.99	5.76	2.03	3.17	5.64	6.44	3.58	4.73
NPPreMod	1.27	1.14	1.02	0.88	1.03	0.86	0.91	0.73	1.21	1.01	1.04	0.87
CpS	0.31	0.5	0.77	0.69	2.11	1.23	1.58	0.86	1.45	1.01	1.19	0.93
CpT	0.27	0.47	0.66	0.66	1.88	1.07	1.49	0.8	1.28	0.8	1.08	0.77
CompNompC	0.67	1.23	1.01	1.08	1.57	1.2	1.09	0.9	1.97	1.51	1.3	1.24
CompNompT	0.8	1.29	1.15	1.13	2.65	1.85	1.52	1.18	2.5	1.85	1.61	1.52
CompTpT	0.02	0.13	0.1	0.3	0.53	0.49	0.37	0.48	0.27	0.44	0.2	0.39
CoordPpC	0.12	0.36	0.06	0.24	0.32	0.52	0.18	0.39	0.45	0.68	0.28	0.52
CoordPpT	0.15	0.41	0.07	0.26	0.51	0.72	0.23	0.47	0.56	0.79	0.34	0.61
DCpC	0.04	0.17	0.12	0.29	0.3	0.29	0.2	0.27	0.16	0.27	0.12	0.24
DCpT	0.02	0.14	0.1	0.32	0.77	0.9	0.45	0.66	0.34	0.62	0.24	0.53
MLC	3.71	6.28	5.83	4.96	12.23	6.89	9.4	4.45	14.63	8.87	10.5	7.5
MLS	12.76	4.46	9.62	2.86	22.76	9.77	13.74	5.12	21.13	10.6	14.67	9.03
MLT	4.62	6.69	6.67	5.02	20.54	10.24	12.96	5.47	18.77	11.09	12.95	9.35
TpS	0.36	0.48	0.7	0.48	1.06	0.39	1	0.27	0.99	0.44	0.88	0.47
VPpT	0.41	0.64	0.93	0.82	2.46	1.42	1.87	1.04	1.56	1.08	1.26	0.98

	Biendata				Newsela				WikiLarge			
	normal		simple		normal		simple		normal		simple	
Feature	M	SD	M	SD	M	SD	M	SD	M	SD	M	SD
ARI	15.98	5.01	11.02	4.62	12.98	5.66	7.45	3.85	12.63	6.14	9.27	6.19
Coleman	54.6	26.05	35.59	16.63	111.87	57.51	58.53	30.06	102.55	62.16	64.31	52.94
DaleChall	10.16	2.13	8.9	2.7	6.2	1.96	5.44	2.3	7.58	2.49	7.48	3.37
DC.PSK	11.41	1.53	10.31	1.95	9.06	1.53	8.01	1.68	9.99	1.8	9.56	2.37
FK Grade	13.23	4.27	8.53	4.05	10.61	4.55	6.16	3.15	10.56	4.97	7.72	5.16
FK Read	22.95	30.03	51.06	29.3	59.52	19.89	75.39	18.56	56.99	23.43	65.85	31.32
FORCAST	13.23	2.14	11.86	2.62	9.79	1.67	9.23	1.96	10.2	1.93	10.08	2.91
Fry.x	202.05	36.22	172.58	35.25	146.84	19.97	138.88	21.31	151.77	25.29	149.05	37.25
Gunning	510.4	178.2	385.0	114.4	910.4	390.9	549.6	204.7	846.5	423.0	587.4	361.1
Lix	61.4	14.53	48.27	16.85	48.26	14.61	35.23	12.96	48.96	15.67	41.45	19.55
Rix	5.9	2.98	5.33	2.51	15.49	6.96	9.91	4.12	13.96	7.55	10.08	6.6
SMOG	8.78	1.64	7.18	2.18	6.26	1.55	5.49	1.86	6.45	1.71	5.88	2.23
Spache	2.25	0.54	1.86	0.34	3.41	1.17	2.33	0.61	3.24	1.27	2.47	1.08

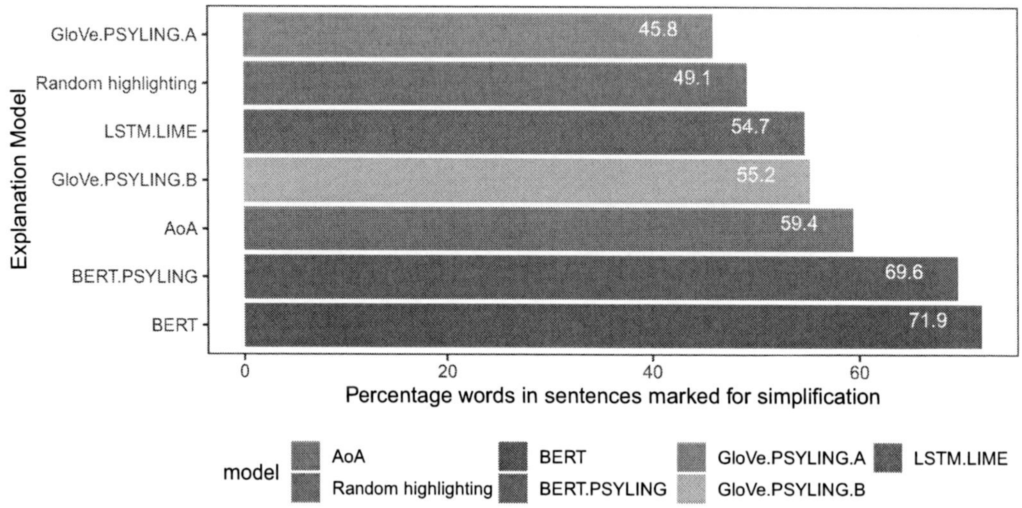

Figure 1: **Complexity explanation:** Differences in mean percentages of highlighted words across the five explanation models compared along with the two baselines: 'Random highlighting' and highlighting based on AoA (=age of acquisition) lexicon (Kuperman et al., 2012).

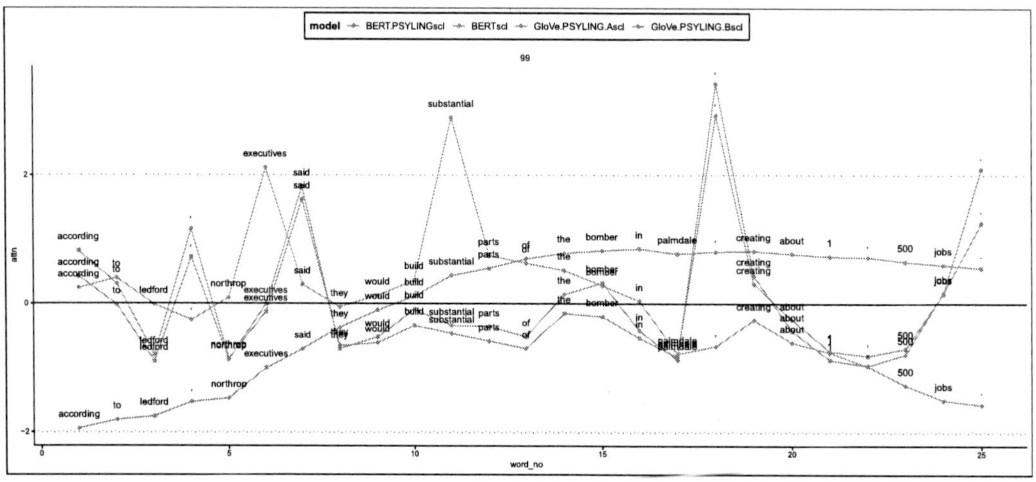

Figure 2: **Complexity explanation:** Distributions of attention weights over words in a randomly selected sentence.

Table 5: **Simplification Generation:** Example pair from WikiLarge corpus (normal, simplified) and source sentence simplified by ACCESS model (including four parameter tokens) and ACCESS-XL (including ten parameter tokens).

Type	Sentence
Source (Wikipedia)	One side of the armed conflicts is composed mainly of the Sudanese military and the Janjaweed, a Sudanese militia group recruited mostly from the Afro-Arab Abbala tribes of the northern Rizeigat region in Sudan.
Target (WikiSimple)	One side of the armed conflicts is made of Sudanese military and the Janjaweed, a Sudanese militia recruited from the Afro-Arab Abbala tribes of the northern Rizeigat region in Sudan.
ACCESS	One side of the armed conflict is made up of the Sudanese military and the Janjaweed, a Sudanese militia group brought mostly from the Afro-Arab Abbala tribes of the northern Rizeigat region in Sudan.
ACCESS-XL	The army of the armed conflicts is mainly made of the Sudanese military and the Janjaweed, a Sudanese militia group. They recruited mostly from the Afro-Arab Abbala tribes of the northern Rizeigat region in Sudan.

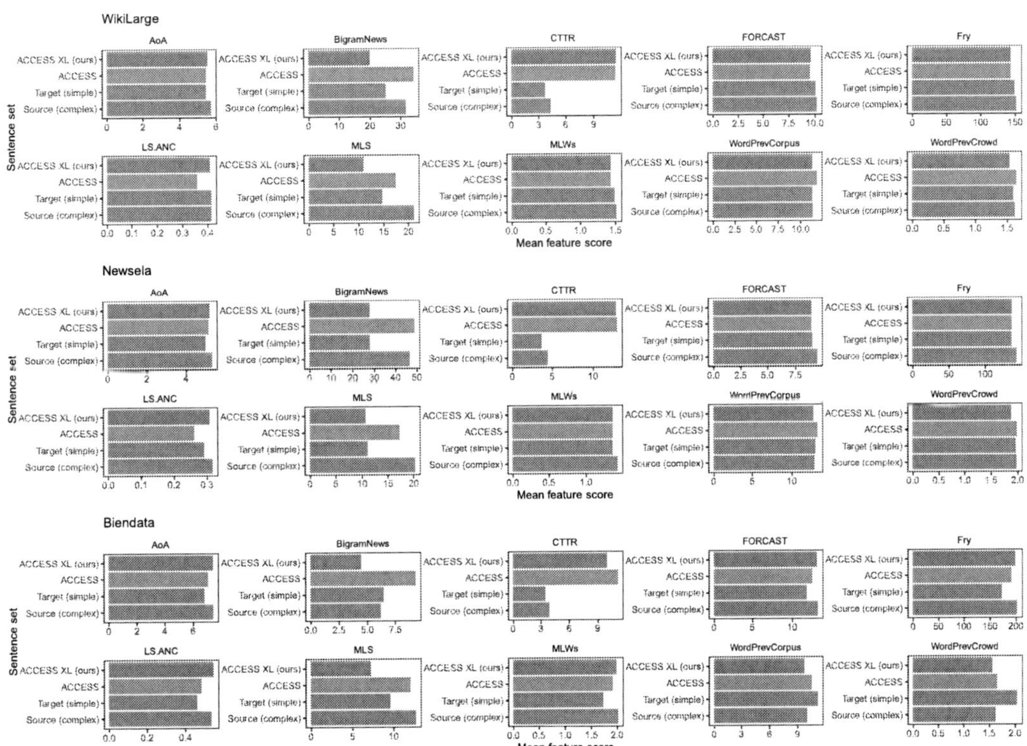

Figure 3: **Simplification Generation:** Mean values of the ten parameter tokens (engineered language features) across sentences sets.

Table 6: ACCESS model performance with prior complexity prediction using different complexity prediction models.

		ACCESS			
		Ours		Martin	
Dataset	Filter	SARI	FKGL	SARI	FKGL
WiKiLarge	BERT	43.01	5.14	40.97	7.21
	BERT_PSYLING	42.84	5.06	40.97	7.17
	GloVe-PSYLING-a	41.38	5.19	39.54	7.24
	GloVe-PSYLING-b	41.53	5.03	39.72	7.22
Biendata	BERT	26.92	10.85	19.93	12.61
	BERT_PSYLING	26.87	10.86	19.87	12.63
	GloVe-PSYLING-a	26.16	11.17	19.31	12.78
	GloVe-PSYLING-b	26.87	10.90	19.89	12.62
Newsela	bert	33.44	5.27	27.33	6.78
	BERT_PSYLING	33.13	5.19	27.30	6.75
	GloVe-PSYLING-a	34.88	3.96	29.41	6.45
	GloVe-PSYLING-b	34.90	3.96	29.43	6.45

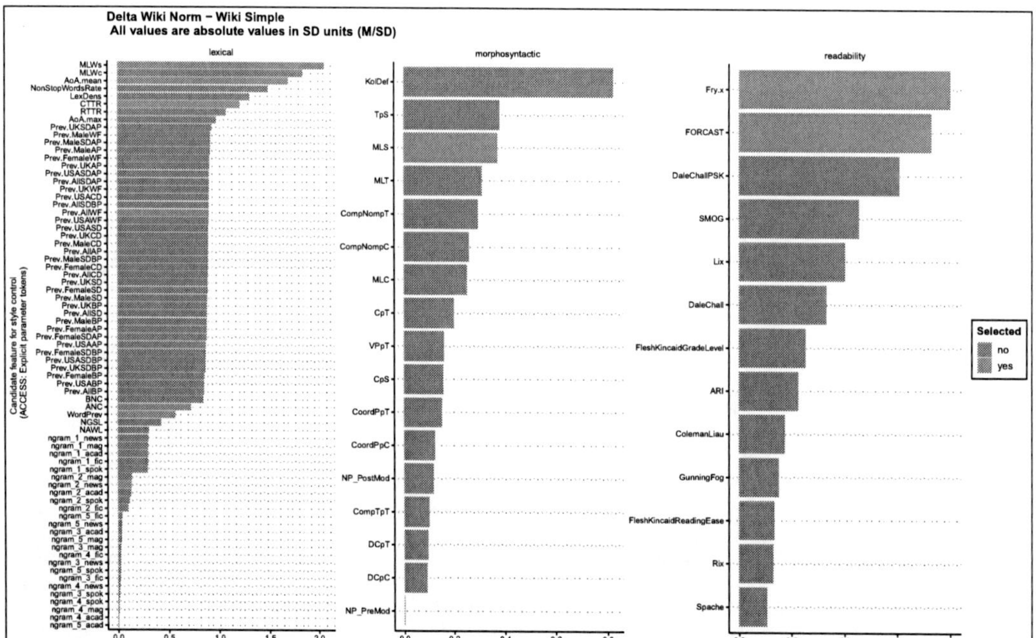

Figure 4: **Simplification Generation:** Differences in mean feature scores (standardized) between 'normal' and 'simple' sentences in WikiLarge corpus. Features in blue were selected for controllable sentence simplification in the ACCESS-XL model.

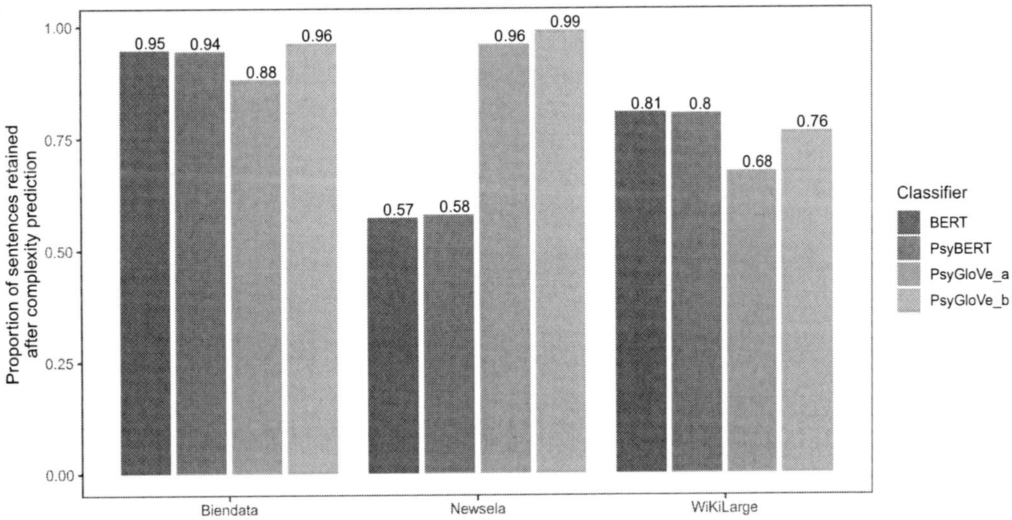

Figure 5: **Simplification Generation:** Proportion of sentences retained after complexity prediction after complexity prediction (step 1) across prediction model and dataset

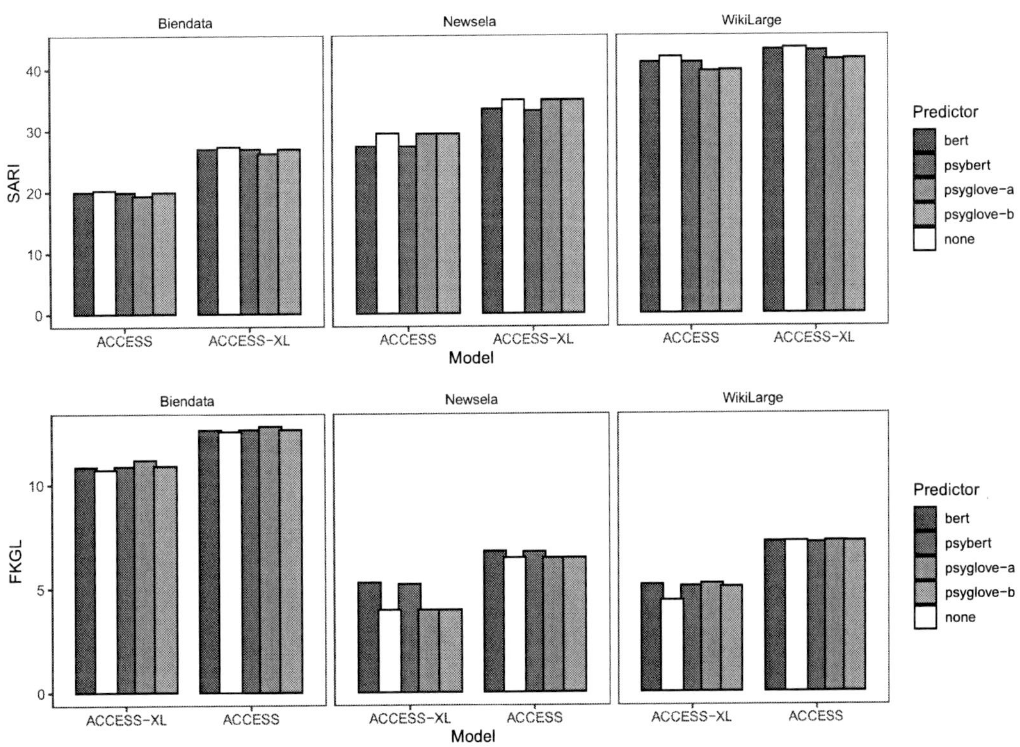

Figure 6: **Simplification Generation:** Performance of text simplification models as measured by SARI (top, higher is better) and Flesch-Kinkaid Grade Level (FKGL, bottom; lower is better) across datasets and use of complexity prediction methods.

Table 7: Average ED between simple sentences and original ACCESS output predictions with and without complexity prediction. ED are calculated using the tseval library, which EASSE relies on.

Dataset	Filter	ED
WiKiLarge	none	15.641
	BERT	15.566
	BERT_PSYLING	15.590
	GloVe-PSYLING_a	15.717
	GloVe-PSYLING_b	15.771
	LSTM	15.705
biendata	none	13.298
	BERT	13.269
	BERT_PSYLING	13.267
	GloVe-PSYLING_a	13.240
	GloVe-PSYLING_b	13.281
	LSTM	13.220
newsela	none	16.378
	BERT	15.958
	BERT_PSYLING	15.957
	GloVe-PSYLING_a	16.377
	GloVe-PSYLING_b	16.376
	LSTM	16.008

Table 8: Avg ED between complex sentences and original ACCESS outputs with/without complexity prediction

Dataset	Filter	ED
WiKiLarge	none	6.684
	BERT	5.916
	BERT_PSYLING	5.979
	GloVe-PSYLING_a	5.639
	GloVe-PSYLING_b	5.765
	LSTM	4.516
biendata	none	2.823
	bert	2.719
	BERT_PSYLING	2.699
	GloVe-PSYLING_a	2.529
	GloVe-PSYLING_b	2.723
	LSTM	1.585
newsela	none	5.368
	BERT	3.918
	BERT_PSYLING	3.960
	GloVe-PSYLING_a	5.358
	GloVe-PSYLING_b	5.363
	LSTM	3.022

Table 9: **Simplification Generation:** Proportion of sentences retained after complexity prediction after complexity prediction (step 1) across prediction model and dataset

	Complexity prediction model			
Dataset	BERT	PsyBERT	PsyGloVe$_a$	PsyGloVe$_b$
Biendata	0.947	0.945	0.881	0.961
Newsela	0.572	0.578	0.959	0.991
WiKiLarge	0.807	0.805	0.675	0.764

Evaluation metrics for simplification generation FKGL is computed as a linear combination of the number of words per simple sentence and the number of syllables per word:

$$FKGL = 0.39\frac{N\ word}{N\ sent} + 11.8\frac{N\ syl}{N\ word} - 15.59$$

SARI compares the predicted simplification with both the source and the target reference. It is an average of F1 scores for three n-gram operations: additions (add), keeps ($keep$) and deletions (del). For each operation, these scores are then averaged for all n-gram orders (from 1 to 4) to get the overall F1 score.

$$f_{ope}(n) = \frac{2 \times p_{ope}(n) \times r_{ope}(n)}{p_{ope}(n) + r_{ope}(n)}$$

$$F_{ope} = \frac{1}{k} \sum_{n=[1,\ldots,k]} f_{ope}(n)$$

$$SARI = \frac{F_{add} + F_{keep} + F_{del}}{3}$$

SARI thus rewards models for adding n-grams that occur in the reference but not in the input, for keeping n-grams both in the output and in the reference, and for not over-deleting n-grams. Xu et al. (2016) show that SARI correlates with human judgments of simplicity gain.

Lexically Constrained Decoding with Edit Operation Prediction for Controllable Text Simplification

Tatsuya Zetsu[†], **Tomoyuki Kajiwara**[‡], **Yuki Arase**[†]
[†]Graduate School of Information Science and Technology, Osaka University, Japan
[‡]Graduate School of Science and Engineering, Ehime University, Japan
[†]{zetsu.tatsuya, arase}@ist.osaka-u.ac.jp
[‡]kajiwara@cs.ehime-u.ac.jp

Abstract

Controllable text simplification assists language learners by automatically rewriting complex sentences into simpler forms of a target level. However, existing methods tend to perform conservative edits that keep complex words intact. To address this problem, we employ lexically constrained decoding to encourage rewriting. Specifically, the proposed method predicts edit operations conditioned to a target level and creates positive/negative constraints for words that should/should not appear in an output sentence. The experimental results confirm that our method significantly outperforms previous methods and demonstrates a new state-of-the-art performance.

1 Introduction

Text simplification (Shardlow, 2014) paraphrases complex sentences into simpler forms. Controllable text simplification (Scarton and Specia, 2018; Nishihara et al., 2019; Agrawal et al., 2021) is a task in text simplification that aims to rewrite a sentence for an audience of a specific level. It is a crucial technique in assisting children and non-native speakers with language learning (Watanabe et al., 2009; Allen, 2009).

Text simplification can be performed based on three approaches: (1) translation-based, (2) edit-based, and (3) hybrid approaches. The translation-based approach, *e.g.*, (Nisioi et al., 2017; Zhang and Lapata, 2017; Kriz et al., 2019; Surya et al., 2019; Martin et al., 2022), formalizes text simplification as monolingual machine translation from complex to simple sentences. This approach can rewrite a sentence flexibly; however, it implicitly learns simplification operations through translation. The infrequent nature of simplification operations hinders a model from learning necessary operations, which makes the model conservative to maintain complex words intact (Zhao et al., 2018; Kajiwara, 2019). In contrast, the edit-based approach (Alva-Manchego et al., 2017; Dong et al., 2019; Kumar et al., 2020; Mallinson et al., 2020; Omelianchuk et al., 2021) rewrites an input by applying edit operations of `add` or `replace`, `keep`, and `delete` to words. This approach can address the conservativeness problem owing to explicit word-by-word edits. However, it lacks the flexibility to rewrite an entire sentence to drastically change its syntactic structure.

Finally, the hybrid approach takes advantages of the above two by applying lexical constraints to translation-based models. Nishihara et al. (2019) added weights to a loss function to bias a sequence-to-sequence (seq2seq) model to output certain words. Agrawal et al. (2021) biased a non-autoregressive simplification model by setting an initial state of decoding, considering the lexical complexity of a source sentence. The constraints in these studies were soft; in contrast, Kajiwara (2019) and Dehghan et al. (2022) applied a hard constraint using lexically constrained decoding to avoid outputting complex words. In spite of their success, these two methods lack flexibility in their constraints. They only use *negative* constraints to avoid outputting specified words. However, *positive* constraints, which encourage the output of specified words, are also valuable for text simplification.

In this study, we propose a hybrid method for controllable text simplification with flexible combinations of positive and negative constraints using NeuroLogic decoding (Lu et al., 2021). The proposed method predicts edit operations conditioned on a target level to generate positive and negative lexical constraints sensible to a target level. Experiments on Newsela (Xu et al., 2015) and Newsela-Auto (Jiang et al., 2020) reveal that the proposed method outperforms previous methods and achieves a new state-of-the-art performance. The codes and outputs of the proposed method will be released at `https://github.com/t-zetsu/ConstrainedTS`.

Proceedings of the Workshop on Text Simplification, Accessibility, and Readability (TSAR-2022), pages 147 - 153
December 8, 2022

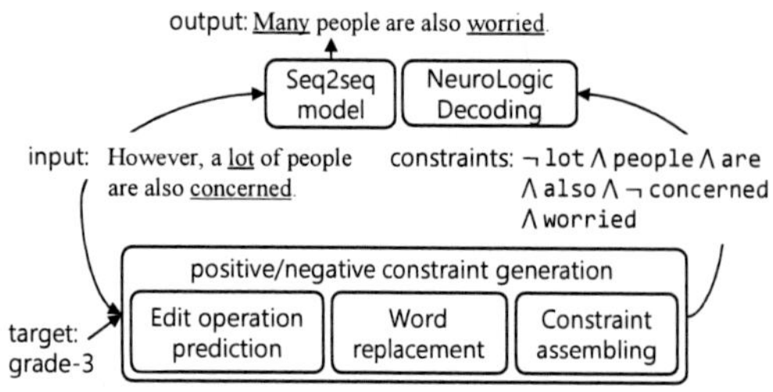

Figure 1: Overview of the proposed method

target level: ℓ	replace	keep	delete
word level $\leq \ell$	—	P	—
word level $> \ell$	N, P	—	N

Table 1: Assembling positive (P) and negative (N) constraints relevant to controlling output levels

2 Proposed Method

Figure 1 illustrates an overview of the proposed method, in which generated constraints are applied to a seq2seq model via NeuroLogic decoding.

2.1 Word Level Lexicon

We create word level lexicons to generate constraints sensible to a target level. We assign word levels based on their frequency in sentences of a certain level, assuming that higher-level words would frequently appear in higher-level sentences. The frequency of a word w in sentences of a level ℓ is as follows: $f(w, \ell) = \frac{n_\ell(w)}{\sum_{\hat{w} \in V_\ell} n_\ell(\hat{w})}$, where $n_\ell(w)$ denotes the number of occurrences of w in ℓ-level sentences, and V_ℓ denotes a set of unique words in those sentences. A word level k is determined as $k = \text{argmax}_\ell f(w, \ell)$. Finally, we collect all ℓ-level words as a lexicon D_ℓ for each level.

2.2 Constraint Generation

Constraints are generated in three steps. The proposed method first predicts all edit operations in an input conditioned on a target level. Following this, it identifies lexical paraphrases for replacing higher-level words. Finally, positive and negative constraints are assembled based on these edit operations, lexical paraphrases, and word level lexicons.

Edit Operation Prediction The proposed method uses a pre-trained language model to predict an edit operation among `replace`, `keep`, and `delete` for each word. These edit operations should depend on a target level. Therefore, the input sentence is tagged with a special token representing the target level, *e.g.*, "sentence <3>."

Manual annotation of these edit operations is costly. Thus, we synthesize a fine-tuning corpus using a state-of-the-art word alignment model (Lan et al., 2021). Specifically, we obtain word alignments between parallel sentences in a simplification corpus. Words with null-alignments are assigned `delete` labels. Among the aligned words, words aligned with identical counterparts are assigned `keep` labels, and the ones aligned to words with different surfaces are assigned `replace` labels. This pseudo-labelled corpus is used for fine-tuning.

Replacement Word Identification The proposed method identifies a word $\hat{w}$ that should replace another word w whose predicted label is `replace`. Given the target level ℓ of simplification, it computes the semantic similarity between w and words in $\{D_k | k \leq \ell\}$ and identifies the replacement word $\hat{w}$ as the one with the highest similarity. For similarity estimation, we fine-tune a pre-trained language model.

Constraint Assembling Finally, we generate positive and negative constraints based on the predicted edit operations and the replacement words. We focus on the edit operations that are relevant to controlling output levels. Note that the predicted edit operations should be a mixture of various edits, including general lexical paraphrasing and omissions. Therefore, we use the word level lexicons to select operations relevant to controlling output levels as summarized in Table 1.

Specifically, words with the `delete` label transform into negative constraints if their levels are higher than the target level ℓ. Words with `keep` labels transform into positive constraints if their levels are lower than or equal to ℓ. Finally, words with `replace` labels transform into negative constraints and their replacement words transform into positive constraints if their levels are higher than ℓ.

The cases where the edit operations and the word level lexicons conflict, *i.e.*, words whose levels are lower than or equal to ℓ but predicted `replace` and `delete` operations, are expected to be independent for controlling output levels and correspond to general lexical paraphrasing and omissions. Therefore, we exclude these operations from the constraints and rely on the seq2seq model for their handling.

3 Experiments

3.1 Dataset

To evaluate the proposed method on the controllable text simplification task, we used Newsela and Newsela-Auto, which provide pairs of complex and simple sentences with K-12 grade levels. These are the only corpora providing fine-grained levels, which makes them standard datasets for evaluating controllable text simplification models. While Newsela-Auto preserves higher quality sentence alignments, we also experimented on Newsela for comprehensive comparison to previous studies. For Newsela, we used the data-split by Zhang and Lapata (2017) consisting of $94,208$ training, $1,129$ validation, and $1,077$ test sentences. For Newsela-Auto, we used the official split of $394,300$ training, $43,317$ validation, and $44,067$ test sentences.

3.2 Implementation Details

We implemented the proposed method using Pytorch[1] and Transformers (Wolf et al., 2020)[2]. All experiments were conducted on an NVIDIA A6000 GPU with a 48 GB memory. Appendix A presents details regarding the fine-tuning settings.

Edit Operation Prediction Model We fine-tuned pre-trained BERT (Devlin et al., 2019) models for an edit operation prediction using the pseudo-labelled corpora created using Newsela and Newsela-Auto, respectively. Table 2 depicts the precision, recall, and F1 of the operation prediction on the test sets. The results indicate that `replace` operations are difficult to predict owing to their infrequency; however, the results confirm that the proposed method improves text simplification even though the edit operation prediction is imperfect.

Lexical Similarity Estimation Model We fine-tuned a pre-trained RoBERTa (Liu et al., 2019) for a lexical similarity estimation using a corpus that provides human assessment of semantic similarities for 26.5k word pairs on a 5-point scale (Pavlick et al., 2015)[3]. Specifically, we concatenate a pair of words w and $\hat{w}$ with start and separator symbols as "<s>w</s></s>$\hat{w}$</s>" and input it in the model. The hidden output of the <s> symbol is then input into a linear layer to predict the similarity. Finally, we obtain a symmetric similarity score based on $(\text{sim}(w, \hat{w}) + \text{sim}(\hat{w}, w))/2$. We randomly split the corpus into 72% for training, 8% for validation, and 20% for testing. The fine-tuned model achieved a sufficiently high Pearson correlation coefficient of 0.86 on the test set. For a comparison, the correlation coefficient of cosine similarities computed using FastText (Bojanowski et al., 2017) was found to be 0.50.

	Newsela			Newsela-Auto		
Edit Operation	P	R	F1	P	R	F1
`replace`	0.28	0.21	0.24	0.28	0.15	0.19
`keep`	0.58	0.57	0.57	0.58	0.57	0.58
`delete`	0.70	0.73	0.72	0.73	0.77	0.75

Table 2: Performance of edit operation prediction on the test sets of Newsela and Newsela-Auto

Seq2seq Model As a seq2seq model to employ NeuroLogic decoding (Lu et al., 2021), we fine-tuned two pre-trained BART-Base (Lewis et al., 2020) models separately for Newsela and Newsela-Auto corpora. The batch size was 64, and the optimizer used was Adam (Kingma and Ba, 2015) with a learning rate of $1e-5$. The fine-tuning continued for 20 epochs, and a checkpoint with the highest SARI (Xu et al., 2016) score on the validation set was used as the final model.

3.3 Comparison

The proposed method is the hybrid of translation-based and edit-based approaches, hence, we compare it with existing methods in these categories. As translation-based methods, We compare our method to DRESS (Zhang and Lapata, 2017), which uses reinforcement learning for maximizing SARI score, as a conventional method. We also compare to MUSS (Martin et al., 2022), which also uses the pre-trained BART and hods the state-of-the-art measured on the Newsela corpus. From strong edit-based methods, we compare the proposed method to EditNTS (Dong et al., 2019) that explicitly learns edit operations using a neural programmer-interpreter model and the model proposed by Kumar et al. (2020) that conducts iterative edits of input sentences. As existing hybrid methods, we compare our method to the models proposed by Kajiwara (2019)[4] and Dehghan et al. (2022), both of which employ negative con-

[1]https://pytorch.org/

[2]https://huggingface.co/docs/transformers/

[3]http://www.seas.upenn.edu/~nlp/resources/ppdb-2.0-human-labels.tgz

[4]For a fair comparison, we employed a fine-tuned BART in (Kajiwara, 2019), which resulted in a higher SARI score.

Model	SARI	Add	Keep	Delete	FKGL	PCC	MSE	ACC	Len
Source	12.24	0.00	36.72	0.00	9.18	0.338	47.2	15.5	23.06
Reference	100.0	100.0	100.0	100.0	3.96	1.000	0.0	100.0	12.75
DRESS (Zhang and Lapata, 2017)†	38.03	2.43	42.20	69.47	4.97	0.388	13.0	24.3	14.37
MUSS (Martin et al., 2022)†	41.20	**6.02**	35.88	**81.70**	2.43	0.362	13.3	20.9	9.23
BART	38.54	3.64	40.59	71.40	4.63	0.350	13.6	26.2	11.26
EditNTS (Dong et al., 2019)⋆	37.05	1.23	36.55	73.37	**3.82**	0.266	16.1	21.4	13.25
(Kumar et al., 2020)†	38.37	1.01	36.51	77.58	2.95	0.334	12.6	25.5	9.61
(Kajiwara, 2019)	38.48 ⋆	4.55	**43.41**	67.47	5.01	0.417	12.2	**28.1**	14.27
(Dehghan et al., 2022)‡	40.01	3.06	36.53	80.43	3.20	–	–	–	11.72
Proposed	**42.65**	4.55	42.49	80.90	3.74	**0.420**	**11.1**	27.9	**12.01**
Proposed (Oracle)	54.73	10.98	66.07	87.14	4.07	0.591	8.0	37.3	12.47

Table 3: Results on the Newsela test set: † indicates that a score was recomputed with EASSE using outputs shared by the authors, ⋆ indicates that a model was trained in this study using the released implementation, and ‡ presents that a score was borrowed from the original papers with the same settings as this experiment.

Model	SARI	Add	Keep	Delete	FKGL	PCC	MSE	ACC	Len
Source	12.04	0.00	36.12	0.00	10.11	**0.393**	57.7	13.9	24.82
Reference	100.0	100.0	100.0	100.0	4.34	1.000	0.0	100.0	13.34
BART	39.66	4.16	39.17	75.65	**4.38**	0.342	16.4	**26.9**	10.33
EditNTS (Dong et al., 2019)	37.43	0.97	34.78	76.53	3.12	0.215	20.4	23.2	11.24
(Kajiwara, 2019)	38.30	**4.42**	40.51	69.96	5.03	0.371	16.0	26.8	**13.79**
Proposed	**43.09**	4.41	**42.74**	**82.13**	3.89	0.391	**15.1**	26.8	11.85
Proposed (Oracle)	51.75	7.45	61.14	86.66	4.64	0.611	9.9	34.5	12.90

Table 4: Results on the Newsela-Auto test set, where all models were trained and evaluated in this study.

straints.[5] In contrast, our method employs both positive and negative constraints on a translation-based model.

3.4 Evaluation Metrics

Following previous studies, we measured the SARI (with F1 scores of Add, Keep, and Delete operations) and FKGL using EASSE (Alva-Manchego et al., 2019), as well as the average output lengths (Len). Note that the FKGL and Len should be closer to those of references. Furthermore, to evaluate simplification controllablity, we measured Pearson's correlation coefficient (PCC), Mean Squared Error (MSE), and Accuracy (ACC) between FKGL scores of outputs and references (Agrawal et al., 2021). The Accuracy represents the percentage of outputs whose grades are within 1-grade difference from those of references.

[5]Due to the heavy dependence on Google Translate to prepare a training corpus, we could not replicate (Agrawal et al., 2021) in this study.

Src	The rest would be preserved as open space.
Ref	The rest would be saved as open space.
BART	The rest would be preserved as open space.
Prop.	The rest would be kept as open space.
- PC	rest, be, kept, open, space
- NC	preserved

Table 5: Example outputs: "PC" and "NC" represent positive and negative constraints, respectively.

3.5 Results

The experimental results on the test sets of Newsela and Newsela-Auto are presented in Tables 3 and 4, respectively. The tables present the performance of representative translation-based (the second set of rows), edit-based (the third set of rows), and hybrid (the last set of rows) methods. The tables also present the performance of source and reference sentences (the first set of rows). "BART"

Src	So Yan, a widow since her husband's death nearly a decade ago, spends every weekday at a modest community center near her home, where she plays mahjong and eats meals prepared by a volunteer staff.
Prop. (Grade 8)	She spends every weekday at a community center near her home.
- PC	husband, at, community, near, staff
- NC	widow, a
Prop. (Grade 5)	Yan's husband died almost 10 years ago.
- PC	–
- NC	widow, nearly, a, every, community, center, and, meals, prepared, by, staff
Prop. (Grade 2)	Yan is a widow.
- PC	–
- NC	widow, husband, nearly, a, ago, at, community, center, near, and, meals, prepared, by, staff

Table 6: Example outputs of controllable simplification; an input sentence of grade-12 was simplified to the grade-8, 5, and 2, respectively.

corresponds to the fine-tuned BART in this study, and "Proposed" represents the proposed method applying our lexical constraint on "BART."

The proposed method achieved the highest SARI and MSE scores with the highest and second-highest PCC scores on Newsela and Newsela-auto, respectively.[6] Furthermore, its output lengths are closest and second-closest to those of the references. A comparison with hybrid methods indicates the effectiveness of the flexible constraints of the proposed method, in spite of the imperfect nature of the edit operation prediction, as shown in Table 2. Among the previous methods, MUSS presents the highest SARI score, which fine-tunes BART using a large-scale data augmentation. The proposed method outperforms it using only the Newsela training set. Finally, a comparison of the `Add`, `Keep`, and `Delete` scores against BART confirms that our lexical constraint successfully improves all of these operations.

Oracle Performance The last rows in Tables 3 and 4 show the proposed method with oracle lexical constraints created using reference sentences as described in Section 2.2. The significantly higher SARI scores indicate that the proposed method can be further enhanced by improved constraint generation, in particular, by more precise edit operation prediction.

Example Outputs Table 5 presents example outputs where the input of grade-5 was simplified to grade-3. The proposed method successfully replaced *preserved* with *kept* owing to the lexical constraints. By contrast, BART ended up preserving it in the output. Table 6 shows example outputs where the input of grade-12 was simplified to the grade-8, 5 and 2, respectively. These outputs indicate that the proposed method can adjust sentence structures while considering lexical complexities according to the target levels.

[6]The highest PCC score of source in Newsela is due to the positive correlation between grades of the source and reference sentences.

4 Conclusion

We proposed a hybrid method for controllable text simplification that takes both advantages of translation- and edit-based methods using the flexible lexically constrained decoding. The experimental results showed that the proposed method conducts high-quality controllable text simplification on Newsela and Newsela-Auto. We expect that the proposed method also works for text simplification in general, *i.e.*, the binary transformation from complex to simple sentences. This investigation is left for our future work. We will also explore complex combinations of constraints allowed by NeuroLogic decoding in the future.

Acknowledgements

We sincerely thank Masato Yoshinaka for his contribution to the lexical similarity estimation model. We appreciate the anonymous reviewers for their insightful comments and suggestions to improve the paper. This work was supported by MHLW AC Program Grant Number JPMW21AC5001.

References

Sweta Agrawal, Weijia Xu, and Marine Carpuat. 2021. A non-autoregressive edit-based approach to controllable text simplification. In *Findings of the Association for Computational Linguistics: ACL-IJCNLP 2021*, pages 3757–3769.

David Allen. 2009. A study of the role of relative clauses in the simplification of news texts for learners of english. *System*, 37(4):585–599.

Fernando Alva-Manchego, Joachim Bingel, Gustavo Paetzold, Carolina Scarton, and Lucia Specia. 2017. Learning how to simplify from explicit labeling of complex-simplified text pairs. In *Proceedings of the Eighth International Joint Conference on Natural Language Processing*, pages 295–305.

Fernando Alva-Manchego, Louis Martin, Carolina Scarton, and Lucia Specia. 2019. EASSE: Easier automatic sentence simplification evaluation. In *Proceedings of the Conference on Empirical Methods in Natural Language Processing and the International Joint Conference on Natural Language Processing (EMNLP-IJCNLP): System Demonstrations*.

Piotr Bojanowski, Edouard Grave, Armand Joulin, and Tomas Mikolov. 2017. Enriching word vectors with subword information. *Transactions of the Association of Computational Linguistics (TACL)*, 5:135–146.

Mohammad Dehghan, Dhruv Kumar, and Lukasz Golab. 2022. GRS: Combining generation and revision in unsupervised sentence simplification. In *Findings of the Association for Computational Linguistics: ACL 2022*, pages 949–960.

Jacob Devlin, Ming-Wei Chang, Kenton Lee, and Kristina Toutanova. 2019. BERT: Pre-training of deep bidirectional transformers for language understanding. In *Proceedings of the Annual Conference of the North American Chapter of the Association for Computational Linguistics: Human Language Technologies (NAACL-HLT)*, pages 4171–4186.

Yue Dong, Zichao Li, Mehdi Rezagholizadeh, and Jackie Chi Kit Cheung. 2019. EditNTS: An neural programmer-interpreter model for sentence simplification through explicit editing. In *Proceedings of the Annual Meeting of the Association for Computational Linguistics (ACL)*, pages 3393–3402.

Chao Jiang, Mounica Maddela, Wuwei Lan, Yang Zhong, and Wei Xu. 2020. Neural CRF model for sentence alignment in text simplification. In *Proceedings of the Annual Meeting of the Association for Computational Linguistics (ACL)*, pages 7943–7960.

Tomoyuki Kajiwara. 2019. Negative lexically constrained decoding for paraphrase generation. In *Proceedings of the Annual Meeting of the Association for Computational Linguistics (ACL)*, pages 6047–6052.

Diederik P. Kingma and Jimmy Ba. 2015. Adam: A method for stochastic optimization. In *Proceedings of the International Conference on Learning Representations (ICLR)*.

Reno Kriz, João Sedoc, Marianna Apidianaki, Carolina Zheng, Gaurav Kumar, Eleni Miltsakaki, and Chris Callison-Burch. 2019. Complexity-weighted loss and diverse reranking for sentence simplification. In *Proceedings of the Annual Conference of the North American Chapter of the Association for Computational Linguistics: Human Language Technologies (NAACL-HLT)*, pages 3137–3147.

Dhruv Kumar, Lili Mou, Lukasz Golab, and Olga Vechtomova. 2020. Iterative edit-based unsupervised sentence simplification. In *Proceedings of the Annual Meeting of the Association for Computational Linguistics (ACL)*, pages 7918–7928.

Wuwei Lan, Chao Jiang, and Wei Xu. 2021. Neural semi-Markov CRF for monolingual word alignment. In *Proceedings of the Annual Meeting of the Association for Computational Linguistics (ACL)*, pages 6815–6828.

Mike Lewis, Yinhan Liu, Naman Goyal, Marjan Ghazvininejad, Abdelrahman Mohamed, Omer Levy, Veselin Stoyanov, and Luke Zettlemoyer. 2020. BART: Denoising sequence-to-sequence pre-training for natural language generation, translation, and comprehension. In *Proceedings of the Annual Meeting of the Association for Computational Linguistics (ACL)*, pages 7871–7880.

Yinhan Liu, Myle Ott, Naman Goyal, Jingfei Du, Mandar Joshi, Danqi Chen, Omer Levy, Mike Lewis, Luke Zettlemoyer, and Veselin Stoyanov. 2019. RoBERTa: A robustly optimized BERT pretraining approach. *arXiv*, 1907.11692.

Ilya Loshchilov and Frank Hutter. 2019. Decoupled weight decay regularization. In *Proceedings of the International Conference on Learning Representations (ICLR)*.

Ximing Lu, Peter West, Rowan Zellers, Ronan Le Bras, Chandra Bhagavatula, and Yejin Choi. 2021. NeuroLogic decoding: (un)supervised neural text generation with predicate logic constraints. In *Proceedings of the Annual Conference of the North American Chapter of the Association for Computational Linguistics: Human Language Technologies (NAACL-HLT)*, pages 4288–4299.

Jonathan Mallinson, Aliaksei Severyn, Eric Malmi, and Guillermo Garrido. 2020. FELIX: Flexible Text Editing Through Tagging and Insertion. In *Proceedings of the Conference on Empirical Methods in Natural Language Processing (EMNLP)*, pages 1244–1255.

Louis Martin, Angela Fan, Éric de la Clergerie, Antoine Bordes, and Benoît Sagot. 2022. MUSS: Multilingual unsupervised sentence simplification by mining paraphrases. In *Proceedings of the Language Resources and Evaluation Conference (LREC)*, pages 1651–1664.

Daiki Nishihara, Tomoyuki Kajiwara, and Yuki Arase. 2019. Controllable text simplification with lexical constraint loss. In *Proceedings of the Annual Meeting of the Association for Computational Linguistics: Student Research Workshop*, pages 260–266.

Sergiu Nisioi, Sanja Štajner, Simone Paolo Ponzetto, and Liviu P. Dinu. 2017. Exploring neural text simplification models. In *Proceedings of the Annual Meeting of the Association for Computational Linguistics (ACL)*, pages 85–91.

Kostiantyn Omelianchuk, Vipul Raheja, and Oleksandr Skurzhanskyi. 2021. Text Simplification by Tagging. In *Proceedings of the 16th Workshop on Innovative Use of NLP for Building Educational Applications*, pages 11–25.

Ellie Pavlick, Pushpendre Rastogi, Juri Ganitkevitch, Benjamin Van Durme, and Chris Callison-Burch. 2015. PPDB 2.0: Better paraphrase ranking, fine-grained entailment relations, word embeddings, and style classification. In *Proceedings of the Joint Conference of the Annual Meeting of the Association for Computational Linguistics and the International Joint Conference on Natural Language Processing (ACL-IJCNLP)*, pages 425–430.

Carolina Scarton and Lucia Specia. 2018. Learning simplifications for specific target audiences. In *Proceedings of the Annual Meeting of the Association for Computational Linguistics (ACL)*, pages 712–718.

Matthew Shardlow. 2014. A survey of automated text simplification. *International Journal of Advanced Computer Science and Applications (IJACSA), Special Issue on Natural Language Processing*, 4(1).

Sai Surya, Abhijit Mishra, Anirban Laha, Parag Jain, and Karthik Sankaranarayanan. 2019. Unsupervised neural text simplification. In *Proceedings of the Annual Meeting of the Association for Computational Linguistics (ACL)*, pages 2058–2068.

Willian Massami Watanabe, Arnaldo Candido Junior, Vinícius Rodriguez Uzêda, Renata Pontin de Mattos Fortes, Thiago Alexandre Salgueiro Pardo, and Sandra Maria Aluísio. 2009. Facilita: Reading assistance for low-literacy readers. In *Proceedings of the ACM international conference on Design of communication*, pages 29–36.

Thomas Wolf, Lysandre Debut, Victor Sanh, Julien Chaumond, Clement Delangue, Anthony Moi, Pierric Cistac, Tim Rault, Remi Louf, Morgan Funtowicz, Joe Davison, Sam Shleifer, Patrick von Platen, Clara Ma, Yacine Jernite, Julien Plu, Canwen Xu, Teven Le Scao, Sylvain Gugger, Mariama Drame, Quentin Lhoest, and Alexander Rush. 2020. Transformers: State-of-the-art natural language processing. In *Proceedings of the Conference on Empirical Methods in Natural Language Processing (EMNLP)*, pages 38–45.

Wei Xu, Chris Callison-Burch, and Courtney Napoles. 2015. Problems in current text simplification research: New data can help. *Transactions of the Association for Computational Linguistics*, 3:283–297.

Wei Xu, Courtney Napoles, Ellie Pavlick, Quanze Chen, and Chris Callison-Burch. 2016. Optimizing statistical machine translation for text simplification. *Transactions of the Association for Computational Linguistics*, 4:401–415.

Xingxing Zhang and Mirella Lapata. 2017. Sentence simplification with deep reinforcement learning. In *Proceedings of the Conference on Empirical Methods in Natural Language Processing (EMNLP)*, pages 584–594.

Sanqiang Zhao, Rui Meng, Daqing He, Andi Saptono, and Bambang Parmanto. 2018. Integrating transformer and paraphrase rules for sentence simplification. In *Proceedings of the Conference on Empirical Methods in Natural Language Processing (EMNLP)*, pages 3164–3173.

A Details Regarding the Fine-Tuning Settings

Edit Operation Prediction Model We fine-tuned the pre-trained BERT-Base, uncased model for edit operation prediction. The batch size was 40, and the optimizer used was AdamW (Loshchilov and Hutter, 2019) with a learning rate of $1e-5$ with linear decay according to steps. We applied early stopping with the patience of 3 epochs to maximize the F1 score on the validation set.

Lexical Similarity Estimation Model We fine-tuned RoBERTa-Large for lexical similarity estimation. The batch size was 256, and the optimizer used was AdamW with a learning rate of $2e-5$ with linear decay according to steps. The training was terminated early with the patience of 7 epochs to minimize the mean squared error in the validation set.

An Investigation into the Effect of Control Tokens on Text Simplification

Zihao LI **Matthew Shardlow** **Saeed-Ul Hassan**
Manchester Metropolitan University
21443696@stu.mmu.ac.uk {m.shardlow,s.ul-hassan}@mmu.ac.uk

Abstract

Recent work on text simplification has focused on the use of control tokens to further the state of the art. However, it is not easy to further improve without an in-depth comprehension of the mechanisms underlying control tokens. One unexplored factor is the tokenization strategy, which we also explore. In this paper, we (1) reimplemented ACCESS, (2) explored the effects of varying control tokens, (3) tested the influences of different tokenization strategies, and (4) demonstrated how separate control tokens affect performance. We show variations of performance in the four control tokens separately. We also uncover how the design of control tokens could influence the performance and propose some suggestions for designing control tokens, which also reaches into other controllable text generation tasks.

1 Introduction

Text simplification (TS) refers to reducing linguistic complexity at both syntactic and lexical levels without losing the main content (Alva-Manchego et al., 2020b). It is commonly used to increase the readability of documents intended for children (De Belder and Moens, 2010), non-native speakers (Petersen and Ostendorf, 2007) and people with dyslexia. The requirements for simplified outcomes may vary among audiences (Xu et al., 2015), for instance, depending on the characteristics of the dataset. The task can be roughly divided into sentence-level simplification (Nishihara et al., 2019; Martin et al., 2020a) and paragraph-level simplification (Sun et al., 2020; Devaraj et al., 2021). The two types of tasks may have different focuses, and this paper only involves sentence-level simplification.

In order to fit the requirements of different user groups, some projects introduced explicit discrete prompts as control tokens to assist the model in learning from datasets and adjusting the simplifications (Martin et al., 2020a; Agrawal et al., 2021).

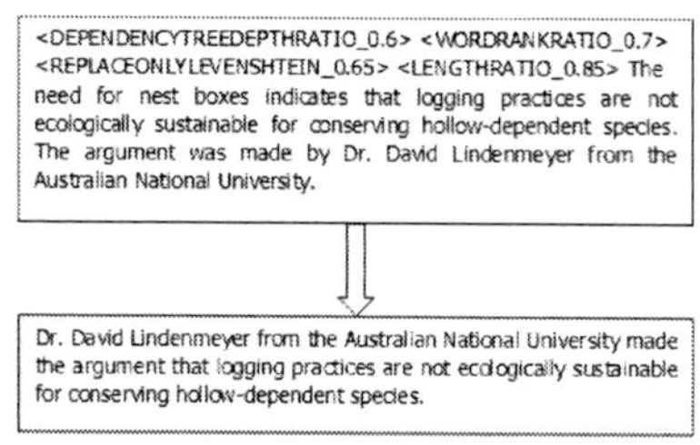

Figure 1: Example of input and output

By adjusting the value in different control tokens, researchers can manually adjust the characteristics of the output, such as length, syntactic and lexical difficulties, etc.

The control tokens are added to the beginning of the complex sentences and represent a relationship between that sentence and the desired input (such as the desired compression ratio). In addition, the numerical value also changes with the demands of the outcome. The format of the control token is: **<Token_*value*>**, where **Token** is a novel extra-vocabulary token with human interpretable meaning, and *value* is a numerical value indicating some relationship between the given input and output as shown in Figure 1 and Appendix A. The design of the control tokens is based on the need for adjustment. Multiple control tokens can be applied simultaneously, and four control tokens are used in this project.

Although the control tokens are manually crafted, how the control tokens change the outcome remains unstudied. To explore the mechanisms of control tokens in simplification, this paper proposes the following: (1) Verify the importance of control tokens in Section 4.2. (2) Reimplement the ACCESS (Martin et al., 2020a) used in the current state-of-the-art (SOTA) in Section 3.3. (3) Explore the influence of the variation of control tokens in the format in Section 4.1. And finally (4) investigate the effects of the tokenization method in Section 4.2.

Proceedings of the Workshop on Text Simplification, Accessibility, and Readability (TSAR-2022), pages 154 - 165
December 8, 2022 ©2022 Association for Computational Linguistics

2 Literature Review

Natural language generation (NLG) is a sub-task in natural language processing. There have been attempts to build an NLG system based on hand-crafted rules and to define the problem and features based on knowledge in the last century (Hovy, 1990; Reiter and Dale, 1997). With the development of computation power and the introduction of neural networks, more neural-network-based statistical methods were applied (Wen et al., 2015; Dušek and Jurčíček, 2016; Lebret et al., 2016; Mei et al., 2016). One important change happened with the publishing of the transformer architecture (Vaswani et al., 2017), which inspired the "pre-train and fine-tune" paradigm. Later, due to the new architecture outperforming existing ones in both performance and computation consumption, the transformer architecture and its derivatives occupied a dominant position in the NLG domain (Yang et al., 2019; Floridi and Chiriatti, 2020; Lewis et al., 2020). As a sub-task of NLG, text simplification can also be regarded as monolingual machine translation (Wubben et al., 2012). With the development of sequence-to-sequence machine translation, text simplification also drew more attention (Guo et al., 2018; Surya et al., 2019; Omelianchuk et al., 2021)

In recent years, researchers tried to introduce explicit parameters to control the simplified output (Nishihara et al., 2019; Martin et al., 2020a; Agrawal et al., 2021). Martin et al. (2020a) introduced four hyper-parameters in the AudienCe-CEntric Sentence Simplification (ACCESS): the number of characters, Levenshtein similarity (Levenshtein et al., 1966), word rank and dependency tree depth, which are used to control the length, similarity, lexical complexity and syntactic complexity respectively. With the help of the parameters, users can modify the generated simplification based on their needs. However, these parameters may be less straightforward for lay users, and Agrawal et al. (2021) replaced the detailed parameters with simplification grades. In addition, a minor change in these parameters may significantly affect the readability and fluency of output. Although the value set that maximises the benchmark scores can be given, it may be of little help to the end-users with specific requirements. Further exploration of the effect and proper parameter preferences needs to be made to guide and help lay users adjust these parameters based on their needs.

Another novel research on the training datasets is multilingual unsupervised sentence simplification (MUSS) (Martin et al., 2020b). They fine-tuned BART (Lewis et al., 2020) on their mined paraphrases datasets instead of complex-simple parallel corpora and found that with the help of ACCESS, the unsupervised model outperformed the other unsupervised text simplification models and became the latest SOTA. As an extension of ACCESS, the authors improved the design of control tokens and changed the tokenization strategy. They showed that performance differences between the two types of datasets might be acceptable only if the mined paraphrase dataset is good enough. Training on paraphrase datasets provides more options than training solely on the supervised datasets and there is a nearly unlimited amount of unlabelled data. They also found that the performance of the combination of unsupervised and supervised training is the best, which is very similar to the pre-train and fine-tune paradigm. Although multilingual tests were made in the MUSS, they were delivered separately and had little interference with the aim of this project. Thus, there is little need to focus on their research in French and Spanish.

The metrics also play a vital role in evaluating the performance of models. Although current metrics can hardly compete with human evaluations, they can still partially reflect the performance in certain indexes. Among the popular metrics, there are reference-based metrics like Bilingual evaluation understudy (BLEU) (Papineni et al., 2002) and Recall-Oriented Understudy for Gisting Evaluation (ROUGE) (Lin, 2004) and non-reference-based metrics like Flesch-Kincaid Grade Level (FKGL) (Flesch, 1948). Currently, the most popular metric for text simplification is the system output against references and against the input sentence (SARI) (Xu et al., 2016). SARI is designed especially for text simplification tasks, which evaluates the outputs in aspects of adding, keeping and deleting. Although it is found to have some deviation from human judgement, SARI is still a valuable metric to evaluate simplicity (Alva-Manchego et al., 2021). As for the non-reference-based metrics, the BERT score is a BERT-based metric that evaluates the similarity between input and output by calculating the correlation in the embedding space (Zhang et al., 2019). It is found to have a high correlation with human judgement (Scialom et al., 2021). By combining the metrics, the performance can be evaluated more comprehensively.

Strategy	Raw Input	'<DEPENDENCYTREEDEPTHRATIO_0.6>'
Default	IDs	[0, 41552, 41372, 9309, 23451, . . . , 2571, 6454, 1215, 288, 4, . . .]
	tokenization	['<s>', '<', 'DEP', 'END', 'ENCY', . . . , '_', '0', '.', '6', '>', . . .]
Joint	IDs	[0, 50265, . . .]
	tokenization	['<s>', '<DEPENDENCYTREEDEPTHRATIO_0.6>', . . .]
Separate	IDs	[0, 50265, 50266, 15698, . . .]
	tokenization	['<s>', '<DEPENDENCYTREEDEPTHRATIO_', '0.6', '>', . . .]

Table 1: Tokenization under differing strategies for the input starting with: '<DEPENDENCYTREEDEPTH-RATIO_0.6>'

3 Experiments

3.1 Quantisation differences

As mentioned in the literature review, there are 4 types of control tokens: <DEPENDENCYTREEDEPTH_x> (DTD), <WORDRANK_x> (WR), <REPLACEONLYLEVENSHTEIN_x> (LV) and <LENGTHRATIO_x> (LR). In the preprocessing step, they are calculated and added to the beginning of complex sentences in the complex dataset. As an augmentation to the control tokens, the calculated values are rounded to the nearest 0.05. However, in the original optimisation process, the calculated values by the algorithm provided by the Nevergrad (Rapin and Teytaud, 2018) API have high precision and verbose digits, just like the first line in Table 2. During the reimplementation, we found that only the first one or two digits are recognised as input values and the remaining digits didn't provide any meaningful instruction. On the contrary, it brought unnecessary information to the system and even lowered the performance of the model. Thus we replaced the continuous values with discrete ones like 0.2, 0.25, 0.3, ..., 1.0 and changed to the corresponding discrete algorithm in Nevergrad (Rapin and Teytaud, 2018).

3.2 Tokenization Strategies

One of the aims of this project is to explore the effects of tokenization strategies. As shown in Table 1, the default tokenization method in the MUSS project is regarding the control tokens as plain text. In comparison, we added 2 more tokenization strategies: One is to regard the whole control token as one token in the tokenizer; the other is to break the control token into a combination of type and value and add them separately to the tokenizer. These 2 strategies are achieved by manually adding all possible control tokens to the dictionary of the tokenizer. This will affect not only the evaluation and optimisation process but also the training process, thus each tokenization strategy requires an independent fine-tuned model.

3.3 Reimplementation of ACCESS

One of the goals of this project is to reimplement and verify the effect of control tokens in the current SOTA. However, since the main focus of this project is on the control tokens, instead of training on both supervised and unsupervised datasets, it would be more practical to claim the reimplementation of ACCESS rather than MUSS. In order to build a unified baseline, this project also applied the BART model (Lewis et al., 2020), which is adopted in the MUSS project. The original project can be divided into the following sections: data mining, preprocessing, training, evaluation and optimisation.

Since the goal is verification, there is no need to rewrite the code for all sections. Thus only the codes related to training and some other peripheral functions have been altered to achieve similar results. The other functions, such as preprocessing and optimisation, still kept most of the original code. The original core API used for training is fairseq. This project replaced it with another open-source API — Huggingface. Huggingface provides a collection of the most popular pre-trained models and datasets, including the BART (Lewis et al., 2020) and a unified, advanced and user-friendly API to achieve the most common applications, which made it easier for future upgrading and modification. The hyper-parameters of models in the reimplementation, including the learning rate and weight decay, are set to be identical to the original project so that the influence of irrelevant factors can be lowered. The last difference between the reimplementation and the original project is the tokeniser. The tokeniser in the reimplementation is the BART-base byte-pair encoding(BPE) tokeniser instead of the GPT2 BPE tokeniser (Radford et al., 2019). Both tokenisers serve the same purpose and perform very similarly to each other. The new one consumes fewer computer resources, which presumably causes only a little effect on the results. Due to the variation of control tokens, the optimisation algorithm has also changed. The original algorithm is the OneplusOne provided by Nevergrad (Rapin and Teytaud, 2018), and the current one is the PortfolioDiscreteOnePlusOne, which fits the discrete values better. As for the metrics, the SARI score is kept as the primary evaluation method (Xu et al., 2016), and the BERT score is introduced as a co-reference.

However, due to the limitation of computation resources and mass fine-tuning demands of models with different tokenization strategies, this project also downgraded the training scale and limited the epochs in both baseline and reimplementation. Here are the changes applied to both the reimplementation and the baseline as follows:

- All results are from models trained in BART-base instead of BART-large.
- All training processes are set to 10 epochs only.
- All models are trained on Wikilarge (Zhang and Lapata, 2017) only.

As explained earlier, each tokenization strategies is corresponding to one model and there is a total of 16 models that need to be fine-tuned. This is why only BART-base is applied and the training epochs are limited. As for the reason for choosing 10 as the targeting epoch number, it is because the training loss for models with combined control tokens has reached 0.85 and decreased very slowly between epochs, while the validation loss started increasing. If continuing training, the over-fitting problem may occur. The results of the baseline shown in the next section can also partially prove the training process is probably long enough.

3.4 Training process

General NLP tasks can be divided into three steps: data preprocessing, training and evaluation. The preprocessing step followed the MUSS project (Martin et al., 2020b). In this project, there is one more step: optimisation. The authors defined four types of prompts used as control tokens to manipulate the features of the outputs. Each control token is designed to represent one character of the sentence. The <DEPENDENCYTREEDEPTH_x> represents the syntactic complexity; The <WORDRANK_x> represents the lexical complexity; The <REPLACEONLYLEVENSHTEIN_x> represents the inverse similarity of input and output at the letter level; The <LENGTHRATIO_x> represents the length ratio of input and output. The value of each control token is calculated based on the reference complex-simple pairs in the training dataset, which is Wikilarge in this project (Zhang and Lapata, 2017). After the calculation, these control tokens will be added to the beginning of complex sentences, and the model will be trained on this preprocessed dataset. In addition to the combined control tokens, this project also explored the effects of a single control token; only the corresponding control tokens are kept in that dataset.

The next step is training. It follows the majority of fine-tuning processes for pretrained language models. By feeding the preprocessed complex-simple sentence pairs to the model, the model is expected to learn how to simplify texts and the meaning of each control token. As explained in the tokenization strategy, each tokenization method demands a separate model. To compare the performance of different tokenization methods, except the baseline, 15 models are fine-tuned in the experiment: 3 models with full control tokens and 12 models with only one control token. The models with one control token are used to verify the importance of combined control tokens and provide supportive evidence for the assumption.

The following step is evaluation. Thanks to Easier Automatic Sentence Simplification Evaluation(EASSE), multiple evaluation metrics can be applied at the same time easily (Alva-Manchego et al., 2019). The SARI score is adopted as the primary metric to compare with the current SOTA, while the BERT score is added as a second reference. Different from the common applications in other projects, the BERT score in this project is the correlation between the output and references. One coefficient array can be used to combine different evaluation metrics and give a weighted score. However, in this project, we also follow the operations in MUSS and maximise the SARI score, so only the SARI score is taken into account, and the corresponding coefficient is set to 1. The models will be evaluated on the ASSET (Alva-Manchego et al., 2020a) test dataset, which contains 359 complex-

Prompts	SARI	BERT	DTD	WR	LV	LR
Baseline	43.83	—	0.249...	0.814...	0.758...	0.858...
Default	44.00±0.05	0.754	0.25	0.8	0.75	0.85
Joint tokens	44.02±0.05	0.769	0.25	0.8	0.75	0.85
Separate tokens	44.04±0.05	0.754	0.25	0.8	0.75	0.85
Default	44.36±0.05	0.733	0.6	0.7	0.65	0.85
Joint tokens	44.58±0.05	0.794	0.35	0.85	0.8	0.85
Separate tokens	44.53±0.05	0.784	0.35	0.75	0.8	0.85
Default	43.34±0.06	0.827	0.6	0.85	0.85	0.85
Joint tokens	43.83±0.06	0.829	0.6	0.85	0.85	0.85
Separate tokens	43.99±0.06	0.828	0.6	0.85	0.85	0.85

Table 2: Results on SARI and BERT score under differing tokenization strategies, with comparison to the baseline (top 4 rows of results), optimised parameter values (middle 3 rows) and values reported on unified parameters (last 3 rows).

simple pairs, and each complex sentence has ten reference simplifications.

The last step is optimisation. As mentioned in previous sections, the value of control tokens is limited to a small range. All options fall between 0.2 to 1.5 except the Levenshtein, whose upper boundary is limited to 1 due to the calculation method that divides the minimum replacement steps to change from the original sentence to the target sentence by the maximum possible steps of replacement. Only these options are provided during optimisation, and the optimisation problem is reduced to finding the best value combination of control tokens within the range. Even though only finite combinations can be applied to the model, the optimisation algorithm is still supported by the Nevergrad (Rapin and Teytaud, 2018) API to compare with the current SOTA. With a budget of limitation to repeat the optimisation process 64 times, the algorithm can find a relatively optimised result. In order to ensure the reliability of the score under the optimised combination, a bootstrapping on the ASSET (Alva-Manchego et al., 2020a) test dataset will be executed by resampling the dataset 200 times and hence generate a 95% confidence interval.

4 Results

4.1 Overall performance

Following the setting in reimplementation, the baseline from the original code of the current SOTA is 43.83 on the ASSET (Alva-Manchego et al., 2020a) test dataset, which is consistent with the reported score in the MUSS in the corresponding scenario, which is 43.63±0.71. There is no confidence interval and BERT score in the baseline because the baseline is generated by rerunning the code in MUSS by altering specific settings only. The actual output lacks these 2 features. As shown in the top 4 rows in the table2, the SARI score with 95% confidence in the reimplementation is slightly higher than the baseline. The middle 3 rows show the best SARI score with optimised options of control tokens. Among the 3 methods, the joint tokens had the highest SARI score. Interestingly, the BERT score is not always proportional to the SARI score, but the BERT score of optimal value is still quite high. The optimised values of control tokens are pretty close in all situations except the DTD. The bottom 3 rows show the performance difference under a unified value of control tokens. The unified value is the average value of all possible values for each control token. Under the unified condition, the separated one outperformed the other two, and the default tokenization method still performs worst. As for the BERT score, the joint tokenization method still outperforms the other two.

4.2 Effects of single control tokens

In order to verify the effects of each single control token, a more detailed investigation of the SARI score was done on control tokens respectively and the results are shown in Figure 2. Except for the Figure 2(b), all 3 tokenization methods show a high consistency in the curves and have a common minimum at the value of 1. As shown in Table 4, it is mainly caused by the low score in both deletion and adding operations.

In addition to the curves, the differences in tokenization methods have marginal effects on the scores while the value of control tokens can change the performance significantly. In Figure 2(a) and

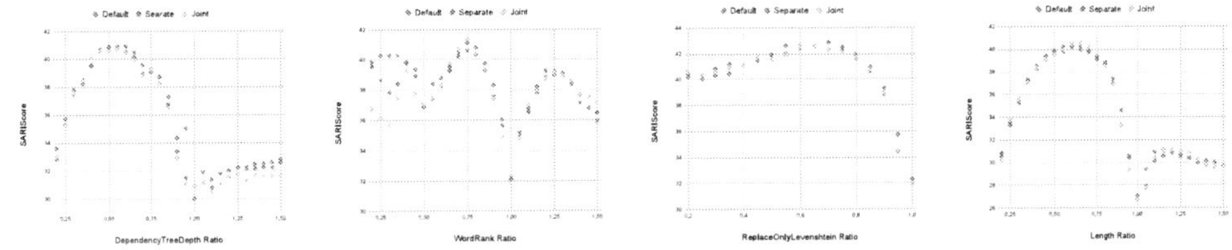

(a) DependencyTreeDepth Ratio (b) WordRank Ratio (c) ReplaceOnlyLevenshtein Ratio (d) Length Ratio

Figure 2: The effect of varying control tokens with different tokenization strategies on SARI Score.

Prompts	SARI	BERT	DTD
Default	40.82 ±0.05	0.805	0.55
	40.54 ±0.05	0.799	0.6
Separate	40.68±0.06	0.804	0.55
	40.87±0.05	0.801	0.6
Joint	40.71±0.06	0.812	0.55
	40.43±0.06	0.800	0.6

Prompts	SARI	BERT	WR
Default	40.61±0.06	0.720	0.75
	40.80±0.06	0.776	0.8
Separate	41.08±0.06	0.738	0.75
	40.32±0.05	0.797	0.8
Joint	**41.42±0.06**	0.733	0.75
	40.43±0.06	0.782	0.8

Prompts	SARI	BERT	LV
Default	42.52±0.06	0.750	0.65
	42.26±0.08	0.785	0.7
Separate	42.55±0.06	0.747	0.65
	42.86±0.06	0.782	0.7
Joint	42.63±0.06	0.761	0.65
	42.31±0.07	0.787	0.7

Prompts	SARI	BERT	LR
Default	40.15±0.06	0.758	0.6
	39.91±0.05	0.782	0.65
Separate	40.25±0.06	0.760	0.6
	40.27±0.05	0.781	0.55
Joint	40.46±0.05	0.758	0.6
	40.64±0.05	0.785	0.65

Table 3: Results on SARI and BERT scores of peak points in different control tokens.

Control Token	Value	SARI_add	SARI_keep	SARI_del	SARI
DTD_joint	0.2	2.71	27.03	69.32	33.02
	0.6	5.24	58.50	57.51	40.41
	1.0	3.30	62.64	26.68	30.87
	1.5	4.41	62.66	27.82	31.63
WR_joint	0.5	5.10	37.47	68.54	37.04
	0.75	6.65	54.91	62.57	41.37
	1.0	3.38	62.04	29.90	31.77
	1.25	4.19	54.88	58.35	39.14
LV_joint	0.2	7.15	50.83	63.83	40.60
	0.7	9.14	60.15	57.60	42.30
	1.0	2.25	61.62	32.17	32.01
LR_joint	0.2	1.80	19.27	69.46	30.18
	0.65	5.54	56.84	59.36	40.56
	1.0	2.43	62.42	15.26	26.70
	1.2	5.80	61.46	26.03	31.10

Table 4: SARI score by operation at turning points in Figure 2.

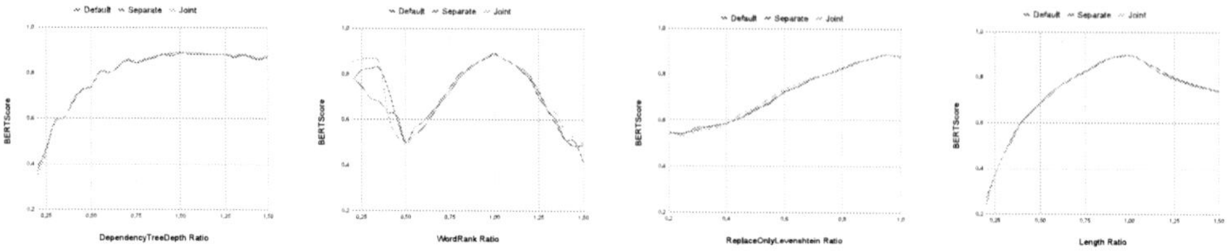

(a) DependencyTreeDepth Ratio (b) WordRank Ratio (c) ReplaceOnlyLevenshtein Ratio (d) Length Ratio

Figure 3: The effect of varying control tokens with different tokenization strategies on BERT score.

2(c), the separate tokenization method shows the highest peak point, while in Figure 2(b) and Figure 2(d), the joint tokenization method has the best performance. The corresponding Table 3 also shows the scores in pairs under a unified value. Although the advantage is not as clear as the combined control tokens, the optimised SARI score of either separate or joint tokenization methods is still slightly higher than the default tokenization method.

The Table 4 is designed to help readers better understand the reason for variations in Figure 2. It shows some local minimum or maximum points within the domain and the corresponding SARI score by operations. The addition score is much lower than the keeping and deletion. It is because there is only limited adding operation in the references and much more expression options to carry a similar meaning, which leads to a low hit rate of the addition operation. At the same time, the keep and deletion are chosen from the existing input and thus have a much bigger hit rate and score.

As for the BERT score, as shown in Figure 3, nearly all 3 tokenization strategies show high similarity to each other except Figure 3(b). The figures show that near all models have the highest BERT score around 1. Since the BERT score calculates the correlation between the output and references, when the control token is set to 1, the model processes nothing, and the output is very similar to the input. Under this situation, as shown in Table 4, the SARI_keep reaches the top. However, the peak of BERT score in 3(c) slightly deviates to the left, which shows that the references and input are not identical.

5 Discussion and Future Directions

One phenomenon found during the optimisation section in the original project is that the score of recommended optimisation is even lower than the default values of control tokens at 0.8. A hypothesis emerged that continuous optimisation is not an ideal option to maximise the score. As shown in the first four rows in Table 2, the score in reimplementation is higher even in similar values. There are several reasons: the algorithm is not working as expected or the optimisation budget is not large enough to find better optimisations. The default tokenization method in the MUSS project that breaks the control tokens into pieces brings more noise and probably lowers the performance. Apart from the verbosity in optimal values, the long tokenization of the control token is another concern of noisy input. Although the results above shows sign of such problem, it may become more serious with the increasing of control tokens, especially for short sentences. It would be wiser to limit the unnecessary noise in the input to a lower level.

Figure 2 and Table 4 expose the reason for variation with the control token and provide a good illustration of nature in each control token. In single control tokens, the peak points mainly fall between 0.6 and 0.7, and the score decreases with the value deviating from the peak point. However, there are still some differences among the control tokens. In the *DependencyTreeDepth Ratio* and *Length Ratio*, the reduction is more dramatic than the other 2. In both graphs, the SARI_add decreases with the value deviating from the peak point and increases slowly when the value is bigger than 1. The SARI_keep and SARI_del fluctuate in the form of 2 half-phase shifted sine functions and the maximum sum is found in between the peaks. The graph of the *WordRank Ratio* shows some diversity in both Figure 2(b) and 3(b) among the tokenization methods. Although there is no explanation for the deviations, the deviations show the potential of combining different tokenization methods. When focusing on the main section from

0.5 to 1, the graph shows characteristics similar to the graphs in the previous 2 control tokens. As for the *ReplaceOnlyLevenshtein Ratio*, the slope is milder on the left side and it seems to have less effect on the SARI score. Unlike the other 3 control tokens, this control token can only indicate the intensity of change but not the direction of change. Although the combined effects are still under research, a more effective control token could be a better solution.

As for the optimal value, the most significant variation between single and combined control tokens is in DependencyTreeDepth Ratio. The optimal value in combined control tokens in the joint and separate tokenization method is 0.35 instead of 0.6. Although no direct comparison is listed in Table 2, comparing the middle and bottom three rows makes it pretty clear that 0.35 has a better SARI score. The correlation among the control tokens presumably causes this variation. There are also deviations in the other three control tokens. If the four control tokens can be designed to work independently, the graph on a single control token can be directly used to find the optimal value. However, the graph of combined control tokens is bound to have some distortions for now. Based on the detailed graph, it is also clear that the value of control tokens can significantly affect the performance of the models trained in this way and should be treated carefully.

Another interesting finding between SARI and BERT in this paper is that most BERT score for optimal value is around 0.78 to 0.8. However, as shown in Figure 3(b) and 3(d), there are more than 1 points that have such value, so the BERT score alone cannot be used to evaluate the text simplification results. It may be a necessary but not sufficient condition for a good simplification. Since the SARI score is not perfect and relies on references, it is important to build non-reference-based metrics to evaluate the model on a different genre of corpora. The BERT score may play a role in these new metrics. Thus, this guess is worth further verification in future work.

In addition to the values, as shown in Table 3, the tokenization methods can also affect the peak score. In the curves, there are different optimised methods for each certain point. Although the performance differences may be caused by the fine-tuned models on a lower training scale, they may still imply performance variations between tokenization methods. Considering the various requirements of lay users, a mixed tokenization method based on the performance curve may maximise the model's performance at different points better than a fixed one. Although it remains unclear whether there will be the same effects in the combined control tokens, the mixed tokenizations method can be still promising with the appearance of more different control tokens. However, a more lightweight and efficient training method should be introduced to solve the problem of balancing cost and effect.

5.1 Future Work

In the future, one of the main tasks is to reimplement control tokens in different models or learning strategies so that training can be more lightweight and less time-consumed. Another goal is to build new non-reference-based metrics and replace SARI, which will significantly contribute to the development. However, it is not easy to understand the relationship between the performance and control tokens. A further investigation of the complex relationship between SARI and combined control tokens is also worth doing. Although the five-dimension graph may be less visualised, it can still provide some guidance on how to apply the control tokens. Designing and introducing new control tokens is another novel direction. The control tokens may be further simplified or optimised with a deeper inspection of the control tokens and SARI score. In addition to that, current optimisation procedure works only on the dataset level and needs more precise prediction on sentence level. A sentence level prediction model to the optimal value of control token may be worth considering. Lastly, whether there is a similar phenomenon of control tokens in other controllable text generation tasks is also an important question.

5.2 Concluding Remarks

In the investigation, we have shown the results and importance of control tokens with different values and tokenization methods, which can be used to balance user intention and performance. We proposed some improvements in quantisation, compared the influences of different tokenization strategies of control tokens and proposed possible further improvement means. Although the proposed suggestions may improve text simplification tasks marginally, they may also be generalised to prompts designing on other controllable NLP tasks.

References

Sweta Agrawal, Weijia Xu, and Marine Carpuat. 2021. A non-autoregressive edit-based approach to controllable text simplification. In *Findings of the Association for Computational Linguistics: ACL-IJCNLP 2021*, pages 3757–3769.

Fernando Alva-Manchego, Louis Martin, Antoine Bordes, Carolina Scarton, Benoît Sagot, and Lucia Specia. 2020a. ASSET: A dataset for tuning and evaluation of sentence simplification models with multiple rewriting transformations. In *Proceedings of the 58th Annual Meeting of the Association for Computational Linguistics*, pages 4668–4679, Online. Association for Computational Linguistics.

Fernando Alva-Manchego, Louis Martin, Carolina Scarton, and Lucia Specia. 2019. EASSE: Easier automatic sentence simplification evaluation. In *Proceedings of the 2019 Conference on Empirical Methods in Natural Language Processing and the 9th International Joint Conference on Natural Language Processing (EMNLP-IJCNLP): System Demonstrations*, pages 49–54, Hong Kong, China. Association for Computational Linguistics.

Fernando Alva-Manchego, Carolina Scarton, and Lucia Specia. 2020b. Data-driven sentence simplification: Survey and benchmark. *Computational Linguistics*, 46(1):135–187.

Fernando Alva-Manchego, Carolina Scarton, and Lucia Specia. 2021. The (un)suitability of automatic evaluation metrics for text simplification. *Computational Linguistics*, 47(4):861–889.

Jan De Belder and Marie-Francine Moens. 2010. Text simplification for children. In *Prroceedings of the SIGIR workshop on accessible search systems*, pages 19–26. ACM; New York.

Ashwin Devaraj, Byron C Wallace, Iain J Marshall, and Junyi Jessy Li. 2021. Paragraph-level simplification of medical texts. In *Proceedings of the conference. Association for Computational Linguistics. North American Chapter. Meeting*, volume 2021, page 4972. NIH Public Access.

Ondřej Dušek and Filip Jurčíček. 2016. Sequence-to-sequence generation for spoken dialogue via deep syntax trees and strings. *arXiv preprint arXiv:1606.05491*.

Rudolph Flesch. 1948. A new readability yardstick. *Journal of applied psychology*, 32(3):221.

Luciano Floridi and Massimo Chiriatti. 2020. Gpt-3: Its nature, scope, limits, and consequences. *Minds and Machines*, 30(4):681–694.

Han Guo, Ramakanth Pasunuru, and Mohit Bansal. 2018. Dynamic multi-level multi-task learning for sentence simplification. *CoRR*, abs/1806.07304.

Eduard H Hovy. 1990. Pragmatics and natural language generation. *Artificial Intelligence*, 43(2):153–197.

Rémi Lebret, David Grangier, and Michael Auli. 2016. Neural text generation from structured data with application to the biography domain. *arXiv preprint arXiv:1603.07771*.

Vladimir I Levenshtein et al. 1966. Binary codes capable of correcting deletions, insertions, and reversals. In *Soviet physics doklady*, volume 10, pages 707–710. Soviet Union.

Mike Lewis, Yinhan Liu, Naman Goyal, Marjan Ghazvininejad, Abdelrahman Mohamed, Omer Levy, Veselin Stoyanov, and Luke Zettlemoyer. 2020. BART: Denoising sequence-to-sequence pre-training for natural language generation, translation, and comprehension. In *Proceedings of the 58th Annual Meeting of the Association for Computational Linguistics*, pages 7871–7880, Online. Association for Computational Linguistics.

Chin-Yew Lin. 2004. ROUGE: A package for automatic evaluation of summaries. In *Text Summarization Branches Out*, pages 74–81, Barcelona, Spain. Association for Computational Linguistics.

Louis Martin, Éric de la Clergerie, Benoît Sagot, and Antoine Bordes. 2020a. Controllable sentence simplification. In *Proceedings of the 12th Language Resources and Evaluation Conference*, pages 4689–4698, Marseille, France. European Language Resources Association.

Louis Martin, Angela Fan, Éric de la Clergerie, Antoine Bordes, and Benoît Sagot. 2020b. Multilingual unsupervised sentence simplification. *arXiv preprint arXiv:2005.00352*.

Hongyuan Mei, Mohit Bansal, and Matthew R Walter. 2016. Listen, attend, and walk: Neural mapping of navigational instructions to action sequences. In *Thirtieth AAAI Conference on Artificial Intelligence*.

Daiki Nishihara, Tomoyuki Kajiwara, and Yuki Arase. 2019. Controllable text simplification with lexical constraint loss. In *Proceedings of the 57th Annual Meeting of the Association for Computational Linguistics: Student Research Workshop*, pages 260–266, Florence, Italy. Association for Computational Linguistics.

Kostiantyn Omelianchuk, Vipul Raheja, and Oleksandr Skurzhanskyi. 2021. Text simplification by tagging. *arXiv preprint arXiv:2103.05070*.

Kishore Papineni, Salim Roukos, Todd Ward, and Wei-Jing Zhu. 2002. Bleu: a method for automatic evaluation of machine translation. In *Proceedings of the 40th Annual Meeting of the Association for Computational Linguistics*, pages 311–318, Philadelphia, Pennsylvania, USA. Association for Computational Linguistics.

Sarah E Petersen and Mari Ostendorf. 2007. Text simplification for language learners: a corpus analysis. In *Workshop on speech and language technology in education*. Citeseer.

Alec Radford, Jeffrey Wu, Rewon Child, David Luan, Dario Amodei, Ilya Sutskever, et al. 2019. Language models are unsupervised multitask learners. *OpenAI blog*, 1(8):9.

J. Rapin and O. Teytaud. 2018. Nevergrad - A gradient-free optimization platform. `https://GitHub.com/FacebookResearch/Nevergrad`.

Ehud Reiter and Robert Dale. 1997. Building applied natural language generation systems. *Natural Language Engineering*, 3(1):57–87.

Thomas Scialom, Louis Martin, Jacopo Staiano, Éric Villemonte de la Clergerie, and Benoît Sagot. 2021. Rethinking automatic evaluation in sentence simplification. *arXiv preprint arXiv:2104.07560*.

Renliang Sun, Zhe Lin, and Xiaojun Wan. 2020. On the helpfulness of document context to sentence simplification. In *Proceedings of the 28th International Conference on Computational Linguistics*, pages 1411–1423, Barcelona, Spain (Online). International Committee on Computational Linguistics.

Sai Surya, Abhijit Mishra, Anirban Laha, Parag Jain, and Karthik Sankaranarayanan. 2019. Unsupervised neural text simplification. In *Proceedings of the 57th Annual Meeting of the Association for Computational Linguistics*, pages 2058–2068, Florence, Italy. Association for Computational Linguistics.

Ashish Vaswani, Noam Shazeer, Niki Parmar, Jakob Uszkoreit, Llion Jones, Aidan N Gomez, Łukasz Kaiser, and Illia Polosukhin. 2017. Attention is all you need. *Advances in neural information processing systems*, 30.

Tsung-Hsien Wen, Milica Gasic, Nikola Mrksic, Pei-Hao Su, David Vandyke, and Steve Young. 2015. Semantically conditioned lstm-based natural language generation for spoken dialogue systems. *arXiv preprint arXiv:1508.01745*.

Sander Wubben, Antal van den Bosch, and Emiel Krahmer. 2012. Sentence simplification by monolingual machine translation. In *Proceedings of the 50th Annual Meeting of the Association for Computational Linguistics (Volume 1: Long Papers)*, pages 1015–1024, Jeju Island, Korea. Association for Computational Linguistics.

Wei Xu, Chris Callison-Burch, and Courtney Napoles. 2015. Problems in current text simplification research: New data can help. *Transactions of the Association for Computational Linguistics*, 3:283–297.

Wei Xu, Courtney Napoles, Ellie Pavlick, Quanze Chen, and Chris Callison-Burch. 2016. Optimizing statistical machine translation for text simplification. *Transactions of the Association for Computational Linguistics*, 4:401–415.

Zhilin Yang, Zihang Dai, Yiming Yang, Jaime Carbonell, Russ R Salakhutdinov, and Quoc V Le. 2019. Xlnet: Generalized autoregressive pretraining for language understanding. *Advances in neural information processing systems*, 32.

Tianyi Zhang, Varsha Kishore, Felix Wu, Kilian Q Weinberger, and Yoav Artzi. 2019. Bertscore: Evaluating text generation with bert. *arXiv preprint arXiv:1904.09675*.

Xingxing Zhang and Mirella Lapata. 2017. Sentence simplification with deep reinforcement learning. *arXiv preprint arXiv:1703.10931*.

Appendices

A

Source	Reflection nebulae are usually blue because the scattering is more efficient for blue light than red (this is the same scattering process that gives us blue skies and red sunsets).
LR_1.2	Reflection nebulae are usually blue because the scattering is more efficient for blue light than red (this is the same scattering process that gives us blue skies and red sunsets) and because the light reflects off of them.
LR_1.0	Reflection nebulae are usually blue because the scattering is more efficient for blue light than red (this is the same scattering process that gives us blue skies and red sunsets).
LR_0.8	Reflection nebulae are usually blue because the scattering is more efficient for blue light than red (this is the same scattering process that gives us blue skies).
LR_0.6	Reflection nebulae are usually blue because the scattering is more efficient for blue light than red.
LR_0.4	Reflection nebulae are usually blue because the scattering is more efficient.
LR_0.2	Reflection nebulae are usually blue in color.

Table 5: Effect of varying Length ratio with the others remain 1.0.

Source	Moderate to severe damage extended up the Atlantic coastline and as far inland as West Virginia.
LV_0.8	Moderate to severe damage happened along the Atlantic coast and as far inland as West Virginia.
LV_0.6	Moderate to severe damage happened along the Atlantic coast and as far inland as West Virginia.
LV_0.4	In West Virginia, the storm caused moderate to severe damage along the Atlantic coast and inland.
LV_0.2	The National Hurricane Center (NHC) said that the storm was a "major hurricane" and not a tropical storm.

Table 6: Effect of varying ReplaceOnlyLevenshtein ratio with the others remain 1.0.

Source	He will abjure his allegiance to the king.
WR_0.8 LV_1.0	He will abjure his allegiance to the king.
WR_0.6 LV_1.0	He will abjure his allegiance to the king.
WR_0.8 LV_0.8	He will not give up his allegiance to the king.
WR_0.6 LV_0.8	He will not give up his power to the king.
WR_0.4 LV_0.8	He will not follow the orders of the king.
WR_0.2 LV_0.8	He will abjure his loyalty to the king.
WR_0.6 LV_0.8 LR_0.75	He will not follow the king anymore.

Table 7: Effect of varying WordRank ratio and some other ratios with the others remain 1.0.

Source	The four canonical texts are the Gospel of Matthew, Gospel of Mark, Gospel of Luke and Gospel of John, probably written between AD 65 and 100 (see also the Gospel according to the Hebrews).
DTD_1.2	The four canonical texts are the Gospel of Matthew, Gospel of Mark and Gospel of Luke , probably written between AD 65 and AD 100 (see also the Gospel according to the Hebrews).
DTD_0.8	The four canonical texts are the Gospel of Matthew, Gospel of Mark and Gospel of Luke. They are probably written between AD 65 and 100 (see also the Gospel according to the Hebrews).
DTD_0.6	The four canonical texts are the Gospel of Matthew, Gospel of Mark and Gospel of Luke. The Gospel of John was probably written between AD 65 and 100 (see also the Gospel according to the Hebrews).
DTD_0.4	The four canonical texts are the Gospel of Matthew, Gospel of Mark and Gospel of Luke. The Gospel of John was probably written between AD 65 and 100 (see also the Gospel according to the Hebrews).

Table 8: Effect of varying DependencyTreeDepth ratio with the others remain 1.0.

Divide-and-Conquer Text Simplification by Scalable Data Enhancement

Sanqiang Zhao
Amazon Alexa AI
sanqiang@amazon.com*

Rui Meng
Salesforce
ruimeng@salesforce.com†

Daqing He
University of Pittsburgh
daqing@pitt.edu

Hui Su
Wechat AI
aaronsu@tencent.com

Abstract

Text simplification, whose aim is to reduce reading difficulty, can be decomposed into four discrete rewriting operations: substitution, deletion, reordering, and splitting. However, due to a large distribution discrepancy between existing training data and human-annotated data, models may learn improper operations, thus lead to poor generalization capabilities. In order to bridge this gap, we propose a novel data enhancement method, SimSim, that generates training pairs by simulating specific simplification operations. Experiments show that the models trained with SimSim outperform multiple strong baselines and achieve the better SARI on the Turk and ASSET datasets. The newly constructed dataset SimSim is available at https://github.com/Sanqiang/sent_simplicaition_data.

1 Introduction & Related Work

Text simplification is a task to reduce the complexity of a text while retain its original meaning. It can facilitate people with low-literacy skills or language impairments, such as children and individuals with dyslexia (Rello et al., 2013) and aphasia (Carroll et al., 1999), to read and understand complicated materials (Watanabe et al., 2009). Normally, substitution, deletion, reordering, and splitting are considered as four core operations for performing text simplification (Zhu et al., 2010). Thus an ideal model should be capable of executing these operations appropriately to simplify a text. However, by examining the degree that each operation is exerted in different datasets, we observe that there is an salient discrepancy between the human annotation and existing training data that is widely used for training simplification models. To alleviate this discrepancy, we propose an unsupervised data construction method that distills each simplifying operation into data via different automatic data enhancement measures. The empirical results demonstrate that the resulting dataset SimSim can support models to achieve better performance by performing all operations properly.

2 Inspecting Simplification Datasets

At its essence, sentence simplification paraphrases a sentence for better readability. It often involves a subset of four rewriting operations/transformations: **splitting**, **dropping**, **reordering**, and **substitution** (Zhu et al., 2010; Zhang and Lapata, 2017). A high-quality sentence simplfication training dataset, which contains many complex-simple sentence pairs, should be well-aligned to provide a wide coverage of different operations, so that the trained models can have good generalizability. Most neural simplification models rely on training with large datasets such as Newela (Xu et al., 2015) and WikiLarge (Zhang and Lapata, 2017), which are automatically collated with paired documents written in different readability levels. The quality of auto-collated data has been questioned in prior work (Jiang et al., 2020), however, it remains unanswered on how well they represent the real simplification distribution and on which aspects they fall short. This motivated us to propose the following five metrics to quantitatively examine common training datasets:

2.1 Measuring Simplification Operations

Alignment between the pair of complex/simplified sentence is a fundamental property since the latter should preserve the meaning of the former. Most datasets are collated from paired complex-simple documents using automatic alignment algorithms (Zhu et al., 2010; Xu et al., 2015), their sentence pairs can be poorly aligned. This is because editors may restructure the words, sentences, or even paragraphs drastically when rewriting a text into different readability level. In consequence, sentences in a paraphrased

*Work was done at University of Pittsburgh
†Work was done at University of Pittsburgh

Proceedings of the Workshop on Text Simplification, Accessibility, and Readability (TSAR-2022), pages 166 - 172
December 8, 2022 ©2022 Association for Computational Linguistics

document may not accurately pair with the original ones. We adopt BERTScore (Zhang* et al., 2020) to measure the semantic alignment between a complex and a simple sentence.

Substitution denotes replacing complicated words or phrases with simplified synonyms. We adopt PPDB (Pavlick et al., 2015) to measure the amount of substitutions between two sentences. PPDB provides extensive substitution rules (see examples in Table 1) and we measure the degree of substitution by checking the ratio of simplified tokens in a sentence pair (normalized by the length of s_{simp})).

Weight	Type	Rule
0.99623	[VP]	recipient → have receive
0.75530	[NN]	recipient → winner
0.58694	[NN]	recipient → receiver

Table 1: Example of simplifying rules in PPDB

Dropping refers to the rewriting transformation by removing unimportant or redundant parts from a sentence. To measure the degree of dropping, we calculate the ratio of the tokens being discarded from a complex sentence.

Reordering denotes the rearrangement of parts in a sentence to simplify its syntax and structure. To measure the reordering, we extract the syntactic structure of each sentence and compare the syntactical change between each pair of sentences.

Concretely, following the method proposed by Xu et al., we use a dependency parser (Honnibal et al., 2020) to extract dependency relations from a sentence. Then Jaccard similarity between the two sets of relations is calculated to measure the degree of reordering transformation.

Splitting divides a long sentence into several shorter ones to reduce syntactic complexity. We count the number of sentences on both sides, and a help from the split is observed when the number of sentences at the simplified side is larger.

2.2 Studies on Existing Datasets

We conducted quantitatively inspections using the five proposed metrics on four mainstream datasets: WikiLarge and Newela, which are commonly used as training data in prior work, as well as the validation set of Turk (Xu et al., 2016) and ASSET (Alva-Manchego et al., 2020). The latter two were annotated by human and are representative of real distribution of text simplification. Figure 1 shows

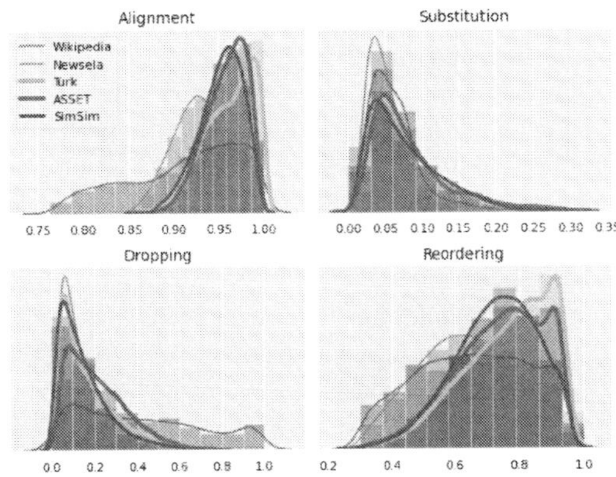

Figure 1: The histograms and density estimates of four property measures in simplification data.

the results on four metrics. On *alignment*, Turk and ASSET contain most aligned sentence pairs and almost all sentence pairs are of high similarity (larger than 0.9), whereas WikiLarge and Newela have a large proportion of poorly aligned pairs with WikiLarge is more problematic. Turk and ASSET also present more *substitution* than the two other datasets, and WikiLarge exhibits a very different distribution of *dropping* from the others, where it discards more words and in certain extreme cases only retains a few words at the simplified side. Lastly, Turk and ASSET contain less *reordering* (leaning towards 1.0), whereas WikiLarge and Newela contain sentences with drastic syntactic changes. Table 2 shows the proportion of sentence pairs contribute to splitting. A large proportion of sentence pairs in ASSET help to split, which indicates the splitting cannot be ignored but all other datasets rarely help to split.

Corpus	Proportion
Wikipedia	0.102
Newsela	0.002
Turk	0.044
ASSET	0.310
SimSim	0.399

Table 2: Proportion of sentence pairs helps to split

Overall, a large discrepancy in the rewriting distributions is shown between Turk, ASSET and the two training datasets, which makes us wonder the validity of the models trained with such biased data. This motivates us to develop novel training data that can better transfer real knowledge of text simplification to models.

3 SimSim: Data Enhancement by Simulating Simplification

We think that a well-generalizable simplification model needs to be trained on high quality training pairs and simplification knowledge. we propose a method to automatically refine/construct existing training pairs and inject knowledge of simplification by simulating various rewriting transformations. Unlike previous datasets (i.e. WikiLarge and Newela) that heavily rely on paired documents of different readabilities and can hardly scale up, our method is capable of exploiting any text data on the Internet as seed thus avoid those limitations. We name the resulting dataset SimSim.

Overview Our method starts with a set of seed sentences, then a series of enhancement steps are performed on each seed sentence to generate a new sentence so that the original seed sentence and the new resulting sentence form a complex-simple pair. Note that this method not only can enhance original training pairs, it can also construct new pairs solely using complex sentences. This method works on other corpora too, but we leave it for future work. To build seed sentences, we apply BERTScore on each sentence pair in WikiLarge and Newela to check their semantic alignment between the complex and simple sentences. For those badly aligned pairs, we remove their simple sentences to eliminate the noise led by the misalignment. We take the rest sentences as seeds for enhancement.

Constructing Paraphrastic Sentences by Back-Translation The bottom line of simplifying a sentence is to paraphrase it without alternating its meaning. Rather than retrieving aligned sentences from paired documents, we propose to create such pairs with the help of back-translation. We expect that the back-translated sentences should preserve the meaning of the original sentences, meanwhile demonstrate more linguistic diversity. The idea has been proven effective for paraphrasing sentences (Wieting et al., 2017) and improving translation with monolingual data (Sennrich et al., 2016).

We employ Google's Neural Machine Translation System (GNMT) (Wu et al., 2016) for this purpose, on account of its overall translation quality and the support of a large number of languages. We translated each seed sentence into 103 pivot languages and translated it back to English. Some examples are shown in Table 3.

Candidate Selection with GPT-2. Paraphrastic sentences generated through back-translation can contain language errors and unnatural expressions. GPT-2, as a powerful neural language model trained with open-domain text (Radford et al., 2019), can help us to evaluate the quality of candidate sentences. GPT-2 gives a score (negative log-likelihood) to a sentence, and we assume that a better GPT-2 score means that the sentence is more likely to be in high quality. Thus among all 103 candidates, we select the best one as the target sentence for further enhancement. Particularly, if GPT-2 deems the back-translated sentence less natural than the original one, it will be discarded. Although, the remaining candidate sentences after GPT-2 scoring can be considered to be well-aligned and natural, they are not ready for training a simplification model since most of them have not been simplified yet. They therefore go through a set of simulating steps as presented below:

Simulating Substitution In order to impose substitution knowledge into the candidate sentences, we applied the paraphrasing rules in PPDB. To ensure the applied rules are proper, we use GPT-2 again to evaluate the quality of the resulting sentences.

Simulating Dropping To distill the dropping operation into data, we follow previous approach (Filippova and Altun, 2013) and augment the data by randomly removing prepositional, adjective or adverb phrases.

Simulating Splitting We find that back-translation rarely splits a sentence into multiple shorter ones. Thus we propose to include WikiSplit (Botha et al., 2018) to incorporate the splitting operation into our data. We put WikiSplit sentence pairs into the seed bank and we apply the above process to the target-side sentences so as to mix the splitting transformation with others.

SimSim Dataset By simulating different operations with the above steps, we present a new corpus SimSim for the task of text simplification. As shown in Figure 1 and Table 2, SimSim demonstrates a closer distribution to the human-annotated Turk and ASSET, from multiple rewriting aspects. This suggests that SimSim may serve as a better dataset for training simplification models.

4 Experiments

Setup We train Transformer-based vanilla Encoder-Decoder models with five datasets. The

Pivot	Sentence	NLL
Original	It is situated at the coast of the Baltic sea , where it encloses the city of stralsund .	3.8020
Chinese	It is located on the coast of the Baltic Sea and surrounds the city of Stralsund .	2.8642
Greek	It is located on the shores of the Baltic Sea, where it encloses the city of Stralsund .	2.8379
Italy	It is located on the Baltic Sea coast, where the city of Stralsund is located .	2.9493
Japanese	It is located on the Baltic Sea coast and surrounds the city of Stralsund .	3.1864
Hindi	It is situated on the banks of the Baltic sea, where it surrounds the town of Stralsund .	3.0487

Table 3: Examples of back-translation with GNMT. The rightmost column shows the Negative log-likelihood (NLL) scores estimated by GPT-2.

first two are `WikiLarge` and `Wiki-Auto`, two common training datasets. **`WikiLarge`** (Zhang and Lapata, 2017) is constructed by automatically aligning sentences in Simple Wikipedia and Wikipedia, with the help of lexical-based features, such as the Jaccard coefficient and TF-IDF. It has 296k complex-simple sentence pairs. **`Wiki-Auto`** (Jiang et al., 2020) uses a neural CRF model in order to achieve a better auto-alignment than the rule-based method used in `WikiLarge`, which contains 488k pairs. The remaining three datasets are the three variants of `SimSim` dataset: (1) `SimSim-S1`, constructed by directly applying 103-language back-translation on candidate sentences, resulting millions of pairs; (2) `SimSim-S2`, constructed by selecting the most natural sentence from translated sentences with GPT-2 (1.67M pairs); (3) `SimSim-S3` further improves `SimSim-S2` by simulating different rewriting operations (1.67M pairs). We use `Turk` (Xu et al., 2016) and `ASSET` (Alva-Manchego et al., 2020) for validation and testing. SARI (Xu et al., 2016) is used as the evaluation measure since it is widely used in the literature.

Train Data	SARI↑ Score	Add	Delete	Keep
SBMT-SARI (Xu et al., 2016)	39.96	5.96	41.42	72.52
DMASS-DCSS (Zhao et al., 2018)	40.45	5.72	42.23	73.41
EditNTS (Dong et al., 2019)	38.23	3.36	39.15	72.13
Edit-Unsup-TS (Kumar et al., 2020)	37.85	2.31	43.65	67.59
WikiLarge	38.84	4.78	41.19	70.53
Wiki-Auto	39.64	5.18	41.61	72.13
SimSim-S1	36.33	4.53	32.79	71.66
SimSim-S2	40.15	7.52	38.64	**74.32**
SimSim-S3	**41.07**	**8.33**	**41.97**	72.89

Table 4: Performance of vanilla Encoder-Decoder models and some other baselines tested on WikiTurk dataset.

Results The experiment results are presented in Table 4 and 5. Between two models trained with `Wiki-Auto` and `WikiLarge` respectively, the one on `Wiki-Auto` achieved better scores than that of `WikiLarge`, which is helped by the improved aligning algorithm. However, `Wiki-Auto` is still limited to the contents in Wikipedia and contains much noise. In comparison, models trained with `SimSim` outperform `WikiLarge` and `Wiki-Auto` consistently. Because `SimSim` is constructed in a more controlled way, the sentences in each pair are more aligned and more rewriting operations are included. Among the three `SimSim` variants, `SimSim-S1`, constructed by only back-translation, performs the worst among the three, and worse than two baselines. Back-translation itself can boost the diversity of sentence pairs, nevertheless it also introduces much noise in language. By utilizing GPT-2 to select the most natural ones from back-translated pairs, the model using `SimSim-S2` outperforms `SimSim-S1` by a large margin. Moreover, the SARI performance can be further boosted with `SimSim-S3`, which applied multiple rewriting operations on each training pair to simulate the real simplification process.

Train Data	SARI↑ Score	Add	Delete	Keep
Wiki-Auto	50.79	16.65	69.58	66.16
SimSim-S1	49.34	17.10	66.48	64.44
SimSim-S2	52.20	**19.34**	69.89	**67.38**
SimSim-S3	**52.37**	19.18	**71.01**	66.92

Table 5: Performance of vanilla Encoder-Decoder models tested on ASSET dataset.

5 Conclusion

In this study, we observe a significant discrepancy exists between the human simplified sentences and common training data and propose an unsupervised data enhancement method, `SimSim`, to explicitly teach the model appropriate operations by distilling the knowledge into training data. The empirical results show that the resulting dataset `SimSim` can support models to achieve better performance by performing all operations properly.

References

Fernando Alva-Manchego, Louis Martin, Antoine Bordes, Carolina Scarton, Benoît Sagot, and Lucia Specia. 2020. Asset: A dataset for tuning and evaluation of sentence simplification models with multiple rewriting transformations. In *Proceedings of the 58th Annual Meeting of the Association for Computational Linguistics*, pages 4668–4679.

Jan A Botha, Manaal Faruqui, John Alex, Jason Baldridge, and Dipanjan Das. 2018. Learning to split and rephrase from wikipedia edit history. *arXiv preprint arXiv:1808.09468.*

John A Carroll, Guido Minnen, Darren Pearce, Yvonne Canning, Siobhan Devlin, and John Tait. 1999. Simplifying text for language-impaired readers. In *EACL*, pages 269–270.

Yue Dong, Zichao Li, Mehdi Rezagholizadeh, and Jackie Chi Kit Cheung. 2019. Editnts: An neural programmer-interpreter model for sentence simplification through explicit editing. *arXiv preprint arXiv:1906.08104.*

Katja Filippova and Yasemin Altun. 2013. Overcoming the lack of parallel data in sentence compression.

Matthew Honnibal, Ines Montani, Sofie Van Landeghem, and Adriane Boyd. 2020. spaCy: Industrial-strength Natural Language Processing in Python.

Chao Jiang, Mounica Maddela, Wuwei Lan, Yang Zhong, and Wei Xu. 2020. Neural crf model for sentence alignment in text simplification. In *Proceedings of the 58th Annual Meeting of the Association for Computational Linguistics*, pages 7943–7960.

Dhruv Kumar, Lili Mou, Lukasz Golab, and Olga Vechtomova. 2020. Iterative edit-based unsupervised sentence simplification. *arXiv preprint arXiv:2006.09639.*

Ellie Pavlick, Pushpendre Rastogi, Juri Ganitkevitch, Benjamin Van Durme, and Chris Callison-Burch. 2015. Ppdb 2.0: Better paraphrase ranking, fine-grained entailment relations, word embeddings, and style classification. In *Proceedings of the 53rd Annual Meeting of the Association for Computational Linguistics and the 7th International Joint Conference on Natural Language Processing (Volume 2: Short Papers)*, volume 2, pages 425–430.

Alec Radford, Jeffrey Wu, Rewon Child, David Luan, Dario Amodei, and Ilya Sutskever. 2019. Language models are unsupervised multitask learners. *URL https://openai. com/blog/better-language-models.*

Luz Rello, Clara Bayarri, Azuki Gòrriz, Ricardo Baeza-Yates, Saurabh Gupta, Gaurang Kanvinde, Horacio Saggion, Stefan Bott, Roberto Carlini, and Vasile Topac. 2013. Dyswebxia 2.0!: more accessible text for people with dyslexia. In *Proceedings of the 10th International Cross-Disciplinary Conference on Web Accessibility*, page 25. ACM.

Rico Sennrich, Barry Haddow, and Alexandra Birch. 2016. Improving neural machine translation models with monolingual data. In *Proceedings of the 54th Annual Meeting of the Association for Computational Linguistics (Volume 1: Long Papers)*, pages 86–96.

Willian Massami Watanabe, Arnaldo Candido Junior, Vinícius Rodriguez Uzêda, Renata Pontin de Mattos Fortes, Thiago Alexandre Salgueiro Pardo, and Sandra Maria Aluísio. 2009. Facilita: reading assistance for low-literacy readers. In *Proceedings of the 27th ACM international conference on Design of communication*, pages 29–36. ACM.

John Wieting, Jonathan Mallinson, and Kevin Gimpel. 2017. Learning paraphrastic sentence embeddings from back-translated bitext. In *Proceedings of the 2017 Conference on Empirical Methods in Natural Language Processing*, pages 274–285.

Yonghui Wu, Mike Schuster, Zhifeng Chen, Quoc V Le, Mohammad Norouzi, Wolfgang Macherey, Maxim Krikun, Yuan Cao, Qin Gao, Klaus Macherey, et al. 2016. Google's neural machine translation system: Bridging the gap between human and machine translation. *arXiv preprint arXiv:1609.08144.*

Wei Xu, Chris Callison-Burch, and Courtney Napoles. 2015. Problems in current text simplification research: New data can help. *Transactions of the Association of Computational Linguistics*, 3(1):283–297.

Wei Xu, Courtney Napoles, Ellie Pavlick, Quanze Chen, and Chris Callison-Burch. 2016. Optimizing statistical machine translation for text simplification. *Transactions of the Association for Computational Linguistics*, 4:401–415.

Yang You, Jing Li, Sashank Reddi, Jonathan Hseu, Sanjiv Kumar, Srinadh Bhojanapalli, Xiaodan Song, James Demmel, Kurt Keutzer, and Cho-Jui Hsieh. 2019. Large batch optimization for deep learning: Training bert in 76 minutes. *arXiv preprint arXiv:1904.00962.*

Tianyi Zhang*, Varsha Kishore*, Felix Wu*, Kilian Q. Weinberger, and Yoav Artzi. 2020. Bertscore: Evaluating text generation with bert. In *International Conference on Learning Representations.*

Xingxing Zhang and Mirella Lapata. 2017. Sentence simplification with deep reinforcement learning. In *Proceedings of the 2017 Conference on Empirical Methods in Natural Language Processing*, pages 584–594.

Sanqiang Zhao, Rui Meng, Daqing He, Saptono Andi, and Parmanto Bambang. 2018. Integrating transformer and paraphrase rules for sentence simplification. *arXiv preprint arXiv:1810.11193.*

Zhemin Zhu, Delphine Bernhard, and Iryna Gurevych. 2010. A monolingual tree-based translation model for sentence simplification. In *Proceedings of the 23rd international conference on computational linguistics*, pages 1353–1361. Association for Computational Linguistics.

A Training Details

Our Transformer architecture uses an embedding dimension of 512, fully connected layers of dimension 2048, 8 attention heads, 6 layers in the encoder and 6 layers in the decoder. we used beam search with a beam size of 8. For optimization, model updates use a batch size of 400 and a LAMB optimizer with learning rate 0.001 (You et al., 2019) and all the models were trained by 250,000 steps (takes around 2-3 days). Training was done on a single Cloud TPU V2.

B Evaluation Details

We computed SARI using the code provided at `https://github.com/cocoxu/simplification` and we mainly compare our results with studies using the same evaluation protocol (Xu et al., 2016; Zhang and Lapata, 2017; Zhao et al., 2018; Dong et al., 2019; Kumar et al., 2020). Note that most studies reported ASSET scores using a different evaluation code and therefore we cannot include their scores for the sake of fair comparison.

C Implementation Details

Our model implementation is based on Tensorflow 1.15 and Tensor2Tensor library `https://github.com/tensorflow/tensor2tensor`.

Improving Text Simplification with Factuality Error Detection

Yuan Ma, Sandaru Seneviratne, Elena Daskalaki
The Australian National University
{u6712879, sandaru.seneviratne, eleni.daskalaki}@anu.edu.au

Abstract

In the past few years, the field of text simplification has been dominated by supervised learning approaches thanks to the appearance of large parallel datasets such as Wikilarge and Newsela. However, these datasets suffer from sentence pairs with factuality errors which compromise the models' performance. In this study we proposed a model-independent factuality error detection mechanism, considering bad simplification and bad alignment, to refine the Wikilarge dataset through reducing the weight of these samples during training. We demonstrated that this approach improved the performance of the state-of-the-art text simplification model TST5 by an FKGL reduction of 0.33 and 0.29 on the TurkCorpus and ASSET testing datasets respectively. Our study illustrates the impact of erroneous samples in TS datasets and highlights the need for automatic methods to improve their quality.

1 Introduction

Text simplification (TS) is a Natural Language Processing (NLP) task that considers the reduction of text's complexity towards increasing its readability and understandability while retaining its original meaning. TS can increase the accessibility of information to a wider audience, including youngsters, those with little literacy, people who are not native speakers, the elderly, and people with disabilities (Inui et al., 2003; Petersen and Ostendorf, 2007; De Belder and Moens, 2010; Suominen et al., 2013). Additionally, numerous studies have also demonstrated that TS can support other NLP tasks as a preprocessing step (Chen et al., 2012; Chatterjee and Agarwal, 2022).

The current TS domain (Zhang and Lapata, 2017; Martin et al., 2020; Omelianchuk et al., 2021) is dominated by fine tuning large sequence-to-sequence language models on existing parallel datasets, the main ones being Wikilarge (Zhang and Lapata, 2017) and Newsela (Xu et al., 2015). However, several studies have revealed that these training datasets suffer from factuality errors. (Xu et al., 2015; Devaraj et al., 2022) Factuality errors occur when the samples provided do not accurately or properly represent the task. In the TS context, two main sources of factuality errors are bad alignment, i.e., loss of content preservation, and bad simplification, i.e., the target sentence is not simpler than the source (Xu et al., 2015). The existence of parallel training samples with factuality errors can impact significantly the performance of the TS models.

In this study, we investigated methods to detect parallel samples with factuality errors in the Wikilarge dataset. We explored the impact of decreasing the loss weight of the detected samples during training in the TS task performance. We re-trained the state-of-the-art (SOTA) TS model TST5 (Sheang and Saggion, 2021) using the modified Wikilarge dataset and observed a significant performance improvement when tested on the TurkCorpus and ASSET datasets.

2 Related Work

2.1 Text simplification

Text simplification is mostly treated as a monolingual translation problem based on existing parallel datasets including Wikilarge and Newsela. While previous models focused on using statistical machine translation (SMT) approaches (Coster and Kauchak, 2011; Wubben et al., 2012; Štajner et al., 2015), current work focuses on using neural machine translation (NMT) approaches (Nisioi et al., 2017; Shen et al., 2017; Zhao et al., 2018; Martin et al., 2020). The Neural Text Simplification (NTS) model proposed by Nisioi et al. (2017) is one of the earliest attempts to apply NMT on TS and showed better performance than other SMT models at that time. After the release of transformers, Zhao et al.

Proceedings of the Workshop on Text Simplification, Accessibility, and Readability (TSAR-2022), pages 173 - 178
December 8, 2022 ©2022 Association for Computational Linguistics

Bad Alignment	Complex: They take up oxygen in the lungs or gills and release it while squeezing through the body 's capillaries . Simple: Red blood cells are very large in number ; in women , there are 4.8 million red blood cells per microliter of blood .
Bad Simplification	Complex: He travelled to Brittany in 1928 to study stone crosses and publish As Cruces de Pedra na Bretaña . Simple: Two years later he published Cousas , and in 1929 he travelled to Brittany to study its stone crosses and publish As Cruces de Pedra na Bretaña .
Real Simplification	Complex: In September 1869 , O'Reilly escaped and was rescued by an American ship . Simple: In September 1869 , O'Reilly escaped with help from an American ship .

Table 1: Examples of bad alignment, bad simplification and real simplification in Wikilarge.

(2018) implemented it in their model DCSS and achieved the SOTA performance, highlighting the promising capability of the transformers framework for TS.

Recently, the addition of control tokens was shown to significantly improve the TS models. Martin et al. (2020) proposed one of the currently benchmark models, named ACCESS. Their model included four tokens to control the amount of compression, paraphrase, lexical, and syntactical complexity separately. Later, Sheang and Saggion (2021) improved this method by adding one more token to control the change of sentence length and fine tuning on the pretrained language model T5 (Raffel et al., 2020), resulting in the TST5 model which has achieved the highest reported SARI score on TurkCorpus dataset until now. These works have shown that adding control tokens can significantly improve the performance of TS models.

2.2 Factuality errors

Factuality errors happen when sample pairings do not accurately represent the job. They can be divided into two categories: bad simplification and bad alignment (Xu et al., 2015). Bad simplification is identified when the target sentence does not simplify the source sentence, while, when the contents of the source sentence and the target sentence disagree, this corresponds to bad alignment. The topic of factuality errors was addressed by Xu et al. (2015) where, through manual examination of 200 sentence pairs from the Parallel Wikipedia Simplification corpus, they found that 33% of sentence pairs were not simplified, and 17% of sentence pairs were not aligned. Thus, they suggested that Simple Wikipedia was a poor training resource and advised using the Newsela dataset instead. However, Devaraj et al. (2022) recently performed a manual quantitative analysis on both Newsela and Wikilarge and demonstrated that, although Newsela dataset made more proactive simplification operations, it faced a more serious problem with bad simplification error.

3 Factuality error detection

In this study, we implemented a rule-based algorithm to detect factuality errors in the Wikilarge dataset. For the detected samples, the loss of the TS model was subsequently scaled down during training to reduce their impact on the model's learning performance.

To detect bad simplification, we utilized the Flesch–Kincaid grade level (FKGL) metric (Kincaid et al., 1975), which was designed for evaluating text readability and has also been used as an evaluation metric in multiple previous works (Martin et al., 2020; Sheang and Saggion, 2021; Omelianchuk et al., 2021). FKGL was originally calculated at the paragraph level based on the average length of the sentence ($\frac{N_{words}}{N_{sentences}}$) and the number of syllables ($\frac{N_{syllables}}{N_{words}}$). To apply FKGL to the sentence level, instead of calculating the average length, the length of the sentence itself was used (Eq. 1). With the assumption that readability reflected simplicity, any sentence pairs for which the source sentence y had higher FKGL score than its target counterpart x were marked as bad simplification pairs.

$$FKGL = 0.39N_{words} + 11.8\frac{N_{syllables}}{N_{words}} - 15.59 \quad (1)$$

Bad alignment was recognized based on named entity recognition. Named entity refers to a phrase that clearly identifies one item from a set of other items that have similar attribute. We identified locations, name, time, and organization in both target and source sentences. This was performed through a pretrained classifier provided by the NLTK library[1] (Bird and Loper, 2009). Here, we assumed that simplification might reduce but should not add entities. According to this, we calculated the cosine similarity between all the entities in source sentences and target sentences. Because each named entity may contain different number of words, we used a contextual embedding model based on transformers to create embeddings for each named entity rather than a word level encoder such as word2vec (Mikolov et al., 2013). Bad alignment was recognized if there existed an entity e_t in the target sentence that did not have a corresponding entity e_s in the source sentence with cosine similarity higher than a predefined threshold T.

For the pairs marked with factuality error, their corresponding weights were scaled down during training as shown in Eq. 2 and 3 for the bad simplification and bad alignment respectively. The effect of the factuality error samples suppression was explored by experimenting with different scaling parameters α_1 and α_2.

$$w_1 = \begin{cases} \alpha_1 & \text{if FKGL(x)<FKGL(y)} \\ 1 & \end{cases} \quad (2)$$

$$w_2 = \begin{cases} 1 & \text{if } \forall_{e_t} \exists_{e_s} cos(e_t, e_s) > T \\ \alpha_2 & \end{cases} \quad (3)$$

The resulting weights of bad simplification and bad alignment were multiplied together, and the outcome was then normalized by the total weight. Thus, sentence pairs that were found to be both unaligned and unsimplified were further suppressed.

$$loss = \frac{\sum CrossEntropy(output, label) w_1 w_2}{\sum w_1 * w_2}. \quad (4)$$

[1]https://www.nltk.org

4 Experiment

4.1 Model

We used the TST5 model to evaluate the efficiency of our approach (Sheang and Saggion, 2021). All the training details were unchanged. The T5-based pretrained model was used as the backbone. Huggingface Transformers library[2] and Pytorch-lighting[3] were used to train the model. NLTK library was used for named entity recognition. Huggingface's sentence encoder all-MiniLM-L6-v2[4] was used to create embeddings for named entities. For comparing cosine similarities, the threshold T was set to 0.6, which was selected after experimenting with different threshold values.

In order to enable controllable simplicity, four control tokens were implemented, including NBChars, LevSim, WordRank, and DepTreeDepth, which were identical to ACCESS (Martin et al., 2020). During testing, the control tokens that produced the highest SARI score in the validation set were used.

We investigated different values for the parameters α_1 and α_2 to explore the impact of the error samples suppression in the model's performance. Specifically, we assessed the model's performance when bad simplification or bad alignment detection was considered with 50% suppression (α_1/α_2 = 0.5), 80% suppression (α_1/α_2 = 0.2), 98% suppression (α_1/α_2 = 0.02), and 100% suppression (α_1/α_2 = 0).

4.2 Datasets

We used WikiLarge for training and TurkCorpus and ASSET for validation and testing. The three datasets are described below.

WikiLarge (Zhang and Lapata, 2017): Contains 29,6402 sentence pairs from Simple Wikipedia and normal Wikipedia. It is the largest and the most commonly used TS dataset.

TurkCorpus (Xu et al., 2016): Contains 2,000 sentence pairs for validation and 359 sentence pairs for testing. Each sentence has 8 references manually simplified by different people.

ASSET (Alva-Manchego et al., 2020): Contains 2,000 sentence pairs for validation and 359 sentence pairs for testing with 10 references.

[2]https://huggingface.co/transformers/model_doc/t5.html

[3]https://pytorchlightning.ai

[4]https://huggingface.co/sentence-transformers/all-MiniLM-L6-v2

	TurkCorpus			ASSET		
	SARI↑	FKGL↓	BLEU↑	SARI↑	FKGL↓	BLEU↑
TST5(Sheang and Saggion, 2021)	42.46	6.28	64.26	45.17	6.31	70.04
+ bad simplification detection ($\alpha_1 = 0.2$)	43.06	6.12	66.07	44.75	6.19	70.87
+ bad simplification detection ($\alpha_1 = 0.02$)	42.87	6.08	65.50	45.10	6.29	71.42
+ bad alignment detection ($\alpha_2 = 0.2$)	42.84	6.38	65.93	45.17	6.27	71.04
+ bad alignment detection ($\alpha_2 = 0.02$)	42.90	6.15	64.91	45.03	6.23	69.42
+ both ($\alpha_1, \alpha_2 = 0.5$)	42.89	6.17	64.48	44.96	6.33	70.23
+ both ($\alpha_1, \alpha_2 = 0.2$)	43.03	5.95	64.97	45.51	6.01	70.03
+ both ($\alpha_1, \alpha_2 = 0.02$)	43.25	5.95	68.32	45.12	6.02	74.03
+ both ($\alpha_1, \alpha_2 = 0$)	43.25	6.19	67.74	45.23	6.28	72.55

Table 2: Performance of the TST5 model trained on the original and modified versions of the Wikilarge and tested on TurkCorpus and ASSET datasets.

To the best of our knowledge, all three datasets were created ethically and are publicly available. No new text data were collected or created as part of this study.

4.3 Evaluation metrics

We evaluated the TST5 model's performance using the SARI, FKGL, and BLEU metrics described below.

SARI (Xu et al., 2016): Averages F1 scores for addition, keep, and deletion operations with references.

FKGL (Kincaid et al., 1975): Evaluates the readability of a sentence.

BLEU (Papineni et al., 2002): Assesses how well one sentence matches multiple references.

As SARI is the most adopted metric for TS we used it as our primary metric while FKGL was used to evaluate the simplicity of our output. Although research has shown that BLEU is not suitable for the TS task (Sulem et al., 2018), we included it in our analysis for comparison with previous works. The Wilcoxon signed-rank test (Wilcoxon, 1992) was used to assess the statistical significance of our results.

4.4 Results

Our proposed factuality error detection algorithm identified $68,237$ (23 %) samples with bad simplification and $93,030$ (31 %) samples with bad alignment. In total, 45% of the total samples of Wikilarge were identified as factuality errors. The proposed dataset modification with the suppression of both bad simplification and bad alignment samples by factors of $\alpha_1, \alpha_2 = 0.02$ resulted in the best statistically significant improvement of the SARI and FKGL scores by 0.79 and 0.33 respectively on TurkCorpus and improvement of FKGL by 0.29 on ASSET (p<0.05). The SARI score on ASSET showed an inconsistent variation, in most of the cases without statistically significant change.

It should be noted that TST5 reported a higher SARI score in the original study(Sheang and Saggion, 2021), but we were unable to reproduce the same results using the code provided by the authors.

5 Discussion

Our factuality detection rate was aligned with the work of Xu et al. (2015)'s experiment on the bad simplification case (23% and 33% respectively), however, it identified a higher number of bad alignment samples (31% in comparison to 17%). This could be due to sensitivity differences between the two approaches.

Our TS results (Table 2) demonstrated that the TST5 model's performance could be enhanced by both bad simplification and bad alignment detection. The combination of both factuality errors detection led to improved results. We observed a significant improvement of SARI on TurkCorpus, but not in ASSET, where the SARI score showed an inconsistent but not statistically significant variation. The reason might be due to the SARI score on ASSET being so close to the reference that it was difficult to improve. These results indicate that that the TST5 model trained on the modified Wikilarge was able to generate simpler sentences compared to the original TST5.

From Table 2, it can also be seen that the model's performance improved as the factuality error sample weights decreased. This indicates that the impact of the erroneous samples in the training performance might be more significant than the reduction of the dataset size.

Our results illustrate that the existence of factuality errors in the training datasets used for TS, can induce a significant impact in the performance of the TS models. This indicates a general need for new reliable datasets exploration. Better error detection methods, including more thorough tuning, and further validation is needed with other TS models and other parallel datasets such as Newsela, which is part of our future work. The trade-off between error detection sensitivity and dataset size reduction is crucial and needs further investigation.

6 Conclusion

In this paper, we designed a model-independent factuality error detection mechanism to support TS model training. We demonstrated that our mechanism could significantly improve the performance of the SOTA TS model (TST5) based on recognized TS metrics. Our study raises the need for high quality parallel datasets, as well as automated factuality error detecton methods to improve the performance of TS models.

7 Limitations

We focused on the Wikilarge dataset and did not include investigation on the Newsela dataset due to lack of access to it at the time of the study. Additionally, we tested our approach on the SOTA TS model TST5 only. However, more models should be tested to assess the generalization of the proposed method. Due to time and resource limitations, we only analyzed our model based on established TS metrics and did not conduct a human evaluation.

8 Acknowledgments

This research was funded in part by and has been delivered in partnership with Our Health in Our Hands, a strategic initiative of the Australian National University (ANU), which aims to transform health care by developing new personalized health technologies and solutions in collaboration with patients, clinicians, and health care providers. We wish to acknowledge the support of the ANU School of Computing for Ms Seneviratne's PhD scholarship. We wish to sincerely thank Prof. Hanna Suominen for her valuable support and comments. We also thank NCI Australia (National Computational Infrastructure) for providing computational resources for the project ij84 and the project yv67.

References

Fernando Alva-Manchego, Louis Martin, Antoine Bordes, Carolina Scarton, Benoît Sagot, and Lucia Specia. 2020. Asset: A dataset for tuning and evaluation of sentence simplification models with multiple rewriting transformations. *arXiv preprint arXiv:2005.00481*.

Klein E. Bird, S. and E. Loper. 2009. *Natural language processing with Python*. O'Reilly.

Niladri Chatterjee and Raksha Agarwal. 2022. Studying the effect of syntactic simplification on text summarization. *IETE Technical Review*, pages 1–12.

Han-Bin Chen, Hen-Hsen Huang, Hsin-Hsi Chen, and Ching-Ting Tan. 2012. A simplification-translation-restoration framework for cross-domain smt applications. In *Proceedings of COLING 2012*, pages 545–560.

Will Coster and David Kauchak. 2011. Learning to simplify sentences using Wikipedia. In *Proceedings of the Workshop on Monolingual Text-To-Text Generation*, pages 1–9, Portland, Oregon. Association for Computational Linguistics.

Jan De Belder and Marie-Francine Moens. 2010. Text simplification for children. In *Proceedings of the SIGIR workshop on accessible search systems*, pages 19–26. ACM; New York.

Ashwin Devaraj, William Sheffield, Byron Wallace, and Junyi Jessy Li. 2022. Evaluating factuality in text simplification. pages 7331–7345.

Kentaro Inui, Atsushi Fujita, Tetsuro Takahashi, Ryu Iida, and Tomoya Iwakura. 2003. Text simplification for reading assistance: a project note. In *Proceedings of the Second International Workshop on Paraphrasing*, pages 9–16.

J Peter Kincaid, Robert P Fishburne Jr, Richard L Rogers, and Brad S Chissom. 1975. Derivation of new readability formulas (automated readability index, fog count and flesch reading ease formula) for navy enlisted personnel. Technical report, Naval Technical Training Command Millington TN Research Branch.

Louis Martin, Éric de la Clergerie, Benoît Sagot, and Antoine Bordes. 2020. Controllable sentence simplification. pages 4689–4698.

Tomas Mikolov, Kai Chen, Greg Corrado, and Jeffrey Dean. 2013. Efficient estimation of word representations in vector space. *arXiv preprint arXiv:1301.3781*.

Sergiu Nisioi, Sanja Štajner, Simone Paolo Ponzetto, and Liviu P. Dinu. 2017. Exploring neural text simplification models. In *Proceedings of the 55th Annual Meeting of the Association for Computational Linguistics (Volume 2: Short Papers)*, pages 85–91, Vancouver, Canada. Association for Computational Linguistics.

Kostiantyn Omelianchuk, Vipul Raheja, and Oleksandr Skurzhanskyi. 2021. Text Simplification by Tagging. pages 11–25.

Kishore Papineni, Salim Roukos, Todd Ward, and Wei-Jing Zhu. 2002. Bleu: a method for automatic evaluation of machine translation. In *Proceedings of the 40th Annual Meeting of the Association for Computational Linguistics*, pages 311–318, Philadelphia, Pennsylvania, USA. Association for Computational Linguistics.

Sarah E Petersen and Mari Ostendorf. 2007. Text simplification for language learners: a corpus analysis. In *Workshop on speech and language technology in education*. Citeseer.

Colin Raffel, Noam Shazeer, Adam Roberts, Katherine Lee, Sharan Narang, Michael Matena, Yanqi Zhou, Wei Li, Peter J Liu, et al. 2020. Exploring the limits of transfer learning with a unified text-to-text transformer. *J. Mach. Learn. Res.*, 21(140):1–67.

Kim Cheng Sheang and Horacio Saggion. 2021. Controllable sentence simplification with a unified text-to-text transfer transformer. In *Proceedings of the 14th International Conference on Natural Language Generation*, pages 341–352, Aberdeen, Scotland, UK. Association for Computational Linguistics.

Tianxiao Shen, Tao Lei, Regina Barzilay, and Tommi Jaakkola. 2017. Style transfer from non-parallel text by cross-alignment. *Advances in neural information processing systems*, 30.

Sanja Štajner, Iacer Calixto, and Horacio Saggion. 2015. Automatic text simplification for Spanish: Comparative evaluation of various simplification strategies. In *Proceedings of the International Conference Recent Advances in Natural Language Processing*, pages 618–626, Hissar, Bulgaria. INCOMA Ltd. Shoumen, BULGARIA.

Elior Sulem, Omri Abend, and Ari Rappoport. 2018. Bleu is not suitable for the evaluation of text simplification. *arXiv preprint arXiv:1810.05995*.

Hanna Suominen, Sanna Salanterä, Sumithra Velupillai, Wendy W Chapman, Guergana Savova, Noemie Elhadad, Sameer Pradhan, Brett R South, Danielle L Mowery, Gareth JF Jones, et al. 2013. Overview of the share/clef ehealth evaluation lab 2013. In *International Conference of the Cross-Language Evaluation Forum for European Languages*, pages 212–231. Springer.

Frank Wilcoxon. 1992. Individual comparisons by ranking methods. In *Breakthroughs in statistics*, pages 196–202. Springer.

Sander Wubben, Antal van den Bosch, and Emiel Krahmer. 2012. Sentence simplification by monolingual machine translation. In *Proceedings of the 50th Annual Meeting of the Association for Computational Linguistics (Volume 1: Long Papers)*, pages 1015–1024, Jeju Island, Korea. Association for Computational Linguistics.

Wei Xu, Chris Callison-Burch, and Courtney Napoles. 2015. Problems in current text simplification research: New data can help. *Transactions of the Association for Computational Linguistics*, 3:283–297.

Wei Xu, Courtney Napoles, Ellie Pavlick, Quanze Chen, and Chris Callison-Burch. 2016. Optimizing Statistical Machine Translation for Text Simplification. *Transactions of the Association for Computational Linguistics*, 4:401–415.

Xingxing Zhang and Mirella Lapata. 2017. Sentence simplification with deep reinforcement learning. In *Proceedings of the 2017 Conference on Empirical Methods in Natural Language Processing*, pages 584–594, Copenhagen, Denmark. Association for Computational Linguistics.

Sanqiang Zhao, Rui Meng, Daqing He, Andi Saptono, and Bambang Parmanto. 2018. Integrating transformer and paraphrase rules for sentence simplification. In *Proceedings of the 2018 Conference on Empirical Methods in Natural Language Processing*, pages 3164–3173, Brussels, Belgium. Association for Computational Linguistics.

JADES: New Text Simplification Dataset in Japanese Targeted at Non-Native Speakers

Akio Hayakawa[1] **Tomoyuki Kajiwara**[2] **Hiroki Ouchi**[1,3] **Taro Watanabe**[1]
[1]Nara Institute of Science and Technology
[2]Ehime University [3]RIKEN AIP
{akio.hayakawa.gv6, hiroki.ouchi, taro}@is.naist.jp
kajiwara@cs.ehime-u.ac.jp

Abstract

The user-dependency of Text Simplification makes its evaluation obscure. A targeted evaluation dataset clarifies the purpose of simplification, though its specification is hard to define. We built JADES (JApanese Dataset for the Evaluation of Simplification), a text simplification dataset targeted at non-native Japanese speakers, according to public vocabulary and grammar profiles. JADES comprises 3,907 complex-simple sentence pairs annotated by an expert. Analysis of JADES shows that wide and multiple rewriting operations were applied through simplification. Furthermore, we analyzed outputs on JADES from several benchmark systems and automatic and manual scores of them. Results of these analyses highlight differences between English and Japanese in operations and evaluations.

1 Introduction

Text Simplification (TS) aims to rewrite texts for easier understanding. Simplified texts can benefit children (Smith et al., 1989), non-native speakers (Paetzold and Specia, 2016), non-specialists (Devaraj et al., 2021; Ivchenko and Grabar, 2022), and people with cognitive disabilities (Rello et al., 2013; Alonzo et al., 2020).

Given the diverse users in various domains, automatic TS has been regarded as an important research area these years (Alva-Manchego et al., 2020b). However, the diversity, in turn, makes the evaluation of TS obscure. As Xu et al. (2015) stated, an appropriate simplification for one type of users will not be appropriate for another. Therefore, the ideal TS system and evaluation is user-dependent, but its specification is difficult to define.

One step to the user-dependent TS could be focusing on a specific population. The validity of the simplification for a specific population can be evaluated using a targeted dataset. Newsela (Xu et al., 2015), available in English and Spanish, can be used in this way when using information about targeted grades on each article. Japanese lacks such a dataset. SNOW (Maruyama and Yamamoto, 2018; Katsuta and Yamamoto, 2018) is a Japanese dataset for TS and limits vocabulary, which comprises the top 2000 words required to understand Japanese. However, this criteria differs from targeting in that no specific populations are considered. For instance, they gave no simplification instructions on grammar to annotators. With a strictly limited vocabulary, this settings causes lengthy expressions. In addition, SNOW is problematic in that its original sentences are already short and simple. Therefore, SNOW may not be suitable for simplifying daily texts such as news articles.

Building a targeted dataset requires criteria for specific populations. In Japanese, Japanese-Language Proficiency Test (JLPT) published vocabulary and grammar profiles for grasping Japanese on each level (Japan-Foundation, 2002). These materials alleviate the difficulties in defining the specification and building a targeted dataset.

In this paper, we introduce a new Japanese TS dataset, **JADES**[1] (**JA**panese **D**ataset for the **E**valuation of **S**implification). JADES is targeted at non-native Japanese speakers capable of everyday communications, following the specification of vocabulary and grammar. JADES comprises 3,907 complex-simple parallel sentence pairs, which an expert of Easy Japanese manually simplifies. Since obtaining manual simplification are costly, JADES is oriented towards tuning and evaluation in size.

We also implemented models as baselines on JADES and rated their outputs automatically and manually. The contributions of this work include: (1) a dataset for TS in Japanese targeted at non-native speakers; (2) analysis of complex-simple text pairs in Japanese; (3) manual scores on simplified sentences.

[1]Our dataset will be available at http://github.com/naist-nlp/jades

Proceedings of the Workshop on Text Simplification, Accessibility, and Readability (TSAR-2022), pages 179 - 187
December 8, 2022 ©2022 Association for Computational Linguistics

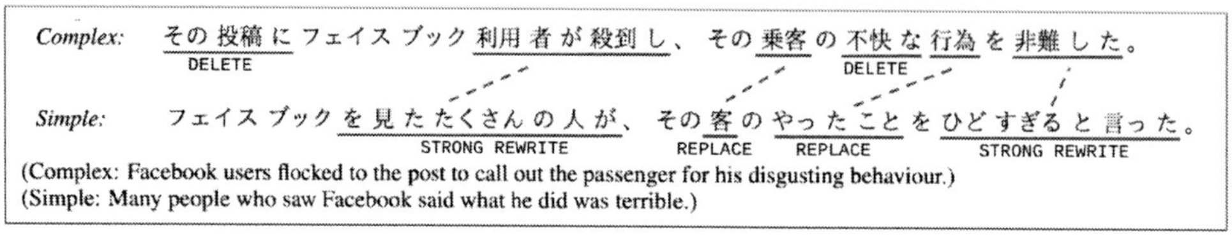

Figure 1: An example sentence pair in JADES with simplification operations.

2 Related Work

2.1 Simplification Dataset for Evaluation

While early works on TS use a subset of a large corpus for evaluation, Xu et al. (2015) pointed out the low quality of automatically aligned sentence pairs. Based on this report, using human-made sentence pairs has become a standard practice for TS evaluation. TurkCorpus (Xu et al., 2016) and ASSET (Alva-Manchego et al., 2020a) are standard datasets for the task comprising multiple reference sentences created by crowdworkers.

Although crowd-sourcing diversifies reference sentences, complex instructions can be difficult for crowdworkers. On the other hand, sentence pairs in Newsela are more valuable in that simplification is done by experts under reliable criteria for multiple levels, though its details are not disclosed. It should be noted that sentence pairs in Newsela dataset are automatically aligned and contains some misalignments.

2.2 Japanese Text Simplification

In addition to works on the typical lexical simplification (Kajiwara and Yamamoto, 2015; Hading et al., 2016), there have been several works for TS in Japanese. Goto et al. (2015) analyzed simplified Japanese news sentences and revealed that more than half of the sentences were reordered through simplification. Kato et al. (2020) focused on simplifying Japanese sentence-ending predicates, which are usually a source of confusion to readers due to their complexity. Each of these works built a dataset for training and evaluation, but unfortunately, they are not publicly available.

For a publicly available corpus, SNOW T15 (Maruyama and Yamamoto, 2018) and SNOW T23 (Katsuta and Yamamoto, 2018) are the largest in size (In the following, we denote them together as SNOW). SNOW extracted 84,400 sentences from Tanaka Corpus[2] and were manually simplified by non-experts. Original sentences in SNOW are mainly from textbooks, and the lengths of those are no more than 16 words, shorter than typical sentences in news and articles.

3 Our New Dataset JADES

We create a new dataset, JADES, for TS in Japanese. JADES contains manually simplified sentences targeted at independent non-native Japanese speakers. JADES comprises 3,907 complex-simple parallel sentence pairs and will help tune and evaluate TS models.

3.1 Simplification Criteria

To build a targeted dataset, we set criteria for the difficulty of simplified sentences. We chose former Level 3 of JLPT as a target level and adopted its vocabulary and grammar profiles as the criteria. Non-native speakers on this level are supposed to understand basic Japanese for everyday communication, which is almost equivalent to CEFR B1. The vocabulary profile contains 1,409 words, but we allowed using named entities and words at the same level as those in the profile. The grammar profile contains basic conjugations and sentence patterns. There is also a profile about Kanji characters, but we ignored it because rewriting Kanji to Hiragana or Katakana can cause misses in tokenization.

Since simplifying sentences based on the strict criteria can require some expertise, we employed an external person with specialized knowledge of Japanese simplification as an annotator. The annotator was asked to simplify sentences according to the criteria and exclude fairly simple sentences with no need for simplification. We asked the annotator to preserve the meaning of sentences on simplification but allowed deletion and addition of words for easier understanding of the main idea of sentences.

[2]http://www.edrdg.org/wiki/index.php/Tanaka_Corpus

	SNOW	JADES
# Sentences	84,400	3,907
# Vocab		
complex	2,610	12,382
simple	1,607	5,633
Avg. # Tokens		
complex	10.89	32.09
simple	11.99	31.51
Avg. Compression Rate	111.03	101.14
% of Identical	25.55	0.00

Table 1: Statistics of SNOW and JADES. Compression rate is calculated by # tokens of a simple sentence / # tokens of a complex sentence.

3.2 Data Source

Complex sentences in JADES were originally extracted from the Japanese-English development and test subsets in WMT20 news translation task (Barrault et al., 2020). These subsets include 3,991 sentences, about half of them are originally Japanese, and the rest are manually translated.

Through simplification under the criteria in Section 3.1, we obtained 3,907 complex-simple sentence pairs. We split these pairs into 2,959/448/500 for a train/valid/test subset, respectively. As multiple sentences in this dataset are originally from a single article, we assigned multiple sentences from the same article to the same subset. Meanwhile, the annotator was asked to treat one sentence as independent of the other sentences.

3.3 Analysis of Corpora

Table 1 shows the statistics of sentences in SNOW and JADES. We tokenized sentences with Sudachi (Takaoka et al., 2018) and calculated the vocabulary size, the number of tokens, and compression rates. The compression rates were calculated by dividing the number of tokens of a complex sentence by that of a simple sentence. One major difference between these two is in the number of tokens, which can derive from the difference in the domain of the original text: SNOW is from textbooks, and JADES is from news articles. The difference is also apparent in the vocabulary size as JADES contains broader topics and many named entities. The ratio of identical simplification, namely the exact match between a complex and a simple sentence, indicates that complex sentences in SNOW are fairly simple already.

We also analyzed how sentences were rewritten. The guideline for Easy Japanese[3], which is a guideline for simplifying Japanese texts published by the Japanese government, includes lexical simplification, syntactic simplification, deletion, and splitting, similar to well-discussed simplification operations in English (Xu et al., 2015; Alva Manchego, 2020). We manually identified the simplification operations applied to the original sentence from each randomly picked 100 sentence pair from SNOW and JADES, excluding identical pairs. We considered seven major simplification operations from Alva Manchego (2020), including `DELETE`, `ADD`, `SPLIT`, `REPLACE`, `SIMPLE REWRITE`, `STRONG REWRITE`, and `REORDER`.

[3]https://www.bunka.go.jp/seisaku/kokugo_nihongo/kyoiku/92484001.html

	N	S	J
`REPLACE`	38.4	80.0	97.0
`SIMPLE REWRITE`	26.0	30.0	76.0
`DELETE`	40.0	3.0	68.0
`STRONG REWRITE`	11.2	19.0	61.0
`ADD`	20.0	25.0	31.0
`REORDER`	11.2	2.0	20.0
`SPLIT`	17.2	1.0	14.0

Table 2: % of sentences from SNOW (S) and JADES (J) in which each operations was performed. Result of Newsela (N) are extracted from Alva Manchego (2020).

The result of manual operation identification in Table 2 indicates that the majority of sentence pairs in JADES have multiple operations. On the other hand, only a few sentence pairs in SNOW have deletion and splitting since sentences are short in length. Compared to Newsela, SNOW and JADES include much more `REPLACE`, which can derive from the vocabulary limitation. On the other hand, JADES include outstanding number of `SIMPLE REWRITE`s and `STRONG REWRITE`s, which implies the large difference in simplicity between sentence pairs. See Appendix A for examples of simplification and operations.

4 Evaluations

We conducted TS in Japanese with several models to investigate the characteristics of our dataset. We also evaluated models automatically and manually.

4.1 Baseline Models

We chose BART (Lewis et al., 2020) and EditNTS (Dong et al., 2019) for model architectures and trained them with sentences from SNOW and JADES.

For BART, we built three models by fine-tuning

System	Model Name	Train / Fine-tune SNOW	Train / Fine-tune JADES	Automatic SNOW BLEU	SNOW SARI	SNOW BS	JADES BLEU	JADES SARI	JADES BS	Manual JADES F	M	S
Reference	`Reference`	-	-	-	-	-	-	-	-	**3.17**	**3.09**	**2.45**
Identical	`Identical`	-	-	57.27	22.58	89.59	29.10	16.27	80.93	-	-	-
BART	`BART-S`	✓	-	**75.85**	**61.06**	**93.25**	26.34	41.21	80.75	-	-	-
	`BART-J`	-	✓	55.58	42.85	88.76	32.50	49.97	82.81	-	-	-
	`BART-SJ`	✓	✓	68.14	59.59	90.18	**36.03**	**58.12**	**83.90**	2.84	2.38	1.95
EditNTS	`EditNTS-S`	✓	-	59.60	47.28	88.97	25.05	36.67	78.38	-	-	-
	`EditNTS-SJ`	✓	✓	51.79	46.86	86.92	30.52	44.30	80.78	2.76	2.36	1.45

Table 3: Automatic and manual evaluation on simplified sentences. In SNOW, multiple references were used for evaluation. F, M, and S stand for Fluency, Meaning Preservation, and Simplicity, respectively.

the Japanese pre-trained model[4]. Two of them were fine-tuned on SNOW and JADES, respectively, and the other was first fine-tuned on SNOW and then fine-tuned again on JADES. For EditNTS, we built two models. One was trained only on SNOW from scratch, and the other was then fine-tuned on JADES. We used the first 80,000 sentence pairs as a training set in SNOW. All models used JADES for their validation.

Subsequently, we generated simplified sentences on the test subset of JADES and SNOW.

In addition to these TS models, we set the identical system, which outputs the input sentences exactly as they are.

4.2 Automatic and Manual Evaluation

Since there are few discussions on suitable automatic metrics for TS in Japanese, we evaluated the outputs of the baseline models with the most commonly used metrics in TS, BLEU (Papineni et al., 2002), SARI (Xu et al., 2016), and BERTScore (Zhang et al., 2020).

In addition to automatic scores, we assessed simplified sentences on JADES by manual scores. We randomly sampled 600 simplified sentences on each of the valid and test subsets, from reference, BART, and EditNTS. We chose the best BART and EditNTS model by automatic evaluation.

Following (Alva-Manchego et al., 2020b), sampled sentences are scored on fluency, meaning preservation, and simplicity. We hired six in-house native Japanese speakers as annotators and asked them to score 300 sentences each from valid and test subsets, respectively. As a result, each sampled sentence was scored by three annotators. Scoring was based on 1-4 Likert scale; see Appendix B for detailed instruction.

[4]`https://github.com/utanaka2000/fairseq/blob/japanese_bart_pretrained_model/JAPANESE_BART_README.md`

	F	M	S
w/ `Reference`			
BLEU	0.308	0.411	0.459
SARI	0.300	0.385	0.493
BERTScore	0.335	0.429	0.474
w/o `Reference`			
BLEU	0.167	0.228	0.177
SARI	0.157	0.142	0.294
BERTScore	0.230	0.275	0.246

Table 4: Correlation between automatic and manual scores on valid/test subsets of JADES.

4.3 Results

Table 3 shows the automatic and manual evaluation of simplified sentences as well as identical outputs. On both SNOW and JADES, fine-tuned BART models are superior to EditNTS models. The best model among BART differs in a test dataset. `BART-SJ` outperforms the other models for JADES and is slightly inferior to `BART-S` for SNOW. This performance implies that two-step fine-tuning works even though the first dataset is rough to some extent.

For manual scores, `BART-SJ` seems able to generate fluent sentences, but lacks the ability to simplify sentences compared to `Reference`. Meanwhile, even `Reference` shows lower scores than expected on simplicity. This result may be because simplification rewritings sometimes euphemize expressions and vocabulary, which are easy to understand for native speakers. Thus, scores by targeted audiences will differ from scores by native Japanese speakers. We calculated Cohen's κ (Cohen, 1960) between each pair of annotators and took the weighted average. κ on fluency, meaning preservation, and simplicity is 0.255, 0.231, and 0.250, respectively. All these values can be assumed as fair agreement (Landis and Koch, 1977).

We also calculated Pearson's correlation coefficients between automatic and manual scores, shown in Table 4. Since `Reference` almost always gains perfect automatic scores, correlation is calculated with and without `Reference` sentences. Although correlations are not much high in all aspects, notably without `Reference`, BERTScore shows the highest correlation in fluency and meaning preservation, while SARI shows the highest in simplicity. The function of SARI differs from Alva-Manchego et al. (2021), which shows that SARI is inferior to BLEU and BERTScore on simplicity for the evaluation of multi-operational simplification.

Focusing on absolute values of automatic scores, `Identical` gains a low score for JADES and a high score for SNOW, which supports that JADES has drastic rewriting. For SARI, although `BART-SJ` and `EditNTS-SJ` show low manual scores, their SARI scores are quite high compared to the fact that state-of-the-art TS models in English, which can outperform even humans, gain just around 45 in SARI (Martin et al., 2020). We found these differences in evaluation between English and Japanese datasets, and will leave them to further research.

5 Conclusion

We have introduced JADES, a new dataset mainly for the evaluation of TS in Japanese. Simplified sentences in JADES are targeted at non-native speakers and made by an expert. This setting may make operations more variant and induce drastic rewriting, as the manual operation identification shows.

We can see the difference between English and Japanese in operations and evaluation metrics, which emphasizes the need for manual datasets in diverse languages.

Since manual scores on automatic TS models are low, TS in Japanese still has room for growth. With manual scores, JADES can also be useful for investigating new evaluation metrics. We believe that JADES facilitates TS in Japanese and its application.

Limitation

JADES has only one reference sentences, which might introduce some biases in simplified sentences since they are created by a single annotator. The heavy workload and quantity of annotation might also impact the overall quality. However, only a few annotators have the expertise to handle such a difficult targeting task. In order to mitigate the current limitations of this work, we are planning to investigate better instructions with detail granularities so that it is easier to expand this task with more annotators. Furthermore, the current dataset is limited in that the qualities are not double-checked by the actual targeted users, and we will leave it as our future studies.

Acknowledgements

The work of H. Ouchi was supported by JSPS KAKENHI grant number 19K20351 and NAIST Foundation.

References

Oliver Alonzo, Matthew Seita, Abraham Glasser, and Matt Huenerfauth. 2020. Automatic text simplification tools for deaf and hard of hearing adults: Benefits of lexical simplification and providing users with autonomy. In *Proceedings of the 2020 CHI Conference on Human Factors in Computing Systems*, pages 1–13.

Fernando Alva-Manchego, Louis Martin, Antoine Bordes, Carolina Scarton, Benoît Sagot, and Lucia Specia. 2020a. ASSET: A dataset for tuning and evaluation of sentence simplification models with multiple rewriting transformations. In *Proceedings of the 58th Annual Meeting of the Association for Computational Linguistics*, pages 4668–4679, Online. Association for Computational Linguistics.

Fernando Alva-Manchego, Carolina Scarton, and Lucia Specia. 2020b. Data-driven sentence simplification: Survey and benchmark. *Computational Linguistics*, 46(1):135–187.

Fernando Alva-Manchego, Carolina Scarton, and Lucia Specia. 2021. The (un)suitability of automatic evaluation metrics for text simplification. *Computational Linguistics*, 47(4):861–889.

Fernando Emilio Alva Manchego. 2020. *Automatic Sentence Simplification with Multiple Rewriting Transformations*. Ph.D. thesis, University of Sheffield.

Loïc Barrault, Magdalena Biesialska, Ondřej Bojar, Marta R. Costa-jussà, Christian Federmann, Yvette Graham, Roman Grundkiewicz, Barry Haddow, Matthias Huck, Eric Joanis, Tom Kocmi, Philipp Koehn, Chi-kiu Lo, Nikola Ljubešić, Christof Monz, Makoto Morishita, Masaaki Nagata, Toshiaki Nakazawa, Santanu Pal, Matt Post, and Marcos Zampieri. 2020. Findings of the 2020 conference on machine translation (WMT20). In *Proceedings of the Fifth Conference on Machine Translation*, pages 1–55, Online. Association for Computational Linguistics.

Jacob Cohen. 1960. A coefficient of agreement for nominal scales. *Educational and Psychological Measurement*, 20(1):37–46.

Ashwin Devaraj, Iain Marshall, Byron Wallace, and Junyi Jessy Li. 2021. Paragraph-level simplification of medical texts. In *Proceedings of the 2021 Conference of the North American Chapter of the Association for Computational Linguistics: Human Language Technologies*, pages 4972–4984, Online. Association for Computational Linguistics.

Yue Dong, Zichao Li, Mehdi Rezagholizadeh, and Jackie Chi Kit Cheung. 2019. EditNTS: An neural programmer-interpreter model for sentence simplification through explicit editing. In *Proceedings of the 57th Annual Meeting of the Association for Computational Linguistics*, pages 3393–3402, Florence, Italy. Association for Computational Linguistics.

Isao Goto, Hideki Tanaka, and Tadashi Kumano. 2015. Japanese news simplification: tak design, data set construction, and analysis of simplified text. In *Proceedings of Machine Translation Summit XV: Papers*, Miami, USA.

Muhaimin Hading, Yuji Matsumoto, and Maki Sakamoto. 2016. Japanese lexical simplification for non-native speakers. In *Proceedings of the 3rd Workshop on Natural Language Processing Techniques for Educational Applications (NLPTEA2016)*, pages 92–96, Osaka, Japan. The COLING 2016 Organizing Committee.

Oksana Ivchenko and Natalia Grabar. 2022. Impact of the text simplification on understanding. *Studies in health technology and informatics*.

The Japan-Foundation. 2002. Japanese-language proficiency test: Test content specification (revised edition).

Tomoyuki Kajiwara and Kazuhide Yamamoto. 2015. Evaluation dataset and system for Japanese lexical simplification. In *Proceedings of the ACL-IJCNLP 2015 Student Research Workshop*, pages 35–40, Beijing, China. Association for Computational Linguistics.

Taichi Kato, Rei Miyata, and Satoshi Sato. 2020. BERT-based simplification of Japanese sentence-ending predicates in descriptive text. In *Proceedings of the 13th International Conference on Natural Language Generation*, pages 242–251, Dublin, Ireland. Association for Computational Linguistics.

Akihiro Katsuta and Kazuhide Yamamoto. 2018. Crowdsourced corpus of sentence simplification with core vocabulary. In *Proceedings of the Eleventh International Conference on Language Resources and Evaluation (LREC 2018)*, Miyazaki, Japan. European Language Resources Association (ELRA).

J. Richard Landis and Gary G. Koch. 1977. The measurement of observer agreement for categorical data. *Biometrics*, 33(1):159–174.

Mike Lewis, Yinhan Liu, Naman Goyal, Marjan Ghazvininejad, Abdelrahman Mohamed, Omer Levy, Veselin Stoyanov, and Luke Zettlemoyer. 2020. BART: Denoising sequence-to-sequence pre-training for natural language generation, translation, and comprehension. In *Proceedings of the 58th Annual Meeting of the Association for Computational Linguistics*, pages 7871–7880, Online. Association for Computational Linguistics.

Louis Martin, Angela Fan, Éric de la Clergerie, Antoine Bordes, and Benoît Sagot. 2020. Muss: Multilingual unsupervised sentence simplification by mining paraphrases.

Takumi Maruyama and Kazuhide Yamamoto. 2018. Simplified corpus with core vocabulary. In *Proceedings of the Eleventh International Conference on Language Resources and Evaluation (LREC 2018)*, Miyazaki, Japan. European Language Resources Association (ELRA).

Gustavo Paetzold and Lucia Specia. 2016. Understanding the lexical simplification needs of non-native speakers of English. In *Proceedings of COLING 2016, the 26th International Conference on Computational Linguistics: Technical Papers*, pages 717–727, Osaka, Japan. The COLING 2016 Organizing Committee.

Kishore Papineni, Salim Roukos, Todd Ward, and Wei-Jing Zhu. 2002. Bleu: a method for automatic evaluation of machine translation. In *Proceedings of the 40th Annual Meeting of the Association for Computational Linguistics*, pages 311–318, Philadelphia, Pennsylvania, USA. Association for Computational Linguistics.

Luz Rello, Ricardo Baeza-Yates, Stefan Bott, and Horacio Saggion. 2013. Simplify or help? text simplification strategies for people with dyslexia. In *Proceedings of the 10th International Cross-Disciplinary Conference on Web Accessibility*, pages 1–10.

Suzanne T Smith, Paul Macaruso, Donald Shankweiler, and Stephen Crain. 1989. Syntactic comprehension in young poor readers. *Applied psycholinguistics*, 10(4):429–454.

Kazuma Takaoka, Sorami Hisamoto, Noriko Kawahara, Miho Sakamoto, Yoshitaka Uchida, and Yuji Matsumoto. 2018. Sudachi: a Japanese tokenizer for business. In *Proceedings of the Eleventh International Conference on Language Resources and Evaluation (LREC 2018)*, Miyazaki, Japan. European Language Resources Association (ELRA).

Wei Xu, Chris Callison-Burch, and Courtney Napoles. 2015. Problems in current text simplification research: New data can help. *Transactions of the Association for Computational Linguistics*, 3:283–297.

Wei Xu, Courtney Napoles, Ellie Pavlick, Quanze Chen, and Chris Callison-Burch. 2016. Optimizing statistical machine translation for text simplification.

Transactions of the Association for Computational Linguistics, 4:401–415.

Tianyi Zhang, Varsha Kishore, Felix Wu, Kilian Q. Weinberger, and Yoav Artzi. 2020. Bertscore: Evaluating text generation with bert. In *International Conference on Learning Representations*.

A Simplification Example

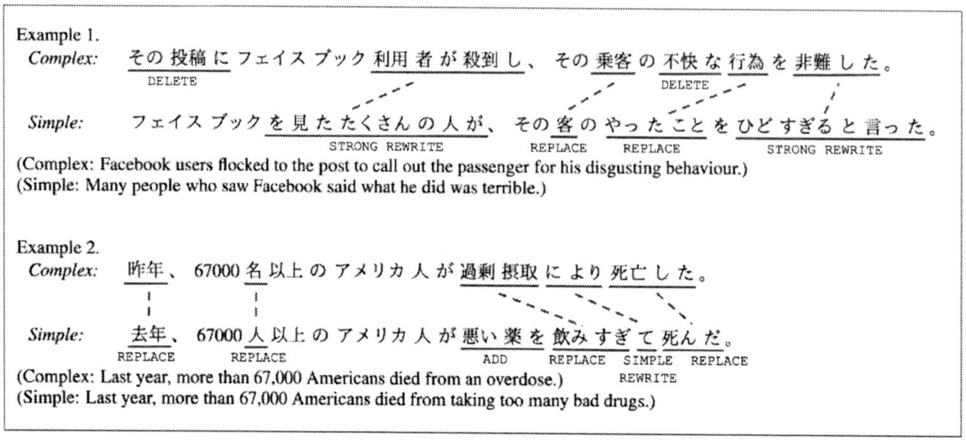

Figure 2: Examples of simplification in JADES.

B Instruction for Manual Scoring

We set 1-4 Likert scale for each of fluency, meaning preservation, and simplicity. Below is a translation of the specific instructions.

Fluency

- (Presenting a simplified sentence) Is the following sentence fluent?
    1. Obviously not fluent
    2. Lack in fluency, and the main idea is hard to understand
    3. Slightly less fluent, but conveys the main idea
    4. Fluent

Meaning Preservation

- (Presenting an original sentence as A and a simplified sentence as B) How much of the meaning of sentence A is retained in sentence B?
    1. Hardly retained (the main idea completely changed)
    2. Not much retained (the main idea changed somewhat)
    3. Largely retained (the main idea is retained)
    4. Almost completely retained

Simplicity

- (Presenting an original sentence as A and a simplified sentence as B) Is sentence B is easier to understand compared to sentence A?
    1. Harder to understand
    2. Almost equal
    3. Slightly easier to understand
    4. Easier to understand

A Benchmark for Neural Readability Assessment of Texts in Spanish

Laura Vásquez-Rodríguez[1], **Pedro-Manuel Cuenca-Jiménez**[2,3],
Sergio Esteban Morales-Esquivel[4], **Fernando Alva-Manchego**[5]
[1]National Centre for Text Mining, The University of Manchester, UK
[2]Universidad Rey Juan Carlos, Fuenlabrada, Madrid, Spain
[3]Hugging Face SAS, Paris, France
[4]School of Software Enigeering, Universidad Cenfotec, San José, Costa Rica
[5]School of Computer Science and Informatics, Cardiff University, UK
laura.vasquezrodriguez@manchester.ac.uk, pedro.cuenca@urjc.es
smorales@ucenfotec.ac.cr, alvamanchegof@cardiff.ac.uk

Abstract

We release a new benchmark for Automated Readability Assessment (ARA) of texts in Spanish. We combined existing corpora with suitable texts collected from the Web, thus creating the largest available dataset for ARA of Spanish texts. All data was pre-processed and categorised to allow experimenting with ARA models that make predictions at two (simple and complex) or three (basic, intermediate, and advanced) readability levels, and at two text granularities (paragraphs and sentences). An analysis based on readability indices shows that our proposed datasets groupings are suitable for their designated readability level. We use our benchmark to train neural ARA models based on BERT in zero-shot, few-shot, and cross-lingual settings. Results show that either a monolingual or multilingual pre-trained model can achieve good results when fine-tuned in language-specific data. In addition, all models decrease their performance when predicting three classes instead of two, showing opportunities for the development of better ARA models for Spanish with existing resources.

1 Introduction

The readability of a text refers to the aggregation of all its elements that affect the reader's understanding, reading speed, and interest in the content (Dale and Chall, 1949). Some of these elements are the words in the text, the grammatical structure of its sentences, and its writing style (Xia et al., 2016). For example, a newspaper article may be more readable than a scientific paper or a novel. Automated Readability Assessment (ARA) aims to exploit these textual elements to predict how "difficult" or comprehensible a text is (Collins-Thompson, 2014). For texts in English, several techniques have been developed, ranging from formulae that relies on surface characteristics such as average word and sentence lengths (Gunning et al., 1952; Kincaid et al., 1975) to machine learning approaches based on feature engineering (François and Miltsakaki, 2012; Vajjala and Meurers, 2012; Howcroft and Demberg, 2017) and, more recently, neural networks and deep learning models (Martinc et al., 2021; Imperial, 2021; Qiu et al., 2021).[1]

Similar to English, some work on ARA for texts in Spanish has developed methods that rely on surface features (Fernández-Huerta, 1959; Szigriszt Pazos, 2001). Others have implemented tools that extract readability indices (e.g. lexical diversity, word information, syntactic complexity) and used them as features to train standard machine learning classifiers to estimate a text's readability (Quispesaravia et al., 2016; López-Anguita et al., 2018; Bengoetxea and Gonzalez-Dios, 2021).

However, these studies were performed on small corpora of at most 300 texts (for both training and testing), limiting its generalisability. In addition, it is unknown to what extend modern neural models are able perform the task for texts in Spanish.

To mitigate the aforementioned issues, we introduce a new benchmark for training and evaluating models for ARA of texts in Spanish. Our benchmark includes the following contributions:[2]

- A collection of 6 datasets aimed to different audiences (e.g. children, Spanish learners as a second language, or people with learning disabilities) and with several "natural" levels of readability. With a total of 31,894 documents, this is the largest collection of texts in Spanish that has been used for ARA research.
- A simple baseline based on TF-IDF and Logistic Regression.

[1]See (Vajjala, 2022) for an up-to-date survey.

[2]Our datasets, models and code are available at: https://github.com/lmvasque/readability-es-benchmark

Proceedings of the Workshop on Text Simplification, Accessibility, and Readability (TSAR-2022), pages 188 - 198
December 8, 2022

- Neural models resulting from fine-tuning BERT (Devlin et al., 2019)-based pre-trained language models in monolingual and multilingual settings. We experimented with classifying texts at two ("simple" and "complex") and three ("basic", "intermediate" and "advanced") readability levels, as well as considering two text granularities (sentence-level and paragraph-level). We have demonstrated a better performance in a 2-class setting and also explain the limitations of working with a 3-class readability.

- An analysis of the performance of the neural models in different settings including zero-shot (no training, test with Spanish), cross-lingual zero-shot (training with English data, test with Spanish), monolingual few-shot (training with Spanish data) and cross-lingual few-shot (training with English and Spanish data, test with Spanish). Our study shows that multilingual models perform better at the paragraph level, while Spanish-specific models are the best at sentence level.

We expect to contribute to the development of ARA models that can help tailor relevant content for wider populations, and even benefit downstream NLP tasks, such as Text Simplification.

2 Related Work

Earlier readability studies focused on readers' background since audiences may have specific needs, and hence individual difficulties when reading a text. These audiences included people with dyslexia who struggle with long and uncommon words (Rello et al., 2013); or second-language learners, who are more affected by grammatical aspects than the content itself (Xia et al., 2016). Other studies focused on methods for readability assessment that relied on surface features, such as character and sentence counts (Dale and Chall, 1949; Collins-Thompson, 2014).

In recent years, researchers have explored alternative methods based on user-oriented studies where scroll interactions are captured to determine a document's easiness to read (Gooding et al., 2021). ARA has also been used in the evaluation of downstream NLP tasks, such as text simplification (Dell'Orletta et al., 2011) and word complexity analysis (Maddela and Xu, 2018).

Readability assessment itself has been approached in multiple ways, including through supervised and unsupervised methodologies (Martinc et al., 2021). The simplest approach is to use traditional metrics such as Gunning Fog Index (GFI, Gunning et al., 1952), Flesch Reading Ease (FRE) and Flesch-Kincaid Grade Level (FKGL, Kincaid et al., 1975), which evaluated the readability of a document based on its characters, words, syllables, and sentences.

While most ARA work is done for texts in English, there is research for other languages such as Portuguese (Evaldo Leal et al., 2020; Scarton and Aluísio, 2010; Scarton et al., 2010), German (Hancke et al., 2012), French (François and Fairon, 2012), Italian (Dell'Orletta et al., 2011; Miliani et al., 2022), Russian (Reynolds, 2016), Vietnamise (Luong et al., 2017) and Swedish (Luong et al., 2017). However, these studies tend to be language and/or domain specific and thus, sparse without benchmarking multiple models.

Recent readability studies in Spanish are focused on specific audiences. These applications include the evaluation of the readability of e-government websites (Morato et al., 2021), the evaluation of the suitability of hearing aid user guides in Spanish (Gaeta et al., 2021) or in more specialised domain such as medical (Rodriguez and Singh, 2018). These studies mostly use traditional metrics (e.g., number of syllables, words, sentences), rather than neural approaches.

Finally, there are limited resources for readability in Spanish and most of them are shared within the domain of Text Simplification (Xu et al., 2015; Saggion et al., 2011; Štajner and Saggion, 2013) and Text Complexity analysis (Quispesaravia et al., 2016). We contribute with the collection of the proposed readability datasets (Section 3) and a benchmark of neural models (Section 4) to this growing field of research in Spanish.

3 Dataset Collection

We describe the data sources and characteristics of each dataset (Section 3.1) in our benchmark, as well as the standardisation process applied to each that allows for ARA experimentation (Section 3.2). We also analyse the readability of the documents and text groupings in our benchmark using readability metrics (Section 3.3), and comment on the datasets limitations (Section 3.4).

Dataset	Documents	Paragraphs	Paragraph/Doc	Sent.	Sent./Paragraph	Words	Words/Sent
CAES	30,935	30,935	1	325,135	11	5,154,567	15.85
Coh-Metrix-Esp	100	100	1	3,066	31	57,459	18.74
Hablacultura.com	217	713	3	2,607	4	62,582	24.01
Kwiziq	206	206	1	3,172	15	61,364	19.35
Newsela-es	243	5,444	22	53,470	10	1,079,921	20.20
Simplext	193	386	2	2,733	7	64,383	23.56
Total	31,894	37,784	31	390,183	77	6,480,276	121.70

Table 1: Datasets statistics including paragraphs and sentences.

3.1 Data Sources

Our benchmark includes resources scraped from the web, as well as datasets previously used for research in ARA and Text Simplification. Table 1 presents some statistics of the datasets, with more detailed descriptions below.

- **Newsela** (Xu et al., 2015): professional translators rewrote news articles (called version 0) to comply with multiple school grade levels (called versions 1 to 4, with higher versions being more readable). Our benchmark considers the Spanish portion of this dataset.
- **Simplext** (Saggion et al., 2011): collection of 200 short news articles that were rewritten following easy-to-read guidelines for wider audiences. While this corpus has been mostly used for Text Simplification research, it naturally provides documents in two levels ("complex" and "simple"), making it suitable for ARA studies.
- **Coh-Metrix-Esp (Cuentos)** (Quispesaravia et al., 2016): collection of 100 documents consisting of 50 children fables ("simple" texts) and 50 stories for adults ("complex" texts) scrapped from the web.
- **CAES**[3] (Parodi, 2015): the "Corpus de Aprendices del Español" (CAES) is a collection of texts created by Spanish L2 learners from Spanish learning centres and universities. Students had different learning levels, different backgrounds (11 native languages) and various levels of experience with the language. We used web scraping techniques to download a portion of the full dataset since its current website only provides content filtered by categories that have to be manually selected. The readability level of each text in CAES follows the Common European Framework of Reference for Languages (CEFR, Uchida et al., 2018). The corpus also includes information about the learners and the type of assignments with which they were assigned to create each text.
- **Other Language Learners Resources**: we collected articles from kwiziq,[4] a website dedicated to aid Spanish learning through automated methods. It also provides articles in different CEFR-based levels. We also collected texts from HablaCultura,[5] a website with resources for Spanish students, labeled by instructors following the CEFR. We scraped the freely available articles from both websites for our benchmark.

These datasets were selected since they inherently provide information about the readability levels of their texts. Although other resources exist (especially aimed at learners of Spanish L2), they have strict data-agreement licenses that prevent their use, or they are not publicly available.

3.2 Data Preprocessing

We used most of the documents from the datasets described in Section 3.1, without discarding any content. Since the documents have different types of readability labels ("complex" and "simple", school grade levels, or CEFR levels), we mapped them into two groups to allow easier and more standardised experimentation. Table 2 summarises this mapping, with further details given below.[6]

- **2-class (simple, complex):** when CEFR information was available, we split texts into "simple" for levels [A1, A2, B1], and "complex" for levels [B2, C1, C2]. For Newsela

[3] `http://galvan.usc.es/caes/`

[4] `https://www.kwiziq.com/`

[5] `https://hablacultura.com/`

[6] In Table 4 we show an example for each of our proposed classifications (2-class and 3-class.)

Group	Readability Label	Newsela	CAES	kwiziq	HablaCultura	Coh Cuentos	Simplext
2-class	simple	versions 3-4		A1, A2, B1		simple	
	complex	versions 0-1		B2, C1, C2		complex	
3-class	basic	grades 2-5		A1, A2		simple	
	intermediate	grades 6-8		B1, B2		-	
	advanced	grades 9-12		C1, C2		complex	

Table 2: Mapping between the original readability labels of each dataset in the benchmark to 2-class and 3-class groups for ARA experimentation.

Text Granularity	Group	Readability Labels	fernandez-huerta↑	szigriszt-pazos ↑	gutierrez-polini↑	crawford ↓
paragraph	2-class	simple	98.049	94.682	43.614	2.647
		complex	83.959	80.698	38.927	3.686
	3-class	basic	99.971	96.588	44.270	2.491
		intermediate	89.273	85.949	40.759	3.420
		advanced	82.909	79.673	38.545	3.746
sentence	2-class	simple	98.700	95.228	43.628	2.542
		complex	81.969	78.495	37.884	3.650
	3-class	basic	99.180	95.729	43.810	2.481
		intermediate	88.527	84.955	40.008	3.417
		advanced	80.953	77.495	37.460	3.689

Table 3: Readability indices for texts in each proposed readability level (2-class or 3-class) and granularity (paragraph or sentence). Arrows indicate if higher (↑) or lower (↓) values can be interpreted as more readable texts.

(with school grade levels), we classified entries as "simple" for simplification degrees [3-4], and "complex" for [0-1]. We skipped level 2 due to its close similarity with texts from versions 1 and 3. Datasets that already had binary labels (i.e. "simple" or "complex") were not modified.

- **3-class (basic, intermediate and advanced):** when school grade levels were available, grades [2-5] were considered as "basic", levels [6-8] as "intermediate", and levels [9-12] as "advanced". For datasets with CEFR information, we considered [A1, A2] as "basic", [B1, B2] as "intermediate", and [C1, C2] as "advanced". We only considered levels "basic" and "advanced" for datasets with only "simple" and "complex" labels, respectively.

We expect our benchmark to be used to develop neural-based ARA models, which are mostly based on BERT (Martinc et al., 2021; Imperial, 2021). As such, due to the input size limitations of BERT-based models, it would be difficult for them to handle full documents from some datasets in the benchmark. Previous work in English dealt with this by chunking documents by a certain number of sentences (Martinc et al., 2021). Instead, we rely on the natural boundaries or structure of documents to split them into paragraphs and sentences. This allows us to implement ARA models at different granularities. For Newsela and HablaCultura, paragraphs could be easily identified, since each one appears as a single line in the files. Documents with no clear paragraph-level divisions (e.g. from CAES, kwiziq and Coh Cuentos) were treated as having a single paragraph. Paragraphs were later split into sentences using NLTK (Bird et al., 2009).

3.3 Readability Assessment

We computed multiple readability indices for Spanish texts in order to validate the splitting of the data into the proposed 2-class and 3-class groups. We used `textstat` to calculate the following indices:[7]

Fernandez-Huerta (Fernández-Huerta, 1959): proposes the implementation of the Flesch Reading Ease (FRE) score for Spanish.[8] This score is given by Equation 1 where P is the number of syllables and F the number of sentences. The values range from 0 to 100, where the lower values correspond to university-level texts.

$$Score = 206.84 - (0.60 * P) - (1.02 * F) \quad (1)$$

[7] `https://github.com/textstat/textstat`

[8] We have used the corrected formula as proposed in `https://linguistlist.org/issues/22/22-2332/#1`.

Granularity	Text	Readability
Paragraph (2-class)	Sevilla es una ciudad de tradiciones, que las celebra con gran devoción y orgullo. Una de estas tradiciones es la ronda de las tunas a la "Inmaculada". Cada siete de diciembre por la noche, diferentes tunas se reúnen en la Plaza del Triunfo, en el centro de la ciudad, para entonar canciones tradicionales que se han cantado durante décadas. [..]	simple
Paragraph (2-class)	Voz de la guitarra mía, al despertar la mañana, quiere cantar su alegría a mi tierra mexicana. Yo le canto a sus volcanes, a sus praderas y flores, que son como talismanes del amor de mis amores. [..]	complex
Paragraph (3-class)	En Nochebuena, 24 de diciembre, cenamos en familia. En la cena típica hay gambas, langostinos, cordero o pavo, vino y champán o cava. Pero lo más típico son los dulces: el turrón, los polvorones, los mantecados y el mazapán.	basic
Paragraph (3-class)	Unos 15 kilómetros al sur de Sidi Ifni, en una de las playas vírgenes que baña el Océano Atlántico en esta parte de la costa, hay un viejo barco encallado. Se trata de una enorme mole oxidada de origen incierto, abandonada en este despoblado punto de la costa. [..]	intermediate
Paragraph (3-class)	Existen artistas con un don, seres únicos elegidos para trasmitir emociones e inquietudes de una manera diferente y a la vez familiar. De aquel niño que escudriñaba a su madre mientras ella interpretaba cartas de amor y de muerte a las vecinas del pueblo, queda la mirada pícara y luminosa del visionario, de aquel que antes de inventar la fábula ya ha imaginado el final. [..]	complex

Table 4: Examples from HablaCultura and Kwiziq paragraph datasets.

Szigriszt-Pazos (Szigriszt Pazos, 1993): measures the "perspicuity" (i.e. intelligibility) of texts using Equation 2, where S is the total of syllables, P is the total of words, and F is the number of sentences.

$$Score = 206.835 - \frac{62.3 * S}{P} - \frac{P}{F} \quad (2)$$

Gutierrez-Polini (Gutiérrez de Polini, 1972): a readability metric designed directly for Spanish, without adapting existing English readability measures. Its value is given by Equation 3, where L is the number of characters, P the number of words, and F the number of sentences.

$$Score = 92.5 - \frac{9.7 * L}{P} - \frac{0.35P}{F} \quad (3)$$

Crawford (Crawford, 1989): this index is limited to measure the difficulty for children at primary school to learn a text. Its value is given by Equation 4, where OP is the number of sentences for every 100 words, and SP the number of syllables for every 100 words. The output refers to the years in primary school needed to understand a text. Therefore, the higher the number of years at school, the less readable the text will be. We are interested in lower values for more legible texts.

$$Score = -0.205OP + 0.049SP - 3.407 \quad (4)$$

Table 3 shows these readability indices for each of the proposed dataset splits for sentences and paragraphs. For both granularities, all scores for texts in each group differ significantly between readability levels. For example, for paragraphs, in the 3-class group, the corresponding fernandez-huerta index for "basic" texts is more than 10 points higher than for "intermerdiate" texts, which in turn is around 7 points higher than for "advanced" texts. Since for this index higher scores indicate more readable texts, this indicates that the split is adequate. In general, these results support our proposed mapping summarised in Table 2.

3.4 Datasets Limitations

Texts from the the Spanish portion of the Newsela dataset are translations from the original English articles.[9] This may impact the quality and generalisation capabilities of the models we created compared to Newsela-based studies in English.

Texts in CAES were written by learners of Spanish with different backgrounds and levels of experience. Therefore, there are grammatical and syntactical errors in their construction. Also, the topics of each text depend on the CEFR levels of the students. For example, A1 students mostly write emails, while B1 students write essays. This could bias the ARA classifiers to learn to identify topics rather than readability levels. For this reason, we did not include CAES in our experiments (Sec. 6). However, this dataset will still be available for further studies where these limitations are not relevant or actually want to be explored.

[9] https://newsela.com/about/blog/how-to-use-spanish-texts-on-newsela/

Group	Subset	Readability Labels	OneStopEnglish	Paragraphs (ES)	Sentences (ES)
2-class	train	complex	-	2,470	9,532
		simple	-	2,096	7,708
	valid	complex	-	313	1,181
		simple	-	258	974
	test	complex	-	317	1,249
		simple	-	254	908
3-class	train	basic	145	1,603	6,147
		intermediate	150	1,975	6,187
		advanced	158	1,512	6,424
	valid	basic	24	201	804
		intermediate	17	256	770
		advanced	16	179	770
	test	basic	20	199	748
		intermediate	22	271	818
		advanced	15	167	779

Table 5: Number of samples for each dataset, stratified by split and readability labels and levels

For our experiments in the next section, we used all the datasets in the benchmark. However, our final release will include only those that are freely available. Researchers would need to request the specific licenses for Newsela and Simplext before we could share with them our specific data splits.

4 Neural ARA Models

Considering the characteristics of our dataset, we treated ARA as a classification task, and used the datasets in our benchmark to implement neural supervised models. Following previous work (Martinc et al., 2021; Lee and Vajjala, 2022), we used BERT (Devlin et al., 2019) models with fully connected layers and softmax outputs. As base BERT models, we experimented with:

- **BERTIN** (De la Rosa et al., 2022): a RoBERTa-based (Liu et al., 2019) pretrained model using Spanish corpora and a perplexity sampling that allowed its fine-tuning with a reduced training time and data.

- **mBERT** (Devlin et al., 2019): a BERT-based model, trained over 102 languages, including Spanish. This model will determine whether a multilingual, general-purpose model is appropriate for this task, in comparison to a dedicated model for Spanish. Also, previous work has relied on these models for multilingual readability assessment in English, French and Spanish (Lee and Vajjala, 2022).

We used the BERTIN[10] and mBERT[11] checkpoints available in HuggingFace (Wolf et al., 2020) to implement six models in the following settings:

Zero-shot. Models based on BERTIN and mBERT are not trained in any task-specific data and are used directly to make predictions in the test set. This aims to explore if pre-trained models (monolingual or multilingual) are by default capable of performing ARA without any fine-tuning. We refer to these models as BERTIN (Zero) and mBERT (Zero).

Cross-lingual Zero-shot. We study if a multilingual model is able to perform ARA after being fine-tuned using task specific data but from a different language. In particular, we fine-tune mBERT using the OneStopEnglish corpus (Vajjala and Lučić, 2018), which includes articles from newspapers rewritten by teachers of English as a second language. Texts in this dataset are divided into elementary, intermediate, and advanced levels. As such, we limit our experiments to the evaluation of the 3-class groups since OneStopEnglish does not have a predefined alignment for 2 levels. Using the intermediate corpus in any of the other categories could be unreliable. In addition, removing the intermediate level to evaluate the 2-class groups would result in a very small dataset. We refer to this model as mBERT (EN).

[10] https://huggingface.co/bertin-project/bertin-roberta-base-spanish

[11] https://huggingface.co/bert-base-multilingual-uncased

Granularity	Model	2-class F1–Score	2-class Precision	2-class Recall	3-class F1–Score	3-class Precision	3-class Recall
Paragraph	Baseline (TF-IDF+LR)	0.829	0.832	0.827	0.556	0.563	0.550
	BERTIN (Zero)	0.308	0.222	0.500	0.227	0.284	0.338
	BERTIN (ES)	0.924	0.923	0.925	0.772	0.776	0.768
	mBERT (Zero)	0.308	0.222	0.500	0.253	0.312	0.368
	mBERT (EN)	-	-	-	0.505	0.560	0.552
	mBERT (ES)	**0.933**	**0.932**	**0.936**	0.776	0.777	0.778
	mBERT (EN+ES)	-	-	-	**0.779**	**0.783**	**0.779**
Sentence	Baseline (TF-IDF+LR)	0.811	0.814	0.808	0.525	0.531	0.521
	BERTIN (Zero)	0.367	0.290	0.500	0.188	0.232	0.335
	BERTIN (ES)	**0.900**	**0.900**	**0.900**	**0.699**	**0.701**	**0.698**
	mBERT (Zero)	0.367	0.290	0.500	0.278	0.329	0.351
	mBERT (EN)	-	-	-	0.521	0.565	0.539
	mBERT (ES)	0.893	0.891	0.896	0.688	0.686	0.691
	mBERT (EN+ES)	-	-	-	0.679	0.676	0.682

Table 6: F1–score, precision, and recall scores for readability baselines. In **bold** we select the best model for each combination of granularity in a group of readability levels.

Monolingual Few-shot. This is the standard supervised setting where BERTIN and mBERT are fine-tuned using the training data from our benchmark. We consider this setting as few-show since the Spanish corpora is not large. We refer to these models as BERTIN (ES) and mBERT (ES).

Cross-lingual Few-shot. We experiment with further fine-tuning the cross-lingual mBERT (EN) model with the language-specific training data from our benchmark (few-shot). We refer to this model as mBERT (EN+ES).

Each of these settings is applied to the two text granularities (paragraph and sentence) and the two groups of readability labels (2-class and 3-class).

5 Experimental Setting

Baseline. We implemented a simple approach based on Logistic Regression and TF-IDF.[12] We extracted the features for each text using TF-IDF algorithm.[13]. Then, we trained a Linear Regression classifier[14] using these features in splits (train/dev).

Data Splits. We randomly split all data into 80% for training, 10% for validation and 10% for testing, consistently across all experiments. We show the data distribution in Table 5.

[12]https://www.kaggle.com/code/kashnitsky/logistic-regression-tf-idf-baseline/notebook

[13]https://scikit-learn.org/stable/modules/generated/sklearn.feature_extraction.text.TfidfVectorizer.html

[14]https://scikit-learn.org/stable/modules/generated/sklearn.linear_model.LogisticRegression.html

Training Details. We performed hyperparameter optimisation and observed training behaviour to select the most stable models (i.e. less variability of the validation loss) as the best for the task. We selected AdamW optimizer, using a beta value of 0.9. For our 2-class and 3-class experiments we used a learning rate of 3e-6, weight_decay of 0.02, batch size of 16 and a number of epochs equal to 10. Once the models were trained, we evaluated the models in the held-out test set. We trained with a 1 Nvidia v100 GPUs (16GB GPU RAM) and training time was about 4 hours for the biggest dataset (sentence-level).

6 Results

Table 6 shows the performance in the test set of the baseline and neural models in all the training settings previously described. In addition, Figure 1 presents representative confusion matrices for our baseline and best performing models. Due to space constraints, we only include matrices for the paragraph-based corpus in the 3-class group and the sentence-based corpus in the 2-class group.

Most BERT-based models are consistently better than the TF-IDF baseline, for all text granularities and readability labels. An exception are mBERT (Zero) and BERTIN (Zero) who had the lowest performance in all cases. This implies that pre-trained models by themselves are unable to perform ARA for Spanish texts in our benchmark.

All models dropped their performance when trained in the 3-class setting compared to the

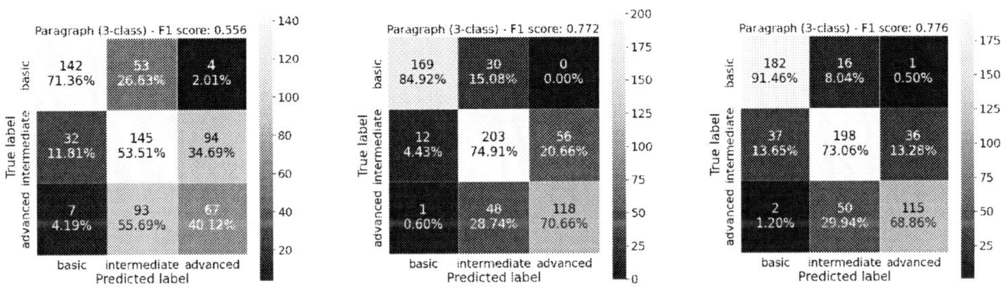

(a) TF-IDF (paragraph, 3-class) (b) BERTIN (ES) (paragraph, 3-class) (c) mBERT (ES) (paragraph, 3-class)

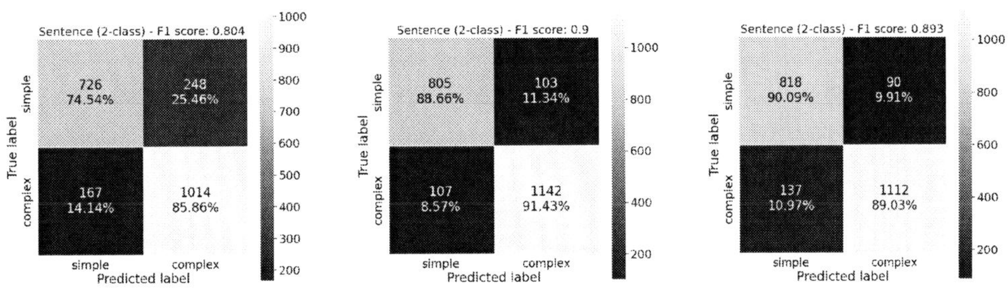

(d) TF-IDF (sentence, 2-class) (e) BERTIN (ES) (sentence, 2-class) (f) mBERT (ES) (sentence, 2-class)

Figure 1: Confusion matrices for LR-TF-IDF, BERTIN (ES) and mBERT (ES) in 2-class and 3-class task setting (paragraphs and sentences).

2-class one, including in the zero-shot models. As shown in Figure 1a, Figure 1b and Figure 1c, an "intermediate" class makes it more difficult to classify the samples, especially in the boundaries ("basic"/"intermediate" and "intermediate"/"advanced"). We can observe that it is easier to distinguish between "basic" and "advanced", evidenced by just having a few misclassified samples (see the matrices corner values). In contrast, there is a significant number of incorrect samples between the "intermediate"-"advanced" boundaries in the 3 models.

The cross-lingual mBERT (EN) models performed comparably to or worse than the baseline in the 3-class group for text granularities. Adding language-specific data, makes the model perform better, making mBERT (EN+ES) comparable to the mBERT (ES) model in all cases. While BERTIN (ES) is still the best in the 3-class paragraph setting, these results suggest that a multilingual pre-trained model can be leveraged for ARA in Spanish is no language-specific model is available.

Overall, we can observe that fine-tuning either BERTIN or mBERT with language-specific data would result in a good performing model for the task, for all the settings we considered. As such, these serve as strong baselines for future research.

7 Discussion

Our zero-shot (cross-lingual) experiments demonstrate that the readability task is not trivial to learn to perform ARA, and that it is directly transferable between languages in the settings we studied. For BERTIN (Zero) and mBERT (Zero), the models were not previously trained for the readability classification task resulting in poor performance.

The decrease in performance between models in the paragraph-based and sentence-based datasets could be attributed to multiple reasons. First, not all texts in the datasets could be mapped to three classes, resulting in fewer instances for training and evaluation. In addition, it may be easier for a model to distinguish between extremes ("simple" or "complex") than to also consider an "intermediate" class. This effect is clearer in the analysis of the confusion matrices in Figure 1.

Regarding our best models, we benefited from the fact that the BERTIN model was trained on

Spanish texts, which contributes for a better "understanding" of readability in this specific language. The multilingual model (mBERT) was trained in multiple languages beside Spanish, which could have contributed to the improvement of its results.

While our results may be encouraging, we state the limitations of our experiments. When short and simple texts are used for training, readability results can easily be related to short sentences and words. However, texts can also be readable in other scenarios, such as using active voice, instead of passive voice, being consistent in the narrative (e.g. following on the same topic) and the use of simpler words, which are not necessarily shorter. These features are harder to learn, as shown in our 3-class experiments, but with the use of more corpora from multiple domains, it may be possible to obtain more robust ARA models. Regarding the models, we could consider that BERTIN model is not uncased, whereas the multilingual model is; this could also be a limitation and a variability factor in the models performance. Overall, current datasets are scarce, and it is advisable to train in wider corpora for the generalisation in multiple domains.

8 Conclusion and Future Work

In this paper, we have introduced a new benchmark for ARA of texts in Spanish. We combined existing datasets for research in ARA and Text Simplification, with other resources scraped from the web. With these data, we trained neural ARA models based on BERT to classify texts into "simple" and "complex" (2-class), or "basic", "intermediate" and "advanced" (3-class), at two levels of text granularities (paragraph and sentence). The neural models proved to be better than simple baselines.

In the future, we plan to include more datasets to the benchmark, such the one used in (López-Anguita et al., 2018). In addition, we plan on training feature-based models for a more comprehensive evaluation of our neural models. Finally, it would be interesting to study the effect that larger multilingual pre-trained models, like XLM-R (Conneau et al., 2020), could have on the performance of neural models.

All of our models are publicly available, as well as demo that showcases their performances. We expect that research communities in Spanish speaking countries will benefit from this effort towards the further development of the field.

References

Kepa Bengoetxea and Itziar Gonzalez-Dios. 2021. Multiaztertest: a multilingual analyzer on multiple levels of language for readability assessment.

Steven Bird, Ewan Klein, and Edward Loper. 2009. *Natural Language Processing with Python: Analyzing Text with the Natural Language Toolkit*. O'Reilly, Beijing.

Kevyn Collins-Thompson. 2014. Computational assessment of text readability: A survey of current and future research. *ITL-International Journal of Applied Linguistics*, 165(2):97–135.

Alexis Conneau, Kartikay Khandelwal, Naman Goyal, Vishrav Chaudhary, Guillaume Wenzek, Francisco Guzmán, Edouard Grave, Myle Ott, Luke Zettlemoyer, and Veselin Stoyanov. 2020. Unsupervised cross-lingual representation learning at scale. In *Proceedings of the 58th Annual Meeting of the Association for Computational Linguistics*, pages 8440–8451, Online. Association for Computational Linguistics.

Alan N Crawford. 1989. *Fórmula y gráfico para determinar la comprensibilidad de textos de nivel primario en castellano*. Lectura y Vida. Revista Latinoamericana de Lectura.

Edgar Dale and Jeanne S. Chall. 1949. The concept of readability. *Elementary English*, 26(1):19–26.

Javier De la Rosa, Eduardo G Ponferrada, Manu Romero, Paulo Villegas, Pablo González de Prado Salas, and María Grandury. 2022. Bertin: Efficient pre-training of a spanish language model using perplexity sampling. *Procesamiento del Lenguaje Natural*, 68.

Felice Dell'Orletta, Simonetta Montemagni, and Giulia Venturi. 2011. READ–IT: Assessing readability of Italian texts with a view to text simplification. In *Proceedings of the Second Workshop on Speech and Language Processing for Assistive Technologies*, pages 73–83, Edinburgh, Scotland, UK. Association for Computational Linguistics.

Jacob Devlin, Ming-Wei Chang, Kenton Lee, and Kristina Toutanova. 2019. BERT: Pre-training of deep bidirectional transformers for language understanding. In *Proceedings of the 2019 Conference of the North American Chapter of the Association for Computational Linguistics: Human Language Technologies, Volume 1 (Long and Short Papers)*, pages 4171–4186, Minneapolis, Minnesota. Association for Computational Linguistics.

Sidney Evaldo Leal, João Marcos Munguba Vieira, Erica dos Santos Rodrigues, Elisângela Nogueira Teixeira, and Sandra Aluísio. 2020. Using eye-tracking data to predict the readability of Brazilian Portuguese sentences in single-task, multi-task and sequential transfer learning approaches. In *Proceedings of the*

28th International Conference on Computational Linguistics, pages 5821–5831, Barcelona, Spain (Online). International Committee on Computational Linguistics.

José Fernández-Huerta. 1959. Medidas sencillas de lecturabilidad. *Consigna*, (214):29–32.

Thomas François and Eleni Miltsakaki. 2012. Do NLP and machine learning improve traditional readability formulas? In *Proceedings of the First Workshop on Predicting and Improving Text Readability for target reader populations*, pages 49–57, Montréal, Canada. Association for Computational Linguistics.

Thomas François and Cedric Fairon. 2012. An "ai readability" formula for french as a foreign language. In *EMNLP*.

Laura Gaeta, Edward Garcia, and Valeria Gonzalez. 2021. Readability and suitability of spanish-language hearing aid user guides. *American Journal of Audiology*, 30(2):452–457.

Sian Gooding, Yevgeni Berzak, Tony Mak, and Matt Sharifi. 2021. Predicting text readability from scrolling interactions. In *Proceedings of the 25th Conference on Computational Natural Language Learning*, pages 380–390, Online. Association for Computational Linguistics.

Robert Gunning et al. 1952. Technique of clear writing.

L.E. Gutiérrez de Polini. 1972. *Investigación sobre lectura en Venezuela*. Documento presentado a las Primeras Jornadas de Educación Primaria, Ministerio de Educación, Caracas.

Julia Hancke, Sowmya Vajjala, and Detmar Meurers. 2012. Readability classification for German using lexical, syntactic, and morphological features. In *Proceedings of COLING 2012*, pages 1063–1080, Mumbai, India. The COLING 2012 Organizing Committee.

David M. Howcroft and Vera Demberg. 2017. Psycholinguistic models of sentence processing improve sentence readability ranking. In *Proceedings of the 15th Conference of the European Chapter of the Association for Computational Linguistics: Volume 1, Long Papers*, pages 958–968, Valencia, Spain. Association for Computational Linguistics.

Joseph Marvin Imperial. 2021. BERT embeddings for automatic readability assessment. In *Proceedings of the International Conference on Recent Advances in Natural Language Processing (RANLP 2021)*, pages 611–618, Held Online. INCOMA Ltd.

J. Peter Kincaid, Robert P. Fishburne, R L Rogers, and Brad S. Chissom. 1975. Derivation of new readability formulas (automated readability index, fog count and flesch reading ease formula) for navy enlisted personnel. In *Institute for Simulation and Training*.

Justin Lee and Sowmya Vajjala. 2022. A neural pairwise ranking model for readability assessment. In *Findings of the Association for Computational Linguistics: ACL 2022*, pages 3802–3813, Dublin, Ireland. Association for Computational Linguistics.

Yinhan Liu, Myle Ott, Naman Goyal, Jingfei Du, Mandar Joshi, Danqi Chen, Omer Levy, Mike Lewis, Luke Zettlemoyer, and Veselin Stoyanov. 2019. Roberta: A robustly optimized BERT pretraining approach. *CoRR*, abs/1907.11692.

An-Vinh Luong, Diep Nguyen, and Dinh Dien. 2017. Examining the text-length factor in evaluating the readability of literary texts in vietnamese textbooks. *2017 9th International Conference on Knowledge and Systems Engineering (KSE)*, pages 36–41.

Rocío López-Anguita, Arturo Montejo-Ráez, Fernando J. Martínez-Santiago, and Manuel Carlos Díaz-Galiano. 2018. Legibilidad del texto, métricas de complejidad y la importancia de las palabras. *Procesamiento del Lenguaje Natural*, 61(0):101–108.

Mounica Maddela and Wei Xu. 2018. A word-complexity lexicon and a neural readability ranking model for lexical simplification. In *Proceedings of the 2018 Conference on Empirical Methods in Natural Language Processing*, pages 3749–3760, Brussels, Belgium. Association for Computational Linguistics.

Matej Martinc, Senja Pollak, and Marko Robnik-Šikonja. 2021. Supervised and unsupervised neural approaches to text readability. *Computational Linguistics*, 47(1):141–179.

Martina Miliani, Serena Auriemma, Fernando Alva-Manchego, and Alessandro Lenci. 2022. Neural readability pairwise ranking for sentences in italian administrative language. In *Proceedings of the 2nd Conference of the Asia-Pacific Chapter of the Association for Computational Linguistics and the 12th International Joint Conference on Natural Language Processing*, Online. Association for Computational Linguistics.

Jorge Morato, Ana Iglesias, Adrián Campillo, and Sonia Sanchez-Cuadrado. 2021. Automated readability assessment for spanish e-government information. *Journal of Information Systems Engineering and Management*, 6:em0137.

Giovanni Parodi. 2015. Corpus de aprendices de español (caes). *Journal of Spanish Language Teaching*, 2(2):194–200.

Xinying Qiu, Yuan Chen, Hanwu Chen, Jian-Yun Nie, Yuming Shen, and Dawei Lu. 2021. Learning syntactic dense embedding with correlation graph for automatic readability assessment. In *Proceedings of the 59th Annual Meeting of the Association for Computational Linguistics and the 11th International Joint Conference on Natural Language Processing (Volume 1: Long Papers)*, pages 3013–3025, Online. Association for Computational Linguistics.

Andre Quispesaravia, Walter Perez, Marco Sobrevilla Cabezudo, and Fernando Alva-Manchego. 2016. Coh-Metrix-Esp: A complexity analysis tool for documents written in Spanish. In *Proceedings of the Tenth International Conference on Language Resources and Evaluation (LREC'16)*, pages 4694–4698, Portorož, Slovenia. European Language Resources Association (ELRA).

Luz Rello, Ricardo Baeza-Yates, Laura Dempere-Marco, and Horacio Saggion. 2013. Frequent words improve readability and short words improve understandability for people with dyslexia. In *INTERACT*.

Robert Joshua Reynolds. 2016. Insights from russian second language readability classification: complexity-dependent training requirements, and feature evaluation of multiple categories. In *BEA@NAACL-HLT*.

Jorge A. Rodriguez and Karandeep Singh. 2018. The spanish availability and readability of diabetes apps. *Journal of Diabetes Science and Technology*, 12(3):719–724. PMID: 29291639.

Horacio Saggion, Elena Gómez-Martínez, Esteban Etayo, Alberto Anula, and Lorena Bourg. 2011. Text simplification in simplext. making text more accessible. *Proces. del Leng. Natural*, 47:341–342.

Carolina Scarton, Caroline Gasperin, and Sandra Aluisio. 2010. Revisiting the readability assessment of texts in portuguese. In *Advances in Artificial Intelligence – IBERAMIA 2010*, pages 306–315, Berlin, Heidelberg. Springer Berlin Heidelberg.

Carolina Evaristo Scarton and Sandra Maria Aluísio. 2010. Coh-metrix-port: a readability assessment tool for texts in brazilian portuguese. In *International Conference on Computational Processing of the Portuguese Language - Propor*. SBC.

Sanja Štajner and Horacio Saggion. 2013. Readability indices for automatic evaluation of text simplification systems: A feasibility study for Spanish. In *Proceedings of the Sixth International Joint Conference on Natural Language Processing*, pages 374–382, Nagoya, Japan. Asian Federation of Natural Language Processing.

Francisco Szigriszt Pazos. 1993. *Sistemas Predictivos de Legibilidad del Mensaje Escrito: Formula de Perspicuidad*. Universidad Complutense de Madrid.

Francisco Szigriszt Pazos. 2001. *Sistemas predictivos de legibilidad del mensaje escrito: fórmula de perspicuidad*. Universidad Complutense de Madrid, Servicio de Publicaciones.

Satoru Uchida, Shohei Takada, and Yuki Arase. 2018. Cefr-based lexical simplification dataset. In *Proceedings of International Conference on Language Resources and Evaluation*, volume 11, pages 3254–3258. European Language Resources Association.

Sowmya Vajjala. 2022. Trends, limitations and open challenges in automatic readability assessment research. In *Proceedings of the 13th Language Resources and Evaluation Conference*, Marseille, France. European Language Resources Association.

Sowmya Vajjala and Ivana Lučić. 2018. OneStopEnglish corpus: A new corpus for automatic readability assessment and text simplification. In *Proceedings of the Thirteenth Workshop on Innovative Use of NLP for Building Educational Applications*, pages 297–304, New Orleans, Louisiana. Association for Computational Linguistics.

Sowmya Vajjala and Detmar Meurers. 2012. On improving the accuracy of readability classification using insights from second language acquisition. In *Proceedings of the Seventh Workshop on Building Educational Applications Using NLP*, pages 163–173, Montréal, Canada. Association for Computational Linguistics.

Thomas Wolf, Lysandre Debut, Victor Sanh, Julien Chaumond, Clement Delangue, Anthony Moi, Pierric Cistac, Tim Rault, Remi Louf, Morgan Funtowicz, Joe Davison, Sam Shleifer, Patrick von Platen, Clara Ma, Yacine Jernite, Julien Plu, Canwen Xu, Teven Le Scao, Sylvain Gugger, Mariama Drame, Quentin Lhoest, and Alexander Rush. 2020. Transformers: State-of-the-art natural language processing. In *Proceedings of the 2020 Conference on Empirical Methods in Natural Language Processing: System Demonstrations*, pages 38–45, Online. Association for Computational Linguistics.

Menglin Xia, Ekaterina Kochmar, and Ted Briscoe. 2016. Text readability assessment for second language learners. In *Proceedings of the 11th Workshop on Innovative Use of NLP for Building Educational Applications*, pages 12–22, San Diego, CA. Association for Computational Linguistics.

Wei Xu, Chris Callison-Burch, and Courtney Napoles. 2015. Problems in current text simplification research: New data can help. *Transactions of the Association for Computational Linguistics*, 3:283–297.

Controllable Lexical Simplification for English

Kim Cheng Sheang, Daniel Ferrés, Horacio Saggion
LaSTUS Lab, TALN Group, Universitat Pompeu Fabra
C/Roc Boronat 138, Barcelona, 08018, Spain
{kimcheng.sheang, daniel.ferres, horacio.saggion}@upf.edu

Abstract

Fine-tuning Transformer-based approaches have recently shown exciting results on sentence simplification task. However, so far, no research has applied similar approaches to the Lexical Simplification (LS) task. In this paper, we present ConLS, a Controllable Lexical Simplification system fine-tuned with T5 (a Transformer-based model pre-trained with a BERT-style approach and several other tasks). The evaluation results on three datasets (LexMTurk, BenchLS, and NNSeval) have shown that our model performs comparable to LSBert (the current state-of-the-art) and even outperforms it in some cases. We also conducted a detailed comparison on the effectiveness of control tokens to give a clear view of how each token contributes to the model.

1 Introduction

Lexical Simplification (LS) is a Natural Language Processing task that modifies texts by substituting difficult words with easier words (or phrases) while keeping the original information and meaning (Shardlow, 2014). Table 1 shows an example of a lexical simplification. On the other hand, Syntactic Simplification (SS) is a similar task that reduces the syntactic complexity of a text. Both LS and SS tasks can be seen as sub-tasks of the broader task of Automatic Text Simplification (Saggion, 2017), which reduces both the lexical and syntactic complexity of texts. Lexical Simplification systems (Paetzold and Specia, 2017a) usually have components for 1) identification of complex words; 2) generation of substitution words; 3) selection of the substitutes that can fit in the context; 4) ranking substitutes by their simplicity; and 5) morphological and contextual adaptation (if necessary). The systems evaluated in this paper do not perform complex word identification. We use datasets that already had a complex word tagged for each instance. Moreover, we do not address the morphological and context adaptation task because neural-based language models usually return a correct inflected candidate.

Complex Sentence:
The Hush Sound is currently on **hiatus**.
Simplified Sentence:
The Hush Sound is currently on **break**.

Table 1: A lexical simplification example taken from the LexMTurk dataset (Horn et al., 2014) with the complex word and the substitute word in bold.

The contributions of this paper are:

- To the best of our knowledge, we are the first to introduce a controllable mechanism for LS and to fine-tune a Transformer-based model for LS. [1]
- We have conducted an extensive evaluation of several metrics. This allows us to better understand the system when applied to real-world scenarios.

The rest of the paper is organized as follows: in Section 2, we describe related work on Lexical Simplification focusing on neural-based systems. Section 3 presents the ConLS approach. Section 4 describes the evaluation metrics and presents the experimental results. Section 5 discusses the results of the experiments, while Section 6 concludes the paper and presents future work.

2 Related Work

Early Lexical Simplification approaches with unsupervised models used: Latent Words Language Models (De Belder and Moens, 2010), Wikipedia-based models/rules (Biran et al., 2011; Yatskar et al., 2010; Horn et al., 2014) and distributional

[1] The code and data are available at `https://github.com/KimChengSHEANG/ConLS`

Proceedings of the Workshop on Text Simplification, Accessibility, and Readability (TSAR-2022), pages 199 - 206
December 8, 2022 ©2022 Association for Computational Linguistics

lexical semantics (Glavaš and Štajner, 2015). (Paetzold and Specia, 2017b) started the use of neural networks for the task combined with a retrofitted context-aware word embedding model.

(Qiang et al., 2020, 2021) presented LSBert, a Lexical Simplification system that uses a pre-trained BERT (Devlin et al., 2019) model for English to generate substitution candidates. LSBert has two main phases: 1) Substitution Generation with the BERT Masked Language Model, and 2) Substitution Filtering and Ranking with several features: BERT prediction order, a BERT language model, PPDB database, corpus-based word frequency, and FastText similarity.

Martin et al. (2020) presented ACCESS a controllable Text Simplification system based on Sequence-to-Sequence models. This system allows explicit control of simplification conditions such as length, amount of paraphrasing, lexical complexity, and syntactic complexity. ACCESS achieved SOTA results in Text Simplification benchmarks on the WikiLarge test set. Later on, Martin et al. (2022) introduced MUSS (an extended version) by fine-tuning BART (Lewis et al., 2019) with ACCESS, and the results were improved. In addition, Sheang and Saggion (2021) took a similar approach, adding another control token (number of words) and fine-tuning it with T5 (Raffel et al., 2020).

3 System Description

Following recent works of Martin et al. (2020), Martin et al. (2022), Sheang and Saggion (2021), and Štajner et al. (2022b), we are inspired to apply a similar approach in lexical simplification task. Specifically, our model is based on Sheang and Saggion (2021), a model originally developed for sentence simplification[2]. We propose a controllable mechanism for LS because we believe that the embedded token values extracted from training data could give additional information to the model about the relations between the source and the target word; so that at inference, we could define different token values that fulfill our objectives, which in this case is to find the best candidates. In the following paragraphs, we describe all the details about each token and the reason why they are chosen.

[2]https://github.com/KimChengSHEANG/TS_T5

Word Length (WL) is the character length ratio between the complex word and the target word. It is the number of characters of the target word divided by the number of characters of the complex word. Based on our analysis of the training dataset (TSAR-EN), 65.71% of the time complex word is longer than the best candidate, 21.30% the complex word is shorter than the best candidate, and 12.99% both are the same length.

Word Rank (WR) is the inverse frequency of the target word divided by that of the complex word. The inverse frequency order is extracted from the FastText pre-trained model. Based on our analysis of the TSAR-EN dataset, 85.45% of the time, the complex word has a lower frequency than the best candidate. Therefore, this token is a good indicator to help guide the model to predict simpler candidates.

Candidate Ranking (CR) is the ranking order extracted from the training data. The values are given to candidates by the ranking order. E.g., the best-ranking candidate is given the value 1.00, the second 0.75, the third 0.50, the fourth 0.25, and starting from the fifth, it is given 0.00. We used only five different values to avoid overloading the model, as the training data is relatively small. In addition, the rationale behind using these values is that we want the model to learn candidates ranking from data through the training process rather than injecting additional information or doing post-processing.

4 Experiments

In our experiments, we compare our model with the current state-of-the-art model LSBert (Qiang et al., 2020). We used the original LSBert configurations and resources, and we made the following changes to have a detailed comparison with our model. By default, LSBert returns only a single best candidate for each complex word, so we made the changes to return the 10 best-ranked candidates. We changed the number of BERT mask selections from 10 to 15 so that after removing duplicate candidates, we still have around 10 candidates. Moreover, we filtered out all the candidates that were equal to the complex word. Due to the fact that all the used datasets have gold annotated simpler substitutions in all instances, we could assume that returning the complex word would be incorrect.

4.1 Datasets

This subsection describes all the Lexical Simplification datasets for English that we used in our experiments. We used LexMTurk (Horn et al., 2014), BenchLS[3] (Paetzold and Specia, 2016a), and NNSeval [4] (Paetzold and Specia, 2016b) for testing and TSAR-EN (Štajner et al., 2022a) dataset for training and validation. LexMTurk has 500 sentences that were obtained from Wikipedia. This dataset contains the marked complex words and their replacements suggested by 50 English-speaking annotators. The BenchLS dataset is a union of the LSeval (De Belder and Moens, 2012) and LexMTurk datasets in which spelling and inflection errors were automatically corrected. The NNSeval dataset is a filtered version of the BenchLS adapted to evaluate LS for non-native English speakers.

Sentence
European Union foreign ministers agreed Monday to impose fresh sanctions on Syria as a U.N.-backed peace plan – along with all other diplomatic efforts – has yet to stop the **carnage** that mounts every day.
Simpler Substitutes
destruction:6, bloodshed:3, massacre:3, slaughter:3, carnage:2, brutality:1, butchering:1, butchery:1, damage:1, death:1, slaying:1, violence:1, war:1

Table 2: An example taken from the TSAR-EN dataset Štajner et al. (2012) with the target word in bold. The numbers after ':' represents the number of workers that suggested the substitution. Each instance has 25 substitutes suggested by 25 crowd-sourced workers.

TSAR-EN dataset has 386 instances with 25 gold-annotated substitutions. Table 2 shows an example. The instances and their target complex words were extracted from the Complex Word Identification shared task 2018 (Yimam et al., 2018). The instances were annotated using Amazon's Mechanical Turk by 25 annotators. A native English annotator reviewed all suggestions.

4.2 Evaluation Metrics

We evaluated the systems with several metrics that could take into account the results for different numbers of K candidates (from 1 up to 10). The metrics used are the following:

- *Accuracy@1*: is the ratio of instances with the top-ranked candidate in the gold standard list of annotated candidates.
- *Accuracy@K@top1*: The ratio of instances where at least one of the top K predicted candidates matches the most frequently suggested synonym/s[5] in the gold list of annotated candidates.
- *Potential@K*: the percentage of instances for which at least one of the top K substitutes predicted is present in the set of gold annotations.
- *Mean Average Precision@K (MAP@K)*: This metric evaluates the relevance and ranking of the top K predicted substitutes.
- Precision@K: the percentage of top K generated candidates that are in the gold standard.
- Recall@K: the percentage of gold-standard substitutions that are included in the top K generated substitutions.

4.3 Experimental Setup

In this section, we describe how the data are preprocessed, the training details of the model, and finally, the generation of candidates.

4.3.1 Data Preprocessing

For each instance, we have a sentence, a complex word, and a list of ranked candidates. We compute all the ratios and the ranking, then prepend it to the source sentence. We also use special tokens [T] and [/T] to mark the boundary of the complex word in the source sentence and the simple word in the target sentence. Moreover, these special tokens help us identify the candidates during the inference. Table 3 shows an example of source and target sentences embedded with token values and boundary tokens.

4.3.2 Training

For our experiments, we fine-tuned T5-Large on the TSAR-EN dataset. We also compared the differences of T5 models; the results are in Table 6. We split the dataset to 90% for training and 10% for validation. This 10% validation set is also used

[3]https://doi.org/10.5281/zenodo.2552393

[4]https://doi.org/10.5281/zenodo.2552381

[5]Ties in the most repeated gold-annotated candidates are taken into account.

Source: <CR_1.00> <WL_0.54> <WR_0.90> The Obama administration has seen what The New York Times calls an [T]unprecedented[/T] crackdown on leaks of government secrets.

Target: The Obama administration has seen what The New York Times calls an [T]unusual[/T] crackdown on leaks of government secrets.

Table 3: A training example. The control token values are extracted from the complex word (unprecedented) and one substitute word (unusual). The word unusual is the best-ranked candidate suggested by annotators, so the CR value is 1.00. We used all the candidates in each instance to generate parallel sentences for training. One candidate per training example.

in the token values search at the inference, as described in the following section. For the training data, we preprocessed by extracting and adding control tokens to the source sentence along with the boundary tokens to the complex word and substitute word, as shown in Table 3. We set the maximum sequence length (number of tokens) to 128, as all our datasets contain less than 128 in tokens length. We used Optuna (Akiba et al., 2019) for hyper-parameters search. For more details about the implementation and hyperparameters, please check Appendix A.

4.3.3 Inference

First, we performed token values search on the validation set that maximizes the Accuracy@1@top1 score using Optuna (Akiba et al., 2019). We searched the values ranging between 0.5 and 1.25; at each iteration, we changed the value by 0.05. We searched only WL and WR, whereas for CR, we set it to 1.00 because we already knew that the best-ranking candidates were given the value of 1.00. Then we kept these values fixed for all sentences at the inference. Finally, at the inference, we set the beam search to 15 and the number of return sequences to 15 so that after filtering out some duplicate candidates, the remaining would be around 10. The ranking order of the candidates is chosen from the return orders of sequences produced by the model.

5 Results and Discussion

In Table 4 we present the results for the metrics: *Accuracy@1*, *Accuracy@k@Top1*, and *Potential@K*. In Table 5 we present the results for the metrics: *MAP@K*, *Precision@K*, and *Recall@K*. The results of ConLS presented here are based T5-Large.

Our experiments show that the modified LSBert had improved its *Accuracy@1* metric results with respect to the ones seen in the original LSBert paper (Qiang et al., 2021): *Accuracy@1* has improved from 79.20 to 84.80 for LexMTurk, from 61.60 to 67.59 for BenchLS, and from 43.60 to 44.76 for NNSeval. On the other hand, for the *Accuracy@1* metric the ConLS system does not improve the results of the modified LSBert system but improves the results of the original LSBert for the LexMturk and BenchLS datasets. The results of the *Accuracy@k@Top1* metric show that the modified LSBert achieves better results at K={1,2} and the ConLS achieves better results at K={3,4,5} for all datasets. This indicates that with more candidates allowed (3, 4, and 5 candidates) the ConLS is able to generate more instances with candidates within the top-1(s) gold annotated substitution(s) with respect to LSBert. The results of the *Potential@K* metric show these facts: 1) in LexMturk and BenchLS, the ConLS is outperforming LSBert gradually and increasingly from k=3 to k=10; 2) in NNSeval, ConLS improves the potential of LSBert only at K=10. For the MAP@K metric, we show that ConLS is able to improve the results of the metric at K={4,5,10} in all the datasets with respect to the modified LSBert. Finally, the results of the *Precision@K* and *Recall@K* metrics show the same pattern: 1) for LexMTurk, ConLS outperforms the LSBert in all K={3,5,10}; 2) for BenchLS and NNSEval, ConLS outperforms the LSBert only in K={5,10}.

We also conducted a comparison on the effect of different T5 models trained with TSAR-EN and evaluated with LexMTurk. Table 6 shows that the T5-Large model performs a lot better than the T5-Base and the T5-Small models in all metrics (Accuracy@1, Accuracy@k@Top1). Therefore, we believe that the performance of our model would improve if we could go with larger model, for example, T5-3b or T5-11b. We have tried with T5-3b model, but unfortunately it was unable to fit into our GPU memory (NVidia RTX 3090) even though we had set the batch size to as small as one.

To evaluate the effectiveness of the control tokens, we conducted further experiments with different set of combinations. We trained and evaluated each set of tokens using T5-Large with TSAR-EN

Dataset	System	ACC@1	ACC@k@Top1					Potential@k				
			@1	@2	@3	@4	@5	@2	@3	@4	@5	@10
BenchLS	LSBert	**67.59**	**40.68**	**51.45**	57.37	59.84	61.57	**77.07**	**81.27**	83.32	84.28	85.47
	ConLS	62.00	37.99	51.34	**59.31**	**64.90**	**68.46**	74.92	**81.27**	**84.82**	**87.08**	**90.31**
NNSeval	LSBert	**44.76**	**28.03**	**38.49**	43.93	46.86	49.79	**59.00**	**64.85**	**67.78**	**71.55**	74.48
	ConLS	41.00	26.77	34.30	**45.18**	**50.20**	**52.71**	53.14	61.09	65.69	69.87	**79.08**
LexMTurk	LSBert	**84.80**	**44.00**	54.80	60.40	61.80	62.80	**91.00**	93.20	94.60	95.00	95.80
	ConLS	80.60	43.80	**56.39**	**65.40**	**71.20**	**76.60**	90.00	**95.60**	**97.40**	**98.20**	**99.60**

Table 4: The results of LSBert and ConLS for the metrics: Accuracy@1, Accuracy@k@Top1, and Potential@K.

Dataset	System	MAP@k					Precision@k			Recall@k		
		@2	@3	@4	@5	@10	@3	@5	@10	@3	@5	@10
BenchLS	LSBert	**52.26**	**42.29**	34.79	29.25	15.74	**46.46**	34.62	24.90	**25.74**	29.80	32.41
	ConLS	49.73	41.37	**35.01**	**30.54**	**18.84**	46.34	**37.11**	**26.20**	25.59	**32.25**	**41.89**
NNSeval	LSBert	**34.93**	**27.84**	23.18	19.97	10.73	32.84	26.16	18.78	**19.55**	23.40	26.14
	ConLS	31.69	27.31	**23.23**	**20.30**	**12.53**	**32.91**	**27.02**	**19.51**	18.80	**23.80**	**32.08**
LexMTurk	LSBert	**67.05**	54.41	45.83	39.01	21.29	58.03	45.25	33.43	20.52	24.61	27.52
	ConLS	65.45	**55.45**	**48.04**	**42.52**	**27.59**	**60.16**	**49.89**	**36.94**	**21.32**	**27.51**	**37.15**

Table 5: The results of LSBert and ConLS for the metrics: *MAP@K*, *Precision@K*, and *Recall@K*.

T5 Model	ACC@1	ACC@k@Top1		
		@1	@2	@3
T5-Small	23.40	7.80	11.80	15.40
T5-Base	60.00	28.80	40.40	48.40
T5-Large	**80.60**	**43.80**	**56.39**	**65.40**

Table 6: The results of ConLS trained all tokens using different T5 models. The models were trained with TSAR-EN and evaluated with LexMTurk.

Tokens	ACC@1	ACC@k@Top1		
		@1	@2	@3
No Tokens	79.20	41.80	55.20	62.60
CR	79.00	41.00	54.40	62.60
WL	79.40	43.00	55.20	65.00
WR	78.60	41.20	54.60	63.20
CR+WL	78.40	41.40	54.40	62.40
CR+WR	78.60	42.80	54.60	62.20
WL+WR	78.60	41.00	54.20	62.20
All Tokens	**80.60**	**43.80**	**56.39**	**65.40**

Table 7: The results of ConLS trained with different set of tokens. Each model was trained with TSAR-EN and evaluated with LexMTurk.

for training and LexMTurk for evaluation. The results on Table 7 have shown that the model trained with no tokens performs lower than the model with all tokens in all metrics, especially for the Accuracy@1@Top1 metric, the model with all tokens perform +2 points higher. Moreover, the **all tokens** model performs better than all other models in all metrics. This indicates that each token contributes to the selection and the ranking of the candidates that leads to better performance.

6 Conclusions and Future Work

This paper presents ConLS, the first approach for Controllable Lexical Simplification. The paper also describes the evaluation of LSBert and ConLS for English with the LexMTurk, BenchLS, and NNSeval datasets for testing and the TSAR-EN dataset for training. The results of our evaluation show that the modified LSBert improves the *Accuracy@1* metric results with respect to the ones seen in the original LSBert paper in all three datasets. ConLS also improves it for the LexMturk and BenchLS datasets. Moreover, the ConLS system is able to achieve: 1) more potential to capture correct answers at K={3,4,5,10} for BenchLS and LexMturk and at K=10 for NNSeval with respect to LSBert, 2) with more candidates retrieved (4 or 5) is able to generate more candidates within the top-1 more frequent gold-annotated suggestions with respect to LSBert, 3) with K={5,10} candidates is able to generate (according to the gold-annotations) more correct and different candidates.

For future work, we plan to build a custom model to predict the best control token values from a given input instance. Having instance-customized control token values seems more adequate, as humans usually select the best candidate based on context.

Limitations

We describe in this Section the limitation of our work. The most probable limiting features are:

- The size of training dataset: the TSAR-EN dataset has 386 instances. Obviously, training with datasets with a large number of instances would be recommended to create better models.
- Quality of the training dataset: although during the creation of the TSAR-EN dataset, it was inspected and the unsuitable substitutions were removed and replaced with suitable ones (Štajner et al., 2022a), it is possible that the dataset quality could be improved by including substitutions not reported by the annotators.
- Quality of the testing datasets: it is also possible that these datasets could be improved by including substitutions not reported by the annotators.
- Successful adaptation to other languages: we could have possible difficulties in achieving similar adaptations and results in non-English languages due to the difficulties in availability of similar resources for other languages and specifically for low-resource languages.

Ethics Statement

We have described the limitations of the proposed method in the previous Section. All the scientific datasets and algorithms used are properly cited.

Acknowledgements

Our work is supported from the project Context-aware Multilingual Text Simplification (ConMuTeS) PID2019-109066GB-I00/AEI/10.13039/501100011033 awarded by Ministerio de Ciencia, Innovación y Universidades (MCIU) and by Agencia Estatal de Investigación (AEI) of Spain. In addition, we would like to thank the anonymous reviewers for their constructive comments and suggestions.

References

Takuya Akiba, Shotaro Sano, Toshihiko Yanase, T. Ohta, and Masanori Koyama. 2019. Optuna: A next-generation hyperparameter optimization framework. In *Proceedings of the 25th ACM SIGKDD International Conference on Knowledge Discovery & Data Mining*.

Or Biran, Samuel Brody, and Noémie Elhadad. 2011. Putting it simply: a context-aware approach to lexical simplification. In *Proceedings of the 49th Annual Meeting of the Association for Computational Linguistics: Human Language Technologies*, pages 496–501, Portland, Oregon, USA. Association for Computational Linguistics.

Jan De Belder and Marie-Francine Moens. 2010. Text Simplification for Children. In *Proceedings of the SIGIR Workshop on Accessible Search Systems*, pages 19–26.

Jan De Belder and Marie-Francine Moens. 2012. A Dataset for the Evaluation of Lexical Simplification. In *Proceedings of the 13th International Conference on Computational Linguistics and Intelligent Text Processing - Volume Part II*, CICLing'12, page 426–437, Berlin, Heidelberg. Springer-Verlag.

Jacob Devlin, Ming-Wei Chang, Kenton Lee, and Kristina Toutanova. 2019. BERT: Pre-training of deep bidirectional transformers for language understanding. In *Proceedings of the 2019 Conference of the North American Chapter of the Association for Computational Linguistics: Human Language Technologies, Volume 1 (Long and Short Papers)*, pages 4171–4186.

Goran Glavaš and Sanja Štajner. 2015. Simplifying Lexical Simplification: Do We Need Simplified Corpora? In *Proceedings of the 53rd Annual Meeting of the Association for Computational Linguistics and the 7th International Joint Conference on Natural Language Processing (Volume 2: Short Papers)*, pages 63–68, Beijing, China. Association for Computational Linguistics.

Colby Horn, Cathryn Manduca, and David Kauchak. 2014. Learning a Lexical Simplifier Using Wikipedia. In *Proceedings of the 52nd Annual Meeting of the Association for Computational Linguistics (Volume 2: Short Papers)*, pages 458–463, Baltimore, Maryland. Association for Computational Linguistics.

Mike Lewis, Yinhan Liu, Naman Goyal, Marjan Ghazvininejad, Abdelrahman Mohamed, Omer Levy, Veselin Stoyanov, and Luke Zettlemoyer. 2019. BART: denoising sequence-to-sequence pre-training for natural language generation, translation, and comprehension. *CoRR*, abs/1910.13461.

Ilya Loshchilov and Frank Hutter. 2019. Decoupled weight decay regularization. In *International Conference on Learning Representations*.

Louis Martin, Éric de la Clergerie, Benoît Sagot, and Antoine Bordes. 2020. Controllable sentence simplification. In *Proceedings of the 12th Language Resources and Evaluation Conference*, pages 4689–4698.

Louis Martin, Angela Fan, Éric de la Clergerie, Antoine Bordes, and Benoît Sagot. 2022. MUSS: Multilingual unsupervised sentence simplification by mining paraphrases. In *Proceedings of the Thirteenth Language Resources and Evaluation Conference*, pages 1651–1664, Marseille, France. European Language Resources Association.

Gustavo Paetzold and Lucia Specia. 2016a. Benchmarking Lexical Simplification Systems. In *Proceedings of LREC-2016*.

Gustavo Paetzold and Lucia Specia. 2016b. Unsupervised Lexical Simplification for Non-Native Speakers. *Proceedings of the AAAI Conference on Artificial Intelligence*, 30(1).

Gustavo Paetzold and Lucia Specia. 2017a. A Survey on Lexical Simplification. *Journal of Artificial Intelligence Research*, 60:549–593.

Gustavo Paetzold and Lucia Specia. 2017b. Lexical simplification with neural ranking. In *Proceedings of the 15th Conference of the European Chapter of the Association for Computational Linguistics: Volume 2, Short Papers*, pages 34–40, Valencia, Spain. Association for Computational Linguistics.

Jipeng Qiang, Yun Li, Zhu Yi, Yunhao Yuan, and Xindong Wu. 2020. Lexical simplification with pretrained encoders. *Thirty-Fourth AAAI Conference on Artificial Intelligence*, pages 8649—-8656.

Jipeng Qiang, Yun Li, Yi Zhu, Yunhao Yuan, Yang Shi, and Xindong Wu. 2021. Lsbert: Lexical simplification based on bert. *IEEE/ACM Transactions on Audio, Speech, and Language Processing*, 29:3064–3076.

Colin Raffel, Noam Shazeer, Adam Roberts, Katherine Lee, Sharan Narang, Michael Matena, Yanqi Zhou, Wei Li, and Peter J. Liu. 2020. Exploring the limits of transfer learning with a unified text-to-text transformer. *Journal of Machine Learning Research*, 21(140):1–67.

Horacio Saggion. 2017. *Automatic Text Simplification*. Synthesis Lectures on Human Language Technologies. Morgan & Claypool Publishers.

Matthew Shardlow. 2014. A Survey of Automated Text Simplification. *International Journal of Advanced Computer Science and Applications*, 4.

Kim Cheng Sheang and Horacio Saggion. 2021. Controllable sentence simplification with a unified text-to-text transfer transformer. In *Proceedings of the 14th International Conference on Natural Language Generation*, pages 341–352, Aberdeen, Scotland, UK. Association for Computational Linguistics.

Thomas Wolf, Lysandre Debut, Victor Sanh, Julien Chaumond, Clement Delangue, Anthony Moi, Pierric Cistac, Tim Rault, Remi Louf, Morgan Funtowicz, Joe Davison, Sam Shleifer, Patrick von Platen, Clara Ma, Yacine Jernite, Julien Plu, Canwen Xu, Teven Le Scao, Sylvain Gugger, Mariama Drame, Quentin Lhoest, and Alexander Rush. 2020. Transformers: State-of-the-art natural language processing. In *Proceedings of the 2020 Conference on Empirical Methods in Natural Language Processing: System Demonstrations*, pages 38–45.

Mark Yatskar, Bo Pang, Cristian Danescu-Niculescu-Mizil, and Lillian Lee. 2010. For the sake of simplicity: Unsupervised extraction of lexical simplifications from Wikipedia. In *Human Language Technologies: The 2010 Annual Conference of the North American Chapter of the Association for Computational Linguistics*, pages 365–368, Los Angeles, California. Association for Computational Linguistics.

Seid Muhie Yimam, Chris Biemann, Shervin Malmasi, Gustavo H. Paetzold, Lucia Specia, Sanja Stajner, Anaïs Tack, and Marcos Zampieri. 2018. A Report on the Complex Word Identification Shared Task 2018. *CoRR*, abs/1804.09132.

Sanja Štajner, Richard Evans, Constantin Orasan, and Ruslan Mitkov. 2012. What can readability measures really tell us about text complexity. In *Proceedings of workshop on natural language processing for improving textual accessibility*, pages 14–22. Citeseer.

Sanja Štajner, Daniel Ferrés, Matthew Shardlow, Kai North, Marcos Zampieri, and Horacio Saggion. 2022a. Lexical Simplification Benchmarks for English, Portuguese, and Spanish. *Frontiers in Artificial Intelligence*, 5.

Sanja Štajner, Kim Cheng Sheang, and Horacio Saggion. 2022b. Sentence simplification capabilities of transfer-based models. *Proceedings of the AAAI Conference on Artificial Intelligence*, 36(11):12172–12180.

A Implementation Details

Our implementation is based on Huggingface Transformers (Wolf et al., 2020) and Pytorch-lightning[6]. We trained the model using T5-Large for 8 epochs. For the optimization, we used AdamW (Loshchilov and Hutter, 2019) optimizer with the learning rate of 1e-5 and adam epsilon of 1e-8. We set the batch size of 8 for both training and testing. For the inference, we used beam search with the size of 15 to get around 10 candidates after filtering out duplicate candidates or the candidates that are the same as the complex word. We trained the model on a machine with an NVidia RTX 3090, Intel core i9 CPU, with 32G of RAM. It took around 2 hours for the whole process: the training and the evaluation on the three datasets.

[6]https://www.pytorchlightning.ai

CILS at TSAR-2022 Shared Task: Investigating the Applicability of Lexical Substitution Methods for Lexical Simplification

Sandaru Seneviratne[1], **Elena Daskalaki**[1], **Hanna Suominen**[1,2]
[1]The Australian National University (ANU) / Canberra, ACT, Australia
[2]University of Turku / Turku, Finland
{sandaru.seneviratne, eleni.daskalaki, hanna.suominen}@anu.edu.au

Abstract

Lexical simplification — which aims to simplify complex text through the replacement of difficult words using simpler alternatives while maintaining the meaning of the given text — is popular as a way of improving text accessibility for both people and computers. First, lexical simplification through substitution can improve the understandability of complex text for, for example, non-native speakers, second language learners, and people with low literacy. Second, its usefulness has been demonstrated in many natural language processing problems like data augmentation, paraphrase generation, or word sense induction. In this paper, we investigated the applicability of existing unsupervised lexical substitution methods based on pre-trained contextual embedding models and WordNet, which incorporate *C*ontext *I*nformation, for *L*exical *S*implification (CILS). Although the performance of this CILS approach has been outstanding in lexical substitution tasks, its usefulness was limited at the TSAR-2022 shared task on lexical simplification. Consequently, a minimally supervised approach with careful tuning to a given simplification task may work better than unsupervised methods. Our investigation also encouraged further work on evaluating the simplicity of potential candidates and incorporating them into the lexical simplification methods.

1 Introduction

Lexical simplification — which aims to simplify complex words and phrases in text while maintaining the meaning of the original text — is an important natural language processing (NLP) problem to improve the understandability of text for, for example, non-native speakers, second language learners, and people with low literacy skills (Gooding and Kochmar, 2019). Due to its importance in achieving complete text simplification with simpler and easier-to-read content, lexical simplification has received rising interest over the years.

Shardlow (2014) has introduced a lexical simplification pipeline, which consists of several sub-problems, including, for instance, complex word identification, simpler substitution generation, substitution selection, and substitution ranking. Out of these four sub-problems, the latter three entirely focus on the generation of relevant and simpler substitutes for better understandability.

Underpinned by Shardlow (2014) among others, over the years researchers have introduced a wide range of methods for simpler substitution generation for the complex words identified in text. Earlier approaches to substitution generation have relied on rule-based methods and lexical resources like WordNet (Miller, 1995) or paraphrase databases (Pavlick and Callison-Burch, 2016). Lexical substitution research has advanced to the use of word embedding models (e.g., word2vec (Mikolov et al., 2013), Glove (Pennington et al., 2014), Embeddings from Language Models (ELMo) (Peters et al., 2018)) to remove the requirement of lexical resources and obtain potential candidates through the cosine similarity of word embeddings.

The introduction of Transformers (Vaswani et al., 2017) has resulted in advanced contextual word and sentence embedding models like Bidirectional Encoder Representations from Transformers (BERT) (Devlin et al., 2019), robustly optimised BERT (RoBERTa) (Liu et al., 2019), and XLNet (Yang et al., 2019) which have been extensively used for NLP, including, but not limited to, lexical simplification and lexical substitution. These models have been useful in generating potential candidates for simplification given a target word and the context, taking the meaning preservation aspect into account; researchers have introduced methods and frameworks for lexical simplification, some of which rely entirely on contextual embeddings (Qiang et al., 2021) whereas some others incorporate lexical resources alongside contextual embedding models (Gooding and Kochmar, 2019).

Proceedings of the Workshop on Text Simplification, Accessibility, and Readability (TSAR-2022), pages 207 - 212
December 8, 2022

Lexical substitution can be identified as a broader problem, which aims to generate alternative substitutes for a target word (McCarthy and Navigli, 2007) whereas lexical simplification specifically focuses on generating simpler substitutes (Shardlow, 2014). Although not identical, the two problems are coupled; both aim to generate substitutes for an identified target word. Hence, also the proposed, studied, and adopted solution techniques have similarities.

In our work, we investigated the applicability of lexical substitution methods for simpler substitution generation in lexical simplification. We applied the *CILex* solution proposed in our previous work (Seneviratne et al., 2022) on *C*ontext *I*nformation for *Lex*ical substitution to lexical simplification[1]. The objective of the research was to evaluate the usefulness of existing substitution methods in a given text simplification task and to identify how these methods can be improved.

2 Related Work

Researchers have used different techniques to achieve lexical simplification; this problem aims to simplify complex content in text while maintaining the meaning, for better understandability.

Earliest lexical simplification approaches relied on rule-based methods and lexical resources (Devlin, 1998) where a set of rules was defined to extract simpler substitutes from lexical resources like WordNet (Miller, 1995) and rank them based on a simplicity metric. Extending beyond these linguistic databases, researchers also used parallel corpora that consisted of complex and simpler sentences to identify simpler substitutes for a target word (Biran et al., 2011; Yatskar et al., 2010). However, given both these approaches were dependent on linguistic databases and parallel corpora, they had limitations with respect to the availability and coverage of simpler alternatives.

To address the limitations of lexical resources, researchers adopted word embedding models for lexical simplification (Glavaš and Štajner, 2015). Further improving on the word embedding models, researchers introduced context-aware lexical simplification methods (Paetzold and Specia, 2016; Gooding and Kochmar, 2019) which also incorporated linguistic features and information from lexical resources. The introduction of Transformer-based language models like BERT, RoBERTa, and XLNet resulted in widely adopting them for downstream NLP problems. To illustrate, Qiang et al. (2020) introduced a recursive simplification method called LSBert based on BERT.

Similar techniques have been used for lexical substitution, which is a broader problem aiming to generate alternative words for a given target word. Early methods, which relied on rule-based systems and lexical resources, have evolved to the methods that use word embeddings (Melamud et al., 2016), contextual embeddings (Zhou et al., 2019; Arefyev et al., 2020) and methods that incorporate additional information from lexical resources (Michalopoulos et al., 2022).

Given the similarities in lexical substitution and simplification problems, we investigated the applicability of the CILex lexical substitution solution also for lexical simplification. This investigation was part of the Text Simplification, Accessibility, and Readability (TSAR) shared task on lexical simplification in 2022 (Saggion et al., 2022).

3 Experiments

3.1 Method

We used the CILex solution proposed in our previous work (Seneviratne et al., 2022) for our experiments, which focused on lexical substitution methods. We based our experiments on pre-trained contextual word embedding models, contextual sentence embedding models, and WordNet. We then defined several metrics to obtain the final set of relevant substitutes and rank them to filter out the most suitable substitutes.

The initial set of substitutes was obtained using the combination of i) a model prediction score $P(w|c)$ computed using the XLNet model given the context c and target word x with any word w in the vocabulary of XLNet and ii) an embedding similarity score $P(w|x)$ by computing the inner product of the embedding of the target word and the embedding of the respective word ($embedding_x \cdot embedding_w^\top$). This followed the approach by Arefyev et al. (2020).

For each word in the XLNet vocabulary, these scores were combined to obtain $S_{\texttt{XLNet}}$ score with α and β being parameters that can be fine-tuned:

$$S_{\texttt{XLNet}} = \alpha P(w|c) + \beta P(w|x). \quad (1)$$

The scoring was then used to rank all the words to filter out the top 20 words.

[1]The implementation is available at https://github.com/sandaruSen/CILex under the MIT license.

For the filtered-out set of potential candidates, we computed a sentence similarity score

$$S_{\texttt{sent}} = \cos(s,\, s') \tag{2}$$

using the cosine similarity between the original and updated sentences $(s,\, s')$ obtained by replacing the target word using each potential candidate (Michalopoulos et al., 2022).

We also used the gloss sentence similarity score $S_{\texttt{gloss}}$ proposed by Michalopoulos et al. (2022) which integrated additional context information from WordNet and BERT (*bert-large-uncased*). We computed the score as follows: first, we obtained lists of potential definitions for target words and possible substitutes from WordNet. Second, for each target word and substitute, we formulated the most suitable definition by computing the cosine similarity between the given sentence and the definition. Third, for each substitute, we calculated the gloss sentence similarity score

$$S_{\texttt{gloss}} = \cos(d_t,\, d_w) \tag{3}$$

using the cosine similarity between the most suitable definition embedding of the target word d_t and the most suitable definition embedding of the substitute d_w.

Similarly to $S_{\texttt{gloss}}$, we computed

$$S_{\texttt{wordnet}} = \cos(d_t,\, s') \tag{4}$$

where lists of potential definitions were obtained only for the possible candidates and the cosine similarity was computed using the updated sentence and the most suitable definition of each substitute.

Additionally, we computed the validation score $S_{\texttt{val}}$ (Zhou et al., 2019) using the cosine similarities of the BERT-based contextual embeddings (*bert-large-uncased*) of the top four layers of every token in the original sentence and the modified sentence was used.

Using these scores, we defined three CILex solutions as

$$\textit{CILex\_1} = \gamma S_{\texttt{XLNet}} + \delta S_{\texttt{sent}}, \tag{5}$$

$$\textit{CILex\_2} = \gamma S_{\texttt{XLNet}} + \delta S_{\texttt{sent}} + \theta S_{\texttt{wordnet}} + \omega S_{\texttt{val}}, \text{ and} \tag{6}$$

$$\textit{CILex\_3} = \gamma S_{\texttt{XLNet}} + \delta S_{\texttt{sent}} + \theta S_{\texttt{gloss}} + \omega S_{\texttt{val}} \tag{7}$$

by interpolating them together using γ and δ as the weights for $S_{\texttt{XLNet}}$ and $S_{\texttt{sent}}$ scores, respectively, for all three CILex solutions. For *CILex_2* and *CILex_3*, ω was used as the weight for $S_{\texttt{val}}$ while θ was used as the weight for $S_{\texttt{wordnet}}$ and $S_{\texttt{gloss}}$ in *CILex_2* and *CILex_3*, respectively. The CILex solutions were specifically proposed for lexical substitution which is a broader problem compared to lexical simplification.

3.2 Datasets

We tested the *CILex* solution on the trial and testing datasets of the English dataset provided at the TSAR-2022 shared task (Štajner et al., 2022). The English dataset was created by manually selecting 400 instances from the 2018 Complex Word Identification Shared task dataset. This set of instances was further filtered based on the quality of the annotations provided by the annotators to obtain the final set of 386 instances with their average number of unique simpler substitutes per instance provided by the annotators being 10.55. The dataset consisted of 10 trial instances and 373 instances in the testing dataset.

3.3 Evaluation metrics

We based our evaluation on the metrics used in the TSAR-2022 shared task (Saggion et al., 2022). $MeanAveragePrecision@K$ (*MAP@K*) score with $K \in \{1,\, 3,\, 5,\, 10\}$ evaluated if the predicted substitutes by the system were relevant and if they were ranked in the top positions. $Potential@K$ and $Accuracy@K$ metrics evaluated the percentage of instances for which at least one of the substitutions predicted was present in the set of gold annotations and the ratio of instances where at least one of the K top predicted candidates matched the most frequently suggested synonym(s) in the gold list of annotated candidates, respectively.

3.4 Experimental Setup

Following Arefyev et al. (2020), we used the XLNet model (Yang et al., 2019) to obtain the initial set of substitutes, RoBERTa (*stsb-roberta-large*) model (Reimers et al., 2019) to obtain the sentence similarity score, and BERT model (*bert-large-uncased*) to obtain the WordNet similarity, gloss sentence similarity, and validation scores. We used the same hyper-parameters introduced in our previous work (Seneviratne et al., 2022) for our experiments without further tuning to the TSAR-2022 shared task. We conducted our experiments

Method	ACC@1	ACC@1@Top1	ACC@3@Top1	MAP@3	MAP@10	Potential@3	Potential@10
LSBert	0.5978	0.3029	0.5308	0.4079	0.1755	0.823	0.9463
CILex_3	0.386	0.1957	0.3083	0.2603	0.1267	0.5656	0.638
CILex_2	0.3806	0.1903	0.3083	0.2597	0.1262	0.563	0.6434
CILex_1	0.3753	0.201	0.3109	0.2555	0.1235	0.5361	0.63
TUNER	0.3404	0.142	0.1823	0.1706	0.0546	0.4343	0.445

Table 1: Results of our proposed three CILex solutions and the LSBert and TUNER baselines for the test subset of the English dataset provided at the TSAR-2022 shared task.

on a RTX 3090 graphics card with 24 GB memory and CUDA 11.4.

3.5 Results

The proposed three solutions outperformed the TUNER-baseline (Table 1). However, they did not perform as well as the LSBert baseline.

Although the performance of our CILex approach has been outstanding in lexical substitution tasks, its usefulness was limited at the TSAR-2022 shared task on lexical simplification. Remembering that lexical substitution and simplification problems are not identical and that also text datasets and their respective annotations have their unique characteristics, a minimally supervised approach with some careful tuning to this specific simplification task could have worked better at TSAR-2022 than our unsupervised lexical substitution methods with pre-trained models.

4 Discussion

In this paper, we have adopted our previous work on lexical substitution for the TSAR-2022 shared task on lexical simplification and experimented with the use of different methods that provide context information. The three methods used for our experiments have not performed as well as the LSBert baseline. However, they have outperformed TUNER-baseline at TSAR-2022 (Štajner et al., 2022) and our approach has excelled in lexical substitution as evidenced by its evaluation using two annotated lexical substitution datasets that are widely used for the broader problem (Seneviratne et al., 2022).

The observed performance difference for lexical simplification and lexical substitution can be explained by the problem differences. The methods used in our experiments were developed to target lexical substitution, which can be identified as a substantially broader problem than lexical simplification. Lexical substitution generally focuses on generating similar rather than simpler substitutes — the narrower focus of lexical simplification. In order to tackle this issue of our lexical substitution approach for lexical simplification, identifying metrics, which can evaluate the simplicity of the potential candidates and using them to rank the potential candidates can be done.

5 Conclusion

We have applied our previous work on lexical substitution for lexical simplification, focusing on the added value of context information for the lexical simplification problem. The results from our methods indicate, that even though the proposed approach has performed well in lexical substitution more broadly, their usefulness in the narrower lexical simplification problem at the TSAR-2022 shared task was limited; a minimally supervised approach with some careful tuning to a given simplification task may have worked better at TSAR-2022 than unsupervised lexical substitution methods with pre-trained models.

Our investigation encourages further work on evaluating the simplicity of potential substitution candidates and incorporating them into lexical substitution methods. This approach should extend these broader methods to lexical simplification by targeting the more specific constraints for substitutes in the narrower text simplification problem.

Acknowledgement

This research was funded by and has been delivered in partnership with Our Health in Our Hands (OHIOH), a strategic initiative of the ANU, which aims to transform health care by developing new personalized health technologies and solutions in collaboration with patients, clinicians and healthcare providers. We gratefully acknowledge the funding from the ANU School of Computing for the first author's PhD studies.

References

Nikolay Arefyev, Boris Sheludko, Alexander Podolskiy, and Alexander Panchenko. 2020. Always keep your target in mind: Studying semantics and improving performance of neural lexical substitution. In *Proceedings of the 28th International Conference on Computational Linguistics*, pages 1242–1255, Barcelona, Spain (Online). International Committee on Computational Linguistics.

Or Biran, Samuel Brody, and Noémie Elhadad. 2011. Putting it simply: a context-aware approach to lexical simplification. In *Proceedings of the 49th Annual Meeting of the Association for Computational Linguistics: Human Language Technologies*, pages 496–501, Portland, Oregon, USA. Association for Computational Linguistics.

Jacob Devlin, Ming-Wei Chang, Kenton Lee, and Kristina Toutanova. 2019. BERT: Pre-training of deep bidirectional transformers for language understanding. In *Proceedings of the 2019 Conference of the North American Chapter of the Association for Computational Linguistics: Human Language Technologies, Volume 1 (Long and Short Papers)*, pages 4171–4186, Minneapolis, Minnesota. Association for Computational Linguistics.

Siobhan Devlin. 1998. The use of a psycholinguistic database in the simplification of text for aphasic readers. *Linguistic Databases*.

Goran Glavaš and Sanja Štajner. 2015. Simplifying lexical simplification: Do we need simplified corpora? In *Proceedings of the 53rd Annual Meeting of the Association for Computational Linguistics and the 7th International Joint Conference on Natural Language Processing (Volume 2: Short Papers)*, pages 63–68, Beijing, China. Association for Computational Linguistics.

Sian Gooding and Ekaterina Kochmar. 2019. Recursive context-aware lexical simplification. In *Proceedings of the 2019 Conference on Empirical Methods in Natural Language Processing and the 9th International Joint Conference on Natural Language Processing (EMNLP-IJCNLP)*, pages 4853–4863, Hong Kong, China. Association for Computational Linguistics.

Yinhan Liu, Myle Ott, Naman Goyal, Jingfei Du, Mandar Joshi, Danqi Chen, Omer Levy, Mike Lewis, Luke Zettlemoyer, and Veselin Stoyanov. 2019. Roberta: A robustly optimized BERT pretraining approach. *arXiv preprint arXiv:1907.11692*.

Diana McCarthy and Roberto Navigli. 2007. SemEval-2007 task 10: English lexical substitution task. In *Proceedings of the Fourth International Workshop on Semantic Evaluations (SemEval-2007)*, pages 48–53. Association for Computational Linguistics.

Oren Melamud, Jacob Goldberger, and Ido Dagan. 2016. context2vec: Learning generic context embedding with bidirectional LSTM. In *Proceedings of The 20th SIGNLL Conference on Computational Natural Language Learning*, pages 51–61, Berlin, Germany. Association for Computational Linguistics.

George Michalopoulos, Ian McKillop, Alexander Wong, and Helen Chen. 2022. LexSubCon: Integrating knowledge from lexical resources into contextual embeddings for lexical substitution. In *Proceedings of the 60th Annual Meeting of the Association for Computational Linguistics (Volume 1: Long Papers)*, pages 1226–1236, Dublin, Ireland. Association for Computational Linguistics.

Tomas Mikolov, Kai Chen, Greg Corrado, and Jeffrey Dean. 2013. Efficient estimation of word representations in vector space. *1st International Conference on Learning Representations, ICLR 2013*.

George A Miller. 1995. WordNet: a lexical database for English. *Communications of the ACM*, 38(11):39–41.

Gustavo Paetzold and Lucia Specia. 2016. Benchmarking lexical simplification systems. In *Proceedings of the Tenth International Conference on Language Resources and Evaluation (LREC'16)*, pages 3074–3080, Portorož, Slovenia. European Language Resources Association (ELRA).

Ellie Pavlick and Chris Callison-Burch. 2016. Simple PPDB: A paraphrase database for simplification. In *Proceedings of the 54th Annual Meeting of the Association for Computational Linguistics (Volume 2: Short Papers)*, pages 143–148, Berlin, Germany. Association for Computational Linguistics.

Jeffrey Pennington, Richard Socher, and Christopher Manning. 2014. GloVe: Global vectors for word representation. In *Proceedings of the 2014 Conference on Empirical Methods in Natural Language Processing (EMNLP)*, pages 1532–1543, Doha, Qatar. Association for Computational Linguistics.

Matthew E. Peters, Mark Neumann, Mohit Iyyer, Matt Gardner, Christopher Clark, Kenton Lee, and Luke Zettlemoyer. 2018. Deep contextualized word representations. In *Proceedings of the 2018 Conference of the North American Chapter of the Association for Computational Linguistics: Human Language Technologies, Volume 1 (Long Papers)*, pages 2227–2237, New Orleans, Louisiana. Association for Computational Linguistics.

Jipeng Qiang, Yun Li, Yi Zhu, Yunhao Yuan, Yang Shi, and Xindong Wu. 2021. LSBert: Lexical simplification based on BERT. *IEEE/ACM Transactions on Audio, Speech, and Language Processing*, 29:3064–3076.

Jipeng Qiang, Yun Li, Yi Zhu, Yunhao Yuan, and Xindong Wu. 2020. Lexical simplification with pretrained encoders. In *Proceedings of the AAAI Conference on Artificial Intelligence*, volume 34, pages 8649–8656.

Nils Reimers, Iryna Gurevych, Nils Reimers, Iryna Gurevych, Nandan Thakur, Nils Reimers, Johannes Daxenberger, Iryna Gurevych, Nils Reimers, Iryna Gurevych, et al. 2019. Sentence-BERT: Sentence embeddings using Siamese BERT-networks. In *Proceedings of the 2019 Conference on Empirical Methods in Natural Language Processing*, pages 671–688. Association for Computational Linguistics.

Horacio Saggion, Sanja Štajner, Daniel Ferrés, Kim Cheng Sheang, Matthew Shardlow, Kai North, and Marcos Zampieri. 2022. Findings of the TSAR-2022 shared task on multilingual lexical simplification. In *Proceedings of TSAR workshop held in conjunction with EMNLP 2022*. Association for Computational Linguistics.

Sandaru Seneviratne, Elena Daskalaki, Artem Lenskiy, and Hanna Suominen. 2022. CILex: An investigation of context information for lexical substitution methods. In *Proceedings of the 29th International Conference on Computational Linguistics*, pages 4124–4135, Gyeongju, Republic of Korea. International Committee on Computational Linguistics.

Matthew Shardlow. 2014. A survey of automated text simplification. *International Journal of Advanced Computer Science and Applications*, 4(1):58–70.

Ashish Vaswani, Noam Shazeer, Niki Parmar, Jakob Uszkoreit, Llion Jones, Aidan N Gomez, Łukasz Kaiser, and Illia Polosukhin. 2017. Attention is all you need. *Advances in Neural Information Processing Systems*, 30:5998–6008.

Sanja Štajner, Daniel Ferrés, Matthew Shardlow, Kai North, Marcos Zampieri, and Horacio Saggion. 2022. Lexical simplification benchmarks for English, Portuguese, and Spanish. *Frontiers in Artificial Intelligence*, 5.

Zhilin Yang, Zihang Dai, Yiming Yang, Jaime Carbonell, Ruslan Salakhutdinov, and Quoc V. Le. 2019. XLNet: Generalized autoregressive pretraining for language understanding. *arXiv preprint arXiv:1906.08237*.

Mark Yatskar, Bo Pang, Cristian Danescu-Niculescu-Mizil, and Lillian Lee. 2010. For the sake of simplicity: Unsupervised extraction of lexical simplifications from Wikipedia. In *Human Language Technologies: The 2010 Annual Conference of the North American Chapter of the Association for Computational Linguistics*, pages 365–368, Los Angeles, California. Association for Computational Linguistics.

Wangchunshu Zhou, Tao Ge, Ke Xu, Furu Wei, and Ming Zhou. 2019. BERT-based lexical substitution. In *Proceedings of the 57th Annual Meeting of the Association for Computational Linguistics*, pages 3368–3373, Florence, Italy. Association for Computational Linguistics.

PresiUniv at TSAR-2022 Shared Task: Generation and Ranking of Simplification Substitutes of Complex Words in Multiple Languages

Peniel John Whistely, Sandeep Mathias and **Galiveeeti Poornima**
Information Retrieval Lab, Department of Computer Science and Engineering
Presidency University, Bangalore
{peniel.20212AIE0002, sandeepalbert, galiveetipoornima}@presidencyuniversity.in

Abstract

In this paper, we describe our system, **PresiUniv**, to generate and rank candidate simplifications using publicly available pre-trained language models (BERT, BETO, and BERTimbeau), word embeddings (Eg. FastText, NILC), and part-of-speech taggers (NLTK PoS Tagger, Stanford PoS Tagger and Mac-Morpho), to generate and rank candidate contextual simplifications for a given complex word. In this shared task, our system was placed **first** in the Spanish track, 5th in the Brazilian-Portuguese track, and 10th in the English track. We upload our codes and data for this project to aid in replication of our results. We also analyze some of the errors and describe design decisions which we took while writing the paper.

1 Introduction

Lexical Simplification (LS) is a task of natural language generation that aims to substitute difficult words and phrases in a sentence for simpler ones that convey the same information (Paetzold and Specia, 2017). This is a challenging task because not only must the substitution retain the original meaning while still adhering to the grammatical requirements of the sentence that is being simplified, but different people may have different needs for simplification (Alva-Manchego et al., 2020). Figure 1 shows the pipeline for lexical simplification (Shardlow, 2014).

In light of this, the TSAR 2022 Workshop organized a shared task on lexical simplification, where participating teams have to generate and rank simplifications for a given complex word (Saggion et al., 2022). Each team is allowed to submit three runs for their system. This paper describes the performance of our team, **PresiUniv**[1] at this shared task.

[1] Code:http://www.github.com/lwsam/TSAR-2022/

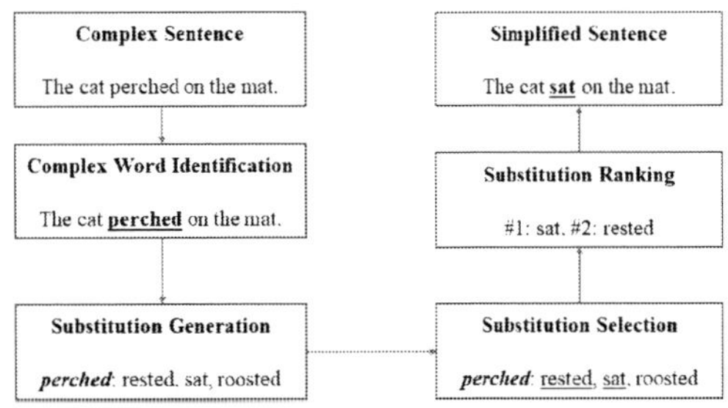

Figure 1: Pipeline of Lexical Simplification

2 Problem Statement

Our problem is defined as follows:

"Given a context and a possible complex word, we need to generate a *ranked list* of candidate simplifications."

Hence, our task is divided into two sub-tasks. The first sub-task involves generating words that would replace a complex word in the target sentence, which would simplify it. The second sub-task consists of ranking the top 10 most suitable words.

3 Related Work

Lexical simplification must identify complex words and choose the optimal replacement (Shardlow, 2014; Paetzold and Specia, 2017). Previous shared tasks have already been done as a part of **SemEval 2016** (Paetzold and Specia, 2016) and **BEA 2018** (Yimam et al., 2018). While the first shared task dealt with a single training and test set in English alone, the second shared task dealt with complex word identification in multiple languages (English, German, and Spanish), as well as a multilingual scenario (where the system is tested in a fourth language, French).

Proceedings of the Workshop on Text Simplification, Accessibility, and Readability (TSAR-2022), pages 213 - 217
December 8, 2022 ©2022 Association for Computational Linguistics

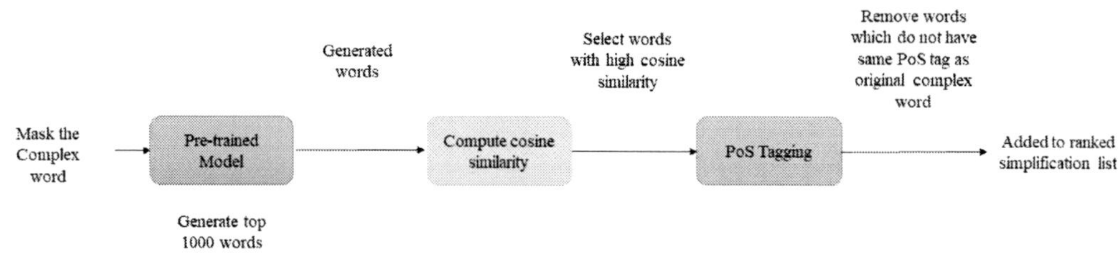

Figure 2: The method that we used for simplification

Language	Pre-trained Language Model	Word Vectors	Part-of-Speech Tagger
English	BERT	FastText	NLTK PoS Tagger
Spanish	BETO	FastText	Stanford PoS Tagger
Brazilian Portuguese	BERTimbeau	NILC Embeddings	Mac-Morpho

Table 1: Resources used for each language

4 Method

Figure 2 shows the different steps that we take to generate and select our candidates. It consists of the following steps:

1. Generation of candidate tokens
2. Candidate word selection
3. Candidate word pruning

Consider the following input sentence: "A Spanish government source, however, later said that banks able to cover by themselves losses on their toxic property assets will not be forced to remove them from their books while it will be **compulsory** for those receiving public help." Let the target word (the one being replaced) be "compulsory"[2].

4.1 Candidate Token Generation

We first generate a list of the top k tokens using a pre-trained language model (Eg. BERT-base-uncased (Devlin et al., 2019)). The pre-trained language model generally selects the most probable word to replace the masked token[3]. Since simpler words are more probable than more complex words (Leroy and Kauchak, 2014), we consider that the words generated are already ranked in order of difficulty from simplest to hardest.

Hence the above example sentence becomes "A Spanish government source, however, later said that banks able to cover by themselves losses on their toxic property assets will not be forced to remove them from their books while it will be **[MASK]** for those receiving public help." The generated tokens (in order of probability) are: "available", "easier", "safe", "beneficial", "provided", "safer", "better", "convenient", "appropriate", "done", "mandatory", ...

4.2 Candidate Word Selection

The next step is to select ***only*** the words which are suitable in meaning to the complex word. For example, the word "done" is not exactly a synonym for the word "compulsory"[4]. On the other hand, the word "mandatory" is a synonym[5]. In order to do that, we select words whose similarity is **above** a threshold value but less than 1 (because a cosine similarity of 1 would imply that the replacement is the same as the original complex word). For a threshold value of 0.50, we select the words "mandatory", "obligatory", "voluntary" and "mandated".

4.3 Candidate Word Pruning

Finally, we prune the selected words selected using a part-of-speech tagger to ensure that the chosen words with the correct inflexion as the complex word are chosen. From the above four words, we see that the word "mandated" is not of the same part of speech as "compulsory" (verb vs adjective)[6], and hence, the final ranked list of words is

[2]This example is taken from the trial dataset of the shared task.

[3]We trim out tokens which are not completely alphabetic, like "##ching"

[4]The cosine similarity using our word embeddings between **done** and **compulsory** is 0.119

[5]The cosine similarity using our word embeddings between **mandatory** and **compulsory** is 0.767

[6]In the given context, "mandated" would behave as an *adjectival*.

Rank	English		Spanish		Brazilian-Portuguese	
	Team	Acc@1	Team	Acc@1	Team	Acc@1
1	UniHD	0.8096	**PresiUniv**	**0.3695**	GMU-WLV	0.4812
2	MANTIS	0.6568	UoM&MMU	0.3668	Cental	0.3689
3	UoM&MMU	0.6353	PolyU-CBS	0.3586	PolyU-CBS	0.3262
4	LSBert	0.5978	GMU-WLV	0.3532	LSBert	0.3262
5	RCML	0.5442	Cental	0.3097	**PresiUniv**	**0.3074**
6	GMU-WLV	0.5174	LSBert	0.2880	TUNER	0.2219
7	CL Lab PICT	0.5067	TUNER	0.1195	UoM&MMU	0.1711
8	teamPN	0.4664	OEG_UPM	0.1032	-	-
9	PolyU-CBS	0.4316	-	-	-	-
10	**PresiUniv**	**0.4021**	-	-	-	-
11	CILS	0.3860	-	-	-	-
12	Cental	0.3619	-	-	-	-
13	TUNER	0.3404	-	-	-	-
14	twinfalls	0.1957	-	-	-	-
15	NU HLT	0.1447	-	-	-	-

Table 2: Comparison of our system with other systems. The ranking of the systems is as per the Accuracy@1 values of the best run submitted by the team. The results also include the performances by a pair of baseline systems - LSBert and TUNER (Štajner et al., 2022).

"mandatory", "obligatory" and "voluntary".

The solution from the gold file (without ties and space separated) is "mandatory required essential forced important necessary obligatory unavoidable".

5 Dataset

There is no training dataset for the TSAR-2022 Shared Task. A sample of 10 or 12 instances with gold standard annotations is provided here as the trial dataset. For the testing data, between 368 to 374 instances were given, with the annotations released upon the completion of the competition.

5.1 Trial dataset

The trial dataset consists of a set of 10 instances (for English and Portuguese) and 12 instances (for Spanish) of a sentence, a target complex word. The trial_none files contain only the sentences and the complex word, while the trial_gold files contain the sentences, the complex word and a set of gold simplifications.

5.2 Test dataset

The test_none files (used for the evaluation benchmark) contain the instances with the sentences and target complex words. The English test_none file had 373 instances, the Spanish test_none file had 368 instances, and the Brazilian Portuguese test_none file had 374 instances. The test_gold files contain the sentences, target complex words, and gold annotations for each of the test_none files.

6 Experimental Setup

6.1 Resources Used

In our experiments, we used the following resources:

- A **pre-trained language model** to generate a list of contextual candidate words to replace the complex word.
- A set of **dense word vectors** to find out which words that were generated earlier are similar in meaning to the complex word.
- A **part-of-speech tagger** to tag the sentence with the replacement and verify that the replacement word is of the same inflexion as the original complex word.

Due to the language requirements, we use a different set of resources for each language. Table 1 shows the different resources used for each language. For English, we used the **BERT** (Devlin et al., 2019) pre-trained language model, 300 dimension FastText (Grave et al., 2018) word vectors, and the default NLTK Part-of-Speech tagger with the Penn Treebank Tagset (Marcus et al., 1994). For Spanish, we used the **BETO** (Cañete et al.,

2020) pre-trained language model, 300 dimension FastText (Grave et al., 2018) word vectors, and the Stanford Part-of-Speech tagger (Toutanova et al., 2003). For Portuguese, we used the **BERTimbeau** (Souza et al., 2020) pre-trained language model, 300 dimension NILC Embeddings (Hartmann et al., 2017) and the Mac-Morpho part-of-speech tagger (Aluísio et al., 2003).

We set the value of k (the number of candidates generated) at **1000**, and we run our experiments for thresholds of similarity as **0.40**, **0.50**, and **0.60**.

6.2 Evaluation Metric

The following evaluation metrics are used for our experiments:

- Mean Accurate Precision - **MAP@K** [K=1,3,5,10]. MAP@K for Lexical Simplification evaluates the following aspects
  - Are the predicted substitutes relevant?
  - Are the top-ranked predicted substitutes at the top positions?
- **Potential@K** [K=1,3,5,10] - The percentage of instances for which at least one of the substitutions predicted is present in the set of gold annotations.
- **Accuracy@K** [K=1,3,5,10] - The ratio of instances where at least one of the K top predicted candidates matches the most frequently suggested synonym/s in the gold list of annotated candidates.

7 Results and Analysis

The results of our experiments on the testing dataset are given in Table 2. These results denote the best performance of a given team based on the MAP@1 for their three runs. While our system performed admirably in the Spanish lexical simplification ranking task (coming **first** overall), we did not do as well overall in the other languages.

7.1 Error Analysis

As we saw in the example in Section 4, ***antonyms*** can also be selected as candidates. For instance, let us consider the words **good** and **bad**, which have a high cosine similarity[7]. Both the words are antonyms, yet they would be selected as a replacement for the other because they have a high cosine similarity and the same part of speech.

7.2 Discussion

In this section, we discuss a couple of important design decisions which we made for our experiments. The first decision that we took was the order of the approaches. One of the approaches which we considered was to first select a similar word and then compute the language model score and rank the output words by the most probable sentences. However, this does not work out because the most similar words are usually ***different forms*** of the original word. For example, the top 5 most similar words for "compulsory" are: "Compulsory", "mandatory", "non-compulsory", "compulsary", and "complusory". As we can see, the most common words are either different forms of "compulsory", or they are spelling mistakes (Eg. "compulsary" and "compulusory"), with very few good candidate words (like "mandatory").

The next design decision is the values of the thresholds for cosine similarity, which we selected. Selecting a very low threshold for candidate selection will ensure that almost all the candidates generated will be selected, while a high threshold will eliminate almost all candidates (Eg. if we had a threshold of 0.8, then even candidates like "mandatory" won't be selected for "compulsory"). This is also why we selected threshold values of 0.40, 0.50 and 0.60 for our experiments.

8 Conclusion and Future Work

In this paper, we describe the participation of our team, **PresiUniv**, in the TSAR 2022 Shared Task on the generation and ranking of lexical simplification substitutes. Overall, we achieved the best performance in the Spanish track but finished 5th in the Portuguese track and 10th in the English track.

In the future, we plan to extend our work towards document-level simplification as well as personalized text simplification (Alva-Manchego et al., 2020).

Acknowledgements

We would like to thank the anonymous reviewers of the shared task for their constructive feedback which helped us improve our paper. We would also like to acknowledge The Presidency University Faculty Seed Grant Award (Ref: **ACC/26/08/2021-2**), dated Autust 26, 2021 for funding this research.

[7]The cosine similarity between **good** and **bad** is 0.752.

References

Sandra Aluísio, Jorge Pelizzoni, Ana Raquel Marchi, Lucélia de Oliveira, Regiana Manenti, and Vanessa Marquiafável. 2003. An account of the challenge of tagging a reference corpus for brazilian portuguese. In *International Workshop on Computational Processing of the Portuguese Language*, pages 110–117. Springer.

Fernando Alva-Manchego, Carolina Scarton, and Lucia Specia. 2020. Data-driven sentence simplification: Survey and benchmark. *Computational Linguistics*, 46(1):135–187.

José Cañete, Gabriel Chaperon, Rodrigo Fuentes, Jou-Hui Ho, Hojin Kang, and Jorge Pérez. 2020. Spanish pre-trained bert model and evaluation data. In *PML4DC at ICLR 2020*.

Jacob Devlin, Ming-Wei Chang, Kenton Lee, and Kristina Toutanova. 2019. BERT: Pre-training of deep bidirectional transformers for language understanding. In *Proceedings of the 2019 Conference of the North American Chapter of the Association for Computational Linguistics: Human Language Technologies, Volume 1 (Long and Short Papers)*, pages 4171–4186, Minneapolis, Minnesota. Association for Computational Linguistics.

Edouard Grave, Piotr Bojanowski, Prakhar Gupta, Armand Joulin, and Tomas Mikolov. 2018. Learning word vectors for 157 languages. In *Proceedings of the Eleventh International Conference on Language Resources and Evaluation (LREC 2018)*, Miyazaki, Japan. European Language Resources Association (ELRA).

Nathan Hartmann, Erick Fonseca, Christopher Shulby, Marcos Treviso, Jéssica Silva, and Sandra Aluísio. 2017. Portuguese word embeddings: Evaluating on word analogies and natural language tasks. In *Proceedings of the 11th Brazilian Symposium in Information and Human Language Technology*, pages 122–131, Uberlândia, Brazil. Sociedade Brasileira de Computação.

Gondy Leroy and David Kauchak. 2014. The effect of word familiarity on actual and perceived text difficulty. *Journal of the American Medical Informatics Association*, 21(e1):e169–e172.

Mitchell Marcus, Grace Kim, Mary Ann Marcinkiewicz, Robert MacIntyre, Ann Bies, Mark Ferguson, Karen Katz, and Britta Schasberger. 1994. The Penn Treebank: Annotating predicate argument structure. In *Human Language Technology: Proceedings of a Workshop held at Plainsboro, New Jersey, March 8-11, 1994*.

Gustavo Paetzold and Lucia Specia. 2016. SemEval 2016 task 11: Complex word identification. In *Proceedings of the 10th International Workshop on Semantic Evaluation (SemEval-2016)*, pages 560–569, San Diego, California. Association for Computational Linguistics.

Gustavo H Paetzold and Lucia Specia. 2017. A survey on lexical simplification. *Journal of Artificial Intelligence Research*, 60:549–593.

Horacio Saggion, Sanja Štajner, Daniel Ferrés, Kim Cheng Sheang, Matthew Shardlow, Kai North, and Marcos Zampieri. 2022. Findings of the tsar-2022 shared task on multilingual lexical simplification. In *Proceedings of TSAR workshop held in conjunction with EMNLP 2022*.

Matthew Shardlow. 2014. A survey of automated text simplification. *International Journal of Advanced Computer Science and Applications*, 4(1):58–70.

Fábio Souza, Rodrigo Nogueira, and Roberto Lotufo. 2020. BERTimbau: pretrained BERT models for Brazilian Portuguese. In *9th Brazilian Conference on Intelligent Systems, BRACIS, Rio Grande do Sul, Brazil, October 20-23 (to appear)*.

Kristina Toutanova, Dan Klein, Christopher D. Manning, and Yoram Singer. 2003. Feature-rich part-of-speech tagging with a cyclic dependency network. In *Proceedings of the 2003 Human Language Technology Conference of the North American Chapter of the Association for Computational Linguistics*, pages 252–259.

Sanja Štajner, Daniel Ferres, Matthew Shardlow, Kai North, Marcos Zampieri, and Horacio Saggion. 2022. Lexical simplification benchmarks for English, Portuguese, and Spanish. *Frontiers in Artificial Intelligence*, 5.

Seid Muhie Yimam, Chris Biemann, Shervin Malmasi, Gustavo Paetzold, Lucia Specia, Sanja Štajner, Anaïs Tack, and Marcos Zampieri. 2018. A report on the complex word identification shared task 2018. In *Proceedings of the Thirteenth Workshop on Innovative Use of NLP for Building Educational Applications*, pages 66–78, New Orleans, Louisiana. Association for Computational Linguistics.

UoM&MMU at TSAR-2022 Shared Task: Prompt Learning for Lexical Simplification

Laura Vásquez-Rodríguez[1], **Nhung T. H. Nguyen**[1], **Matthew Shardlow**[2], **Sophia Ananiadou**[1]
[1]National Centre for Text Mining,
The University of Manchester, Manchester, United Kingdom
[2]Department of Computing and Mathematics,
Manchester Metropolitan University, Manchester, United Kingdom
{laura.vasquezrodriguez,nhung.nguyen,sophia.ananiadou}@manchester.ac.uk
m.shardlow@mmu.ac.uk

Abstract

We present PromptLS, a method for fine-tuning large pre-trained Language Models (LM) to perform the task of Lexical Simplification. We use a predefined template to attain appropriate replacements for a term, and fine-tune a LM using this template on language specific datasets. We filter candidate lists in post-processing to improve accuracy. We demonstrate that our model can work in a) a zero shot setting (where we only require a pre-trained LM), b) a fine-tuned setting (where language-specific data is required), and c) a multilingual setting (where the model is pre-trained across multiple languages and fine-tuned in an specific language). Experimental results show that, although the zero-shot setting is competitive, its performance is still far from the fine-tuned setting. Also, the multilingual is unsurprisingly worse than the fine-tuned model. Among all TSAR-2022 Shared Task participants, our team was ranked second in Spanish and third in English.

1 Introduction

We present our system submission for the TSAR-2022 Shared Task (ST) on Lexical Simplification (Saggion et al., 2022). The task required participants to develop a lexical simplification system capable of taking a word in context and returning a list of candidate substitutions. The task provided test data in English (EN), Spanish (ES) and Brazilian Portuguese (PT). We chose to submit for all three tracks a system based on the concept of Prompt Learning. Whereas the previous state of the art for Lexical Simplification, LSBert (Qiang et al., 2020), masked the token in context, our approach, namely PromptLS, injects prompts within the context that forces the model to generate appropriate substitutions as in Table 1. We experimented with multiple prompts, varying the syntax and lexicon of the prompt, selecting the best-performing variants.

Context	Training sentences
No	a simple word for **classified** is [MASK] .
5 words (left and right)	triangles can also be classified *(a simple word for **classified** is [MASK])* according to their internal angles
All context	triangles can also be classified *(a simple word for **classified** is [MASK])* according to their internal angles , measured here in degrees .

Table 1: Data examples generated for fine tuning the LMs for the prompt template: *"a simple word for [MASK] is"*. We show the complex word in **bold**.

To fine-tune a language model using prompts, we firstly collected labelled data from different sources corresponding to the three languages. We then combined them and split the data into training and validation subsets. We also tested our prompts with a zero-shot and multilingual settings. As a result, PromptLS performed the best fine-tuned, compared to the multilingual and zero-shot settings.

We finally selected the best configurations to run on the official testing sets. Hence, we could observe the same pattern in the testing set as in our validation subsets, i.e., the fine-tuned setting still produced the best performance across languages.

2 Related Work

Lexical simplification arose as a form of assistive technology (Devlin, 1999; Carroll et al., 1999) for people with aphasia. Early systems used dictionary based replacement methods (Bott et al., 2012), with disambiguation methods to improve the selection of candidates (Paetzold and Specia, 2015).

Recently, simplification systems have focused on the use of transformer architecture to identify

Proceedings of the Workshop on Text Simplification, Accessibility, and Readability (TSAR-2022), pages 218 - 224
December 8, 2022

appropriate replacements for a given word (Qiang et al., 2021). This can be applied at a single or multi-word level (Przybyła and Shardlow, 2020).

Prompt learning is a method of leveraging the learnt probabilities in a large pre-trained language model to solve NLP tasks (Brown et al., 2020; Liu et al., 2022). This can be done in a zero shot (Sun et al., 2021; Ni and Kao, 2022), or fine-tuned setting (Jiang et al., 2020). Prompt learning requires the design of a prompt (Ding et al., 2022), which can be engineered (Ding et al., 2021), or generated (Shin et al., 2020).

3 Methodology

In this section, we start by the description of our selected datasets (Section 3.1) and the design of our prompts (Section 3.2). We then describe our proposed method **PromptLS** that consists of three modules: 1) a large language model (LM) that generates candidates based on a given prompt (Section 3.3), 2) a fine-tuning module that guides the LM to select more appropriate substitutes (Section 3.4) and 3) a candidate filtering module which removes incorrect or inappropriate candidates (Section 3.5).

3.1 Data Collection

In this section we describe our collected state-of-the-art Lexical Simplification (LS) datasets for EN, ES and PT. We include a summary in Table 2.

- **(EN) LexMTurk** (Horn et al., 2014): a dataset obtained from the alignment of 137K sentences from English Wikipedia and Simple English Wikipedia. The LexMTurk corpus represents a random sample of 500 candidates, where each sentence was manually annotated by 50 MTurk[1] workers.
- **(EN) NNSEval** (Paetzold and Specia, 2016b): a dataset based on an user study of 400 non-native speakers who judged simplification samples from Wikipedia, LSEval and LexMTurk. The NNSEval datasets is a subset of 239 instances from LSEval (De Belder and Moens, 2012) and LexMTurk, which was improved and refined for LS using complexity annotations.
- **(EN) BenchLS** (Paetzold and Specia, 2016a): is a combined dataset of 929 instances based on LexMTurk and LSeval. All lexical candidates were improved and ranked by native speakers from the United States.

[1]https://www.mturk.com/

Language	Datasets	Instances
EN	LexMTurk	500
	NNSEval	239
	BenchLS	929
	CEFR	414
ES	EASIER	5,130
PT	SIMPLEX-PB-3.0	1,582

Table 2: All labelled datasets used in this work.

- **(EN) CEFR dataset** (Uchida et al., 2018): a dataset of 414 instances based on the Common European Framework of References for Languages (CEFR).[2] Sentences were extracted from university textbooks and words were filtered with the corresponding level based on words lists. Candidates were selected and ranked with the support online thesaurus and CEFR levels annotations.
- **(ES) EASIER corpus** (Alarcon et al., 2021): a collection 260 documents annotated by a linguist and verified by experts and a target audience. As a result, a LS Spanish dataset of 5130 instances was created, with at least one candidate per target word.
- **(PT) SIMPLEX-PB-3.0** (Hartmann and Aluisio, 2021): a Brazilian Portuguese corpus of 1582 instances which has been iterative improved from SIMPLEX-PB (Hartmann et al., 2018) and SIMPLEX-PB 2.0 (Hartmann et al., 2020) with manual annotations adapted to children needs as a main audience. These annotations include 52 different features including complex words definitions and linguistic information.

3.2 Template Design

For the implementation of prompt-learning in Lexical Simplification we have designed a template using equivalent keywords or substitutes appropriate for each language. For example, in English, we used a template composed by two prompts as follows:

A(n) <Prompt1> <Prompt2> for <target_word>

The templates for Spanish and Portuguese are translations of the English template, which resulted better with performance in comparison with other alternatives evaluated. The selected prompts for each language are listed in Table 3.

[2]https://www.coe.int/en/web/common-european-framework-reference-languages

LN	Prompt1	Prompt2
EN	easier, simple	word, synonym
ES	palabra, sinónimo	fácil, simple
PT	palavra, sinônimo	fácil, simples

Table 3: All prompts used in our work. Notice that for ES and PT, the equivalent prompts has to be inverted with respect to English due to grammar rules.

We used the masked token tailored to each model (e.g., [MASK] token) to predict less complex words instead. We also investigate the impact of context around a target word on the model by adding context words into the training sentences. Table 1 illustrates our selected prompts in English for 3 defined scenarios: no context, context within a window size (delimited by a number of characters on each side) and all context, where all the sentence is considered. We selected the best-performing prompts after experimenting with multiple templates.

3.3 Language Models

We selected our models based on their language, size and performance to evaluate a prompt-learning setting. These models were trained for Masked language modeling (MLM) objective.[3]

- (multiL[4]) **mBERT** (Devlin et al., 2019): a BERT-based model trained over a large multilingual corpus using Wikipedia in 102 languages in a unsupervised way.
- (EN) **RoBERTa-large** (Liu et al., 2019): an improved version of BERT (Devlin et al., 2019) model, trained in a large English corpus (160GB of uncompressed data) with no labels (i.e., unsupervised).
- (ES) **BERTIN** (De la Rosa et al., 2022): a RoBERTa-based model trained in a the Spanish portion of mC4 dataset (Raffel et al., 2022), which has 1 TB of uncompressed data. Due to the difficulties of using such a large corpus, a subsection of the dataset was selected using perplexity sampling.
- (PT) **BR_BERTo**[5]: a roBERTa-based model trained on 6.9M of sentences in PT.

3.4 Fine Tuning

To fine tune our LMs, given a sentence from the original dataset and its target word (i.e., complex), we generate a source sentence by masking the target word in our prompt. Then, we generate the target sentence by replacing the masked token ([MASK]) in the source sentence with its top-k simplified candidates. As a result, for each sentence containing a complex word, we have k target sentences. For example, with the training sentence in the first row of Table 1, with $k = 3$ we have the following target sentences:

a simple word for **classified** is *grouped* .
a simple word for **classified** is *organized* .
a simple word for **classified** is *categorized* .

We performed similarly with the other scenarios (n-words context, all-context). Then, we repeated this generation process with all our templates (see Section 3.2) and across the three languages.

3.5 Candidate Filtering

To maximise the accuracy of our model, we implemented a post-processing step to remove unsuitable candidates. To decide best on the filtering strategies, we performed a manual analysis of the results from the trial data provided by the ST.[6] For all three languages, we remove characters that could represent an undefined candidate such as "unknown" or "[UNK]". Also, we removed the complex candidate and any non-words that could be suggested by the model. For Spanish and Portuguese, we lowercased all candidates and kept only those words of length higher than 2. We also removed duplicated candidates. Finally, for English, we filtered antonyms using Wordnet.[7]

4 Experiments

4.1 Datasets

For English, we concatenated all the datasets and removed duplicates in the combined corpus. For Spanish and Portuguese, we used the EASIER and SIMPLEX corpora, respectively. In all languages, the corpus was split in two portions: 90% for training and 10% for validation, using a random sampling. We used the official release of the gold-standard from the ST as the testing set.

4.2 Training Settings

We test PromptLS in three different settings:

1. **Zero-shot**: we input the source sentences templates with the complex candidate into the MLM and obtain top-k simple candidates.

[3]Please refer to the Appendix A for additional systems that we considered for our benchmarks.

[4]We refer to our multilingual models as multiL.

[5]`https://huggingface.co/rdenadai/BR_BERTo`

[6]`https://github.com/LaSTUS-TALN-UPF/TSAR-2022-Shared-Task/tree/main/datasets`

[7]`https://www.nltk.org/howto/wordnet.html`

LN	Model	Setting	Prompt1	Prompt2	w	k	Acc@1	A@3	M@3	P@3
EN	RoBERTa-L	zero-shot	easier	word	all	0	0.378	0.303	0.251	0.606
			easier	word	10	0	0.356	0.553	0.251	0.612
		fine-tune	simple	word	5	5	0.830	0.899	0.644	0.941
			easier	word	5	5	0.803	0.904	0.644	0.941
	mBERT	multiL	easier	word	10	10	0.681	0.718	0.503	0.824
			easier	synonym	5	7	0.644	0.739	0.510	0.840
ES	BETO	zero-shot	palabra	simple	10	10	0.064	0.115	0.031	0.115
			palabra	fácil	10	2	0.053	0.103	0.030	0.103
	BERTIN	fine-tune	sinónimo	fácil	all	3	0.396	0.589	0.191	0.589
			palabra	simple	all	3	0.402	0.559	0.184	0.559
	XLM-RoBERTa-L	multiL	sinónimo	fácil	5	10	0.304	0.409	0.136	0.409
			sinónimo	simple	10	10	0.302	0.404	0.135	0.406
PT	ALBERT-pt	zero-shot	sinônimo	fácil	5	1	0.013	0.045	0.010	0.045
			sinônimo	simples	10	3	0.013	0.039	0.008	0.039
	BR_BERTo	fine-tune	palavra	simples	all	8	0.497	0.594	0.420	0.600
			sinônimo	fácil	all	10	0.516	0.574	0.433	0.594
	XLM-RoBERTa-L	multiL	sinônimo	sinônimo	10	5	0.271	0.406	0.180	0.439
			sinônimo	simples	5	5	0.277	0.419	0.188	0.452

Table 4: Best-performing configurations on the validation set for each model. **LN** refers to "Language", ***w*** to the number of tokens in the context window, ***k*** is the number of candidates used to augment the training data, **Acc@1** refers to MAP@1/Potential@1/Precision@1, **A@3** to Accuracy@3@top_gold_1, **M@3** to MAP@3, and **P@3** to Potential@3.

2. **Fine-tuned MLM**: we train the model with the augmented source sentences and their corresponding labels to fine-tune the MLM. At inference step, the steps are similar to the zero-shot setting.

3. **Multilingual**: We run both (i) and (ii) scenarios using multilingual MLMs.

We also combine the three settings with different sizes of the window context including 5, 10, and all context. The performance of PromptLS was additionally evaluated with different k numbers of top-k candidates used to generate the training data ($k = 1, 3, 5, 7, 10$).

In all experiments, we used the evaluation script provided by the organiser (Saggion et al., 2022) to calculate the following metrics: **MAP@K** (Mean Average Precision @ K) with K=1,3,5,10; **Potential@K** with K=1,3,5,10; **Accuracy@K@top1** with K=1,2,3.

4.3 Training Details

We performed our training using 2 NVIDIA v100 GPU (16GB RAM) using the HuggingFace (Wolf et al., 2020) framework for the implementation of our models. Our models were trained for 5 epochs, with a learning rate of 5e-5 using AdamW optimizer, a batch size of 8, a linear scheduler with no warm-up steps and a Cross Entropy loss. We did not perform further variations on these hyperparameters due to the increased variability of our prompt-based experiments.[8]

5 Results

For English, we executed 48 runs in a zero-shot setting, 240 for the fine-tuned MLM, and 192 for the multilingual settings. For Spanish, we executed 160 runs for the zero-shot and fine-tuned model and 140 for the multilingual setting. Similarly, for Portuguese, we ran 106 runs for zero-shot, 169 for fine-tuned setting and 144 for our multilingual setting.

Overall, we ran more than 600 experiments for each language with multiple combinations of prompts, context windows, number of candidates for data augmentation, models and settings for the selection of our submitted system.[9] In Table 4, we include the best two configurations of each model

[8]Our code is available on Github: `https://github.com/lmvasque/ls-prompt-tsar2022`

[9]We publish our settings selection scripts on Github: `https://github.com/lmvasque/ls-prompt-tsar2022/tree/main/scripts/benchmark`

LN	#	Model	Setup	Prompt1	Prompt2	w	k	Acc@1	A@3	M@3	P@3
EN	1	RoBERTa-L	fine	simple	word	5	5	**0.6353**	**0.5308**	**0.4244**	**0.8739**
	2	mBERT	multi	easier	word	10	10	0.4959	0.4235	0.3273	0.7560
	3	RoBERTa-L	zero	easier	word	5	0	0.2654	0.268	0.1820	0.4906
ES	1	BERTIN	fine	sinónimo	fácil	0	3	0.3451	**0.2907**	**0.2238**	**0.5543**
	2			palabra	simple	0	10	0.3614	**0.2907**	0.2225	0.538
	3			sinónimo	fácil	10	10	**0.3668**	0.269	0.2128	0.5326
PT	1	BR_BERTo	fine	palavra	simples	0	8	**0.1711**	0.1096	0.1011	0.2486
	2			sinônimo	fácil	0	10	0.1363	0.0962	0.0944	0.2379
	3			sinônimo	simples	5	10	0.1577	**0.1283**	**0.1071**	**0.2834**

Table 5: Results on the official testing set. "LN" refers to Language, "#" to the number of submission, "fine" to fine-tune and "zero" to zero-shot.

in the benchmark for each language. Nevertheless, for our ST submission, we selected the three best-performing runs in the development set using a ranking of all the models results. We show our final systems in Table 5.

6 Discussion

In Table 4, we showed that in the case of English, using zero-shot combined with context produced a relatively reasonable performance. Meanwhile, it is not the case for Spanish and Portuguese, which scored significantly lower. Such performance can be attributed to the size of the MLMs. In contrast, the fine-tuning setting led to a higher performance although we used small annotated corpora to fine-tune the MLMs. The performance gap between zero-shot and fine-tuning ones is between 0.3 and 0.4 across metrics and languages. It is unsurprising that the multilingual LMs did not outperform the monolingual ones.

Candidates for the prompts (e.g., "easier", "word") affected the performance of PromptLS. In the English language, the best prompts are composed by "easier word" and "simple word". Meanwhile, it was more suitable to use "palabra simple" and "palabra fácil" for the Spanish model and "palavra simples" and "sinônimo simples" for the Portuguese model. Our selections in Portuguese were done based on the knowledge of a second-language learner without the support of a native Brazilian Portuguese speaker. Therefore, there might be space for improvement on the selected settings of this model.

In addition, we observed that context words around a complex word are important in this task. In all the settings reported in Table 4, we had to use at least a window of 5 words to obtain good performance. Using multiple candidates for a complex word to augment the training data helps improve the performance as well. Finally, we selected the best settings and applied them to the official testing set. The results (Saggion et al., 2022) of our three runs in each language are reported in Table 5.

Concerning the model selection, it is noted that T5 model (Raffel et al., 2022) is also a suitable baseline for a prompt-based setting. However, unlike the experimental MLMs, T5 has a decoder, which requires additional effort to apply it to Lexical Simplification. We therefore leave this implementation for future work.

7 Conclusion

In this paper, we presented the implementation of a prompt-learning system for LS. Our experiments indicate we can obtain reasonable results even in zero-shot settings, especially for full resourced languages such as English. We demonstrate that by fine-tuning our prompt templates, we obtain competitive results in all languages. As future work, we intend to experiment with better datasets, including better filtering and ranking methods for LS.

8 CRediT author statement

Laura Vásquez-Rodríguez: Methodology, Software, Validation, Writing - Original Draft, Writing – Review & Editing. **Nhung T. H. Nguyen**: Methodology, Software, Validation, Writing - Original Draft, Writing – Review & Editing. **Matthew Shardlow**: Conceptualization, Methodology, Software, Writing - Original Draft, Writing – Review & Editing. **Sophia Ananiadou**: Funding acquisition, Supervision.

References

Rodrigo Alarcon, Lourdes Moreno, and Paloma Martinez. 2021. Lexical simplification system to improve web accessibility. *IEEE Access*, PP:1–1.

Stefan Bott, Luz Rello, Biljana Drndarevic, and Horacio Saggion. 2012. Can Spanish be simpler? LexSiS: Lexical simplification for Spanish. In *Proceedings of COLING 2012*, pages 357–374, Mumbai, India. The COLING 2012 Organizing Committee.

Tom B. Brown, Benjamin Mann, Nick Ryder, Melanie Subbiah, Jared Kaplan, Prafulla Dhariwal, Arvind Neelakantan, Pranav Shyam, Girish Sastry, Amanda Askell, Sandhini Agarwal, Ariel Herbert-Voss, Gretchen Krueger, Tom Henighan, Rewon Child, Aditya Ramesh, Daniel M. Ziegler, Jeffrey Wu, Clemens Winter, Christopher Hesse, Mark Chen, Eric Sigler, Mateusz Litwin, Scott Gray, Benjamin Chess, Jack Clark, Christopher Berner, Sam McCandlish, Alec Radford, Ilya Sutskever, and Dario Amodei. 2020. Language models are few-shot learners. In *Proceedings of the 34th International Conference on Neural Information Processing Systems*, NIPS'20, Red Hook, NY, USA. Curran Associates Inc.

John Carroll, Guido Minnen, Darren Pearce, Yvonne Canning, Siobhan Devlin, and John Tait. 1999. Simplifying text for language-impaired readers. In *Ninth Conference of the European Chapter of the Association for Computational Linguistics*, pages 269–270, Bergen, Norway. Association for Computational Linguistics.

José Cañete, Gabriel Chaperon, Rodrigo Fuentes, Jou-Hui Ho, Hojin Kang, and Jorge Pérez. 2020. Spanish pre-trained bert model and evaluation data. In *PML4DC at ICLR 2020*.

Alexis Conneau, Kartikay Khandelwal, Naman Goyal, Vishrav Chaudhary, Guillaume Wenzek, Francisco Guzmán, Edouard Grave, Myle Ott, Luke Zettlemoyer, and Veselin Stoyanov. 2020. Unsupervised cross-lingual representation learning at scale. In *Proceedings of the 58th Annual Meeting of the Association for Computational Linguistics*, pages 8440–8451, Online. Association for Computational Linguistics.

Jan De Belder and Marie-Francine Moens. 2012. A dataset for the evaluation of lexical simplification. In *Computational Linguistics and Intelligent Text Processing*, pages 426–437, Berlin, Heidelberg. Springer Berlin Heidelberg.

Javier De la Rosa, Eduardo G Ponferrada, Manu Romero, Paulo Villegas, Pablo González de Prado Salas, and María Grandury. 2022. Bertin: Efficient pre-training of a spanish language model using perplexity sampling. *Procesamiento del Lenguaje Natural*, 68.

Jacob Devlin, Ming-Wei Chang, Kenton Lee, and Kristina Toutanova. 2019. BERT: Pre-training of deep bidirectional transformers for language understanding. In *Proceedings of the 2019 Conference of the North American Chapter of the Association for Computational Linguistics: Human Language Technologies, Volume 1 (Long and Short Papers)*, pages 4171–4186, Minneapolis, Minnesota. Association for Computational Linguistics.

Siobhan Lucy Devlin. 1999. *Simplifying natural language for aphasic readers*. Ph.D. thesis, University of Sunderland.

Ning Ding, Yulin Chen, Xu Han, Guangwei Xu, Pengjun Xie, Hai-Tao Zheng, Zhiyuan Liu, Juanzi Li, and Hong-Gee Kim. 2021. Prompt-learning for fine-grained entity typing. *arXiv preprint arXiv:2108.10604*.

Ning Ding, Shengding Hu, Weilin Zhao, Yulin Chen, Zhiyuan Liu, Haitao Zheng, and Maosong Sun. 2022. OpenPrompt: An open-source framework for prompt-learning. In *Proceedings of the 60th Annual Meeting of the Association for Computational Linguistics: System Demonstrations*, pages 105–113, Dublin, Ireland. Association for Computational Linguistics.

Nathan S. Hartmann, Gustavo H. Paetzold, and Sandra M. Aluísio. 2018. Simplex-pb: A lexical simplification database and benchmark for portuguese. In *Computational Processing of the Portuguese Language*, pages 272–283, Cham. Springer International Publishing.

Nathan S. Hartmann, Gustavo H. Paetzold, and Sandra M. Aluísio. 2020. A dataset for the evaluation of lexical simplification in portuguese for children. In *Computational Processing of the Portuguese Language*, pages 55–64, Cham. Springer International Publishing.

Nathan Siegle Hartmann and Sandra Maria Aluisio. 2021. Automatic lexical adaptation in brazilian portuguese informative texts for elementary education. *Linguamatica*, 12(2).

Colby Horn, Cathryn Manduca, and David Kauchak. 2014. Learning a lexical simplifier using Wikipedia. In *Proceedings of the 52nd Annual Meeting of the Association for Computational Linguistics (Volume 2: Short Papers)*, pages 458–463, Baltimore, Maryland. Association for Computational Linguistics.

Zhengbao Jiang, Frank F. Xu, Jun Araki, and Graham Neubig. 2020. How can we know what language models know? *Transactions of the Association for Computational Linguistics*, 8:423–438.

Zhenzhong Lan, Mingda Chen, Sebastian Goodman, Kevin Gimpel, Piyush Sharma, and Radu Soricut. 2020. Albert: A lite bert for self-supervised learning of language representations.

Pengfei Liu, Weizhe Yuan, Jinlan Fu, Zhengbao Jiang, Hiroaki Hayashi, and Graham Neubig. 2022. Pre-train, prompt, and predict: A systematic survey of prompting methods in natural language processing. *ACM Computing Surveys*. Just Accepted.

Yinhan Liu, Myle Ott, Naman Goyal, Jingfei Du, Mandar Joshi, Danqi Chen, Omer Levy, Mike Lewis, Luke Zettlemoyer, and Veselin Stoyanov. 2019. Roberta: A robustly optimized bert pretraining approach.

Shiwen Ni and Hung-Yu Kao. 2022. Electra is a zero-shot learner, too.

Gustavo Paetzold and Lucia Specia. 2015. LEXenstein: A framework for lexical simplification. In *Proceedings of ACL-IJCNLP 2015 System Demonstrations*, pages 85–90, Beijing, China. Association for Computational Linguistics and The Asian Federation of Natural Language Processing.

Gustavo Paetzold and Lucia Specia. 2016a. Benchmarking lexical simplification systems. In *Proceedings of the Tenth International Conference on Language Resources and Evaluation (LREC'16)*, pages 3074–3080, Portorož, Slovenia. European Language Resources Association (ELRA).

Gustavo Paetzold and Lucia Specia. 2016b. Unsupervised lexical simplification for non-native speakers. *Proceedings of the AAAI Conference on Artificial Intelligence*, 30(1).

Piotr Przybyła and Matthew Shardlow. 2020. Multi-word lexical simplification. In *Proceedings of the 28th International Conference on Computational Linguistics*, pages 1435–1446, Barcelona, Spain (Online). International Committee on Computational Linguistics.

Jipeng Qiang, Yun Li, Zhu Yi, Yunhao Yuan, and Xindong Wu. 2020. Lexical simplification with pretrained encoders. *Thirty-Fourth AAAI Conference on Artificial Intelligence*, page 8649–8656.

Jipeng Qiang, Yun Li, Yi Zhu, Yunhao Yuan, Yang Shi, and Xindong Wu. 2021. Lsbert: Lexical simplification based on bert. *IEEE/ACM Transactions on Audio, Speech, and Language Processing*, 29:3064–3076.

Colin Raffel, Noam Shazeer, Adam Roberts, Katherine Lee, Sharan Narang, Michael Matena, Yanqi Zhou, Wei Li, and Peter J. Liu. 2022. Exploring the limits of transfer learning with a unified text-to-text transformer. *J. Mach. Learn. Res.*, 21(1).

Horacio Saggion, Sanja Štajner, Daniel Ferrés, Kim Cheng Sheang, Matthew Shardlow, Kai North, and Marcos Zampieri. 2022. Findings of the tsar-2022 shared task on multilingual lexical simplification. In *Proceedings of TSAR workshop held in conjunction with EMNLP 2022*.

Taylor Shin, Yasaman Razeghi, Robert L. Logan IV, Eric Wallace, and Sameer Singh. 2020. AutoPrompt: Eliciting Knowledge from Language Models with Automatically Generated Prompts. In *Proceedings of the 2020 Conference on Empirical Methods in Natural Language Processing (EMNLP)*, pages 4222–4235, Online. Association for Computational Linguistics.

Yi Sun, Yu Zheng, Chao Hao, and Hangping Qiu. 2021. Nsp-bert: A prompt-based zero-shot learner through an original pre-training task–next sentence prediction.

Satoru Uchida, Shohei Takada, and Yuki Arase. 2018. CEFR-based lexical simplification dataset. In *Proceedings of the Eleventh International Conference on Language Resources and Evaluation (LREC 2018)*, Miyazaki, Japan. European Language Resources Association (ELRA).

Thomas Wolf, Lysandre Debut, Victor Sanh, Julien Chaumond, Clement Delangue, Anthony Moi, Pierric Cistac, Tim Rault, Remi Louf, Morgan Funtowicz, Joe Davison, Sam Shleifer, Patrick von Platen, Clara Ma, Yacine Jernite, Julien Plu, Canwen Xu, Teven Le Scao, Sylvain Gugger, Mariama Drame, Quentin Lhoest, and Alexander Rush. 2020. Transformers: State-of-the-art natural language processing. In *Proceedings of the 2020 Conference on Empirical Methods in Natural Language Processing: System Demonstrations*, pages 38–45, Online. Association for Computational Linguistics.

A Baselines

In addition to the submitted baselines, we also considered the following systems:

- (multiL) **XLM-RoBERTa-large** (Conneau et al., 2020): a multilingual RoBERTa-based model trained over 2.5T of data from the CommonCrawl in 102 languages in an unsupervised way.
- (EN) **bert-large-uncased** (Devlin et al., 2019): a BERT-based model trained on the BookCorpus, a dataset of 11,038 books and English Wikipedia.
- (EN) **ALBERT-large** (Lan et al., 2020): a BERT-based model optimised to consume less memory with reduced training time. It is also trained for sentence order prediction task with a self-supervised loss to compensate its performance drop from the parameters reduction.
- (ES) **BETO** (Cañete et al., 2020): a BERT-based model trained in large (300M lines) Spanish corpora from different sources[10].
- (PT) **ALBERT-pt-br**[11]: an ALBERT-based model trained in Brazilian Portuguese data.
- (PT) **RoBERTa-pt-br**[12]: a roBERTa-based model trained in Brazilian Portuguese data.

[10] https://github.com/josecannete/spanish-corpora

[11] https://huggingface.co/josu/albert-br

[12] https://huggingface.co/josu/roberta-pt-br

PolyU-CBS at TSAR-2022 Shared Task: A Simple, Rank-Based Method for Complex Word Substitution in Two Steps

Emmanuele Chersoni and **Yu-Yin Hsu**
The Hong Kong Polytechnic University
Department of Chinese and Bilingual Studies
Yuk Choi Road 11, Hung Hom, Kowloon, Hong Kong, China
emmanuelechersoni@gmail.com, yu-yin.hsu@polyu.edu.hk

Abstract

In this paper, we describe the system we present at the Workshop on Text Simplification, Accessibility, and Readability (TSAR-2022) regarding the shared task on Lexical Simplification for English, Portuguese, and Spanish. We proposed an unsupervised approach in two steps: First, we used a masked language model with word masking for each language to extract possible candidates for the replacement of a difficult word; second, we ranked the candidates according to three different Transformer-based metrics. Finally, we determined our list of candidates based on the lowest average rank across different metrics. The results show that our method, based on two simple steps and rankings, can effectively improve the scores among datasets for the task of lexical simplification.

1 Introduction

The notion of *linguistic complexity* has been widely debated in both theoretical and computational linguistics, and has been interpreted very differently depending on the discipline. Specifically, in the field of natural language processing (NLP), complexity has often been associated with the difficulties that language users encounter while processing concrete linguistic productions (e.g., sentences, utterances, etc.) (Blache, 2011; Chersoni et al., 2016, 2017, 2021; Sarti et al., 2021; Iavarone et al., 2021), with research focusing on applications that aim to simplify challenging texts and to make them more easily readable for a wider variety of users (North et al., 2022b).

Previously, NLP shared tasks focused on the problem of identifying a complex word in a sentence, or assigning a difficulty score to it (Yimam et al., 2018; Shardlow et al., 2021). The TSAR-2022 shared task (Saggion et al., 2022) instead focused on the next step; that is, how to find simpler words as replacement candidates for a given target word in a multilingual setting. Consequently, the task can be seen as similar to lexical substitution in context (McCarthy and Navigli, 2009).

In this paper, we describe our contribution to the TSAR-2022 shared task, which is a system for English, Portuguese, and Spanish that i) generates replacement candidates for a given word via masked language modeling, and ii) assigns scores to the candidates by averaging the ranks assigned by different Transformer-based metrics.

2 Related Work

The goal of the previous shared tasks regarding lexical complexity was to identify complex words in a sentence context, and complexity was defined as a binary variable (Paetzold and Specia, 2016b; Yimam et al., 2018). However, these tasks were oversimplified because there is no clear-cut choice in many contexts, and human annotators prefer to assign a score based on a continuous scale of difficulty. Shardlow et al. (2020) introduced the CompLex corpus, a gold-standard benchmark for lexical complexity in English, in which words and multiword expressions are extracted from different text genres (legal, religious, and biomedical genres) and are annotated with continuous scores that reflect their difficulty in the sentence context. The same corpus was then used as the source material for the SemEval-2021 shared task regarding lexical complexity in context (Shardlow et al., 2021).

The estimation of lexical complexity is only one component in the lexical simplification pipeline, which also involves generating candidates for substitution, ranking them, and assessing their degree of fitness in the given sentence context. Datasets focusing on the latter parts of the pipeline have been published for English (Specia et al., 2012; Horn et al., 2014; Paetzold and Specia, 2016a; Štajner et al., 2022), Japanese (Kajiwara and Yamamoto, 2015; Hading et al., 2016), Portuguese (Hartmann and Aluísio, 2020; North et al., 2022a; Štajner et al., 2022), French (Rolin et al., 2021), Spanish (Alar-

Proceedings of the Workshop on Text Simplification, Accessibility, and Readability (TSAR-2022), pages 225 - 230
December 8, 2022 ©2022 Association for Computational Linguistics

Language	Sentence	Target	Substitutes
English (EN)	Brevard County was the scene of six homicides in 2011, Goodyear said.	homicides	murders deaths killings
Portuguese (PT)	o nosso é brasileiro colorido é um menino alegre com pontos de melancolia	melancolia	tristeza tédio abatimento
Spanish (ES)	Antes de aquello, el estadio albergaba una capacidad para más de 130.000 espectadores.	albergaba	alojaba tiene aloja

Table 1: Dataset examples for each of the three languages.

con, 2021; Ferrés and Saggion, 2022; Štajner et al., 2022), and Chinese (Qiang et al., 2021).

The current state-of-the-art system for English, LSBert, was introduced by Qiang et al. (2020). The system first generates a list of possible replacement candidates via the masked language modeling function of BERT (Devlin et al., 2019) by being fed the original sentence concatenated with a copy of the sentence in which the original word has been masked. The system then performs a re-ranking using different features, e.g. frequency, vector-based semantic similarity, and/or language model probability. Studies using LSBert (Przybyła and Shardlow, 2020; Štajner et al., 2022) have shown that the approach could easily be adapted to other languages and still achieve state-of-the-art results.

3 Experimental Settings

3.1 Datasets

The shared task organizers provided a testing dataset (Štajner et al., 2022) with a combined number of 1115 instances: 373 for English, 374 for Portuguese, and 368 for Spanish. Each instance consisted of a sentence, a target word, and a list with a variable number of gold replacement words, all obtained from human native speakers on Amazon Mechanical Turk. Each instance was annotated by 25 different annotators, and each annotator had to simplify the sentence by proposing a simpler candidate word for substitution. An example for each target language is displayed in Table 1.

3.2 Methodology

3.2.1 Candidate Generation

For each of the three target languages, we masked each target word in the dataset instances and used a masked language model – a variant of the BERT Base model (Devlin et al., 2019) – to generate a list of candidate words (the original word itself was filtered out). For English, we simply used the original BERT Base;[1] for Portuguese, we used the BERT Base BERTimbau model by Souza et al. (2020);[2] for Spanish, we used the BETO model by Canete et al. (2020).[3] For our experiments, the number n of generated candidates was used as a system parameter, and was fixed at $n = 30$. Importantly, for each candidate word we saved the $rank$; that is, the position that the word occupies in the list of candidates sorted by decreasing probability score. We refer to this method, before any re-ranking step, as the **Base** and used it as a baseline method.

3.2.2 Candidate Re-Ranking

Using the n candidate words identified in the candidate generation step, we extracted three Transformer-based metrics for re-ranking. The idea behind our approach is that words that achieve higher scores and lower rankings for multiple metrics are strong candidates for replacement.

We considered three metrics, which we extracted via the `minicons` library (Misra, 2022):

- *Sentence probability via autoregressive language modeling*. For each item, we replaced the target word with a candidate substitute word, and computed a probability for the whole sentence via a variant of the GPT2 model (Radford et al., 2019). For English, we used the original GPT2-Base;[4] for Portuguese, the GPorTuguese-2 Small (Guillou, 2020);[5]

[1]https://huggingface.co/bert-base-uncased

[2]https://huggingface.co/neuralmind/bert-base-portuguese-cased

[3]https://huggingface.co/dccuchile/bert-base-spanish-wwm-uncased

[4]https://huggingface.co/gpt2

[5]https://huggingface.co/pierreguillou/gpt2-small-portuguese

Method	Acc@1	Acc(1,2,3)@Top1	Pot(3,5,10)	MAP(3,5,10)
Base	0.27	0.12 / 0.19 / 0.22	0.49 / 0.57 / 0.68	0.17 / 0.13 / 0.08
Base + LMProb *	0.32	0.14 / 0.20 / 0.26	0.51 / 0.60 / 0.71	0.19 / 0.15 / 0.09
Base + PLL	0.29	0.12 / 0.17 / 0.22	0.5 / 0.6 / 0.72	0.18 / 0.14 / 0.08
Base + cosSim *	0.43	0.2 / 0.28 / 0.33	0.61 /0.7 / 0.77	0.27 / 0.2 / 0.11
Base + All *	0.4	0.18 / 0.26 / 0.3	0.59 / 0.68 / 0.75	0.25 / 0.18 / 0.11
TUNER	0.34	0.14 / 0.17 / 0.18	0.43 / 0.44 / 0.44	0.17 / 0.1 / 0.05
LSBert	**0.6**	**0.3 / 0.44 / 0.53**	**0.82 / 0.87 / 0.94**	**0.40 / 0.29 / 0.17**

Table 2: Scores for the English dataset. * indicates the systems submitted to the shared task.

and for Spanish, a GPT2 Base model trained on the BETO corpus (Canete et al., 2020).[6]

- *Sentence probability via masked language modeling*. Similar to the previous metric, we computed the probability of the sentence via estimating the pseudo-log-likelihood (PLL) with a masked language model (the scores were obtained by masking the tokens one-by-one) (Salazar et al., 2020). For this metric, we adopted the same versions of BERT Base used in the step of candidate generation.

- *Contextualized embedding similarity*. By always using the same BERT Base models, we measured the cosine similarity of i) the contextualized embedding of the target word in the context of the original sentence, and ii) the contextualized embedding of each candidate word after replacing the target word in the original sentence.

$$score(w) = \frac{rank_{Base}(w) + rank_{metric}(w)}{2} \quad (1)$$

After computing the scores for each of the three metrics in our pool of n candidates, we sorted them to obtain their respective rankings. We call these rankings, respectively, *LMProb*, *PLL* and *cosSim*. Then, for each candidate word w, we computed its score by averaging the rank in the **Base** model and the rank in one of the metrics (see Equation 1). This resulted in three different scores: 1) **Base + LMProb**; 2) **Base + PLL**; and 3) **Base + cosSim**. We then computed one last score, which averaged the ranks of the four rankings together for each candidate word. We call this score **Base + All**. The scores of the candidate words are finally sorted in ascending order (the ones with the lowest ranks are the top candidates for replacement).

[6]https://huggingface.co/mrm8488/spanish-gpt2

3.3 Baselines and State-of-the-Art

We presented the scores for a simple baseline method, based on the mere candidate generation by a BERT masked language model, without any further re-ranking (**Base**). Moreover, the scores for two state-of-the-art systems were provided by the shared task organizers for comparison:

- **TUNER**, an unsupervised system introduced by Ferrés et al. (2017) for Spanish, and further adapted to English and Portuguese. The system relies on the identification of a list of candidate synonyms via a word sense disambiguation algorithm and a distributional thesaurus.[7] Candidates are then re-ranked based on their frequencies in the Wikipedia of each language. Finally, a morphological generator component ensures that the correct form of the word is selected for the final replacement;

- The above-mentioned **LSBert** system (Qiang et al., 2020), with its adaptations to Spanish and Portuguese.

3.4 Evaluation

Evaluation metrics for lexical simplification were introduced by Paetzold and Specia (2016a):

- *Accuracy (Acc)*: $Acc@1$ is the ratio of instances for which the top substitute is in the gold standard, regardless of the order, and it is the main metric for ranking the shared task systems; $AccK$ measures instead the ratio of instances for which at least one of the top K predicted candidates matches the most frequently suggested candidate synonym in the gold standard (we made our system return up to 10 candidates per instance);

[7]Both tools rely on the Freeling text analysis tool (Padró and Stanilovsky, 2012), available at: https://nlp.lsi.upc.edu/freeling/index.php/node/1.

Method	Acc@1	Acc(1,2,3)@Top1	Pot(3,5,10)	MAP(3,5,10)
Base	0.23	0.1 / 0.12 / 0.15	0.34 / 0.39 / 0.49	0.12 / 0.08 / 0.05
Base + LMProb *	0.22	0.09 / 0.12 / 0.15	0.33 / 0.38 / 0.49	0.11 / 0.08 / 0.05
Base + PLL	0.22	0.09 / 0.13 / 0.14	0.34 / 0.4 / 0.48	0.12 / 0.08 / 0.05
Base + cosSim *	0.32	0.14 / 0.19 / 0.21	0.45 / 0.51 / 0.57	0.17 / 0.12 / 0.07
Base + All *	0.28	0.11 / 0.14 / 0.17	0.4 / 0.47 / 0.55	0.15 / 0.1 / 0.06
TUNER	0.22	0.13 / 0.16 / 0.16	0.27 / 0.27 / 0.27	0.1 / 0.06 / 0.03
LSBert	**0.32**	**0.16 / 0.23 / 0.28**	**0.49 / 0.58 / 0.67**	**0.19 / 0.13 / 0.07**

Table 3: Scores for the Portuguese dataset. * indicates the systems submitted to the shared task.

Method	Acc@1	Acc(1,2,3)@Top1	Pot(3,5,10)	MAP(3,5,10)
Base	0.24	0.1 / 0.14 / 0.18	0.45 / 0.53 / 0.62	0.15 / 0.11 / 0.06
Base + LMProb *	0.2	0.08 / 0.13 / 0.17	0.41 / 0.5 / 0.64	0.14 / 0.1 / 0.06
Base + PLL	0.23	0.08 / 0.15 / 0.2	0.44 / 0.54 / 0.64	0.16 / 0.11 / 0.06
Base + cosSim *	**0.36**	**0.16 / 0.2 / 0.23**	**0.52 / 0.6 / 0.68**	**0.2 / 0.14 / 0.08**
Base + All *	0.28	0.11 / 0.18 / 0.22	0.5 / 0.6 / 0.68	0.18 / 0.13 / 0.07
TUNER	0.12	0.06 / 0.08 / 0.08	0.14 / 0.14 / 0.15	0.06 / 0.03 / 0.02
LSBert	0.28	0.09 / 0.14 / 0.18	0.49 / 0.61 / 0.74	0.19 / 0.13 / 0.07

Table 4: Scores for the Spanish dataset. * indicates the systems submitted to the shared task.

- *Potential (Pot)*: the ratio of instances for which at least one of the generated candidates is present in the gold standard.
- *Mean Average Precision (MAP)*: a commonly-used metric in information retrieval, which assesses how many of the predicted candidates are relevant (i.e., how many of them are present in the gold standard annotations).

In the official results, the metrics are computed based on different values of K: for Accuracy, $K = 1, 2, 3$, while for Potential and MAP, $K = 3, 5, 10$.

4 Results and Conclusion

The results for English, Portuguese and Spanish can be seen, respectively, in Table 2, 3 and 4. On the basis of preliminary results on the trial dataset, we submitted the scores for Base + All, Base + LMProb, and Base + cosSim in all the three language tracks. At a glance, it can be seen that the combination of the Base ranking with the ranking based on cosine similarity is the only one that consistently improves over the baseline performance. A possible reason is that the initial selection of the candidates is already based on a Transformer language model, so it could be the case that the information coming from the language model-based rankings is redundant, or tend to suggest the same subset of candidates. On the other hand, the cosine metric between the contextualized embeddings is assessing a paradigmatic type of similarity between the target and the candidate word: this is not necessarily taken into account by the other metrics, which are more focused on the syntagmatic axis.

Our method relying on Base + cosSim, which was submitted as PolyU-CBS3, was the one reporting the best scores on all the three datasets (15th overall on English, 5th on Spanish, 3rd on Portuguese). It is noticeable that our methods always outperform TUNER on the metrics of Potential and MAP. The LSBert is the best performing method on English and Portuguese datasets, although our Base + cosSim is a close match to the latter. Finally, Base + cosSim outperforms both TUNER and LSBert on Spanish. We take the results as a preliminary evidence that our method, based on two simple steps and ranking, can be highly effective for the task of lexical simplification. A possible way to further improve the methodology will be to introduce different methods of extracting candidate words. In our preliminary experiments, we found that a similarity ranking based on traditional, static embedding model alone can lead to improvements of the performance on English. However, for languages with a richer morphology like the Romance ones, a morphological adapter would be needed to generate the form that best fits the target sentence. Another possible direction could be using a generative model treating the task as a text-to-text problem (Raffel et al., 2020), which could be fine-tuned on supervised lexical substitution data and combined with a frequency filter to ensure that the proposed replacement is actually a simpler word.

Acknowledgements

This study was supported by the Startup fund (1-BD8S) by the Hong Kong Polytechnic University.

References

Rodrigo Alarcon. 2021. Dataset of Sentences Annotated With Complex Words and Their Synonyms to Support Lexical Simplification. *Mendeley Data*.

Philippe Blache. 2011. Evaluating Language Complexity in Context: New Parameters for a Constraint-based Model. In *Proceedings of the International Workshop on Constraints and Language Processing*.

José Canete, Gabriel Chaperon, Rodrigo Fuentes, Jou-Hui Ho, Hojin Kang, and Jorge Pérez. 2020. Spanish Pre-Trained BERT Model and Evaluation Data. In *Proceedings of the ICLR Workshop on Practical Machine Learning for Developing Countries*.

Emmanuele Chersoni, Philippe Blache, and Alessandro Lenci. 2016. Towards a Distributional Model of Semantic Complexity. In *Proceedings of the COLING Workshop on Computational Linguistics for Linguistic Complexity*.

Emmanuele Chersoni, Alessandro Lenci, and Philippe Blache. 2017. Logical Metonymy in a Distributional Model of Sentence Comprehension. In *Proceedings of *SEM*.

Emmanuele Chersoni, Enrico Santus, Alessandro Lenci, Philippe Blache, and Chu-Ren Huang. 2021. Not All Arguments Are Processed Equally: A Distributional Model of Argument Complexity. *Language Resources and Evaluation*, 55(4):873–900.

Jacob Devlin, Ming-Wei Chang, Kenton Lee, and Kristina Toutanova. 2019. BERT: Pre-training of Deep Bidirectional Transformers for Language Understanding. In *Proceedings of NAACL*.

Daniel Ferrés and Horacio Saggion. 2022. ALEXSIS: A Dataset for Lexical Simplification in Spanish. In *Proceedings of LREC*.

Daniel Ferrés, Horacio Saggion, and Xavier Gómez Guinovart. 2017. An Adaptable Lexical Simplification Architecture for Major Ibero-Romance Languages. In *Proceedings of the EMNLP Workshop on Building Linguistically Generalizable NLP Systems*.

Pierre Guillou. 2020. GPorTuguese-2 (Portuguese GPT-2 Small): A Language Model for Portuguese Text Generation (and More NLP Tasks...).

Muhaimin Hading, Yuji Matsumoto, and Maki Sakamoto. 2016. Japanese Lexical Simplification for Non-native Speakers. In *Proceedings of the COLING Workshop on Natural Language Processing Techniques for Educational Applications*.

Nathan Siegle Hartmann and Sandra Maria Aluísio. 2020. Adaptaçao Lexical Automática em Textos Informativos do Português Brasileiro para o Ensino Fundamental. *Linguamática*, 12(2):3–27.

Colby Horn, Cathryn Manduca, and David Kauchak. 2014. Learning a Lexical Simplifier Using Wikipedia. In *Proceedings of ACL*.

Benedetta Iavarone, Dominique Brunato, and Felice Dell'Orletta. 2021. Sentence Complexity in Context. In *Proceedings of the NAACL Workshop on Cognitive Modeling and Computational Linguistics*.

Tomoyuki Kajiwara and Kazuhide Yamamoto. 2015. Evaluation Dataset and System for Japanese Lexical Simplification. In *Proceedings of the ACL-IJCNLP 2015 Student Research Workshop*.

Diana McCarthy and Roberto Navigli. 2009. The English Lexical Substitution Task. *Language Resources and Evaluation*, 43(2):139–159.

Kanishka Misra. 2022. minicons: Enabling Flexible Behavioral and Representational Analyses of Transformer Language Models. *arXiv preprint arXiv:2203.13112*.

Kai North, Marcos Zampieri, and Tharindu Ranasinghe. 2022a. ALEXSIS-PT: A New Resource for Portuguese Lexical Simplification. *arXiv preprint arXiv:2209.09034*.

Kai North, Marcos Zampieri, and Matthew Shardlow. 2022b. Lexical Complexity Prediction: An Overview. *ACM Computing Surveys (CSUR)*.

Lluís Padró and Evgeny Stanilovsky. 2012. Freeling 3.0: Towards Wider Multilinguality. In *Proceedings of LREC*.

Gustavo Paetzold and Lucia Specia. 2016a. Benchmarking Lexical Simplification Systems. In *Proceedings of LREC*.

Gustavo Paetzold and Lucia Specia. 2016b. SemEval 2016 Task 11: Complex Word Identification. In *Proceedings of SemEval*.

Piotr Przybyła and Matthew Shardlow. 2020. Multi-Word Lexical Simplification. In *Proceedings of COLING*.

Jipeng Qiang, Yun Li, Yi Zhu, Yunhao Yuan, and Xindong Wu. 2020. LSBert: A Simple Framework for Lexical Simplification. *arXiv preprint arXiv:2006.14939*.

Jipeng Qiang, Xinyu Lu, Yun Li, Yunhao Yuan, and Xindong Wu. 2021. Chinese Lexical Simplification. *IEEE/ACM Transactions on Audio, Speech and Language Processing*, 29:1819–1828.

Alec Radford, Jeffrey Wu, Rewon Child, David Luan, Dario Amodei, and Ilya Sutskever. 2019. Language Models Are Unsupervised Multitask Learners. *OpenAI Blog*, 1(8):9.

Colin Raffel, Noam Shazeer, Adam Roberts, Katherine Lee, Sharan Narang, Michael Matena, Yanqi Zhou, Wei Li, Peter J Liu, et al. 2020. Exploring the Limits of Transfer Learning with a Unified Text-to-text

Transformer. *Journal of Machine Learning Research*, 21(140):1–67.

Eva Rolin, Quentin Langlois, Patrick Watrin, and Thomas François. 2021. FrenLyS: A Tool for the Automatic Simplification of French General Language Texts. In *Proceedings of RANLP*.

Horacio Saggion, Sanja Štajner, Daniel Ferrés, Kim Cheng Sheang, Matthew Shardlow, Kai North, and Marcos Zampieri. 2022. Findings of the TSAR-2022 Shared Task on Multilingual Lexical Simplification. In *Proceedings of the EMNLP Workshop on Text Simplification, Accessibility, and Readability*.

Julian Salazar, Davis Liang, Toan Q Nguyen, and Katrin Kirchhoff. 2020. Masked Language Model Scoring. In *Proceedings of ACL*.

Gabriele Sarti, Dominique Brunato, and Felice Dell'Orletta. 2021. That Looks Hard: Characterizing Linguistic Complexity in Humans and Language Models. In *Proceedings of the NAACL Workshop on Cognitive Modeling and Computational Linguistics*.

Matthew Shardlow, Michael Cooper, and Marcos Zampieri. 2020. Complex: A New Corpus for Lexical Complexity Prediction from Likert Scale Data. In *Proceedings of the LREC Workshop on Tools and Resources to Empower People with REAding DIfficulties (READI)*.

Matthew Shardlow, Richard Evans, Gustavo Paetzold, and Marcos Zampieri. 2021. SemEval-2021 Task 1: Lexical Complexity Prediction. In *Proceedings of SemEval*.

Fábio Souza, Rodrigo Nogueira, and Roberto Lotufo. 2020. BERTimbau: Pretrained BERT Models for Brazilian Portuguese. In *Brazilian Conference on Intelligent Systems*.

Lucia Specia, Sujay Kumar Jauhar, and Rada Mihalcea. 2012. Semeval-2012 Task 1: English Lexical Simplification. In *Proceedings of SemEval*.

Sanja Štajner, Daniel FerrĂŹes, Matthew Shardlow, Kai North, Marcos Zampieri, and Horacio Saggion. 2022. Lexical Simplification Benchmarks for English, Portuguese, and Spanish. *Frontiers in Artificial Intelligence*, 5.

Seid Muhie Yimam, Chris Biemann, Shervin Malmasi, Gustavo H Paetzold, Lucia Specia, Sanja Štajner, Anaïs Tack, and Marcos Zampieri. 2018. A Report on the Complex Word Identification Shared Task 2018. In *Proceedings of the NAACL Workshop on Innovative Use of NLP for Building Educational Applications*.

CENTAL at TSAR-2022 Shared Task: How Does Context Impact BERT-Generated Substitutions for Lexical Simplification?

Rodrigo Wilkens[1], **David Alfter**, **Rémi Cardon**[1], **Isabelle Gribomont**[1,2], **Adrien Bibal**[1], **Patrick Watrin**[1], **Marie-Catherine de Marneffe**[1], **Thomas François**[1]

[1]CENTAL, IL&C, University of Louvain, Belgium

[2]Royal Library of Belgium (KBR)

{first name dot last name}@uclouvain.be

Abstract

Lexical simplification is the task of substituting a difficult word with a simpler equivalent for a target audience. This is currently commonly done by modeling lexical complexity on a continuous scale to identify simpler alternatives to difficult words. In the TSAR shared task, the organizers call for systems capable of generating substitutions in a zero-shot-task context, for English, Spanish and Portuguese. In this paper, we present the solution we (the CENTAL team) proposed for the task. We explore the ability of BERT-like models to generate substitution words by masking the difficult word. To do so, we investigate various context enhancement strategies, that we combined into an ensemble method. We also explore different substitution ranking methods. We report on a post-submission analysis of the results and present our insights for potential improvements. The code for all our experiments is available at `https://gitlab.com/Cental-FR/cental-tsar2022`.

1 Introduction

Lexical Simplification (LS) aims at identifying words that are considered too difficult for a given audience and replacing them with simpler substitutes.[1] Following Housen and Simoens (2016, 166), we distinguish the notion of *absolute complexity* that refers to "inherent linguistic properties of a language feature" from the notion of *difficulty*, which depends on "how costly, demanding, or difficult a given language feature is for a given language learner in a given learning context, particularly in terms of the mental resources allocated and cognitive mechanisms."

The TSAR shared task (Saggion et al., 2022) asks for solutions generating and ranking substitutes for predefined difficult words in sentences in English, Spanish and Portuguese. This paper describes the CENTAL team solution to the TSAR shared task, which takes advantage of pretrained neural language models and is easy to use in any language for which such models exist. Our solution has two steps: Substitution Generation (SG) and Substitution Ranking (SR). For SG, we use an ensemble of BERT-like models to generate candidate words to replace the difficult word. We assume language models can produce correct substitutes but are noisy (i.e., they also produce wrong substitutes). We try to mitigate this issue by combining the output of different language models in an SR step. We explore three strategies for combining and ranking the output of our SG methods. We propose a simple voting strategy for the substitutions generated by each model. We also use a standard ranking method, assuming that the ensemble of models can generate relevant substitution words, but the models do not agree on them. The third strategy uses a model trained for one language and ranks in the other two. It assumes we have poor resources for a given language and explores the use of cross-lingual transfer learning.

The remainder of this paper is organized as follows: Section 2 describes the task proposed in the TSAR shared task, their corpora and the additional corpora that we use. Section 3 details the proposed solution for generating and ranking substitutions while their results are shown in Section 4. Finally, in Section 5, we present the error analysis and possible solutions for improving the performance of the proposed methods.

2 Task and Corpora

The TSAR shared task proposes a zero-shot task, where a trial set composed of only 10 trial sentences with difficult words and their substitutions and later assessed the systems on a test corpus for English, Spanish and Portuguese. The corpus consists of sentences with one difficult word per sentence to be substituted. The TSAR corpus is consti-

[1]For a recent description of Text Simplification and Lexical Complexity, see North et al. (2022).

Proceedings of the Workshop on Text Simplification, Accessibility, and Readability (TSAR-2022), pages 231 - 238
December 8, 2022 ©2022 Association for Computational Linguistics

tuted of 1,115 sentences with target words (373 for English, 368 for Spanish and 374 for Portuguese) annotated by 25 crowdsourced workers, whose sociodemographics are not provided. They proposed simpler substitutions for the difficult words, taking the sentence as context. An expert later selected the proposals and only non-multiword expressions were kept (Saggion et al., 2022).[2]

We used additional corpora for parameter optimization and hyperparameter tuning of the classification algorithm used in our ranking approach, given the zero-shot nature of the task. For English, we used a monolingual lexical simplification corpus (Specia et al., 2012) constituted of 2,010 English sentences annotated with difficult words and their ranked substitute words or phrases. For Spanish, we selected a cross-lingual lexical substitution corpus (Mihalcea et al., 2010) constituted of 1,300 English sentences, which are a subset of the monolingual corpus, in which the substitutes are in Spanish. To obtain both sentences and substitutions in Spanish and Portuguese, we used the Google Vision Translation API to translate the English sentences from the cross-lingual corpus to Spanish and the sentences and substitutions from the monolingual corpus to Portuguese. After translating the corpora, we automatically marked the difficult words using the list of substitutions (i.e., simpler words).[3] We divided this corpus into 80% for training and hyperparameter tuning (using cross-validation) and 20% for testing. The testing part is used for internal comparison of the methods described in Sections 3.1 and 3.2 and the training part is used in the ranking method (Section 3.2).

3 Our Approach

We detail here the runs submitted (2 for English and 3 for Spanish and Portuguese each). Figure 1 illustrates our pipeline, and Table 6, in Appendix A, shows outputs of the different strategies.

3.1 Substitution Generation

For this step, we explored whether masked BERT as a word-level "generative" model – i.e., pretrained BERT – is able to produce a suitable list of substitution candidates. Simply masking the difficult word gave unsatisfactory results in our preliminary tests. We thus investigated different ways of providing context to help the model generate adequate substitutions. All runs had words proposed by a BERT-like model, which was fed the original sentence with a mask replacing the difficult word, preceded by more context. We truncated the number of contexts generated when the concatenation of the context and the original sentence is longer than BERT models' input size limit (512 tokens). To generate that context, we explored three strategies: *Copy*, *Query Expansion*, and *Paraphrase*.

The *Copy* strategy is inspired by LSBERT (Qiang et al., 2021). The extra context preceding the sentence is simply a copy of the sentence itself. In this approach, we tested using the [SEP] token for splitting the sentences, but our experiments showed that using it led to worse results.

The *Query Expansion* (QE) strategy consists in applying the technique with the same name from the Information Retrieval domain. In our case, we produced 5 related words for the difficult word using FastText models in addition to the original sentence. We explored two variations: (1) repeating the entire sentence for each alternative, using the generated word instead of the original word, and (2) only using the proposed words.

The *Paraphrase* strategy generates a context composed of paraphrases of the original sentence. We generated up to 10 paraphrases for each sentence. The number of paraphrases is limited so that the entire prompt fits within the limit of 512 tokens imposed by BERT. This method was only applied to the English part of the shared task because, to our knowledge, there is no equivalent of the applied model for Portuguese and Spanish.

In our experiments, we compared various models available on HuggingFace[4] and observed different behaviors depending on the strategy.[5] For the official submission, we chose those that produced the best results on the test corpus. Thus, we combined the Large and Base models in the QE strategy and employed only Large models in the Copy strategy,[6]

[2]The original sentences came from three different datasets: the PorSimplesSent dataset for Portuguese (Leal et al., 2018) and the CWI Shared Task 2018 dataset for Spanish and English (Yimam et al., 2017).

[3]The sentences in which the difficult word could no longer be isolated in translation were dropped.

[4]`https://huggingface.co/`

[5]We tested the following models in addition to those we submitted: bert-base-multilingual-cased, skimai/spanberta-base-cased, PlanTL-GOB-ES/roberta-base-bne, josu/roberta-pt-br and rdenadai/BR_BERTo.

[6]The Large and Base models used are bert-large-uncased, bert-base-uncased, roberta-large and roberta-base for English, dccuchile/bert-base-spanish-wwm-cased and dccuchile/bert-base-spanish-wwm-uncased for Spanish, and neuralmind_bert-large-portuguese-cased and neuralmind_bert-base-portuguese-

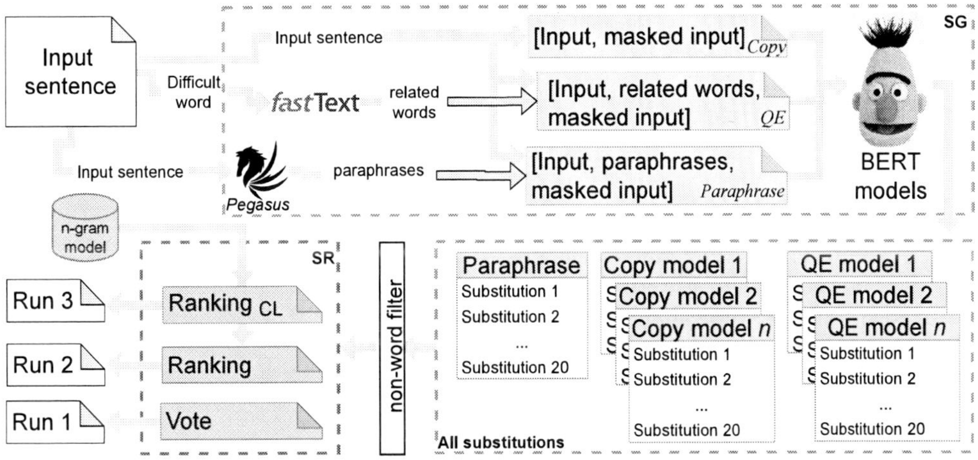

Figure 1: Pipeline of the proposed solutions.

while we used a specialized model[7] (i.e., (Zhang et al., 2020)) for the Paraphrase strategy. For the Paraphrase strategy, we used 10 beams: as we generated up to 10 paraphrases, the number of beams cannot be below 10, and there was not much difference between 10 beams and more.

The three substitution generation strategies yielded 20 items for each model. Predictions that contained non-alphabetic characters (e.g., BERT subtokens) were automatically discarded.

3.2 Substitution Ranking

All substitutions generated by the substitution generation strategies must be grouped into a single sorted list of 10 words, following the shared task guidelines. We thus combined and ranked the substitutions, selecting the top 10.

The first ranking method is a simple vote (*Vote*): we count the number of methods that generated a given substitution and rank them from most frequently proposed to least frequently proposed. This method is exemplified in Table 6.

The two other ranking methods we explored use a model of lexical complexity. High word frequency is a generally good predictor of simplicity (Brysbaert et al., 2018). However, frequencies from corpus- and list-based lookups suffer from the *out-of-vocabulary* (OOV) problem; instead, we use character-based n-gram language models to represent words (Wieting et al., 2016; Bojanowski et al., 2017). For each language, we create a character-based n-gram language model with $1 \leq n \leq 4$. The English model was trained on the *British National Corpus* (BNC Consortium, 2007). The Spanish model was trained on *Corpus lingüístico de referencia de la lengua española en Chile* (Marcos Marín, 1991). The Portuguese model was trained on *PorPopular* (Silva, 2010). We use the probabilities of each n-gram model to represent words as input for the model.

In the second ranking method (*Ranking*), we train a binary classifier on the SemEval train corpus (Section 2) predicting which one of two words is easier. For training, we concatenate the vector representations (n-gram probabilities) of two words. We opted for XGBoost (Chen and Guestrin, 2016) – with hyperparameter tuning – as the classification algorithm. We tested RandomForest, ExtraTrees, MLP, DecisionTree, AdaBoost, and Bagging classifier, all from the scikit-learn package (Pedregosa et al., 2011), including hyperparameter tuning, and found that XGBoost outperformed the other algorithms. It calculates scores based on pairwise comparisons between words and produces a ranking over a list of substitution words.

As a third ranking method (*Ranking$_{CL}$*), we explore the cross-linguistic applicability of the English classifier model. In this setup, Spanish and Portuguese words are vectorized by their respective language model (similarly to the *monolingual ranking* method), but the ranking is performed by the English ranking model.

For all rankings, if the difficult word itself is found within the final list of ten substitutions, the list is truncated up to the difficult word, otherwise we take the top 10 substitutions. In a ranking in-

cased for Portuguese.

[7] google/pegasus-xsum model

cluding the difficult word, all words ranked after the difficult word are considered more difficult than the original difficult word itself, and are thus not good substitutions for simplification.

4 Evaluation

Our evaluation of the 8 runs submitted (one for each ranking method[8]) focuses on the MAP/Potential@1 metric (@1 in our tables). All official metrics adopted by the shared task are in Appendix A.

Lang	Method	@1	Rank
EN	QE_{BERT_L} 1	.4155	21
	QE_{BERT_L} 2	**.5281**	8
ES	$QE_{RoBERTa_L}$ 1	.3109	10
	$QE_{RoBERTa_L}$ 2	**.4477**	1
PT	QE_{BERT} 1	.4090	5
	QE_{BERT} 2	**.4759**	2
EN	$Copy_{B\ U}$	.4959	12
	$Copy_{L\ U}$	.5040	11
	$Copy_{RoBERTa_B}$	.4772	14
	$Copy_{RoBERTa_L}$	.3994	23
ES	$Copy_C$	.4211	2
	$Copy_U$	.2989	12
PT	$Copy_B$	.4331	4
	$Copy_L$	.4705	3
EN	Paraphrase	.2171	36

Table 1: MAP/Potential@1 of our substitution generation techniques (U: uncased, C: cased, B: base, L: large; 1 and 2 refer to the first and second variations of QE)

Table 1 shows the MAP/Potential@1 of each substitution generation strategy. *Paraphrase* gives the worst result. This method did not provide many correct substitutions (see the potential in Appendix A, Table 4). Still, the proportion between the scores is similar to the other prompt-based methods (i.e., the value of potential is about twice as high as other metrics). Overall *QE* achieved better results than *Copy*. In addition, only using the words from FastText (ignoring the sentence) as additional context (i.e., variant 2) outperforms the use of the entire sentence. In general, large (L) models tend to outperform base (B) models.[9] For the three languages, *QE* achieved the best results in terms of @1 and MAP scoring methods. It also reached the best potential for Spanish and Portuguese.

Table 2 shows the results of each run. Interestingly, *Vote* tends to provide the best results for Spanish and Portuguese. It implies that the models tend to propose the correct words. For English, the ranking method achieved the best results. It is likely due to a strong disagreement between the models for this language.

Lang	Method	@1	Rank
EN	Vote	.2761	28
	Ranking	**.3619**	23
ES	Vote	**.3097**	8
	Ranking	.1983	17
	$Ranking_{CL}$	.2201	14
PT	Vote	**.3689**	2
	Ranking	.2058	15
	$Ranking_{CL}$	.2245	10

Table 2: Official results

5 Error analysis

To better understand our results, we evaluated the substitution generation and the ranking strategies. We also measure the gap between our best ranking model (*Vote*) and a perfect substitution generation step (i.e., an oracle).

For the SG step, our methods rely on providing BERT models with a single mask, but they cannot produce multiword expressions. To identify the impact of this limitation, we calculated their proportion in the gold standard: 3.35% for English, 6.27% for Spanish, and 2.97% for Portuguese.

We also studied the extent to which substitutions generated by our methods were grammatically correct regarding the context. To do so, we compared the morpho-syntactic information of each candidate against its respective difficult word, after analyzing the sentences with Stanza (Qi et al., 2020), assuming the parser output is correct. Out of all the candidates present in our submitted runs, there was a mismatch in 10.68% of the cases for English, 6.09% for Spanish, and 12.28% for Portuguese. We corrected those mismatches by using DELA dictionaries (Courtois, 1990).[10] Whenever

[8]The cross-lingual ranking method is not used for English because we only use this language as a pivot.

[9]The superior performance of the large models is in line with our experiments. However, we note that we identify exceptions such as $Repeat_{B\ U}$ for English.

[10]https://github.com/UnitexGramLab/

a mismatch was detected, we converted the Stanza information to the DELA format. Using the candidate's lemma, we checked whether an inflected form with the same morpho-syntactic information existed. If it did, we replaced the candidate with the correct form, otherwise, we deleted the candidate from the list. We can see that there is a slight improvement (up to .03 on MAP/Potential@1), indicating that while it solves issues, inflection is not the main shortcoming of the submitted lists.[11] In future work, we would like to apply this correction phase to each individual model's output in order to apply the ranking to morpho-syntactically correct candidates. In Table 6, the impact of the parser combined with the dictionary-based correction is illustrated in the line "POS filtered out", which indicates the percentage of reduction in the number of responses.

As for the ranking methods, we see that for Spanish and Portuguese, voting produces better results than ranking, while for English, ranking produces better results than voting. We hypothesize that voting prioritizes frequent and contextually suitable words that are generated by multiple methods, while ranking performs better on the tail end of the distribution. To test it, we used the ranking system exclusively to break ties created by the vote. This produces slightly better results than a full ranking in all cases, indicating that the ranking does indeed learn about simple words, yet does not have enough information on its own to rank a full list in the order given by the gold standard.

We also explored the importance of a substitution selection method, instead of a simple filter. To do so, we analyze the best possible results using all the generated substitutions for the voting method. So, we drop all generated words that are not in the gold standard and apply the same voting method. This substitution selection is exemplified in the line "Oracle+SS" in Table 6. This showed a considerable increase in voting performance (a gain of 0.7212 for English, 0.5544 for Spanish and 0.5268 for Portuguese).[12] This improvement points out the need for substitution selection methods and improvement of the ranking.

It is interesting to note that the results of the substitution generation methods outperform our ranking methods, including *Vote*, which only counts the agreement between the models. However, the previous analysis showed that the different strategies produce the correct words. This apparent contradiction is mostly due to the fact that the models can individually predict some of the correct words, but they also predict several unrelated words at the same time. Moreover, the proposed strategies share common key elements (e.g., the BERT-like model), and the *Copy* strategy, our worst result, is also present in the other two strategies. Therefore, the models' ensemble, despite agreeing on the correct words, also agree on the incorrect words. This effect is illustrated in the line "Oracle SS step filter", which indicates the percentage of removed words when applying the oracle substitution selection.

6 Conclusion

This paper presented the solution proposed by the CENTAL team in the TSAR shared task on lexical simplification. We proposed three substitution generation strategies, where we saw that Query Expansion is superior. Moreover, generation strategies can produce and sort suggestions with good performance. The Query Expansion strategy could achieve 8th, 1st and 2nd positions for English, Spanish and Portuguese respectively by itself. We also identified that the voting method might produce promising results, but a good substitution selection step is required. This step would improve morphologically incorrect substitutions and remove semantically/contextually inappropriate substitutions. In addition, the ranking methods can be useful for breaking ties in voting.[13]

Acknowledgements

We would like to thank the anonymous reviewers for their comments that helped improve the presentation of our approach and results. Rodrigo Wilkens is supported by a research convention with France Education International (FEI). David Alfter is supported by the Fonds de la Recherche Scientifique de Belgique (F.R.S-FNRS) under grant MIS/PGY F.4518.21. Rémi Cardon is supported by the FSR Incoming Postdoc Fellowship program of the FSR - Université catholique de Louvain. Isabelle Gribomont is supported by the FED-tWIN program from BELSPO. Adrien Bibal is supported by the Walloon region with a Win2Wal funding.

`unitex-lingua/tree/master/`

[11]Table 5 shows the results obtained for our submitted runs after applying this method.

[12]See Table 4 for all metrics.

[13]The code for our models is available at `https://gitlab.com/Cental-FR/cental-tsar2022`.

Marie-Catherine de Marneffe is a Research Associate of the Fonds de la Recherche Scientifique – FNRS.

References

BNC Consortium. 2007. British National Corpus. *Oxford Text Archive Core Collection.*

Piotr Bojanowski, Edouard Grave, Armand Joulin, and Tomas Mikolov. 2017. Enriching word vectors with subword information. *Transactions of the Association for Computational Linguistics*, 5:135–146.

Marc Brysbaert, Paweł Mandera, and Emmanuel Keuleers. 2018. The word frequency effect in word processing: An updated review. *Current Directions in Psychological Science*, 27(1):45–50.

Tianqi Chen and Carlos Guestrin. 2016. XGBoost: A Scalable Tree Boosting System. In *Proceedings of the 22nd ACM SIGKDD International Conference on Knowledge Discovery and Data Mining*, KDD '16, pages 785–794, New York, NY, USA. ACM.

Blandine Courtois. 1990. Un système de dictionnaires électroniques pour les mots simples du français. *Langue Francaise*, 87:11–22.

Alex Housen and Hannelore Simoens. 2016. Introduction: Cognitive perspectives on difficulty and complexity in l2 acquisition. *Studies in Second Language Acquisition*, 38(2):163–175.

Sidney Evaldo Leal, Magali Sanches Duran, and Sandra Aluísio. 2018. A nontrivial sentence corpus for the task of sentence readability assessment in portuguese. In *Proceedings of the 27th International Conference on Computational Linguistics*, pages 401–413.

Francisco Marcos Marín. 1991. Corpus lingüístico de referencia de la lengua española. *Boletín de la Academia Argentina de Letras*, 56(1991):129–155.

Rada Mihalcea, Ravi Sinha, and Diana McCarthy. 2010. SemEval-2010 task 2: Cross-lingual lexical substitution. In *Proceedings of the 5th International Workshop on Semantic Evaluation*, pages 9–14, Uppsala, Sweden. Association for Computational Linguistics.

Kai North, Marcos Zampieri, and Matthew Shardlow. 2022. Lexical complexity prediction: An overview. *ACM Computing Surveys (CSUR)*.

Fabian Pedregosa, Gaël Varoquaux, Alexandre Gramfort, Vincent Michel, Bertrand Thirion, Olivier Grisel, Mathieu Blondel, Peter Prettenhofer, Ron Weiss, Vincent Dubourg, et al. 2011. Scikit-learn: Machine learning in Python. *the Journal of machine Learning research*, 12:2825–2830.

Peng Qi, Yuhao Zhang, Yuhui Zhang, Jason Bolton, and Christopher D Manning. 2020. Stanza: A Python natural language processing toolkit for many human languages. *arXiv preprint arXiv:2003.07082*.

Jipeng Qiang, Yun Li, Yi Zhu, Yunhao Yuan, Yang Shi, and Xindong Wu. 2021. Lsbert: Lexical simplification based on bert. *IEEE/ACM Transactions on Audio, Speech, and Language Processing*, 29:3064–3076.

Horacio Saggion, Sanja Štajner, Daniel Ferrés, Kim Cheng Sheang, Matthew Shardlow, Kai North, and Marcos Zampieri. 2022. Findings of the TSAR-2022 Shared Task on Multilingual Lexical Simplification. In *Proceedings of TSAR workshop held in conjunction with EMNLP 2022*.

Bruna Rodrigues da Silva. 2010. PorPopular: o português popular escrito em um objeto de aprendizagem.

Lucia Specia, Sujay Kumar Jauhar, and Rada Mihalcea. 2012. SemEval-2012 task 1: English lexical simplification. In **SEM 2012: The First Joint Conference on Lexical and Computational Semantics – Volume 1: Proceedings of the main conference and the shared task, and Volume 2: Proceedings of the Sixth International Workshop on Semantic Evaluation (SemEval 2012)*, pages 347–355, Montréal, Canada. Association for Computational Linguistics.

John Wieting, Mohit Bansal, Kevin Gimpel, and Karen Livescu. 2016. Charagram: Embedding words and sentences via character n-grams. *arXiv preprint arXiv:1607.02789*.

Seid Muhie Yimam, Sanja Štajner, Martin Riedl, and Chris Biemann. 2017. Cwig3g2-complex word identification task across three text genres and two user groups. In *Proceedings of the Eighth International Joint Conference on Natural Language Processing (Volume 2: Short Papers)*, pages 401–407.

Jingqing Zhang, Yao Zhao, Mohammad Saleh, and Peter J. Liu. 2020. Pegasus: Pre-training with extracted gap-sentences for abstractive summarization. In *Proceedings of the 37th International Conference on Machine Learning*, ICML'20. JMLR.org.

A Appendix

The Appendix presents a complete version of the results, which have been shortened in the main text due to space constraints. Table 3 shows the results from the Substitution Generation strategies discussed in Section 3. Table 4 shows the results of the submitted runs, as presented in Section 4, as well as the value we would obtain with a perfect substitution filtering step before ranking. This upper bound is calculated by removing all words that are not in the gold standard before the ranking. Table 5 shows the results after automatically correcting the results presented in Table 4. In these tables, the best results of each language are in bold (the statistical significance is not calculated). We also indicate the rank of each method (based on the @1 column) in comparison with the official results. Moreover, the MAP/Potential@1 is titled "@1".

In addition, Table 6 presents some examples of outputs of the different strategies and the results of the voting method presented in Section 3. It also illustrates the impact of the substitution selection method discussed in Sections 4 and 5.

				MAP			Potential			Accuracy		
Lang	**Method**	**@1**	@3	@5	@10	@3	@5	@10	@1	@2	@3	**Rank**
EN	QE_{Bert_L} 1	.4155	.2752	.2142	.1365	.7050	.7855	.8873	.1903	.3029	.3753	21
	QE_{Bert_L} 2	**.5281**	**.3431**	**.2554**	**.1640**	.7640	.8659	.9195	**.2627**	**.3914**	.4611	8
ES	$QE_{Roberta_L}$ 1	.3109	.2397	.1867	.1208	.5898	.7345	.8632	.1179	.2091	.2868	10
	$QE_{Roberta_L}$ 2	**.4477**	**.2983**	**.2222**	**.1410**	**.7265**	**.8364**	**.9383**	**.2037**	**.3029**	**.3860**	1
PT	QE_{Bert} 1	.4090	.2473	.1794	.1041	.6577	.7433	.8101	.2112	.3235	.3716	5
	QE_{Bert} 2	**.4759**	**.2892**	**.2055**	**.1189**	**.7139**	.7727	**.8422**	**.2540**	.3609	.4090	2
EN	$Repeat_{B\ U}$	.4959	.3296	.2496	.1587	.7479	.8525	.9276	**.2627**	.3833	.4611	12
	$Repeat_{L\ U}$	.5040	.3245	.2466	.1579	.7506	.8552	.9302	.2520	.3619	.4450	11
	$Repeat_{Robert_B}$	.4772	.3263	.2497	.1604	**.7962**	**.8793**	**.9490**	.2359	.3753	**.4745**	14
	$Repeat_{Roberta_L}$	.3994	.2634	.1996	.1216	.7131	.8069	.8981	.1581	.2654	.3565	23
ES	$Repeat_C$	.4211	.2601	.1952	.1111	.6467	.7255	.7880	.1956	.2744	.3396	2
	$Repeat_U$	.2989	.1840	.1298	.0744	.4809	.5489	.6250	.1413	.2092	.2364	12
PT	$Repeat_B$	.4331	.2693	.1985	.1176	.6925	.7513	.8208	.2513	.3342	.3957	4
	$Repeat_L$	.4705	.2843	.1984	.1158	.7032	**.7807**	.8395	.2513	**.3689**	**.4144**	3
EN	Paraphrase	.2171	.1407	.1069	.0650	.3833	.4638	.5603	.0938	.1581	.1849	36

Table 3: Results of each candidate generation strategy. @1 indicates the MAP/Potential@1 (U: uncased, C: cased, B: base, L: large; 1 and 2 refer to the first and second variations of QE)

				MAP			Potential			Accuracy		
Lang	**Method**	**@1**	@3	@5	@10	@3	@5	@10	@1	@2	@3	**Rank**
EN	SS+Vote	.9973	.9678	.8643	.5182	.9973	.9973	.9973	.3833	.6219	.7372	1
	Vote	.2761	.1635	.1183	.0707	.3780	.4021	.4182	**.1313**	.1930	.2117	29
	Ranking	**.3619**	**.2573**	**.2056**	**.1271**	**.6541**	**.7667**	**.8418**	.1152	**.2091**	**.2788**	24
ES	SS+Vote	.8641	.7083	.5103	.2649	.8641	.8641	.8641	.9097	.4211	.5244	1
	Vote	**.3097**	**.1826**	**.1327**	**.0779**	**.5000**	.5923	.6358	**.1467**	**.2092**	**.2391**	9
	Ranking	.1983	.1265	.0979	.0695	.4184	.5570	.7282	.0652	.1114	.1657	18
	$Ranking_{CL}$	.2201	.1416	.1122	.0745	.4646	**.6086**	**.7581**	.0407	.0896	.1331	15
PT	SS+Vote	.8957	.7103	.5235	.2737	.8957	.8957	.8957	.3101	.4786	.5401	1
	Vote	**.3689**	**.1983**	**.1344**	.0766	**.5240**	.5641	.6096	**.1737**	**.2433**	**.2673**	3
	Ranking	.2058	.1470	.1103	.0726	.4786	.6016	.7673	.0641	.1203	.1898	16
	$Ranking_{CL}$	.2245	.1478	.1143	**.0769**	.4705	**.6096**	**.8021**	.0614	.1310	.1925	11

Table 4: Results of the candidate ranking strategies. @1 indicates the MAP/Potential@1 Official results (CL: cross-language). SS+Vote refers to the study of an oracle substitution selection combined with voting.

Lang	Method	MAP @1	MAP @3	MAP @5	MAP @10	Potential @3	Potential @5	Potential @10	Accuracy @1	Accuracy @2	Accuracy @3
EN	Vote	.2815	.165	.1204	.0708	.3753	.3994	.4128	.1367	.193	.2117
	Ranking	.3646	.2622	.2084	.1267	.6541	.764	.8257	.1152	.2091	.2815
ES	Vote	.3179	.1911	.1389	.0815	.5135	.6086	.6603	.1467	.2119	.25
	Ranking	.2201	.1394	.1061	.0741	.451	.5788	.7527	.076	.1222	.182
	Ranking$_{CL}$	.2282	.1493	.118	.078	.4864	.6304	.7826	.0489	.1005	.1467
PT	Vote	.3877	.2039	.1401	.0792	.5427	.5775	.6229	.1818	.254	.2754
	Ranking	.2192	.1552	.1175	.0758	.4946	.6256	.7807	.0721	.1336	.2058
	Ranking$_{CL}$	.2326	.1555	.1206	.0799	.4973	.6417	.8155	.0721	.147	.2112

Table 5: Results obtained by applying the DELA correction method to the submitted runs (Table 2). @1 indicates the MAP/Potential@1 (CL: cross-language).

	Lebanon is sharply split along **sectarian** lines, with 18 religious sects.	The **motive** for the killings was not known.
QE BERT$_{L\,1}$	religious sunni secular islamist islamic [...] shia	motive reason motivation motives purpose [...] impetus
QE BERT$_{L\,2}$	religious ideological ethnic regional national [...] tribal	motive reason motivation motives purpose [...] plan
Copy$_{U}$	religious ethnic secular national islamic [...] shia	motive reason motivation cause motives [...] blame
Copy$_{RoBERTa\,L}$	sectarian religious theological spiritual sunni [...] dramatic	motive reason rationale motives cause [...] target
Paraphrase	religious ethnic ideological cultural religion [...] many	the punishment location a information [...] reasons
Non-word filtered	-	. " (
Vote	religious (5) secular (5) ethnic (4) regional (4) protestant (4)	motive (5) reason (5) motivation (4) motives (4) purpose (4)
POS filtered out	80% of words removed	98% of words removed
Vote after POS filter	religious (5) secular (5) ethnic (4) regional (4) political (4)	reason (5) motive (4) cause (4) intention (2) inspiration (1)
Oracle SS step filter	92% of words removed	90% of words removed
Oracle SS+Vote	religious (5) sectarian (1) provincial (1) party (1)	criminals (4)

Table 6: Outputs of the substitution generation (SG) methods and the Vote ranking strategy (Section 3) for two examples, as well as the evaluation and analysis performed in Sections 4 and 5. We give the top 5 candidates and the last for each SG method.

teamPN at TSAR-2022 Shared Task: Lexical Simplification Using Multi-Level and Modular Approach

Nikita Katyal
nikita18katyal@gmail.com

Pawan Kumar Rajpoot
pawan.rajpoot2411@gmail.com

Abstract

Lexical Simplification is the process of reducing the lexical complexity of a text by replacing difficult words with easier to read (or understand) expressions while preserving the original information and meaning. This paper explains the work done by our team "teamPN" for English track of TSAR 2022 Shared Task of Lexical Simplification. We created a modular pipeline which combines transformers based models with traditional NLP methods like paraphrasing and verb sense disambiguation. We created a multi level and modular pipeline where the target text is treated according to its semantics (Part of Speech Tag). Pipeline is multi level as we utilize multiple source models to find potential candidates for replacement. It is modular as we can switch the source models and their weighting in the final re-ranking.

1 Introduction

As per TSAR-2022 Workshop Shared Task the problem definition is: "Given a sentence containing a complex word, systems should return an ordered list of simpler valid substitutes for the complex word in its original context. The list of simpler words (up to a maximum of 10) returned by the system should be ordered by the confidence the system has in its prediction (best predictions first) and it must not contain ties." One example is shown in Table 1. The English data-set consists of 373 sentences, with 1 complex word per sentence. No training data was provided and the teams were free to create supervised or unsupervised model. We found that majority of the complex words were verbs or nouns (see Table 2). If not noun or verb, we consider the POS to be of "Others" type. This motivated us to build a pipeline where we first disambiguate the words and then find optimal substitutes. Verbs and nouns are generally more ambiguous in the senses which they are used when compared to other Part of Speech tags. We based our whole idea on this assumption and hence treated verbs and nouns with an additional module. Other than verb/noun only module we have 2 modules which we use for all the POS tags. First common to all module uses Distil BERT based word prediction, while the second one uses Paraphrase Database to do a standard lookup for finding potential substitute candidates. Verb only module is based around Verbnet where we do verb sense disambiguation and then as per predicted verb class we collect potential substitute candidates.

Noun only module first grounds the noun entity to a standard knowledge graph. Once entity is grounded we parse the surrounding neighbours from the KG and collect potential substitute candidates.

Once all modules individually run, all potential candidates are combined and re-ranked using Transformer based model.

Sentence	Substitutes
That prompted the military to deploy its largest warship, the BRP Gregorio del Pilar.	send, post, use, position, employ, extend, launch

Table 1: Example sentence with complex word (in red) and substitutes (in teal).

Nouns	Verbs	Others
162	145	66

Table 2: POS tags of complex words in TSAR 2022 Shared Task en evaluation data.

2 Approach

We parse the sentence using spacy (Honnibal and Montani, 2017) and run different sets of modules for verb, noun and others respectively. Our modules are explained in in detail as follows. See Algorithm 1 for pseudo code of the pipeline.

Proceedings of the Workshop on Text Simplification, Accessibility, and Readability (TSAR-2022), pages 239 - 242
December 8, 2022 ©2022 Association for Computational Linguistics

2.1 Potential Candidate Collection

2.1.1 Verb Sense Disambiguation

Verbnet is a lexicon which is an extension to Levin's original verb classifications (Levin, 1993) in 1993. Semantically similar verbs are placed in same class. We use Verbnet 3.1 (Schuler, 2005) to ground the verb and get possible classes. For class prediction we do not rely on traditional VSD work (Abend et al., 2008; Dligach and Palmer, 2008; Kawahara and Palmer, 2014) as the data which is used in model training is Wall Street Journal historical text data (Loper et al., 2007) which is biased towards fintech domain. For instance the verb "rise" has 6 possible classes in verbnet, but in WSJ data 93 percent of the examples have "rise" related to "calibration" class, as in "Stocks rise from 10 to 12". There have been related research where efficiency of BERT (Devlin et al., 2018) model to capture English syntactic phenomena is studied (Goldberg, 2019), this motivated us to instead do transformer based VSD (see Figure 1) . We first mask the target word and use FitBERT (Havens and Stal, 2019) to rank the top possible words among all possible classes member verbs. As per the work[1] "FitBERT is trained to look at a sentence with a blank, and output an ordered list of every possible word that could fill in that blank, and a score indicating how likely that word is". We choose the verbnet class with maximum representations in top k predicted words. Once the class is fixed we return the class members as potential candidates.

2.1.2 Paraphrase DataBase

We directly query PPDB (Ganitkevitch et al., 2013) and return the retrieved result list as potential candidates. We use lexical version and small size dictionary of PPDB as it contains the highest quality paraphrases. We use PPDB python library[2] for loading and querying the database.

2.1.3 Distil BERT

DistilBERT (Sanh et al., 2019) is a transformers model which is smaller and faster than BERT, which was pretrained on the same corpus in a self-supervised manner. It is based on Knowledge distillation (teacher student) (Bucila et al., 2006; Hinton et al., 2015) method. Rather than training with a cross-entropy over the hard targets (one-hot encoding of the gold class), knowledge is transfered from the teacher (BERT) to the student (DistilBERT) with a cross-entropy over the soft targets (probabilities of the teacher). We mask the complex word in the context and then use DistilBERT model to predict the words (fill-mask pipeline) then return the result list as the potential candidates. Due to computational resource restrictions we were not able to use complex Transformer models.

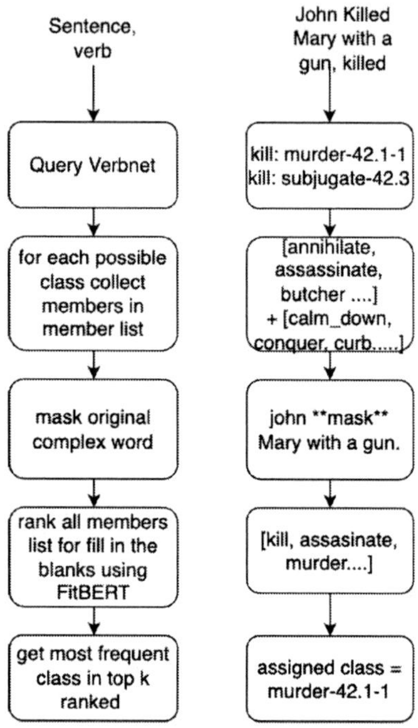

Figure 1: Verb Sense Disambiguation Module. Left part explains overall flow. Right part shows how one example passes through the module.

2.1.4 Knowledge Graph

We use Multi Modal Knowledge Graph VisualSem (Alberts et al., 2020) to do text entity extraction and grounding to KG for the target complex word. For entity extraction, CLIP textual embedding (Radford et al., 2021) were used as defined in original paper. Retrieval is implemented with k nearest neighbour where the dot-product between the sentence vector and all nodes' gloss matrix for VisualSem graph is calculated. Top-k unique nodes associated to the most relevant glosses are retrieved and if they are same as complex word, the corresponding synonym neighbours are added to the potential candidate list.

[1] https://medium.com/@samhavens/introducing-fitbert-4b047af860fd

[2] https://github.com/erickrf/ppdb

2.2 Aggregation and re-ranking

See Table 3 for usage of modules as per POS tags. Once all potential candidate list is created first we combine all together, then we adjust all the inflections. For inflection correction we use pattern[3] library. We inflect the all candidate words with same tense and quantity (singular/plural) as complex word. Then we again use FitBERT (Havens and Stal, 2019) to rank the combined candidates. For the submissions we used 5 top words.

Algorithm 1 teamPN: Text Simplification

```
Require: m1 = vsdModule
Require: m2 = PPDBModule
Require: m3 = distilBertModule
Require: m4 = kgModule
  for each sentence and complexWord do
    pos = getPos(complexWord)
    if pos == verb then
      candidates = m1 + m2 + m3 + m4
    end if
    if pos == noun then
      candidates = m2 + m3 + m4
    end if
    if pos == Others then
      candidates = m2 + m3
    end if
    candidates = fixInflection(candidates)
    rankCandidates = rerankUsingFitBERT
  end for
```

POS/Module	VSD	PPDB	distil BERT	KG
VERB	Y	Y	Y	N
NOUN	N	Y	Y	Y
Others	N	Y	Y	N

Table 3: Use of Candidate collection modules as per part of Speech of complex word.

3 Results

As per TSAR definition (Štajner et al., 2022) The evaluation metrics to be applied in the TSAR-2022 Shared Task are the following:
MAP@K (Mean Average Precision @ K): K=1,3,5,10. The MAP@K metric is used to check whether the predicted word can be matched (relevant) or not matched (irrelevant) against the set of the gold-standard annotations for evaluation. MAP@K for Lexical Simplification evaluates the following aspects: 1) are the predicted substitutes relevant?, and 2) are the predicted substitutes at the top positions?

Potential@K: K=1,3,5,10. The percentage of instances for which at least one of the substitutions predicted is present in the set of gold annotations.

Accuracy@K@top1: K=1,2,3. The ratio of instances where at least one of the K top predicted candidates matches the most frequently suggested synonym/s in the gold list of annotated candidates.

We stand 12th, on the official results[4] (Saggion et al., 2022) of TSAR-2022 Shared Task. We outperform one of the baseline models TUNER (Štajner et al., 2022). See Table 4 for our scores. We submitted output from 3 different runs, the only difference between the 3 versions was the value for threshold for DistilBERT unmasker module. This threshold corresponds for the minimum confidence cut off for the words predicted. See Table 5 for the threshold values used.

Metric	Run 1	Run 2	Run 3
ACC@1	0.4477	**0.4664**	0.4504
ACC@1@Top1	0.1769	**0.1823**	0.1769
ACC@2@Top1	0.2815	**0.3056**	0.2841
ACC@3@Top1	0.3297	**0.3378**	0.3297
MAP@3	0.2666	**0.2743**	0.2676
MAP@5	0.1874	**0.195**	0.1872
MAP@10	0.0937	**0.0975**	0.0936
Potential@3	0.6621	**0.6729**	0.6648
Potential@5	0.7453	**0.7506**	0.7399
Potential@10	0.7453	**0.7506**	0.7399

Table 4: Our scores for TSAR 2022 Shared Task -EN track

Run 1	Run 2	Run 3
0.02	0.03	0.01

Table 5: DitilBERT Threshold values for 3 runs.

[3] https://github.com/clips/pattern

[4] https://taln.upf.edu/pages/tsar2022-st/#results

4 Conclusion and Future Work

We presented a novel approach where we combine power of transformer based models with traditional NLP. Our work was restricted by computing resources. We would further like to improve on using more modules built out from complex transformers. Also apart from PPDB we did not work with any other synonym dictionaries, adding more open source dictionary modules will bring on more variety. All of our code and documentation is available on Github[5].

Acknowledgements

We would like to acknowledge TSAR organizing committee and EMNLP 2022 for their support and also organizing the Workshop event.

References

Omri Abend, Roi Reichart, and Ari Rappoport. 2008. A supervised algorithm for verb disambiguation into verbnet classes. In *Proceedings of the 22nd International Conference on Computational Linguistics (COLING 2008)*, pages 9–16.

Houda Alberts, Teresa Huang, Yash Deshpande, Yibo Liu, Kyunghyun Cho, Clara Vania, and Iacer Calixto. 2020. Visualsem: a high-quality knowledge graph for vision and language. *CoRR*, abs/2008.09150.

Cristian Bucila, Rich Caruana, and Alexandru Niculescu-Mizil. 2006. Model compression. In *KDD*, pages 535–541. ACM.

Jacob Devlin, Ming-Wei Chang, Kenton Lee, and Kristina Toutanova. 2018. BERT: pre-training of deep bidirectional transformers for language understanding. *CoRR*, abs/1810.04805.

Dmitriy Dligach and Martha Palmer. 2008. Novel semantic features for verb sense disambiguation. In *Proceedings of ACL-08: HLT, Short Papers*, pages 29–32.

Juri Ganitkevitch, Benjamin Van Durme, and Chris Callison-Burch. 2013. Ppdb: The paraphrase database. In *Proceedings of the 2013 Conference of the North American Chapter of the Association for Computational Linguistics: Human Language Technologies*, pages 758–764.

Yoav Goldberg. 2019. Assessing bert's syntactic abilities. *CoRR*, abs/1901.05287.

Sam Havens and Aneta Stal. 2019. Use bert to fill in the blanks.

[5]https://github.com/katyalnikita/TSAR-2022-teamPN

Geoffrey Hinton, Oriol Vinyals, and Jeff Dean. 2015. Distilling the knowledge in a neural network.

Matthew Honnibal and Ines Montani. 2017. spaCy 2: Natural language understanding with Bloom embeddings, convolutional neural networks and incremental parsing. To appear.

Daisuke Kawahara and Martha Palmer. 2014. Single classifier approach for verb sense disambiguation based on generalized features. In *Proceedings of the Ninth International Conference on Language Resources and Evaluation (LREC'14)*, pages 4210–4213.

Beth Levin. 1993. *English verb classes and alternations: A preliminary investigation*. University of Chicago press.

Edward Loper, Szu-Ting Yi, and Martha Palmer. 2007. Combining lexical resources: mapping between propbank and verbnet. In *Proceedings of the 7th International Workshop on Computational Linguistics, Tilburg, the Netherlands.*

Alec Radford, Jong Wook Kim, Chris Hallacy, Aditya Ramesh, Gabriel Goh, Sandhini Agarwal, Girish Sastry, Amanda Askell, Pamela Mishkin, Jack Clark, Gretchen Krueger, and Ilya Sutskever. 2021. Learning transferable visual models from natural language supervision. *CoRR*, abs/2103.00020.

Horacio Saggion, Sanja Štajner, Daniel Ferrés, Kim Cheng Sheang, Matthew Shardlow, Kai North, and Marcos Zampieri. 2022. Findings of the tsar-2022 shared task on multilingual lexical simplification. In *Proceedings of TSAR workshop held in conjunction with EMNLP 2022.*

Victor Sanh, Lysandre Debut, Julien Chaumond, and Thomas Wolf. 2019. Distilbert, a distilled version of bert: smaller, faster, cheaper and lighter.

Karin Kipper Schuler. 2005. *VerbNet: A broad-coverage, comprehensive verb lexicon*. University of Pennsylvania.

Sanja Štajner, Daniel Ferrés, Matthew Shardlow, Kai North, Marcos Zampieri, and Horacio Saggion. 2022. Lexical simplification benchmarks for English, Portuguese, and Spanish. *Frontiers in Artificial Intelligence*, 5.

MANTIS at TSAR-2022 Shared Task: Improved Unsupervised Lexical Simplification with Pretrained Encoders

Xiaofei Li[1], **Daniel Wiechmann**[2], **Yu Qiao**[1], **Elma Kerz**[1]
[1] RWTH Aachen University
[2] University of Amsterdam
{xiaofei.li1,yu.qiao}@rwth-aachen.de
d.wiechmann@uva.nl, elma.kerz@ifaar.rwth-aachen.de

Abstract

In this paper we present our contribution to the TSAR-2022 Shared Task on Lexical Simplification of the EMNLP 2022 Workshop on Text Simplification, Accessibility, and Readability. Our approach builds on and extends the unsupervised lexical simplification system with pretrained encoders (LSBert) system introduced in Qiang et al. (2020) in the following ways: For the subtask of simplification candidate selection, it utilizes a RoBERTa transformer language model and expands the size of the generated candidate list. For subsequent substitution ranking, it introduces a new feature weighting scheme and adopts a candidate filtering method based on textual entailment to maximize semantic similarity between the target word and its simplification. Our best-performing system improves LSBert by 5.9% accuracy and achieves second place out of 33 ranked solutions.

1 Introduction

Lexical simplification (LS) is a natural language processing (NLP) task that involves automatically reducing the lexical complexity of a given text, while retaining its original meaning (Shardlow, 2014; Paetzold and Specia, 2017b). Since LS has a high potential for social benefit and improving social inclusion for many people, it has attracted increasing attention in the NLP community (Štajner, 2021). LS systems are commonly framed as a pipeline of three main steps (Paetzold and Specia, 2017a): (1) Complex Word Identification (CWI), (2) Substitute Generation (SG), and (3) Substitute Ranking (SR), with CWI often being treated as an independent task.

In this paper, we present our contributions to the English track of the TSAR-2022 Shared Task on LS (Saggion et al., 2022). Focusing on steps (2) and (3) in the pipeline above, the task was defined as follows: Given a sentence containing a complex word, systems should return an ordered list of "simpler" valid substitutes for the complex word in its original context. The list of simpler words (up to a maximum of 10) returned by the system should be ordered by the confidence the system has in its prediction (best predictions first). The ordered list must not contain ties. The task employed a new benchmark dataset for lexical simplification in English, Spanish, and (Brazilian) Portuguese. The gold annotations consists of all simpler substitutes suggested by crowdsourced workers and checked for quality by at least one computational linguist who is native speaker of the respective language (for details, see Štajner et al. (2022)). Contributing teams were provided with a small sample with gold standard annotations as a trial dataset. For English, this trial dataset consists of 10 instances of a sentence, a target complex word and a list of substitution candidates. The English test dataset consisted of 373 instances of sentence/complex word pairs. Submission were evaluated in terms of ten performance metrics that fall into three groups: (1) MAP@K (Mean Average Precision@K) for $K = 1, 3, 5, 10$ candidate words. This metric evaluates a ranked list of predicted substitutes that is matched (relevant) and not matched (irrelevant) terms against the set of the gold-standard annotations for evaluation. (2) Potential@K: $K = 1, 3, 5, 10$. Potential scores quantify the percentage of instances for which at least one of the substitutions predicted is present in the set of gold annotations and (3) Accuracy@K@top1: $K = 1, 2, 3$. Accuracy scores represent the ratio of instances where at least one of the K top predicted candidates matches the most frequently suggested synonym/s in the gold list of annotated candidates.

2 System Description

Our contributions to the TSAR shared task builds on and extends the approach to unsupervised lexical simplification with pretrained encoders – LSBert – described in Qiang et al. (2020) and Qiang

Proceedings of the Workshop on Text Simplification, Accessibility, and Readability (TSAR-2022), pages 243 - 250
December 8, 2022 ©2022 Association for Computational Linguistics

et al. (2021). This approach leverages a pretrained transformer language models to generate context-aware simplifications for complex words. The LSBert simplification algorithm addresses two of three principal subtasks of LS: simplification candidate generation and substitution ranking.

Our approach extends LSBert in the following ways: (1) It utilizes a RoBERTa transformer language model for simplification candidate generation and expands the size of the generated candidate list. (2) It introduces new substitution ranking methods that involve (i) a re-weighting of the ranking features used by LSBert and (ii) the adoption of equivalence scores based on textual entailment to maximize semantic similarity between the target word and its simplification. In submissions (runs) 2 and 3, we further explore the utility of crowdsourcing- and corpus-based measure of word prevalence for substitution ranking. The simplification algorithm underlying the three submissions described in this paper is shown in Algorithm 1. In the following we describe the details of simplification candidate generation (2.1), substitution ranking (2.2) and obtaining equivalence scores (2.3).

Algorithm 1 Lexical Simplification

Input: sentence S, Complex word w
Output: sorted suggestion list $word\_list$

Replace word w of S into <mask> as S'
Concatenate S and S' using <s> and </s>
$p(\cdot|S, S' \setminus \{w\}) \leftarrow RoBERTa(S, S')$
$scs \leftarrow top\_probability(p(\cdot|S, S' \setminus \{w\}))$
$all\_ranks \leftarrow \emptyset$
for each feature f and its weight c_f **do**
    $scores \leftarrow \emptyset$
    for each $sc \in scs$ **do**
        $scores \leftarrow scores \cup f(sc)$
    end for
    $rank \leftarrow c_f \times rank\_numbers(scores)$
    $all\_ranks \leftarrow all\_ranks \cup rank$
end for
$tot\_rank \leftarrow sum(all\_ranks)$
$word\_list' \leftarrow sort\_ascending(tot\_rank)$
$word\_list \leftarrow postproc(word\_list')$
return $word\_list$

2.1 Simplification Candidate Generation

During candidate generation, for each pair of sentence S and complex word w, the LSBert algorithm first generates new sequence S' in which w is masked. The two sentences S and S' are then concatenated and fed into a pretrained transformer language model (PTLM) to obtain the probability distribution of the vocabulary that can fill the masked position, $p(\cdot|S, S' \setminus \{w\})$. The top 10 words from this distribution are considered as the list of simplification candidates.[1] Our simplification candidate generation method differs from the one used in LSBert in two ways: (1) the choice of PTLM and (2) the size of the candidate list. Qiang et al. (2021) performed experiments with three BERT models: (i) BERT-based, uncased: 12-layer, 768-hidden, 12-heads, 110 M parameters. (ii) BERT-large, uncased: 24-layer, 1024-hidden, 16-heads, 340 M parameters, and (iii) BERT-large, uncased, Whole Word Masking (WWM): 24-layer, 1024-hidden, 16-heads, 340 M parameters. The results of their experiments indicated that the WWM model obtains the highest accuracy and precision. Here we extended these PTLM-experiments to include RoBERTa models (Liu et al., 2019) and also experimented with the combined use of BERT and RoBERTa to enlarge the list of substitution candidates. The results of our experiments indicated that optimal results are obtained using the RoBERTa-md: 12-layer, 768-hidden, 12-heads, 125M parameters. To maximize the chance of obtaining at least ten suitable substitution candidates after rigorous filtering based on semantic criteria (see below), we increased the size of the candidate list generated in this step from 10 to 30 candidates.

2.2 Substitution Ranking

In LSBert, candidate substitutions are ranked based on four features each of which is designed to capture one aspect of the suitability of the candidate word to replace the complex word. These features are rank orders of candidate substitutions based on four scores: (1) 'Pretrained LM (PTLM) prediction' ($B_{PTLM}(sc)$, in LSBert, PTLM = Bert) representing the probability derived from PTLM that the candidate substitution word sc presents at the masked position given the rest of a sentence. (2) 'Language model feature' ($L_{PLM}(sc)$) representing the average loss of the context of sc, $w_{-m}^{m} = (w_{-m}, w_{-m+1}, \ldots, w_0, \ldots, w_{m-1}, w_m)$, where $w_0 = sc$. (3) 'Semantic similarity' ($S(sc)$) expressed as the cosine similarity between the fastText vector of the original word and the that of the sc. (4) 'Word frequency' ($F(sc)$) as estimated from the top 12 million texts from Wikipedia and

[1] Morphological derivations of w are excluded.

the Children's Book Test corpus.[2] In LSBert, the rank of a sc, $R(sc)$, is based on an equal weighting of these four features, as shown in equation (1) and (2).

$$Score(sc) = \frac{1}{4} \sum_{f \in \{B_{Bert}, -L_{Bert}, S, F\}} rank_f(sc) \quad (1)$$

$$R(sc) = rank_{Score}(sc) \quad (2)$$

where $rank_f : SCS \rightarrow \mathbb{Z}$:

$$sc \mapsto |\{w \in SCS | f(w) > f(sc)\}| + 1$$

and SCS is the set of all substitution candidates.

In our three submissions to the shared task, we considered three different strategies to derive the above $Score(sc)$: In the first submission (Mantis_1), we adapted the ranking method as shown in equation (3). c_f is the feature weight for feature f and $c_{B_{Roberta}} = c_F = 1, c_S = 3$.

$$Score_{run1}(sc) = \sum_{f \in \{B_{Roberta}, S, F\}} c_f \cdot rank_f(sc) \quad (3)$$

This ranking method introduces a re-weighting of the features so as to (i) increase the relative importance of the semantic similarity between the target word w and a substitute candidate sc and (ii) decrease the relative importance of the probability-based PTLM prediction. With regard to the former, the value of $S(sc)$, corresponding to ranked cosine similarity, was increased by a factor of 3 to penalize candidates with low similarity to the target word. With regard to the latter, we decided to drop the language model feature $L_{PTLM}(sc)$ as its correlation with $B_{PTLM}(sc)$ would yield an up-weighting of the importance assigned to the probability of sc to appear in the masked position.

In the second and third submissions (Mantis_2 and Mantis_3), we experimented with alternative features for substitution ranking: To this end, we first computed lexical complexity scores for the sentences in the trial data for each substitution candidate using 77 indicators (see Table 2 in the appendix). All scores were obtained using an automated text analysis system developed by our group (for its recent applications, see e.g. Wiechmann et al. (2022) or Kerz et al. (2022)). Tokenization, sentence splitting, part-of-speech tagging, lemmatization and syntactic PCFG parsing were performed using Stanford CoreNLP (Manning et al., 2014).

[2] `https://github.com/google-research/bert`

We then used each feature to obtain a rank order of substitution candidates and correlated reach ranking with the rank order of substitution candidates provided in the trial data. The top-2 lexical features yielding the largest correlations with the gold standard ranking were selected for substitution ranking for Mantis_2 and Mantis_3, respectively. Both of these lexical features concern word prevalence (WP), i.e. they refer to the number of people who know the word: WP_{crowd} estimates the proportion of the population that knows a given word based on a crowdsourcing study involving over 220,000 people (Brysbaert et al., 2019). $WP_{corp.SDBP}$ is an corpus-derived estimate of the number of books that a word appears in (Johns et al., 2020). The corresponding rankings were obtained as shown in equations (4) and (5):

$$Score_{run2}(sc) = \sum_{f \in \{WP_{crowd}, Eq\}} rank_f(sc) \quad (4)$$

$$Score_{run2}(sc) = \sum_{f \in \{WP_{corp.SDBP}, Eq\}} rank_f(sc) \quad (5)$$

Apart from these WP-features, the substitution ranking in runs 2 and 3 was determined by a semantic feature, referred to as the 'equivalence score' $Eq(sc)$ (see section 2.3). This score was evoked based on the consideration that semantic similarity measured by cosine similarity of embeddings is not expressive enough (Kim et al., 2016): Any two words that are frequently used in similar contexts will have a low cosine similarity between the embeddings. Thus cosine similarity often fails to recognize antonyms, such as "fast" and "slow". The next section will provide more details on how equivalence score were obtained.

2.3 Obtaining Equivalence Scores

Lexical simplification needs to preserve the original meaning of the target word. As cosine similarity between embedding vectors can be too permissive, we introduced a stricter criterion based on textual entailment. To achieve this we utilized a language model explicitly trained to the natural language inference (NLI) task of evaluating logical connections between sentences. The central idea is to compute for each substitute word sc a score that quantifies the textual entailment of the original sentence S and its variant S' that contains sc. Textual entailment is a directional relation between text fragment that holds whenever the truth of one text fragment follows from another text. The entailing and en-

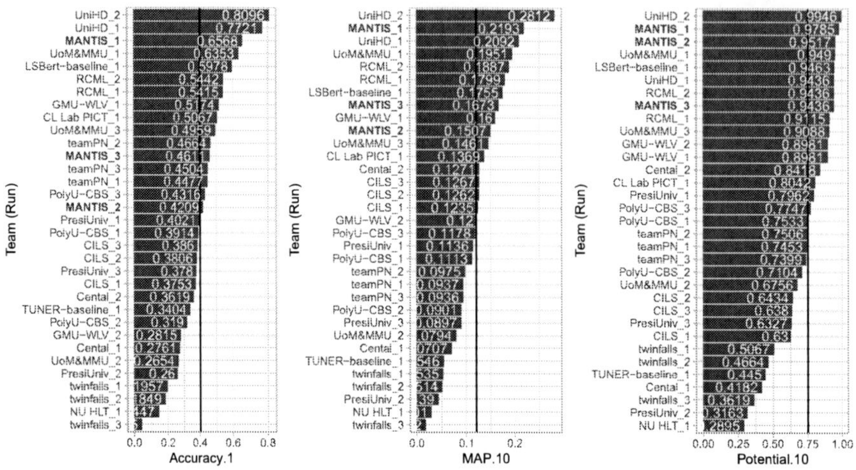

Figure 1: Performance ranking based on Accuracy, Mean Average Precision, and Potential scores (k=10). Vertical lines represent the median performance across the 33 submission for each metric.

tailed texts are termed premise (p) and hypothesis (h), respectively. The relation between p and h can be one of entailment, contradictory or neutral (neither entailment nor contradictory). To the extent that p and h mutually entail each other, they are considered equivalent. In this paper, the entailment scores were obtained from the 'roberta-large-mnli' model from the Hugginface transformer library.[3] Roberta-large-mnli is a RoBERTa large model fine-tuned on the Multi-Genre Natural Language Inference corpus using a masked language modeling objective (Williams et al., 2018). The entailment score is defined as the probability that p entails h:

$$En(p,h) = Prob_\theta(entailment \mid p,h) \quad (6)$$

where θ is the parameters of trained roberta-large-mnli. We quantify the degree of equivalence of two sentences (*equivalence score*) as the product of the entailment scores in both directions. For a given sentence S and the corresponding simplified sentence S', the equivalence score is defined as:

$$Eq(S,S') = En(S,S') \cdot En(S',S) \quad (7)$$

Apart from their use in the substitution ranking in Mantis_2 and Mantis_3, equivalent scores were also used in a postprocessing step in Mantis_1: Here the list of substitution candidates was pruned after ranking by removing candidates whose equivalence scores were smaller than the mean equivalence score of all candidates.

[3] https://huggingface.co/roberta-large-mnli

3 End-to-end System Performance

The official results across seven performance metrics[4] are presented in Table 1 in the appendix (for details, see Saggion et al. (2022)). As the performance metrics are strongly intercorrelated (mean correlation across all metrics = 0.920, sd = 0.071, see also Figure 2 in the appendix), we focus our discussion here on the results of one metric from each of the three groups: (1) Accuracy.1, (2) MAP.10 and (3) Potential.10 (see Figure 1). Our best-performing system was 'Mantis_1'. This system reached 2nd rank on both MAP.10 and Potential.10 and 3rd rank on accuracy. Mantis_1 displayed an improvement over the median performance of +25.56% on accuracy, +24.13% on potential.10 and +9.93% MAP.10. It outperformed the LSBert baseline by +5.9% accuracy, +4.38 MAP.10 and 3.49% Potential.10. The two systems whose substitution ranking was based solely on word prevalence and an equivalence score lagged behind the LSBert baseline on two of the performance metrics shown here, suggesting that the improvements of our system over LSBert was mainly due to better substitution ranking, rather than candidate selection. However, Mantis_2 outperformed LSBert on the Potential.10 metric, suggesting that the inclusion of word prevalence can be fruitfully employed to improve LS systems. In future work, we intend to explore the role these and additional indicators of lexical sophistication for substitution ranking.

[4] Four of the ten performance metrics, Acc@1, MAP@1, Potential@1, and Precision@1, give the same results as per their definitions.

References

Marc Brysbaert, Paweł Mandera, Samantha F McCormick, and Emmanuel Keuleers. 2019. Word prevalence norms for 62,000 english lemmas. *Behavior research methods*, 51(2):467–479.

Mark Davies. 2008. The Corpus of Contemporary American English (COCA): 560 million words, 1990-present.

Brendan T Johns, Melody Dye, and Michael N Jones. 2020. Estimating the prevalence and diversity of words in written language. *Quarterly Journal of Experimental Psychology*, 73(6):841–855.

Elma Kerz, Yu Qiao, Sourabh Zanwar, and Daniel Wiechmann. 2022. Pushing on personality detection from verbal behavior: A transformer meets text contours of psycholinguistic features. In *Proceedings of the 12th Workshop on Computational Approaches to Subjectivity, Sentiment & Social Media Analysis*, pages 182–194, Dublin, Ireland. Association for Computational Linguistics.

Joo-Kyung Kim, Gokhan Tur, Asli Celikyilmaz, Bin Cao, and Ye-Yi Wang. 2016. Intent detection using semantically enriched word embeddings. In *2016 IEEE spoken language technology workshop (SLT)*, pages 414–419. IEEE.

Yinhan Liu, Myle Ott, Naman Goyal, Jingfei Du, Mandar Joshi, Danqi Chen, Omer Levy, Mike Lewis, Luke Zettlemoyer, and Veselin Stoyanov. 2019. Roberta: A robustly optimized bert pretraining approach. *arXiv preprint arXiv:1907.11692*.

Christopher D Manning, Mihai Surdeanu, John Bauer, Jenny Rose Finkel, Steven Bethard, and David McClosky. 2014. The stanford corenlp natural language processing toolkit. In *Proceedings of 52nd annual meeting of the association for computational linguistics: system demonstrations*, pages 55–60.

Gustavo Paetzold and Lucia Specia. 2017a. Lexical simplification with neural ranking. In *Proceedings of the 15th Conference of the European Chapter of the Association for Computational Linguistics: Volume 2, Short Papers*, pages 34–40.

Gustavo H Paetzold and Lucia Specia. 2017b. A survey on lexical simplification. *Journal of Artificial Intelligence Research*, 60:549–593.

Jipeng Qiang, Yun Li, Yi Zhu, Yunhao Yuan, Yang Shi, and Xindong Wu. 2021. Lsbert: Lexical simplification based on bert. *IEEE/ACM Transactions on Audio, Speech, and Language Processing*, 29:3064–3076.

Jipeng Qiang, Yun Li, Yi Zhu, Yunhao Yuan, and Xindong Wu. 2020. Lexical simplification with pretrained encoders. In *Proceedings of the AAAI Conference on Artificial Intelligence*, volume 34, pages 8649–8656.

Horacio Saggion, Sanja Štajner, Daniel Ferrés, Kim Cheng Sheang, Matthew Shardlow, Kai North, and Marcos Zampieri. 2022. Findings of the tsar-2022 shared task on multilingual lexical simplification. In *Proceedings of TSAR workshop held in conjunction with EMNLP 2022*.

Matthew Shardlow. 2014. A survey of automated text simplification. *International Journal of Advanced Computer Science and Applications*, 4(1):58–70.

Sanja Štajner. 2021. Automatic text simplification for social good: Progress and challenges. *Findings of the Association for Computational Linguistics: ACL-IJCNLP 2021*, pages 2637–2652.

Sanja Štajner, Daniel Ferres, Matthew Shardlow, Kai North, Marcos Zampieri, and Horacio Saggion. 2022. Lexical simplification benchmarks for English, Portuguese, and Spanish. *Frontiers in Artificial Intelligence*, 5.

Daniel Wiechmann, Yu Qiao, Elma Kerz, and Justus Mattern. 2022. Measuring the impact of (psycho-) linguistic and readability features and their spill over effects on the prediction of eye movement patterns. *arXiv preprint arXiv:2203.08085*.

Adina Williams, Nikita Nangia, and Samuel Bowman. 2018. A broad-coverage challenge corpus for sentence understanding through inference. In *Proceedings of the 2018 Conference of the North American Chapter of the Association for Computational Linguistics: Human Language Technologies, Volume 1 (Long Papers)*, pages 1112–1122. Association for Computational Linguistics.

A Appendix

Table 1: Official results across 7 performance metrics (Acc@1, MAP@1, Potential@1, and Precision@1 give the same results as per their definitions)

Rank	Team	Run	ACC@1	ACC@1.1	ACC@3.1	MAP@3	MAP@10	Pot@3	Pot@10
1	UniHD	2	0.8096	0.4289	0.6863	0.5834	0.2812	0.9624	0.9946
2	UniHD	1	0.7721	0.4262	0.571	0.509	0.2092	0.89	0.9436
3	**MANTIS**	1	**0.6568**	0.319	0.5388	0.473	0.2193	0.8766	0.9785
4	UoM&MMU	1	0.6353	0.2895	0.5308	0.4244	0.1951	0.8739	0.949
5	**LSBert-baseline**	1	**0.5978**	0.3029	0.5308	0.4079	0.1755	0.823	0.9463
6	RCML	2	0.5442	0.2359	0.4664	0.3823	0.1887	0.831	0.9436
7	RCML	1	0.5415	0.2466	0.4691	0.3716	0.1799	0.8016	0.9115
8	GMU-WLV	1	0.5174	0.2493	0.4477	0.3522	0.16	0.7533	0.8981
9	CLLabPICT	1	0.5067	0.2064	0.4021	0.3278	0.1369	0.7265	0.8042
10	UoM&MMU	3	0.4959	0.2439	0.4235	0.3273	0.1461	0.756	0.9088
11	teamPN	2	0.4664	0.1823	0.3378	0.2743	0.0975	0.6729	0.7506
12	**MANTIS**	3	0.4611	0.2117	0.4235	0.3227	0.1673	0.7747	0.9436
13	teamPN	3	0.4504	0.1769	0.3297	0.2676	0.0936	0.6648	0.7399
14	teamPN	1	0.4477	0.1769	0.3297	0.2666	0.0937	0.6621	0.7453
15	PolyU-CBS	3	0.4316	0.2064	0.3297	0.2683	0.1178	0.6139	0.7747
16	**MANTIS**	2	0.4209	0.1662	0.3565	0.2745	0.1507	0.7131	0.9517
17	PresiUniv	1	0.4021	0.1581	0.3002	0.2603	0.1136	0.6568	0.7962
18	PolyU-CBS	1	0.3914	0.1823	0.3002	0.2576	0.1113	0.5924	0.7533
19	CILS	3	0.386	0.1957	0.3083	0.2603	0.1267	0.5656	0.638
20	CILS	2	0.3806	0.1903	0.3083	0.2597	0.1262	0.563	0.6434
21	PresiUniv	3	0.378	0.1474	0.2573	0.2277	0.0897	0.5656	0.6327
22	CILS	1	0.3753	0.201	0.3109	0.2555	0.1235	0.5361	0.63
23	Cental	2	0.3619	0.1152	0.2788	0.2573	0.1271	0.6541	0.8418
24	TUNER-baseline	1	0.3404	0.142	0.1823	0.1706	0.0546	0.4343	0.445
25	PolyU-CBS	2	0.319	0.1447	0.2573	0.1973	0.0901	0.512	0.7104
26	GMU-WLV	2	0.2815	0.0804	0.2493	0.1899	0.12	0.563	0.8981
27	Cental	1	0.2761	0.1313	0.2117	0.1635	0.0707	0.378	0.4182
28	UoM&MMU	2	0.2654	0.1367	0.268	0.182	0.0794	0.4906	0.6756
29	PresiUniv	2	0.26	0.1018	0.1554	0.135	0.0439	0.3136	0.3163
30	twinfalls	1	0.1957	0.0509	0.1233	0.1175	0.0535	0.3485	0.5067
31	twinfalls	2	0.1849	0.0643	0.1367	0.1182	0.0514	0.3565	0.4664
32	NUHLT	1	0.1447	0.067	0.1179	0.0902	0.0301	0.26	0.2895
33	twinfalls	3	0.0455	0.0107	0.0455	0.037	0.0182	0.1474	0.3619

Table 2: An example instance from the trial dataset with gold annotation candidate list provided by the organizers

Sentence	A Spanish government source, however, later said that banks able to cover by themselves losses on their toxic property assets will not be forced to remove them from their books while it will be compulsory for those receiving public help.
Complex word	compulsory
Gold annotations	mandatory, mandatory, mandatory, mandatory, mandatory, mandatory, mandatory, mandatory, mandatory, mandatory, mandatory, required, required, required, required, required, required, required, essential, forced, important, manadatory, necessary, obligatory, unavoidable

Table 3: Overview of the 77 features considered for Substitution Ranking

Feature group	N	Examples/description
Lexical Sophistication Density and Diversity	14	Mean length/word, N Words on NGSL, Corrected TTR
Register-based N-gram Frequency	25	N-gram freq. (N = 1-5) five subcorpora from COCA (Davies, 2008)
Psycholinguistic	38	Age of Acquisition, Word Prevalence (corpus-based), Word Prevalence (crowdsourced)

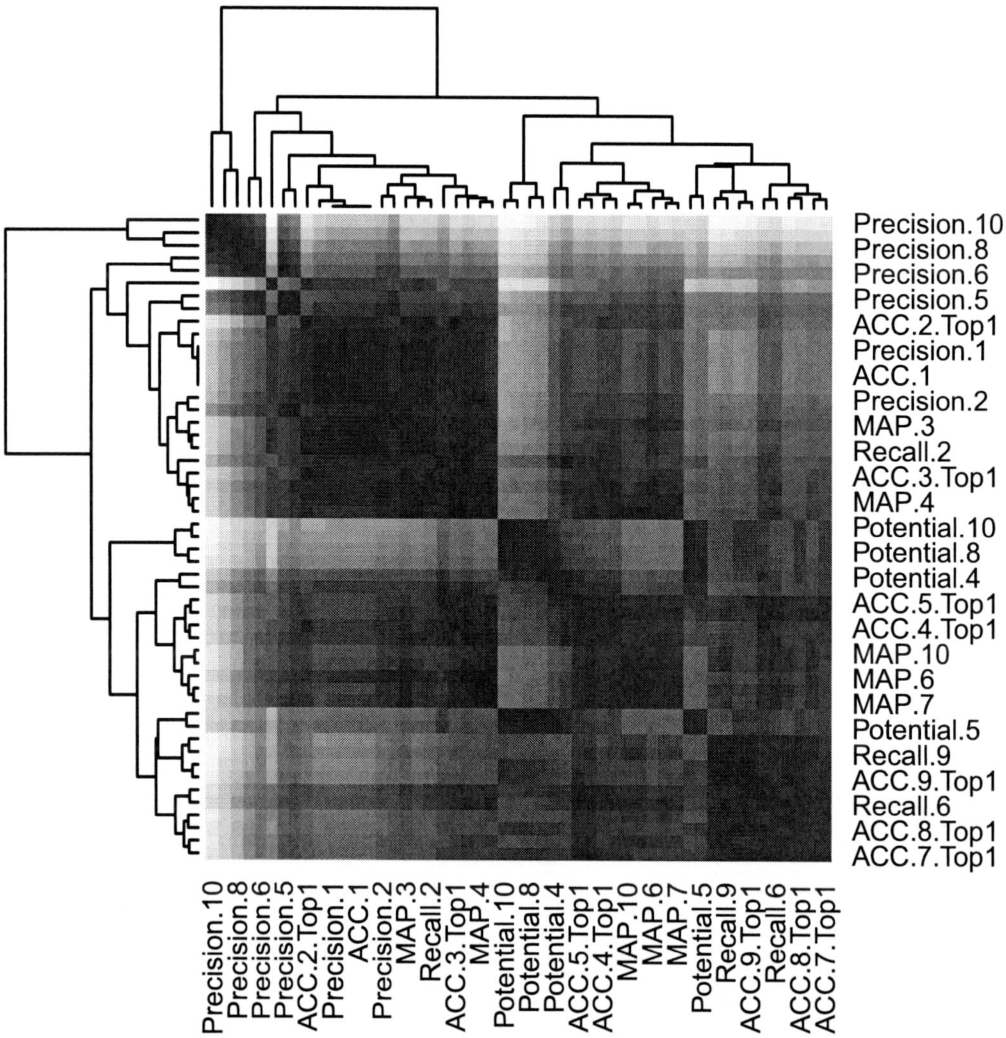

Figure 2: Heatplot of intercorrelations (Pearson r) of evaluation metrics (ns=50). Mean r = 0.920, sd = 0.071. Ranks of the three runs submitted were constant across metrics (run1 = 3, run2 = 12, run3 = 16).

UniHD at TSAR-2022 Shared Task: Is Compute All We Need for Lexical Simplification?

Dennis Aumiller and **Michael Gertz**
Institute of Computer Science
Heidelberg University
{aumiller, gertz}@informatik.uni-heidelberg.de

Abstract

Previous state-of-the-art models for lexical simplification consist of complex pipelines with several components, each of which requires deep technical knowledge and fine-tuned interaction to achieve its full potential. As an alternative, we describe a frustratingly simple pipeline based on prompted GPT-3 responses, beating competing approaches by a wide margin in settings with few training instances. Our best-performing submission to the English language track of the TSAR-2022 shared task consists of an "ensemble" of six different prompt templates with varying context levels. As a late-breaking result, we further detail a language transfer technique that allows simplification in languages other than English. Applied to the Spanish and Portuguese subset, we achieve state-of-the-art results with only minor modification to the original prompts. Aside from detailing the implementation and setup, we spend the remainder of this work discussing the particularities of prompting and implications for future work. Code for the experiments is available online.[1]

1 Introduction

With recent advancements in Machine Learning (ML) research coming largely from increasing compute budgets, Richard Sutton coined the idea of a "bitter lesson", wherein more computational power will ultimately supersede a hand-crafted solution (Sutton, 2019). More recently, increasing compute power on a general purpose architecture has also shown to be wildly successful in the Natural Language Processing (NLP) community (Vaswani et al., 2017; Wei et al., 2022). In particular, emergent capabilities in very large language models (vLLMs) have made it possible to approach a variety of tasks wherein only few (if any) samples are labeled, and no further fine-tuning on task-specific data is required at all.

In stark contrast to the complex pipelines in modern lexical simplification systems (Ferrés et al., 2017; Qiang et al., 2020; Štajner et al., 2022), we present a simplistic approach utilizing few-shot prompts based on a vLLM with basic instructions on simplification, which returns frustratingly good results considering the overall complexity of the approach, which utilizes a grand total of four hand-labeled instances. We present our results on the TSAR-2022 shared task (Saggion et al., 2022), which evaluates lexical simplification systems in three available languages (English, Spanish and Portuguese), with ten labeled instances and around 350 unlabeled test samples provided per language. For the English subset, official results rank our model as the best-performing submission, indicating that this approach may be another instance of the bitter lesson. While the initial findings are indeed promising, we want to carefully evaluate erroneous instances on the test set to analyze potential pitfalls, and further detail some of our experiences in hand-crafting prompts. We also acknowledge the technical challenges in reproducing (and deploying) systems based on vLLMs, especially given that suitable models exceed traditional computing budgets.

2 Prompt-based Lexical Simplification

With the public release of the GPT-3 language model (Brown et al., 2020), OpenAI has started the run on a series of now-available vLLMs for general-purpose text generation (Thoppilan et al., 2022; BigScience, 2022; Zhang et al., 2022). Across these models, a general trend in scaling beyond a particular parameter size can be observed, while keeping the underlying architectural design close to existing smaller models. Through exhibiting zero-shot transfer capabilities, such models have also become more attractive for lower-resourced tasks; oftentimes, models are able to answer questions formulated in natural language with somewhat sen-

[1] https://github.com/dennlinger/TSAR-2022-Shared-Task

Proceedings of the Workshop on Text Simplification, Accessibility, and Readability (TSAR-2022), pages 251 - 258
December 8, 2022 ©2022 Association for Computational Linguistics

sible results. Particular template patterns (so-called *prompts*) are frequently used to guide models towards predicting a particularly desirable output or answer format, without requiring a dedicated training on labeled examples.
Utilizing this paradigm shift, we experimented with different prompts issued to OpenAI's largest available model, `text-davinici-002`, which totals 176B parameters. Our first approach uses a singular prompt template in a zero-shot setting to obtain predictions for the shared task; we further improve upon these results by combining predictions from different prompt templates later on.

2.1 Run 1: Zero-shot Prediction

Upon inspecting the provided trial data, we noted that the simplification operations required a vastly different contextualization within the provided sample sentence. Whereas some instances can be solved with pure synonym look-ups (e.g., "compulsory" and "mandatory"), others require a more nuanced look at the context sentence (e.g., replacing "disguised" with "dressed"). To avoid biasing system predictions by providing samples as a prompt template, we provide a baseline that is entirely based on a single zero-shot query; it provides the context sentence and identifies the complex word, asking the model for ten simplified synonyms of the complex word in the given context. Given that no additional knowledge is provided to the model, the zero-shot contextual query also provides a reasonable lower-bound for the task setting. A secondary advantage of minimal provided context in zero-shot settings is the reduced computational cost, which will be discussed in more detail in Section 3.4.

2.2 Filtering Predictions

Model suggestions are returned as free-form text predictions, generally in the form of comma-separated lists or enumerations. This requires the additional step of parsing the output prediction into the more structured ranked predictions required for the shared task, which varies between the models used. In our experience, no clear pattern can be expected from the model and seems to be non-deterministic even with set template structures. We additionally employ a list of simple filters to ensure the quality of predictions, as detailed in Appendix C. The resulting model suggestions are considered in ranked order, and no prediction confidence scores or similar information was used to re-rank single-prompt predictions.

2.3 Run 2: Ensemble Predictions

Upon inspecting the results from the first run, we noticed that in some instances, predictions were almost fully discarded due to filtering. Simultaneously, we had already previously encountered strong variability in system generations when changing the prompt template or altering the context setting. To this extent, an ensemble of predictions from multiple different prompt templates was utilized to broaden the spectrum of possible generations, as well as ensuring that a minimum number of suggestions survives the filtering step.

2.3.1 Prompt Variations

The exact prompts are detailed in Table 3. Utilized variations can be grouped into *with context* (the context sentence is provided), or *without context* (synonyms are generated from the complex word alone). Simultaneously, different prompts also contain between zero and two examples taken from the trial data, including their expected outputs. This can be interpreted as a few-shot setting in which the model is demonstrated on what correct answers may look like for the particular task. We further vary the generation temperature, where a higher value increases the likelihood of a more creative (but not always correct) prediction, enabling a more diverse candidate set.

2.3.2 Combining Predictions

For each of the six prompts p, we ask the model to suggest ten alternative simplified expressions S_p and filter them with the exact same rules as the single prompt system in Run 1. In order to combine and re-rank suggestions s, we assign a combination score V to each distinct prediction $s \in \bigcup_p S_p$:

$$V(s) = \sum_p \max(5.5 - 0.5 \cdot \text{rank}_{S_p}(s), 0), \quad (1)$$

where $\text{rank}_{S_p}(s)$ is the ranked position of suggestion s in the resulting ranking from prompt p. If $s \notin S_p$, we set $\text{rank}_{S_p}(s) = \infty$. The scaling parameters are chosen arbitrarily and can be adjusted to account for the expected number of suggestions per prompt. We estimate that the biggest performance improvement is coming simply from providing enough predictions post filtering. As a secondary gain, we see more consistent behavior in the top-most prediction slots, boosting especially the @1 performance of the ensemble.

Run	ACC@1	Acc@k@Top1 $k=1$	$k=2$	$k=3$	MAP@k $k=3$	$k=5$	$k=10$	Potential@k $k=3$	$k=5$	$k=10$
Ensemble (Ours)	**0.8096**	**0.4289**	**0.6112**	**0.6863**	**0.5834**	**0.4491**	**0.2812**	**0.9624**	**0.9812**	**0.9946**
Single (Ours)	0.7721	0.4262	0.5335	0.5710	0.5090	0.3653	0.2092	0.8900	0.9302	0.9436
MANTIS-1	0.6568	0.319	0.4504	0.5388	0.473	0.3599	0.2193	0.8766	0.9463	0.9785
UoM&MMU-1	0.6353	0.2895	0.4530	0.5308	0.4244	0.3173	0.1951	0.8739	0.9115	0.9490
LSBert	0.5978	0.3029	0.4450	0.5308	0.4079	0.2957	0.1755	0.8230	0.8766	0.9463
TUNER	0.3404	0.1420	0.1689	0.1823	0.1706	0.1087	0.0546	0.4343	0.4450	0.4450

Table 1: Results on the English language test set of the TSAR-2022 shared task, ranked by *ACC@1* scores. Listed are our own results (*Ensemble* and *Single*), the two best-performing competing systems (*MANTIS* and *UoM&MMU*), as well as provided baselines (*LSBert* (Qiang et al., 2020) and TUNER (Ferrés et al., 2017)).

3 Results and Limitations

3.1 Results for English

For the official runs, we initially only submitted predictions for the English subset; an excerpt of the results can be seen in Table 1. While the zero-shot single prompt run has consistently better results on most metrics, it does not outperform all systems for large candidate sets; e.g., Potential@10 is lower than that of competing approaches, including the LSBert baseline. We attribute this to the previously mentioned issue of filtering predictions, and can see a consequent improvement especially for larger k by using the proposed ensemble method. Here, the Potential@10 scores indicate that at least one viable prediction is present in *all but three samples*.

3.2 Results for Spanish and Portuguese

Given the surprisingly good results on the English subset, we decided to extend our experiments to the Spanish and Portuguese tracks as well. Transferring the prompts to Spanish or Portuguese is surprisingly simple. We alter the prompt to: *"Given the above context, list ten alternative* ***Spanish*** *words for* 'complex_word' *that are easier to understand."* (bold highlight indicates change).

Without this adaption, returned suggestions generally tend to be in English, which could be an attractive opportunity to mine cross-lingual simplifications in future work. By adding the output language explicitly, we ensure that the suggestions match the expected results. For Portuguese, the prompt can be adapted accordingly.

We find that our system also outperforms all competing submitted approaches in the shared task; result comparisons can be found in Table 4 and 5 in the Appendix, respectively. Notably, predictions for Portuguese perform slightly better, which goes against intuition, given that Spanish is usually a highly represented language in multilingual corpora. We suspect that a more literal wording of synonyms in Portuguese, compared to multi-word expressions in Spanish, could be the cause.

3.3 Error Analysis

As is common for sequence-to-sequence tasks, crafting an approach centered around a LM requires consideration of the particular challenges arising. We detail some of the errors we have encountered in our predictions that are unlikely to appear in more stringently designed pipelines. Instances for particular failure cases can be found in Table 2.

Unstable Prompts One of the primary challenges, particularly for zero-shot prompt settings, is the unreasonable variance observed in results based on even just slightly altered prompt templates. For example, when removing the explicit mention of *Context:*, *Question:* and *Answer:* in the prompt template, the model is frequently predicting fewer than the ten requested answers. Practical limitations in our computational budget also mean that we have no guarantee that these prompts are yielding the best possible results; given the variability, multiple runs should be compared for a thorough pattern of a "best" prompt.

Lack of Context Instances with longer (or subtly enforced) context cues show issues where these hints are not properly recognized. In Table 2, we can see the model changing the term *"collision"* to a particular mode of transportation, such as *"car crash"*, while an explicit context clue is given through the word *"flight"* in the original sentence.

Enforcing Language While the transfer to Spanish and Portuguese is largely successful, the model's capabilities seem to be still limited in maintaining the language throughout all samples.

Error Type	Context (complex word in bold)	Model Predictions
Lack of Context	#7-8 Despite the fog, other flights are reported to have landed safely leading up to the **collision**.	car crash, train wreck, ...
Hallucinations	The larva grows to about 120-130 mm, and **pupates** in an underground chamber.	Transforms into a pupa, ...
Language	[...] propiciado la **decadencia** de la Revolución francesa.	decline, deterioration, ...

Table 2: Instances of observed failure classes in our system's predictions.

For instances with particularly rare complex terms, the predictions are sometimes still in English, despite the specific prompt request to return Spanish/Portuguese results.

Hallucinations The necessity for post-filtering of suggestions stems largely from the spontaneous occurrence of hallucinations in responses. While hallucinations in vLLMs are less about invalid vocabulary terms, we observe instances where unnecessary multi-word suggestions were chosen over a simple synonymous single-word expression, or random inflections (such as the infinitive form with an additional "to") were generated.
Similar to the issues with language enforcing, this occurs more frequently with particularly complex words; in this sense, the system conversely fails at instances that are most in need of simplification. However, we note that some of the generated multi-word expressions are actually more helpful for understanding, even though the generations are not precisely matching expected outputs.

3.4 Computational Limitations

Running a vLLM in practice, even for inference-only settings, is non-trivial and requires compute resources that are far beyond many public institution's hardware budget. For the largest models with publicly available checkpoints[2], a total of around **325GB GPU memory** is required, assuming efficient storage in `bfloat16` or similar precision levels. The common alternative is to obtain predictions through a (generally paid) API, as was the case in this work. Especially for the ensemble model, which issues six individual requests to the API per sample, this can further bloat the net cost of a single prediction. To give context of the total cost, we incurred a total charge of slightly over $7 for computing predictions across the entire test set of 373 English samples, which comes out to about 1000 tokens per sample, or around $0.02 at the current OpenAI pricing scheme.[3] For the Spanish subset and language-dependent prompt development, the total cost came to about $10, primarily due to longer sample contexts. Costs for Portuguese processing were around $6.50. While the singular prompt approach is cheaper at around 1/6 of the total cost, even then a continuously deployed model has to be supplied with a large enough budget. Aside from monetary concerns, environmental impacts are also to be considered for larger-scale deployments of this kind (Lacoste et al., 2019).

[2]At the time of writing, this would be the 176B Bloom model (BigScience, 2022), which has a similar parameter count to OpenAI's davinci-002 model.

4 Conclusion and Future Work

Utilizing prompted responses from vLLMs seems to be a promising direction for lexical simplification; particularly in the constrained setting with pre-identified complex words the model performs exceptionally well, even when presented with a severely restricted budget of labeled training data. While the approach also offers promising directions for multi- and cross-lingual approaches, obtaining state-of-the-art results in other languages, we are presented with a prohibitive amount of computation per sample instance. It would therefore be an interesting addition to deal with resource-constraint systems, putting the prediction power into a slightly different perspective. Finally, we are reminded of the unstable nature of neural LMs; given similar inputs, quality can vary greatly between samples, including a complete breakdown in performance.
For future work, we are considering approaches to generate static resources from vLLMs (Schick and Schütze, 2021), which may require only a one-time commitment to spending on datasets, which can then used as training data for cheaper systems. Exploration of prompt tuning approaches for automated search of suitable prompt templates would also greatly accelerate the development process of domain-specific applications (Lester et al., 2021).

[3]`https://openai.com/api/pricing/`, last accessed: 2022-10-01

References

Workshop BigScience. 2022. BLOOM (revision 4ab0472).

Tom Brown, Benjamin Mann, Nick Ryder, Melanie Subbiah, Jared D Kaplan, Prafulla Dhariwal, Arvind Neelakantan, Pranav Shyam, Girish Sastry, Amanda Askell, Sandhini Agarwal, Ariel Herbert-Voss, Gretchen Krueger, Tom Henighan, Rewon Child, Aditya Ramesh, Daniel Ziegler, Jeffrey Wu, Clemens Winter, Chris Hesse, Mark Chen, Eric Sigler, Mateusz Litwin, Scott Gray, Benjamin Chess, Jack Clark, Christopher Berner, Sam McCandlish, Alec Radford, Ilya Sutskever, and Dario Amodei. 2020. Language models are few-shot learners. In *Advances in Neural Information Processing Systems*, volume 33, pages 1877–1901. Curran Associates, Inc.

Daniel Ferrés, Horacio Saggion, and Xavier Gómez Guinovart. 2017. An adaptable lexical simplification architecture for major Ibero-Romance languages. In *Proceedings of the First Workshop on Building Linguistically Generalizable NLP Systems*, pages 40–47, Copenhagen, Denmark. Association for Computational Linguistics.

Alexandre Lacoste, Alexandra Luccioni, Victor Schmidt, and Thomas Dandres. 2019. Quantifying the carbon emissions of machine learning. *CoRR*, abs/1910.09700.

Brian Lester, Rami Al-Rfou, and Noah Constant. 2021. The power of scale for parameter-efficient prompt tuning. In *Proceedings of the 2021 Conference on Empirical Methods in Natural Language Processing*, pages 3045–3059, Online and Punta Cana, Dominican Republic. Association for Computational Linguistics.

Jipeng Qiang, Yun Li, Zhu Yi, Yunhao Yuan, and Xindong Wu. 2020. Lexical simplification with pretrained encoders. *Thirty-Fourth AAAI Conference on Artificial Intelligence*, page 8649–8656.

Horacio Saggion, Sanja Štajner, Daniel Ferrés, Kim Cheng Sheang, Matthew Shardlow, Kai North, and Marcos Zampieri. 2022. Findings of the tsar-2022 shared task on multilingual lexical simplification. In *Proceedings of TSAR workshop held in conjunction with EMNLP 2022*.

Timo Schick and Hinrich Schütze. 2021. Generating datasets with pretrained language models. In *Proceedings of the 2021 Conference on Empirical Methods in Natural Language Processing*, pages 6943–6951, Online and Punta Cana, Dominican Republic. Association for Computational Linguistics.

Richard Sutton. 2019. The bitter lesson. *Incomplete Ideas (blog)*, 13:12.

Romal Thoppilan, Daniel De Freitas, Jamie Hall, Noam Shazeer, Apoorv Kulshreshtha, Heng-Tze Cheng, Alicia Jin, Taylor Bos, Leslie Baker, Yu Du, YaGuang Li, Hongrae Lee, Huaixiu Steven Zheng, Amin Ghafouri, Marcelo Menegali, Yanping Huang, Maxim Krikun, Dmitry Lepikhin, James Qin, Dehao Chen, Yuanzhong Xu, Zhifeng Chen, Adam Roberts, Maarten Bosma, Yanqi Zhou, Chung-Ching Chang, Igor Krivokon, Will Rusch, Marc Pickett, Kathleen S. Meier-Hellstern, Meredith Ringel Morris, Tulsee Doshi, Renelito Delos Santos, Toju Duke, Johnny Soraker, Ben Zevenbergen, Vinodkumar Prabhakaran, Mark Diaz, Ben Hutchinson, Kristen Olson, Alejandra Molina, Erin Hoffman-John, Josh Lee, Lora Aroyo, Ravi Rajakumar, Alena Butryna, Matthew Lamm, Viktoriya Kuzmina, Joe Fenton, Aaron Cohen, Rachel Bernstein, Ray Kurzweil, Blaise Aguera-Arcas, Claire Cui, Marian Croak, Ed H. Chi, and Quoc Le. 2022. Lamda: Language models for dialog applications. *CoRR*, abs/2201.08239.

Ashish Vaswani, Noam Shazeer, Niki Parmar, Jakob Uszkoreit, Llion Jones, Aidan N. Gomez, Lukasz Kaiser, and Illia Polosukhin. 2017. Attention is all you need. In *Advances in Neural Information Processing Systems 30: Annual Conference on Neural Information Processing Systems 2017, December 4-9, 2017, Long Beach, CA, USA*, pages 5998–6008.

Sanja Štajner, Daniel Ferrés, Matthew Shardlow, Kai North, Marcos Zampieri, and Horacio Saggion. 2022. Lexical simplification benchmarks for English, Portuguese, and Spanish. *Frontiers in Artificial Intelligence*, 5.

Jason Wei, Yi Tay, Rishi Bommasani, Colin Raffel, Barret Zoph, Sebastian Borgeaud, Dani Yogatama, Maarten Bosma, Denny Zhou, Donald Metzler, Ed H. Chi, Tatsunori Hashimoto, Oriol Vinyals, Percy Liang, Jeff Dean, and William Fedus. 2022. Emergent abilities of large language models. *CoRR*, abs/2206.07682.

Susan Zhang, Stephen Roller, Naman Goyal, Mikel Artetxe, Moya Chen, Shuohui Chen, Christopher Dewan, Mona T. Diab, Xian Li, Xi Victoria Lin, Todor Mihaylov, Myle Ott, Sam Shleifer, Kurt Shuster, Daniel Simig, Punit Singh Koura, Anjali Sridhar, Tianlu Wang, and Luke Zettlemoyer. 2022. OPT: open pre-trained transformer language models. *CoRR*, abs/2205.01068.

A Prompt Templates

Table 3 provides the exact prompt templates used in the submission. Notably, the *zero-shot with context* prompt is included twice, but with different generation temperatures; with this we increase the likelihood of strong candidates being retained. For few-shot prompts, we have taken samples from the previously published trial set for the respective language. In instances where less than 10 distinctly different suggestions were provided by annotators, we manually extended the list of examples to match exactly ten results based on our own judgment. For instances with more provided suggestions, we limit ourselves to the ten most frequently occurring ones. The reason for this is that GPT-3 otherwise tended to return an inconsistent number of suggestions in our preliminary testing. The exact prompts for the Spanish and Portuguese runs can be found in our repository.

B Hyperparameters

We use the OpenAI Python package[4] version 0.23.0 for our experiments. For generation, the function `openai.Completion.create()` is used, where most hyperparameters remain fixed across all prompts. We explicitly list those hyperparameters below that differ from their respective default values.

1. `model="text-davinci-002"`, which is the latest and biggest available model for text completion.

2. `max_tokens=256`, to ensure sufficient room for generated outputs. In practice, most completions are vastly below the limit.

3. `frequency_penalty=0.5`, as well as `presence_penalty=0.3`, which jointly penalize present tokens and token repetitions. The values are well below the maximum (values can range from -2 to 2), since individual subword tokens might indeed be present several times across multiple (valid) predictions. A more detailed computation can be found in the documentation of OpenAI.[5]

Outside of the repetition penalties, the most influential parameter choice for generation is the sampling temperature. We generally take a more measured approach than the default (`temperature=1.0`), but vary temperature across our ensemble prompts to ensure a more diverse result set overall. We list the used temperatures in Table 3. *Zero-shot with context* is used twice in the ensemble, once with a more conservative temperature, and once with a more "creative" (higher) temperature. For the singular prompt run, we use the conservative *zero-shot with context* variant.

C Post-Filtering Operations

Given the uncertain nature of predictions by a language model, we employ a series of post-filtering steps to ensure high quality outputs. This includes stripping newlines/spaces/punctuation (`\n :;.?!`), lower-casing, removing infinitive forms (in some instances, we observed predictions in the form of "to deploy" instead of simply "deploy"), as well as removing identity predictions (e.g., the prediction being the same as the original complex word) and deduplicating suggestions. Additionally, we noticed that for some instances, generated synonyms resemble more of a "description" rather than truly synonymous expressions (example: "people that are crazy" as a suggestion for "maniacs"). Given the nature of provided data, we removed extreme multi-word expressions (for English, any suggestion with more than two words, for Spanish and Portuguese more than three words in a single expression).

[4] https://github.com/openai/openai-python

[5] https://beta.openai.com/docs/api-reference/parameter-details

Prompt Type	Template
Zero-shot /w context temperature: 0.3 (conservative), 0.8 (creative)	Context: {context_sentence}\n Question: Given the above context, list ten alternatives for “{complex_word}” that are easier to understand.\n Answer:
Single-shot /w context temperature: 0.5	Context: A local witness said a separate group of attackers disguisedin burqas – the head-to-toe robes worn by conservative Afghan women – then tried to storm the compound.\n Question: Given the above context, list ten alternative words for “disguised” that are easier to understand.\n Answer:\n1. concealed\n2. dressed\n3. hidden\n4. camouflaged\n 5. changed\n6. covered\n7. masked\n8. unrecognizable\n 9. converted\n10. impersonated\n\n Context: {context_sentence}\n Question: Given the above context, list ten alternatives for “{complex_word}” that are easier to understand.\n Answer:
Two-shot /w context temperature: 0.5	Context: That prompted the military to deploy its largest warship, the BRP Gregorio del Pilar, which was recently acquired from the United States.\n Question: Given the above context, list ten alternative words for “deploy” that are easier to understand.\n Answer:\n1. send\n2. post\n3. use\n4. position\n5. send out\n 6. employ\n7. extend\n8. launch\n9. let loose\n10. organize\n\n Context: The daily death toll in Syria has declined as the number of observers has risen, but few experts expect the U.N. plan to succeed in its entirety.\n Question: Given the above context, list ten alternative words for “observers” that are easier to understand.\n Answer:\n1. watchers\n2. spectators\n3. audience\n4. viewers\n 5. witnesses\n6. patrons\n7. followers\n8. detectives\n 9. reporters\n10. onlookers\n\n Context: {context_sentence}\n Question: Given the above context, list ten alternatives for “{complex_word}” that are easier to understand.\n Answer:
Zero-shot w/o context temperature: 0.7	Give me ten simplified synonyms for the following word: {complex_word}
Single-shot w/o context temperature: 0.6	Question: Find ten easier words for “compulsory”.\n Answer:\n1. mandatory\n2. required\n3. essential\n4. forced\n 5. important\n6. necessary\n7. obligatory\n8. unavoidable\n 9. binding\n10. prescribed\n\n Question: Find ten easier words for “{complex_word}”.\n Answer:

Table 3: The English prompt templates used for querying the OpenAI model, including associated generation temperatures. Only written out “\n” symbols indicate newlines, visible line breaks are inserted for better legibility. Only top-most prompt template with conservative temperature was used in the single prompt (Run 1), as well as in the ensemble run (Run 2). All other prompts were only included in the ensemble submission.

Run	ACC@1	Acc@k@Top1			MAP@k			Potential@k		
		$k=1$	$k=2$	$k=3$	$k=3$	$k=5$	$k=10$	$k=3$	$k=5$	$k=10$
Ensemble (Ours)	**0.6521**	**0.3505**	**0.5108**	**0.5788**	**0.4281**	**0.3239**	**0.1967**	**0.8206**	**0.8885**	**0.9402**
Single (Ours)	0.5706	0.3070	0.3967	0.4510	0.3526	0.2449	0.1376	0.6902	0.7146	0.7445
PresiUniv-1	0.3695	0.2038	0.2771	0.3288	0.2145	0.1499	0.0832	0.5842	0.6467	0.7255
UoM&MMU-3	0.3668	0.1603	0.2282	0.269	0.2128	0.1506	0.0899	0.5326	0.6005	0.6929
LSBert	0.2880	0.0951	0.1440	0.1820	0.1868	0.1346	0.0795	0.4945	0.6114	0.7472
TUNER	0.1195	0.0625	0.0788	0.0842	0.0575	0.0356	0.0184	0.144	0.1467	0.1494

Table 4: Results on the Spanish language test set of the TSAR-2022 shared task, ranked by *ACC@1* scores. Listed are our own results (*Ensemble* and *Single*), the two best-performing competing systems (*PresiUniv* and *UoM&MMU*), as well as provided baselines (*LSBert* (Qiang et al., 2020) and TUNER (Ferrés et al., 2017)).

Run	ACC@1	Acc@k@Top1			MAP@k			Potential@k		
		$k=1$	$k=2$	$k=3$	$k=3$	$k=5$	$k=10$	$k=3$	$k=5$	$k=10$
Ensemble (Ours)	**0.7700**	**0.4358**	**0.5347**	**0.6229**	**0.5014**	**0.3620**	**0.2167**	**0.9171**	**0.9491**	**0.9786**
Single (Ours)	0.6363	0.3716	0.4625	0.5160	0.4105	0.2889	0.1615	0.7860	0.8181	0.8422
GMU-WLV-1	0.4812	0.2540	0.3716	0.3957	0.2816	0.1966	0.1153	0.6871	0.7566	0.8395
Cental-1	0.3689	0.1737	0.2433	0.2673	0.1983	0.1344	0.0766	0.524	0.5641	0.6096
LSBert	0.3262	0.1577	0.2326	0.286	0.1904	0.1313	0.0775	0.4946	0.5802	0.6737
TUNER	0.2219	0.1336	0.1604	0.1604	0.1005	0.0623	0.0311	0.2673	0.2673	0.2673

Table 5: Results on the Portuguese language test set of the TSAR-2022 shared task, ranked by *ACC@1* scores. Listed are our own results (*Ensemble* and *Single*), the two best-performing competing systems (*GMU-WLV* and *Cental*), as well as provided baselines (*LSBert* (Qiang et al., 2020) and TUNER (Ferrés et al., 2017)).

RCML at TSAR-2022 Shared Task: Lexical Simplification With Modular Substitution Candidate Ranking

Desislava Aleksandrova and **Olivier Brochu Dufour**
CBC/Radio-Canada
dessy.aleksandrova@radio-canada.ca, olivier.brochu.dufour@radio-canada.ca

Abstract

This paper describes the lexical simplification system RCML submitted to the English language track of the TSAR-2022 Shared Task. The system leverages a pre-trained language model to generate contextually plausible substitution candidates which are then ranked according to their simplicity as well as their grammatical and semantic similarity to the target complex word. Our submissions secure 6th and 7th places out of 33, improving over the SOTA baseline for 27 out of the 51 metrics.

1 Introduction

Lexical Simplification (LS) is a means to facilitate reading comprehension for different target audiences such as second language learners, native speakers with low literacy levels or various kinds of neurodivergent conditions and reading impairments.

1.1 Task description

The task of lexical simplification (LS) consists in reducing the lexical complexity of a sentence by replacing one (or more) difficult words or multiword expressions (MWE) with easier to read and understand vocabulary all the while preserving the original sense.

Normally, LS includes the task of complex word identification (CWI) (Paetzold and Specia, 2016) but in the context of the TSAR-2022 Shared Task (Saggion et al., 2022), the word to be simplified is provided. Given a sentence containing a complex word, a system should then return an ordered list (best predictions first) of substitutes (min 0, max 10) for the complex word in its original context. The ordered list of predicted candidates must not contain ties, repetitions or the complex word itself. Predicted candidates must be good contextual fits (semantically and syntactically) as well as have the same morphological inflection as the complex word in the original sentence. A team is allowed to submit 3 runs per track.

Our team participated in the English track and made 2 submissions.

Despite the fog, other flights are reported to have landed safely leading up to the ***collision.***
GOLD: *crash, impact, accident, collision*
RCML: *accident, crash, tragedy, incident*

Figure 1: A complex word in context with gold annotations and predicted substitution candidates

1.2 Dataset description

The TSAR-2022 Shared Task has provided participants with a trial and test sets (.tsv) from a new multilingual lexical simplification dataset (Stajner et al., 2022) in English, Spanish and Portuguese. The trial set of each language contains 10 sentences accompanied by the complex word to simplify (in the second column) and the suggested substitution candidates (24 or 25) in the remaining columns. The test set, in contrast, contains only the first two columns (sentence and complex word). The English test set contains 373 instances (rather than the initially stated 386). The gold test set in English contains multiple simplification suggestions provided by annotators (25 or 26 in some cases).

To produce the dataset, crowdsourced workers were presented with instances (sentences) in which a single token (and never a MWE) is marked as requiring simplification. They were asked to provide simpler synonyms for the marked words, taking into account that the original meaning of the sentence should be preserved. Annotators were allowed to return multiple words if they could not think of a relevant single-word simplification. A number of suggestions match the complex word, since annotators were instructed to submit the com-

Proceedings of the Workshop on Text Simplification, Accessibility, and Readability (TSAR-2022), pages 259 - 263
December 8, 2022 ©2022 Association for Computational Linguistics

plex word whenever they couldn't find a simpler substitution. However, the evaluation script ignores such suggestions when calculating the scores.

1.3 Evaluation metrics

The evaluation metrics used in the TSAR-2022 Shared Task are the following:

Mean Average Precision @ K: K={1,3,5,10}. MAP@K evaluates the relevance of the predicted substitutes as well as the position of the relevant candidates compared to the gold annotations.

Potential@K: K={1,3,5,10}. Potential@K evaluates the percentage of instances for which at least one of the substitutions predicted is present in the set of gold annotations.

Accuracy@K@top1: K={1,2,3}. ACC@K@top1 evaluates the ratio of instances where at least one of the K top predicted candidates matches the most frequently suggested substitute in the gold list of annotated candidates.

2 System Description

We propose a modular system for lexical simplification which requires no training data and allows to fine-tune each module separately in order to improve the final result. Since the dataset already provides complex word annotations, RCML is composed of only two modules: one for candidate generation and one for candidate ranking.

2.1 Candidate Generation

To generate substitution candidates, we used the lexical substitution framework LexSubGen (Arefyev et al., 2020) and in particular, the best performing estimator XLNet+emb which employs a target word injection method different to LSBert's (Qiang et al., 2020). To produce a list of substitutes with their probabilities from the XLNet-large-cased model, LexSubGen combines a representation of the original input sentence (without masking) with the product of two distributions modelling the fitness of a substitute to the context and to the target. The proximity of each candidate to the target word is computed as the inner product between the respective embeddings, followed by a softmax to get a probability distribution.

We modified the post-processing of the original system to exclude the candidate lemmatization and get inflected suggestions, rather than lemmas. We kept the lowercase post-processor followed by target exclusion which uses lemmatization to detect and exclude all forms of the target word. Finally, we increased the number of suggestions to 20 which we found increased the chances of finding a suitable simpler substitution candidate.

2.2 Candidate Ranking

We selected and ranked candidates based on a combination of their grammaticality, meaning preservation and simplicity scores (for which we provide detailed descriptions further down in this section). Despite a large number of metrics aiming to evaluate one or more aspects of a simplification at a time (BLEU (Papineni et al., 2002), METEOR (Banerjee and Lavie, 2005), SARI (Xu et al., 2016), SAMSA (Sulem et al., 2018), Simple-QE (Kriz et al., 2020), ISiM (Mucida et al., 2022), Flesch Reading Ease Score (Kincaid et al., 1975), BERTScore (Zhang* et al., 2020), language model perplexity, etc.), not a single one of them excels at accurately measuring all three while also being publicly available. To rank the substitution candidates we thus chose to evaluate each aspect separately and to combine the scores through a simple heuristic giving twice as much weight to the simplicity score.

$$rank\ w_{n \leq N} = G_w \times (S_w \times 2 + M_w)$$

The rank of each substitution w_n of the $N = 20$ generated candidates is calculated as a function of its grammaticality $G \in \{0, 1\}$, simplicity $S \in [1, 6]$ and meaning preservation $M \in [1, N]$ scores. The top 10 ranking candidates (or less) are those included in the submission.

Grammaticality To evaluate the grammaticality of a sentence given a substitute candidate, we compare the coarse-grained part-of-speech (POS) and morphological features of both complex word and candidate in context. We use spaCy [1] to tokenize and parse the sentence, making sure not to split hyphenated complex words, since LexSubGen does not support multi-word expressions. We assign a score of 1 to all candidates whose features (person, number, mood, tense, etc.) correspond to those of the target word and 0 otherwise.

Meaning Preservation To evaluate the effect of a substitution candidate on the meaning of the original sentence we compute the similarity of the two sentences as a sum of the cosine similarities between their tokens' embeddings using BERTScore (Zhang* et al., 2020). The higher the similarity

[1] https://spacy.io/ | v. 3.1.3 | en-core-web-lg

between source and target sentences, the higher the chances that the substitution candidate's meaning is close to the one of the complex word. Candidates are ranked by decreasing $F1$ score with the best candidate receiving a score of 1 and the last one - a score equal to N.

Simplicity Arguably the most important aspect to evaluate of a given substitution candidate is whether or not it is simpler than the original complex word. Many synonyms a system (or even annotators) suggests may very well be grammatical, but if they do not simplify the concept within an acceptable degree of semantic variability, they fail to render the phrase easier to understand. The metric often times employed as a proxy for complexity is frequency, but frequency alone does not explain all the variation in lexical complexity datasets.

Our main contribution to this LS system is a more accurate measure of lexical complexity, notably a CEFR[2] vocabulary classifier, which we use to assign a complexity level to each substitution candidate. The lower the difficulty level, the higher a word's final rank.

The classifier is trained on data from the English Vocabulary Profile [3] (EVP) (Capel, 2012, 2015), a rich resource in British and American English which associates single words, phrasal verbs, phrases, and idioms not only with a CEFR level but with part of speech tags, definitions, dictionary examples and examples from learner essays. The corpus also contains distinct entries for distinct meanings of polysemous words, each associated with its own difficulty level. For example, we find 10 entries for the word form *run* in the American English section of the corpus, two noun forms and eight verbs, whose difficulty varies between A1 (*He can **run** very fast.*) and C2 (*He would like to **run** for mayor.*)

Rather than representing the vocabulary items by their frequency and/or surface-level characteristics (number of characters, number of syllables, etc.), we extract a semantic, contextual, dense vector representation of each item from a pre-trained masked language model [4] (Devlin et al., 2018) by first encoding the target word or MWE in context (using the dictionary and learner examples) and then aggregating all 12 hidden layers for all WordPieces.

This representation of the dataset is then used to train a support vector classifier [5] (Platt et al., 1999).

The resulting model is able to assign a difficulty level between $1 \equiv A1$ and $6 \equiv C2$ to the meaning of any word or MWE as determined by its context.

3 Results and Discussion

We submitted results from two runs of the same system with the only difference being the grammaticality score. In our second submission, we disabled the filtering of morphologically inconsistent substitution candidates (in other words, we assign G_w a score of 1 for all w) after noticing that in some cases, some very appropriate candidates get filtered out following an erroneous morphological analysis. Both submissions achieve very similar results (Saggion et al., 2022), but the second one improves on the first on all but two metrics: ACC@1@Top1 and ACC@3@Top1 despite generating inappropriate candidates (both semantically and syntactically) in some rare cases.

Team	ACC@1	MAP@3	Pot@3
UniHD	0.809	0.583	0.962
UniHD	0.772	0.509	0.89
MANTIS	0.656	0.473	0.876
UoM&MMU	0.635	0.424	0.873
LSBert-baseline	0.597	0.407	0.823
RCML	0.544	0.382	**0.831**
RCML	0.541	0.371	0.801
GMU-WLV	0.517	0.352	0.753

Table 1: Top of the leaderboard for the English track

RCML outperforms the state-of-the-art LSBert baseline on 27 out of the total 51 metrics (including Precision and Recall). Table 1 shows the top of the leaderboard including our team's two submissions. RCML has Potential@3 of 0.831 which is higher than LSBert's (Qiang et al., 2020) and comparable to the top-scoring systems. This result suggests a potential for our system to assist human editors in the task of lexical simplification by proposing a few simpler synonyms to choose from. The system's Accuracy@1@top1 doubles when $K = 3$ which means that in 46% of the time, the most commonly suggested substitute is among our top 3 predictions.

[2]The Common European Framework of Reference for Languages (CEFR) organizes language proficiency in six levels, A1 to C2.

[3]https://www.englishprofile.org/american-english

[4]https://huggingface.co/bert-base-uncased

[5]sklearn.svm.SVC

Sentence	**Gold@1**	**System@1**
Putin was expected to formally register later in the day to run for president, [...] a period in which he grew more **authoritarian**.	dictatorial	nationalist
In Japan, rice with azuki beans [...] is traditionally cooked for **auspicious** occasions.	favorable	important
Police are appealing for information about anyone seen acting **suspiciously** lately at Bidston Hill, Bidston, to come forward.	doubtfully	strangely
And in the capital Damascus, regime forces raided [...] while **snipers** were stationed on the roofs of some buildings.	sharpshooters	guns

Table 2: Sentences with complex gold substitution candidates

Sentence	**Gold@1**	**System@1**
It **decomposes** to arsenic trioxide, elemental arsenic and iodine when heated in air at 200°C.	decays	changes
Lebanon is sharply split along **sectarian** lines, with 18 religious sects.	divided	religious
The stretch of DNA transcribed into an RNA molecule is called a transcription unit and **encodes** at least one gene .	encrypts	codes
Obama earlier dropped from night skies into Kabul [...], **cementing** 10 years of U.S. aid for Afghanistan after NATO combat troops leave in 2014.	bonding	securing

Table 3: Sentences with erroneous gold substitution candidates

3.1 Error Analysis

We analyzed manually the first 100 sentences of the test set, comparing the most popular substitution candidate among annotators with the most probable candidate suggested by RCML. We identified 15 sentences for which the best Gold annotation is more complex than the system's top candidate, vs. 3 cases where the roles are reversed. Table 2 provides a few examples of our tentative observations. Admittedly, choosing a lexical simplification candidate requires to strike a balance between simplicity and synonymy, but we would argue that simplicity should be the guiding factor.

In a number of cases (six in the gold annotations and ten in the system predictions) the top substitution candidate is semantically and/or morphologically incoherent. Table 3 lists some of the cases where we believe the annotators confused the meaning of the target complex word, while RCML provided a suitable candidate.

The error analysis of RCML allowed us to notice that its current version does not exclude or penalize candidates introducing repetitions in the sentence, while human annotators avoid those naturally.

Another examined sentence illustrates well the limits of distributional semantics and the pitfalls of structural ambiguity. The complex word in the sentence below is a predicate whose argument is the noun *fighters*, but RCML first suggests predicates compatible with *explosives — hidden, positioned, stored*.

> The unsophisticated nature of the attack suggests little planning beyond having fighters and some explosives **prepositioned** in the vicinity of Kabul.

4 Conclusion

In this paper, we describe a modular lexical simplification system for English which requires no training data. RCML uses LexSubGen to generate substitution candidates before evaluating their grammaticality, meaning and simplicity. The latter is predicted by a 6-class contextual CEFR vocabulary classifier. The system is easily adaptable to other languages provided a trained CEFR vocabulary classifier in the languages in question. It also has the capacity to perform personalized lexical simplification, a particularly relevant approach when simplifying text for language learners at different proficiency levels.

References

Nikolay Arefyev, Boris Sheludko, Alexander Podolskiy, and Alexander Panchenko. 2020. Always keep your target in mind: Studying semantics and improving performance of neural lexical substitution. In *Proceedings of the 28th International Conference on Computational Linguistics*, pages 1242–1255, Barcelona, Spain (Online). International Committee on Computational Linguistics.

Satanjeev Banerjee and Alon Lavie. 2005. Meteor: An automatic metric for mt evaluation with improved correlation with human judgments. In *Proceedings of the acl workshop on intrinsic and extrinsic evaluation measures for machine translation and/or summarization*, pages 65–72.

Annette Capel. 2012. Completing the english vocabulary profile: C1 and c2 vocabulary. *English Profile Journal*, 3.

Annette Capel. 2015. The english vocabulary profile. *English profile in practice*, 5:9–27.

Jacob Devlin, Ming-Wei Chang, Kenton Lee, and Kristina Toutanova. 2018. BERT: pre-training of deep bidirectional transformers for language understanding. *CoRR*, abs/1810.04805.

J Peter Kincaid, Robert P Fishburne Jr, Richard L Rogers, and Brad S Chissom. 1975. Derivation of new readability formulas (automated readability index, fog count and flesch reading ease formula) for navy enlisted personnel. Technical report, Naval Technical Training Command Millington TN Research Branch.

Reno Kriz, Marianna Apidianaki, and Chris Callison-Burch. 2020. Simple-qe: Better automatic quality estimation for text simplification. *arXiv preprint arXiv:2012.12382*.

Lucas Mucida, Alcione Oliveira, and Maurilio Possi. 2022. A language-independent metric for measuring text simplification that does not require a parallel corpus. In *The International FLAIRS Conference Proceedings*, volume 35.

Gustavo Paetzold and Lucia Specia. 2016. Semeval 2016 task 11: Complex word identification. In *Proceedings of the 10th International Workshop on Semantic Evaluation (SemEval-2016)*, pages 560–569.

Kishore Papineni, Salim Roukos, Todd Ward, and Wei-Jing Zhu. 2002. Bleu: a method for automatic evaluation of machine translation. In *Proceedings of the 40th annual meeting of the Association for Computational Linguistics*, pages 311–318.

John Platt et al. 1999. Probabilistic outputs for support vector machines and comparisons to regularized likelihood methods. *Advances in large margin classifiers*, 10(3):61–74.

Jipeng Qiang, Yun Li, Yi Zhu, Yunhao Yuan, and Xindong Wu. 2020. Lexical simplification with pretrained encoders. *AAAI*, 34(05):8649–8656.

Horacio Saggion, Sanja Stajner, Daniel Ferres, Kim Cheng Sheang, Matthew Shardlow, Kai North, and Marcos Zampieri. 2022. Findings of the tsar-2022 shared task on multilingual lexical simplification. In *Proceedings of TSAR workshop held in conjunction with EMNLP 2022*.

Sanja Stajner, Daniel Ferres, Matthew Shardlow, Kai North, Marcos Zampieri, and Horacio Saggion. 2022. Lexical simplification benchmarks for English, Portuguese, and Spanish. *Frontiers in Artificial Intelligence*, 5.

Elior Sulem, Omri Abend, and Ari Rappoport. 2018. Semantic structural evaluation for text simplification. In *Proceedings of the 2018 Conference of the North American Chapter of the Association for Computational Linguistics: Human Language Technologies, Volume 1 (Long Papers)*, pages 685–696, New Orleans, Louisiana. Association for Computational Linguistics.

Wei Xu, Courtney Napoles, Ellie Pavlick, Quanze Chen, and Chris Callison-Burch. 2016. Optimizing statistical machine translation for text simplification. *Transactions of the Association for Computational Linguistics*, 4:401–415.

Tianyi Zhang*, Varsha Kishore*, Felix Wu*, Kilian Q. Weinberger, and Yoav Artzi. 2020. Bertscore: Evaluating text generation with bert. In *International Conference on Learning Representations*.

GMU-WLV at TSAR-2022 Shared Task: Evaluating Lexical Simplification Models

Kai North[1], Alphaeus Dmonte[2], Tharindu Ranasinghe[3], Marcos Zampieri[1]

[1]George Mason University, USA

[2]Rochester Institute of Technology, USA

[3]University of Wolverhampton, UK

knorth8@gmu.edu

Abstract

This paper describes team GMU-WLV submission to the TSAR shared-task on multilingual lexical simplification. The goal of the task is to automatically provide a set of candidate substitutions for complex words in context. The organizers provided participants with ALEXSIS, a manually annotated lexical simplification dataset in English, Portuguese, and Spanish. Instances in ALEXSIS were split between a small trial set with a dozen instances in each of the three languages of the competition and a test set with over 300 instances in the three aforementioned languages. To cope with the lack of training data, participants had to either use alternative data sources or pre-trained language models. We experimented with monolingual models: BERTimbau, ELECTRA, and RoBERTA-large-BNE. Our best system achieved 1st place out of sixteen systems for Portuguese, 8th out of thirty-three systems for English, and 6th out of twelve systems for Spanish.

1 Introduction

Text simplification (TS) is an important NLP application that consists of applying automatic methods to make texts more accessible to various target populations, such as children (Kajiwara et al., 2013), second language learners (Lee and Yeung, 2018), individuals with low-literacy levels (Watanabe et al., 2009; Gasperin et al., 2009), and individuals with reading disabilities (Devlin and Tait, 1998; Carroll et al., 1998; Rello et al., 2013). The core component of TS systems is lexical simplification (LS) which addresses the simplification of single complex words, complex multi-word expressions or both.

LS is a multi-stage process. In the first step, systems need to recognize words that are likely considered to be hard to understand by a given target population. This step is known as complex word identification (CWI) (Paetzold and Specia, 2016) or lexical complexity prediction (LCP) (Shardlow et al., 2020, 2021; North et al., 2022c). The second step in LS systems is to provide suitable candidate substitutions for complex words also known as substitute generation (SG) (Qiang et al., 2020; North et al., 2022a; Ferres and Saggion, 2022). These candidate substitutions are then filtered in regards to their suitability, known as substitute selection (SS) (Shardlow, 2014; Paetzold and Specia, 2017b), and then ranked in accordance to their simplicity, referred to as substitute ranking (SR) (Specia et al., 2012; Paetzold and Specia, 2017a; Maddela and Xu, 2018). The most appropriate candidate is then selected to replace the complex word.

While most of the work in LS deals with English, recent advances in multilingual and cross-lingual NLP models have motivated the study of multilingual models and datasets for LS with the goal of improving performance for languages other than English (Yimam et al.; Finnimore et al., 2019; Štajner et al., 2022). The Text Simplification, Accessibility, and Readability (TSAR-2022) shared-task (Saggion et al., 2022) follows this trend by providing participants with a multilingual LS dataset containing annotated data in English, Portuguese, and Spanish following the ALEXIS protocol (Ferres and Saggion, 2022). In this paper, we present team GMU-WLV's submissions to TSAR-2022 where we evaluate multiple models for this task. We describe prior methods of SG (Section 2), the task and data (Section 3), our model architecture (Section 4), and results (Section 5).

2 Related Work

As discussed by Paetzold and Specia (2017b), various approaches have been used for LS. Early approaches relied on predefined lists of complex words with candidate substitutions (Ong et al.,

Proceedings of the Workshop on Text Simplification, Accessibility, and Readability (TSAR-2022), pages 264 - 270
December 8, 2022 ©2022 Association for Computational Linguistics

2008; Kandula et al., 2010). WordNet (Fellbaum, 2010) is another widely used resource. Numerous SG systems take the synonyms provided by WordNet as valid simplifications of a complex word (Devlin and Tait, 1998; Carroll et al., 1998, 1999) while others use WordNet's list of hyponyms and hypernyms to identify and rank suitable replacements (Sinha, 2012; Nunes et al., 2013). Finally, some combine WordNet with other datasets consisting of linguistic features indicative of a word's complexity, such as the Psycholinguistic Database (Wilson, 1988).

More recent approaches have used transformer-based models that are able to more effectively capture and utilize contextual information as described by Vaswani et al. (2017). Qiang et al. (2020) used a pretrained BERT model to generate candidate substitutions using masked language modelling (MLM) (Devlin et al., 2019). Ferres and Saggion (2022) experimented with multiple pre-trained multilingual and monolingual transformers for MLM to generate Spanish candidate substitutions, including BETO (Cañete et al., 2020), mBERT (Devlin et al., 2019), BERTIN (De la Rosa and Fernández, 2022), RoBERTa-base-BNE, and RoBERTA-large-BNE (Fandiño et al., 2022).

3 Task and Data

The TSAR-2022 shared task was hosted at the Empirical Methods in Natural Language Processing (EMNLP) conference. Participants were tasked with creating an LS system that returns an ordered list of a maximum of 10 potential candidate substitutions for a given complex word. TSAR-2022 supplied participants with datasets in English, Portuguese (North et al., 2022a), and Spanish (Ferres and Saggion, 2022) each having their own track within the competition (Saggion et al., 2022). The task received 33, 17 and 16 entries in the English, Spanish, and Portuguese tracks respectively. The datasets contained excerpts from journalistic texts and Wikipedia articles. The English and Spanish datasets contained extracts from WikiNews and Wikipedia articles, whereas the Portuguese dataset contained extracts from locally sourced Brazilian newspapers. The Portuguese dataset is the only variety-specific dataset of the three containing only Brazilian Portuguese texts.

The three datasets are comparable in terms of size. The English dataset consisted of 386 instances, the Spanish dataset contained 381 instances, and the Portuguese dataset had 386 instances. Each dataset was split into trial and test sets and were provided to the participants with the trial set being released approximately 2 months prior. The trial set had only 10-12 instances per language, whereas the test set contained 369-376 instances per language. The test set did not contain the candidate substitution for each instance's complex word. The datasets were formatted as follows: *<sentence><complex.word>*, providing the original context for each complex word.

4 GMU-WLV: System Description

We approached this task with two model architectures inspired by the performance of large pre-trained monolingual transformers (Ferres and Saggion, 2022). We submitted two unsupervised models for each track due to the limited size of the development and train sets. The first model consisted of a pre-trained monolingual transformer with substitute ranking of the probabilities produced by MLM, which we name *GMU-WLV-vanilla*. The second model consisted of the same transformer model but with Zipf frequency for additional substitute ranking, which we name *GMU-WLV-zipf*. Both GMU-WLV-vanilla and GMU-WLV-zipf models conducted MLM similar to that described in Qiang et al. (2020). We masked the complex word of the original sentence and fed both the original sentence and the masked sentence separated by a [SEP] token to predict the masked token or in this case, the candidate substitution.

RoBERTA-large-BNE[1] was seen to perform well for Spanish by Ferres and Saggion (2022). As such, we selected several large pre-trained monolingual models for each track. For English, we used ELECTRA[2] (Clark et al., 2020), for Spanish we used RoBERTA-large-BNE (Fandiño et al., 2022), and for Portuguese we used the BERTimbau model[3] (Souza et al., 2020). RoBERTA-large-BNE was pre-trained on the National Library of Spain (Biblioteca Nacional de España) corpus (Fandiño et al., 2022) containing 135 billion Spanish tokens extracted from crawling all .es domains. ELECTRA was pre-trained on English Wikipedia data with a vocabulary size of 30522 tokens (Clark

[1]https://huggingface.co/BSC-TeMU/roberta-large-bne

[2]https://huggingface.co/google/electra-base-generator

[3]https://huggingface.co/neuralmind/bert-large-portuguese-cased

Track	Rank	Model	Top-k=1 Accuracy	Top-k=1 MAP	Top-k=1 Potential	Top-k=5 Accuracy	Top-k=5 MAP	Top-k=5 Potential	Top-k=10 Accuracy	Top-k=10 MAP	Top-k=10 Potential
	1	**GMU-WLV-vanilla**	**0.254**	**0.481**	**0.481**	**0.446**	**0.197**	**0.757**	**0.505**	**0.115**	**0.84**
	2	Central-1	0.174	0.369	0.369	0.286	0.134	0.564	0.324	0.077	0.61
PT	4	LSBert-Baseline	0.158	0.326	0.326	0.326	0.131	0.58	0.401	0.078	0.674
	12	GMU-WLV-zipf	0.07	0.216	0.216	0.324	0.124	0.655	0.505	0.084	0.84
	16	UoM&MMU-2	0.045	0.136	0.136	0.136	0.071	0.297	0.168	0.042	0.361
	1	UniHD-2	0.429	0.81	0.81	0.751	0.449	0.981	0.842	0.281	0.995
	5	LSBert-Baseline	0.303	0.598	0.598	0.611	0.296	0.877	0.684	0.176	0.946
EN	**8**	**GMU-WLV-vanilla**	**0.249**	**0.517**	**0.517**	**0.523**	**0.263**	**0.834**	**0.633**	**0.16**	**0.898**
	26	GMU-WLV-zipf	0.08	0.282	0.282	0.41	0.159	0.74	0.633	0.12	0.898
	33	twinfalls-3	0.011	0.046	0.046	0.067	0.028	0.23	0.107	0.018	0.362
	1	PresiUniv-1	0.204	0.37	0.37	0.361	0.15	0.647	0.402	0.083	0.726
	6	**GMU-WLV-vanilla**	**0.182**	**0.353**	**0.353**	**0.413**	**0.166**	**0.679**	**0.492**	**0.099**	**0.772**
ES	9	LSBert-Baseline	0.095	0.288	0.288	0.25	0.135	0.611	0.348	0.08	0.747
	12	GMU-WLV-zipf	0.068	0.236	0.236	0.307	0.126	0.617	0.492	0.083	0.772
	17	OEG_UPM-1	0.043	0.103	0.103	0.141	0.059	0.334	0.217	0.039	0.446

Table 1: A snapshot of SG performances on the PT, EN, and ES tracks per Saggion et al. (2022). We list our two models (GMU-WLV-vanilla and GMU-WLV-zipf), the LSBert-Baseline, as well as the highest and lowest scoring entries in each track for comparison. Run numbers are provided with a hyphen (e.g. -1) next to the model/team name. Our best system in each track is presented in bold.

et al., 2020). BERTimbau was pre-trained on the Brazilian Web as Corpus (Wagner Filho et al., 2018) that contains 2.7 billion Portuguese tokens annotated with tagging and parsing information and being derived from a diverse selection of Brazilian websites.

In regards to Zipf frequency ranking, we used the *wordfreq* Python library (Speer et al., 2018) to rank candidate substitutions. Inspired by previous work in CWI and LCP (Zampieri et al., 2016; Quijada and Medero, 2016; Shardlow et al., 2021), we pose that those candidate substitutions with a higher Zipf frequency would be considered more familiar to the user and therefore would be considered less complex than compared to those with a lower Zipf frequency.

5 Results

The results obtained by GMU-WLV-vanilla are presented in Table 1 and Table 2. GMU-WLV-vanilla's top-k = 1 accuracy placed it first among the sixteen submissions in the Portuguese track, whereas for the English and Spanish tracks, its top-k = 1 accuracy placed it eighth among thirty-three submissions and sixth among seventeen submissions respectively.

The accuracies achieved by our GMU-WLV-vanilla model for its top-k = [1, 2, 3] candidate substitutions for Portuguese were 0.254, 0.372 and 0.396 respectively (Table 2). Their MAP scores were 0.481, 0.364 and 0.282, whereas their potential scores were 0.481, 0.642 and 0.687 respectively. As such, a positive correlation was found between performance and number of candidate substitutions generated with this positive correlation increasing up to top-k = 10 candidate substitutions (Table 1). For the English track, our GMU-WLV-vanilla model generated top-k = [1, 2, 3] candidate substitutions with accuracies of 0.249, 0.354 and 0.448 respectively. Their MAP scores were 0.517, 0.414 and 0.352, whereas their potential scores were 0.517, 0.649, and 0.753 respectively. For the Spanish track, the accuracies achieved by this model's top-k = [1, 2, 3] candidate substitutions were 0.182, 0.264 and 0.329 respectively. Their MAP scores were 0.353, 0.266 and 0.22, whereas their potential scores were 0.353, 0.497, and 0.568 respectively. A positive correlation was therefore found to exist between performance and number of candidate substitutions generated, regardless of the language in question.

The performance of our second model: GMU-WLV-zipf was less promising (Table 1). GMU-WLV-zipf ranked twelfth among the sixteen submissions in the Portuguese track, it was placed twenty-sixth among thirty three submissions for the English track, and twelfth among seventeen submissions for the Spanish track. GMU-WLV-zipf performed noticeably worst on the Portuguese track in comparison to our GMU-WLV-vanilla model. Its top-k = [1, 2, 3] candidate substitutions achieved accuracies of 0.07, 0.136, and 0.216 respectively (Table 2). Their MAP scores were 0.216, 0.18 and 0.156, whereas its potential scores were 0.216, 0.382 and 0.513 respectively.

GMU-WLV-zipf also performed less well on

		GMU-WLV-vanilla					GMU-WLV-zipf				
Track	Top-k=n	Accuracy	MAP	Precision	Recall	Potential	Accuracy	MAP	Precision	Recall	Potential
PT	1	0.254	0.481	0.481	0.072	0.481	0.07	0.216	0.216	0.029	0.216
	2	0.372	0.364	0.404	0.118	0.642	0.136	0.18	0.222	0.059	0.382
	3	0.396	0.282	0.329	0.141	0.687	0.216	0.156	0.221	0.089	0.513
	4	0.43	0.232	0.287	0.16	0.727	0.273	0.14	0.22	0.12	0.612
	5	0.446	0.197	0.255	0.176	0.757	0.324	0.124	0.207	0.138	0.655
	6	0.46	0.172	0.233	0.193	0.783	0.39	0.113	0.203	0.163	0.741
	7	0.489	0.155	0.22	0.211	0.799	0.43	0.104	0.197	0.185	0.781
	8	0.495	0.139	0.202	0.221	0.807	0.462	0.098	0.195	0.213	0.81
	9	0.5	0.127	0.191	0.234	0.824	0.481	0.091	0.187	0.23	0.826
	10	0.505	0.115	0.178	0.242	0.84	0.505	0.084	0.178	0.242	0.84
EN	1	0.249	0.517	0.517	0.064	0.517	0.08	0.282	0.282	0.033	0.282
	2	0.354	0.414	0.446	0.107	0.649	0.169	0.223	0.263	0.062	0.44
	3	0.448	0.352	0.412	0.146	0.753	0.249	0.19	0.255	0.09	0.563
	4	0.496	0.304	0.377	0.178	0.81	0.33	0.174	0.259	0.122	0.662
	5	0.523	0.263	0.338	0.2	0.834	0.41	0.159	0.256	0.15	0.74
	6	0.547	0.23	0.305	0.214	0.842	0.472	0.148	0.253	0.176	0.786
	7	0.574	0.207	0.283	0.232	0.858	0.512	0.139	0.249	0.2	0.828
	8	0.603	0.19	0.269	0.249	0.874	0.566	0.132	0.247	0.227	0.86
	9	0.619	0.174	0.254	0.262	0.89	0.617	0.126	0.244	0.252	0.885
	10	0.633	0.16	0.239	0.272	0.898	0.633	0.12	0.239	0.272	0.898
ES	1	0.182	0.353	0.353	0.047	0.353	0.068	0.236	0.236	0.031	0.236
	2	0.264	0.266	0.302	0.08	0.497	0.13	0.189	0.223	0.057	0.372
	3	0.329	0.22	0.273	0.107	0.568	0.188	0.156	0.206	0.079	0.465
	4	0.375	0.191	0.257	0.135	0.641	0.253	0.14	0.209	0.105	0.56
	5	0.413	0.166	0.237	0.154	0.679	0.307	0.126	0.202	0.126	0.617
	6	0.438	0.148	0.22	0.169	0.715	0.364	0.113	0.195	0.147	0.679
	7	0.462	0.132	0.203	0.179	0.739	0.408	0.106	0.191	0.169	0.715
	8	0.47	0.12	0.19	0.19	0.753	0.435	0.098	0.182	0.184	0.728
	9	0.486	0.11	0.178	0.2	0.766	0.473	0.091	0.177	0.199	0.761
	10	0.492	0.099	0.173	0.204	0.772	0.492	0.083	0.173	0.204	0.772

Table 2: Full list of our models' performances for different number of top-k candidate substitutions generated on the PT, EN, and ES tracks.

the English and Spanish tracks with its top-k = [1, 2, 3] candidate substitutions achieving less impressive results across all evaluation metrics. For the English track, these candidate substitutions achieved accuracies of 0.08, 0.169, and 0.249, MAP scores of 0.282, 0.223, and 0.19, and potential scores of 0.282, 0.44, and 0.563 respectively (Table 2). For the Spanish track, these candidate substitutions showed accuracies of 0.068, 0.13, and 0.188, MAP scores of 0.236, 0.189, and 0.156, and potential scores of 0.236, 0.372, and 0.465 respectively.

6 Discussion

We believe that our GMU-WLV-vanilla model's performance on the Portuguese track was a result of it being a large pre-trained model trained only on Brazilian Portuguese data (Souza et al., 2020). GMU-WLV-vanilla model's competitive performance on the English and Spanish tracks was also likely due to the use of large monolingual models.

We were hoping that multilingual models may be able to transfer useful information learned from the vector representations of multiple or similar languages, such as Spanish, to the target language, for instance, Portuguese. However, during our experimentation, multilingual models, such as mBERT (Devlin et al., 2019) or XLM-R (Conneau et al., 2020), were found to produce candidate substitutions in languages other than the target language. Removing these words still resulted in a list of candidate substitutions that appeared to be less suitable than those produced by the monolingual models. This was also found to be the case after having applied Zipf frequency ranking.

We had previously theorised that ranking candidate substitutions per their zipf-frequency would produce a list of candidate substitutions ordered from most to least familiar for a specific or general target audience. Nevertheless, given that the performance of our GMU-WLV-zipf model was worst than that of our GMU-WLV-vanilla model, we concluded that zipf-frequency ranking was not in alignment with the annotators' notion of simplicity, regardless of language.

Table 2 shows that the top-k = 5 candidate substitutions ordered without zipf-frequency ranking achieved on average +0.114, +0.090, and +0.086 better accuracy, MAP, and potential scores across all three languages. The problem with Zipf frequency ranking is that it assumes that shorter words are innately less complex since they are more frequent than longer words and therefore make better simplifications. This is not always the case as it does not take into consideration context. Consider the following example shown in both Spanish (a) and English (b):

(a). El sistema prehispánico se **colapsó** bajo la conquista española en el siglo XVI.

(b). The pre-Hispanic system **collapsed** under the Spanish conquest in the 16th century.

Given the complex word "colapsó" (collapsed), our GMU-WLV-zipf model generated several candidate substitutions, including "hizo" (made), "puso" (put), "detuvo" (stopped), and "acabara" (finished). Without taking the meaning of the complex word or its context into consideration, "hizo" (made) or "puso" (put) would be the most logical candidate substitutions as they are shorter and more common in comparison to the other candidates. However, they do not have the desired meaning in this context. On the other hand, "detuvo" (stopped) or "acabara" (finished) are more semantically similar to the complex word despite being longer and less common. For this reason, zipf-frequency is not always a useful feature for substitute ranking.

7 Conclusion and Future Work

This paper presents GMU-WLV's submission to the TSAR shared-task on multilingual lexical simplification. Our GMU-WLV-vanilla model came first place at generating candidate substitutions for Portuguese, eighth for English, and sixth for Spanish. We demonstrate the importance of relying upon monolingual models for SG with pretrain models, such as BERTimbau and RoBERTA-large-BNE, performing exceptionally well. We also show that the use of zipf-frequency ranking for substitute ranking may result in inferior candidate substitutions being selected for simplification.

Transfer learning allows for the utilization of large pre-existing datasets to under-resourced NLP-related tasks, such as LS of Portuguese or Spanish. We hope to experiment with transfer learning on a number of datasets related to LS but are not formatted in such a way as to allow for the direct training of SG models, including datasets such as the CompLex dataset (Shardlow et al., 2020), a large pre-exsisting dataset containing continuous lexical complexity values, or the binary comparative CompLex dataset (North et al., 2022b), a somewhat smaller dataset consisting of comparative judgements between lexical complexities. We hypothesize that transfer learning will substantially increase the performance of our models.

Acknowledgements

We would like to thank the TSAR shared-task organizers for proposing this interesting shared-task and for replying promptly to all our inquiries. We further thank the anonymous reviewers for their insightful feedback.

References

John Carroll, Guido Minnen, Yvonne Canning, Siobhan Devlin, and John Tait. 1998. Practical Simplification of English Newspaper Text to Assist Aphasic Readers. In *Proceedings of AAAI*.

John Carroll, Guido Minnen, Darren Pearce, Yvonne Canning, Siobhan Devlin, and John Tait. 1999. Simplifying text for language-impaired readers. In *Proceedings of EACL*.

José Cañete, Gabriel Chaperon, Rodrigo Fuentes, Jou-Hui Ho, Hojin Kang, and Jorge Pérez. 2020. Spanish pre-trained bert model and evaluation data. In *PML4DC at ICLR*.

Kevin Clark, Minh-Thang Luong, Quoc Le, and Christopher Manning. 2020. ELECTRA: Pre-training text encoders as discriminators rather than generators. In *Proceedings of ICLR*.

Alexis Conneau, Kartikay Khandelwal, Naman Goyal, Vishrav Chaudhary, Guillaume Wenzek, Francisco Guzmán, Edouard Grave, Myle Ott, Luke Zettlemoyer, and Veselin Stoyanov. 2020. Unsupervised cross-lingual representation learning at scale. In *Proceedings of ACL*.

Javier De la Rosa and Andres Fernández. 2022. Zero-shot reading comprehension and reasoning for spanish with BERTIN GPT-J-6B. In *Proceedings of the SEPLN*.

Jacob Devlin, Ming-Wei Chang, Kenton Lee, and Kristina Toutanova. 2019. BERT: Pre-training of deep bidirectional transformers for language understanding. In *Proceedings of NAACL*.

Siobhan Devlin and John Tait. 1998. The use of a psycholinguistic database in the simplification of text for aphasic readers. *Linguistic Databases*, pages 161–173.

Asier Gutiérrez Fandiño, Jordi Armengol Estapé, Marc Pàmies, Joan Llop Palao, Joaquin Silveira Ocampo, Casimiro Pio Carrino, Carme Armentano Oller, Carlos Rodriguez Penagos, Aitor Gonzalez Agirre, and Marta Villegas. 2022. Maria: Spanish language models. *Procesamiento del Lenguaje Natural*, 68.

Christiane Fellbaum. 2010. Wordnet. In *Theory and applications of ontology: computer applications*, pages 231–243. Springer.

Daniel Ferres and Horacio Saggion. 2022. ALEXSIS: A dataset for lexical simplification in Spanish. In *Proceedings of LREC*.

Pierre Finnimore, Elisabeth Fritzsch, Daniel King, Alison Sneyd, Aneeq Ur Rehman, Fernando Alva-Manchego, and Andreas Vlachos. 2019. Strong baselines for complex word identification across multiple languages. In *Proceedings of NAACL*.

Caroline Gasperin, Lucia Specia, Tiago F. Pereira, and Sandra M. Aluisio. 2009. Learning when to simplify sentences for natural text simplification. *Encontro Nacional de Inteligencia Artificial*, pages 809–818.

Tomoyuki Kajiwara, Hiroshi Matsumoto, and Kazuhide Yamamoto. 2013. Selecting proper lexical paraphrase for children. In *Proceedings of ROCLING*.

Sasikiran Kandula, Dorothy W. Curtis, and Qing Zeng-Treitler. 2010. A semantic and syntactic text simplification tool for health content. *AMIA ... Annual Symposium proceedings. AMIA Symposium*, 2010:366–370.

John Lee and Chak Yan Yeung. 2018. Personalizing lexical simplification. In *Proceedings of COLING*.

Mounica Maddela and Wei Xu. 2018. A word-complexity lexicon and a neural readability ranking model for lexical simplification. In *Proceedings of EMNLP*.

Kai North, Marcos Zampieri, and Tharindu Ranasinghe. 2022a. ALEXSIS-PT: A new resource for portuguese lexical simplification. In *Proceedings of COLING*.

Kai North, Marcos Zampieri, and Matthew Shardlow. 2022b. An evaluation of binary comparative lexical complexity models. In *Proceedings of BEA*.

Kai North, Marcos Zampieri, and Matthew Shardlow. 2022c. Lexical complexity prediction: An overview. *ACM Computing Surveys*.

Bernardo Pereira Nunes, Ricardo Kawase, Patrick Siehndel, Marco A. Casanova, and Stefan Dietze. 2013. As simple as it gets - a sentence simplifier for different learning levels and contexts. *Proceedings of ICALT*.

Ethel Ong, J. Damay, Gerard Jaime D. Lojico, Kimberly Lu, and Dex Tarantan. 2008. Simplifying text in medical literature. *Journal of Research in Science, Computing and Engineering*, 4:1–1.

Gustavo Paetzold and Lucia Specia. 2016. SemEval 2016 Task 11: Complex Word Identification. In *Proceedings of SemEval*.

Gustavo Paetzold and Lucia Specia. 2017a. Lexical simplification with neural ranking. In *Proceedings of EACL*.

Gustavo H. Paetzold and Lucia Specia. 2017b. A survey on lexical simplification. *J. Artif. Int. Res.*, 60(1):549–593.

Jipeng Qiang, Yun Li, Zhu Yi, Yunhao Yuan, and Xindong Wu. 2020. Lexical simplification with pretrained encoders. In *Proceedings of AAAI*.

Maury Quijada and Julie Medero. 2016. HMC at SemEval-2016 Task 11: Identifying Complex Words Using Depth-limited Decision Trees. In *Proceedings of SemEval*.

Luz Rello, Ricardo Baeza-Yates, Laura Dempere-Marco, and Horacio Saggion. 2013. Frequent words improve readability and short words improve understandability for people with dyslexia. In *Proceedings of INTERACT*.

Horacio Saggion, Sanja Štajner, Daniel Ferrés, Kim Cheng Sheang, Matthew Shardlow, Kai North, and Marcos Zampieri. 2022. Findings of the TSAR-2022 shared task on multilingual lexical simplification. In *Proceedings of TSAR*.

Matthew Shardlow. 2014. Out in the Open: Finding and Categorising Errors in the Lexical Simplification Pipeline. In *Proceedings of LREC*.

Matthew Shardlow, Michael Cooper, and Marcos Zampieri. 2020. CompLex — a new corpus for lexical complexity prediction from Likert Scale data. In *Proceedings of READI*.

Matthew Shardlow, Richard Evans, and Marcos Zampieri. 2021. Predicting lexical complexity in english texts. In *Proceedings of LREC*.

Ravi Sinha. 2012. UNT-SimpRank: Systems for lexical simplification ranking. In *Proceedings of SemEval*.

Fábio Souza, Rodrigo Nogueira, and Roberto Lotufo. 2020. BERTimbau: pretrained BERT models for Brazilian Portuguese. In *Proceedings of BRACIS*.

Lucia Specia, Kumar Jauhar, Sujay, and Rada Mihalcea. 2012. Semeval - 2012 task 1: English lexical simplification. In *Proceedings of SemEval*.

Robyn Speer, Joshua Chin, Andrew Lin, Sara Jewett, and Lance Nathan. 2018. Luminosoinsight/wordfreq: v2.2.

Sanja Štajner, Daniel Ferrés, Matthew Shardlow, Kai North, Marcos Zampieri, and Horacio Saggion. 2022. Lexical Simplification Benchmarks for English, Portuguese, and Spanish. *Frontiers in Artificial Intelligence*.

Ashish Vaswani, Noam Shazeer, Niki Parmar, Jakob Uszkoreit, Llion Jones, Aidan N Gomez, Łukasz Kaiser, and Illia Polosukhin. 2017. Attention is all you need. In *Proceedings of NIPS*.

Jorge A. Wagner Filho, Rodrigo Wilkens, Marco Idiart, and Aline Villavicencio. 2018. The brWaC corpus: A new open resource for Brazilian Portuguese. In *Proceedings of LREC*.

Willian Massami Watanabe, Arnaldo Candido Junior, Vinícius Rodriguez Uzêda, Renata Pontin de Mattos Fortes, Thiago Alexandre Salgueiro Pardo, and Sandra Maria Aluísio. 2009. Facilita: Reading assistance for low-literacy readers. In *Proceedings ACM*.

Michael Wilson. 1988. Mrc psycholinguistic database: Machine-usable dictionary, version 2.00. *Behavior research methods, instruments, & computers*, 20(1):6–10.

Seid Muhie Yimam, Chris Biemann, Shervin Malmasi, Gustavo Paetzold, Luci Specia, Sanja Štajner, Anaïs Tack, and Marcos Zampieri. A Report on the Complex Word Identification Shared Task 2018. In *Proceedings of BEA*.

Marcos Zampieri, Liling Tan, and Josef van Genabith. 2016. MacSaar at SemEval-2016 Task 11: Zipfian and Character Features for ComplexWord Identification. In *Proceedings of SemEval*.

Findings of the TSAR-2022 Shared Task on Multilingual Lexical Simplification

Horacio Saggion[1], **Sanja Štajner**[2], **Daniel Ferrés**[1], **Kim Cheng Sheang**[1]
Matthew Shardlow[3], **Kai North**[4], **Marcos Zampieri**[4]
[1]Universitat Pompeu Fabra, Barcelona, Spain
[2]Karlsruhe, Germany
[3]Manchester Metropolitan University, Manchester, UK
[4]George Mason University, Fairfax, VA, USA
horacio.saggion@upf.edu

Abstract

We report findings of the TSAR-2022 shared task on multilingual lexical simplification, organized as part of the Workshop on Text Simplification, Accessibility, and Readability TSAR-2022 held in conjunction with EMNLP 2022. The task called the Natural Language Processing research community to contribute with methods to advance the state of the art in multilingual lexical simplification for English, Portuguese, and Spanish. A total of 14 teams submitted the results of their lexical simplification systems for the provided test data. Results of the shared task indicate new benchmarks in Lexical Simplification with English lexical simplification quantitative results noticeably higher than those obtained for Spanish and (Brazilian) Portuguese.

1 Introduction

Lexical Simplification (Shardlow, 2014; Paetzold and Specia, 2017a) is a sub-task of Automatic Text Simplification (Saggion, 2017) that aims at replacing difficult words with easier to read (or understand) synonyms while preserving the information and meaning of the original text. This is a key task to facilitate reading comprehension to different target readerships such as foreign language learners, native speakers with low literacy levels or people with different reading impairments (e.g. dyslexic individuals). As such, it has gained considerable attention in the past few years (Štajner, 2021).

Although Lexical Simplification systems can be developed following different architectural precepts, several studies have suggested the following pipe-lined approach:

1. identification of complex terms (Complex Word Identification - CWI),
2. generation of substitution words (Substitute Generation - SG),
3. selection of the substitutes that can fit in the context (Substitute Selection - SS),
4. ranking substitutes by their simplicity (Substitute Ranking - SR), and
5. morphological generation and context adaptation (e.g. agreement).

There exists a considerable body of research in lexical simplification for English (Horn et al., 2014; Glavaš and Štajner, 2015; Paetzold and Specia, 2017b; Qiang et al., 2020a). However, and in spite of several lexical simplification studies for languages other than English notably (Bott et al., 2012; Baeza-Yates et al., 2015; Ferrés et al., 2017; Ferrés and Saggion, 2022) for Spanish, (Hartmann et al., 2018; North et al., 2022b) for Portuguese, (Hmida et al., 2018) for French, (Qiang et al., 2021) for Chinese, (Kajiwara and Yamamoto, 2015; Hading et al., 2016) for Japanese and (Abrahamsson et al., 2014) for Swedish, there is a clear need to broaden the scope of lexical simplification in terms of language coverage. Moreover, given its social relevance in making information accessible to broader audiences, we believe it is important to understand how far automatic systems can go in this task.

We therefore established this first Shared Task on Multilingual Lexical Simplification calling the NLP research community to contribute with methods to advance the state of the art. The task called for systems able to simplify words in context in (one or more of) three languages, namely English, Portuguese, and Spanish. Systems have to deal with steps 2-5 above to generate, select, rank, and adapt to context substitutes for a given complex word in a sentence. As the result of our call for systems, of the 22 teams registered to the task, 14 sent their system outputs for evaluation. There were 31

Proceedings of the Workshop on Text Simplification, Accessibility, and Readability (TSAR-2022), pages 271 - 283
December 8, 2022

different runs for English, 15 for Spanish, and 14 for Portuguese.

This paper overviews the first Shared Task on Multilingual Lexical Simplification. We describe in detail the task, the trial and test data used, the evaluation metrics, and the results. We also provide an analysis of the results and consider possible ways to expand the current scope of the task.

1.1 State-of-the-Art Lexical Simplification

In recent years, researchers have turned to large off-the-shelf word embedding models, instead of pre-compiled lists of synonyms or lexical databases, for retrieving (or generating) substitution candidates (Glavaš and Štajner, 2015; Paetzold and Specia, 2016), ranking them for simplicity and context using several sorting factors such as frequency, target context similarity, language model probabilities, etc. These approaches demonstrated better coverage than previous systems. Before the TSAR 2022 Shared Task, the state of the art for English lexical simplification was the LSBert system (Qiang et al., 2020a), which used the pre-trained transformer language model BERT (Devlin et al., 2019) and a masking technique for finding suitable simplifications for complex words, resorting, as previous approaches, to unsupervised ranking using several feature combinations.

Lexical simplification in languages other than English attracted less attention, however several systems for Spanish have been proposed since the initial work of (Bott et al., 2012). As it is with the case of English, here the use of neural systems is also observed. For example, Alarcón et al. (2021) leverages pretrained word embedding vectors and BERT models. Subsystems were developed for CWI, SG, and SS; in particular, the CWI sub-task was evaluated using the CWI 2018 shared task dataset for Spanish (Yimam et al., 2018) where it was found that traditional algorithms (i.e. Support vector Machines) are still competitive in this task. The SG and SS sub-tasks were evaluated using a portion of 500 instances of the EASIER corpus (Alarcon et al., 2021). Each instance of this portion contains a sentence, a target word and three substitutions. More recently, Ferrés and Saggion (2022) presented ALEXSIS, a dataset for benchmarking Lexical Simplification in Spanish, and performed experiments with several neural and unsupervised systems for the different phases of the simplification pipeline. They also performed the first evaluation of an adaptation of LSBERT (Qiang et al., 2020a) software for Spanish for SG and Full Pipeline with the ALEXSIS and EASIER datasets, achieveing state of the art.

For Brazilian Portuguese, a data-driven machine translation approach has been proposed in (Specia, 2010). In the current neural paradigm, North et al. (2022b) developed and evaluated, on a new corpus for Portuguese based on ALEXSIS (Ferrés and Saggion, 2022), four transformer models for substitute generation following the BERT masked approach (Qiang et al., 2020a). Somehow related is the work of (Hartmann et al., 2020) that describe a Portuguese datasets which is designed for simplification of texts for children.

1.2 Previous Lexical Simplification Shared Tasks

The first shared task in lexical simplification was proposed for SemEval 2012. It addressed English Lexical Simplification (Specia et al., 2012) and offered the opportunity to evaluate systems able to rank substitution candidates in relation to their simplicity. It was, therefore, concentrating just on step number 4 in the lexical simplification pipeline we have described in the Introduction. The dataset used was taken from the Lexical Substitution task at SemEval 2007 which was enriched with simplicity rankings provided by second language learners with high proficiency levels in English, rankings per instance were aggregated to obtain a final gold annotation. The task attracted 5 different institutions which provided nine systems in total.

Complex word identification (CWI), which is not addressed in the current TSAR challenge, has been explored in two shared tasks: SemEval 2016 CWI for English (Paetzold and Specia, 2016), and the BEA 2018 CWI shared task for multiple languages (Yimam et al., 2018). In SemEval 2016 CWI task, participants were requested to predict which words in a given sentence would be considered complex by a non-native English speaker. A CWI dataset composed of 9,200 instances was created with sentences from different datasets which have already been used in text simplification research and it was, for the task objectives, annotated by non-native speakers of English. The task attracted 21 teams which produced a total of 42 systems. The BEA 2018 CWI shared task proposed to tackle CWI in English, German, and Spanish (training and test data were provided), together with a multilingual task with French as a target language without training data. Teams were asked to produce systems to classify words as either complex or simple (binary) and/or provide a probability for the complexity of each word. The shared task attracted 11 teams. The SemEval 2021 shared task on lexical complexity prediction (Shardlow et al., 2021) also provided a new dataset for complexity detection for single words and multi-word expressions in English attracting 55 teams. Additionally, the IberLef 2020 forum proposed a shared task on Spanish complex word identification (Zambrano and Montejo-Ráez, 2020) but attracted few participants.

2 Task Description

The TSAR-2022 shared task featured three tracks:

- Lexical simplification in English;
- Lexical simplification in Spanish;
- Lexical simplification in (Brazilian) Portuguese.

In all tracks, the task was the same. Given a sentence/context and one target (complex) word in it, provide substitutes for the target word that would make the sentence easier to understand. It was allowed to submit up to 10 substitutes, ordered from the best to the least fitting/simple one. Ties were not allowed.

Participants were provided with several trial examples in each language. Training datasets were not provided. However, participants were allowed to use any external resources for building their lexical simplification systems. Participating systems were evaluated on test sets using several metrics.[1]

2.1 Datasets

Datasets for all three languages were compiled using comparable procedures.

2.1.1 Context and Target Word Selection

For English and Spanish, the sentences/contexts and target words were selected from respective datasets used in the BEA-2018 shared task on complex word identification (Yimam et al., 2018).[2] For (Brazilian) Portuguese, the sentences and target words were selected from the PorSimplesSent dataset (Leal et al., 2018). In the (English and Spanish) CWI-2018 datasets, complex words were marked based on a crowdsourcing experiment with 10 native and 10 non-native speakers in each language. Words that were highlighted by at least one crowdsourced annotator as difficult to understand in a given context (paragraph containing several sentences), were marked as complex in the final CWI-2018 datasets (Yimam et al., 2018). The PorSimplesSent dataset, used for selecting sentences and target words for (Brazilian) Portuguese, is a corpus of original and manually simplified news articles. To identify complex words in the original sentences, the following procedure was used. An automatic word alignment tool was applied which marked inconsistencies between the original and simplified sentences. These were further checked by a native Brazilian-Portuguese speaker, who identified among them the complex words which contained simpler substitutes in the simplified sentences.

In all three datasets (English portion of CWI-2018, Spanish portion of CWI-2018, and PorSimplesSent for Portuguese), sentences often had several words marked as complex. For compiling the TSAR-2022 shared task datasets, we chose only one of the marked complex words as the target word, in each selected sentence. This made the task easier for participants, as they only had to take into account how the proposed simpler substitute fit the context (i.e., whether or not it preserves the original meaning) instead of additionally taking into account interactions among the proposed substitutes of different target words within the same sentence.

2.1.2 Dataset Annotation

To obtain a list of simpler substitutes for each target word, selected sentences (386 in English, 381 in Spanish, and 386 in Brazilian Portuguese) with marked target words were presented to crowdsourced workers who had a task of proposing a simpler substitute which would preserve the meaning of the original sentence. For English and Brazilian Portuguese, this crowdsourcing annotation task was done on Amazon Mechanical Turk,[3] while for Spanish, it was done on Prolific platform.[4] The annotation was first done for the Spanish dataset. The guidelines used for the Spanish annotation were then translated into English and Portuguese with

[1] Compilation of the datasets used in the TSAR-2022 shared task, their limitations, and strong baselines for English, Spanish, and (Brazilian) Portuguese are described in detail in (Štajner et al., 2022).

[2] https://sites.google.com/view/cwisharedtask2018

[3] https://www.mturk.com/

[4] https://www.prolific.co/

Language	Instances	Substitutes per target		
		Min	Max	Avg
EN	386	2	22	10.55
ES	381	2	19	10.28
PT-BR	386	1	16	8.10

Table 1: Statistics on the TSAR-ST 2022 multilingual lexical simplification dataset.

Language	Test	Trial	Total
EN	373	10	383
ES	368	12	380
PT-BR	374	10	384

Table 2: Dataset splits for TSAR-2022 shared task. Instances with two or more repetitions of the complex word were excluded from the test set.

minimal editing to ensure that the task remained the same across languages. Details about dataset compilation and annotation across the three languages can be found in the work by Štajner et al. (2022). Additional details about Spanish and Portuguese portions of the dataset can be found in the works by Ferrés and Saggion (2022) and North et al. (2022b), respectively. The total number of annotated instances, the minimal, the maximal, and average number of proposed simpler substitutes per target word in each language are given in Table 1.

2.1.3 Test Sets and Examples

Annotated sentences in each language were split into trial and test datasets (Table 2).[5] Datasets are available under the Creative Commons Attribution-NonCommercial-ShareAlike 4.0 International License (CC-BY-NC-SA-4.0).[6] Examples of instances from trial portion of the dataset are given in Table 3.

2.2 Baselines

We provided two strong baselines: TSAR-TUNER and TSAR-LSBert. TSAR-TUNER is an adaptation of the TUNER Lexical Simplification system (Ferrés et al., 2017), which is a state-of-the-art non-neural Spanish lexical simplification system. TSAR-TUNER differs from TUNER in that it omits the complex word identification and context adaptation phases. Instead, it returns an ordered list of substitution candidates. TSAR-TUNER sequentially executes four tasks: (1) sentence analysis, (2) word sense disambiguation, (3) synonyms ranking, and (4) morphological generation. Details of TSAR-TUNER and its adaptation to English, and Portuguese can be found in (Štajner et al., 2022).

TSAR-LSBert is an adaptation of LSBert (Qiang et al., 2020b), the state-of-the-art neural lexical simplification for English. LSBert uses the masked language model (MLM) of BERT to predict a set of candidate substitution words and their substitution probabilities. It combines five features to rank substitute candidates according to their simplicity: BERT prediction order, a BERT-based language model, the PPDB database, word frequency, and semantic word similarity from fastText word embeddings. Our TSAR-LSBert uses the same resources as the original system for lexical simplification in English. For lexical simplification in Spanish and Portuguese, all language-dependent components are adapted using the best available resources in corresponding languages. Details of TSAR-LSBert system and its adaptation to Spanish and Portuguese can be found in (Štajner et al., 2022).

2.3 Evaluation Metrics

To allow for fairer comparison of systems that propose a different number of substitution candidates, i.e., not to penalize systems which return fewer candidates, all evaluation metrics are applied on a fixed number of k top-ranked candidates.

To account for various aspects of systems' performances, ten metrics were used as the official metrics of the shared task: ACC@1, MAP@k, potential@k, accuracy@n@top1 where k $\in$ {3, 5, 10} and n $\in$ {1, 2, 3}.[7]

Potential@k is defined as the percentage of instances for which at least one of the k top-ranked substitutes is also present in the gold data.

Accuracy@k@top1 is defined as the percentage of instances where at least one of the k top-ranked substitutes matches the most frequently suggested synonym in the gold data. Here is important to note that Accuracy@1@top1 was denoted as Accuracy@1 in (Štajner et al., 2022).

[5]Note that some instances had two repetitions of the complex word in the same sentence but were not included in the TSAR-2022 Shared Task splits of the Evaluation Benchmark. There was one such case in Spanish, three in English, and two in Portuguese.

[6]https://github.com/LaSTUS-TALN-UPF/TSAR-2022-Shared-Task/

[7]ACC@1, MAP@1, and Potential@1 give the same results per definition. We thus used ACC@1 to denote them all in the official results.

Data	Context/Sentence	Target	(Gold) Substitutes Ranked
EN	A local witness said a separate group of attackers disguised in burqas — the head-to-toe robes worn by conservative Afghan women — then tried to storm the compound.	disguised	concealed:4, dressed:4, hidden:3, camouflaged:2, changed:2, covered:2, disguised:2, masked:2, unrecognizable:2, converted:1, impersonated:1
ES	Floreció en la época clásica y tenía una reputada escuela de filosofía.	reputada	prestigiosa:6, famosa:4, reconocida:2, afamada:2, conocida:2, renombrada:2, respetada:2, prestigioso:1, muy reconocida:1, valorada:1, acreditada:1, prestigiada:1
PT	naquele país a ave é considerada uma praga	praga	peste:9, epidemia:5, maldição:3, doença:2, desgraça:2, tragédia:1, infestação:1

Table 3: Examples from the trial part of the TSAR 2022 dataset. The number after the ":" indicates the number of repetitions.

MAP@k: The MAP metric is used commonly for evaluating information retrieval models and recommender systems (Beitzel et al., 2018; Valcarce et al., 2020). In the context of lexical simplification, instead of using a ranked list of relevant and irrelevant documents, we use a ranked list of generated substitutes, which can either be matched (relevant) or not matched (irrelevant) against the set of the gold-standard substitutes. Unlike Precision@k, which only measures which percentage of the k top-ranked substitutes can be found among the gold-standard substitutes, MAP@k additionally takes into account the position of the relevant substitutes among the first k generated candidates (i.e., whether or not the relevant candidates are at the top positions).

The evaluation script was provided to the participants and the research community.[8]

3 Participating Systems

We received the outputs of 13 teams for English, 6 for Spanish, and 5 for (Brazilian) Portuguese. Each team was allowed to submit outputs of up to 3 systems. This totaled to 31 submitted outputs for English, 15 for Spanish, and 14 for Portuguese.

CILS (Seneviratne et al., 2022) submitted three systems for the English track. All systems use the Model Prediction Score and Embedding Similarity Score for candidate generation. A model prediction score is computed using the XLNet model (Yang et al., 2019) given the context and the target word with any word in the vocabulary of XLNet. The Embedding Similarity Score is the inner product of the embedding of the target word and the embedding of the respective word. The three systems differ in the ranking module. They rank the candidates based on different combinations of scores such as 1) the score from the candidate generation; 2) sentence similarity score (cosine similarity between the source and target sentence); 3) gloss sentence similarity score (the cosine similarity between the target word and the candidate); 4) WordNet score (a cosine similarity between the target word and the candidate extracted from WordNet); and 5) Validation score (a cosine similarity of the BERT-base between the source and target sentence).

PresiUniv (Whistely et al., 2022) uses masked language model (follows LSBert) for candidate generation, ranks candidates by cosine similarity (extracted from FastText), and then filter them out by checking part-of-speech. The systems for the three languages are the same, except that the language model is specific for each language. It is interesting that this approach works the best on Spanish dataset, but not so well on the Portuguese and English datasets (lower than the baseline).

UoM&MMU (Vásquez-Rodríguez et al., 2022) uses an approach that consists of three steps: 1) candidate generation based on different prompt templates (e.g., <easier, simple> <word, synonym> for <target_word>); 2) fine-tuning of a language model (BERT-based model) to select and rank can-

[8] https://github.com/LaSTUS-TALN-UPF/TSAR-2022-Shared-Task

didates; and 3) post-processing to filter out noise and antonyms. This approach achieves the second rank on the Spanish dataset and the third rank on the English dataset, but to our surprise, the model ranks the lowest on the Portuguese dataset.

PolyU-CBS (Chersoni and Hsu, 2022) proposes three approaches for the candidate ranking. In all three approaches, the candidates are generated using a masked language model. Then, the first approach ranks candidates based on the probability received from the candidate generation (base probability) and sentence probability extracted from GPT-2 pre-trained model by replacing the target word with its candidate. The second approach ranks candidates by base probability and masked language model scoring (Salazar et al., 2020). The third model ranks candidates by base probability and contextualized embedding similarity (cosine similarity between the target word and its candidate in the context of the original sentence). Based on the official results, the third approach performs better than the other two in all languages.

CENTAL (Wilkens et al., 2022) explored the use of masked language model for candidate generation with three strategies for context expansion: Copy, Query Expansion, and Paraphrase. The Copy strategy is a copy of the sentence itself (follows that of LSBert). The Query Expansion strategy extracts alternative words for the target word from FastText and then replaces the original sentence with each alternative word. The Paraphrase strategy (English only) extracts paraphrases from Pegasus (Zhang et al., 2020). The authors propose three ranking approaches: 1) using the frequency of words generated by the three strategies; 2) training a binary classifier (English only) for the ranking; 3) the English ranking module (the binary classifier) performs cross-lingual ranking for Spanish and Portuguese.

teamPN (Nikita and Rajpoot, 2022) proposes a model that extract candidates through a combination of modules such as verb sense disambiguation module (candidates are extracted from VerbNet (Schuler, 2005) and filtered by FitBERT (Havens and Stal, 2019)), paraphrase database module (PPDB) (Ganitkevitch et al., 2013), DistilBERT module (Sanh et al., 2019) (uses masked language model), and Knowledge Graph module (Alberts et al., 2021). Modules are combined depending on the part-of-speech of the target word. All extracted candidates are checked for correct inflection and ranked by FitBERT (Havens and Stal, 2019).

MANTIS (Li et al., 2022) adapts masked language model (RoBERTa) for candidate generation and performs the candidate ranking with three different approaches. The first ranking approach uses three features with different weights to rank the candidates: 1) pre-trained language model feature (the probability of the candidate extracted during the candidate generation), 2) Word Frequency, and 3) semantic similarity (cosine similarity between the FastText vector of the target word and the candidate). The second and third approaches rank candidates by word prevalence and equivalence score. The second approach uses crowd-sourcing word prevalence, which is a proportion of the population that knows a given word based on a crowd-sourcing study involving 220,000 people (Brysbaert et al., 2019). The third approach uses corpus-derived word prevalence, which is an estimate of the number of books that a word appears in (Johns et al., 2020). The equivalence score is the entailment score of the original sentence and the sentence replaced with the candidate. The experimental results have shown that the first approach performs better than the other two.

UniHD (Aumiller and Gertz, 2022) submitted two systems. The first system was a zero-shot prompted GPT-3 with a prompt asking for simplified synonyms given a particular context. Simplifications are then ranked. The second system was an ensemble over six different GPT-3 prompts/configurations with average rank aggregation. The second system attained the highest score for English on all metrics. The approach is simplistic in nature, relying heavily on the underlying language model which is only available for research through a paid interface.

RCML (Aleksandrova and Brochu Dufour, 2022) proposes a system (English only) by applying the lexical substitution framework LexSubGen (based on XLNet) for candidate generation and ranks the candidates based on grammaticality (POS + morphological features), meaning preservation (BERTScore of the source and target sentences), and simplicity (predicted by an SVM classifier trained on CEFR level data).

GMU-WLV (North et al., 2022a) submitted two models for each of the three languages. These two models follow the approach of LSBert, except the second model uses an additional Zipf frequency in the candidate ranking module. The first model performs the best on the Portuguese dataset.

Team	Language	Approach
CILS	EN	SG: Language Model (LM) probability and similarity score, SR: SG score, cosine similarity scores
PresiUniv	EN, ES, PT	SG: Masked Language Model (MLM), SR: cosine similarity, POS check
UoM&MMU	EN, ES, PT	SG: LM with prompt, SR: fined-tuned Bert model as classifier
PolyU-CBS	EN, ES, PT	SG: MLM, SR: MLM probability, GPT-2 probability, sentence probability, cosine similarity
CENTAL	EN, ES, PT	SG: MLM, SR: word frequency, binary classifier
teamPN	EN	SG: MLM, VerbNet, PPDB, Knowledge Graph, SR: MLM probability
MANTIS	EN	SG: MLM, SR: MLM probability, word frequency, cosine similarity
UniHD	EN	GTP-3 prompts: zero-shot, few-shot
RCML	EN	SG: lexical substitution, SR: POS, BERTScore, SVM classifier
GMU-WLV	EN, ES, PT	SG: MLM, SR: MLM probability, word frequency

Table 4: The approaches taken by each team, categorised according to substitution generation (SG) and substitution ranking (SR) strategy.

A comparative of system approaches is provided in Table 4.

4 Results and Discussions

In the following subsections we describe the results obtained by the participant teams for each of the tracks in the TSAR 2022 Multilingual Lexical Simplification shared task.[9] Note that we will base our description on the ranking obtained by sorting submissions according to the ACC@1 metric as well as summarizing methods for which a paper has been submitted and accepted for the Shared Task (see Section 3).

We also provided an extended version of the results,[10] which included ACC@1, Potential@k, MAP@k, macro-averaged Precision@k, macro-averaged Recall@k, and Accuracy@k@top1, for k $\in \{1, 2, ..., 10\}$. Precision@k and Recall @k were defined as follows:

- **Precision@k**: the percentage of k top-ranked substitutes that are present also in the gold data;
- **Recall@k**: the percentage of substitutions provided in the gold data that are included in the top k generated substitutions.

Overall, we observe that several systems achieved new state-of-the-art results in the different tracks overtaking a previous competitive Neural Language Model for lexical simplification (LSBert).

4.1 English Track

In table 5 the results for English are presented sorted by ACC@1.[11] In this track, and of the 31 submitted runs, only four (from 3 teams: UniHD, MANTIS, and UoM&MMU) performed better than the LSBert baseline according to ACC@1. Moreover, UniHD run number 2 achieved the best performance in all the reported metrics. UniHD run number 2 outperforms the other teams' systems in more than 15 points in ACC@1 achieving a score of 0.8096 in this metric. This indicates that it is able to retrieve a correct synonym in the 80,96% of instances of the dataset. Moreover, UniHD's run number 2 achieves a 99,46% of Potential@10. This indicates that it has the potential to retrieve at least one correct substitution in the top-10 predictions of almost all the instances. In fact, it achieves 0.9624 in Potential@3 metric, which is almost nine points higher than the second best official result (MANTIS with 0.8900) and indicates also a great performance obtaining at least one correct substitution in the top-3 predictions.

It is important to highlight that the UniHD's system relies on a pre-trained *pay-per-query* GPT-3 model to obtain candidate substitutions by prompting the model with 6 versions of zero, one, and two shot prompts, based on the provided trial data, finally combining the predicted candidate ranks to select the best substitutions. In contrast, team MANTIS relied on a freely available masked language model to obtain substitutions and an adaptation of the ranking procedure of LSBert. While UoM&MMU also relying on freely available pre-

[9]Please note that official results can also be queried at https://taln.upf.edu/pages/tsar2022-st/#results

[10]https://github.com/LaSTUS-TALN-UPF/TSAR-2022-Shared-Task/tree/main/results/extended

[11]Note that the data to sort the results is available at https://github.com/LaSTUS-TALN-UPF/TSAR-2022-Shared-Task/tree/main/results/official

Team	Run	ACC @1	ACC@1 @Top1	ACC@2 @Top1	ACC@3 @Top1	MAP @3	MAP @5	MAP @10	Potential @3	Potential @5	Potential @10
UniHD	2	**0.8096**	**0.4289**	**0.6112**	**0.6863**	**0.5834**	**0.4491**	**0.2812**	**0.9624**	**0.9812**	**0.9946**
UniHD	1	0.7721	0.4262	0.5335	0.5710	0.5090	0.3653	0.2092	0.8900	0.9302	0.9436
MANTIS	1	0.6568	0.3190	0.4504	0.5388	0.4730	0.3599	0.2193	0.8766	0.9463	0.9785
UoM&MMU	1	0.6353	0.2895	0.4530	0.5308	0.4244	0.3173	0.1951	0.8739	0.9115	0.9490
LSBert-baseline	1	0.5978	0.3029	0.4450	0.5308	0.4079	0.2957	0.1755	0.8230	0.8766	0.9463
RCML	2	0.5442	0.2359	0.3941	0.4664	0.3823	0.2961	0.1887	0.8310	0.8927	0.9436
RCML	1	0.5415	0.2466	0.3887	0.4691	0.3716	0.2850	0.1799	0.8016	0.8847	0.9115
GMU-WLV	1	0.5174	0.2493	0.3538	0.4477	0.3522	0.2626	0.1600	0.7533	0.8337	0.8981
CL Lab PICT	1	0.5067	0.2064	0.3297	0.4021	0.3278	0.2331	0.1369	0.7265	0.7828	0.8042
UoM&MMU	3	0.4959	0.2439	0.3458	0.4235	0.3273	0.2411	0.1461	0.7560	0.8310	0.9088
teamPN	2	0.4664	0.1823	0.3056	0.3378	0.2743	0.1950	0.0975	0.6729	0.7506	0.7506
MANTIS	3	0.4611	0.2117	0.3351	0.4235	0.3227	0.2553	0.1673	0.7747	0.8793	0.9436
teamPN	3	0.4504	0.1769	0.2841	0.3297	0.2676	0.1872	0.0936	0.6648	0.7399	0.7399
teamPN	1	0.4477	0.1769	0.2815	0.3297	0.2666	0.1874	0.0937	0.6621	0.7453	0.7453
PolyU-CBS	3	0.4316	0.2064	0.2788	0.3297	0.2683	0.1995	0.1178	0.6139	0.6997	0.7747
MANTIS	2	0.4209	0.1662	0.2654	0.3565	0.2745	0.2193	0.1507	0.7131	0.8391	0.9517
PresiUniv	1	0.4021	0.1581	0.2305	0.3002	0.2603	0.1932	0.1136	0.6568	0.7399	0.7962
PolyU-CBS	1	0.3914	0.1823	0.2627	0.3002	0.2576	0.1883	0.1113	0.5924	0.6836	0.7533
CILS	3	0.3860	0.1957	0.2627	0.3083	0.2603	0.2014	0.1267	0.5656	0.6005	0.6380
CILS	2	0.3806	0.1903	0.2600	0.3083	0.2597	0.1997	0.1262	0.5630	0.6005	0.6434
PresiUniv	3	0.3780	0.1474	0.2010	0.2573	0.2277	0.1609	0.0897	0.5656	0.6058	0.6327
CILS	1	0.3753	0.2010	0.2788	0.3109	0.2555	0.1964	0.1235	0.5361	0.5898	0.6300
CENTAL	2	0.3619	0.1152	0.2091	0.2788	0.2573	0.2056	0.1271	0.6541	0.7667	0.8418
TUNER-baseline	1	0.3404	0.1420	0.1689	0.1823	0.1706	0.1087	0.0546	0.4343	0.4450	0.4450
PolyU-CBS	2	0.3190	0.1447	0.2091	0.2573	0.1973	0.1490	0.0901	0.5120	0.6032	0.7104
GMU-WLV	2	0.2815	0.0804	0.1689	0.2493	0.1899	0.1589	0.1200	0.5630	0.7399	0.8981
CENTAL	1	0.2761	0.1313	0.1930	0.2117	0.1635	0.1183	0.0707	0.3780	0.4021	0.4182
UoM&MMU	2	0.2654	0.1367	0.2171	0.2680	0.1820	0.1307	0.0794	0.4906	0.5817	0.6756
PresiUniv	2	0.2600	0.1018	0.1313	0.1554	0.1350	0.0862	0.0439	0.3136	0.3163	0.3163
twinfalls	1	0.1957	0.0509	0.0884	0.1233	0.1175	0.0879	0.0535	0.3485	0.4235	0.5067
twinfalls	2	0.1849	0.0643	0.0911	0.1367	0.1182	0.0857	0.0514	0.3565	0.4075	0.4664
NU HLT	1	0.1447	0.0670	0.1018	0.1179	0.0902	0.0583	0.0301	0.2600	0.2815	0.2895
twinfalls	3	0.0455	0.0107	0.0348	0.0455	0.0370	0.0277	0.0182	0.1474	0.2305	0.3619

Table 5: Results submitted for the English track in comparison with the baselines (LSBert, TUNER). The best performances are in bold. Note: ACC@1, MAP@1, Potential@1, and Precision@1 give the same results as per their definitions

trained masked language models fine tuned with prompts to select the most appropriate substitutes and filtering substitution candidates by checking several resources (e.g. WordNet, corpora). Also noticeable in the results of the task is that several "neural" systems under-perform the "non-neural" TUNER baseline in terms of ACC@1. Overall, it seems that the use of pre-trained masked language models fine-tuned to the task together with extra lexical resources or corpora produce very competitive approaches.

4.2 Portuguese Track

Table 6, presents the results for Portuguese, also sorted by ACC@1. In this track, and of the 14 submitted runs, only two (from two teams: GMU-WLV and CENTAL) performed better than the LSBert baseline (as observed in the table, one team performed equally to LSBert in terms of ACC@1, but worst in the other metrics). The displayed results indicate that there is a clear top performing (considering all metrics) system produced by team GMU-WLV. Surprisingly, they have relied on a simple approach to substitute generation and ranking by adopting a pre-trained Portuguese masked language model, BERTimbau (Souza et al., 2020). The second best performing system according to ACC@1 is by the CENTAL team which also relied on a pre-trained masked language model in which several strategies were used to provide context to the target sentence, followed by a ranking procedure based on voting. Similar as in the English track, in this track, several systems under-perform, in terms of ACC@1, the shared task non-neural TUNER baseline.

Team	Run	ACC @1	ACC@1 @Top1	ACC@2 @Top1	ACC@3 @Top1	MAP @3	MAP @5	MAP @10	Potential @3	Potential @5	Potential @10
GMU-WLV	1	**0.4812**	**0.2540**	**0.3716**	**0.3957**	**0.2816**	**0.1966**	**0.1153**	**0.6871**	**0.7566**	**0.8395**
CENTAL	1	0.3689	0.1737	0.2433	0.2673	0.1983	0.1344	0.0766	0.5240	0.5641	0.6096
PolyU-CBS	3	0.3262	0.1390	0.1871	0.2139	0.1755	0.1256	0.0732	0.4491	0.5106	0.5748
LSBert-baseline	1	0.3262	0.1577	0.2326	0.2860	0.1904	0.1313	0.0775	0.4946	0.5802	0.6737
PresiUniv	1	0.3074	0.1604	0.2032	0.2379	0.1573	0.1077	0.0580	0.4598	0.5320	0.5935
PresiUniv	3	0.3048	0.1604	0.2032	0.2379	0.1555	0.1062	0.0571	0.4572	0.5294	0.5855
PresiUniv	2	0.2941	0.1604	0.1978	0.2326	0.1494	0.1020	0.0549	0.4411	0.5026	0.5588
PolyU-CBS	1	0.2807	0.1122	0.1470	0.1711	0.1515	0.1059	0.0629	0.3983	0.4705	0.5534
CENTAL	3	0.2245	0.0614	0.1310	0.1925	0.1478	0.1143	0.0769	0.4705	0.6096	0.8021
PolyU-CBS	2	0.2219	0.0882	0.1203	0.1497	0.1112	0.0797	0.0478	0.3315	0.3850	0.4919
TUNER-baseline	1	0.2219	0.1336	0.1604	0.1604	0.1005	0.0623	0.0311	0.2673	0.2673	0.2673
GMU-WLV	2	0.2165	0.0695	0.1363	0.2165	0.1559	0.1243	0.0845	0.5133	0.6550	**0.8395**
CENTAL	2	0.2058	0.0641	0.1203	0.1898	0.1470	0.1103	0.0726	0.4786	0.6016	0.7673
UoM&MMU	1	0.1711	0.0695	0.0855	0.1096	0.1011	0.0747	0.0430	0.2486	0.2914	0.3636
UoM&MMU	3	0.1577	0.0748	0.1016	0.1283	0.1071	0.0785	0.0461	0.2834	0.3262	0.4171
UoM&MMU	2	0.1363	0.0454	0.0721	0.0962	0.0944	0.0711	0.0418	0.2379	0.2967	0.3609

Table 6: Results submitted for the Portuguese track in comparison with the baselines (LSBert, TUNER). The best performances are in bold. Note: ACC@1, MAP@1, Potential@1, and Precision@1 give the same results as per their definitions

4.3 Spanish Track

Results for the Spanish track are presented in Table 7. The systems' runs are sorted by ACC@1. Several systems outperformed the LSBert baseline. In particular, the PresiUniv team produced two competitive approaches which ranked first and third (tied with team UoM&MMU). However, the approach did not reach top performance in several of the official metrics. The PresiUniv lexical simplifier relies on a masked language model approach for substitute selection combined with a word-embbeding similarity model for meaning preservation and a filtering stage based on POS-tagging. The UoM&MMU, GMU-WLV and CENTAL (with approaches already described for English or Portuguese) also performed well in the Spanish track, with UoM&MMU and GMU-WLV achieving top scores for some of the metrics. The PolyU-CBS team produced a competitive system which used a Spanish specific masked language model to generate substitutes and a ranking based on a combination of sentence language model probabilities and word-embedding similarities. Best performing systems in this track rely on Spanish-specific masked language models, corpus-based information, language model prompts, and syntactic information, among others.

5 Conclusions and Further Work

Lexical Simplification, the task of replacing difficult words in a sentence by easier to read or understand synonyms preserving the meaning of the original sentence is an important problem which has gained considerable attention in the past few years. In spite of its popularity for English, the task has attracted less research for other languages. Considering its social relevance in today's digital world, we put forward the first Shared Task on Multilingual Lexical Simplification addressing three languages: English, (Brazilian) Portuguese, and Spanish, and called the research community to challenge the state of the art. To carry out the task, we have prepared three datasets, one per each language, following similar data collection and data annotation approaches, leading the way to the development of future datasets for additional languages. The datasets are composed of sentences each containing a single complex word which needs to be simplified. Although the datasets were intended only for testing the participating systems, a small (between 10 and 12 instances) portion was released as trial data. This was particularly useful for several teams to fine-tune their computational methods or prompts. The task also featured two baselines: one based on a competitive neural approach, and another one on a traditional (dictionary-based) pipe-lined architecture. The Shared Task attracted a considerable number of participants with a total of 60 systems' runs submitted across the three tracks. Several systems outperformed the competition, setting a new benchmark in Lexical Simplification. It is observed that pre-trained masked language models when fine-tuned to the lexical simplification task produce very competitive approaches in combina-

Team	Run	ACC @1	ACC@1 @Top1	ACC@2 @Top1	ACC@3 @Top1	MAP @3	MAP @5	MAP @10	Potential @3	Potential @5	Potential @10
PresiUniv	1	**0.3695**	**0.2038**	**0.2771**	**0.3288**	0.2145	0.1499	0.0832	**0.5842**	0.6467	0.7255
UoM&MMU	3	0.3668	0.1603	0.2282	0.2690	0.2128	0.1506	0.0899	0.5326	0.6005	0.6929
PresiUniv	3	0.3614	0.2038	0.2581	0.2961	0.1944	0.1318	0.0706	0.5163	0.5543	0.5815
UoM&MMU	2	0.3614	0.1603	0.2445	0.2907	0.2225	0.1657	0.0958	0.5380	0.6168	0.7010
PolyU-CBS	3	0.3586	0.1630	0.2010	0.2364	0.2068	0.1456	0.0850	0.5244	0.5978	0.6793
GMU-WLV	1	0.3532	0.1820	0.2635	**0.3288**	0.2202	**0.1664**	**0.0994**	0.5679	**0.6793**	**0.7717**
UoM&MMU	1	0.3451	0.1494	0.2364	0.2907	**0.2238**	0.1614	0.0949	0.5543	0.6385	0.7038
CENTAL	1	0.3097	0.1467	0.2092	0.2391	0.1826	0.1327	0.0779	0.5000	0.5923	0.6358
LSBert-baseline	1	0.2880	0.0951	0.1440	0.1820	0.1868	0.1346	0.0795	0.4945	0.6114	0.7472
PolyU-CBS	1	0.2826	0.1141	0.1820	0.2255	0.1820	0.1320	0.0780	0.5000	0.5978	0.6820
PresiUniv	2	0.2500	0.1576	0.1793	0.1956	0.1197	0.0740	0.0371	0.3125	0.3152	0.3152
GMU-WLV	2	0.2364	0.0679	0.1304	0.1875	0.1557	0.1256	0.0833	0.4646	0.6168	**0.7717**
CENTAL	3	0.2201	0.0407	0.0896	0.1331	0.1416	0.1122	0.0745	0.4646	0.6086	0.7581
PolyU-CBS	2	0.2010	0.0869	0.1331	0.1739	0.1417	0.1025	0.0615	0.4103	0.4972	0.6413
CENTAL	2	0.1983	0.0652	0.1114	0.1657	0.1265	0.0979	0.0695	0.4184	0.5570	0.7282
TUNER-baseline	1	0.1195	0.0625	0.0788	0.0842	0.0575	0.0356	0.0184	0.1440	0.1467	0.1494
OEG_UPM	1	0.1032	0.0434	0.0842	0.1086	0.0772	0.0594	0.0389	0.2527	0.3342	0.4456

Table 7: Results submitted for the Spanish track in comparison with the baselines (LSBert, TUNER). The best performances are in bold. Note: ACC@1, MAP@1, Potential@1, and Precision@1 give the same results as per their definitions

tion with additional syntactic/lexical resources or corpora.

The submitted systems relied heavily on pre-trained language models, which are known to hallucinate (i.e., generate non-factual statements based on previously seen contexts). In the context of substitution generation, hallucination may indicate that incorrect simplifications are returned when the context is under-specified or unfamiliar. Further work to ensure that the simplifications generated by such systems are faithful to the original text and are factual in nature will help to engender a culture of security and trust in simplification research.

In our dataset, we have not considered a key aspect of simplification, which is the user. Our datasets assume that there is one correct simplification that is the best simplification for all users. In fact, our 'best' simplification is collected from many users and is based on the most frequently returned simplification. It is interesting to note that when asked to simplify the same word in the same context, users will answer differently. It is logical to conclude then, that a simplification system must return a term which is appropriate to a user.

Concerning the selected evaluation metrics, although the MAP@K metric takes into account the order of returned items and it is very useful for cases when multiple relevant items are expected, it has the disadvantage that the relevance of the returned items is binary. So, in further work, it could be included a metric that could take into account the possibility of graded or weighted relevance allowing the participants to submit a weight associated to each prediction and allow ties.

Finally, we note that our evaluation methodology is entirely automated, due to the constraints of a shared task environment. Whilst this is very useful for developing systems for lexical simplification, we strongly encourage those working on in-production systems to directly evaluate the resulting systems with the user bases that they are intended for. Automated evaluation is secondary to human evaluation, and this is especially true in simplification where the goal is to enable the user to better understand the original information.

Acknowledgements

We thank all the teams who registered and sent submissions to the Shared Task. We acknowledge partial support from the individual project Context-aware Multilingual Text Simplification (ConMuTeS) PID2019-109066GB-I00/AEI/10.13039/501100011033 awarded by Ministerio de Ciencia, Innovación y Universidades (MCIU) and by Agencia Estatal de Investigación (AEI) of Spain.

References

Emil Abrahamsson, Timothy Forni, Maria Skeppstedt, and Maria Kvist. 2014. Medical text simplification using synonym replacement: Adapting assessment of word difficulty to a compounding language. In

Proceedings of the 3rd Workshop on Predicting and Improving Text Readability for Target Reader Populations (PITR), pages 57–65, Gothenburg, Sweden. Association for Computational Linguistics.

Rodrigo Alarcón, Lourdes Moreno, and Paloma Martínez. 2021. Exploration of Spanish Word Embeddings for Lexical Simplification. In *Proceedings of the First Workshop on Current Trends in Text Simplification (CTTS 2021)*, volume 2944 of *CEUR Workshop Proceedings*. CEUR-WS.org.

Rodrigo Alarcon, Lourdes Moreno, and Paloma Martínez. 2021. Lexical Simplification System to Improve Web Accessibility. *IEEE Access*, 9:58755–58767.

Houda Alberts, Ningyuan Huang, Yash Deshpande, Yibo Liu, Kyunghyun Cho, Clara Vania, and Iacer Calixto. 2021. VisualSem: a high-quality knowledge graph for vision and language. In *Proceedings of the 1st Workshop on Multilingual Representation Learning*, pages 138–152, Punta Cana, Dominican Republic. Association for Computational Linguistics.

Desislava Aleksandrova and Olivier Brochu Dufour. 2022. RCML at TSAR-2022 Shared Task: Lexical Simplification With Modular Substitution Candidate Ranking. In *Proceedings of the Workshop on Text Simplification, Accessibility, and Readability (TSAR-2022)*, Abu Dhabi, United Arab Emirates (Virtual). Association for Computational Linguistics.

Dennis Aumiller and Michael Gertz. 2022. UniHD at TSAR-2022 Shared Task: Is Compute All We Need for Lexical Simplification? In *Proceedings of the Workshop on Text Simplification, Accessibility, and Readability (TSAR-2022)*, Abu Dhabi, United Arab Emirates (Virtual). Association for Computational Linguistics.

Ricardo A. Baeza-Yates, Luz Rello, and Julia Dembowski. 2015. CASSA: A Context-Aware Synonym Simplification Algorithm. In *NAACL HLT 2015*, pages 1380–1385.

Steven M. Beitzel, Eric C. Jensen, and Ophir Frieder. 2018. *MAP*, pages 2200–2201. Springer New York, New York, NY.

Stefan Bott, Luz Rello, Biljana Drndarevic, and Horacio Saggion. 2012. Can Spanish Be Simpler? LexSiS: Lexical Simplification for Spanish. In *COLING*, pages 357–374. Indian Institute of Technology Bombay.

Marc Brysbaert, Paweł Mandera, Samantha F McCormick, and Emmanuel Keuleers. 2019. Word prevalence norms for 62,000 english lemmas. *Behavior research methods*, 51(2):467–479.

Emmanuele Chersoni and Yu-Yin Hsu. 2022. PolyU-CBS at TSAR-2022 Shared Task: A Simple, Rank-Based Method for Complex Word Substitution in Two Steps. In *Proceedings of the Workshop on Text Simplification, Accessibility, and Readability (TSAR-2022)*, Abu Dhabi, United Arab Emirates (Virtual). Association for Computational Linguistics.

Jacob Devlin, Ming-Wei Chang, Kenton Lee, and Kristina Toutanova. 2019. BERT: Pre-training of Deep Bidirectional Transformers for Language Understanding. In *Proceedings of the 2019 Conference of the North American Chapter of the Association for Computational Linguistics: Human Language Technologies, Volume 1 (Long and Short Papers)*, pages 4171–4186, Minneapolis, Minnesota. Association for Computational Linguistics.

Daniel Ferrés and Horacio Saggion. 2022. ALEXSIS: A Dataset for Lexical Simplification in Spanish. In *Proceedings of the Language Resources and Evaluation Conference*, pages 3582–3594, Marseille, France. European Language Resources Association.

Daniel Ferrés, Horacio Saggion, and Xavier Gómez Guinovart. 2017. An Adaptable Lexical Simplification Architecture for Major Ibero-Romance Languages. In *Proceedings of the First Workshop on Building Linguistically Generalizable NLP Systems*, pages 40–47, Copenhagen, Denmark. Association for Computational Linguistics.

Juri Ganitkevitch, Benjamin Van Durme, and Chris Callison-Burch. 2013. Ppdb: The paraphrase database. In *Proceedings of the 2013 Conference of the North American Chapter of the Association for Computational Linguistics: Human Language Technologies*, pages 758–764.

Goran Glavaš and Sanja Štajner. 2015. Simplifying Lexical Simplification: Do We Need Simplified Corpora? In *Proceedings of the 53rd Annual Meeting of the Association for Computational Linguistics and the 7th International Joint Conference on Natural Language Processing of the Asian Federation of Natural Language Processing*, ACL, pages 63–68.

Muhaimin Hading, Yuji Matsumoto, and Maki Sakamoto. 2016. Japanese lexical simplification for non-native speakers. In *Proceedings of the 3rd Workshop on Natural Language Processing Techniques for Educational Applications (NLPTEA)*, pages 92–96.

Nathan S. Hartmann, Gustavo H. Paetzold, and Sandra M. Aluísio. 2020. A dataset for the evaluation of lexical simplification in portuguese for children. In *Computational Processing of the Portuguese Language: 14th International Conference, PROPOR 2020, Evora, Portugal, March 2–4, 2020, Proceedings*, page 55–64, Berlin, Heidelberg. Springer-Verlag.

Nathan S. Hartmann, Gustavo H. Paetzold, and Sandra M. Aluísio. 2018. SIMPLEX-PB: A Lexical Simplification Database and Benchmark for Portuguese. In *Proceedings of the International Conference on Computational Processing of the Portuguese Language*.

Sam Havens and Aneta Stal. 2019. Use bert to fill in the blanks.

Firas Hmida, Mokhtar B. Billami, Thomas François, and Núria Gala. 2018. Assisted lexical simplification for French native children with reading difficulties. In *Proceedings of the 1st Workshop on Automatic Text Adaptation (ATA)*, pages 21–28, Tilburg, the Netherlands. Association for Computational Linguistics.

Colby Horn, Cathryn Manduca, and David Kauchak. 2014. Learning a Lexical Simplifier Using Wikipedia. In *Proceedings of ACL (Short Papers)*, pages 458–463.

Brendan T Johns, Melody Dye, and Michael N Jones. 2020. Estimating the prevalence and diversity of words in written language. *Quarterly Journal of Experimental Psychology*, 73(6):841–855.

Tomoyuki Kajiwara and Kazuhide Yamamoto. 2015. Evaluation dataset and system for Japanese lexical simplification. In *Proceedings of the ACL-IJCNLP 2015 Student Research Workshop*, pages 35–40, Beijing, China. Association for Computational Linguistics.

Sidney Evaldo Leal, Magali Sanches Duran, and Sandra Maria Aluísio. 2018. A nontrivial sentence corpus for the task of sentence readability assessment in Portuguese. In *Proceedings of COLING*, pages 401–413.

Xiaofei Li, Daniel Wiechmann, Yu Qiao, and Elma Kerz. 2022. MANTIS at TSAR-2022 Shared Task: Improved Unsupervised Lexical Simplification with Pretrained Encoders. In *Proceedings of the Workshop on Text Simplification, Accessibility, and Readability (TSAR-2022)*, Abu Dhabi, United Arab Emirates (Virtual). Association for Computational Linguistics.

Nikita Nikita and Pawan Kumar Rajpoot. 2022. teamPN at TSAR-2022 Shared Task: Lexical Simplification using Multi-Level and Modular Approach. In *Proceedings of the Workshop on Text Simplification, Accessibility, and Readability (TSAR-2022)*, Abu Dhabi, United Arab Emirates (Virtual). Association for Computational Linguistics.

Kai North, Alphaeus Dmonte, Tharindu Ranasinghe, and Marcos Zampieri. 2022a. GMU-WLV at TSAR-2022 Shared Task: Evaluating Lexical Simplification Models. In *Proceedings of the Workshop on Text Simplification, Accessibility, and Readability (TSAR-2022)*, Abu Dhabi, United Arab Emirates (Virtual). Association for Computational Linguistics.

Kai North, Marcos Zampieri, and Tharindu Ranasinghe. 2022b. ALEXSIS-PT: A New Resource for Portuguese Lexical Simplification. In *Proceedings of COLING.*

Gustavo Paetzold and Lucia Specia. 2016. Semeval 2016 task 11: Complex word identification. In *Proceedings of the 10th International Workshop on Semantic Evaluation, SemEval@NAACL-HLT 2016, San Diego, CA, USA, June 16-17, 2016*, pages 560–569. The Association for Computer Linguistics.

Gustavo Paetzold and Lucia Specia. 2017a. A Survey on Lexical Simplification. *Journal of Artificial Intelligence Research*, 60:549–593.

Gustavo Paetzold and Lucia Specia. 2017b. Lexical simplification with neural ranking. In *Proceedings of the 15th Conference of the European Chapter of the Association for Computational Linguistics: Volume 2, Short Papers*, pages 34–40, Valencia, Spain. Association for Computational Linguistics.

Jipeng Qiang, Yun Li, Zhu Yi, Yunhao Yuan, and Xindong Wu. 2020a. Lexical simplification with pretrained encoders. *Thirty-Fourth AAAI Conference on Artificial Intelligence*, pages 8649—-8656.

Jipeng Qiang, Yun Li, Yi Zhu, Yunhao Yuan, and Xindong Wu. 2020b. LSBert: A Simple Framework for Lexical Simplification. *arXiv preprint arXiv:2006.14939.*

Jipeng Qiang, Xinyu Lu, Yun Li, Yunhao Yuan, and Xindong Wu. 2021. Chinese lexical simplification. *IEEE/ACM Transactions on Audio, Speech, and Language Processing*, 29:1819–1828.

Horacio Saggion. 2017. *Automatic Text Simplification.* Synthesis Lectures on Human Language Technologies. Morgan & Claypool Publishers.

Julian Salazar, Davis Liang, Toan Q. Nguyen, and Katrin Kirchhoff. 2020. Masked language model scoring. In *Proceedings of the 58th Annual Meeting of the Association for Computational Linguistics*. Association for Computational Linguistics.

Victor Sanh, Lysandre Debut, Julien Chaumond, and Thomas Wolf. 2019. Distilbert, a distilled version of bert: smaller, faster, cheaper and lighter. In *NeurIPS* EMC^2 *Workshop.*

Karin Kipper Schuler. 2005. *VerbNet: A broad-coverage, comprehensive verb lexicon.* University of Pennsylvania.

Sandaru Seneviratne, Elena Daskalaki, and Hanna Suominen. 2022. CILS at TSAR-2022 Shared Task: Investigating the Applicability of Lexical Substitution Methods for Lexical Simplification. In *Proceedings of the Workshop on Text Simplification, Accessibility, and Readability (TSAR-2022)*, Abu Dhabi, United Arab Emirates (Virtual). Association for Computational Linguistics.

Matthew Shardlow. 2014. A Survey of Automated Text Simplification. *International Journal of Advanced Computer Science and Applications*, 4.

Matthew Shardlow, Richard Evans, Gustavo Henrique Paetzold, and Marcos Zampieri. 2021. SemEval-2021 task 1: Lexical complexity prediction. In *Proceedings of the 15th International Workshop on Semantic Evaluation (SemEval-2021)*, pages 1–16, Online. Association for Computational Linguistics.

Fábio Souza, Rodrigo Nogueira, and Roberto Lotufo. 2020. BERTimbau: pretrained BERT models for Brazilian Portuguese. In *Proceedings of BRACIS*.

Lucia Specia. 2010. Translating from complex to simplified sentences. In *Proceedings of the 9th international conference on Computational Processing of the Portuguese Language (PROPOR)*, volume 6001 of *Lecture Notes in Computer Science*, pages 30–39. Springer Berlin Heidelberg.

Lucia Specia, Sujay Kumar Jauhar, and Rada Mihalcea. 2012. Semeval-2012 task 1: English lexical simplification. In *Proceedings of the First Joint Conference on Lexical and Computational Semantics - Volume 1: Proceedings of the Main Conference and the Shared Task, and Volume 2: Proceedings of the Sixth International Workshop on Semantic Evaluation*, SemEval '12, page 347–355, USA. Association for Computational Linguistics.

Daniel Valcarce, Alejandro Bellogín, Javier Parapar, and Pablo Castells. 2020. Assessing ranking metrics in top-n recommendation. *Information Retrieval Journal*, 23:411–448.

Sanja Štajner. 2021. Automatic text simplification for social good: Progress and challenges. In *Findings of the Association for Computational Linguistics: ACL-IJCNLP 2021*, pages 2637–2652, Online. Association for Computational Linguistics.

Sanja Štajner, Daniel Ferrés, Matthew Shardlow, Kai North, Marcos Zampieri, and Horacio Saggion. 2022. Lexical simplification benchmarks for English, Portuguese, and Spanish. *Frontiers in Artificial Intelligence*, 5.

Laura Vásquez-Rodríguez, Nhung Nguyen, Sophia Ananiadou, and Matthew Shardlow. 2022. UoM&MMU at TSAR-2022 Shared Task: Prompt Learning for Lexical Simplification. In *Proceedings of the Workshop on Text Simplification, Accessibility, and Readability (TSAR-2022)*, Abu Dhabi, United Arab Emirates (Virtual). Association for Computational Linguistics.

Peniel John Whistely, Sandeep Mathias, and Galiveeti Poornima. 2022. PresiUniv at TSAR-2022 Shared Task: Generation and Ranking of Simplification Substitutes of Complex Words in Multiple Languages. In *Proceedings of the Workshop on Text Simplification, Accessibility, and Readability (TSAR-2022)*, Abu Dhabi, United Arab Emirates (Virtual). Association for Computational Linguistics.

Rodrigo Wilkens, David Alfter, Rémi Cardon, Isabelle Gribomont, Adrien Bibal, Watrin Patrick, Marie-Catherine de Marneffe, and Thomas François. 2022. CENTAL at TSAR-2022 Shared Task: How Does Context Impact BERT-Generated Substitutions for Lexical Simplification? In *Proceedings of the Workshop on Text Simplification, Accessibility, and Readability (TSAR-2022)*, Abu Dhabi, United Arab Emirates (Virtual). Association for Computational Linguistics.

Zhilin Yang, Zihang Dai, Yiming Yang, Jaime Carbonell, Russ R Salakhutdinov, and Quoc V Le. 2019. XLNet: Generalized Autoregressive Pretraining for Language Understanding. In *Advances in Neural Information Processing Systems*, volume 32. Curran Associates, Inc.

Seid Muhie Yimam, Chris Biemann, Shervin Malmasi, Gustavo Paetzold, Lucia Specia, Sanja Štajner, Anaïs Tack, and Marcos Zampieri. 2018. A Report on the Complex Word Identification Shared Task 2018. In *Proceedings of the Thirteenth Workshop on Innovative Use of NLP for Building Educational Applications*, pages 66–78, New Orleans, Louisiana. Association for Computational Linguistics.

Jenny Alexandra Ortiz Zambrano and Arturo Montejo-Ráez. 2020. Overview of alexs 2020: First workshop on lexical analysis at SEPLN. In *Proceedings of the Iberian Languages Evaluation Forum (IberLEF 2020) co-located with 36th Conference of the Spanish Society for Natural Language Processing (SEPLN 2020), Málaga, Spain, September 23th, 2020*, volume 2664 of *CEUR Workshop Proceedings*, pages 1–6. CEUR-WS.org.

Jingqing Zhang, Yao Zhao, Mohammad Saleh, and Peter Liu. 2020. Pegasus: Pre-training with extracted gap-sentences for abstractive summarization. In *International Conference on Machine Learning*, pages 11328–11339. PMLR.

Author Index

Association for Computational Linguistics
209 N. Eighth Street
Stroudsburg, Pennsylvania 18360

ISBN 978-1-7138-9150-5

CURRAN ASSOCIATES INC.
proceedings.com